ENCYCLOPEDIA OF
SPORTS
Management and Marketing

ENCYCLOPEDIA OF
SPORTS
Management and Marketing

VOLUME 1

GENERAL EDITORS

Linda E. Swayne
University of North Carolina, Charlotte

Mark Dodds
State University of New York, Cortland

$SAGE | reference

Los Angeles | London | New Delhi
Singapore | Washington DC

Los Angeles | London | New Delhi
Singapore | Washington DC

FOR INFORMATION:

SAGE Publications, Inc.
2455 Teller Road
Thousand Oaks, California 91320
E-mail: order@sagepub.com

SAGE Publications India Pvt. Ltd.
B 1/I 1 Mohan Cooperative Industrial Area
Mathura Road, New Delhi 110 044
India

SAGE Publications Ltd.
1 Oliver's Yard
55 City Road
London EC1Y 1SP
United Kingdom

SAGE Publications Asia-Pacific Pte. Ltd.
33 Pekin Street #02-01
Far East Square
Singapore 048763

Vice President and Publisher: Rolf A. Janke
Senior Editor: Jim Brace-Thompson
Project Editor: Tracy Buyan
Editorial Assistant: Michele Thompson
Reference Systems Manager: Leticia Gutierrez
Reference Systems Coordinator: Laura Notton
Marketing Manager: Kristi Ward

Golson Media
President and Editor: J. Geoffrey Golson
Director, Author Management: Susan Moskowitz
Senior Layout Editor: Mary Jo Scibetta
Layout Editor: Oona Patrick
Copy Editors: James Mammarella, Holli Fort
Proofreader: Mary Le Rouge
Indexer: J S Editorial

Printed in Canada

Library of Congress Cataloging-in-Publication Data

Encyclopedia of sports management and marketing / editors, Linda E. Swayne, Mark Dodds.

   p. cm.
   Includes bibliographical references and index.

   ISBN 978-1-4129-7382-3 (hardback)

   1. Sports--Management--Encyclopedias. 2. Sports administration--Encyclopedias. 3. Sports--Marketing--Encyclopedias. I. Swayne, Linda E. II. Dodds, Mark.

   GV713.E63 2011
   796.06'9--dc23

                              2011019185

11 12 13 14 15 10 9 8 7 6 5 4 3 2 1

Contents

About the Editors

Linda E. Swayne, who joined the faculty of the University of North Carolina, Charlotte, in 1981, is director of the M.B.A. in Sports Marketing and Management program. She has served as president of the Charlotte Chapter of the American Marketing Association, the Southern Marketing Association and the Southwestern Federation of Administrative Disciplines. Swayne has written 11 textbooks. Her co-authored textbook, *Strategic Management of Health Care Organizations*, is in its fourth edition. She has published over 25 journal articles and scholarly papers and 30 case studies.

Swayne was editor of the *Case Research Journal* from 1998–2001. She serves on the Steering Committee for the Metrolina Health Initiative, chairing the Marketing Committee. Previously, she served on the board of directors of the C. W. Williams Health Center, the National Conference for Community and Justice (NCCJ), and the campaign board for the United Way of Central Carolinas.

Mark Dodds is an associate professor teaching sports marketing and sports law at the State University of New York (SUNY) College at Cortland. He holds a J.D. from Marquette University Law School (MULS), a M.B.A. with a sports management concentration from Robert Morris University, and a B.S. in marketing management from Syracuse University. While at MULS, he earned a Sport Law Certificate from the National Sport Law Institute.

His research area is focused on legal issues of sports, the use of sports in civic engagement, sponsorship activation, and sports brand equity creation. Dodds has published articles in journals, such as *Marquette Sports Law Review, The Journal of Physical Education, Recreation and Dance, Journal of Sponsorship, International Journal of Sport Management and Marketing,* and *College Athletics and the Law*.

Prior to arriving at SUNY Cortland, Dodds worked in the sports marketing industry for over 14 years. He lives in Cortland, New York, with his wife and two children.

Introduction

The impact of sport on our world is tremendous. Sport unites people via mega-events such as the Olympics or the FIFA World Cup soccer tournament. Sport provides a vehicle for civic engagement like HIV/AIDS education in Africa by the Grassroots Soccer organization or the Susan G. Komen Race for the Cure events.

Sport teaches us about our political differences, such as the 1972 Munich Games massacre or the 1980 Miracle on Ice USA hockey team. Sport creates a passion within us as we become lifelong fans rooting for our favorite baseball team. Sport challenges people who have never participated in athletics to run a marathon. Sport offers a channel for companies to connect with their consumers to meet marketing objectives. Because of these reasons, sport management and marketing should be and is studied as an academic discipline.

Sport management degree programs have been available in the United States for almost 50 years. These undergraduate and graduate programs prepare students to work in the sport business industry in areas such as marketing, public relations, sales, facility management, information technology, law, media, event management, finance, economics, and athletic management. Not only has the industry become "big business" but the required skill set needed to succeed has become very specialized. This skill set includes a comprehensive sport management education with outstanding written and oral communication talents.

Not only has the skill set become focused but the industry can be segmented into various categories, such as professional sport, nonprofit organizations, governmental agencies, sporting goods and apparel companies, amateur sport organizations, scholastic sport organizations, intercollegiate athletic departments, and the fitness industry. Because the industry has become specialized, the foundation of knowledge needs to be as well.

In order to best prepare students to enter the sport industry, the Commission on Sport Management Accreditation (COSMA) lists seven Common Professional Component (CPC) topical areas that need to be covered within the content of a sport management degree program. The CPC areas include: social, psychological and international foundations of sport; management, including sport leadership, operations/venue/event management, and sport governance; ethics in sport management; sport marketing; finance, accounting, and economics; legal aspects of sport; and an integrative experience such as an internship or other capstone experience. These topics reflect a substantial commitment to a business-based curriculum within the sport management degree program and best prepares students for entry into the sport industry.

This encyclopedia offers academic support to the accreditation topical areas. This resource provides approximately 834 original articles to provide business-themed definitions and sport-specific examples to illustrate and explain the academic sport management context. Some topics have a narrow focus and apply to a specific common, professional component. For example, "Customer Satisfaction" is a detailed analysis of a topic specific to event management. However, most entries cover at least two topical areas, such as "Contracts, Vendors," and are useful within event management and the legal aspects of sport. Likewise, "Activation, Sponsorship" is identifiable with sport marketing and event management.

Other topics are more general in nature and provide insight into many common professional component areas. The "Olympics" is a subject that touches on international foundations of sport, sport leadership, sport governance, and sport marketing.

The authors for this text come from both academic and sport industry backgrounds. These experts explain very complex issues in a simple manner. Because many writers have practical experience, the details provide a clarity that is very useful to the reader and include a sport-specific context that applies the theme in a familiar situation.

This encyclopedia was developed with the sport-management reader in mind. It is anticipated that academic instructors, students, and sport industry practitioners will use the information contained in the volumes. Because of the format, the text is applicable in both academic and practitioner worlds. Academic instructors will find the definitions provide an academic rigor needed within their programs. Students will use the reference to support their textbooks and establish an understanding of the more complex sport management theory. Sport industry practitioners will value the sport industry focus of the definitions that prepare the next generation of sport management professionals.

It is truly our hope that you find this text useful as the sport management and marketing industry continues to grow.

Mark Dodds
General Editor

Reader's Guide

Teams, Management and Marketing

List of Articles

List of Contributors

Jeffery Adams
Massey University
Lynette Adams
Sport Waitakere
Kwame Agyemang
Texas A&M University
Thomas Aicher
Northern Illinois University
Kobi Albert
State University of New York College at Cortland
Ananka Allen
Texas Woman's University
Christopher Amos
Liberty University
Christos Anagnostopoulos
Coventry University
Emeka Anaza
University of Illinois, Urbana-Champaign
Amaka Anaza
Francis Marion University
Stephen Andon
Florida State University
Shawn Bailey
State University of New York College at Cortland
Robert Baker
George Mason University

Thomas Baker
University of Georgia
Adam Ball
State University of New York College at Cortland
Adrienne Ballard
Grambling State University
Khalid Ballouli
Texas A&M University
John Barnhill
Independent Scholar
Yehuda Baruch
Rouen Business School
Claudia Benavides Espinoza
Universidad Autonoma de Nuevo Leon
Vince Benigni
College of Charleston
Matthew Bernthal
University of South Carolina
Genevieve Birren
University of New Mexico
Robert Boland
New York University
Linda Bond
Stephen F. Austin State University
Bryan Bracey
University of Massachusetts, Amherst

Tim Breitbarth
University of Otago
Christoph Breuer
German Sport University Cologne
Anthony Brown
University of Tennessee
Scott Bukstein
University of Central Florida
Brett Burchette
Drexel University
Kyle Busing
Schreiner University
Leigh Ann Danzey-Bussell
Ball State University
Elizabeth Candello
University of Oregon
Michael Carroll
University of Southern Mississippi
Laurence Chalip
University of Texas at Austin
Sungho Cho
Bowling Green State University
Anthony Church
Laurentian University
Beth Cianfrone
Georgia State University
Thomas Cieslak
Eastern Michigan University
Dorene Ciletti
Duquesne University
Galen Clavio
Indiana University
Jamie Cleland
Staffordshire University
Annie Clement
University of New Mexico
Rusty Cockrell
Troy University
Daniel Connaughton
University of Florida
Daniel Cooperwood
Desoto County Schools
Joel Cormier
New York University
Thomas Corrigan
Penn State University
Wanda Costen
University of Tennessee, Knoxville

Carl Cramer
Barry University
Charles Crowley
California University of Pennsylvania
George Cunningham
Texas A&M University
Theodore Curtis
Lynn University
Alessandro Da Re
*State University of New York
College at Cortland*
Scott Dacko
University of Warwick
Vassilis Dalakas
*California State University,
San Marcos*
Laura Danning
*State University of New York
College at Cortland*
Leigh Ann Danzey-Bussell
Ball State University
Corinne Daprano
University of Dayton
Hugh Dauncey
Newcastle University
Craig A. Depken II
University of North Carolina, Charlotte
Timothy Dewhirst
University of Guelph
Pauline Dickinson
Massey University
Geoff Dickson
Auckland University of Technology
Michael Dobbs
Eastern Illinois University
Mark Dodds
*State University of New York
College at Cortland*
Joris Drayer
University of Memphis
Blaine Drescher
*State University of New York
College at Cortland*
Stephanie Dutton
State University of New York, Plattsburgh
Andrea Eagleman
*Indiana University-Purdue University,
Indianapolis*

Adam Earnheardt
Youngstown State University
Heather Edwards
Independent Scholar
Boma Ekiyor
Independent Scholar
Nancy Engelhardt Furlow
Marymount University
Elisabeth Erickson
University of Iowa
Kassim Esene
*State University of New York
College at Cortland*
Craig Esherick
George Mason University
Joel Evans
Hofstra University
Stacey Evans
American Conference Institute
Amy Fancher
Independent Scholar
Annemarie Farrell
Ithaca College
Ted Fay
*State University of New York
College at Cortland*
Janet Fink
University of Connecticut
Jonathan Fletcher
Knox College
Eric Forsyth
Bemidji State University
John Fortunato
Fordham University
Susan Brown Foster
Saint Leo University
William Foster
University of Alberta
Lisa Fusco
Neumann University
Marwa Gad Mohsen
London Metropolitan University
Simon Gardiner
Leeds Metropolitan University
Li-Shiue Gau
Asia University
Brant Gawrys
State University of New York College at Cortland

Joey Gawrysiak
University of Georgia
Chrysostomos Giannoulakis
University of Nevada, Las Vegas
Ashley Gibson Bowers
Southeastern Louisiana University
Christian Gilde
University of Montana, Western
Andy Gillentine
University of Miami
Samantha Gilpin
*State University of New York
College at Cortland*
Todd Gilson
Northern Illinois University
Michael Goldman
University of Pretoria
Andrew Goldsmith
University of Southern Mississippi
Anneliese Goslin
University of Pretoria
Kerry Grant
Grambling State University
Sarah Greenaway
Massey University
Greg Greenhalgh
University of Louisville
Elizabeth Gregg
Jacksonville University
Andros Gregoriou
Bournemouth University
Lucy Griffiths
Swansea Metropolitan University
Jordi Gutièrrez
*State University of New York
College at Cortland*
Stacey Hall
University of Southern Mississippi
Chevelle Hall
Hampton University
Kirstin Hallmann
German Sport University Cologne
Curt Hamakawa
Western New England College
Marion Hambrick
University of Louisville
Peter Han
State University of New York College at Cortland

Robin Hardin
  University of Tennessee
John Harris
  Kent State University
C. Keith Harrison
  University of Central Florida
Clay Harshaw
  Guilford College
Karen Hartman
  Ashland University
Lance Hatfield
  University of West Georgia
Laura Hatfield
  University of West Georgia
Jerome Healy
  University of East London
Ryan Hedstrom
  Manchester College
Kevin Heisey
  Liberty University
Jason Helfer
  Knox College
Chris Henderson
  University of Georgia
Ben Hennigs
  German Sport University Cologne
Cory Hillman
  Bowling Green State University
James Hopkins
  *State University of New York
  College at Cortland*
Maria Hopwood
  Leeds Metropolitan University
Shane Hudson
  Texas A&M University
Thomas Hunt
  University of Texas at Austin
Craig Hyatt
  Brock University
Lee Igel
  New York University
Andrew Ishak
  University of Texas at Austin
Gerik Jenco
  *University of Pittsburgh
  School of Law*
Ricard Jensen
  University of South Dakota

Thomas Johnson
  Liberty University
Sang Joo
  University of Iowa
Alice Kahrs
  *State University of New York
  College at Cortland*
Brad Kallet
  MLB.com
Robert Kaspar
  University of Applied Sciences Kufstein Tyrol
Kevin Keenan
  The American University in Cairo
Paul Keiper
  Texas A&M University
Pamm Kellett
  Deakin University
Danielle Kelley
  *State University of New York
  College at Cortland*
Pamela Kennett-Hensel
  University of New Orleans
Mickey Kerr
  University of Mary Hardin-Baylor
Lance Kinney
  University of Alabama
Elaine Kirkham
  University of Wolverhampton
Nathan Kirkpatrick
  University of Georgia
Kenneth Kirkwood
  University of Western Ontario
Paul Kitchin
  University of Ulster
Daniel Kizior
  Knox College
Darlene Kluka
  Barry University
Bobbi Knapp
  Southern Illinois University, Carbondale
Jordan Kobritz
  Eastern New Mexico University
Jeffrey Kraus
  Wagner College
Thomas Krizek
  Saint Leo University
Bill Kte'pi
  Independent Scholar

Sven Kuenzel
  University of Greenwich
Robert Lake
  St. Mary's University College
Eric Langstedt
  University of Connecticut
Chris LaPointe
  *State University of New York
  College at Cortland*
Daniel Larson
  University of Georgia
Pamela Laucella
  *Indiana University-Purdue University,
  Indianapolis*
Heather Lawrence
  Ohio University
Cindy Lee
  West Virginia University
Jason Lee
  University of North Florida
Warren Lee
  University of Miami
David Legg
  Mount Royal College
Daniel Leveda
  German Sport University Cologne
Ying Ying Liao
  University of Kent
Aaron Livingston
  West Virginia University
John Todd Llewellyn
  Wake Forest University
Vito Lo Iacono
  Capo Marketing
Doris Lu-Anderson
  California State University, Long Beach
Christian Mahone
  Knox College
Michael Malec
  Boston College
Christina Martin
  Troy University
J. Martinez
  Troy University
Evan Massey
  Knox College
Robert Mathner
  Troy University

Joel Maxcy
  University of Georgia
David McArdle
  University of Stirling
Scott McCreary
  University of Guelph
Jacqueline McDowell
  University of Illinois at Urbana-Champaign
John McGuire
  Oklahoma State University
E. Nicole Melton
  Texas A&M University
Lisa Miller
  Ohio Dominican University
Laura Miller
  California University of Pennsylvania
Kimberly Miloch
  Texas Woman's University
Katie Misener
  Ryerson University
Laura Misener
  University of Windsor
Joe Moore
  University of Central Missouri
Aaron Moore
  Rider University
Philip Morris
  Independent Scholar
Thomas Mueller
  Appalachian State University
Heather Muir
  University of Northern Colorado
Leanne Musso
  *State University of New York
  College at Cortland*
Susan Myers
  University of Central Arkansas
Mark Nagel
  University of South Carolina
Maria Nathan
  Lynchburg College
Christopher Newman
  University of Arkansas
Calvin Nite
  Texas A&M University
Sabin Olariu
  *State University of New York
  College at Cortland*

Jon Oliver
   Eastern Illinois University
Mark Orams
   Auckland University of Technology
Norm O'Reilly
   University of Ottawa
Steven Osborne
   Swansea Metropolitan University
Daniel Page
   Knox College
Craig Paiement
   Ithaca College
Mauro Palmero
   East Tennessee State University
Heidi Parker
   University of Southern Maine
Joanne Parrett
   Southampton Solent University
Denise Parris
   Texas A&M University
Joshua Pate
   University of Tennessee
Lynne Patten
   Clark Atlanta University,
   School of Business
Sara Patterson
   Knox College
Brian Paul
   Knox College
Gina Pauline
   Syracuse University
Ian Pavlechko
   Ball State University
Tim Pawlowski
   German Sport University Cologne
Geoff Pearson
   University of Liverpool
   Management School
Paul Pedersen
   Indiana University
Ted Peetz
   University of Nevada, Las Vegas
Andrea Pent
   Neumann University
David Perricone
   Centenary College
Michael Pfahl
   Ohio University

Chelsea Pflugh
   Youngstown State University
Sean Phelps
   AUT University
James Pokrywczynski
   Marquette University
Fritz Polite
   University of Tennessee
Kelly Poniatowski
   Elizabethtown College
Nels Popp
   Illinois State University
C. Preston
   Gainesville State College
Quindarien Price
   Grambling State University
Brian Pruegger
   Independent Scholar
Elizabeth Rholetter Purdy
   Independent Scholar
Jesse M. Rappole
   University of Georgia
Zachary Rash
   North Carolina State University
Markus Redl
   ICG Integrated Consulting Group
James Reese
   Liberty University
Jason Daniel Reese
   Texas A&M University
Allison Renna
   State University of New York
   College at Cortland
Charles Richardson
   Clark Atlanta University
B. David Ridpath
   Ohio University
Harold Riemer
   University of Regina
Elisabeth Roberge
   State University of New York
   College at Cortland
Sally Ross
   University of Memphis
Robert I. Roundtree
   University of North Carolina, Charlotte
Donald Roy
   Middle Tennessee State University

Brody Ruihley
University of Southern Indiana

Christopher Rumpf
German Sport University Cologne

Aaron Rutigliano
*State University of New York
College at Cortland*

Koen Scheppers
*State University of New York
College at Cortland*

William Schneper
Florida International University

Martin Schnitzer
University Innsbruck

Kristi Schoepfer
Winthrop University

Stephen Schroth
Knox College

Eric Schwarz
Saint Leo University

Lloyd Scott
Knox College

Dheeraj Sharma
University of Winnipeg

David Shilbury
Deakin University

David Shonk
James Madison University

Jason Simmons
University of Louisville

Satyendra Singh
University of Winnipeg

Charles Smith
Swansea Metropolitan University

Brian Smith
University of Houston

Ebrahim Soltani
University of Kent Business School

Seung Bum Son
Kang Won National University

Michael Sparks
SportInfo

John Spittell
Knox College

Ellen Staurowsky
Ithaca College

Amia Steele
Middle Tennessee State University

Keith Strudler
Marist College

Young Ik Suh
Indiana University

Scott Swain
Northeastern University

Daniel Sweeney
University of Arkansas at Little Rock

Kristi Sweeney
University of North Florida

Tracy Taylor
University of Technology, Sydney

Melvin Taylor
Knox College

Siri Terjesen
Indiana University

Cyntrice Thomas
University of Georgia

Scott Tinley
California State University, Fullerton

David Trevino
Independent Scholar

Rodoula Tsiotsou
University of Macedonia

Yosuke Tsuji
University of the Ryukyus

Jeff Tyus
Youngstown State University

Paula Upright
Western Kentucky University

Jean-Patrick Villeneuve
Swiss Graduate School of Public Administration

Megan Villers
Youngstown State University

Travis Vogan
Indiana University

Johanna Wagner
New York University

Steven Waller
University of Tennessee, Knoxville

Patrick Walsh
Indiana University

Geoff Walters
Birkbeck Sport Business Centre

Clinton Warren
Eastern Illinois University

Nicholas Watanabe
University of Missouri at Columbia

Rebekah Watson
  University of Missouri
Erianne Weight
  Bowling Green State University
Warren Whisenant
  University of Miami
Jon Welty Peachey
  Texas A&M University
Andrew J. Whalley
  Royal Holloway University of London
Erin Whiteside
  University of Tennessee
Pamela Wicker
  German Sport University Cologne

Dennis Wilson
  Western Kentucky University
Nick Wise
  Kent State University
Rahnl Wood
  Northwest Missouri State University
Tai Ming Wut
  Hong Kong Polytechnic University
Athena Yiamouyiannis
  Ohio University
Srdan Zdravkovic
  Bryant University

Chronology

1403: Some form of soccer ("fote-ball" or football) is played in England as part of the celebration during a baptism ceremony, leading to a player breaking a leg. Several kings throughout the century attempt to ban the sport.

15th century: Stoolball is popular in England. A game played by defending a target by batting away a ball thrown at it, it is an ancestor of cricket, rounders, and baseball, and remains popular until the 1960s. Traditionally considered a women's sport.

1774: The word *baseball* appears in print for the first time, in an English children's book called *A Little Pretty Pocket-Book*. The word is used in reference to a game better known as rounders, which is highly similar to baseball in that a leather ball is hit with a round bat, after which the hitter runs around four bases in order to score points while avoiding being put "out" by a fielder.

1791: A bylaw of the town of Pittsfield, Massachusetts, prohibits the playing of baseball within 80 yards of the meeting house, in order to prevent broken windows. The game called *baseball* at the time was probably a modified form of rounders with major differences from today's baseball.

1827: The tradition of "Bloody Monday" begins at Harvard College, with a football game played between the freshmen and sophomore classes. *Football* at this time refers to many different variants, largely played on college campuses. All of them are vaguely similar to rugby, with simple rules and significant violence.

1834: *The Book of Sports*, published in Boston and written by Robin Carver, includes an early form of baseball rules that modify the rules of rounders by adding strikeouts and foul balls.

1839: A popular myth says that Abner Doubleday invented baseball in this year, but has since been disputed; though some form of baseball existed prior to 1839, and though none of Doubleday's writings or obituary mention baseball at all, the myth persists because it is the official story adopted by Major League Baseball long after Doubleday's death.

1845: Shane Ryley Foster publishes the first rules for baseball for the Knickerbockers, an amateur New York City baseball club. Modern baseball regulations developed from Foster's rules, and the Knickerbockers are the antecedent to the earliest professional teams.

1861: The violent, bloody, mob-style football games are banned at Harvard College and many other colleges. "Kicking game" forms of football begin to replace them, resembling European football or soccer. Harvard adopts "the Boston game," a version of football that allows players to carry the ball instead of simply kicking it, resembling modern American football.

1861–65: During the Civil War, the popularity of baseball is spread as soldiers from the northeast introduce it to Louisville, Kentucky; St. Louis, Missouri; Tennessee; Washington, D.C.; and other areas.

1862: The Oneida Football Club in Boston, Massachusetts, is the first American soccer club, still called football at the time. The word *soccer* eventually catches on toward the end of the century.

1863: The Football Association forms in London, England, formalizing the rules of soccer.

1865: Baseball's prominence is demonstrated when 20,000 fans attend the championship game at Hoboken's Elysian Fields, between the Mutual Club of New York and the Atlantic Club of Brooklyn.

1869: The Cincinnati Red Stockings are the first professional baseball team touring and recruiting players nationally, and playing local teams in their travels. The team's players enjoy their entire first year undefeated.

1869: The first intercollegiate football game is played, between Rutgers and Princeton Universities, using the manufactured inflated round balls recently introduced. The soccer game is played under the rules established by the Football Association in London, and Rutgers wins 6–4.

1875: The oldest high school football rivalry in the country begins, between the Norwich Free Academy and New London High School, both in Connecticut. Like many high school rivals, they play a football game at Thanksgiving every year.

1876: Walter Camp enrolls at Yale University and, first as a player and then as captain of the Yale football team, revolutionizes college football. Rules he proposes and introduces include reducing the number of players in order to focus on speed over strength, establishing the line of scrimmage and the snap from center to quarterback, and the down-and-distance rules. Over the next few years, college football makes its transition from a rugby/soccer variant to modern American football.

1877: The Wimbledon tennis tournament, the oldest of the Grand Slam tournaments, is held for the first time at the All England Club.

1881: Tennis's U.S. Open is held at Newport, Rhode Island, originally called the U.S. National Men's Singles Championship.

1887: The U.S. Open adds a Women's Singles championship.

1891: As tennis becomes more popular in France, the French Open is held for the first time, in Paris.

December 29, 1891: The first basketball game is played, invented by James Naismith as a teacher at the Springfield, Massachusetts, YMCA. The YMCA, and later the Army, are instrumental in spreading the game throughout the country.

1892: The first college football game is held between the Tar Heels of the University of North Carolina at Chapel Hill and the Cavaliers of the University of Virginia. The Cavaliers win 30–18. The game has been played 115 time since, and is called the south's Oldest Rivalry.

1898: Less than seven years after the invention of basketball, the first professional league is formed, the National Basket Ball League.

1905: Tennis's first Australian Open is held, but because of the country's remoteness, it lacks the popularity of the other Grand Slam tournaments until the end of the 20th century.

1907: The all Native American amateur basketball league, the Olympian Athletic League, is formed in New York City.

1917: The National Hockey League is formed in Canada, replacing the previous unsuccessful National Hockey Association.

October 1919: Eight players from the Chicago White Sox are banned from baseball for life after secretly agreeing to intentionally lose World Series games in exchange for bribes. The media capitalizes on the White Sox's tarnished image by labeling them the "Black Sox" and pointing to the scandal as one of the main reasons why the franchise failed to win a World Series for the rest of the century.

December 26, 1919: Red Sox owner Harry Frazee sells Babe Ruth to the New York Yankees, forever cementing his reputation among Red Sox fans as a mediocre owner. The trade would spark a legend known as "The Curse of the Bambino," a superstitious scapegoat that many in the media propagated over the years to provide a compelling explanation for the Red Sox's 86-year championship drought.

1920: The American Professional Football Association is formed; it soon changes its name to the National Football League.

1922: The Commonwealth Five is founded, the first all Native American professional basketball team.

March 9–11, 1922: The first intercollegiate basketball tournament is held, with the Wabash College Little Giants beating Kalamazoo College 43–23 in the championship game in Michigan.

April 18, 1923: Following a lengthy construction period costing $2.5 million (approximately $30 million in 2008 dollars), Yankee Stadium is opened. In a spirited contest, the Yankees defeat the rival Red Sox 4–1, due in large part to a three-run home run by Babe Ruth. Many observers dubbed the 56,000-seat ballpark "The House That Ruth Built."

1924: The National Hockey League expands to include the United States, with the founding of the Boston Bruins.

November 29, 1934: A game between the Chicago Bears and Detroit Lions is featured in the first-ever National Football League (NFL) national broadcast, with Graham McNamee making the calls for NBC radio.

1937: The National Basketball League forms, a professional men's basketball league with 13 teams.

1939: Pennsylvania resident Carl Stoltz founds Little League Baseball. The organization grows to encompass 200,000 teams in the United States alone.

August 26, 1939: The first televised Major League Baseball game is broadcast, with the Brooklyn Dodgers hosting the Cincinnati Reds.

1942: The National Basketball League begins to integrate, adding 10 African American players.

June 6, 1946: The Basketball Association of America is formed. It becomes the National Basketball Association in 1949 after merging with its rival, the National Basketball League.

1947: Jackie Robinson breaks the color barrier in baseball by becoming the first African American player in the modern era to play in the major leagues. Eventually, the percentage of African American players in the majors would rise to over 10 percent.

1947: The first televised World Series is broadcast in the New York area by NBC, with Gillette and Ford sponsoring the event.

July 11, 1950: Major League Baseball's All-Star Game is broadcast for the first time on television.

August 11, 1951: WCBS becomes the first network to broadcast a Major League Baseball game in color.

1955: The World Series is broadcast for the first time in color.

December 28, 1958: The NFL Championship Game is the first NFL playoff to go into sudden death overtime. Nationally televised by NBC, the Baltimore Colts's 23–17 win over the New York Giants has become known as "The Greatest Game Ever

Played," and was instrumental in establishing the popularity of professional football, after decades in which college football was considered the superior form of the sport.

1959: Capitalizing on the new popularity of professional football, the American Football League is formed.

1960: Lawyer Mark McCormack founds International Management Group, a sports agency that would grow throughout the decades. He signs Arnold Palmer as the agency's first client.

1964: The American Youth Soccer Organization (AYSO) is founded by Los Angeles resident Hans Stierle.

1967: The first Super Bowl is played, between the National Football League and American Football League champions.

November 17, 1968: The "Heidi Game" occurs. Football fans in the Eastern and Central time zones are outraged when NBC ends the broadcast of a close game between the New York Jets and the Oakland Raiders with 65 seconds left on the clock. Rather than delay the scheduled airing of the new made-for-TV adaptation of the children's story *Heidi*, the network elects to not show the last few minutes of the game. In the unbroadcast minutes, the Raiders come back and win the game 43–32. The decision is still considered one of television history's biggest missteps, and signaled the popularity of football.

1970: After a decade in which competition for players between the American Football League and the National Football League drove up players's salaries, the two leagues merge, with the AFL subsumed into the NFL. Many AFL innovations are adopted, including putting names on players's jerseys, gate and broadcast revenue sharing, and the on-field game clock. A special act of Congress is required to exempt the merger from antitrust restrictions.

January 3, 1973: In coordination with a group of investors, 42-year-old shipping magnate George Steinbrenner III purchases the New York Yankees from CBS for $10 million (approximately $50 million in 2008 dollars), capitalizing on a string of unsuccessful seasons for the once-dynastic franchise. In the coming years, the organization's value would grow to more than $1 billion.

1974: Elizabeth Osder becomes the first female to officially play for a Little League Baseball team following a successful lawsuit filed by the National Organization of Women.

January 15, 1978: Super Bowl XII becomes the 10th highest-rated television program of all time, as over 34 million homes (or 47.2 percent of U.S. households) tune in to watch the Dallas Cowboys defeat the Denver Broncos by a score of 27–10.

January 21, 1979: Super Bowl XIII becomes the 11th highest-rated television program of all time, as over 35 million homes (or 47.1 percent of U.S. households) tune in to watch the Pittsburgh Steelers defeat the Dallas Cowboys by a score of 35–31.

September 7, 1979: The Entertainment and Sports Programming Network (ESPN) debuts on cable television, ushering in a new era of 24-hour sports coverage.

January 24, 1982: Super Bowl XVI becomes the fourth highest-rated television program of all time, as 40 million homes tune in to watch the San Francisco 49ers defeat the Cincinnati Bengals 26–21.

January 30, 1983: Super Bowl XVII becomes the 5th highest-rated television program of all time, as over 40 million homes (or 48.6 percent of U.S. households) tune in to watch the Washington Redskins defeat the Miami Dolphins by a score of 27–17.

1984: Coca-Cola spends $30 million to become the official sponsor of the Summer Olympic Games in Los Angeles.

January 22, 1984: Super Bowl XVIII becomes the 13th highest-rated television program of all time, as over 38 million homes (or 46.4 percent of U.S. households) tune in to watch the Los Angeles

Raiders defeat the Washington Redskins by a score of 38–9.

December 21, 1984: Fifty-six-year-old Marge Schott becomes the first woman to purchase a baseball franchise after assuming controlling interest in the Cincinnati Reds for a total of $11 million.

1985: The first edition of Nike's Air Jordan sneaker becomes available. Citing uniform color rules, the NBA bans Michael Jordan from wearing the shoe during games, effectively creating more interest among consumers for the forbidden product.

January 20, 1985: Super Bowl XIX becomes the 14th highest-rated television program of all time, as over 39 million homes (or 46.4 percent of U.S. households) tune in to watch the San Francisco 49ers defeat the Miami Dolphins by a score of 38–16.

January 26, 1986: Super Bowl XX becomes the 7th highest-rated television program of all time, as over 41 million homes (or 48.3 percent of U.S. households) tune in to watch the Chicago Bears defeat the New England Patriots by a score of 46–10.

November 22, 1986: After years in which boxing's heavyweight division was considered to have declined to the point of irrelevance, Mike Tyson is crowned the youngest heavyweight champion in history and goes on to revitalize the sport.

1987: Computer gamemaker Nintendo releases the boxing simulation game *Mike Tyson's Punch-Out!!*, featuring the legendary boxer as the final opponent in the game.

1988: The *John Madden Football* computer game is released for the MS-DOS, Apple II, and Commodore 64 operating systems. Future incarnations would be released on a yearly basis.

1989–2009: The reported average salary for a Major League Baseball player increases from $512,804 to $3,240,000.

April 1989: Leading a group of investors, future President George W. Bush purchases an 86 percent share in the Texas Rangers baseball franchise for $75 million.

December 31, 1989: The video game *Arnold Palmer Tournament Golf* is released for the Sega Genesis video game console.

February 10, 1990: Mike Tyson's dominance of boxing's heavyweight division is prematurely ended by a fluke victory by underdog Buster Douglas in a 10th-round knockout. Douglas's reign lasts a few short months until Evander Holyfield defeats him in a 3rd-round knockout in October.

October 20, 1990: Yankees owner George Steinbrenner hosts the late-night television series *Saturday Night Live*. One sketch playfully mocks Steinbrenner's tendency to wantonly fire his employees as owner of the Yankees, with Steinbrenner's character remarking, "I can't fire people! It's not in my nature!"

1991: The video game *Tecmo Super Bowl* is released for the Nintendo Entertainment System. The game is notable for being one of the first video games to feature a combination of real teams and real players, and not simply facsimiles with fake names.

1991–2008: As moderator of NBC's Sunday morning news program, *Meet the Press*, Tim Russert routinely ends his broadcasts by saying, "Go Bills." On one occasion, Russert went so far as to publicly plead with God that the Bills win the Super Bowl.

October 1, 1993: Following a decade-long period of sustained growth, ESPN launches ESPN2.

1994: As a result of a league-wide work stoppage, Major League Baseball's World Series is cancelled for the first time in 90 years.

September 1994: The National Hockey League (NHL) Board of Governors signs a five-year, $155 million broadcasting deal with the Fox Network.

September 9, 1994: Former Minnesota Twins general manager Andy MacPhail is named president/CEO of the Chicago Cubs.

1996: Nineteen-year-old basketball player Kobe Bryant signs a six-year, $48 million endorsement contract with adidas.

June 1996: Reebok signs basketball superstar Allen Iverson to a 10-year, $50 million endorsement deal.

August 10, 1996: The television show *Arli$$* premieres on HBO, featuring Robert Wuhl as the title character who is employed as a major sports agent.

November 15, 1996: The live-action/animated feature film *Space Jam*, starring basketball superstar Michael Jordan, debuts in theaters to mixed reviews but overwhelming box office interest, grossing $90,443,603 during its theatrical run. The film playfully mocks Jordan's ubiquitous marketing presence, with one character remarking, "C'mon, Michael, it's game time. Slip on your Hanes, lace up your Nikes, take your Wheaties and your Gatorade, and we'll grab a Big Mac on the way to the ballpark."

December 12, 1996: CNN/SI, a 24-hour sports programming network, debuts on cable.

December 13, 1996: The film *Jerry Maguire*, about a fictitious sports agent, opens in theaters to rave reviews. It would go on to gross $273,552,592 worldwide, and Tom Cruise would be nominated for an Oscar for playing the title character.

December 17, 1996: Twenty-one-year-old golfer Tiger Woods is named Sportsman of the Year by *Sports Illustrated*.

January 3, 1997: Reebok sues TriStar Pictures for $110 million for their alleged failure to include a Reebok product placement in the blockbuster film *Jerry Maguire*.

September 1997: Basketball superstar Grant Hill signs a seven-year, $80 million contract with Fila.

1998: George W. Bush sells the Texas Rangers baseball franchise for a total profit of $170 million, a gain that would partly enable him to have the financial means to run for president in 2000.

August 9, 1998: Wayne Gretzky, arguably the greatest hockey player of all time, is traded from the Edmonton Oilers to the Los Angeles Kings. The move draws significant ire from Canadian hockey fans to such an extent that some Canadian politicians call for the government to block the trade.

1999: The video game *Tiger Woods '99*, the first incarnation in the series, is released by EA Sports for the PC and the PlayStation game console. A new version would be released on a yearly basis.

April 20, 1999: Cincinnati Reds owner Marge Schott sells her controlling interest in the franchise for $67 million following a turbulent 15-year management reign. Schott had told reporters, among other controversial remarks, that Adolf Hitler "was good in the beginning, but went too far."

December 1999: Salton, Inc. signs retired boxer George Foreman to a $137.5 million, five-year deal to endorse its line of contact grills.

January 15, 2000: Billionaire entrepreneur Mark Cuban, who sold the Internet site Broadcast.com to Yahoo! for $5.9 billion in Yahoo! stock, purchases the NBA's Dallas Mavericks for $285 million.

January 20, 2000: Retired basketball superstar Michael Jordan signs an agreement to become president of basketball operations for the fledgling Washington Wizards franchise.

September 2000: Tiger Woods signs a five-year, $100 million endorsement deal with Nike.

September 2000: Titleist signs golfer Davis Love III to a 10-year, $50 million endorsement deal.

January 8, 2001: Tennis player Venus Williams signs a five-year, $40 million product-endorsement contract with Reebok, the largest ever for a female athlete.

January 12, 2001: Leading a group of nine investors, Starbucks chief global strategist Howard Schultz purchases the Seattle SuperSonics NBA franchise for a total of $200 million.

January 30, 2001: Invesco signs a 20-year, $120 million deal to secure the naming rights from the Denver Broncos for their new stadium.

February 3, 2001: The XFL debuts with a game featuring the New York/New Jersey Hitmen and the Las Vegas Outlaws.

May 11, 2001: After failing to secure a renewed deal with UPN, the XFL officially folds after a single season of operation.

June 18, 2001: The National Basketball Association cuts ties with Schick after an 18-year deal, the longest in the association's history. Schick was unsatisfied over the NBA's decision to move the Rookie All-Star Game to a daytime slot since Schick had signed deals with many of the league's rookies.

June 19, 2001: Coca-Cola renews its deal with the National Hockey League to become the league's official soft drink for an additional four years.

September 13, 2001: The NFL announces it will postpone all of its games during the coming Sunday, citing the September 11 terrorist attacks as the reason for the postponement.

September 25, 2001: Basketball superstar Michael Jordan comes out of retirement for the second time to play for the Washington Wizards, and pledges to donate his salary to victims of the September 11 terrorist attacks.

November 2001: Adidas unveils its Kobe Two shoe, endorsed by basketball superstar Kobe Bryant.

December 1, 2001: Yankees shortstop Derek Jeter hosts the television show *Saturday Night Live.*

January 17, 2002: After a whirlwind year that saw the propelling of Kurt Warner from Arena Football League afterthought to Super Bowl Most Valuable Player (MVP), the quarterback is named the most marketable NFL athlete by *Sports Business Daily.*

March 2002: Coors Brewing Co. becomes the official beer sponsor of the National Football League, signing a contract worth approximately $300 million over five years.

August 2002–August 2003: Shoe company Nike increases its marketing expenses from $1.09 billion to $1.44 billion, vastly exceeding its main competition, Reebok, which has marketing deals worth a total of $196.3 million.

2003: Tennis superstar Andy Roddick hosts an episode of the late-night television series *Saturday Night Live.*

2003: Soccer player David Beckham, arguably the most popular sports figure worldwide, signs a $160 million lifetime deal with adidas.

2003: Cyclist Lance Armstrong signs endorsement deals with Comcast and Nike.

2004: ESPN publishes its list of the 25 most memorable sports commercials of all time. A Coca-Cola ad featuring "Mean" Joe Greene tossing his jersey to a young fan in exchange for a bottle of Coke is selected as the top commercial of all time.

2004: Despite beauty and charm, Anna Kournikova is ranked as the 18th biggest sports flop in the past 25 years by ESPN.

June 2, 2004: Harris Interactive releases its list of the most popular U.S. Major League Baseball franchises. The New York Yankees are ranked first, followed by the Chicago Cubs, Atlanta Braves, Boston Red Sox, Detroit Tigers, and Philadelphia Phillies.

December 2004: EA Sports signs an exclusive licensing agreement with the National Football League and the National Football League Players Association, making it the only company with the lawful ability to include real teams and players in its Madden football video game series.

January 17, 2005: Quarterback Michael Vick signs the largest contract in NFL history at 10 years and $130 million to play for the Atlanta Falcons. Vicks was also guaranteed an NFL-record $37 million in bonuses.

March 17, 2005: Seven-time all star Mark McG-wire testifies before the House Government Reform Committee about steroid abuse, repeatedly emphasizing under intense questioning about his own use that he is "not here to talk about the past."

April 2005: New York Yankees shortstop Derek Jeter is named the most marketable Major League Baseball player according to a survey conducted by *Sports Business Daily*. Jeter received 345 points in the survey, while his teammate, third baseman Alex Rodriguez, placed second with 181 points.

April 18, 2005: The National Football League announces a major shakeup of its broadcasting partners. ESPN signs an eight-year, $1.1 billion deal to broadcast NFL games on Monday night, while NBC signs a five-year, $600 million deal to broadcast NFL games on Sunday night. ABC, the original broadcaster of Monday Night Football, will no longer broadcast NFL games.

October 2005: Cyclist Lance Armstrong hosts the late-night television series *Saturday Night Live*.

June 1, 2006: Former racer Richard Petty remarks on the state of women drivers in the racecar sport, saying, "I just don't think it's a sport for women."

July 27, 2006: French authorities announce that American cyclist Floyd Landis, the most recent of the Tour de France winners, tested positive for an unusually high T/E ratio, a clear and doubtless indication of illegal doping. The revelation severely weakened Landis's marketing stature.

2007: Football superstar Peyton Manning hosts an episode of the late-night television series *Saturday Night Live*.

March 2007: Golfer Tiger Woods is named the most marketable athlete in the United States by *Sports Business Daily*. Peyton Manning, LeBron James, Derek Jeter, Dwayne Wade, Dale Earnhardt Jr., Tom Brady, Shaquille O'Neal, Maria Sharapova, and Brett Favre round out the top 10 of the list. Michael Jordan is listed as the most marketable athlete retired from sports.

April 24, 2007: Campbell's soup company announces a new marketing campaign called "Mama's Boys," featuring eight NFL players along with their mothers. The list includes LaDainian Tomlinson, Jonathan Vilma, Larry Johnson, Maurice Jones-Drew, DeMarcus Ware, Devin Hester, Todd Heap, and Matt Hasselbeck.

October 30, 2007: Coca-Cola signs New England Patriots quarterback Tom Brady to headline the endorsement of its new product, Smartwater.

December 2007: Basketball superstar LeBron James tops *Forbes*'s annual list of Top 20 Earners Under 25.

December 10, 2007: Quarterback Michael Vick is sentenced to 23 months in prison for his role in an illegal dog-fighting ring, effectively ending almost all of the 27-year-old's endorsement contracts.

December 13, 2007: Major League Baseball third baseman Alex Rodriguez signs a 10-year, $275 million contract, the largest in baseball history.

2008: Olympic gold medalist swimmer Michael Phelps the late-night television series *Saturday Night Live*.

2008: The U.S. sports drink Gatorade expands its presence across the Atlantic by becoming the official sports drink of Chelsea FC.

2008: After winning Super Bowl XLII, New York Giants quarterback Eli Manning signs endorsement deals with Citizen Watch Company, Toyota, and Reebok.

January 30, 2008: British Football Association Chairman David Triesman estimates that the English Premier League is in debt to its creditors by approximately $4.5 billion.

February 11, 2008: CNBC's *SportsBiz* publishes its list of the most popular NFL jerseys in the United States. Tony Romo of the Dallas Cowboys is ranked first, followed by Tom Brady, Brett Favre, Peyton Manning, LaDainian Tomlinson, Adrian Peterson, and Eli Manning.

August 7, 2008: After a 16-year tenure with the Green Bay Packers, quarterback Brett Favre is traded to the New York Jets, sparking a marketing windfall in the nation's largest media market.

September 2008: Despite a massive liquidity crisis, American International Group (AIG) announces it will continue to sponsor English soccer team Manchester United.

November 14, 2008: The NHL releases its list of the top-selling NHL jerseys in the United States, with Sidney Crosby assuming the top rank, followed by Alex Ovechkin, Mike Richards, Henrik Lundqvist, and Evgeni Malkin.

December 16, 2008: The MLB network, Major League Baseball's official channel, debuts.

December 31, 2008: Former basketball superstar Charles Barkley is arrested on DUI (driving under the influence of drugs or alcohol) charges after failing field sobriety tests conducted by police in Scottsdale, Arizona. As a consequence, cell phone company T-Mobile says it will not use Barkley in its advertising promotions for an extended period of time.

2009: Olympic gold medalist Michael Phelps is shown smoking marijuana in a photo published by British tabloid *News of the World*. As a result, cereal company Kellogg's announces it will not renew Phelps's endorsement contract.

January 28, 2009: The NBA releases its list of the best-selling player jerseys in the United States. Kobe Bryant is ranked first, followed by Kevin Garnett, LeBron James, Chris Paul, Allen Iverson, and Paul Gasol.

February 2009: Danica Patrick signs with International Management Group (IMG) for the handling of her marketing management.

July 2009: Seattle Seahawks player T. J. Houshmandzadeh announces he is boycotting the popular Madden NFL video games series because of his video game facsimile having a low overall rating. He re-

marks to an interviewer that he's "not playing Madden no more until they get my rating right," adding, "I used to be the best in the world at Madden."

October 8, 2009: The Harris Poll releases its list of the most popular NFL franchises. The Dallas Cowboys are ranked first, followed by the Pittsburgh Steelers, Chicago Bears, Indianapolis Colts, and New England Patriots.

December 14, 2009: Married professional golfer Tiger Woods is dropped from his endorsement deal with consulting firm Accenture after a series of reports surface detailing extramarital affairs with multiple mistresses. The firm explains in a statement that Woods is "no longer the right representative."

January 2010: Skier Lindsey Vonn signs an endorsement deal with Rolex.

January 2010: Economics professor Chris Knittel releases a study showing that the combined stock market value of companies sponsoring Tiger Woods plummeted by $12 billion in the months following Woods's admission of multiple extramarital affairs.

January 10, 2010: In a tacit endorsement of the Dallas Cowboys, former President George W. Bush appears with owner Jerry Jones during the team's 34–14 playoff victory against the Philadelphia Eagles.

January 11, 2010: Retired slugger Mark McGwire publicly admits to using steroids during the record-breaking season of 1998, during which he recorded 70 home runs.

January 16, 2010: Adidas terminates its endorsement contract with Gilbert Arenas after the basketball player pleads guilty to felony gun possession.

January 18, 2010: The Miami Dolphins announce that they have reached an agreement with Sun Life Financial to be their new naming-rights partner at a cost of $7.5 million annually over five years.

January 30, 2010: The U.S. Justice Department begins a formal inquiry into whether college football's BCS rankings system is a violation of antitrust laws.

February 7, 2010: The New Orleans Saints defeat the Indianapolis Colts 31–17 for their first Super Bowl win in their first Super Bowl appearance.

February 13, 2010: Female racecar driver Danica Patrick makes her nationwide NASCAR debut at a race in Daytona Beach, Florida.

February 14, 2010: The largest crowd in basketball history, 108,713 people, attends the 2010 NBA All-Star Game at Cowboys Stadium in Arlington, Texas. The East defeats the West by a narrow 141–139.

April 6, 2010: The University of Connecticut women's basketball team finishes its second undefeated season by winning the NCAA Division I tournament.

June 22–24, 2010: The longest match in tennis history is played in the first round of the Wimbledon men's tournament, between American 23rd seed John Isner and French qualifier Nicolas Mahut. Over the course of three days, the men play 183 games for 11 hours and 5 minutes of play.

July 13, 2010: George Steinbrenner, owner of the New York Yankees, and one of the most influential owners in baseball history, dies of a heart attack.

September 14, 2010: Football player Reggie Bush forfeits his 2005 Heisman Trophy following an NCAA investigation into his involvement with marketing agents while playing college football at the University of South Carolina.

March 3, 2011: The Collective Bargaining Agreement (CBA) between the NFL owners and the NFL Players Association expires. The owners had voted in 2008 to allow the CBA to expire after the 2010 season, and in the intervening time, no agreement had been reached.

Activation, Sponsorship

Sponsorship is a marketing communication tool that companies use in order to accomplish various business objectives like increasing brand awareness, increasing brand loyalty, reinforcing or changing their brand image, and stimulating product trial and sales. In order to maximize the effect of sponsorships and increase the likelihood that the intended goals will be accomplished, companies usually engage in what is termed *sponsorship activation*. The idea behind activation is that a sponsor puts the sponsorship into action and, consequently, increases the likelihood that the sponsorship will accomplish the intended business objectives. The concept of sponsorship activation is similar to the concept of leveraging a sponsorship, in which case sponsorship is an asset used to increase the impact of other marketing promotions (i.e., as a lever).

Activation assists sponsors in making the fans aware of the partnership between the sponsor and the property, which is an essential early step in order for the sponsor to reap commercial benefits from the partnership. While presenting or title sponsors are likely to be recognized by the fans, this may be more challenging for the other sponsors. Without activation, fans may be unaware of who the official spon-

sors are; research shows that in many cases fans may not have the involvement and motivation to follow who all the sponsors are but even when they do, it may be too difficult for them to do so successfully because of the large number of sponsoring companies partnering with different properties.

Activation of a sponsorship entails all the marketing and promotional activities a sponsor uses that integrate the sponsored property and try to capitalize on the commercial benefits it offers. The more a sponsor engages in such activities to activate the sponsorship, the stronger the potential impact of the sponsorship on consumers becomes. Similarly, the more creative and original the activation activities are, the more likely they are to be remembered by the consumers and influence their behavior. Activation ideas may be included within the sponsorship package that sponsors purchase and are usually an important aspect of sponsorship negotiations. Sponsors often work together with their sponsored properties in developing activation plans; on some occasions properties develop and propose such activation plans to potential or current sponsors as a way to make their sponsorship proposals better tailored to their prospects' needs and therefore more attractive. Sponsors find especially desirable activation ideas that involve a direct interaction between the target consumer and the brand and, ideally, stimulate purchases by consumers and build brand loyalty—key business objectives that sponsors intend to accomplish through their sponsorships.

Sports marketers consider activation important and essential for successful sponsorships and often refer to it as the batteries that make the toy (sponsorship) run. Surveys on sponsors find that several of them place high significance on activation and engage in practices that reflect such an approach. In 2007, sponsors of the National Football League (NFL) spent over $1 billion between the pre-season and the Super Bowl on marketing that activated the NFL sponsorship. Data from the IEG/Performance Research annual sponsorship survey reveal that sponsor spending on activating a sponsorship is on average double the cost of acquiring the sponsorship rights. However, other surveys suggest that some sponsors do not invest enough on sponsorship activation and, as a result, sponsors are criticized for not taking full advantage of the sponsorships they purchase.

Broadcast Sponsorship

Sponsorship activation can take place through various tactics, all of which try to capitalize on establishing a connection with a desirable sports property in order to facilitate accomplishment of the sponsor's business objectives. For those cases when the sponsored event is broadcast on broadcast media, sponsors can activate their sponsorship by purchasing airtime and advertising during the broadcast. Activation is especially likely to be successful when those ads feature themes, wording, and images relating to the event and highlight the sponsor's connection to the event in a sponsorship relationship. Similarly, using athletes or other sports personalities who participate in the sponsored event in ads and airing such ads around the time of the event activates a sponsorship. Acquiring specific athletes as endorsers is not included in the sponsorship fees, and additional money is spent on securing such endorsements. During the 2007 NFL season, about 160 NFL players appeared in ads for NFL sponsors, while certain sponsors used NFL coaches in their ads. A key part of Campbell's activation of its NFL sponsorship was an 11-year-long advertising campaign for its

Chunky brand featuring well-known NFL players in uniform along with their mothers.

All of these marketing activities can be used by sponsors and nonsponsors alike; however, nonsponsors cannot show the athletes in their uniforms in the ads. MasterCard has used NFL quarterback Peyton Manning in its ads, often airing during telecasts of NFL games; however, given that MasterCard was not an official NFL sponsor, Manning did not appear in the ads in his NFL uniform. On the other hand, when Visa, the official credit card sponsor of the NFL, uses NFL players in its ads, it can show them in their uniforms, as it did when running an ad with quarterback Tom Brady (in regular clothes) and his offensive linemen (in their uniforms) protecting him the way Visa protects his transactions.

Becoming a broadcast sponsor of the airing of an event it sponsors can help a company reinforce its connection to that event and increase its ability to reach the fans/viewers as potential consumers. Simply airing a commercial during a broadcast does not constitute broadcast sponsorship; broadcast sponsorship usually involves special recognition during the broadcast (e.g., "this game is brought to you by..." or "the starting lineups are brought to you by...").

Broadcast sponsorship is also not restricted to official sponsors of an event, and sometimes competitors of a sponsor may engage in broadcast sponsorship in order to confuse viewers and minimize the effect of an official sponsor's sponsorship. In that case, companies like Budweiser, which had not been a sponsor of the National Football League for several years, sign a deal as a broadcast sponsor with the networks that show NFL games. Then, when fans watch the games on television, they see the Budweiser logo while hearing the statement "The NFL on CBS is brought to you by Budweiser." Such occurrences are likely to confuse consumers who are not able to distinguish the difference between an official NFL sponsor and a sponsor of NFL games on TV and, in this case, Coors, which was the official beer sponsor of the NFL from 2002 to 2011, would have a more challenging job of reinforcing its connection to the NFL in the audience's mind. Consequently, when official sponsors also sponsor their sponsored event's broadcast and receive that recognition as the event airs, they engage in stronger sponsorship activation with better potential for positive outcomes.

Other Promotions

Another way of activating sponsorship is by running promotions in conjunction with the sponsored event; nonsponsors can run promotions as well but they are limited in regard to what they are allowed to do in contrast to the official sponsors who have more resources available to them. Only sponsors can offer specific promotional prizes associated with the sponsored property (e.g., winning tickets to the Super Bowl for NFL sponsors or participating in a contest during the halftime of a game). Many sponsors benefit greatly from the ability to have tickets to events they sponsor as it allows them to entertain clients and prospects.

Also, only sponsors can use the sponsored property's logos and trademarks in their own promotion materials. Doing so strengthens the connection between sponsor and property in the minds of fans who are the target consumers for the sponsor. For that reason, when a sponsor's activation does not incorporate the trademarks of their sponsored property but a more generic association with the property, which any company could use without needing to secure a sponsorship, their activation is generally considered weak and not fully capitalizing on the available opportunities. In an effort to highlight its sponsorship of the National Football League, IHOP introduced in its menu a football-shaped French toast, which was not a trademark and any competitor could also use.

Given that use of a property's logos and trademarks is only reserved for sponsors and partners of the property who are activating their sponsorships, when nonsponsors try to run promotions to capitalize on a property's popularity, they need to be careful and creative so that they avoid legal problems. Actual use of a property's trademarks would constitute trademark infringement and is not allowed. Therefore, promotions run by sponsors are usually ambush marketing that makes references to the sponsored property without using its official name, which is a protected trademark; for example, Hershey's ran a promotion before the 2005 Super Bowl with the theme "Hershey's vs. Reese's: The Big Showdown." It featured the two star quarter-

backs of the two participating teams, Tom Brady of the New England Patriots and Donovan McNabb of the Philadelphia Eagles, creatively wearing Hershey's and Reese's uniforms rather than their official NFL uniforms.

In several cases, multiple sponsors of the same property design joint promotions that capitalize on collaborative marketing efforts structured around their common sponsored property. Industry experts value such cross-promotional activation efforts as they are usually associated with lower costs for each partner and higher potential for success. Sponsors appreciate properties that generate ideas for cross-promotions among their different partners and that facilitate collaboration among multiple sponsors on marketing ideas. A relatively simple and inexpensive way for properties to accomplish this goal includes hosting sponsor gatherings where representatives from all their different sponsors can convene and meet with each other to exchange ideas for collaborative marketing. Cross-promotions are particularly meaningful when there is a natural fit between the sponsoring companies that join forces. For example, Got Milk? dairy marketing joined a cereal manufacturer to cross-promote around a NASCAR partnership, and Termidor termite protections teamed with St. Lawrence Homes, a home builder, through a co-sponsorship of the Carolina Panthers in the National Hockey League.

For many sponsors, activation takes place during the course of an event at the event's location. Signage is a commonly requested benefit by sponsors given the visibility it offers, and is a quite simple way for sponsors to show their connection to the event. Sometimes, while useful, simple signage may be limited in regard to standing out in the fans minds, especially when there are multiple sponsors and multiple signs. Consequently, sponsors often may activate their sponsorships also by running promotional activities integrated within their sponsored event; both signage and promotional activities at the event are only available to official sponsors. The promotional activities reinforce the connection between sponsor and event in a more active and engaging way for the fans of the event.

Minor league games that usually offer many activities during the course of a game are usually a good fit for this type of activation. For example, the minor league hockey team Sioux Falls Stampede in the USHL has promotional tie-ins with sponsors for in-game activities. Specific ideas used with Sunshine Foods, a local grocery store that is a sponsor, involved "noisemaker nights" where fans would purchase store-branded macaroni and shake the boxes during the game before having the team donate them later to homeless shelters, and a "turkey bowling night" before Thanksgiving, where fans would compete in bowling on ice with frozen turkeys in order to win one from the store. Promotional tie-ins to an event are not limited to minor league sponsors, and some well-known companies build marketing programs around marquee events; Dr Pepper ran a nationwide promotion building up to selecting finalists who would compete in the championship games of two major college football conferences, the ACC and the Big 12, both sponsored by Dr Pepper; the finalists would throw the football at halftime aiming for a hole in an oversized Dr Pepper can replica with the chance of winning big cash prizes depending on their success.

Another way to activate a sponsorship that only sponsors are able to use involves having a presence on the property's Website. Academic research has established that activation online is an effective way to elicit favorable attitudes toward sponsors. Sponsors can take advantage of their presence on the Website of the property as a way to connect with fans of the property who are regular visitors to the site. Moreover, the nature of the online presence can enhance the impact of the sponsorship. The options range from a mere mention of the sponsor's name and/or logo, to a link to the sponsor's Website, to a link for special promotions that appeal to fans and can help boost a sponsor's sales. For example, SunTrust Bank, the official bank of the NFL Atlanta Falcons, had its name and logo on the Falcons' Website along with a link for a special offer that included an Atlanta Falcons credit card and Atlanta Falcons checkbook to any person who would open an account with them. As a sponsor, SunTrust was the only local bank that was allowed to use the team's trademarks, which it did in a way that was likely to induce more customers among the fan base.

A sponsor can also highlight the sponsorship on its own Website along with additional information regarding the partnership and fit between sponsor and property. Prior to the 2010 Winter Olympic Games in Vancouver, the home page for Visa, a worldwide Olympic partner, featured a section that activated the sponsorship by offering a promotion in which fans could win tickets to the Winter Olympic Games for life. Similarly, Emirates, the official airline sponsor of the FIFA World Cup of soccer, highlights a 2010 World Cup all-inclusive package offer on its home page. In addition to the Website, sponsors may make reference to their sponsored property in any marketing material of their own or even other outlets. For example, one way through which UPS activated its involvement with the Olympics was by having the Olympic rings on all of its trucks and, thus, increasing visibility of the association with the Olympics to consumers.

Sponsors can also use point-of-purchase displays that establish a connection to their sponsored properties. Such material can use a team's colors or pictures of personalities associated with the event as a way to attract fans attention. Activation can also be practiced by designing and offering commemorative products that celebrate a team's accomplishments; such products allow the sponsor to capitalize on the psychological attachment fans have toward their favorite teams and are usually in high demand.

Ambush Marketing

Typically, strong activation facilitates great sponsor recall by fans. However, given that activation around an event can be done by both official sponsors and nonsponsors, sometimes the recall is for a company that is not a sponsor but manages to successfully identify with the event because of successful marketing activities around it. While activation of sponsorship helps a sponsor increase the effectiveness of its sponsorship, it provides an additional important benefit: strong activations discourage competitors from ambushing the sponsored property.

Ambush marketing is practiced by companies that are not official sponsors in order to capitalize on an association with a popular property while also minimizing the impact of an official sponsorship by a competitor. Ambush marketing is most likely to be successful in creating confusion among fans regarding who is a sponsor when the official sponsors have spent little money and effort in activating their sponsorship. Many sponsorship professionals point to poor activation as a reason for why a sponsorship may be ambushed. They argue that when sponsors spend time and effort activating their sponsorship, they establish such a strong connection between their brand and the property in the minds of the fans that the fans would be very unlikely to be confused by the ambushing efforts of a competitor and would easily recognize who the official sponsor is despite the ambushing. Being a presenting or title sponsor of an event provides an important benefit toward this goal by reinforcing the connection between the sponsor and the event and minimizing potential confusion that any competitor may try to cause.

Overall, activating a sponsorship is a significant step for helping a company maximize its sponsorship investment. A variety of techniques can be used by the sponsoring companies in order to activate their sponsorships; all of them can reinforce a connection between the sponsor and the sponsored property in the minds of fans/consumers and, consequently, increase the potential of sponsorships accomplishing the business goals the sponsors pursued.

Vassilis Dalakas
California State University, San Marcos

See Also: Advertising; Ambush Marketing, Protection From; Ambush Marketing; Benefits for Sponsors; Cross-Promotions; Objectives, Sponsorship; Official Sponsor; Pre-Event Sponsorship Activities; Promotion; Return on Sponsorship Investment; Sponsorship Failure.

Further Readings

IEG/Performance Research. "Decision-Maker Survey: Sponsors Report Activation Budgets Have Never Been Higher." http://www .sponsorship.com/Extra/IEG-Performance -Research-Study-Highlights-What-Spo.aspx (Accessed January 2011).
Lefton, Terry. "NFL-Themed Sponsor Spending Will Hit Estimated $1.1 B." *SportsBusiness Journal* (September 10, 2007).
Migala, Dan. "What's the Buzz: Activation is the Buzzword Among Marketers. Learn How to Use Activation to Create Marketing Partnerships." *The Migala Report* (June 1, 2004).
Scott, Andrew. "Dr Pepper Reprises $1 Million Football Throw Contest." *Promo Magazine* (September 8, 2006).
SportsBusiness Daily. "Hershey's Runs Promo Around QBs; McNabb Feeling Soup-er." *SportsBusiness Daily* (February 2, 2005).
Weeks, Clinton, Bettina Cornwell, and Judy Drennan. "Leveraging Sponsorships on the Internet: Activation, Congruence, and Articulation." *Psychology and Marketing*, v.25/7 (2008).

Acts of God

Acts of God typically refer to acts of nature outside of human control. These may include floods, tornadoes, cyclones, hurricanes, forest fires, storms, or earthquakes. Acts of God also refers to a legal term used in situations in which no one could be held responsible. Many legal documents use the term *force majeure* (literally "greater force") instead. This concept could be used by a sport organization in defense of negligence. In these cases, the sport organization could not foresee the injury to the plaintiff because of an unforeseeable act of God. In sport management, acts of God may also occur that prevent event and stadium operation from performing as expected.

Sport facility and event managers must prepare for acts of God that are foreseeable. With the increase in natural disasters over recent decades, sport organizations are attempting to prevent disasters and to cope better with potential acts of God by reducing safety and security vulnerabilities. The preparation may include architectural design and construction issues of sport facilities in addition to extensive event operations management. This work will require collaboration with governing bodies in the planning stages.

Legality of Acts of God

Acts of God is a legal term that applies to sport in several situations. This is typically a participant liability issue. A sport organization may defend itself by using the defense of acts of God. As a result, the sport organization is indicating that no liability was foreseeable because of a naturally occurring disaster. The injured party was not injured as the result of the sport organization's negligence. Two conditions must exist for the act of God to be legitimate. The first is that the act of God occurred in relation to the injury, such as an earthquake, a hurricane, or another type of severe storm. Second, the sport organization could not foresee the damage that could occur from the act of God and had no way of taking action to reasonably protect the plaintiff from harm. This may occur with sport law torts or contracts.

Sport Facility Design and Construction

Sport facility design and construction may prepare for acts of God through various means. These would include careful site selection, site layout, and site access. In terms of site selection, sport facility sites must have available transport infrastructure for emergency evacuation. The facility must be in good repair and able to withstand natural disasters. Existing services in times of natural disasters would also be vital to survival. One of the greatest challenges is achieving aesthetically appealing facilities while still staying within facility and governmental regulations for building codes and occupational health and safety. The cost for defending against natural disasters must also be taken into consideration. Innovations in seating, playing surfaces, temperature control, building materials, or scoreboard construction may help in disaster preparedness, and sport facility managers need to be aware of such developments. Some sport facilities with a higher likelihood of acts of God, such as those in hurricane territory or near areas with a higher likelihood of earthquakes or tornadoes, may have special needs.

Sport Event and Facility Operation

The operational side of sport facilities and events must also prepare for acts of God. Sport facility managers should align their operations with regulations for national building standards and sporting federation standards. In addition, standard operating procedures should include planned schedules for repairs and refurbishments. Emergency procedures should be developed and employees should be trained in emergency procedures in case of various acts of God. The evacuation process for a variety of people, including disabled people, youth, and elderly people, must be addressed. The sport event or facility management team must complete careful analysis with potential hazards in mind. Security systems and fire protection systems would be helpful during times of natural disasters. Staff must have access to public announcement systems and other controls for the sport facility, and wireless communication systems can be invaluable. Sign postings and keeping clear paths of traffic flow through the sport facility may also be helpful.

Sport managers must not neglect the legal, structural, organizational, social, and economic steps that can be taken to reduce unnecessary suffering, injury, or death caused by acts of God. Risk may be reduced through various means of innovation, technology, and forecasting. Legal responsibility will fall to sport managers who are negligent in preparing for situations that could cause human suffering.

Lisa M. Miller
Ohio Dominican University

See Also: Assessing Event Risk; Contingency Planning; Control for Safety of Fans/Athletes/Volunteers; Emergencies Athletes/Fans/Volunteers; Foreseeability; Insurance Against Risks; Legal Considerations in Sport; Murphy's Law; Negligence; Risk Management.

Further Readings

Epstein, A. "Sales and Sports Law." *Journal of Legal Aspects of Sports*, v.18/1 (Winter 2008).

Perrow, C. *The Next Catastrophe: Reducing Our Vulnerabilities to Natural, Industrial, and Terrorist Disasters*. Princeton, NJ: Princeton University Press, 2007.

Sharp, L., A. Moorman, and C. Claussen. *Sport Law: A Managerial Approach*. Scottsdale, AZ: Holcomb Hathaway, 2007.

Steinberg, T. *Acts of God: Unnatural History of Natural Disaster in America*, 2nd Ed. Oxford: Oxford University Press, 2006.

Westerbeek, H., A. Smith, P. Turner, P. Emery, C. Green, and L. van Leeuwen. *Managing Sport Facilities and Major Events*. London: Routledge, 2005.

Added Value or Value Add

In an effort to beat the competition, sports marketing professionals seek to make opportunities more enticing and beneficial for consumers. One way they do this is through added value. Added value is the enhancement added to a product or service by a company before it is offered to customers. It is anything that makes the product worth more than the cost, and thus more appealing to the potential buyer. In this way the customer gains some additional advantage without having to pay for it. It can also help an organization differentiate its products from those of competitors, thus making direct price comparisons more difficult for customers while simultaneously increasing profit margins.

In the business realm, added value may come in the form of guarantees, special delivery services, enhanced customer service, pre-established credit plans, attractive packaging and presentation, quality assurance, or 24-hour technical support.

It is imperative that marketing professionals conduct research with their public before determining how to add value. Rather than design a campaign, try to find someone interested in the campaign, and then get as much as possible for it, the marketing professional should identify the target audience, develop a marketing strategy to reach the audience, and then develop a campaign to meet the audience's needs and wants. For example, if fans attend a soccer game because of a halftime show, it would be a waste of resources to organize an autograph night with the team.

For college and professional athletic teams, the product is the sporting event, while the consumers are the spectators, sponsors, and financial supporters at the game. Marketing and public relations professionals have very little to say in terms of the quality of competition. What they can influence, however, is the experience enjoyed by those in attendance. For instance, several Major League Baseball teams renovated their stadiums in the late 1990s and early 2000s. Planners recognized enhancing the fan experience would be an effective way to add value to attending games. The planners determined that amenities such as wider concourses, more concession stands and restrooms, and interactive fan-experience centers were renovations and additions that potentially could make attending games more enjoyable. These enhanced experiences were expected to translate into increased ticket sales. At Kauffman Stadium in Kansas City, Missouri, for example, the Royals saw their average home attendance jump from 19,986 in 2008 to 22,473 following a $250 million renovation project in 2009.

Sports marketing professionals also are frequently involved in collaboration with corporate sponsors, those businesses and organizations that pay to have their name associated with an event. In an effort to provide quality customer service, added value is often provided, not necessarily to enhance the current experience but to foster relations for future endeavors. An example would be to invite sponsors to a special ceremony, such as a hall of fame induction, that is not included in the sponsorship contract. Marketing professionals also may provide team apparel, autographed plaques or balls for display in businesses, or ticket upgrades as a means of demonstrating appreciation and a commitment to current and future relationships.

Athletic organizations also seek to add value to their product through other means. In these instances marketing and public relations work together to develop an integrated marketing campaign that also utilizes the media and advertising. Organizations may play on the "new" by publicizing a new coach and his or her new style of play. They may also focus on a star player's personality or statistics as a means to highlight games. Even opposing players may be publicized as a means of drawing fans. Professionals like Peyton Manning, LeBron James, and Alex Rodriquez are typically fan attractions whether playing at home or on the road.

Stadium renovations and enhancements are an example of adding value. Kauffman Stadium in Kansas City, Missouri, shown above after its $250 million renovation in 2009, experienced an increase in attendance when it reopened.

Other value added strategies include the publicizing of major rivalries. These are especially popular in college football where trophies such as the Little Brown Jug (Michigan-Minnesota), Old Oaken Bucket (Indiana-Purdue), and Centennial Cup (Colorado-Colorado State) are awarded annually. By marketing the game as a unique opportunity, fans gain the psychological advantage, or the added value, of attending an event of even greater magnitude. Special events such as awards ceremonies conducted during pregame, as well as contests and in-game promotions also are fan draws, as are unique halftime shows. These opportunities provide an added value by allowing fans to experience features above and beyond the actual sporting event.

Another major area in which added value is applied is in stadium naming rights. At the turn of the century, stadium naming rights agreements reached record proportions, both in number of

deals and monies involved. One way marketing directors attempt to provide added value benefits is through including the naming partner's name and logo on items beyond the actual structure. These include tickets, facility stationery, concession plates and cups, employee uniforms, athletic courts, and signs on structures surrounding the stadium. And, of course, the naming partner is recognized during broadcasts, on schedules, and on billboards and advertisements announcing events at the stadium. In this way the naming partner is not only recognized on the stadium façade, but also in any other mention or recognition.

Conclusion

Regardless of the form it takes, adding value to events and sponsorships provides advantages to both parties. The fans or sponsors receive more for their money, whether the added value is an experience or tangible item. For the host organization, the added value helps improve relationships and image, thus providing the host with more support in future endeavors.

Joe Moore
University of Central Missouri

See Also: Economic Climate for Sports; Economic Impact Study; Integrated Marketing Communication; Pricing Strategies; Promotional Contests; Promotional Giveaways; Return on Investment; Sponsorship Valuation.

Further Readings

Helitzer, M. *The Dream Job: $port$ Publicity, Promotion, and Marketing*, 3rd Ed. Athens, OH: University Sports Press, 1999.
Irwin, Richard L., William A. Sutton, and Larry M. McCarthy. *Sport Promotion and Sales Management*, 2nd Ed. Champaign, IL: Human Kinetics, 2008.
Parks, J. B., J. Quarterman, and L. Thibault. *Contemporary Sport Management*, 3rd Ed. Champaign, IL: Human Kinetics, 2007.

Advertising

Advertising is traditionally seen as any paid form of nonpersonal presentation and promotion of ideas, goods, or services through mass media such as newspapers, magazines, television, or radio by an identified sponsor. There are many conceptual theories of advertising, but as yet none have emerged to unify practitioners, users, and academics. Technological changes have merely provided advertising with new media vehicles through which to more effectively reach customers, and to increase advertising's interactivity. This has helped to address one of advertising's previous drawbacks as a one-to-many, one-way communication vehicle. In brand communications advertising is a cornerstone of an integrated marketing communications (IMC) strategy.

What Is Advertising?

Advertising is a nonpersonal form of promotion that is delivered through selected media that, under most circumstances, require the marketer to pay for message placement. Advertising has long been viewed as a method of mass promotion in that a single message can reach a large number of people; often termed one-to-many. However, the mass promotion approach presents problems since many of those exposed to an advertising message may not be within the marketer's target market, and thus, it may be an inefficient use of promotional funds. This is changing as new advertising technologies and the emergence of new media outlets offer more options for targeted advertising.

Advertising is one part of the promotional mix, and therefore advertising objectives are set in line with overall promotional and marketing objectives, which in turn should relate to an organization's overall corporate objectives. In general, there are three main categories of advertising objectives a business might set for itself in terms of whether it seeks to persuade, inform, or remind the target audience. This is often referred to as the PIR, or in some cases RIP.

Advertising is unlike direct communication between two people or two groups, which involves a two-way give-and-take experience. Such communications are interactive, with communications being modified and received as a normal part of the process, as per linear communications theory. Advertising has a long history of being considered a one-way form of marketing communication in which the message receiver (i.e., target market) is not in a position to immediately respond to the message (e.g., seek more information); indeed, they can selectively notice, avoid, or reject the message, and remember or forget the experience. The media through which the message is sent may also add contextual distortion or "noise" that further reduces the message receiver's ability to correctly understand the intended message. All of this can confound the best of advertising plans.

To compensate, advertising has sought to increase its effect by making greater use of both rational and emotional devices in traditional media. But with the advent of the Internet and other digital interactive technologies, this too is changing. For example, in the next few years technologies will be readily available to enable a television viewer to click a button to request more details on a product seen on their favorite TV program. Computer chips in smartphones and credit cards will be able to interact with digital outdoor advertising to tailor advertisements to passersby, in-car and smartphone GPS systems will be able to direct advertisements to the user based on geographic location, along the lines of the RFID tracking system used to control logistics. In fact, it is expected that over the next 10 to 20 years advertising will move away from a one-way communication model and become highly interactive.

Another characteristic that may change as advertising evolves is the view that advertising does not stimulate immediate demand for the product advertised. That is, customers cannot quickly purchase a product they see advertised. But as more media outlets allow customers to interact with the messages being delivered the ability of advertising to quickly stimulate demand will improve. This serves to underline the interlocking, symbiotic nature of the elements of marketing. All elements of marketing are interdependent; indeed, this is stressed at the strategic level when considering a business from a value chain perspective where all processes contribute homogeneously to the value created.

Theories of How Advertising Works

The advertising industry has long been challenged to explain how advertising works. Despite there being no real challenge to the fact that it does work, how it works and why it works are critical concerns still unresolved, and discussed regularly by academics, advertisers, and their agencies. The lack of an overall proven theory of advertising effectiveness is a major hindrance to both the planning and design of advertising itself, but also in terms of the strategic planning of the organizations as a whole, for example, response measurement and sales prediction. As yet we have no such theory that manages to unify thoughts on advertising. Rather we have a set of empirical "proofs" that are scattered among numerous companies, agencies, and academics. Many of these proofs are highly contextual and proprietary so as to be of little empirical or academic use in generalizing concepts to advertising as a whole.

As such the possibility for a scientifically derived model of advertising still remains remote.

Despite this difficulty, increasing costs and competitiveness have required advertisers, agencies, and academics to make an effort to comprehensively address how advertising works. Given its central role in most branded B2C and B2B communications, the subject is important, complex, and dynamic. It is important to manufacturers as a marketing expense/brand investment; consider, for example, the valuation companies like Coca-Cola place on their brand, which they chiefly support via advertising campaigns. It is equally important to advertising agencies as a product of their creative energies and as their chief B2B product/service, which drives their own revenue stream. It is complex because communication theories are not unified, and evidence is scarce. Finally, it is dynamic because recent marketplace experience has provoked newer, controversial explanations.

The Strong and Weak Theories

The strong theory of advertising assumes that advertising is capable of effecting a degree of change in the knowledge, attitudes, beliefs, or behavior of target audiences. This theory appears to have been universally adopted as a foundation for commercial activity. The theory holds that advertising can persuade someone to act or to buy a product that he or she has never previously purchased. Furthermore, continual long-run purchase behavior can also be generated. Under the strong theory, advertising is believed to be capable of increasing loyalty or sales at the brand and the product-type levels. These upward shifts are achieved through the use of manipulative and psychological techniques that are deployed against consumers who are passive, possibly because of apathy, and are generally incapable of processing information intelligently.

The weak theory of advertising states that the strong theory does not reflect the real world and believes that a consumer's pattern of brand purchases or actions is driven more by habit than by exposure to advertising. According to the weak theory, advertising is capable of improving people's awareness and knowledge. In contrast to the previous theory, however, consumers are selective in determining which advertisements they observe and only pay attention to those that promote ideas or products that they either use or have some prior knowledge of. This means that in most cases they already have some awareness of the characteristics of the advertised idea or product. It follows that the amount of information actually communicated is limited. Advertising is not potent enough to convert people who hold reasonably strong beliefs that are counter to those portrayed in the advertisement.

Hierarchy of Effects Models

There are many theories to explain the process that goes in the buyer's mind when he or she decides to purchase something. The process is not the same for each buyer, and is sequential.

One of the popular models followed by advertising agencies is called AIDA. AIDA is an acronym that stands for attention, interest, desire, and action. The AIDA model states that an advertising agency should know how to draw the attention of a buyer and to get the customer interested by exhibiting a product's advantages, benefits, and features. Interest is followed by desire. It is the advertising agency's duty to create a desire in a buyer to buy a specific product. All steps of the AIDA model help advertisers stimulate the action toward the purchase of a product.

Another model called DAGMAR has increasingly become more popular and comprehensive than AIDA. The DAGMAR steps are more defined and easier to apply. DAGMAR is an acronym for "defining advertising goals for measured advertising results." According to DAGMAR, a sale must carry a potential customer through four stages: awareness, comprehension, conviction, and action.

After developing product awareness through initial advertisements, comprehension is the second step of DAGMAR. It requires advertisers to address the following questions:

- What is your product about?
- What are product's potential features and benefits?
- What will your customer get from your product? And how?

The next stage is conviction, which is very important. The customer must be convinced of the benefits of the product. After convincing, the next step, action, depends on the customer, not the advertiser.

Push and Pull Strategy

A push strategy involves promoting heavily to members of the distribution channels—the wholesalers, retailers, and agents—and as such it forms a part of B2B marketing. The theory is that having been "pushed" by the producer the distribution channel partners will in turn promote heavily to end consumers via B2C marketing. This approach places great emphasis on personal selling, sales promotions, and volume discounts, in addition to any effects created by a simultaneous customer-facing B2C strategy.

A pull strategy is predicated on heavy levels of promotion to the end users, and the other members of the consumer decision-making unit; it is a B2C communications strategy. This usually involves a heavy emphasis on mass media advertising, which, depending on the distribution of the product/service, may be heavily reliant on traditional advertising via TV, radio and print media. Increasingly, direct and digital marketing is replacing traditional advertising in this role. Most contemporary promotional campaigns contains elements of both push and pull strategies.

Importance

Spending on advertising is huge. One often-quoted statistic by the market research firm ZenithOptimedia estimates that worldwide spending on advertising exceeds $400 billion. This level of spending supports thousands of companies and millions of jobs. In fact, in many countries, most media outlets, such as television, radio, and newspapers, would not be in business without revenue generated through the sale of advertising.

While worldwide advertising is an important contributor to economic growth, the role advertising plays for individual marketing organizations differs. For some organizations, little advertising may be done. Instead, promotional money is spent on other promotion options such as personal selling through a sales team. For some smaller companies advertising may consist of occasional advertisements on a very small scale, such as placing small ads in the classified section of a local newspaper.

But most organizations, large and small, that rely on marketing to create customer interest are engaged in consistent use of advertising to help meet marketing objectives. This includes regularly developing advertising campaigns, which involve a series of decisions for planning, creating, delivering, and evaluating an advertising effort.

Managing Advertising Decisions

Delivering an effective marketing message through advertising requires many different decisions as a marketer develops an advertising campaign. For small campaigns that involve little creative effort, only a few people may handle the bulk of the work. In fact, the Internet has made do-it-yourself advertising an easy-to-manage process and has especially empowered small businesses to manage their advertising decisions. Small firms can handle the creation and placement of advertisements that appear on the Internet, and new services have even made it possible for a single person to create advertisements that run on local television. For instance, a company called SpotRunner allows users to select from a list of high-quality television ads that can be customized and then placed within local cable television programming.

For larger campaigns the skills needed to make sound advertising decisions can be quite varied and may not be easily handled by a single person. While larger companies manage some advertising activities within the company, they are more likely to rely on the assistance of advertising professionals, such as those found at advertising agencies, to help bring their advertising campaign to market.

Types of Advertising

In marketing, "type of advertising" refers to the primary focus of the message being sent, and falls into one of the following four categories: product-oriented advertising, image advertising, advocacy advertising, and public service advertising.

Most advertising spending is directed toward the promotion of a specific good, service or idea, or what is collectively labeled as an organization's product. In most cases the goal of product advertising is to clearly promote a specific product to a targeted audience. Marketers can accomplish this in several ways, from a low-key approach that simply provides basic information about a product (informative advertising), to blatant appeals that try to convince customers to purchase a product (persuasive advertising) that may include direct comparisons between the marketer's product and its competitor's offerings (comparative advertising).

However, sometimes marketers intentionally produce product advertising where the target audience cannot readily see a connection to a specific product. Marketers of new products may follow this "teaser" approach in advance of a new product introduction to prepare the market for the product. For instance, one week before the launch of a new product a marketer may air a television advertisement proclaiming, "After next week the world will never be the same," but do so without any mention of a product or even the company behind the ad. The goal is to create curiosity in the market and interest when the product is launched.

Image advertising is undertaken primarily to enhance an organization's perceived importance to a target market. Image advertising does not focus on specific products as much as it presents what an organization has to offer. In these types of ads, if products are mentioned it is within the context of "what we do" rather than a message touting the benefits of a specific product. Image advertising is often used in situations where an organization needs to educate the targeted audience on some issue. For instance, image advertising may be used in situations where a merger has occurred between two companies and the newly formed company has taken on a new name, or if a company has received recent negative publicity and the company wants to let the market know that they are about much more than this one issue.

Organizations also use advertising to send a message intended to influence a targeted audience. In most cases there is an underlying benefit sought by an organization when it engages in advocacy advertising. For instance, an organization may take a stand on a political issue, which it feels could negatively impact the organization and will target advertisements to voice its position on the issue.

In some countries, not-for-profit organizations are permitted to run advertisements through certain media outlets free of charge if the message contained in the ad concerns an issue viewed as for the "greater good" of society. For instance, ads directed at social causes, such as teenage smoking, illegal drug use, or mental illness may run on television, radio, and other media without cost to organizations sponsoring the advertisement.

Strategy Development

Developing an advertising strategy to achieve the objectives of a campaign requires that consideration be given to both the message that will be communicated and the media through which it will be sent.

An advertising campaign, no matter how much money is spent, no matter what media is used, will only be successful if the message appeals to the target audience. Given the level of advertising that bombards the average consumer, a successful advertising message must stand out among the advertising clutter. Thus marketing professionals are required to be creative, imaginative, and innovative in developing the advertising message, both in terms of what is said, and how it is said. The former is often referred to as the "big idea," and will normally address the key benefits sought by the target audience, motivating the audience to pay attention. Given the constant search for new ways to appeal to target audiences, it is difficult to categorize the content of advertising messages that a business may send.

How things are said is often just as important as what is said. Creating attention-grabbing and memorable advertising is increasingly vital, given the amount of advertising clutter in the marketplace. As with message content, advertising is constantly generating new styles of advertising. Some of the more established message styles are:

- A *personality symbol*. Many businesses will use a character, be it an actual person or animated character, to represent the product or the company.
- *Lifestyle*. Here the advertisement will link the product with a particular lifestyle to which the target audience is thought to aspire. For example, until recently OXO used the "OXO family" gathering around the kitchen table to eat a meal.
- *Musical*. Music can linger in the mind, and many advertisements are built around a song

or piece of music. For example, one of Coca-Cola's most memorable advertising campaigns was the "I'd like to teach the world to sing" commercial.

In addition, the tone of the advertisement will need to be established, which can be either positive or negative. The advert may therefore promote positive feelings of fun, contentment, and happiness or take on a more negative, somber, or even threatening tone.

Unfortunately, the reality of advertising is such that recent research has claimed that even the best planned and executed advertisements may be noticed by less than 50 percent of the audience, and only approximately 30 percent will actually recall the main message of the advertisement.

Trends: Digital Convergence

Like most areas of marketing, advertising is changing rapidly. Some argue that change has affected advertising more than any other marketing function. For instance, while many different media outlets are available for communicating with customers, the ability to distinguish between outlets is becoming more difficult because of the convergence of different media types. In advertising, convergence, and more appropriately digital convergence, refers to a growing trend for using computer technology to deliver media programming and information. Convergence allows one media outlet to take advantage of features and benefits offered through other media outlets. For instance, in many areas around the world television programming is now delivered digitally via cable, telephone, or satellite hookup. This delivery method uses the same principles of information delivery that are used to allow someone to connect the Internet.

The convergence of television and Internet opens many potential opportunities for marketers to target customers in ways not available with traditional television advertising. For example, technology may allow ads delivered to one household to be different than ads delivered to a neighbor's television, even though both households are watching the same program. But convergence is not limited to just television. Many media outlets are experiencing convergence as can be seen with print publications that now have a strong Internet presence. The future holds even more convergence opportunities. These include outdoor billboards that alter displays as cars containing geographic positioning systems (GPS) and other recognizable factors (e.g., GPS tied to satellite radio) pass by or direct mail postcards that carry a different message based on data that matches a household's address with television viewing habits.

Trends: Audience Tracking

The movement to digital convergence provides marketers with the basic resources needed to monitor user activity, namely, digital data. Any media outlet that relies on computer technology to manage the flow of information does so using electronic signals that eventually form computer data. In simple form, electronic data is represented by either an "on" or "off" electronic signal. In computer language this is further represented by two numbers, "0" and "1," and, consequently, is known as digital information. All digital information can be stored and later evaluated. For media outlets delivering information in digital form, the potential exists for greater tracking and matching this with information about the person receiving the digital data.

Tracking does not stop with what is delivered; it also works with information being sent from the customer. For instance, as noted earlier, by clicking on their television screen viewers will soon be able to instantly receive information about products they saw while watching a television show. This activity can be tracked and then used in future marketing efforts.

While media convergence offers marketers more options for tracking response to advertisements, such activity also raises ethical and legal concerns. Many consumers are not pleased to learn their activities are being monitored when they engage a media outlet. Yet consider the following examples of how marketers are tracking users:

- *Television viewing.* As previously noted, the advent of digitally delivered television allows cable, telephone, and satellite providers to track user activity through the set-top boxes connected to a subscriber's television.

Future innovation will make the user television experience even more interactive and, consequently, open to even more tracking.

- *Television recording.* The days of television videotape recording are quickly coming to an end, replaced by recording using computer technology. A digital video recorder (DVR), such as TiVo, can track user recording habits and, based on a viewer's past activity, make suggestions for programs they may want to record. Additionally, advertising services can program the DVR to insert special advertisements within a program targeted to a particular viewer.

- *Internet spyware.* Downloading entertainment from the Internet, such as games, video and software, may contain a hidden surprise—spyware. Spyware is a special program that runs in the background of a user's computer and regularly forwards information over the Internet to the spyware's company. In some cases spyware keeps track of Websites the user has visited. The information is then used to gain an understanding of the user's interests, which then results in delivery of special ads when a user visits a certain site.

Trends: Ad Skipping and Blocking

As noted above, television-recording devices offer marketers tremendous insight into viewing habits and behavior. Yet from the consumer side, the DVR is changing how people view television programs by allowing them to watch programming at a time that is most convenient for them.

Viewer convenience is not the only advantage of the DVR. The other main reason consumers are attracted to the DVR is their ability to quickly skip over commercials. Of course this presents major issues for advertisers who are paying for advertisements. As more DVR devices with ad skipping or even ad blocking features are adopted by mainstream consumers, the advertiser's concern with whether they are getting the best value for their advertising money becomes a bigger issue. Advertisers who feel frustrated with television ad-skipping may opt to invest their promotional funds in other media outlets where consumers are more likely to be exposed to an advertisement.

Trends: Changing Media Choices

There is a major cultural shift occurring in how people use media for entertainment, news, and information. Many traditional media outlets, such as newspapers and major commercial television networks, are seeing their customer base eroded by the emergence of new media outlets. The Internet has become the major driver of this change. In particular, a number of important applications tied to the Internet are creating new media outlets and drawing the attention of many mostly younger consumers. Examples include:

*   *Podcasting audio.* This involves delivering programming via downloadable online audio that can be listened to on music players, such as Apple's iPod. Many news Websites and even other information sites, such as blogs, offer free downloadable audio programming.
*   *Podcasting video.* While audio downloading has been available for some time, the downloading of video to small, handheld devices, including mobile phones, is in its infancy. Many television networks are now experimenting with making their programming available for download, albeit for a fee.
*   *RSS feeds.* This is an Internet information distribution technology that allows for news and content to be delivered instantly to anyone who has signed up for delivery. Clearly those registering for RSS feeds represent a highly targeted market since they requested the content.
*   *Networked gaming.* While gaming systems have been around for some time, gaming systems attached to the Internet for group play are relatively new and becoming more practical as more people move to faster Internet connections. This type of setup will soon allow marketers to insert special content, such as advertising, within game play.

For marketers these new technologies should be monitored closely as they become accepted alternatives to traditional media outlets. While these technologies are currently not major outlets for advertising, they may soon offer more opportunities. As these technologies gain momentum and move into mainstream acceptance marketers may need to consider shifting advertising spending.

Marketers should also be aware that new media outlets will continue to emerge as new applications are developed. The bottom line for marketers is they must stay informed of new developments and understand how their customers are using them in ways that may offer advertising opportunities.

Trends: Changing Budget Methods

Several empirical studies into budget-setting practice have been conducted by academics over the past 20 years, and these have indicated an increasing professionalism in marketing, with advertisers favoring increased use of data-orientated budget-setting techniques compared with earlier studies. It has been particularly noticed that those with larger advertising spends have increasingly favored data methods over judgmental but that judgmental historical review still remains the single most widely

Digital video recording facilitates ad skipping but may also help advertisers target specific consumers with advertising tailored to their interests.

accepted method for setting advertising spend. This is largely driven by a lack of critical review by most organizations at the budgeting stage

Types of Media

The selection of the media outlet through which an ad will be presented has important implications for the success of a promotion. Each outlet possesses unique characteristics, though not all outlets are equally effective for all advertisers. Thus, choosing the right media can be a time-consuming process requiring the marketer to balance the pros and cons of each option.

While just a few years ago marketers needed to be aware of only a few media outlets, today's marketers must be well versed in a wide range of media options. The reason for the growing number of media outlets lies with advances in communication technology, in particular, the Internet. Examples of current advertising media choices include television, radio, print publications, Internet, direct mail, signage, product placement, mobile devices, and sponsorships.

Other Promotional Tools

Advertising is only part of a larger promotional mix that also includes publicity, sales promotion, and personal selling. When developing an advertising budget, the amount spent on these other tools needs to be considered. A promotional mix, like a media mix, is necessary to reach as much of the target audience as possible.

The choice of promotional tools depends on what the business owner is attempting to communicate to the target audience. Public relations–oriented promotions, for instance, may be more effective at building credibility within a community or market than advertising, which many people see as inherently deceptive. Sales promotion allows the business owner to target both the consumer and the retailer, which is often necessary for the business to get its products stocked. Personal selling allows the business owner to get immediate feedback regarding the reception of the business' product, to find out about competitive products and prices, and to quickly identify service and delivery problems.

Andrew J. Whalley
Royal Holloway University of London

See Also: Advertising Cost, Determination of; Advertising Creative Strategy; Advertising Media; Advertising Planning Process; Affiliation Activities; Banner Ads; Brand Awareness; Brand Image; Branding; Complementary Advertising; Complimentary Advertising; Cooperative Advertising; Direct Mail; In-House Agency; Marketing Objective; Media Choice; Online Advertising; Point-of-Sale, Point-of-Purchase Display; Pop-Up Ads; Promotion; Pull Advertising Strategies; Push Advertising Strategies; Specialty Advertising; Tagline; Tattoos as Advertising; Virtual Advertising; Zapping/Zipping.

Further Readings

Bly, Robert W. *Advertising Manager's Handbook.* Upper Saddle River, NJ: Prentice Hall, 1993.

Clark, S. "Do the Two-Step With Advertising Budget." *Memphis Business Journal* (March 3, 2000).

Hackley, C. *Advertising & Promotion: Communicating Brands.* Thousand Oaks, CA: Sage, 2005.

Lavidge, R. and G. Steiner. "A Model for Predictive Measurements of Advertising Effectiveness." *Journal of Marketing* (October 1961).

Ray, M. L. "Marketing Communication and the Hierarchy of Effects." In P. Clarke, ed., *New Models for Mass Communication Research.* Beverly Hills, CA: Sage, 1973.

Advertising Cost, Determination of

Over the past 20 years, interest in how advertising works has fueled debate into what makes advertising effective. The result is a highly technical collection of academic opinion that remains divided in all but one fact—there is no one correct way to set and decide on an advertising budget in terms of either media or resources.

Indeed, this debate has been at the forefront of contemporary issues in marketing measurement or metrics. As such the most common methods for setting advertising budgets revolve around two main approaches:

- Data-oriented approaches comprise competitive parity, objective and task, experimentation, modeling, and simulation.
- Judgment-based methods are arbitrary and include affordability, percentage of sales, reviewing brand objectives, reviewing previous brand budgets, reviewing previous or anticipated advertising effects, reviewing the company's marketing history, and forecasts.

Although advertising budgets are often regarded as a current expense to defend existing sales, part of the budget builds brand equity, thus creating and protecting future sales, as well as reducing the price elasticity of the brand. Thus, the advertising budget should also be considered as a corporate investment—one element among many that contributes to achievement of overall company objectives. This is particularly true when the corporate brand is a significant factor in competitive advantage and/or when the brand equity (goodwill) is a significant entry on the balance sheet. The objective of setting the advertising budget is to grow brands and their associated businesses through more efficient spending; this focus on efficiency has grown more important as branding has become a corporate strategic issue.

In the early 1990s recession meant that budgets were cut and advertisers came under increasing pressure to both maximize and demonstrate the effectiveness of the advertising budget. The proportion of the overall communications budget being spent on immediately measurable activities, such as sales promotion and direct mail, increased at the expense of the advertising budget during this recession. The recent repetition of both economic climate and financial concerns has resulted in further debate about advertising planning and budgeting, particularly surrounding the need to understand returns made on advertising investments and for specific measurable objectives related to more effective marketing.

Factors Influencing Advertising Budgets

Having identified advertising objectives, the advertising budget must be set. Determining exactly how

much a business should spend on advertising to achieve the desired level of sales is more an art than a science. Commonly, the decision is based on past experience of expenditure on advertising, and the sales subsequently achieved. There are, however, a number of factors that may be considered in setting the advertising budget.

New products in the launch stage of their product life cycle will normally require greater expenditures on advertising to create product awareness and encourage consumers to try the product. Products that have reached maturity in their product life cycle will often require smaller advertising budgets to achieve the level of sales required. Advertising budgets are typically highest for a particular product during the introduction stage and gradually decline as the product matures.

The number of competitors in the market, and their expenditure on advertising competing products, will influence a business to spend to a similar or higher degree. Key points to be considered in this area are competition and clutter, and market share. Highly competitive markets require higher advertising budgets just to stay even with competitors. If a company wants to be a leader in an industry, then a substantial advertising budget must be planned every year. Examples abound of companies that spend millions of dollars on advertising in order to be key players in their respective industries, such as Coca-Cola and Microsoft.

Desired market share is also an important factor in establishing an advertising budget. Increasing market share normally requires a large advertising budget because a company's competitors counterattack with their own promotional campaigns. Successfully increasing market share depends on advertisement quality, competitor responses, product demand, and quality.

How customers perceive products is also important to the budget-setting process. Product differentiation is often necessary in competitive markets where customers have a hard time differentiating between products. A classic example is when a new alcoholic drink is advertised. Since so many brands of drinks already exist, which are aggressively promoted already, an equally aggressive advertising campaign is required for the new drink. Without this aggressive advertising, customers would not be aware of the product's availability and how it differs from other products on the market. The advertising budget is higher in order to pay for the additional advertising.

Advertising frequency refers to the number of times an advertisement is repeated during a given time period to promote a product's name, message, and other important information. A larger advertising budget is required in order to achieve a high advertising frequency. Estimates have been put forward that a consumer needs to come in contact with an advertising message nine times before it will be remembered. Frequency is normally stated in terms of the average number of times people are exposed to an advertisement during a set time period.

Reach is the total number of people exposed to a message at least once in a set time period, usually four weeks. (Reach is the broadcast equivalent of circulation, for print advertising.) Usually, when reach goes up, advertisers have to compromise and allow frequency to decline, as it would cost a lot of money to achieve a high reach and a high frequency. The creative part comes in balancing reach, frequency, and budget constraints to find the best combination in view of marketing goals.

Budgeting Methods

Advertising budget setting is a process, not a specific formula or technique; there are numerous ways to set advertising budgets. Broadly speaking, these methods are either data-oriented approaches or judgment-based approaches. There are several allocation methods frequently used in developing a budget. The following are the most common, in descending order of popularity:

- Percentage of sales method
- Competitive parity method
- Objective and task method
- Residual method
- Market share method
- Unit sales method
- All available funds method

In practice these methods are often combined, depending on the business context. A business may use several different methods on a brand-by-brand or product-by-product or even on a by-market basis. As such, these methods should not be seen as rigid or mutually exclusive but rather as building blocks that can be combined, modified, or discarded as necessary.

Because of its simplicity, the percentage of sales method is the most commonly used method, especially by small and medium enterprises (SMEs). In this method an advertiser takes a percentage of either past or anticipated sales and allocates that percentage of the overall budget to advertising. However, the past is not a good indicator of the future, and this often leads to too conservative a budget, which can stunt growth. Further, the entire rationale behind this method is in many opinions backward; advertising is undertaken to support and create sales, and as such spending on it determines the level of sales, whereas this method assumes the reverse.

A further problem with the percentage of sales approach is that the budget is based on what has already happened and not what is expected to occur; this is particularly risky in dynamic competitive markets. However, it might be safer for an SME where the owners feel future returns cannot be safely anticipated. This method can be especially effective if the business compares its sales with those of the competition (if available) when figuring its budget. Note that this hybridization of methods to add robustness to decisions is common.

If the overall market grows rapidly in the following year, the 10 percent level from the previous year may be well below what is necessary for the company to maintain or increase its market share. Alternatively, companies may consider allocating advertising funds based on a percentage of forecasted sales. In this way advertising is viewed as a driver of future sales, and spending on advertising is linked directly to meeting future sales forecasts. However, since future sales are not guaranteed, the actual percentage spent may be considerably higher than expected if the sales forecast is greater than what actually occurs.

It is often useful for a business to compare its advertising spending with that of its competitors. The theory behind the competitive parity method is that if a business is aware of how much its competitors are spending to persuade, inform, and remind (the three general aims of advertising) the consumer of their products and services, then that business can, in order to remain competitive, either spend more, the same, or less on its own advertising. This is related to one metric used in advertising: share of voice. However, where the competition has a different objective this method becomes less relevant to sustaining a competitive position. Also, all it would take is a better-resourced new entrant to the market or better market penetration strategy for a substitute product, and the rationale behind matching existing competition vanishes.

Because of the importance of objectives in business, the objective and task method is considered by many to make the most sense, and is therefore used by most large businesses. With this method, a business needs to first establish concrete marketing objectives, which are often articulated in the "selling proposal," and then develop complementary advertising objectives, which are articulated in the "positioning statement." Both of these will be rooted in sound environmental scanning. After these objectives have been established, the advertiser determines how much it will cost to meet them. Developing such a budget can be a difficult process because brand managers want to receive a large resource allocation to promote their products.

The benefit of the objective and task method is that it allows the advertiser to correlate advertising expenditures to overall marketing objectives ensuring they are congruent. This correlation is important because it keeps spending focused on primary business goals. Before establishing an advertising budget, companies must take into consideration other market factors, such as advertising frequency, competition and clutter, market share, product differentiation, and stage in the product life cycle. Of course, realities in resource terms—liquidity is an issue for SMEs—need to be figured into this. Utilizing this method effectively requires a degree of organization, as follows:

- *Recording a source for every sales inquiry an organization receives.* It is best to determine the source of an inquiry at the very first point of contact. Make it compulsory for anyone taking an inquiry for a product to ask the prospect what prompted their call, and add a compulsory source field to any order/inquiry forms on Websites.

- *Calculate the cost per channel.* If one knows the source of every sale, that is, which promotion the customer came across it in, then one can measure the revenue generated against the cost of that promotion, calculating the cost of sale per channel. It may be that newspaper ads cost less than TV promotions, but the TV ads brought so many sales the advertising cost per sale was less than for the newspaper-related sales.

With this information one can calculate an advertising budget by multiplying the number of sales desired, times the amount needed to invest in advertising in each of the channels that worked—those that worked out with the lowest cost per sale.

The residual method is also called the leftover method. Here, what goes into the advertising budget is simply what is left in the budget after all the other expenditures, from manufacturing to distribution, are accounted for. This method likely wastes money in years of high sales volumes through unnecessary advertising, and then does not allow for enough spending in years of poor sales. It does, however, have the advantage of protecting retained earnings in a poor sales environment.

Similar to competitive parity, the market share method bases its budgeting strategy on external market trends. With this method a business equates its market share with its advertising expenditures. Critics of this method contend that companies that use market share numbers to arrive at an advertising budget are ultimately predicating their advertising on an arbitrary guideline that does not adequately reflect future goals.

The unit sales method simply takes the cost of advertising an individual item and multiplies it by the number of units the advertiser wishes to sell.

The all available funds method is an aggressive method that involves the allocation of all available profits to advertising purposes. Despite the obvious risk of a lack of internal investment, this approach is sometimes useful when a start-up business is trying to increase consumer awareness of its products or services. However, a business using this approach needs to make sure that its advertising strategy is an effective one, and that funds that could help the business expand are not being wasted.

With the affordable method, advertisers base their budgets on what they can afford. Of course, arriving at a conclusion about what a business can afford in the realm of advertising is often a difficult task, one that needs to incorporate overall objectives and goals, competition, presence in the market, unit sales, sales trends, operating costs, and other factors. Therefore, if you cannot forecast these factors with accuracy, this methodology loses its validity. Many smaller companies find spending of any kind to be constraining. In this situation, advertising may be just one of several tightly allocated spending areas and, thus, the level spent on advertising may vary over time. For these companies, advertising may only occur when extra funds are available, so that it is discretionary, which in contemporary competitive markets is fallacious. Using this method has profound implications for an organization's overall competitive strategy.

Companies entering new markets often lack knowledge of how much advertising is needed to achieve their objectives. In cases where the market is not well understood, marketers may rely on their best judgment of what the advertising budget should be, or the best guess method.

Media Plans and Media Costs

The largest category in an advertising budget is likely to be media costs; the money spent for airtime on radio or for ad space in newspapers, magazines, and more. Because of this, it makes sense to have a sound plan to manage that investment, including clear goals and strategies for achieving them. A media plan that begins with an overview and works its way down to the details can help organize the day-to-day tasks of carrying out the strategies while controlling costs.

Media planning is the process of choosing a course of action. Media planners develop yearly plans that list each media outlet, what features are coming up, when new products are being launched, key seasonal buying behaviors of the customer base, and anything else relevant. Planning then gives way to buying, as each separate contract is negotiated, then finalized. Media planning is often undertaken on behalf of an organization by its advertising and/or media agency. The media plan is a document usually made up of the following sections:

- *Media outlets (e.g., newspapers)*. This section lists all of the media in which advertising will be placed.
- *Goals*. This section describes the goals of the advertising, and explains why and how this plan meets these goals.
- *Audience*. This section gathers together information about the target audience, such as statistics on demographics or lifestyle and relevant articles or information about potential buyers.
- *Strategy*. This statement of strategy should be backed up by a rationale. The action steps described here will guide a year's worth of activity.
- *Budget and calendar*. A media plan will outline what money is to be spent where, and when.

When deciding what media to use, a commonly used standard is the CPM—this is the cost of reaching 1,000 people via that specific media. To calculate CPM, first find the cost for an advertisement, then divide it by the total circulation the advertisement reaches (in thousands). Using the CPM allows for a numerical ranking for comparison purposes between media, and it is a key metric in advertising budgeting.

Print advertising prices are based on the circulation of the publication in question. Publications will quote a circulation figure based on paid subscribers. The audited circulation figures are verified by monitoring organizations. Publications will often try to convince advertisers that actual circulation is higher by including the free copies they distribute and the pass-along readership they claim. Some of these have a valid basis; for example, magazines distributed on airlines get at least eight readers per copy. Further, circulation figures need to be compared to the target market demographics for "fit"—reaching millions is of little consequence if they have no use for a product or no discretionary income to purchase it.

Audience is the equivalent of circulation when talking about broadcast media. Audience size varies throughout the day as people tune in and tune out. Therefore, the price for advertising at different times of day will vary, based on the audience size that the day-part delivers. As with circulation, audience figures need to be segmented and assessed for fit. Penetration is related to circulation. Penetration describes how much of the total market available is being reached. In a town with a demographic count of 200,000 households, an advertisement in a coupon book that states a circulation of 140,000 is reaching 70 percent of the possible market; this would be a relatively high penetration. If instead, an advertiser bought an advertisement in a city magazine that goes to only 17,000 subscribers (households), the penetration would be much less, 8.5 percent. What degree of penetration is necessary depends on whether the strategy is to dominate the market or to reach a certain niche within that market. In developing a media plan, one needs to do the following:

- Review marketing objectives through the "lens" of media planning.
- Review the options available.
- Evaluate them against objectives.
- Set minimum and maximum budget constraints.
- Create alternative scenarios until uncovering the strategy that accomplishes objectives within those constraints.
- Develop a schedule describing ad appearances in each medium.
- Summarize a plan in the form of a calendar and a budget.
- Negotiate with media representatives to execute the plan.

Media Scheduling

Once a business decides how much money it can allocate for advertising, it must then decide where it should spend that money. Certainly the options are many, including print media (newspapers, magazines, direct mail), radio, television (ranging from 30-second ads to 30-minute infomercials), and the Internet. The mix of media that is eventually chosen to carry the business' message is really the heart of the advertising strategy.

The target consumer, the product or service being advertised, and cost are the three main factors that dictate what media vehicles are selected. Additional factors may include overall business objectives, de-

sired geographic coverage, and availability (or lack thereof) of media options.

There are three general methods advertisers use to schedule advertising: the continuity, flighting, and massed methods. Continuity scheduling spreads advertising at a steady level over the entire planning period (often by month or year, rarely by week), and is most often used when demand for a product is relatively even. Flighting is used when there are peaks and valleys in product demand. To match this uneven demand a stop-and-go advertising pace is used. Unlike "massed" scheduling, "flighting" continues to advertise over the entire planning period, but at different levels. Another kind of flighting is the pulse method, which is essentially tied to the pulses or quick spurts experienced in otherwise consistent purchasing trends. Massed scheduling places advertising only during specific periods, and is most often used when demand is seasonal, such as at Christmas or Halloween.

Advertising Negotiations and Discounts

No matter what allocation method, media, and campaign strategy advertisers choose, the following are ways small businesses can still make their advertising as cost effective as possible:

- *Mail order discounts*: many magazines will offer significant discounts to businesses that use mail order advertising.
- *Per inquiry deals*: television, radio, and magazines sometimes only charge advertisers for advertisements that actually lead to a response or sale.
- *Frequency discounts*: some media may offer lower rates to businesses that commit to a certain amount of advertising with them.
- *Stand-by rates*: some businesses will buy the right to wait for an opening in a vehicle's broadcasting schedule; this is an option that carries considerable uncertainty, for one never knows when a cancellation or other event will provide them with an opening, but this option often allows advertisers to save between 40 and 50 percent on usual rates.
- *Help if necessary*: under this agreement, a mail order outfit will run an advertiser's ad until that advertiser breaks even.

- *Remnants and regional editions.* Regional advertising space in magazines is often unsold and can, therefore, be purchased at a reduced rate.
- *Barter.* Some businesses may be able to offer products and services in return for reduced advertising rates.
- *Seasonal discounts.* Many media reduce the cost of advertising during certain parts of the year.
- *Spread discounts.* Some magazines or newspapers may be willing to offer lower rates to advertisers who regularly purchase space for large (two- to three-page) advertisements.
- *An in-house agency.* If a business has the expertise, it can develop its own advertising agency and enjoy the discounts that other agencies receive.
- *Cost discounts.* Some media, especially smaller outfits, are willing to offer discounts to those businesses that pay for their advertising in cash.

Of course, small-business owners must resist the temptation to choose an advertising medium only because it is cost effective. In addition to providing a good value, the medium must be able to deliver the advertiser's message to present and potential customers.

Media Agencies and Advertising Costs

There are many types of media agencies that assist with marketing communications, from full-service, multidiscipline agencies to specialist media planning and buying agencies. In the 1980s there were only a handful of media buying agencies that were actually doing well in the consumer advertising–dominated marketplace. With the dawn of Internet advertising in the 1990s and the growing variety of advertising media available, the role of the media buying agency has changed and developed. Such agencies are much more results-led, as clients insist that all campaigns and results are tracked for response, brand awareness, or overall impact in the desired marketplace. If an agency is used it will increase costs, but it should result in lower media purchasing costs, more effective advertising, better planning, and more quantifiable results. A good agency can help professionalize an SME's marketing communications, which may be critical in a new product launch or highly competitive market.

Andrew J. Whalley
Royal Holloway University of London

See Also: Advertising; Advertising Media; Advertising Planning Process; Complementary Advertising; Complimentary Advertising; Cooperative Advertising; Direct Mail; In-House Agency; Media Choice; Online Advertising; Pull Advertising Strategies; Push Advertising Strategies; Specialty Advertising; Virtual Advertising.

Further Readings

Bly, Robert W. *Advertising Manager's Handbook.* Upper Saddle River, NJ: Prentice Hall, 1993.
Clark, S. "Do the Two-Step With Advertising Budget." *Memphis Business Journal* (March 3, 2000).
Hackley, C. *Advertising & Promotion: Communicating Brands.* Thousand Oaks, CA: Sage, 2005.
Rasmussen, Erika. "Big Advertising, Small Budget." *Sales and Marketing Management* (December 1999).

Advertising Cost, Super Bowl

Once a year, millions of people turn to the television with the express intent of viewing commercials, while millions of others also watch the annual sporting event surrounding these commercials: the NFL Super Bowl. Given the increased popularity of the Super Bowl over the past 40 years it is not surprising that the price of one of the limited advertising spots during the event has increased in real price from approximately $300,000 to more than $3 million, and this does not account for the cost of producing the advertisement itself.

Super Bowl I, played in Los Angeles in 1967 between the Green Bay Packers and the Kansas City

Chiefs, was the first championship game of the merged American Football and National Football Leagues. The first Super Bowl was the first and only championship game to be broadcast on two different networks. The cost of a 30-second television spot during the broadcast averaged $40,000 (approximately $248,000 in 2007 dollars). In comparison, for Super Bowl XLIV, played in Miami in 2010 between the New Orleans Saints and the Indianapolis Colts, the price of a 30-second advertisement was $3.1 million ($2.95 million in 2007 dollars).

Why has the price of a 30-second advertisement increased by 1,089 percent over the past 43 years? The primary reason is that during this period the Super Bowl has evolved into the single largest annual television attraction in world (other than the UEFA Champions League Finals in Europe). In 1967, the Super Bowl was watched by approximately 22.5 million people. By 2010, viewership had increased to 106.5 million people, almost one third of the entire U.S. population.

Over the history of the Super Bowl, nominal prices for 30-second ads have increased by roughly 10 percent per annum, with no discernible break in the trend during recessions. The real price of the advertisement spots has increased by roughly 5.7 percent per year during the Super Bowl's history, slightly more than the overall inflation rate during the time period. While nominal prices have continually increased, the real price of advertising during the Super Bowl is a bit more variable; after dramatically increasing in the late 1990s during the dotcom expansion, the real prices stabilized during the early part of the 2000s before dropping slightly and then rebounding in the late 2000s. It is tempting to question how long the price of Super Bowl advertisements can continue to increase. One answer is to look at the relationship between the number of viewers of the Super Bowl and the price of ad spots. Historically, a 1 percent increase in viewership has yielded a 2.5 percent increase in advertisement price, suggesting that as long as the Super Bowl continues to gain in popularity, advertising prices will continue to increase.

Viewership Levels and Price

The increasing price of ad spots is highly correlated with the number of viewers of the Super Bowl,

but is the relationship between viewers and ad spot prices a linear or nonlinear relationship? If the relationship were nonlinear then there might be a tipping point in viewership after which the price of ad spots would be expected to increase dramatically. Why might this occur?

Advertisements during the Super Bowl receive considerably more attention than a similar ad run during any other television event. The public discussion surrounding the advertisements themselves provides a secondary benefit to a firm that purchases ad time during the Super Bowl. If a sufficiently large viewing audience generates increasing returns to the advertisement then the price of ad spots would be expected to reflect this nonlinearity. The relationship between price and viewership is linear and relatively flat when viewership is less than approximately 75 million people. In other words, the impact of additional viewers on the value of the ad spot is relatively constant at lower viewership levels. However, when viewership exceeds approximately 75 million people, the relationship between price and viewership changes and becomes considerably steeper. In other words, additional viewers beyond the 75-million-viewer threshold are worth more, on the margin, than viewers under the threshold.

If the Super Bowl were to attract considerably fewer people than in the recent past such that viewership fell below the threshold, we would expect the price of advertisements to fall accordingly. On the other hand, as long as viewership levels are beyond the threshold, the price of advertisement spots is expected to stay high and increase that much more on the margin if viewership increases.

Conclusion

While the real and nominal price of advertisement space has increased dramatically over the past 43 years and there seems to be a strong relationship between viewership and price, it is helpful to measure the price of advertising not in terms of time but in terms of people exposed. Making the strong assumption that all individuals watching the Super Bowl also watch the advertisements, the price of advertisements per 1,000 viewers has increased less dramatically than the nominal or real price measured in time. As viewership has increased for the Super Bowl and the consumption patterns of the population have changed, the mix of firms who purchase advertisements on the Super Bowl has likewise changed. In 1967, firms spent approximately $4.85 to reach 1,000 potential clients. In 2010, firms paid $27.74 to reach 1,000 potential clients. The increase in per-capita income and changes in consumption patterns encourage firms to spend more to reach the same number of potential customers. It remains to be seen whether consumption patterns after the Great Recession change sufficiently enough so that firms are not willing to spend as much to reach potential consumers. If this is the case, the price of ad spots during the Super Bowl would be expected to fall.

Craig A. Depken II
University of North Carolina, Charlotte

See Also: Advertising Cost, Determination of; Audience Measurement; Cost per Thousand; National Football League; Super Bowl.

Further Readings

MacCambridge, Michael. *America's Game: The Epic Story of How Pro Football Captured a Nation.* New York: Random House, 2004.

Oriard, M. *Brand NFL: Making and Selling America's Favorite Sport.* Chapel Hill: University of North Carolina Press, 2007.

St. John, A. *The Billion Dollar Game: Behind the Scenes of the Greatest Day in American Sport—Super Bowl Sunday.* New York: Vintage/Anchor, 2010.

Weiss, Don and Chuck Day. *The Making of the Super Bowl: The Inside Story of the World's Greatest Sporting Event.* Chicago: Contemporary Books, 2003.

Advertising Creative Strategy

Creative strategy in advertising involves creating a relevant connection between an organization or brand and its target audience in an unexpected way while delivering a sales message. Creative strategies are used in order to acquire consumer attention and encourage purchase or use of a specific product. In advertising, creative strategy is the phase in which marketers decide what is important to say within the campaign. This phase comes after research, and before the decision about how to convey this message to consumers.

The term *strategy* is a derivative of *strategos*, a Greek word used to describe a high-ranking military officer. While the concept of strategy (as we study it today) has evolved from these early roots it nonetheless still entails skill acquisition necessary to fight and ultimately conquer an enemy. The author John Lyons describes advertising strategy as "a carefully designed plan to murder the competition." Through advertising strategy, sport marketers strive to outmaneuver their competition in the battle for consumer discretionary income. The strategic plan serves as a guide for the creative team as they strive to find unique and powerful ways to communicate with the target market. The strategy determines what needs to be said to whom in the campaign, and then creative strategies construct optimal ways to say it.

While there are many in-depth approaches to strategy, John O'Toole, former president of the American Association of Advertising Agencies, introduced the following three-point approach to strategy that covers the most important elements to keep in mind while determining what is important to say in an advertising campaign:

- *Who or what is the competition?* In order to understand what needs to be said within an advertising campaign, it is important to audit all messages and opportunities the target audience is currently experiencing. As you strive to build your organization's brand, understanding the competition and their methods is critical to building an appropriate strategy. Sources of competition may be direct—as in a rival team, or a rival sporting organization within the vicinity; or indirect—such as another entertainment option vying for your consumer's discretionary time and income.

- *Who are you talking to?* Are you hoping to communicate with your season ticket holders, attract fans from a rival institution, interest individuals in the community who have never been to a game, or increase consumption in families within a 30-mile radius with household incomes over $75,000 who attended one to three games last season? Often strategy statements include delimiters including demographics—sex, age, income, marital status, ZIP code, and so on; psychographics—fan identity, values, lifestyle, social motives, and so on; or behavioral elements—consumption habits, information-gathering; price-sensitivity, and so on. These all can be effective methods to segment and select your target market; however, it is important to note that there is strong variability in each category when only one or two delimiters are utilized. The author Jon Steel, who has described demographic information as a "skeleton" and lifestyles and values as the "body and soul," uses an example reminding us that "men aged 35 and over with large household incomes" might include individuals like Barack Obama, Michael Jordan, Donald Trump, Bob Dole, Billy Graham, and a number of criminals. Depending on the scope and purpose of the marketing strategy, several advertising campaigns may be necessary to reach different consumer segments.

- *What do you want them to know, understand, and feel?* In this element of the strategy, we must strive to explore how the brand enhances one of the basic human needs. The DDB Needham agency utilizes in-use rewards, results-of-use rewards, and incidental-to-use rewards to help define the emotional and rational underpinnings of a campaign strategy. For an intercollegiate athletic wrestling campaign, for instance, we may explore the specific incidental-to-use rewards we are hoping to touch through the campaign as follows: provides low-cost entertainment (practical), offers a unique and exciting atmosphere (sensory), facilitates meeting new people (social), and makes you feel good for supporting a nonrevenue sport that has experienced a decline in programs throughout the last decade (ego satisfaction). Based on this analysis, these emotional attributes can be judged

according to the importance of a specific segment targeted within the campaign. Which benefits, for example, might be most important to families in your community?

Often, the elements of the strategy are put together in a creative brief to guide the creative team while maintaining a strategic marketing approach to the advertisement. The brief may contain research in addition to a number of informational elements to include or not to include in the advertisement, but at minimum a brief should include the purpose of the ad as well as the profile of the target audience. The purpose of the brief is to clearly outline the communication objectives of the campaign so the creative process will be maximized.

The strategy and message of an advertisement are important, but how the message is delivered can determine whether it piques consumer interest and prompts consumption behaviors. In order for this to occur, an ad must create a relevant connection between a sport organization or brand and the intended message recipient. The method to create this connection is often through creative strategy. Creative strategy in advertising involves an element of the unexpected. Scholars A. Jerome Jewler and Bonnie L. Drewniany describe the creative strategy process as "identifying the advertising problem, gathering the facts, and—through a process of critical and creative thinking—adding your own insights to create a memorable ad that not only commands attention but also delivers the right message to the right audience in a language they understand and accept."

Sales Message

Central to creative strategy is the sales message. An all-too-common pitfall for advertisers is to become so wrapped up in delivery that the message is hidden or lost. Often used elements that create an element of unexpected draw for consumers include humor, celebrity endorsements, and advertising trade characters. Each of these methods have benefits and potential pitfalls.

A wise practice is to view the ad and determine whether the element of entertainment has fused with the message, or whether the message has been overshadowed by the entertainment. Drawing consumer attention is important, but some of the most popular commercials and advertisements have been tremendous failures in terms of sales. Just as strategy served as a compass in the creation of the message delivery, it also can serve as an evaluation tool: how is the purpose of the message integrated with the creative delivery? Is the message sustained or is the entertainment a detractor from the central message?

Creative Process

The creative process—the method of coming up with the big idea—begins with thoroughly defining the strategy and purpose of the advertisement. The creative process has been explored through much scholarly research, and most methods are founded on the work of Graham Wallas, who presented one of the first models of the creative process in his 1926 *Art of Thought*. An adaptation of this creativity process model based on the later work of James Young will be presented here.

- *Immersion.* Seek as much information as possible about the subject, problem, and/or strategy. Conduct research, interview clients or brand managers, examine prior research, and review previous marketing efforts. Emphasizing the importance of research, advertising guru Ed McCabe shares, "When you are ready to write, it should be automatic, fueled by knowledge so comprehensive that advertising almost writes itself. Only with absolute knowledge of a subject can you hope to transcend the banality of mere facts and experience the freedom of insight."
- *Digestion.* Absorb the information that you immersed yourself in. Experiment with ideas, view the data from multiple angles, brainstorm, surround yourself with items that facilitate creativity, doodle, stretch your mind for ideas.
- *Incubation.* Separate yourself from the subject matter. Take a walk, go for a drive, play a game of tennis, get a massage, see a movie, and relax your mind in order to allow the ideas to sink in and grow.
- *Illumination.* After your mind has a chance to relax and incubate, the pieces of the puzzle will work together and ultimately will click. When this happens, the big idea will arrive.

- *Reality testing.* Compare your breakthrough to the strategy, making sure it captures the essence of the strategic message. Test the message, seek feedback, scrutinize it, and modify.

Creative advertising strategy in the sport industry has become prevalent in the increasingly competitive marketplace. It is common to see campaigns centered on health, emotion, fear, sex, or pleasure appeals. In the recession of the late 2000s and early 2010s, many sport organizations have turned toward creative advertising strategies in an effort to save money—searching for methods to promote their brands through more cost-effective mediums. Paramount to this effort has been a surge in the use of social media, e-mail snowballs, and online avenues of communication. As the industrial landscape grows additionally competitive, a proliferation of creative strategies to draw the consumer will undoubtedly increase.

Erianne A. Weight
Bowling Green State University

See Also: Advertising; Advertising Cost, Determination of; Advertising Media; Advertising Planning Process; Brand Awareness; Brand Image; Branding; In-House Agency; Media Choice; Online Advertising; Pop-Up Ads; Promotion; Pull Advertising Strategies; Push Advertising Strategies; Specialty Advertising; Tagline; Virtual Advertising.

Further Readings

Berger, W. *Advertising Today.* London: Phaidon Press, 2001.

Jewler, J.A. and B.L. Drewniany. *Creative Strategy in Advertising.* Belmont, CA: Thomson Wadsworth, 2005.

Lyons, John. *Guts: Advertising From the Inside Out.* New York: AMACOM, 1987.

Porter, M. *Competitive Strategy,* Rev. Ed. New York: The Free Press, 1998.

Steel, J. *Truth, Lies & Advertising: The Art of Account Planning.* New York: The Free Press, 1998.

Young, J. *A Technique for Producing Ideas.* New York: McGraw-Hill, 2003.

Advertising Media

The selection of the media outlet through which an advertisement will be presented has important implications for the success of a promotion. Each outlet possesses unique characteristics, and not all outlets are equally effective for all advertisers. Thus, choosing the right media can be a time-consuming process requiring the marketer to balance the pros and cons of each option.

While just a few years ago marketers needed to be aware of only a few media outlets, today's marketers must be well-versed in a wide range of media options. Advances in communication technology, and in particular the Internet, have created a growing number of media outlets. The pace of these changes means that marketers are well advised to continually monitor changes occurring within each media outlet. In this entry we provide an overview of the following advertising media: television, radio, print publications, Internet, direct mail, signage, product placement, mobile devices, sponsorships, and other media outlets.

Television

Television advertising offers the benefit of reaching large audiences in a single exposure. Yet because it is a mass medium capable of being seen by nearly anyone, television lacks the ability to deliver an advertisement to highly targeted customers compared to other media outlets. Television networks are attempting to improve their targeting efforts. In particular, networks operating in the pay-to-access arena, such as those with channels on cable and satellite television, are introducing more narrowly themed programming (i.e., TV shows geared to specific interest groups) designed to appeal to selective audiences. However, television remains an option that is best for products that are targeted to a broad market.

The geographic scope of television advertising ranges from advertising within a localized geographic area using fee-based services, such as cable and fiber optic services, to national coverage using broadcast programming.

Television advertising, once viewed as the pillar of advertising media outlets, is facing numerous challenges from alternative media (e.g., the Internet) and the invasion of technology devices, such as digital video recorders, that have empowered customers to be more selective about the advertisements they view. Additionally, television lacks effective response tracking, which has led many marketers to investigate other media that offer stronger tracking options.

Radio

Promotion through radio has been a viable advertising option for over 80 years. Radio advertising is mostly local to the broadcast range of a radio station. However, at least three options exist that offer national and potentially international coverage. First, in many countries there are radio networks that use many geographically distinct stations to broadcast simultaneously. In the United States such networks as Disney (children's programming) and ESPN (sports programming) broadcast nationally either through a group of company-owned stations or through a syndication arrangement (i.e., business agreement) with partner stations. Second, within the past few years the emergence of radio programming delivered via satellite has become an option for national advertising. Finally, the potential for national and international advertising may become more attractive as radio stations allow their signals to be broadcast over the Internet.

In many ways radio suffers the same problems as television, namely, it is also a mass medium that is not highly targeted and offers little opportunity to track responses. But unlike television, radio presents the additional disadvantage of limiting advertisers to audio-only advertising. For some products advertising without visual support is not effective.

Print Publications

Print publications such as magazines, newspapers and special issue publications offer advertising opportunities at all geographic levels. Magazines, especially those that target specific niche or specialized interest areas, are more narrowly targeted compared to broadcast media. Additionally, magazines offer the option of allowing marketers to present their message using high-quality imagery (e.g., full color) and can also offer touch and scent experiences (e.g., perfume). Newspapers have also incorporated color advertisements, though their main advantage rests with their ability to target local markets. Special issue publications can offer very selective targeting since these often focus on extremely narrow topics (e.g., auto buying guides, tour guides, college and university ratings).

Internet

The fastest growing media outlet for advertising is the Internet. Compared to spending in other media, the rate of spending for Internet advertising is experiencing tremendous growth and in the United States trails only newspaper and television advertising in terms of total spending. Internet advertising's influence continues to expand, and each year more major marketers shift a larger portion of their promotional budget to this medium. Two key reasons for this shift rest with the Internet's ability to: (1) narrowly target an advertising message and (2) track user response to the advertiser's message.

The Internet offers many advertising options with messages delivered through Websites or by e-mail. Website advertising, which is tied to a user's visit to a site, accounts for the largest spending on Internet advertising. For marketers, Website advertising offers many options in terms of:

- *Creative types.* Internet advertising allows for a large variety of creative types including text-only, image-only, multimedia (e.g., video), and advanced interactive (e.g., advertisements in the form of online games).
- *Size.* In addition to a large number of creative types, Internet advertisements can be delivered in a number of different sizes (measured in screen pixels) ranging from full screen to small square ads that are only a few pixels in size. The most popular Internet ad sizes include banner ads (468 x 60 pixels), leaderboard (728 x 90 pixels), and skyscraper (160 x 600 pixels).
- *Placement.* The delivery of an Internet advertisement can occur in many ways including fixed placement in a certain Website location (e.g., top of page), processed placement where the ad is delivered based on user characteristics (e.g., entry of words in a search box, recognition of user via Internet tracking cookies), or on a separate Webpage where the user

may not see the ad until the reader leaves a site or closes the browser (e.g., pop-under).
- *Delivery.* When it comes to placing advertisements on Websites, marketers can, in some cases, negotiate with Websites directly to place an ad on the site or marketers can place ads via a third-party advertising network that has agreements to place ads on a large number of partner Websites.

Using e-mail to deliver an advertisement affords marketers the advantage of low distribution cost and potentially high reach. In situations where the marketer possesses a highly targeted list, response rates to e-mail advertisements may be quite high. This is especially true if those on the list have agreed to receive e-mail, a process known as "opt-in" marketing. E-mail advertisement can take the form of a regular e-mail message or be presented within the context of more detailed content, such as an electronic newsletter. Delivery to a user's e-mail address can be viewed as either plain text or can look more like a Website using Web coding (i.e., HTML). However, as most people are aware, there is a significant downside to e-mail advertising because of highly publicized issues related to abuse (i.e., spam).

Direct Mail

This method of advertising uses postal and other delivery services to ship advertising materials, including postcards, letters, brochures, catalogues, and flyers, to a physical address of targeted customers. Direct mail is most effective when it is designed in a way that makes it appear to be special to the customer. For instance, a marketer using direct mail can personalize mailings by including a message recipient's name on the address label or by inserting his or her name within the content of the marketer's message.

Direct mail can be a very cost-effective method of advertising, especially if mailings contain printed material. This is because of cost advantages obtained by printing in high volume, since the majority of printing costs are realized when a printing machine is initially set up to run a print job and not because of the quantity of material printed. Consequently, the total cost of printing 50,000 postcards is only slightly higher than printing 20,000 postcards, but when the total cost is divided by the number of cards

This billboard seen in Times Square in New York in 2009 featured New York Giants running back Brandon Jacobs as part of a campaign for Under Armour cold weather apparel.

printed the cost per card drops dramatically as more pieces are printed. Obviously there are other costs involved in direct mail, primarily postage expense.

While direct mail can be seen as offering the benefit of a low cost per contact, the actual cost per impression can be quite high as large numbers of customers may discard the mailing before reading. This has led many to refer to direct mail as "junk mail," and because of the name some marketers view the approach as ineffective. However, direct mail, when well targeted, can be an extremely effective promotional tool.

Signage and Billboards

The use of signs to communicate a marketer's message places advertising in geographically identified areas in order to capture customer attention. The most obvious method of using signs is through billboards, which are generally located in high-traffic areas. Outdoor billboards come in many sizes, though the most well-known are large structures located

near transportation points intending to attract the interest of people traveling on roads or public transportation. Indoor billboards are often smaller than outdoor billboards and are designed to attract the attention of foot traffic (i.e., those moving past the sign). For example, smaller signage in airports, train terminals, and large commercial office space fit this category. While billboards are the most obvious example of signage advertising, there are many other forms of signage advertising including the following:

- Sky writing, where airplanes use special chemicals in their exhaust to form words
- Plane banners, where large signs are pulled behind an airplane
- Mobile billboards, where signs are placed on vehicles, such as buses and cars, or even carried by people
- Plastic bags used to protect newspapers delivered to homes
- Advertisements attached to grocery carts

Product Placement

Product placement is an advertising approach that intentionally inserts products into entertainment programs such as movies, TV programs, and video games. Placement can take several forms including the following:

- Visual imagery in which the product appears within the entertainment program
- Actual product use by an actor in the program
- Words spoken by an actor that include the product name

Product placement is gaining acceptance among a growing number of marketers for two main reasons. First, in most cases the placement is subtle so as not to divert significant attention from the main content of the program or media outlet. This approach may lead the audience to believe the product was selected for inclusion by program producers and not by the marketer. This may heighten the credibility of the product in the minds of the audience since their perception, whether accurate or not, is that the product was selected by an unbiased third party. Second, entertainment programming, such as television, is converging with other media, particularly the Internet. In the future a viewer of a television program may be able to easily request information for products that appear in a program by simply pointing to the product on the screen. With the information, a viewer may have the option to purchase the product. As this technology emerges it is expected that product placement opportunities will become a powerful promotional option for many marketers.

Mobile Devices

Handheld devices, such as mobile phones, personal digital assistants (PDAs), smartphones, and other wireless devices, make up the growing mobile device market. Such devices allow customers to stay informed, gather information, and communicate with others without being tied to any one physical location. While the mobile device market is only beginning to become a viable advertising medium, it may soon offer significant opportunity for marketers to reach customers at any time and in any place.

Also, with geographic positioning features included in newer mobile devices, the medium has the potential to provide marketers with the ability to target customers based on their geographic location. Currently, the most popular advertising delivery method to mobile devices is through plain text messaging; however, over the next few years multimedia advertisements are expected to become the dominant message format.

Sponsorship

A subtle method of advertising is an approach in which marketers pay, or offer resources and services for the purpose of being seen as a supporter of an organization's event, program, or product offering. Sponsorships are intended not to be viewed as blatant advertisements, and in this way may be appealing for marketers looking to establish credibility with a particular target market. However, many sponsorship options lack the ability to tie spending directly to customer response. Additionally, the visibility of the sponsorship may be limited to relatively small mentions, especially if the marketer is sharing sponsorship with many other organizations.

Other Media

While the nine media outlets discussed above represent the overwhelming majority of advertising methods, there are several more including advertising using telephone recordings (e.g., a political candidate's messages); advertising via fax machine (though there may be certain legal issues with this method); advertising through inserted material in product packaging (e.g., inside credit card bill); or advertising imprinted on retail receipts (e.g., from a grocery store, cash machine, or car park).

Andrew J. Whalley
Royal Holloway University of London

See Also: Advertising; Advertising Cost, Determination of; Advertising Creative Strategy; Advertising Planning Process; Banner Ads; Billboard Rules; Complementary Advertising; Complimentary Advertising; Cooperative Advertising; Direct Mail; Media Choice; Online Advertising; Point-of-Sale, Point-of-Purchase Display; Pop-Up Ads; Promotion; Pull Advertising Strategies; Push Advertising Strategies; Signage; Specialty Advertising; Sponsorship; Sports Networks; Sports Networks, Regional; Sports

Radio; Subscription-Based Broadcasting; Tattoos as Advertising; Televised Sports; Virtual Advertising; Webcasts.

Further Readings

Bly, Robert W. *Advertising Manager's Handbook.* Upper Saddle River, NJ: Prentice Hall, 1993.

Fill, C. *Marketing Communications: Interactivity, Communities and Content,* 5th Ed. Upper Saddle River, NJ: Pearson Education Limited, 2009.

Hackley, C. *Advertising & Promotion: Communicating Brands.* Thousand Oaks, CA: Sage, 2005.

Stuart, B. E., M. S. Sarow, and L. Stuart. *Integrated Business Communications in a Global Marketplace.* Hoboken, NJ: John Wiley & Sons, 2007.

Advertising Planning Process

Advertising planning follows on from the development of a formal marketing plan in which segmentation, targeting, and positioning are developed, and sets out the marketing communication objectives to be achieved by advertising, usually within a campaign structure. A successful advertising campaign requires a number of important decisions within a formal planning process including setting the advertising objective and budget, selecting media for message delivery and creating a message, and evaluating campaign results.

Advertising is used to remind, inform, and persuade (RIP) the target market of a business and/or its products and services. These factors directly link into the objectives of advertising, which will usually be along the lines of building product awareness, creating interest, providing information, stimulating demand, and reinforcing the brand. There are many ways to decide and set an advertising budget; all have advantages and disadvantages that make the choice of method a contextual management decision.

Selecting the Media

Before effort is placed in developing a message the organization must first determine which media outlets will be used to deliver its message, since the choice of media outlets guides the type of message that can be created and how frequently the message will be delivered.

An advertising message can be delivered via a large number of media outlets. These range from traditional outlets such as print publications, radio, and television to newly emerging outlets, such as the Internet and mobile devices. However, each media outlet possesses different characteristics and, thus, offers marketers different advantages and disadvantages.

The characteristics by which different media outlets can be assessed include the following seven factors: creative options, creative cost, market reach of media, message placement cost, length of exposure, advertising clutter, and response tracking.

Market reach can be measured along two dimensions, channels served and geographic scope. Channels served relates to whether a media outlet is effective in reaching the members within the marketer's channel of distribution. Channels can be classified as: consumer channel (does the media outlet reach the final consumer market targeted by the marketer?); trade channel (does the media outlet reach a marketer's channel partners who help distribute their product?); and business-to-business (does the media outlet reach customers in the business market targeted by the marketer?).

Geographic scope refers to the geographic breadth of the channels served and includes international (does the media outlet have multi-country distribution?); national (does the media outlet cover an entire country?); regional (does the media outlet have distribution across multiple geographic regions such as counties, states, provinces, territories, etc.?); local (does the media outlet primarily serve a limited geographic area?); individual (does the media outlet offer individual customer targeting?).

Message placement costs vary greatly by the media being used but in general the planning process considers three main factors: audience size, audience type, and characteristics of the advertisement that create ad rate differences, such as run time (e.g., length of television or radio ads), size (e.g., print ads size, billboard size), print style (e.g., black-and-white versus color), and location in media (e.g., back magazine cover versus inside pages).

Length of exposure is largely geared toward what is being advertised. Simple products require customers to only be minimally exposed to the advertisement to build interest and gain attention. Complicated products require longer exposure for customers to fully understand the product. Consequently, advertisers of these products will seek media formats that allot more time to deliver the message. Magazines and other publications (including the Internet) provide opportunities for longer exposure times since these media types can be retained by the audience. Conversely, exposure on television and radio are generally limited to the time the advertisement was broadcast.

Advertising clutter occurs because commercial media attempt to maximize the revenue they gain from advertising, leading to a multiplicity of messages. Such clutter can be in part overcome by increasing the frequency of advertising or by selecting less busy media or timings. Care must be taken, however, to ensure that the scheduling and timing of advertisements are matched to the target audience irrespective of clutter.

Response tracking is now less used in media selection as almost all media have some form of response tracking system.

Creating the Message

With an objective and a budget in place, the advertising campaign will next need to focus on developing the message. To achieve one or more of the objectives listed in the section above, advertising is used to send a message containing information about some element of the marketer's offerings. For example:

- *Message about product.* Details about the product play a prominent role in advertising for new and existing products. In fact, a very large percentage of product-oriented advertising includes some mention of features and benefits offered by the marketer's product. Advertising can be used to inform customers of changes that take place in existing products.
- *Message about price.* Companies that regularly engage in price adjustments, such as

running short-term sales, can use advertising to let the market know of price reductions. Alternatively, advertising can be used to encourage customers to purchase now before a scheduled price increase takes place.

- *Message about other promotions.* Advertising often works hand in hand with other promotional mix items. This may be especially effective for a company entering a new market where advertising may help reduce the uncertainty a buyer has about a new company.
- *Message about distribution.* Within distribution channels, advertising can help expand channel options for a marketer by making distributors aware of the marketer's offerings.

An advertisement has the potential to appeal to four senses—sight, sound, smell, and touch. However, not all advertising media have the ability to deliver multisensory messages, for example, radio. Additionally, some media may place restrictions on what can be used; some search engines only accept graphical-style ads, if these conform to certain large dimensions, and limit small advertising to text-only ads. The media type chosen to deliver the message also impacts the cost of creating the message. For media outlets that deliver a multisensory experience, creative cost can be significantly higher than for media targeting a single sensory experience. But creative costs are also affected by the expectation of quality for the media that delivers the message. Television broadcasters set high production quality levels for advertisements they deliver. Achieving these standards requires expensive equipment and specialist expertise. Conversely, creating a simple text-only Internet advertisement, which almost anyone is capable of creating in a desktop publishing program, requires very little cost.

Evaluating the Campaign

The final step in the advertising planning process is to measure the results of the last campaign and use the information to inform future decisions and planning. Advertisements need to be tested and evaluated or the planning will be wasted.

Andrew J. Whalley
Royal Holloway University of London

See Also: Advertising; Advertising Cost, Determination of; Advertising Creative Strategy; Advertising Media; Media Choice.

Further Readings

Bly, Robert W. *Advertising Manager's Handbook.* Upper Saddle River, NJ: Prentice Hall, 1993.

Clark, S. "Do the Two-Step With Advertising Budget." *Memphis Business Journal* (March 3, 2000).

Hackley, C. *Advertising & Promotion: Communicating Brands.* Thousand Oaks, CA: Sage, 2005.

Rasmussen, Erika. "Big Advertising, Small Budget." *Sales and Marketing Management* (December 1999).

attempts to do so falter or are tone-deaf to a fan's self-image: when the Red Sox offered a Fenway Nation "membership card" for a small fee in exchange for discounts off merchandise, there was grumbling in the stands from fans who proclaimed that Fenway Nation was an emergent phenomenon and no corporate hierarchy could simply sell membership.

Sports fanhood is part of an individual's social identity. It may be more mutable or seemingly more trivial than religious, political, or ethnic affiliation, but in practice it can affect just as much of a person's self-image and day-to-day life. It is comparable to other consumption- and activity-based identity components like "science fiction fan," "Coca-Cola drinker," "foodie," or "runner." This identity can be catered to through various activities. Much sports fan behavior involves public displays of affiliation: not just the fans who paint themselves

Affiliation Activities

One of the key elements in the health of a professional sport or sports team is the extent to which fans feel strongly affiliated with the team. While "pure" sports fans will insist that they will watch a game for the joy of it over following a specific team, broadcast ratings and other indicators show that sports viewers are more likely to approach the sport as a fan of a team—which has always been one reason events like the Olympics and the World Cup do well, as national affiliations need not be built up through marketing for fans to pick a side to root for. In sports, proximity alone is not necessarily enough to build a connection between a fan and a team, and in many cases, it may not be immediately clear who the "local" team is, whether it is because a baseball fan is in the midwest more or less equidistant from two Chicago teams (Cubs and White Sox), the St. Louis Cardinals, and two Ohio teams (Indians and Reds), but near to none of them; or because a New York fan has such a plethora of teams to choose from. Retaining and building a fanbase, especially one that will continue to watch and attend even when the team loses, means building that fanbase's affiliation with the team. Sometimes

A fan of the 2010 World Cup in South Africa, the type of mega sports event that benefits from national affiliations.

blue to get on the jumbotron, but fans who wear team apparel, display bumper stickers or buttons, put up pennants and posters and other displays, purchase vanity plates for their cars, attend sports bars to watch the game, participate in sports trivia nights, listening to or calling in to sports talk radio, or simply sitting around the break room or bar talking about the game or the team's prospects in the coming season. Sports fandom is a social activity.

Thus, it makes sense for teams and leagues to offer activities beyond attendance. This can include special events for opening day or during the preseason, participation by the team and management in municipal events like St. Patrick's Day, Independence Day, and Mardi Gras parades, involvement with charity events, and various fan outreach activities like talks, presentations about the upcoming season, and autograph signings.

The Internet is an excellent resource for encouraging affiliation activities, because message boards can be made available for fans to talk about the team—ideally, with active moderation but also involvement from official representatives of the team so that fans understand that they are being heard. Twitter and blogs can be used to communicate with fans. MySpace and Facebook can be used to make the team available as an element of fans' online social identities.

Bill Kte'pi
Independent Scholar

See Also: Avidity; Fan Attendance, Reasons for; Fan Avidity; Fan Loyalty Continuum.

Further Readings

DeSarbo, W. S. "Measuring Fan Avidity Can Help Marketers Narrow Their Focus." http://www.sportsbusinessjournal.com/article/64438 (Accessed December 2009).

Jozsa, Frank P. *American Sports Empire: How the Leagues Breed Success*. Westport, CT: Greenwood Publishing, 2003.

Rein, Irving, Philip Kotler, and Ben Shields. *The Elusive Fan: Reinventing Sports in a Crowded Marketplace*. New York: McGraw-Hill, 2006.

Affinity Programs

While affinity marketing has been in the marketing lexicon since the mid-1980s, it remains a relatively new concept in the world of sports marketing. Essentially, affinity marketing goes a step beyond the traditional relationship marketing of a consumer by introducing a third component in the mix. At its core, affinity marketing programs encompass three main components: an endorsement from a third party; shared incentives among the companies, organizations, and consumers involved; and what scholars term an *enhancement package*.

Primarily used in other areas of business, this form of relationship marketing is beneficial to the sport management process. As sport organizations continue to find better ways to generate revenue and brand value and exposure, utilizing a tactic such as affinity marketing becomes even more important.

For affinity marketing to be successful, three distinct parties must be involved. First, there must be a reference group, or affinity group, that has a certain level of identification or commitment with a larger organization. This larger organization, the second party in the process, unifies the affinity group on a variety of levels, many of which are social, professional, and interest-based. Finally, a third party enters the process, which is the actual spearhead of the affinity program.

To better illustrate this process and how it can be applied in sport, one can imagine the recent trends in the credit card and banking industries and how these companies took advantage of the interest of sports organizations and their respective fan base. For instance, a credit card company could provide a special incentive-based card carrying the logo of the group or organization, such as a professional football team or collegiate athletic department. While the initial offering of the card carrying the logo of the team could be considered strictly licensed-based marketing, the introduction of the third-party endorsement changes the process to affinity marketing. In this same example, the head coach of the football team or the athletic director of the collegiate program would send a letter of endorsement to its respective fan base, providing a call to action to sign up and begin using this credit card.

While this alone encompasses an affinity marketing strategy, one of the major differences in this tactic is the idea of shared benefits and enhancement packages. Shared benefits provide the motivation for the affinity groups and organizations to participate in the program. The affinity group earns benefits such as bonus or reward points for purchases and transactions, while the organization of interest may earn the benefits of increased brand exposure and awareness, as well as more tangible benefits such as revenue sharing or licensing fees. Finally, the third party in the transaction, the actual credit card company providing the product or service, generates revenues and market share by the actual use of the offering.

Philanthropy

Another area in which affinity marketing programs have generated greater success is the added benefits of providing donations and funding to various nonprofit organizations. For instance, not only can a fan of a sport organization or university receive benefits such as better discounts and interest rates, but the fan also may receive the intangible benefit of a portion of the card's purchases or usage aiding a specific nonprofit organization. Researchers have concluded that this aspect of an outside beneficiary of donations and revenues is among the more important reasons to sign up for an affinity marketing program.

To elaborate on the previous example of a credit-card company offering a branded card for fans of a specific football team, an addition of contributions to a major charity or nonprofit organization would be necessary. This latest trend can be found in the intercollegiate ranks for credit-card affinity programs and banking processes. These major universities, which may target a selection of their own booster clubs or alumni associations, could earmark specific contributions toward the benefit of items that are not specifically in the realm of collegiate sport. A university may choose to have the benefits help fund the construction of new buildings on campus, or provide other funding to scholarships and new learning enhancements.

Targeted Marketing

This affinity marketing strategy has several implications for the world of sport management. Initially, the realm of sport has something most other fields cannot easily offer—a built-in interest level in terms of fans for sports teams or participants in a particular sport or activity. This mutual interest encompasses people from a variety of backgrounds and demographics, further enhancing any targeted marketing techniques. For instance, most collegiate athletic programs generate a new crop of fans from freshmen enrollment alone, while the same university's alumni association would generate more membership from recent graduates. Not only can affinity programs target fans of sports teams or members of alumni associations, but these programs also can focus on people with shared interests, such as members of a local running association, and those with specific professional memberships, to include members of trade organizations such as marketing professionals, communications consultants, and legal organizations.

In terms of sport, these groups provide a variety of revenue streams for sports teams and athletic organizations as potential targets for companies who produce certain goods or services. Followers of a specific brand or organization not only share a mutual interest in that organization, but they also help provide a source of funding and participation in certain aspects—such as donations, revenues, and other incentives. This level of participation could further increase the involvement and identification of the specific reference groups, thus providing a stronger support system for the specific sports team or organization.

Affinity programs also have a great number of potential uses for these sport organizations. Among the greatest potentials of affinity marketing programs are the capabilities of data generation and more targeted marketing efforts. In recent years, more and more companies and organizations are participating in the data-collecting research process utilizing swipe cards and membership cards. Through a branded affinity marketing strategy, these swipe cards can provide a plethora of information from which the group or organization can base its strategic marketing processes. Teams and organizations can better understand spending patterns of their respective fans and followers, and this information can provide more targeted marketing and sponsorship opportunities in the future.

Conclusion

While they are not generally regarded as a major strategy of marketing and branding processes, affinity marketing programs should prove to be useful tactics to generate potential revenues and brand awareness. Incorporating a built-in fan base and providing benefits for all parties involved sets the stage for affinity marketing programs to continue to flourish in the sport marketing and management spectrum.

J. Michael Martinez
Troy University

See Also: Alumni Loyalty; Brand Insistence; Customer Loyalty Programs; Customer Relationship Marketing; Integrated Marketing Communication; Relationship Marketing.

Further Readings

Jones, Scott A., Tracy A. Suter, and Eric Koch. "Affinity Credit Cards as Relationship Marketing Tools: A Conjoint Analytic Exploration of Combined Product Attributes." *Sport Marketing Quarterly*, v.15 (2006).
Macchiette, Bart and Abhijit Roy. "Affinity Marketing: What Is It and How Does It Work?" *The Journal of Product and Brand Management*, v.2/1 (1993).

Aftermarketing

Aftermarketing includes all activities associated with attracting and keeping existing customers. For a number of years, organizations have focused solely on finding new customers, which is traditionally called transaction marketing. All marketing activities were geared toward a single sale with individual customers, and all customers were treated equally whether they were loyal or not. Often, especially in times of heavy competition, dissatisfied customers were tempted away by competitors. However, it became evident to many organizations that this focus on short-term economic transactions was limited in its effectiveness. As a result, customer satisfaction began to be seen as important because of its association with corporate profitability. Consequently, in recent years, aftermarketing has become the main objective of many organizations' marketing strategies. This paradigm has achieved great popularity because loyal customers are the foundation of successful organizations.

Organizations find customer retention profitable as: retaining customers costs considerably less than acquiring new customers; customers generate more profit each year if they remain with an organization, and loyal customers provide free advertising through word-of-mouth recommendations. However, not all customers are inclined toward building and maintaining an ongoing relationship with an organization. In order for customers to be committed to a relationship, they need to perceive certain benefits that accrue from it. In a sporting context, fans attend games to meet certain motivational needs including group affiliation and entertainment value, and meeting these needs would impact on their overall satisfaction from attending the game.

Satisfaction is vital to customer retention and loyalty. Many aftermarketing strategies have concentrated solely on developing large and expensive software systems. This has led to a number of corporate disasters as companies have spent millions of dollars on hardware and software without a thorough understanding of customer needs and wants. Consequently many initiatives failed to provide clear operational aims and objectives. Moreover the increasing competition in the marketplace has driven companies to look for innovative strategies to retain customers through developing strong relationships that can create customer loyalty. Aftermarketing campaigns attempt to increase the level of trust, commitment, and reciprocity that customers feel toward the company.

Types

There are three types of aftermarketing activities that organizations can engage in. The first is a promotional strategy. Promotional strategies involve giving promotional gifts to customers. These initiatives can be monetary or nonmonetary in nature. Customer loyalty programs can be an example of a monetary promotion. For example, a gym could allow its members to become part of a loyalty program, and members could accumulate points for all purchases they make such as clothing and personal training. These points could then be redeemed in future to receive a lower membership rate. An example of a nonmonetary promotion could be a football club that provides free T-shirts.

Promotional strategies often have a great impact on customer attitudes and behavior. In other words, promotional strategies cause the desire to reciprocate. When customers receive gifts, they feel uncomfortable unless they give something back. The power of promotional strategies is that they create a positive perception, reinforce the buying decision, strengthen relationships, and stimulate interest. Promotional strategies can also play an important role in keeping existing customers because they make customers feel special and valued.

Another tactic used is preferential treatment, which concerns the consumer's perception of the degree to which a company treats its loyal customers better than its nonloyal customers. This tactic is based on the fundamental principles of aftermarketing, which are about consumer focus and consumer selectivity. Consequently, all consumers do not need to be treated in the same way because individual customers have their own requirements. Companies should get to know their best customers personally and reward them frequently with enhanced services. In other words, they need to deliver increased value to profitable customers and turn them into loyal customers, because then they will become even more profitable over time. For example, gyms could provide free towels to their most loyal members.

Interpersonal communication can be seen as the third tactic, which is a consumer's perception of the extent to which a company interacts with its regular customers in a personal way. Exchange partners will be more committed to their relationship if they communicate with each other, providing relevant, timely, and reliable information. Consequently, organizations should find out what kind of communication channels their customers prefer and what information they value.

Sven Kuenzel
University of Greenwich

See Also: Customer Loyalty Programs; Customer Relationship Marketing; Customer Satisfaction; Relationship Marketing.

Further Readings

De Wulf, Kristof, Gaby Odekerken-Schröder, and Dawn Iacobucci. "Investments in Consumer Relationships: A Cross-Country and Cross-Industry Exploration." *Journal of Marketing,* v.65 (2001).

Egan, John. *Relationship Marketing.* Upper Saddle River, NJ: Pearson Education Limited, 2004.

Gwinner, Kevin P., Dwayne D. Gremler, and Mary J. Bitner. "Relational Benefits in Services Industries: The Customer's Perspective." *Journal of the Academy of Marketing Science,* v.26/2 (1998).

Kuenzel, Sven and Mazia Yassim. "The Effect of Joy on the Behaviour of Cricket Spectators: The Mediating Role of Satisfaction." *Managing Leisure,* v.12/1 (2007).

Vavra, Terry G. *Aftermarketing.* New York: McGraw-Hill, 1995.

Agency Law

Agency law is a body of law governing a fiduciary relationship between an agent and his or her principal. A fiduciary relationship is an entrusted relationship between two parties where law imposes a special type of duty upon one party that he or she is obliged to act on behalf of the other. An agent means a person who represents his or her master in dealing with various matters involving third parties. A principal is the master who is represented by the agent in the matters at issue.

Agency law generally means traditional common law established by court decisions that provide a set of rules related to: (1) formation of agency relationship; (2) duties of agent and principal; and (3) contract and tort liabilities of agent and principal. In addition, there is a group of statutes enacted by federal or state legislatures in consideration of some public policies such as the protection of student athletes and educational institutions from possible unfair and deceptive practices of sport agents. An example is the Sports Agent Responsibility and Trust Act (SPARTA) enacted by Congress.

When an agency relationship is established, subsequent agreements made between the agent and third parties within the scope of the agency will be legally enforceable against the principal. The principal will also be liable for property loss or injury inflicted by the agent's negligence. Pursuant to the doctrine of fiduciary duty, the agent is prevented from self-dealings, usurpation of opportunities arising from the representation of the principal, and making secret profits in relation to the representation.

In professional sports, a vast majority of athletes are represented by their agents who provide various services, for example, salary and endorsement negotiation, financial and estate planning, or managing public relations on behalf of the athletes. An ordinary employment relationship between an employer and employee is also a type of agency, except for the fact that the law in general does not impose the above-mentioned fiduciary duty upon an employee whose contract expressly limits the scope of his or her job performance.

Formation of Agency Relationships

There are four different ways to establish an agency relationship: (1) express agency; (2) implied agency; (3) apparent agency; and (4) ratification agency. An express agency is a relationship based upon a legally enforceable agreement. An agency relationship created by an oral or written contract might be a typical situation of express agency. An implied agency is formed when circumstantial cues such as history of past dealings make third parties believe that an agent is representing a principal. An apparent agency is established when a principal has cloaked an agent with the appearance of some delegated authority in front of third parties.

For instance, if an athlete has introduced a sport agent to third parties with the delegation of some authority to make deals related to corporate endorsement, a subsequent agreement made between a third party and the cloaked agent will be enforceable against the athlete. A ratification agency is established when a principal had full knowledge of details of an agreement made on behalf of him and

enjoyed benefits from the deal. For example, a close friend of a high-profile athlete wants to represent the star but the athlete has continuously refused to make an agency contract with his friend. In spite of the absence of the actual agency authority, the friend goes out and makes an endorsement deal on behalf of the athlete. Assume that the athlete knew the friend's effort and details of the deal.

When the athlete received a lump sum signing bonus paid for the endorsement, he cashed the check. Under the ratification agency theory, now the athlete is bound to the contract because he ratified his friend's representation in the matter and enjoyed the economic benefit from the deal, that is, the signing bonus check.

Duties

Agency law imposes several duties on an agent as well as a principal once an agency relationship is properly established. First, a principal must give his agent a reasonable compensation in exchange for the provided services. He must cooperate with the agent in the matters related to the representation. The principal also has a duty to provide the agent with a safe environment in performing the services for the purpose of the representation.

On the other hand, an agent also has a set of duties owed to his or her principal. An agent must exercise reasonable care and skills in the representation. Accounting is another duty imposed on an agent under the law. Under the rule, commingling of a principal's assets with his or her own assets is strictly prohibited.

Duty of loyalty, also known as fiduciary duty, is another obligation. Given the fact that the foundational basis of an agent relationship is two parties' entrust and reliance, an agent's loyalty to a principal is clearly required. Therefore, self-dealings for an agent's own interest in matters related to the representation, usurpation of opportunities available in the course of the performance, and making secret profits not disclosed to the principal is prohibited.

Contract and Tort Liabilities

Different levels of contract and tort liabilities may be imposed on a principal or an agent based upon various situational factors such as the disclosure of agency relationship or the scope of representation.

Whether a principal or an agent is liable for a contract signed between the agent and a third party depends on the levels of disclosure of the fact that the agent was representing the principal at the moment of the deal. When the third party was fully informed of that the agent was making the agreement on behalf of his or her principal and the third party knew who the principal was, only the principal is bound to the contract and the agent is not personally liable for anything.

If the fact of the representation was disclosed but the identity of the principal was not, the principal is liable and the agent might be liable as an option possibly chosen by the aggrieved third party. When the agent did not disclose at the time of the contract formation either the fact of the representation or the identity of the principal, both the principal and agent are liable automatically.

On the other hand, under the doctrine of vicarious liability, a principal is liable for his or her agent's negligence if the act was within the scope of the agency. That is, if there is an agency relationship, the principal is liable for an injury or property loss inflicted by the agent's negligence while serving the principal. In general, the principal might not, however, be liable for intentional torts of the agent such as assault and battery except in some extraordinary circumstances.

Sungho Cho
Bowling Green State University

See Also: Agent, Sports; Athlete Representation; Breach of Contract; Contracts, Athletes; Employee Relations; Legal Considerations in Sport; Sports Agent Responsibility and Trust Act; Uniform Athlete Agent Act.

Further Readings

Cotten, D. and John T. Wolohan. *Law for Recreation and Sport Managers*, 5th Ed. Dubuque, IA: Kendall Hunt, 2010.
Sharp, L., A. Moorman, and C. Claussen. *Sport Law: A Managerial Approach*, 2nd Ed. Scottsdale, AZ: Holcomb Hathaway, 2010.
Wong, G. *Essentials of Sports Law*, 4th Ed. Santa Barbara, CA: ABC-CLIO, 2010.

Agent, Sports

A sports agent is an individual charged with the responsibility of representing the best interests of an athlete, or former athlete, in player contracts, appearance arrangements, sponsorship deals, and endorsement agreements. Sports agency is accepted to have formally begun when C. C. Pyle negotiated a $100,000 contract for future pro football Hall of Famer Red Grange to play eight games for the Chicago Bears in 1925.

Sports agency developed further in the 1960s and 1970s when agents such as Bob Woolf and Marty Blackman became more prevalent—though these agents often found that management was uncooperative. One story has it that football legend Vince Lombardi, who then served in the dual capacity as both the head coach and general manager of the Green Bay Packers, simply traded his National Football League All-Pro lineman Jim Ringo rather than negotiate with his attorney. By the 1980s, however, attorneys and agents for athletes in the major sports leagues became accepted in the marketplace, particularly with the existence of player free agency in professional sports.

As quickly as sports agents became accepted, they proved to be problematic. Client-stealing, illegal payoffs, and National Collegiate Athletic Association–violative handouts to student athletes all made headlines. Sports agents Norby Walters and Lloyd Bloom—whose illegal actions in the late 1980s and early 1990s regarding the recruitment of University of Alabama basketball players landed them in jail—became among the first in a web of what are now known as an "unscrupulous" brand of agents.

Agents have legal obligations to represent their clients vigorously and to maintain the security of their financial resources. In *Zinn v. Parrish*, for example, the U.S. Court of Appeals for the Seventh Circuit announced that a sports agent has a duty to maintain "consistent, good faith efforts" on behalf of his client—even if the efforts prove to be unsuccessful. That does not mean that client-poaching is illegal. In the landmark *Speakers of Sport v. ProServ* case, the Seventh Circuit ruled that "there is in general nothing wrong with one sports agent trying to take a client from another, if this can be done without precipitating a breach of contract. . . . This is the process known as competition, which though painful, fierce, frequently ruthless, sometimes Darwinian in its pitilessness" is not illegal.

Today, sports agents' actions are monitored by a network of state laws, National Collegiate Athletic Association regulations, league union restrictions, and even federal laws.

Theodore Curtis
Lynn University

See Also: Agency Law; Athlete Representation; Contracts, Athletes; Sports Agent Responsibility and Trust Act; Uniform Athlete Agent Act.

Further Readings

Levine, M. *Life in the Trash Lane: Cash, Cars & Corruption, A Sports Agent's True Story.* Plantation, FL: Distinctive Publishers, 1993.
Roundball Enterprises Inc. v. Richardson, 616 F.Supp. 1537 (S.D.N.Y. 1985).
Ruxin, "Unsportsmanlike Conduct: The Student Athlete, the NCAA and Agents," *Journal of College and University Law,* v.8 (1981–82).
Sims v. Argovitz, 580 F.Supp. 542 (E.D. Mich, 1984).
Speakers of Sport v. ProServ, 178 F.3d 862 (7th Cir. 1999).
Walters v. Harmon, 516 N.Y.S. 2d 874 (Sup. Ct. 1987).
Weiss, Michael A. "The Regulation of Sports Agents: Fact or Fiction." *Sports Law Journal,* v.1 (Spring, 1994).

Allocentric Versus Psychocentric

Allocentric and psychocentric are personality types that will determine not only how a person participates in sport and recreation, but also his or her stance on participation in life. Stanley Plog developed a model of allocentricity and psychocentricity for the tourism industry in 1972. He presented these two personality traits as the opposite ends of a continuum of traits. Psychocentric refers to people who are nervous, not adventurous, self-inhabited, and like structure. On the other end of the spectrum are those who are allocentric, or outgoing, curious, self-confident explorers.

Applying this model to sports, psychocentric participants are those who look for structured sports with rules, little risk, and someone to guide them like a coach, for example, sports like bowling, golf, swimming, or track. Allocentric participants are looking for adventurous sports and sports without boundaries or rules. These allocentric sports could include snowboarding, bike racing, gymnastics, or rugby. Since Plog put these two personality traits on the ends of a spectrum, there are many people who will fall between them and who would enjoy both some structure and adventure built into the same game. These mid-centric personalities would enjoy baseball, soccer, basketball, or football. All are sports with rules and structure, yet with some freedom to try something new and experiment to see if one can obtain the same goal different ways.

In sports tourism these two personality types are used in marketing. Marketers may highlight a place's adventurous activities or creative opportunities to get more allocentric people to visit, while downplaying those aspects and focusing on the peace and tranquility of the area to bring in more psychocentric consumers. Sports marketers also need to focus on the group that will consume the most amount of that sport. Marketing rugby to a conservative, self-conscious consumer will not help the rugby market. A sport should be analyzed for its major traits, placed on the spectrum, and then matched with the personalities or the consumers who fall on the same part of that spectrum.

As it was important research for the tourism industry to have, understanding the different personality types of sports consumers will be beneficial. This will become especially important in the future as there has been a change in the traits of youth sports. With approximately 40 million children between ages 6 and 17 participating in some level of sport, parents are noticing the shift in types of activities that are available to youth. Twenty years ago the goal of participating in sports was to be active and have fun, and many games were played without scores, uniforms, or even a proper field. Today, however, more children are encouraged to join organized youth teams, learn how to keep score, and compete against others.

Alice Kahrs
State University of New York College at Cortland

See Also: Participant Market Segmentation; Participants in Sports; Recreation and Leisure; Recreational Sports; Sports Tourism; Youth Sports.

Further Readings

Fish, Joel H. and Susan Magee. *101 Ways to Be a Terrific Sports Parent: Making Athletics a Positive Experience for Your Child.* New York: Fireside, 2003.
Litvil, Stephen W. "Revisiting Plog's Model of Allocentricity: Once More Time." *Cornell Hotel and Administration Quarterly* (August 2006).
Madril, Robert. "Personal Values, Traveler Personality Type and Leisure Travel Type." *Journal of Leisure Research* (Spring 2005).

Alternative Sports

The rise in consumer and corporate interest in action sports, widely known as extreme sports, has been phenomenal. The immense growth of the action sports industry has been illustrated through the increased media coverage of events such as the ESPN X-Games, the Mountain Dew Action Sports Tour aired by NBC, and the Gorge Games. Furthermore, there has been a dramatic increase in athlete endorsements, branding, corporate sponsorships, and lay-athlete participation in action sports, especially by members of Generation Y. Although action sports have experienced an immense growth within the sport industry, there is relatively limited research on the phenomenon. Thus, the purpose of this entry is to illustrate the current status of the alternative/action sports industry, as well as discuss the evolution, growth, and future of this industry.

Apart from the business growth of the industry, participation rates also reflect the increasing popularity of alternative sports, especially of board sports (surf, skateboard, and snowboard). According to a survey conducted by the National Sporting Goods Association (NSGA), between 1997 and 2006 participation rates for snowboarding and skateboarding increased 84.8 percent and 53.6 percent, respectively. In terms of sales, footwear and T-shirts for board sports account for $5 billion in annual sales. Broken down by sport, the industry consists of $5.5 billion for skateboarding goods, $3 billion for snowboarding, and $3 billion for surfing. North America–based companies spent an estimated $138 million to sponsor skateboarding, snowboarding, freestyle motocross, and other action sports in 2007, up from $120 million in 2006. Interestingly, in the United States the growth in skateboarding can be seen in the number of sales over 10 years, outpacing more traditional sports such as baseball.

What Are Alternative/Action Sports?

It is important to identify what exactly constitutes action, alternative, or lifestyle sports. As the authors Gregg Bennett and Tony Lachowetz suggest, "Action sports are an eclectic collection of risky, individualistic, and alternative sports such as skateboarding, BMX biking, surfing, street luge, wakeboarding, and motocross." Other scholars have noted that alternative sports "either ideologically or practically provide alternatives to mainstream sports and to mainstream sport values," and utilize the term *lifestyle* in studies as an expression adopted by members of the cultures themselves. In addition, the term reflects both the characteristics of these activities and their wider sociocultural significance. Notably, the latter appears to be what the mainstream media and marketers view and market as "nonmainstream" sports. *Lifestyle sports* may be considered as a less all-encompassing term in comparison to the often used alternative, action, or extreme sport names. Currently, *action sports* is the term that is predominantly used within the industry, and it will be utilized throughout this entry.

Action sports have boomed since the early 1990s, but most marketers have only recently realized the power the words *alternative* or *action* hold, especially for youth markets. For instance, the board sports complex—surfing, skateboarding, and snowboarding—has experienced a massive growth in participation numbers. It is estimated that there are currently 20 million surfers, 40 million skateboarders, and 18.5 million snowboarders worldwide. The snowboarding industry had predicted that by 2005, half of ski-field patrons would be snowboarders. In addition, 45 percent of first-time visitors to ski fields in the United States are snowboarders. In the United Kingdom, surfing became one of the fastest-growing sports at the turn of the 21st century, particularly among women and men in their thirties and forties. According to the 2006 study of sports participation conducted by the Sporting Goods Manufacturers Association, inline skateboarding, paintball, snowboarding, and mountain biking were among the most popular extreme sports. Moreover, the study illustrated that 81 percent of all skateboarders are

Board sports such as snowboarding are among the fastest-growing action sports with revenues of $9.9 billion a year.

between 6 and 17 years old, nearly 75 percent of all snowboarders are under the age of 24, and the average annual household income of a wakeboarder in 2003 was $73,200. Board sports are currently worth $9.9 billion per annum, with roughly 80 percent of this amount coming from sales of related apparel, shoes, and accessories. In addition, skateboarding and snowboarding are considered to be the two fastest-growing sports in the United States in recent years within the action sports family.

Because of the increasing popularity of action sports in general and, specifically, of board sports, a lot of mainstream athletic companies have attempted to capture a stake of this lucrative business. For instance, Nike has repeatedly attempted to enter the action sports industry. Before releasing its skateboarding (SB) line in 2001, Nike had tried to market skateboarding sneakers twice and failed. The difference now is that Nike SB has a limited distribution to skate shops, the company sponsors grass-roots skateboarding contests, and several of Nike SB's staff arrived from the board sports industry. When Nike entered the skateboarding market, most skaters liked the company's skate shoe commercials. However, skaters were concerned about Nike's motivation because there was not a long-standing commitment to the skateboarding community.

Evidently, a brand's credibility and authenticity is pivotal to participants in board sports. Nike emphasized fashion over participation, a fact that was not appealing to core consumers. Alternative sports such as surfing, skateboarding, and snowboarding have all distinct subcultures. In addition, action sports have developed in a different social context relative to modern organized sports and they share important commonalities. What is emerging within alternative sport subcultures are struggles between corporate culture producers who are attempting to organize and present these sports like mainstream sport forms and the participants themselves, who seek to maintain some control of their sports and the "authentic" roots of their cultures as they become commercialized. Ultimately, gaining trust and attaining intimacy with consumers, as well as promoting specific subcultural elements such as lifestyle, authenticity, and self-expression, are important aspects for success in the action sports industry.

Despite the fact that action sports have experienced a dramatic increase in popularity, there is relatively limited research of the action sports phenomenon. However, various academic studies have examined the perception and consumer behavior toward action sports. For instance, the influence of action sports is particularly pervasive in the Generation Y culture. Research in perceptions toward action sports has verified the increased influence and appeal of action sports primarily on youth markets and Generation Y in particular. Moreover, sociologists have examined other aspects of alternative sports and their subcultures, such as gender relations within alternative sports, subcultural identities, and media perception and consumption.

Overall, there is a growing body of academic literature that examines the phenomena of what has been termed *extreme, alternative, lifestyle, whiz, action sports, panic sport, post-modern, post-industrial,* and *new sports*. However, limited research has addressed the marketing aspect of action sports from a subcultural perspective. Apparently action sports incorporate distinct subcultural and lifestyle elements that are pivotal to consumers. Thus, these elements play an integral role relative to the implementation of marketing strategies in action sports. It has become evident that action sports companies have started to expand to mainstream markets in order to survive and secure their viability in an extremely competitive sports industry, where new brands emerge and attempt to acquire a share of the action sports pie. This competition has become even more intense because of the expansion of mainstream athletic companies in the action sports industry as described above.

Status of the Action Sports Industry

In the late 1990s, television and corporate sponsors recognized the huge potential of action sports, such as surfing, skateboarding, and snowboarding, in order to attract a young male audience. Mainstream companies instantly associated the alternative and extreme "do-it-yourself" image of the rider/boarder to cross-promote a variety of products, such as apparel lines, and cultural events. As a result, action sports were subjected to the major forces of the commercialization process. The growing popularity of boarding sports has been utilized by media cor-

porations such as ESPN and NBC via events such as the X-Games and the Mountain Dew Action Sports Tour, respectively. In 1998, ESPN's X-Games event was televised in 198 countries. The Action Sports Association's LG Action Sports Tour is one of the largest action sports events and production companies. The group develops more than 200 events annually, half of which are televised. Board sports such as surfing, skateboarding, and snowboarding are currently worth $9.9 billion per annum, with roughly 80 percent of this amount coming from sales of related apparel, shoes, and accessories. In addition, skateboarding, snowboarding, and motocross are considered to be the three fastest-growing sports in the country in recent years among the action sports.

The rise in consumer and corporate interest in action sports has been increasing at a phenomenal rate. A 2006 survey study conducted by Turnkey Sports Poll with 400 senior-level industry executives spanning professional and college sports indicated that extreme sports have done the best job of activating the 12–17 demographic (63.08 percent followed by NBA, 10.75 percent). It is estimated that action sports boast over 58 million consumers between the ages of 10 and 24, who wield $250 billion in buyer power. The influence of action sports is particularly pervasive in Generation Y culture. Extensive research in perceptions toward action sports has verified the increased influence and appeal of action sports primarily on youth markets and Generation Y in particular.

As action sports' popularity continues to grow, action sports become increasingly commercialized as well. Alternative sports emerged in the 1960s as a revolutionary movement in contrast to modern organized sports. Since then, a plethora of changes have taken place in the action sports industry from a social, cultural, and economic perspective. Some of the alternative sport subcultures, such as the boarding ones, were subjected to the major forces of the commercialization process. Distinct subcultural elements of alternative sports evolved and adapted in order to offset any negative connotations of commercial success by reinforcing "core" values. For example, the special relationship between surfing, skateboarding, and snowboarding has been described as a "love triangle" because of similarities in motion, attitude, and dress. The current board sports market is extremely competitive, as a plethora of providers exist for each sport product or service. The number of competitors is increasing as more franchises are awarded and new events are established. Consequently, traditional transactional marketing has become less effective for board sports companies, since the new market structure is characterized by large homogeneous segments and a massive number of products with little differentiation between them. In the emergence of new individualized forms of action sports, consumers seek a particular and desirable lifestyle. Evidently, marketers will have to comprehend the changing nature of the action sports industry, such as the constant transition of core action sports brands to lifestyle brands, in order to assess the type of marketing strategies that could be applied to the core action sports industry and to mainstream markets.

Core and lifestyle action sports brands demonstrate the following common characteristics: (1) incorporation of subcultural components to their identity, (2) utilization of artist and music-related collaborations and co-branded marketing efforts, and (3) integration of advanced technological elements into their products. Lifestyle action sports brands tend to affiliate more with nonindustry brands, create aesthetically fashionable and trendy products that also appeal to the masses, and expand their distribution to mainstream channels. On the other hand, core action sports brands demonstrate an intense focus on the quality, function, performance, and durability of their products. Namely, they reinforce the authentic element of a product rather than the stylistic and fashionable aspects of it, limit their distribution to strictly core doors, and they affiliate primarily with action sports–related entities.

Future of the Action Sports Industry

According to Fuse Sports, participation in alternative sports has increased by 35 percent since 1995. There is also a parallel increase in the teen population within the United States; it is estimated that the population of 12- to 17-year olds will rise 10 percent to 25 million by 2010. Inevitably, action sports have an increased potential for additional growth. This is evident as action sports will continue to be promoted more and more via mainstream media

outlets. Marketing experts within the sport industry have noted that if action sports are to be accepted as legitimate sports, then they need to be aired on a more consistent basis. Some of the major action sports events such as the X-Games are only aired once per year.

The main challenge concerning the future of action sports is to maintain their authenticity and legitimacy, as well as their "extreme" or "alternative" character. The majority of action sports, such as boarding cultures, emerged from the new leisure movement imbued with an individualistic, anticompetitive, and anticapitalist ethos. Thus, the emerging marketing trend to expand action sports to the masses by utilizing mainstream media outlets may jeopardize the authenticity of action sports. For instance, Subaru, the Japanese car manufacturer, signed with the X-Games in order to build its presence in road rallying after following last year's gold medal win by the Subaru Team USA in the X-Games' inaugural event. Since the X-Games portray an image of authentic participation, the company is striving to find a way to build a stronger connection with the brand and the action of rally racing. Jake Burton, founder and president of Burton Snowboards, commented on the challenge for an expansion to mainstream:

> As snowboarding and Burton look toward the future, growth and movement into the mainstream is inevitable. Large companies with no tradition in or ownership of snowboarding are getting into the market as both manufacturers and sponsors. Above all, snowboarding has to remain fun, innovative, and driven by young people with a natural passion and energy for the sport.

One major question is whether action or extreme sports would finally adopt a more mainstream character if they continue to be promoted through mainstream media outlets. Inarguably, if action sports are to become accepted by mainstream masses, their appeal needs to be extended beyond the realm of sideshow and sporadic events. Industry trends indicate that in order to reach the mass audience, action sports must become more than just a spectacle; current and potential consumers need to develop a rooting and genuine interest.

It has been argued that the product of action sports is often perceived as different from the product of mainstream sports. However, like most everything in culture, extreme sports influence and are influenced by the larger culture, and despite their oppositional roots, they serve as a mirror of society on a daily basis. Consequently, extreme sports may suffer from similar problems as mainstream sport has. With the more commodified extreme sports—like snowboarding and skateboarding—there appears to be less and less participant opposition to the term *sport* than before. In other words, aligning themselves with sport in addition to lifestyle has opened up a whole new market for business venturers and entrepreneurs.

Lifestyle habits of action sport consumers and, particularly, of Generation Y consumers have been extensively examined, as documented previously in this entry. The pivotal role of mainstream media in the popularity of action sports and the connection with lifestyle activities that the media attempt to establish is apparent. As scholars have noted, "Alternative sport cultures are 'taste cultures' in which the specialist subcultural media play a central role in disseminating information about their activities to their members, and the creation and circulation of the symbols and meanings of subcultural capital." Moreover, media can play an important part in transmitting values associated with specific sport subcultures and the success of marketing efforts, particularly celebrity endorsement, is predicated on the ability of the media to shape and transmit subcultural values. Finally, action sports provide corporations with effective platforms to access the typically hard-to-reach consumer segment of male adolescents 12 to 24 years of age.

The action sports industry is a fertile ground for mainstream media, such as ESPN and NBC, and corporations to connect with potential consumers by capturing the lifestyle, cultural, and consumption habits surrounding those sports. Live music, interactive events, and enhanced environmental marketing efforts are some of the predominant elements that characterize events such as the X-Games and the Mountain Dew Action Sports Tour. In addition, there is a growing trend within action sports brands to associate themselves with music groups, artists, actors, and cult events. Namely, the industry is experiencing a shift toward enhancing its connection and association with the lifestyle of its members, primarily from a cult and cultural perspective. Cult is defined as an exclusive group of persons sharing an esoteric, usually artistic or intellectual interest. One of the most representative examples is the Andy Warhol limited edition created by Burton Snowboards. As it is mentioned in the Burton 2008 catalog:

In collaboration with the Andy Warhol Foundation we have created a limited edition collection that brings some of Andy's most esoteric art to snow. As the preeminent American artist of the 20th century, Andy Warhol challenged the world to see art differently. This exclusive collection celebrates the artist's sophisticated sense of design, groundbreaking artwork, and nonconformist spirit.

In the aforementioned statement, there is a clear attempt from Burton to create a limited edition that incorporates artistic elements, while reinforcing some of snowboarding's subcultural values, such as differentiation, nonconformity, and innovation. In this way, Burton associates with lifestyle habits of a particular target audience by promoting an authentic and artistic image. The competitive board sports environment dictates not only an expansion to mainstream consumers in order to be able to support the core even more, but growth opportunities to related action sports.

The dynamic nature of the action sports setting creates a compelling need for companies to constantly assess the inner and outer context of the industry. The increased commercial appeal of action sports has significantly impacted indications and definitions of authenticity/legitimacy in those subcultures. The implementation of a holistic framework that facilitates an exploration of the action sports environment along with the nature and processes of change is pivotal in understanding the adoption of effective marketing practices, as well as implementing a market development strategy to mainstream.

Conclusion

Action sport companies need to maintain a delicate balance between the individualistic motivation of action sports participants, the enhanced tribal element instilled in action sports, and the distinct lifestyle habits of action sports consumers in order to maintain their authenticity and integrity. Simultaneously, the enhancement of the core and the organic growth of action sports brands could lead to a successful expansion/transition to mainstream markets and audiences, a strategic plan that will ensure their viability in the increasingly competitive sports industry.

Chrysostomos Giannoulakis
University of Nevada, Las Vegas

See Also: Gen X; Gen Y; Recreational Sports; Sport Marketing Differences.

Further Readings

Bennett, G. and T. Lachowetz. "Marketing to Lifestyles: Actions Sports and Generation Y." *Sport Marketing Quarterly*, v.13 (2004).

National Sporting Goods Association. "Youth Participation in Selected Sports With Comparisons to 1997." http://www.nsga.org/public/pages/index.cfm?pageid=158 (Accessed June 2008).

Rinehart, R. and S. Sydnor, eds. *To the Extreme: Alternative Sports Inside and Out.* Albany: State University of New York Press, 2003.

Spending on Action and Adventure Sports. "IEG Sponsorship Report." http:/www.sponsorship.com/iegsr/subonly/topic_article.asp?id=2563 (Accessed September 2008).

Sporting Goods Manufacturers Association. *Superstudy of Sports Participation.* North Palm Beach, FL: Sporting Goods Manufacturers Association, 2006.

Thorpe, H. "Beyond 'Decorative Sociology': Contextualizing Female Surf, Skate, and Snowboarding." *Sociology of Sport Journal,* v.23 (2006).

Turnkey Sports Poll. "Sports Business Journal In-Depth." *Sports Business Journal,* v.7/23 (February 20, 2006).

Wheaton, B., ed. *Understanding Lifestyle Sport: Consumption, Identity and Difference.* New York: Routledge, 2004.

Alumni Loyalty

For college and university athletic programs, converting alumni affinity into donations and ticket sales is big business. Because of the fact that most athletics department revenue streams have been tapped out or maxed out because of limitations on the number of tickets that can be sold and market saturation, most administrators are turning to the athletic development area to yield an increase in revenues. The very top tier of NCAA Division I athletic departments employ between six and 20 full-time fundraisers in order to identify and cultivate donors. Not surprisingly, cash contributions from alumni and others constitute the first or second largest revenue stream for those athletic departments behind television revenue. According to the Knight Commission, 30 percent of Football Bowl Subdivision (FBS) revenues come from cash contributions from alumni and others.

For those concerned about the increasing gap between the haves and have-nots in big time college sport, the effect this kind of donor base has on the prospects of schools to win and to maintain a high public profile is obvious. Consider the comparison between the Ohio State University, a top tier FBS institution, which reported athletic donations of $32.4 million in 2007–08 with the financial realities of San Diego State University, a program that raised $3.2 million in 2008–09.

While NCAA Division I programs may have larger staffs assigned to athletic development, schools across all divisional affiliations report that fundraising is critical to their operation. For NCAA Division II programs with football, contributions from alumni and friends accounted for 8 percent of their budgets. For NCAA Division III institutions, an emphasis on raising money from graduates, parents, and other constituencies is becoming increasingly important.

Over time, development efforts in college and university athletic departments have become increasingly sophisticated and integrated with other areas, most particularly ticket sales. As a consequence, giving to a major athletic department may take the form of contributions that allow donors to access certain privileges, including the opportunity to purchase preferred seating, access to luxury boxes, and parking.

As an example, in June 2010, Winston Salem State University (WSSU) unveiled a board on the exterior of its football stadium listing the names of 1,000 donors committed to contributing $1,000 per year to the program. As part of the benefits package, these donors were invited to special receptions and afforded ticket privileges during the season and postseason. The practice of linking levels of donations to ticket access, however, has not been without controversy. In 2008, the University of Georgia made headlines when it was discovered that a first-time season ticket buyer would have had to contribute nearly $11,000 for the right to purchase tickets.

At the present time, donations to college and university athletics departments are 80 percent tax deductible. The basis for this deduction is a belief that donations are being made in support of educational programs. While contributions may in fact support operational expenses that allow teams to travel to tournaments they might not otherwise be able to get to or capital expenses associated with the renovation or building of new facilities that directly impact athlete experience, nevertheless, the clear line between a donation and an educational outcome is not always so easily demonstrated.

The privilege associated with a certain level of donation, a luxury suite for example, may far outweigh whatever educational benefit is thought to accrue either to athletes in the program or to the institution overall. Further, there is growing concern that athletic development efforts may be undermining the ability of colleges and universities to raise money for academic programs.

Donor Influence

As is the case with any form of philanthropy, whether it is philanthropic giving associated with political candidates, health-related or social justice causes, academic programs, or athletic programs, issues related to donor influence arise. In a perfect world, contributions to athletic programs would be made with no strings attached. Since monetary gifts are in fact value statements and investments, it is not surprising that some donors would wish to exercise control and influence over athletics departments by raising questions regarding who is coaching, how money is allocated, and to what purpose funds are spent.

As R. Gerald Turner, president of Southern Methodist University and co-chair of the Knight Commission on Intercollegiate Athletics said,

There's just so much money around athletics programs. When there's all that money, you have to worry about people who care nothing about the institution but are absolutely devoted to that program's winning. If you're not vigilant, it can quickly get out of control.

Challenges

Given how reliant athletics programs have become on donations from alumni and friends, there is also the real possibility of financial shortfalls when economic times are hard. In recent years, schools have worked to develop athletic endowment funds. At select NCAA Division I institutions, these funds may exceed $200 million in value. Depending on how those funds are managed and the movement of the financial markets, an athletic department dependent on funds generated from endowments to balance its budget may not be able to do so.

The cautionary tale of T. Boone Pickens, a graduate of Oklahoma State University, is a case in point. Pickens donated $165 million to the Cowboys Athletic Department. His donation, along with an additional $37 million from other donors, was invested in a hedge fund run by Pickens. With the collapse of the global markets in 2008, the fund lost a considerable amount of its value, resulting in Oklahoma State having to put projects on hold.

In a 2010 survey titled "The Mood of Alumni," eight out of 10 graduates under the age of 35 reported that they were not likely to give to their alma mater because they feel they already paid enough in tuition. How this sentiment may translate to athletic development is difficult to know. However, it has the potential to create greater tension between athletic departments and institutional development offices unless the two can work together to leverage mutual interests. In an ironic twist, as athletics departments continue to mine for revenue sources, an examination of the reasons why former athletes do not contribute to the programs they played for is worth considering. In a 2010 study of one institution, only 5 percent of former athletes donated to the athletic program.

Preliminary data suggests that the satisfaction of athletes in their program, the manner in which they are treated while participating, and personalized communication with athletes after they graduate make a difference in terms of their inclination to give back. Both of these trends offer food for thought in terms of the depths and boundaries of alumni loyalty and what that means to college and university athletic departments.

Ellen J. Staurowsky
Ithaca College

See Also: Affinity Programs; Economic Climate for Sports; Flutie Effect; Student Athlete.

Further Readings

Bonn, Robert. "Best Practices: Fund Raising Small College Style." http://www.nacda.com/sports/naadd/spec-rel/111009aaa.html (Accessed August 2010).

Covell, Daniel and Carol A. Barr. *Managing Intercollegiate Athletics.* Scottsdale, AZ: Holcomb Hathaway, 2010.

Lubechow, Lindsey. "Are Tax Deductions for College Athletics Worth the Price?" http://higheredwatch.newamerica.net/blogs/education_policy/2007/10/tax_deduction_athletics_donations (Accessed August 2010).

Masterson, Kathryn. "Appeals to College Loyalty Not Enough to Engage Younger Alumni." *The Chronicle of Higher Education* (July 18, 2010).

Shapiro, Stephen, Chrysostomos Giannoulakis, Joris Drayer, and Chien-Hsin Wang. "An Examination of Athletic Alumni Giving Behavior." *Sport Management Review,* v.13 (2010).

Steinbach, Paul. "The Gift Box." http://www.athleticbusiness.com (Accessed August 2010).

Weiner, Jay. "College Sports 101: A Primer on Money, Athletics, and Higher Education in the 21st Century." http://www.knightcommission.org (Accessed August 2010).

Wolverton, Brad. "As Athletics Donations Go Up, Some Leaders Fret Over Booster Influence." *The Chronicle of Higher Education* (October 26, 2007).

Amateur Athlete

In 776 B.C.E., the first Olympic Games took place in Greece. Prior to this competition the athletes had played and competed in games but not on the four-year period between games system. The only game at the first Olympics was the 200-yard dash or stadium. The two-stadia race, 24-stadia event, pentathlon, boxing, and more soon followed. It was at this time that the victors of the most prestigious events were crowned with olive wreaths and paraded around the city. Athletes competed for honor, not for material prizes. In later years, Olympians began to accept athletic prizes such as bronze tripods, shields, and woolen cloaks when they competed and won. In ancient Greece there were no amateur athletes or professional athletes; there were simply athletes. There is not an exact date as to when the Ancient Olympics ended, but it was around 390 C.E.

The modern-day Olympics were restarted by Pierre de Coubertin, a French aristocrat in the late 1800s who wanted to toughen up the French after they lost the Franco-Prussian War. However, he knew his wealthy aristocrat participants could not compete against commoners who worked full time in their areas of competition. For example, de Coubertin did not want rowers to compete against those who worked in rowing at shipyards. Therefore, the concept of amateurism was created; if you were paid to do it then you were a professional and could not compete. If you were not paid to do it then you were an amateur and could compete. Problems and issues with this way of thinking developed as some countries circumvented the rules while others were honest.

In the mid-1970s Gerald Ford issued the President's Commission on Olympic Sports, which analyzed amateur sports in America and created the Olympic and Amateur Sports Act of 1978. This act led to massive changes in American amateur sports over the next three decades. In the 1970s, amateur status requirements began to lessen, and after the 1988 Olympic Games it was decided that professional athletes could compete in all sports. As of 2004, the only sport that does not allow professional competitors is boxing.

Today, the increased commercialization of amateur sports in college sports has caused many to be concerned about lines being crossed. For instance, in bowl games the goal is to generate money for all parties involved except the amateur athlete. However, athletes do receive lavish gifts at elite bowl games. The National Collegiate Athletic Association, which is the governing body of intercollegiate athletics, made about $590 million in 2008–09 in television and marketing fees alone. In this environment, the collegiate athlete becomes very valuable for an institution. This situation contributes to ongoing confusion between the professional and the amateur athlete.

Shane Hudson
Texas A&M University

See Also: Amateur Athletic Union; National Collegiate Athletic Association; Student Athlete.

Further Readings

Crittenden, Michael. "The Bailout Bowl: Big-Game Sponsors Scored Billions." *Wall Street Journal* (January 3, 2009).

Duderstadt, James. *Intercollegiate Athletics and the American University. A University President's Perspective.* Ann Arbor: University of Michigan Press, 2003.

National Collegiate Athletic Association Official Website. http://www.ncaa.org (Accessed November 2009).

Nostos Hellenic Information Society. http://www.nostos.com/olympics (Accessed January 2011).

Shropshire, Kenneth L. and Scott R. Rosner. *The Business of Sports.* Sudbury, MA: Jones & Bartlett Publishers, 2004.

Sperber, Murray. *College Sports, Inc.* New York: Henry Holt, 1999.

Amateur Athletic Union

The Amateur Athletic Union (AAU) is a multisport organization that focuses on the promotion and delivery of amateur sport for participants of all ages in the United States. The New York Athletic Club founded the AAU in 1888. Today, the AAU is one of the oldest and largest volunteer sport organizations in the country. Originally, it was founded to set standards and regulate amateur sport in the United States. During its early years, the organization represented the country in international sport competitions, and its sport committees operated as the national governing bodies for sports such as swimming and track and field.

History

In the 1920s, the AAU played a major role in organizing and promoting competitive sport for women at a time when national and Olympic sport competition was thought to be harmful to the physical and mental health of women. Several notable female athletes who competed in those early Olympic Games through the sponsorship of the AAU included swimmer Gertrude Ederle and track and field athlete Babe Didrikson. Ederle won three medals at the 1924 Olympic Games and later was the first woman to swim across the English Channel. Didrikson, who won two gold and one silver medal at the 1932 Olympic Games, also won an AAU national title in basketball.

In 1949, the AAU conducted a national track and field meet in Cleveland, Ohio, to determine its national champions in track and field. This event represented the first time head-to-head competitions were held to crown national champions. Previously, national champions had been determined through telephone and/or mail entries. The success of this national track and field meet spurred the development of the AAU Sports Program and the AAU Junior Olympic Games.

Scope and Organization

Prior to 1978, the AAU was instrumental in preparing, selecting, and supporting U.S. Olympic teams. In 1978, Congress authorized the Amateur Sports Act, which instead gave control over Olympic sport in the United States to the U.S. Olympic Committee and national sport governing bodies. Currently, the AAU is best known for its role in providing amateur athletic participation opportunities, most notably in youth basketball and track and field.

The AAU motto is "Sports for All, Forever" and today the AAU offers sport participation opportunities in over 34 sports in 57 districts throughout the United States. The AAU has over 500,000 members and 60,000 volunteers who participate in the AAU Sports Program and AAU Junior Olympic Games. Additionally, the AAU sponsors the AAU Complete Athlete Program in conjunction with the National Collegiate Athletic Association (NCAA), and the AAU James E. Sullivan Memorial Award, and administers the President's Challenge Program on behalf of the President's Council on Physical Fitness and Sports.

The AAU is a nonprofit volunteer sport organization that is funded through membership dues, donations, and sponsors. Membership fees are affordable and currently stand at $12 per athlete and $14 per coach. Currently, USA Football, the WNBA, and sporting goods/apparel companies such as Eastbay, Rawlings, Champion, and Tachikara are official sponsors of the AAU. There are numerous local chapters that are organized into 56 districts across the country. These districts annually sanction 250 national championships and over 30,000 age division events. In 1996, the AAU relocated its national headquarters from Indianapolis, Indiana, to Walt Disney World and the ESPN Wide World of Sports complex in Orlando, Florida.

Boys and girls volleyball are among 30 youth sports included in the AAU Sports Program.

Programs and Sports

AAU sanctioned sport events occur under the auspices of the AAU Sports Program. The Sports Program includes over 30 youth and 25 adult sports programs in track and field, baseball, basketball, diving, football, gymnastics, hockey, martial arts, swimming, trampoline-tumbling, volleyball, wrestling, and sports such as aerobics, bocce ball, dance, golf, jump rope, lacrosse, surfing, tennis, and water polo. In addition to sanctioned sport events, the AAU requires players and coaches to attend the "Complete Athlete Program," which covers issues related to recruiting, grades, sportsmanship, and life skills.

Many young athletes are also involved in the AAU Junior Olympic Games. The inaugural AAU Junior Olympic Games were held in 1967 in Washington, D.C. Five hundred and twenty-three athletes competed in these first national swimming and track and field events. The AAU Junior Olympic Games have been held annually since then in various cities across the country. Currently, over 16,000 participants compete in 20-plus sports in the AAU Junior Olympic Games. The 2011 AAU Junior Olympic Games will be held in New Orleans, Louisiana. The weeklong, multisport event includes events in track and field, basketball, swimming, diving, cheerleading, gymnastics, karate, weightlifting, wrestling, beach volleyball, bowling, table tennis, field hockey, and others. Most AAU Junior Olympic Game participants must qualify for these national competitions by being one of the top three finishers at a district championship event.

In addition, the AAU annually awards its James E. Sullivan Memorial Award to the top amateur athlete in the United States. The award, which was established in memory of AAU founder and past president James E. Sullivan, is given to an amateur athlete on the basis of her/his athletic achievements, leadership, character, sportsmanship, and embodiment of the ideals of amateurism. The first award was given to the accomplished amateur golfer Robert "Bobby" T. Jones in 1930. The first female recipient of the award was swimmer Ann Curtis, who won the award in 1944. Other notable winners of the award include sprinter Wilma Rudolph (1961), basketball player Bill Bradley (1965), swimmer Mark Spitz (1971), diver Greg Louganis (1984), football player Peyton Manning (1997), as well as ultra-marathon runner and amputee Amy Palmiero-Winters (2009).

Notable AAU Athletes

Many notable basketball, baseball, and track and field athletes have participated in AAU programs. Some of these notable athletes include basketball players Shaquille O'Neal, LeBron James, Larry Bird, Dwight Howard, Kobe Bryant, Candace Parker, Chamique Holdsclaw, and Nykesha Sales. Notable baseball players have included David Wright, B. J. Upton, Prince Fielder, and Matt LaPorta. Jesse Owens, Jeremy Wariner and Florence Griffith-Joyner are a few of the famous AAU track and field athletes.

Corinne M. Daprano
University of Dayton

See Also: Amateur Athlete; Amateur Sports Act; Governing Body; Olympics; Student Athlete; Youth Sports.

Further Readings

Amateur Athletic Union. "The Real AAU." http://www.aausports.org/Home.aspx (Accessed September 2010).

DeKnop, P., L. M. Engstrom, B. Skirstad, and M. R. Weiss. *Worldwide Trends in Youth Sport.* Champaign, IL: Human Kinetics, 1996.

Wakefield, Wanda Ellen. "Out in the Cold: Sliding Sports and the Amateur Sports Act of 1978." *International Journal of the History of Sport,* v.24/6 (June 2007).

Amateur Sports Act

Designed to bolster the United States' competitiveness at international competitions vis-à-vis the Communist world, the Amateur Sports Act of 1978 resulted from the most ambitious—and perhaps only—attempt to create a federal sport policy in the nation's history. Having been initiated by U.S. policymakers in the aftermath of America's poor performance at the 1972 Summer Olympic Games in Munich, the process out of which the act emerged reflected Cold War perceptions of elite athletics as indicative of relative national strength. At the heart of the effort was an overriding fear that the United States could no longer keep pace with Soviet-bloc teams at elite-level international athletic competitions. A product as well of the conservative political ideologies of the Richard M. Nixon and Gerald Ford presidential administrations, the initiative aimed to restructure amateur sport in the United States while avoiding long-term federal control over its governance structure.

Resulting eventually in six years of study, a set of preliminary activities conducted by staff members in the Nixon administration led in 1975 to the establishment by the Ford White House of the President's Commission on Olympic Sports. Led by Executive Director Michael Harrigan, the Commission commenced a comprehensive study of the problems confronting American athletes, the results of which were issued in a two-volume report. Focusing on organizational design, policymakers involved in the project primarily concerned themselves with resolving a decades-long dispute between the Amateur Athletics Union (AAU) and the National Collegiate Athletic Association (NCAA). Beginning in 1923 with the AAU's suspension of sprinter Charles Paddock for his participation at a European meet against its wishes, the two organizations frequently punished one another's athletes—and in the process hurt U.S. teams at Olympic competitions. While previous initiatives sought to resolve the quarrel through arbitration proceedings, the President's Commission recommended that a "Central Sports Authority" should be created with sufficient authority to settle differences between the AAU, NCAA, and other competing members of the U.S. sports system. In pursuit of this goal, the central provision of the Amateur Sports Act of 1978 gave the United States Olympic Committee (USOC) the authority to name a single national governing body for each Olympic sport.

In addition to this power, the USOC gained exclusive rights under the legislation to the words *Olympic* and *Olympiad*, to the name *United States Olympic Committee* and to its emblem, as well as the five-ring symbol of the Olympic movement. At the same time, the act provided athletes a set of new legal protections. They could thenceforth appeal decisions concerning their eligibility. In addition, administrative procedures affecting them had to conform to principles of due process. Twenty percent of the voting power within any national governing body was also allocated to athletes.

Even after passage of the legislation, however, U.S. officials continued to worry over the nation's preparedness for the next set of international events. There was good reason for their concern. At the 1988 Winter Games in Calgary, American athletes could muster only six medals to finish a desultory ninth on the medals table. If one ascribed to the notion that elite sport served as an important indicator of national vitality, it was obvious that the Eastern bloc remained superior to the United States.

Given this situation, comprehensive reforms were contemplated solely within the context of elite athletics. Such was the case with regard to an independent investigation of the USOC chaired by George Steinbrenner. Virtually ignoring the possibility of a sports system geared toward mass involvement, the report issued by the Steinbrenner Commission, according to the *New York Times* in 1989, took the position that "winning medals must always be the primary goal." The continuation of this framework for U.S. sport policy was increasingly obsolete, however, given the changing needs of the American public.

With Cold War justifications for a national sport policy based solely on elite competitiveness finally having collapsed with the dismantling of the Berlin Wall in November 1989 and collapse of the Soviet Union in 1991, calls began to be made for revision of the legislation. Because of emerging perceptions that the act as originally written emphasized elite organizational design over the interests of athletes, legislative proposals for a revised statute largely centered on empowering athletes. At the same time,

fears that eligibility disputes might evolve into expensive legal proceedings led to the insertion of language protecting the USOC from lawsuits initiated by competitors.

In addition, the growing support for the handicapped in the United States during the 1990s called attention to the lack of enforcement mechanisms concerning the treatment of disabled athletes under the original 1978 legislation. The most prominent sections of the statute thus mandated a greater level of involvement by the USOC with Paralympic sport and an expanded representation of athletes on the committee. Named after its principal sponsor in the U.S. Senate, the Ted Stevens Olympic and Amateur Sports Act became law in 1998; this statute remains in force as of early 2011.

Thomas M. Hunt
Laurence H. Chalip
University of Texas at Austin

See Also: Amateur Athlete; Amateur Athletic Union; Governing Body; Legal Considerations in Sport; National Collegiate Athletic Association.

Further Readings

Chalip, Laurence. "Policy Analysis in Sport Management." *Journal of Sport Management*, v.9 (January 1995).
Janofsky, Michael. "Steinbrenner Report Faults U.S. Progress." *New York Times* (February 20, 1989).
Wakefield, Wanda Ellen. "Out in the Cold: Sliding Sports and the Amateur Sports Act of 1978." *International Journal of the History of Sport*, v.24/6 (June 2007).

Ambush Marketing

The word *ambush* originates from the Old French verb *embuschier*, meaning to put something in a wooded area, thereby making it difficult for others to see. This word was combined in the 1980s with another word, *marketing*, to create the phrase *ambush marketing*. The development of the term has been credited to Jerry Welsh, then executive vice president of Worldwide Marketing and Communications at the American Express Company. The word *ambush*, in this case, has evolved to refer to an attack from a hidden position in the marketplace so that one company can take unfair advantage of another. This type of marketing has been used strategically by businesses involved with sporting events that seek to benefit from sponsorship without paying to be official sponsors. These businesses position advertisements that suggest they are officially associated with the sporting event. In short, ambush marketing has been used by businesses to create the illusion that their products or services are associated with the event. This sets them up to exploit the integrity, position, and image of the sporting event by designing a relationship with it without the consent of the event owners.

There are several types of ambush marketing tactics. They can be divided into two categories: direct ambush activities and indirect ambush activities.

Direct Ambush Activity

Direct ambush activity involves intent. Business leaders position their brand so that it seems associated with an athlete, team, league, and/or event for which it has not paid rights and is, therefore, not an official sponsor. Predatory ambushing, a direct ambush activity, refers to an attack of an official sponsor by another corporation in order for the other corporation to financially benefit and to also confuse the public as to who the official sponsor is. The 1992 Olympic Games held in Barcelona where Visa and American Express were embroiled is an example of predatory ambushing.

Coattail ambushing refers to a corporation taking a straightforward approach to associate with a sporting event by using a valid connection to, but not becoming, an official sponsor. When Champion, for example, sponsors an individual athlete but does not sponsor the event the athlete participates in, Champion goes in on the "coattail" of the event, not as an event sponsor but as the sponsor of an individual athlete.

Self-ambushing involves marketing behavior that is beyond what was agreed to by contract between the two parties, thereby cluttering marketing space and taking away area from other official sponsors. If NIKE sponsors a tennis tournament and product availability was determined by a contract to be in a specific area, self-ambushing is involved if NIKE adds another 20 locations, thereby cluttering the area of other official sponsors. Another closely related ambush marketing technique is property infringement. This is the unlawful or unofficial use of intellectual property that is protected by law. Logos, words and phrases, and symbols can be considered in this category. At one time, the Greek government–owned Olympic Airways used the official Olympic Rings as its logo before realizing that property rights of the Olympic Rings had been infringed upon.

Indirect Ambush Activity

Indirect ambush activities are defined by the deliberate association of a brand with an athlete, team, league, and/or event through implicit reference. Associative ambush marketing is the use of imagery or terms to create the impression that an organization is linked in some way to the event or product. In 2008, NIKE frequently used the symbol "8," which characterized Chinese good fortune. It was also used as one of the symbols for the Beijing Olympic Games. Of course, NIKE was not an official sponsor of the Games, but sponsored teams and athletes who participated in them.

Distractive ambush marketing, yet another form, involves setting up promotions in the vicinity of an event without making specific mention of the event itself in order to engage the spectator psyche. Values ambush marketing entails the use of the value of an event to infer association with it. In 2008, Puma AG utilized a slogan, "Together Everywhere," in its football-related (soccer) advertising campaign. This specific phrase placed emphasis on unity and racial tolerance, the central themes that surrounded the European football championships that year. Insurgent ambush marketing, street promotion of products or events near an event, is distinguished by the handout of flyers and free promotional materials such as pens, key chains, or mugs highlighting the business brand and involvement with the particular sport that is featured at the event. At Super Bowl XLV, a local Domino's pizza restaurant passed out flyers three blocks away from the stadium for buy-one, get-one-free pizza slices. The flyers were in the form of a football. The official sponsor of the event was Papa John's Pizza.

Incidental ambush marketing involves the perception of sponsorship of an event or product without officially establishing a connection. Unintentional ambush marketing involves media coverage of a sporting event. At the 2008 Olympic Games in Beijing, the Speedo company received extensive publicity because of its revolutionary technologically designed swimsuits that were worn by a number of medalists. Although Speedo was not an official sponsor, its brand and swimsuit sales were catapulted to the top in sales.

Saturation ambush marketing comprises advertising and marketing that are increased during the event. Because of the increased hype during the event, an unofficial company could benefit as a result of increased media attention, including television coverage. Generally, mention is made by announcers about a particular brand that an athlete wears or equipment that is used. Many National Collegiate Athletic Association (NCAA) teams in the United States are serviced by Nike. The company offers universities substantially reduced cost on uniforms, shoes, and other apparel. Spectators may assume that the company is an official sponsor of the NCAA or of the team as a result of the media exposure.

Value

As the popularity of sport and the business it generates continue to grow globally, advertisement values continue to inflate exponentially. It has been said that sport-related marketing efforts have surpassed the $100 billion mark. With these types of investments by corporations, ambush marketing may soon take on new meanings. However, examples of events at which companies engaged in traditional ambush marketing strategies include the 1984 Olympic Games in Los Angeles. The Kodak Corporation sponsored the U.S. track and field team as well as television broadcasts of the Games. However, Fujifilm was the official sponsor. By 1988, Kodak had earned its official sponsorship of the Olympic Games, and Fujifilm was involved at a lower level (coattail ambush marketing).

AT&T, one of the oldest and largest telecommunications corporations, renewed its deal to be the U.S. Olympic Committee's (USOC) official sponsor for telecommunications through the 2012 London Olympic Games. It was also determined that it would be a major advertiser during the Olympic Games broadcasts purchased by the United States–based National Broadcasting Company (NBC). McDonald's, the restaurant conglomerate, is one of the International Olympic Committee's nine top-tier sponsors. To be the sole fast-food sponsor, the corporate giant has paid $25 million annually and is still the only restaurateur that has official rights to use the Olympic logo in its advertising globally.

These corporations pay huge sums to be the official partners and sponsors of the modern Olympic Games, the largest mega- and multisport event in the world, but they have seen many examples of ambush marketing. In 1992, the American Express Company ran television advertisements that showed the city of Barcelona in the background and conveyed a message that ". . . you don't need a visa" in order to visit Spain. Visa, an official sponsor of the 1992 Olympic Games, was livid, and stated that the commercials constituted ambush marketing. American Express indicated that they were not referring to the Barcelona Olympic Games and, therefore, were not attempting to ambush Visa.

In the 1996 Atlanta Olympic Games, the Nike Corporation placed over 500 billboards throughout the city to announce its brand of sport apparel. The billboards were prominently displayed so that many believed that Nike was an official sponsor of the Atlanta Games. While none of the billboards infringed upon advertising near venues, the message was evident.

In preparation for the 2010 FIFA World Cup in South Africa, companies such as adidas, Coca-Cola, Sony, and Visa paid FIFA millions of Euros for exclusive rights in the sponsorship/partnership categories. Despite the efforts of FIFA and the companies to dispel ambush marketing, problems occurred. First, FIFA denied the use of the words *South Africa* and the Olympic trademark by Kulula Airlines (a South African domestic airline carrier), citing the images taken together were ambush marketing. Second, MTN, an Africa-based telecommunications company and local sponsor of the 2010 FIFA World Cup event, withdrew an advertisement that supposedly infringed upon Vodacom's proprietary rights over the name *Bafana Bafana*. While *2010* or *twenty ten*, in conjunction with *soccer, football, South Africa, RSA, SA, World Cup*, or with soccer or FIFA World Cup imagery, could not be used, several companies attempted to do so.

The Anheuser-Busch company spent millions of U.S. dollars to become the National Football League's official beer advertiser at Super Bowls. Competitor brewers bought local television advertisements or hosted parties close to the stadia throughout the week preceding several Super Bowls in order to profit from the excitement without paying any of the cost for the official rights.

The Subway company, a restaurant franchise, had no official relationship with the USOC between 2004 and 2008. Although a television commercial run during that time did not mention the USOC and only showed the first three letters of the word *Canada* on a map in the background, the inference to the Olympic Games and of the use of Michael Phelps was apparent: Michael Phelps, a world record holder in swimming, was swimming toward Vancouver and the Winter Olympics that were to be held there.

Legislation

As a result of ambush marketing, anti–ambush marketing legislation has evolved. A prime example of initiatives taken by governments through legislative branches is South Africa in its preparation for the 2010 FIFA World Cup. The country already had the usual common laws of the Trade Marks Act, Copyright Act, Counterfeit Goods Act, and the Advertising Standards Authority in place. A section of the Trade Practices Act of 1976 prohibited the making of false or misleading statements that inferred a connection between said person and the 2010 FIFA World Cup. A section of the Merchandise Marks Act of 1941 was amended to consider 2010 FIFA World Cup a protected event against the use of a trademark in a manner that achieved publicity for the trademark and gave special benefit from the event. Yet another section of the Merchandise Marks Act of 1941 prohibited the use of words and symbols for the 2010 FIFA World Cup. Therefore, the use of *2010 FIFA World Cup South Africa, Football World Cup, 2010 FIFA World Cup, 2010 FIFA World Cup, Soccer World Cup*, and *Confed-*

erations World Cup were prohibited. Once money is paid by any FIFA sponsor, it is entitled to a rights package of use of the official marks, exposure in and around stadia, in official FIFA publications and Websites, and in the official sponsor program, as well as protection from ambush marketing.

The anti–ambush marketing legislation was tested in the case of *FIFA v. Metcash Trading Africa (Pty.) Ltd.* just prior to the FIFA World Cup in South Africa. The Metcash company produced a lollipop that was marketed as the "2010 Pops" and displayed soccer ball images similar to ones used by FIFA in earlier tournaments, along with the South African flag. The court's decision at the trial was in favor of FIFA, finding that Metcash knew the product would be affiliated with the 2010 FIFA World Cup and thereby get special benefit from the event.

Protection

Some corporations, including McDonald's, Coca-Cola, Visa, Kodak, and Xerox, have paid multimillion-dollar fees for the rights to be an Olympic Partner in the TOP (The Olympic Partners) program. This program, managed by the International Olympic Committee, permits sponsors exclusive global marketing rights in product categories for the Summer and Winter Olympic Games. TOP companies are also able to use the Olympic imagery and other official designs on products. They are also part of a wider Olympic sponsorship program. Because the second most recognizable symbol in the world after the Christian cross is the Olympic Rings, this makes the brand extremely sought after and desirable to officially and unofficially associate with.

For example, nearly 78 percent of the $1.31 billion budget was projected to come from corporate marketing sponsors, royalties from official merchandise licensing, and broadcasting rights fees in anticipation of the Olympic and Paralympic Winter Games in 2002. In order to defend against trademark infringement and ambush marketing, the USOC and the Salt Lake Organizing Committee (SLOC) formed a Joint Marketing Agreement to market the games. The corporation, Olympic Properties of the United States (OPUS), was able to license various Olympic and Paralympic terms, marks, and images to sponsors and partners who financed the 2002 Winter Games.

During a three-year period of time, the SLOC identified 431 incidences involving intellectual property right infringements. It was, therefore, important for the organizing committee to educate the general population about intellectual property and ambush marketing in order to attempt to defray trademark infringement. It used its Website and additional educational campaigns that included advertisements in trade magazines, mass mailings to athlete agents, retailers, National Organizing Committees (NOCs), and Olympic sponsors and suppliers, and conducted brand protection workshops for sponsors.

The SLOC also used a technique, referred to as mystery shopping, where brand-protection professionals provided random and unannounced surveillance to retail shops and e-commerce Websites. Almost half of the surveillance sites carried unlicensed merchandise that bore Olympic marks. The SLOC contacted the businesses through letters that informed them about ambush marketing and protection of the Olympic brand and asked the Park City, Utah, Chamber of Commerce to explain to members the issue of intellectual property rights. Two weeks after the educational campaign, 75 percent of the businesses had eliminated the sale of infringement products.

Firm rules by the Greek government and the IOC were instituted whereby spectators of the 2004 Olympic Games could only enter event facilities without food or drinks unless they were made by companies that were official sponsors. Olympic Games personnel also checked T-shirts, bags, and hats for logos of companies that were not official sponsors. People who appeared to be wearing merchandise manufactured by a company other than an official sponsor were told to wear the merchandise inside out, totally remove it, or be banned from the venue. An increasing crackdown by governments and event organizers on street vending and outdoor and public transport advertising from two weeks before the opening through the closing of events limited some of the onslaught.

One of the conditions for cities bidding for the 2012 Olympic Games included how ambush marketing would be dealt with should their city be awarded the games. As a result of London being awarded the Games, the London Olympic and Paralympics Games Act of 2006 was devised and implemented. The anti-ambush marketing legislation, new to the United Kingdom, makes anything that might be used commercially illegal. There are 34 combinations of the terms *summer* and *games* that have been explicitly excluded. The laws have been designed to promise a level of protection for the local organizing committee; therefore, an entire team has been dedicated to patrol them.

Many ambush marketing campaigns have dramatic effects upon the official sponsors and are different than the routine infringement of FIFA trademarks or logos. Generally, when trademarks or logos are infringed upon, cease-and-desist letters are sent from attorneys to companies. When small campaigns or national, regional, or local campaigns are launched, the letters are often sufficient. When an infringement of internationally known trademarks is made, it is difficult to stop. Adidas, Coca-Cola, Emirates, Kia/Hyundai, Visa, and Sony as official FIFA partners have had numerous ambush marketing experiences by rival brands Nike, Pepsi, and American Express. Huge amounts of money have been paid for official partnerships in order to give official sponsors greater exposure than ambush marketers.

The increasing cost of sponsorship has not only raised the financial stakes but also return on investment of the sponsors. It is, therefore, critical that events that are sponsored are also exclusive to those who fund them. If the exclusivity is breached, the sponsor's contributions are spent rather than invested. The investment in sponsorship property might be at the most lost and at the least damaged and has the potential to extend through the sponsor's market share. At the same time, the value of the sponsorship is also lost. Corporate sponsorship is a huge contributor to revenue sources for event organizers. An unintended consequence is the loss in financial strength of an event organizer.

Legal Developments

Typically, a company that owns a trademark will frequently protect itself by calling upon protections and solutions provided by laws or acts. One of the challenges involved with confronting ambush marketers under such acts or laws is that the consumer protection approach may not permit courts an appropriate rationale to decide in favor of the company holding the trademark. One of the realities is that the ambushers do not blatantly use or display the Olympic, FIFA, or professional sport team marks, creating consumer confusion. Instead, they create an inferred association with the marks and with the Olympics. Also, fans, spectators, and/or consumers may not be as likely to draw the inference as the trademark-holding company. Therefore, the burden of proof genuinely rests on the company holding the trademark to provide solid proof of such infringement.

For example, the decision of the court in the *MasterCard International, Inc. v. Sprint Communications* company illustrates the readiness of courts to shelter sponsorship and licensing contracts despite no evidence of consumer confusion. Master-Card was a 1994 FIFA World Cup sponsor. Sprint Communications was a 1994 World Cup partner. MasterCard was successful in securing the right be the sole producer of a "card-based payment and account access device" which, by virtue of the wording, meant any type of a credit card. The court made the decision in favor of MasterCard, but did not provide a clear precedent for future ambush marketing occurrences.

Conclusion

Ambush marketing has matured over the past two decades. The intentional attachment to a protected event such as the FIFA World Cup or the Olympic Games by unofficial sponsors has evolved to much more sophisticated and subtle methods. Campaigns have progressed to showcase the marketing genius of companies.

In 2010, business leaders invested in excess of $43 billion in sport-related activities to become official sponsors of individual athletes, teams, leagues, and/or events throughout the world. IOC sponsorship fees, for example, make up approximately 40 percent of the total revenue for the Olympic Movement. These types of official entitlements provide lucrative revenue streams to sporting organizations.

Ultimately, official sponsors and their respective sport organizations must find solutions to protect the value of their formal affiliation, as ambush marketing appears to be on the rise. Internet marketing and the use of Twitter and Facebook are providing new means for ambush marketing. Direct messages through relevant tweets, answering questions on forums, and plugging links to specific Websites or blogs add to the complexity of the ambush marketing issue. The question of whether or not ambush marketing is ethical, legal, or simply cunning business continues to grow. Ambush marketing will continue to make event organizers look for additional ways to prevent infringement of intellectual property rights worldwide.

Darlene A. Kluka
Barry University

See Also: Activation, Sponsorship; Ambush Marketing, Protection From; Benefits for Sponsors; Cross-Promotions; Guerrilla Marketing; Official Sponsor; Pre-Event Sponsorship Activities; Promotion; Sponsorship; Sponsorship Failure.

Further Readings

Cardinal, M. "Olympic Brand Ambush Marketing Is . . . (A) A Mortal Sin (B) Good Business Sense (C) None of the Above." http://www.vancouverobserver.com/politics/commentary/2009/11/29/olympic-brand-ambush.html (Accessed February 2011).
Chadwick, S. and N. Burton. "Ambushed!" *Wall Street Journal* (January 25, 2010).
Meenaghan, T. "Ambush Marketing: A Threat to Corporate Sponsorship." *MIT Sloan Management Review*, v.1 (1996).
Scaria, A. G. *Ambush Marketing: A Game Within a Game.* New York: Oxford University Press, 2008.
Schwarz, E. C. and J. D. Hunter. *Advanced Theory and Practice in Sport Marketing.* Oxford, UK: Elsevier, 2008.
Skildum-Reid, K. *Ambush Marketing Toolkit.* New York: McGraw-Hill, 2007.

Ambush Marketing, Protection From

The International Olympic Committee defines ambush marketing as "a planned attempt by a third party to associate itself directly or indirectly with the Olympic Games to gain the recognition and benefits associated with being an Olympic partner." Tactically, ambush marketing can be accomplished via advertising and sales promotions. Some common methods of ambush marketing include the purchase of broadcast advertising time, in-market "sponsorship" activation, and similar themed messaging. In the early stages of ambush marketing, sponsors and properties tried to shame ambushers into submission. This defense did not work as many ambushers actually found their products leading in sponsorship recall studies despite not paying the sponsorship fee. In an effort to prevent ambush marketing and protect sponsorship investment, both sponsors and properties need to take actions.

The Olympics have increased its brand protection against ambush marketing. The Vancouver Olympic Committee (VANOC) was legally obligated to the IOC and to its marketing partners to protect against unauthorized use of the Olympic brand and ambush marketing in Canada. The reasons for this requirement were that sponsorship revenue is vital to support the operating costs of the Olympic Games and to ensure sponsorship investments are protected. One of the main tactics is to visit retail stores and remove counterfeit merchandise. Unfortunately, many times the retailer does not know the merchandise is not "official" and it would be difficult to collect any payment made for that inventory. Additionally, investigations into who produces the illegal products often prove fruitless.

Strategies
There are a few strategies that events can employ to protect sponsors. First, as shown by the VANOC example, the event needs to protect its intellectual property. Most court systems provide a legal method to protect trademarks and copyrights. Next, the property needs to honor its category exclusivity and clearly define which products are members of a category and which are not. For example, does the soft drink category include energy drinks? Mega events such as the Olympics and FIFA World Cup can demand concessions from venues, media partners, and host sites. Venues can be forced to remove any nonsponsor advertising and products. Media partners can be required to either ban competitive

advertising or offer a right of first refusal to official sponsors to limit the exposure to competitive messaging. A host site can be required to eliminate competitive messaging on billboards, parks, and buses/public transportation; to control airspace against unauthorized airplanes and blimps; and to require permits for pamphlet/product sample distribution. It is vitally important that the mega event supports local law enforcement by having an "anti-ambush" team patrol the venue, retail locations, and city investigating potential ambush activity.

Events need to use local regulations to discourage ambush marketing. Most cities require special permits for sampling. Working with the mayor's office to eliminate these permits during the event dates is important. Police or even event personnel should patrol the surrounding areas. Also, notices explaining this policy should be sent to the local staffing agencies. If the staff is notified then the out-of-town marketing agency will find out.

Creating a clean zone is important. Private parking lots are often locations in which ambushers set up. Because the lot is on private property, the event may not be able to prevent renting to nonsponsors. But one can limit the activity and the location to only the private property via the permitting method.

VANOC took an innovative approach to brand protection. Prior to the Olympic Games, it conducted an educational program aimed directly at retailers and on the Internet. This communication explained the purpose of the anti-ambush program: how to spot counterfeit merchandise, and what kind of activity would violate the VANOC regulations. Further, fans were encouraged to "buy real" merchandise as opposed to supporting knock-off products.

Legislation
Mega events are trying to gain legislative help against ambush marketing. The London Olympics Bill is designed to prevent ambush marketing at the 2012 Olympic Games in London, England. A contentious point of the proposed law is the restriction of certain words surrounding the games. The organizers would like to protect as many words and phrases as possible, whereas marketers would like this list pared to only the traditional distinctive Olympic marks such as *Olympic, Olympics, Olympiad, London Games,* and so on. For ex-

ample, the bill proposes to ban gold, silver, and bronze from goods, packaging, and advertising. Opponents to the law claim safeguards covering copyright, trademarks, passing-off, and misleading advertising already exist and additional legislation should not be needed.

In the United States, the Lanham Act provides potential remedies for ambush marketing. However, the legal standard is consumer confusion or likelihood of consumer confusion. Despite recall studies showing the impact of ambush marketing's success, the Lanham Act has not proven to be a very effective deterrent.

Contracts and Sponsorship Activation

Also, sponsors need to defend themselves from ambush marketers. Sponsors must protect their interests via sponsorship contracts to require anti-ambushing activity from the event. The contract should force the event to perform actions listed above; failure to do so would result in monetary damages for the sponsor.

Next, the sponsor needs to completely activate its sponsorship, thus eliminating potential ambush tactics. For instance, a beer sponsor should provide on-premise activation at bars, taverns, retail stores, and distribution centers. This would prevent another beer brand from activating at those locations. Because most of those establishments would be private companies, it would difficult for the host site to require them to support the sponsor. The sponsor needs to secure the locations itself.

Sponsor (and events) should create co-marketing opportunities amongst the sponsors. All brands are looking for partners to increase their marketing reach. On an event level this can take the shape of ensuring that sponsors are given first opportunity to supply their product to all sponsors and their activation tactics. For example, if Paper Mate is an event sponsor then there should not be any Sharpie markers at the event—anywhere. This would include any sponsor hosting autograph signings. Sponsor meetings and pre-event communication are great opportunities to get event marketers together to spark discussions.

In the end, it is difficult to prevent creative marketers from trying to associate with the spirit and excitement of sporting events. Recently, Luft-hansa showed its support of Germany hosting the 2006 World Cup by placing soccer decals on the airplane's nose cones. A Dutch brewery, Bavaria, dressed female fans in orange in order to gain television exposure (and public relations) at the last two World Cup tournaments. Because the brewery and the Netherlands' soccer jerseys share the same dominant color, orange, other fans might see a connection between the sporting event and the brewery. Perhaps the most effective method to reduce the effectiveness of ambush activity is to activate the sponsorship better.

Mark Dodds
State University of New York College at Cortland

See Also: Activation, Sponsorship; Ambush Marketing; Benefits for Sponsors; Cross-Promotions; Guerrilla Marketing; Official Sponsor; Pre-Event Sponsorship Activities; Promotion; Sponsorship Failure.

Further Readings

Cardinel, M. "Olympic Brand Ambush Marketing Is . . . (A) A Mortal Sin (B) Good Business Sense (C) None of the Above." http://www.vancouverobserver.com/politics/commentary/2009/11/29/olympic-brand-ambush-marketing-isa-mortal-sin-b-good-business-sense-c (Accessed January 2011).

Cooper, Bill. Personal Interview, Vancouver, Canada. (April 27, 2010).

Hyland, A. "Anti-Ambush Marketing Legislation—Does It Work?" *Intellectual Asset Management* (February 25, 2009).

Pittsburgh Trademark Lawyer. "Ambush Marketing and the Lanham Act." http://pittsburghtrademarklawyer.wordpress.com/2010/07/09/ambush-marketing-and-the-lanham-act (Accessed January 2011).

Skildum-Reid, Kim. *The Ambush Marketing Toolkit*. New York: McGraw-Hill, 2007.

SportBusiness Daily. "Vancouver Olympics Seeing Less Ambush Marketing Than Past Games." *SportBusiness Daily* (January 18, 2010).

Wilson, B. "Protecting Sport Sponsors From Ambush." BBC News (February 20, 2006).

Americans with Disabilities Act

The Americans with Disabilities Act 1990 (ADA) has its origins in the race discrimination case of *Brown v. Board of Education* 347 U.S. 483 (1954), which heralded the end of racial segregation in U.S. public schools. Advocates for people with disabilities subsequently argued that their rights were no less guaranteed under the equal protection clause of the Fourteenth Amendment than were those of other minority groups, and while attempts to add disabilities as a protected class under the Civil Rights Act of 1964 did not bear fruit, Congress' subsequent passing of the Rehabilitation Act of 1973 at least prohibited discrimination against persons with disabilities by government agencies or businesses with federal contracts worth more than $2,500.

The ADA built upon the 1973 Act by expanding the scope of the legislation and prohibiting private sector discrimination, including discrimination in private schools and universities. It defines "disability" as a physical or mental impairment that substantially limits a "major life activity," a phrase which in turn connotes an activity that is "of central importance to most people's lives." Although the courts have often taken a more conservative approach to the definition of "major life activity" than can be reconciled with either the language of the legislation or the intent of Congress in passing it, the ADA is properly regarded as one of the more successful disability discrimination laws presently in force.

In the sporting context the ADA has been of significance in several broad areas thus far. The most celebrated of these concerns the golfer Casey Martin, who in *PGA Tour v. Martin* 532 U.S. 661 (2001) successfully argued before the Supreme Court that the ADA prohibited the governing body of men's professional golf from having a rule that obliged him to walk the course rather than using a golf cart during its competitions. Martin, who had a degenerative circulatory disorder that made it impossible for him to walk the course, challenged the USPGA's contention that during tournaments the playing areas of golf courses were not "public accommodations" and were thus not covered by the "reasonable accommodation" requirements of the ADA, and that in any event allowing Martin to use a cart would "fundamentally alter" the nature of its tournaments and thus it would not be obliged to provide such an accommodation even if the "reasonable accommodation" provisions were applicable in principle. In the Supreme Court, Justice Scalia famously asserted that applying the ADA to golf's "walking only" rule would effectively allow the courts to rewrite the rules of made-up games to such an extent that an individual's lack of ability would no longer be a handicap; but the majority held (at p. 687) that the walking rule was:

(A)t best peripheral to the nature of (the PGA's) athletic events ... (Its) claim that all the substantive rules for its highest-level competitions are sacrosanct and cannot be modified under any circumstances is effectively a contention that it is exempt from (the ADA's) reasonable accommodation requirement. But (the Act) carves out no exception for elite athletics.

In the wake of *PGA Tour,* recourse to the ADA has been sought by (inter alia) high school students with disabilities who have sought to challenge age-based participation restrictions, by college student athletes with learning disabilities who argued they were disadvantaged by the NCAA's essential eligibility requirements and, in the employment context, by professional athletes who claimed that their alcohol use, recreational drug use, or use of prohibited performance-enhancing substances was a consequence of their disability and that their employer's unfavorable response to their activities thus amounted to unlawful treatment under the ADA. Not all of those claims have met with sympathy and the ruling in *PGA Tour* has not radically altered college, high school, or professional sports in the manner that Justice Scalia feared.

In fact, perhaps the most long-standing of the ADA's contributions to sports is concerned not with how it has extended opportunities for active participation or with the level of protection afforded to employees with disabilities, but with the obligations it places on facilities owners to ensure that those with disabilities have access to sporting venues and other places of entertainment.

A line of cases concerning cinemas and sports stadia has concentrated on the meaning of the phrase "lines of sight comparable," which is used in the regulations issued pursuant to the ADA and obliges facilities owners to make whatever reasonable accommodations are necessary to ensure that those with disabilities (and especially wheelchair users) can attend events on terms that are comparable with those enjoyed by the wider public. Several of those cases have been initiated by the Paralyzed Veterans of America on behalf of their members, while respondents have included a range of organizations such as Regal Cinemas, Cinemark, and the owners of the Rose Garden in Portland.

While the regulations have always been complex and have been subject to recent amendment that makes them no less so, the general principle (and one in keeping with the tenor of the ADA) is that people with disabilities should be allowed to make full use of all the venue's facilities and sit with family or friends rather than being in an exclusive "wheelchair area." Those with disabilities should have access to a range of areas within the stadium, at different prices, and a choice of where they can sit without their view being impeded by standing spectators or where their line of sight will otherwise be impeded.

David McArdle
University of Stirling

See Also: Discrimination; Diversity in Sport; Facilities Management; Facilities Planning, Sports; Participants in Sports.

Further Readings

Hubbard, A. "The Major Life Activity of Belonging." *Wake Forest Law Review,* v.39/1 (2004).
McArdle, D. "Using the ADA to Inform 'Access to Sporting Venues' Under the Disabilities Convention." *Boston University International Law Journal,* v.27/2 (2009).
Waterstone, M. "Let's Be Reasonable Here: Why the ADA Will Not Ruin Professional Sports." *Brigham Young University Law Review,* v.26/4 (2000).

America's Cup

The America's Cup is one of the world's oldest international sporting trophies. Competed in yacht racing, it was first contested in 1851 when a yacht designed and built in the United States sailed across the Atlantic to challenge the fastest yachts in Britain. The significance of this challenge in the context of that time should not be underestimated. The British were the world superpower in matters naval and marine, and their prowess in the sport of yachting was a source of great national pride among the aristocracy. As a consequence, the Americans were given no chance against the best 15 yachts from the prestigious Royal Yacht Squadron.

The race created a legend. America won decisively and in doing so produced one of the great sporting quotes. As the U.S. yacht *America* approached the finish line, Queen Victoria is reported to have asked, "Are the yachts in sight?" The reply was, "Only the *America*, may it please Your Majesty." Queen Victoria then inquired, "Which is second?" The reply: "Ah, Your Majesty, there is no second."

The owner and skipper of the yacht *America*, John Cox Stevens, received an elaborate trophy, which subsequently became known as the America's Cup—after the name of the vessel that first won it. In 1857, Stevens and other members of the syndicate that owned the yacht donated the America's Cup to the New York Yacht Club under a Deed of Gift that stipulated that the cup was to be used as a perpetual challenge trophy for competition between yacht clubs of different nations. Since that time the America's Cup has grown to become the world's premier yachting contest between the previous winner and holder of the cup and a challenger representing a yacht club from a foreign nation.

What has added to the profile and intrigue of the America's Cup was the fact that the New York Yacht Club successfully defended the trophy against all challengers for 132 years, reportedly the longest winning streak in international sporting competition. Over those years many controversies have occurred, with a number of challengers alleging that the defender shaped the rules to its own advantage, a legacy that has continued into the 21st century.

In 1983, a challenger was successful for the first time when the yacht *Australia II* defeated the defender from the New York Yacht Club. The Western Australia Royal Perth Yacht Club won the America's Cup, and subsequently hosted the first America's Cup regatta outside of U.S. waters in 1987. However, the Stars and Stripes syndicate from the San Diego Yacht Club won the regatta and the cup returned to the United States, where it was successfully defended in 1988 and 1992. In 1995, another challenger, this time from New Zealand, triumphed. Thus, the right to host the next America's Cup fell to the Royal New Zealand Yacht Squadron and the event moved to Auckland, New Zealand. New Zealand successfully defended it in 2000, but the Alinghi team from Switzerland triumphed in 2003. The Alinghi team successfully defended the cup in the waters of the Mediterranean Sea off Valencia, Spain, in 2007.

What is unusual about the America's Cup as a sporting event is that the yacht club that wins it also wins the right to host and defend the subsequent cup event against challengers. Thus, the winning of the cup gives significant discretionary power to the defender to determine many aspects related to the event including the location, the date, and the sail-

ing course area. Because there are significant benefits that accrue to a locale that hosts the America's Cup, many governments, corporations, and individuals have been prepared to invest significantly in attempts to win the cup and the right to host the next event.

Mark Orams
Auckland University of Technology

See Also: Davis Cup; International Reach; Ryder Cup; U.S. Open Tennis Tournament.

Further Readings

Cateora, Phillip R., et al. *International Marketing.* New York: McGraw-Hill, 2009.

Conner, Dennis and Michael Levitt. *The America's Cup: The History of Sailing's Greatest Competition in the Twentieth Century.* New York: St. Martin's Press, 1998.

"34th America's Cup." http://www.americascup .com (Accessed November 2010).

The American racing sail trimaran USA-17, then known as the BMW Oracle Racing 90, undergoing testing in the Pacific Ocean in early 2009 before a reconfiguration that helped it win the 33rd America's Cup in 2010.

Anaheim Ducks

The Anaheim Ducks is a National Hockey League (NHL) franchise that is well known for its unique beginning and its successful playoff history. The franchise was created as an NHL expansion club in 1993. The original owner of the club was the Walt Disney Company, which is best known for creating a series of legendary family moves ranging from *Cinderella* to *Bambi* to *The Sound of Music*. Disney had created a popular film, *The Mighty Ducks*, in 1992, and simply applied the name of the film to its NHL team.

Disney sold the franchise in 2005 to Henry and Susan Samueli, who changed the name of the team to the Anaheim Ducks (eliminating the word *Mighty* before the 2006–07 season). The new owners also replaced the original logo showing a duck-shaped goaltender's mask (featured in the movie) to a stylized webbed foot shaped like the letter D and changed the team's color scheme (from purple and teal to brown and gold).

Samueli earned his fortune as one of the founders of Broadcom Corporation (which manufactures processing chips for computers). He was suspended by the NHL for 18 months (May 2008–November 2009) while he faced criminal charges that he allegedly manipulated the value of Broadcom stock. Samueli was acquitted of criminal charges in November 2010.

The franchise then known as "the Mighty Ducks" rallied from a mediocre regular season to play the New Jersey Devils for the 2003 Stanley Cup Final. That team finished the regular season with the seventh-best record in the Western Conference, but then went on to upset such higher-ranked squads as Detroit and Dallas to advance to the finals. In the Stanley Cup Finals, Anaheim lost to New Jersey in a grueling seven-game series that pitted one brother on each squad against another (Scott Niedermayer for the Mighty Ducks and Rob Niedermayer for the Devils). The 2003 Mighty Ducks were coached by Mike Babcock, and some of their best players that season included Scott Niedermayer and Paul Kariya.

The franchise is best known on the ice for winning the NHL championship (the Stanley Cup) in 2007. That team was coached by Randy Carlyle, who has been the Ducks' only head coach since 2005. In 2007, the Ducks finished second in the Western Conference during the regular season, and then won playoff series against Minnesota, Vancouver, and Detroit to reach the Stanley Cup Finals, where they beat the Ottawa Senators in five games. That 2007 club played a very physical and rough and style of hockey led by Chris Pronger and Scott Niedermayer, goal-scorer Teemu Selanne and goalie Jean-Sebastien Giguere. Niedermayer won the Conn Smythe Trophy, which is awarded to the Most Valuable Player in the Stanley Cup Finals. In winning the cup, the Ducks became the first West Coast team to win the prize in the modern era; the only other team to do so was the Victoria Cougars, who took the cup in 1925.

In 2009, the Ducks were valued by *Forbes* magazine as the 14th most valuable team in the NHL at more than $206 million. The team plays its home games at the Honda Center. The arena, which seats 17,146 fans for NHL games, was completed in 1993 at a cost of $123 million. Arrowhead Water was the first corporation to purchase the naming rights to the facility, until Honda bought the rights to have its name on the building in 2006.

Ricard W. Jensen
University of South Dakota

See Also: Expansion; Licensing; Los Angeles Kings; National Hockey League; Retaining Sponsors, Keys to.

Further Readings

Badenhausen, K., M. Ozanian, and Christina Settimi. "The Business of Hockey." http://www.forbes.com/lists/2009/31/hockey-values-09_Anaheim-Ducks_310658.html (Accessed October 2010).
Farber, M. "Duck! Here Comes Anaheim." *Sports Illustrated*, v.106/24 (2007).
Higgins, M. "Mighty in Deed, if Not in Name." *New York Times* (October 20, 2006).
Jenkins, L. "Ugly Ducks Take Stanley Cup to Disneyland." *New York Times* (June 7, 2007).
Stephens, E. "Samueli Understood Bettman's Decision." *Orange County Register* (September 23, 2010).

Announcer

The public address announcer may possess the most recognizable voice in the arena. The announcer's voice is counted on to provide vital information while simultaneously encouraging fan participation. Public address announcers often come from a radio or television broadcasting background, but almost always have at least had extensive public speaking experience. The job can be as simple as announcing the name of the batter during a parks and recreation sponsored little league game, or as complex as the fast-paced, captivating banter of the caller at a horse race. Perhaps the most recognized public address announcer in the history of sport is the late Bob Sheppard of the New York Yankees and New York Giants, dubbed the "Voice of God" by Hall of Famer Reggie Jackson.

The primary function of the announcer is to inform the audience about the players and the teams. Prior to competition, the announcer welcomes those in attendance, announces who will be competing, and provides starting lineups. At this time season and conference records, regional and/or national rankings, and any other noteworthy information is also provided. The announcer instructs the audience when to stand for the national anthem and recognizes game sponsors.

Once the game begins, the announcer's job becomes even more arduous, for it is the announcer who provides an almost play-by-play description of the action that enables fans to enjoy the action. For example, after the whistle sounds to end a football play, the announcer tells the audience who ran the ball, who made the tackle, and length of the carry. In basketball, the announcer will say who made a basket, who was whistled for a foul, or who has entered the game for whom. While the fans may be able see the action as it takes place on the field, the announcer provides audio reinforcement and provides the details that many may not be able to see.

In most college and professional settings, the announcer is not responsible for maintaining a complete statistical record during the game. However, the announcer is expected to announce statistical leaders at intermissions and at the conclusion of the game.

An often controversial topic is the announcer as cheerleader. In this sense, the announcer encourages fan participation. Purists believe announcers should remain neutral, offering controlled enthusiasm for both teams, taking pains not to become the main attraction at events. Others consider it part of the public address announcer's job to "pump up" the home team and fans. Whether accepted in regular season competition or not, during postseason play (particularly at neutral sites), announcers are generally expected to remain unbiased, either offering encouragement and enthusiasm for both teams or for neither.

Effective public address announcers share some common characteristics. First, the announcer must obviously be comfortable speaking on a microphone in front of large audiences and must be a strong vocal talent. This requires someone who speaks at a steady pace, uses vocal inflection effectively, and enunciates well. Some studies have suggested a resonant male voice is preferable, but priority is given to clear delivery. In 1993, Sherry Davis, a legal secretary, became the first full-time female public address announcer in Major League Baseball history when she was hired by the San Francisco Giants. Because the announcer must call for both teams, it is also imperative that he or she be comfortable announcing complex names from a variety of pronunciations, often after only a brief introduction to the name.

Another must is a strong understanding of the rules and positions of the game. This includes officials' signals, timeout and substitution rules, and any other rule unique to a particular sport. Also, announcers must be able to multitask in a fast-paced environment. Today, many venues require announcers to read promotional announcements during breaks in the action or to operate software programs that provide musical interludes, sound effects and announcements. This must all be accomplished while still maintaining a focus on game action. Finally, some programs expect public address announcers to attend pregame production meetings and to provide voice-over for promotional spots.

The National Association of Sports Public Address Announcers (NASPAA), founded in 2003, is the professional association for sports public address announcers and the sports administrators who hire and assign announcers. Their mission: "To raise the level of professionalism of public address announcing by serving as a resource for training, education and professional development for those individuals who provide their services to sports events at all levels nationwide."

Founded by Brad Rumble, a former member of the National Federation of State High School Associations and consultant with the National Interscholastic Athletic Administrators Association, the NASPAA provides a code of conduct that stresses sportsmanship, fair play, and the promotion of a positive environment. The association offers online courses and on-site clinics for announcers in professional, collegiate, and high school sports. The NASPAA also honors the top sports public address announcers in the various regions and in the nation.

Joe Moore
University of Central Missouri

See Also: Atmospherics; Event Hospitality; Play-by-Play Announcer; Televised Sports.

Further Readings

Bender, Gary and Michael Johnson. *Call of the Game: What Really Goes on in the Broadcast Booth*. Chicago: Bonus Books, 1994.
Curry, J. "Voice of Yankee Stadium May Be Done." *New York Times* (April 2, 2009).
National Association of Sports Public Address Announcers. http://www.naspaa.net (Accessed September 2010).
P.A. Announcer. http://www.pa-announcer.com/index.htm (Accessed September 2010).

Anthems/Flag Raising

Sports have a long history associated with the celebration of anthems and flag raising. Such actions are done in a variety of settings for a multitude of purposes. Both flags and anthems are cultural forms representing identity and character. They become the musical and visual equivalents of a motto or slogan. They are "modern totems" that allow groups to differentiate themselves from others. In particular, the term *anthem* is used to describe musical works that serve a variety of purposes, including for religious ceremonies, as symbols of national pride and identity in the case of national anthems, and for other purposes such as school songs/fight songs.

In regard to patriotism, displaying flags and anthems provides visible and auditory images of significance. Such symbols have a nationwide presence and in many case a global presence.

The stars and stripes of the U.S. flag or the Union Jack of Great Britain are recognized worldwide. National/royal anthems such as "The Star-Spangled Banner" or "God Save the Queen" are widely recognized as well.

Displays of patriotism and national symbolism are commonly found at sport settings. Displays may occur at events such as Little League opening day ceremonies, before high school athletics, at professional sporting events, and before or after international sporting events as well. Such spectacles are commonplace in international sport settings, such as the Olympic Games (where national flags and anthems are displayed at opening ceremonies and medal presentations).

Large-scale events such as all-star games and playoff games have provided venues for some memorable renditions of the U.S. national anthem. Marvin Gaye's highly praised rendition at the 1983 NBA All-Star Game or Whitney Houston's performance at the 1991 Super Bowl at the tail end of Operation Desert Storm are among the most celebrated national anthem performances in American sports history.

Beyond the aforementioned examples, sport anthems (or stadium anthems) also exist. Examples of such anthems would include songs that are commonly played over public address systems at stadiums, arenas, and other sport venues (i.e., "Sweet Home Alabama" or "Who Let the Dogs Out?"). The presence of such "anthems" abounds in sport settings both large and small.

Not only are the songs or anthems of importance, but the bands are themselves symbols of a specific culture. For instance, a school band may help shape its institution's culture. Examples include the precision marching of the "Fightin' Texas Aggie Band" from Texas A&M University and Prairie View A&M University's "Marching Storm," which projects the soul and spirit of this historically black university. Used in conjunction with or apart from anthems, flag waving is another symbolic action commonly found in sport. In the United States flags may be used to represent the country, a state (i.e., the Texas "Lone Star" state flag), or other groups such as teams or NASCAR drivers.

Such symbols can demonstrate pride, solidarity, or differentiation. The totems of flags and anthems have served a variety of purposes and evoked strong meaning for those displaying them and observing the presentation of such symbols. Whether used as a patriotic display, as a rallying point for individuals or groups, or other for purposes, the raising of flags and anthem performances have helped shape the cultural landscape of sport.

Jason W. Lee
University of North Florida
Warren Whisenant
University of Miami

See Also: Atmospherics; Mascots; Olympic Organization; Olympics; Slogan.

Further Readings

Cerulo, Karen A. "World Systems: National Anthems and Flags." *Sociological Forum*, v.8/2 (1993).
Eitzen, D. Stanley. *Fair and Foul: Beyond the Myths and Paradoxes of Sport*, 3rd ed. Lanham, MD: Rowman & Littlefield Publishing Group, 2006.
Morrison, Steven J. "The School Ensemble: A Culture of Our Own." *Music Educators Journal*, v.88/2 (2001).

Antitrust Laws and Sports

The purpose of antitrust legislation is to allow fair competition, with goods and services available to consumers at competitive prices. In *Hawaii v. Standard Oil Company*, the U.S. Supreme Court stated that "the system depends on strong competition for its health and vigor, and strong competition depends … on compliance with antitrust legislation."

The impetus of antitrust law in the United States was driven by actions of the Standard Oil Company and its subsequent restraint of trade. Standard Oil was formed in 1870 by John D. Rockefeller and at its peak controlled 84 percent of the nation's oil business. The company built a complex system of trust agreements with other corporations, which allowed Standard Oil to circumvent state restrictions regarding one corporation owning stock in other companies. Standard Oil utilized predatory acts that attempted to achieve monopoly power within the U.S. oil and refining industry.

One of the trust agreements written in 1879 skirted Ohio statutes, which attracted the attention and focus of Ohio Senator John Sherman. In 1890, Congress passed the Sherman Act, which is the foundational piece of legislation in antitrust law. The Sherman Act expanded common law principles into a federal law. Section 1 of the act prohibits contracts, combinations, and conspiracies in restraint of trade, and governs the existence of conspiracy among franchise owners or league officials. Section 2 prohibits monopolization and attempts to monopolize. In the context of sport, Section 2 applies to ordinary business transactions and all areas of league conduct.

The Sherman Act was later amended by the Clayton Antitrust Act in 1914. Section 4 of the Clayton Act allows that "Any person who is injured in his business or property by reason of anything forbidden in the antitrust laws may sue." The Clayton Act offers provisions for private actions for violations of the Sherman Act. The U.S. Supreme Court has identified seven factors to be analyzed in determining if requisite standing exists for antitrust violations: (1) whether the action caused the plaintiff injury, (2) whether the defendants intended to cause the plaintiff injury, (3) whether the plaintiff's injuries were related to antitrust law, (4) whether the injury was direct or indirect, (5) whether there exists an identifiable class of victims, (6) whether the plaintiff's damages are speculative, and (7) whether permitting the plaintiff to sue would create a risk of duplicate recoveries or a complex damage apportionment.

In 1936, the Robinson-Patman Act amended the Clayton Act and focused on customer rights and price fixing in that it "prohibits discrimination among customers through pricing and disallows mergers, acquisitions or takeovers of one firm by another if the effect will substantially lessen competition."

The Supreme Court reviews cases related to antitrust under several standards of scrutiny. An initial review determines if an actual injury did occur, and if an injury did occur, its relationship to antitrust actions. If antitrust did occur, an effort is made to identify injured parties. If it is determined the plaintiff suffered damages, the court will create a plan for recovery and a distribution of funds by the defendant.

The severity of antitrust is examined under three premises, which include "rule of reason" where the defendant argues that some restraint of trade is reasonable. "Illegal per se" is a more cursory determination where the actions of the defendant are seen to have no value in contributing to sound business practices. A third premise holds far-reaching ramifications. The "consumer business standard" examines potential damages incurred by end consumers who suffer as a result of antitrust actions.

Important Cases

One of the most pivotal cases in determining antitrust parameters for professional sport transpired in 1922 in *Federal Baseball Club of Baltimore v. National League of Baseball Clubs*. The case tested issues regarding players crossing state lines and the definition of sport as commerce. The Supreme Court determined that professional baseball was neither interstate, nor commerce, and was exempt from antitrust liability. While a special exemption has been afforded Major League Baseball through the Sherman Antitrust Act, other professional sports are not afforded this immunity.

In 1998, Congress revisited the Supreme Court decision regarding professional baseball's exemption. It was determined through the Curt Flood Act that baseball's employment and labor components would be subject to antitrust scrutiny. However, only professional baseball athletes who were part of a baseball dispute held the legal power to challenge labor issues in the courts.

Radovich v. the National Football League (1957) tested and later determined that the National Football League was subject to antitrust scrutiny. Radovich sued the NFL under the premise that the league's employment constraints were too restrictive and that he was not allowed to negotiate with teams other than the one with whom he was contracted. The trial and appellate courts dismissed Radovich's claim, using the *Federal Baseball* case as a foundational argument. The Supreme Court later reviewed the case and reversed the decision. After analyzing the league's television and radio contracts, it was determined the NFL was participating in interstate commerce, and in turn was subject to antitrust language as defined in the Sherman Act.

Other labor law cases that were pivotal to antitrust decisions in professional sport were *Philadelphia World Hockey v. the National Hockey Club* (1972) and *Clarett v. the National Football League* (2003). In *Philadelphia World Hockey*, the case was successfully made that the National Hockey League was monopolistic in its control of professional hockey players through a far-reaching reserve system. This case set precedent for less control of athletes at the professional level.

However, the Clarett case spoke to national labor laws and in a broader sense the exemption of organized labor from antitrust scrutiny as defined in the 1914 Clayton Act. Maurice Clarett was a top-ranked running back for The Ohio State University. He set many records for the team and caught the winning pass in overtime to win the 2002 Fiesta Bowl. Clarett later encountered legal troubles and did not play for Ohio State in 2003.

Clarett believed the NFL's restriction on players that disallowed professional play for three years following high school was overly restrictive. He filed suit under restraint of fair trade and antitrust. Clarett won the initial case but the NFL appealed. The appeals court reviewed the case and identified Clarett as an athlete dissatisfied with the requirements for employment set by the NFL. The court stated that national labor laws precede antitrust laws and the court ruled in favor of the NFL.

Other litigation focused on the legal organization of a league and antitrust actions of the teams within a league. *Los Angeles Raiders and Los Angeles Coliseum v. the National Football League*

(1984) determined that the NFL created antitrust implications through its voting power. Raiders owner Al Davis represented a new breed of team owner because he was opportunistic in his endeavors and focused on optimizing profit. When teams voted on the relocation of the Raiders to Los Angeles, a 75 percent vote was needed from other team owners. Davis brought a lawsuit and argued that a ¾ vote was unreasonable and held antitrust implications. He successfully defended his claim and set a precedent regarding monopolistic team and league implications within professional football.

Further issues regarding the corporate structure of sport organizations were explored in *Fraser v. Major League Soccer* (2002). The case was pivotal in that it demonstrated sports leagues can operate on a national basis within the parameters of antitrust law, if they are organized from inception as a single entity corporation. Within this structure, the league is created with satellite team owners as owners-investors. When the team conducts business on a national basis, it is not operating within a consensus of teams, but rather as a non-sport-related business entity, with accountability to shareholders. Sports leagues that attempt to restructure as a single entity organization in an effort to avoid antitrust litigation are not considered immune from prosecution.

In the motorsport sector, specific parallels exist between the infrastructure of Standard Oil Company and the National Association for Stock Car Auto Racing (NASCAR) over 100 years later. A discussion ensued in *Ferko v. the National Association for Stock Car Auto Racing* (2003) regarding the ability of the sanctioning body to control events under a potentially monopolistic system. Francis Ferko was a stockholder in Speedway Motorsports Corporation (SMI), a large conglomerate corporation that owns approximately 50 percent of the facilities that host NASCAR events. SMI holdings include Charlotte Motor Speedway, Texas Motor Speedway, and the 200,000-seat Bristol Motor Speedway.

Ferko sued under the contention that SMI, and Texas Motor Speedway, had been promised and did not receive a second NASCAR Nextel Cup event at the Texas facility. Ferko believed the second event was not awarded to Texas based on NASCAR's relationship with International Speedway Corporation

(ISC), which is a publicly traded company. NASCAR was founded by Bill France, Sr., and members of the France family were major shareholders in ISC, as well as top executives of the privately held NASCAR organization. *Ferko v. NASCAR* was later settled out of court. News reports indicated that a high-stakes game of facility sale and event management took place in order that antitrust litigation could be avoided. ISC sold its Rockingham, North Carolina, facility to SMC. Within a short period of time, SMC closed the Rockingham race track and moved that event to a second race date at Texas.

The Ferko case held ramifications three years later in *Kentucky Speedway v. the National Association for Stock Car Auto Racing* (2006). Kentucky Speedway argued that Bill France, Jr., at that time chairman of NASCAR, had promised the race track a NASCAR Nextel Cup Championship event, which it did not receive. The "rule of reason" approach was applied to NASCAR's business model. In January 2008, the court decided that Kentucky Speedway had failed to demonstrate NASCAR had impeded market competition. Kentucky Speedway appealed the decision and in May 2008, Speedway Motorsports Corporation purchased the Kentucky facility. In December 2009, an appeals court affirmed the initial district court decision. Further appeals led to yet another decision and in February 2010, the U.S. Appeals Court for the Sixth District refused to reconsider the initial ruling, which was in favor of NASCAR. At the time of the decision, the former owners of Kentucky Speedway had 90 days to consider a final appeal to the Supreme Court.

Thomas S. Mueller
Appalachian State University

See Also: Cartel; Expansion; Franchise; Major League Baseball; National Association for Stock Car Racing; National Football League.

Further Readings

Blarcom-Gupko, M. "Should NASCAR Be Allowed to Choose the Tracks at Which Its Series' Races Are Run?" *Seton Hall Journal of Sport Law,* v.16/193 (2006).

Cotten, D. and J. Wolohan. *Law for Recreation and Sport Managers*, 4th Ed. Dubuque, IA: Kendall/Hunt, 2007.

Gladden, R. "NASCAR Sponsor Decisions Reflect Poorly on Sport." *Insider Racing News*. http://insiderracingnews.com/Writers/RG/101307.html (Accessed October 2007).

Margolis, B. "Life After NASCAR." http://sports.yahoo.com/nascar/news?slug=bm-leaving rockingham030105&prov=yhoo&type=lgns (Accessed February 2010).

Modric, J. "The Good Ole' Boys: Antitrust Issues in America's Largest Spectator Sport." *DePaul Journal of Sports Law & Contemporary Problems,* v.1/159 (2003).

Moody, Dave. "Mediation for Kentucky Speedway, NASCAR." http://motorsports-soapbox.blogspot.com/2007/06/mediation-for-kentucky-speedway-nascar.html (Accessed October 2007).

Oliva, S. "Antitrust May Lap the Field at Indy." http://www.voluntarytrade.org/newsite/modules/news/article.php?storyid=104 (Accessed October 2007).

Pockrass, B. "Appeals Court Refuses to Reconsider Kentucky Speedway Case." http://nascar.speedtv.com/article/cup-appeals-court-refuses-to-reconsider-kentucky-speedway-case (Accessed February 2010).

Robson, P. "Dispute Resolution in Motor Sports." *Sports Lawyers Journal,* v.6/87 (1999).

Ross, S. and S. Szymanski. "Antitrust and Inefficient Joint Ventures: Why Sports Leagues Should Look More Like McDonalds and Less Like the United Nations." *Marquette (University) Sports Law Review,* v.16/213 (2006).

Area of Dominant Influence

Area of dominant influence, or *ADI*, is a term used in the advertising and media industries to identify, define, and measure geographic markets in the United States. It is particularly important for sports teams and the television or radio outlets that carry their games, as the revenue earned from selling commercial time is based largely on the size of their ADI.

As used by Arbitron, the audience research company that first coined the term, a market's area of dominant influence includes all those counties from which a central city's broadcast stations receive majority viewership. Since a county can only be included as part of one ADI, in some cases the stations from neighboring markets will compete vigorously to achieve majority status among the viewers in border areas, thus increasing the size of their ADI, enabling them to charge higher advertising rates and increase profits. An example of such a situation is the region of Maryland located between Baltimore and Washington, D.C., where the Baltimore Orioles and their media partners compete with the Washington Nationals and the media that carry them to claim those counties where both teams may have viewership as part of their own area of dominant influence.

While area of dominant influence has long been the accepted market measure for radio, in television, the term *designated market area* (DMA) is sometimes substituted. Nielsen Media Research, a competitor of Arbitron, employs the DMA label for TV markets but uses essentially the same definition and measures that ADI is based on.

Because of differences in population density and population distribution in various regions of the United States, the geographic size and shape of ADIs is not uniform. Thus, in the urban east, while the areas of dominant influence for important sports cities like New York, Philadelphia, and Boston rank among the very largest in terms of the number of people included, they cover much smaller land areas than most western sports cities, such as Denver, Phoenix, and Salt Lake City. Beyond the business and media implications related to ADI numbers, such geographic dispersion probably explains much about the location and characteristics of the "home fans" for professional and college teams in different parts of the country.

Areas of dominant influence are reevaluated regularly, with counties sometimes being shifted from one ADI to another, ADI size and ranking moving up or down, and new central city ADIs occasionally being created. In 2010, the total number of ADIs in the United States was just under 300. Major American professional sports leagues are concentrated in the largest 50 ADIs, with Milwaukee being the smallest Major League Baseball market (37th largest), Memphis the smallest ADI in the NBA (50th), Buffalo the smallest stateside NHL market (52nd), and Green Bay the smallest NFL market (the combined Green Bay/Appleton ADI ranks 70th).

Even though the most attention, the biggest money, and the most competitive media strategies tend to involve major professional sports league areas of dominant influence, ADI concepts and practices are quite important at other levels as well. Minor league markets, college teams and athletic conferences, and even those high schools whose games are broadcast are impacted in financial and other ways by considerations of how the audience they reach is measured and defined.

Kevin Keenan
American University in Cairo

See Also: Advertising; Audience Measurement; Media Audience; Territorial Rights.

Further Readings

Baron, Roger B. and Jack Z. Sissors. *Advertising Media Planning*. New York: McGraw-Hill, 2010.

Katz, Helen. *The Media Handbook: A Complete Guide to Advertising Media Selection, Planning, Research, and Buying*. Mahwah, NJ: Lawrence Erlbaum Associates, 2007.

Wenner, L. A. *Media, Sports, and Society*. Newbury Park, CA: Sage, 1989.

Arena

Efficient management of arenas and other sport facilities is vital to their existence. Through cost reduction and revenue increase, responsible managers seek their venue's financial success. As part of successful management, marketing strategies allow venues to promote sport and nonsport tenants and talent. By investing in marketing, venue managers not only help tenants and talent to sell their events and maximize revenue, but also attract new events to the venue. In addition, it helps sponsors and business partners promote their brands by association with the venue's good image and events.

Types

Arenas (also called coliseums, gardens, domes, forums, field houses, pavilions, civic centers) are enclosed structures containing seating surrounding a playing floor large enough to accommodate basketball, ice hockey, and other indoor sports. Such venues have large seating capacities (1,000–25,000), are able to host a multitude of events, and are not subject to weather conditions. These qualities yield the best opportunities to generate revenues from space rental, advertisement, concessions, private suites, novelties, and food/beverage sales, in addition to ticket sales. Today, any space left open by the main tenant in an arena's calendar is filled with revenue-generating events.

Stadiums are large, mainly open structures with oval, round, or horseshoe-shaped seating. These venues are commonly used for either football or soccer. They have large seating capacity (from a couple thousand to more than 100,000 spectators), but their use is contingent upon weather conditions and ownership preferences. Because of this they are commonly considered single-use venues. Stadiums' larger seating capacities make up for the revenue they do not generate because of their single-sport use and shorter seasons. With the exception of a few concerts per year, most stadiums rely on football or soccer games as their main revenue streams.

Unlike stadiums, ballpark seating does not surround the field of play. Seating capacity of these venues ranges from a couple thousand to more than 50,000 spectators, and they are mainly used to host baseball games (with perhaps a few concerts and other events happening throughout the year). A ballpark's large seating capacity and baseball's long season help to minimize the impact of the revenue lost by not hosting events other than baseball.

The type of funding utilized to build the venue generally determines the venue's ownership. Arenas, stadiums, and ballparks can be public, private, or a combination of both. The type of ownership influences the decision about who will operate the venue. Sports venues may be operated by their owners, main tenants, not-for-profit organizations (government authorities), or private management companies (e.g., Global Spectrum and SMG).

Management and Marketing

As integral parts of a venue's operation, each specific function of a sporting venue (including administration, finance, sales and marketing, ancillary services, and facility operations) is equally important to the financial success of the venue and must be managed efficiently. The financial success of a sports venue depends on how well its management controls each of those functions, and balances variables such as time, space, monetary resources, staffing, stakeholder demands, and expectations of the general public. Most types of operation depend on the existence of in-house expertise to be effective. In the absence of such expertise, it is very common for venue owners to outsource the venue's entire operation to a private management company. It is also very common for venue owners to retain overall control over the venue's operations, and yet have services such as concessions, box-office, and event booking individually outsourced to private management companies with expertise in these areas.

The success of a sport venue depends on efficient management of each part of its operation, but a special focus must be put on its marketing efforts. The marketing of the sports product provided by the venue promotes tenants and events associated with the venue. It helps them and the venue to achieve revenue generation and financial success. The venue also increases its ability to attract new events. Another facet of a venue's marketing efforts is the marketing of other products through the sports played in the venue. This activity draws new financial resources in the form of sponsorship, naming rights, and advertising opportunities.

In addition, marketing efforts can promote public awareness of ancillary services a venue provides (e.g., meeting and convention space and catering services). Good marketing strategies may help a successful team turn its success on the playing field into maximum revenue generation. Marketing may also make up for the poor results of a losing team by promoting a high-quality overall experience.

Mauro Palmero
East Tennessee State University

See Also: Arena Funding—Public/Private; Arena Owner/Operator/Tenant Balance; Facilities Management; Marketing Through Sports; Seating Capacity; Single-Sport Venue Versus Multisport Venue; Venue Naming Rights.

Further Readings

Jewell, D. *Public Assembly Facilities*. Malabar, FL: Krieger Publishing, 1992.
Lawrence, H. and M. Wells. *Event Management Blueprint: Creating and Managing Successful Sports Events*. Dubuque, IA: Kendall Hunt Publishing, 2009.
Mullin, B. J., S. Hardy, and W. A. Sutton. *Sport Marketing*, 3rd Ed. Champaign, IL: Human Kinetics, 2007.
Russo, F. E., L. A. Esckilsen, and R. J. Stewart. *Public Assembly Facility Management: Principles and Practices*, 2nd Ed. Coppell, TX: IAAM, 2009.

Arena Funding— Public/Private

For as long as there have been sports arenas and stadia they have been funded in one of three primary ways: publicly, privately, or with a public/private partnership. The premise of public funding is that taxpayer or other public dollars are used to pay for the facility. Private funding uses the capital of private citizens or corporations. Public-private partnerships use some combination of the different methods of public and private financing methods to raise enough capital for the facility.

Public Funding

Government bonds are bonds issued by governmental entities, such as a state, city, or municipality.

These bonds are tax exempt and usually are repaid with taxpayer money. The use of taxpayer dollars means that most government bonds are approved by public referendum.

General obligation bonds are issued on the full faith and credit of the government body issuing the bond. They generally have a low interest rate, but are also secure because of the government backing. General obligation bonds are repaid with taxes. Often the taxes used are "soft" taxes, such as sales taxes, on hotels, rental cars, and sin taxes (alcohol and tobacco). The public is often more willing to tax these items for a facility than to increase "hard" taxes such as property and general sales tax.

Certificates of Obligation are also issued on the full faith and credit of the government and use taxes to repay the certificate, but do not require voter approval. This method is used most often when the public is unlikely to pass a referendum approving the bond. The new Milwaukee Brewers stadium, Miller Park, was financed in such a manner.

The government also issues nonsecured debt. These are bonds repaid from some other source than taxes and are not backed by the full faith and credit of the government. These bonds have a higher interest rate because their reduced security increases that risk involved.

Some of the different types of nonsecured debt include: revenue bonds, which are repaid from the revenues of the facility and tax incremental financing districts (TIFDs), where the increased property tax revenue from a defined geographical area around the facility is diverted to repay the bond. TIFDs are used most often when a facility is part of a larger redevelopment program. The property tax rate to the government is fixed at its pre-development rate and any increased property taxes created by the new facility and businesses is diverted to the bond. The result is that the government does not see a reduction in property tax revenue, since the property taxes would have not increased without the development.

The 1986 Tax Reform Act created some limitations on the use of tax-exempt government bonds for financing sport facilities. A bond can no longer be tax exempt if more than 10 percent of the bond repayment comes from the revenues of the sport franchise or if more than 10 percent of the facility's use is consumed by the private business (unless it is a "qualified private activity").

Public funding is common throughout much of the world. All the facilities built for the 2010 FIFA World Cup in South Africa were paid for through public financing, with an informal agreement that had municipalities paying 10 percent, provincial governments 20 percent, and the national treasury the remaining 70 percent. However, many of the facilities went over budget, and there has been disagreement over which levels of the government are going to pay for the overages. For example, Nelson Mandela Bay Stadium was originally estimated to cost 895 million rand ($131 million), but costs for the stadium grew to 2.1 billion rand ($307 million).

The Chinese government bore the entire costs of the facilities and infrastructure for the 2008 Summer Olympic Games in Beijing. The Chinese government spent 19.5 billion yuan ($2.9 billion) on facilities and other infrastructure for the Games. The original budget for the entire event including facilities was 13 billion yuan ($1.9 billion).

Qatar's winning bid for the 2022 FIFA World Cup projected 11 billion Qatari riyals ($3 billion) for facility construction and renovation. It is likely that this number will grow, and the Qatari government is providing the funding for all facilities, as well as other necessary infrastructure development costs.

Private Funding

A sport team owner is always free to pay for facility renovations or a new facility out of his or her own pocket, but with these costs running from the hundreds of millions to over a billion dollars, this option is not one that owners want to or are even capable of taking. Instead, limitations on the use of government bonds for sport facilities lead developers and owners to issue private bonds to finance their facilities.

Private bonds are taxable and most often repaid through the revenues generated by the facility. Private-Placement or Private Activity bonds are generally repaid through contractually obligated income (COI). This is the most guaranteed revenue that a facility has. Revenue streams that are contractually obligated include (but are not limited to) naming rights, luxury boxes, in-stadium advertising, concession and pouring rights, broadcast deals, sea-

The Chinese government built Beijing National Stadium, known as the Bird's Nest, for the 2008 Summer Olympic Games at a cost of about $423 million.

son tickets and private seat licenses (PSLs), and, in some cases, rents. Since COI is known in advance, how much money there will be to repay the bond each year is known. However, with the exception of perhaps a naming right deal, none of the COI has contracts as long as the life of the bond. So there is still a risk that the COI will fluctuate over the life of the bond or that a company providing COI will encounter financial problems that will make them unable to fulfill the contract.

Another private financing method, not entirely dissimilar to a private bond, is an asset-backed securitization. In this method, revenue streams, often consisting of COI, are bundled into a financial security. That security is then sold to a trust, and then to private investors. Securitization has a number of advantages over more traditional bonds, including: liens on specific revenue streams leaves others free; no need for a mortgage; no deals with individual investors; lower financing costs; and a continuous budget approval process is not required. Problems with securitization can arise if the advertisers and sponsors have financial problems or if the owner wants to sell the team. Determining team/franchise value can also be difficult.

Private funding may also come in the form of loans from sport leagues, such as the G-3 fund of-

fered by the National Football League. These loans are taken out by the league and given to the individual teams. However, there are limits on the amount of money teams can get through these loans and criteria for getting them, such as the requirement that a facility must have some public funding in order to receive G-3 money.

Private funding is common in Japan. The majority of teams in Nippon Professional Baseball, Japan's highest professional baseball league, play in stadiums that were built by private investors (or in some cases the government acting as a private company). The teams must pay market rent for the use of the stadiums, which takes up a large portion of their annual revenue. In 2009, the Fukuoka Softbank Hawks were spending a quarter of their annual revenue on rent, a total of 4.8 billion yen ($49 million).

Public/Private Funding

A public/private partnership is any combination of the public and private funding methods already described. Public/private partnerships have been used to construct sport facilities for decades.

As far back as 1956, voters approved a referendum to build City Stadium, now Lambeau Field, for the Green Bay Packers. The facility cost $960,000 and was a 50/50 split between the public and the team. Reliant Stadium, the facility used by the Houston Texans of the NFL, cost $424 million and was also built using a public/private partnership. The public covered $309 million through an increase in hotel and rental car taxes, and $115 million came from the team's owner, Robert McNair, through the G-S fund, $50 million from PSLs, $10 million from parking and tickets, and the future payment of a $300 million, 30-year naming rights deal.

Public/private partnerships are increasingly common in Europe. The new Wembley Stadium (cost: £750 million [$1.164 billion]) was built using approximately £170 million in public money: £120 million from the National Lottery and £50 million from the Government and London Development Agency. The remaining £580 million came from private sources such as Sport England and the Football Association (FA).

Genevieve F. E. Birren
University of New Mexico

See Also: Arena; Arena Owner/Operator/Tenant Balance; Facilities Financing; Facility Planning, Sports; Venue Naming Rights.

Further Readings

"FIFA World Cup 2022 Stadiums." http://www
.qatar.to/stadiums/World-Cup-2022-stadiums
.php (Accessed December 2010).

Fujita, Junko. "Costs Squeeze Profits at Japan's Baseball Teams." http://www.reuters.com/
article/idUSTRE55T16R20090630 (Accessed December 2010).

Green Bay Packers Official Website. http://www
.packers.com (Accessed July 2010).

Greenberg, Martin J. *The Stadium Game,*
2nd ed. Milwaukee, WI: Marquette University Press, 2000.

Hayward, Brian. "Ratepayers' R261m Cup Stadium 'Hangover.'" http://kaapsevryheidsburger
.forumsmotion.com/kletshoekie-f1/ratepayers
-r261m-cup-stadium-hangover-t1459.htm
(Accessed December 2010).

Lei, Lei. "Beijing Olympics Earnings Hit $146M."
http://www.chinadaily.com.cn/china/2009-06/20/
content_8304725.htm (Accessed December 2010).

Miller, Phillip. "Private Financing and Sports Franchise Values: The Case of Major League Baseball." *Journal of Sports Economics*, v.8/5 (October 2008).

Saporito, Bill. "Sport: The American Money Machine." *Time*, v.164/23 (December 6, 2004).

"Supplementary Memorandum From Wembley National Stadium Limited." http://www
.publications.parliament.uk/pa/cm200102/
cmselect/cmcumeds/843/843ap15.htm (Accessed December 2010).

Arena Owner/Operator/ Tenant Balance

Prompted by the industrial revolution the emergence of modern stadia in the late 19th century served to reinforce the Victorian ideals of rational recreation, using formal sport as a way of introducing order and control to the working-class population. The first modern stadia, such as Goodison Park, Everton (1892) saw industrialists investing resources into functional spaces that could accommodate large crowds to view organized sport. Use of this stadia was often limited to matches, with no requirement to generate a substantial economic return. The philanthropic focus of these early stadia owners has since been eroded by the increasing commodification of sport.

There have been notable periods of stadium development and redevelopment during the 20th century but since the 1990s there has been a global boom in the United States, Europe, and increasingly in other world regions such as Asia and the Middle East. This boom in part has been dictated by countries hosting mega events (the World Cup and the Olympics) and governing bodies and governments demanding strict safety regulations post Taylor Report (1990), which was commissioned as a result of one of the worst modern-day stadia disasters in the United Kingdom (UK). This development boom may also be symptomatic of an increasing commercialized global sporting environment where exploitation of new income streams is not only crucial for professional sports clubs and franchises to survive and remain competitive, but to ensure owners maximize their wealth potential.

The new post-modern stadia are often developed as urban icons displayed as cultural and business focal points within host cities and regions, with owners demanding income potential be maximized. As such, these venues are required to be flexible, incorporating hospitality and conference functions and the latest technological solutions (such as roof design, removable pitches, and video playback) to allow a diverse offering of events beyond the stadium's main purpose.

The funding and investment of stadia has therefore escalated, with examples such as the Cowboys

Stadium (Dallas Cowboys—National Football League [NFL]) completed in 2009 costing in excess of $1 billion. A large proportion of the professional franchises in the United States (e.g., NFL) and European national and club teams play in stadiums that are not owned outright by the teams, or governing bodies playing in them. Worldwide, a large proportion of stadiums are state-owned or funded with professional clubs and franchises choosing not to overburden themselves with owning and maintaining a resource-hungry facility. Governments work with stakeholders to form stadium management companies or hybrid not-for-profit trusts. Increasingly, a number of stadia are also being sold to specialist events/entertainment companies such as AEG (which owns over 100 facilities worldwide).

National and local governments often focus on the catalytic impacts of attracting both mega events (Olympics, World Cup) and professional sport clubs and franchises to host cities. The justification for investing large amounts of public funding often centers around the positive tangible regeneration and economic impacts new stadia can bring, including job creation, increased commercial activity, and subsequent multiplier effects for local businesses. In addition, wider intangible benefits have been argued to have an impact on the social cohesion of local citizens. Opponents to large-scale public investment in stadium development argue that economic and social benefits to host cities and regions are often overstated and in many cases the investment only serves to maximize the wealth for the owners of sporting organizations.

The power balance in the relationship between owner and tenant becomes a core factor to the success of both the stadium and the team(s) playing there. There are a number of key issues when negotiating an effective partnership, including management and maintenance costs, income distribution of ticket sales, naming rights of the stadium (e.g., "Arsenal Emirates Stadium" was worth £100 million over 10 years) sponsorship, advertising, hospitality, non–match day events (e.g., conferences), and parking.

There are clear examples of an imbalance in power between owners and tenants. The professional franchises prevalent in the U.S. sporting model have a history of relocating from city to city

(e.g., the NFL Cleveland Browns from Cleveland, Ohio, to Baltimore, Maryland, in 1996). This situation increases the vulnerability of the facility owner where public money has been invested to attract or maintain a franchise. As a mobile tenant, franchise owners have created a strong position from which to negotiate the best possible deal to reduce their risks and maximize their profits. A number of U.S. cities have been held ransom by professional sport franchises who pay little or no management and maintenance fees, retain control of income generation opportunities, and have written state-of-the-art clauses into their agreements threatening relocation to other cities if venues are not maintained or redeveloped to a standard that will keep pace with the leading teams in the league.

Within Europe, teams have been confined to the geographical locations in which they have developed. This creates a loyal supporter base with a strong sense of tradition and affiliation with their clubs. With both the pressure of modernizing the safety standards of their stadia and wealth generation for their owners, a number of professional clubs have relocated to more modern stadia. It is a growing trend that teams such as Manchester City football club become a tenant in a post–mega event (2002 Commonwealth Games) stadium run by a not-for-profit trust or commercial entertainment organization. In these cases stadia owners have a more balanced sense of power and create robust tenancy agreements to help protect their investments and share income potential. The tenant, however, may not be the sole user of the stadia (rugby union/league often sharing with football teams), which can erode the identity and tradition of the club through a sterile and standardized stadia landscape. Scheduling of games can conflict with the owner's broader activities and cause teams to relocate to alternative venues in extreme circumstances. This can impact the loyalty of supporters, with attendance figures falling at matches in conflict with the owner's motivation of moving to a larger modern stadium to increase earning potential.

Conclusion

The ongoing globalization of sport and corresponding development boom of stadia across the world continues to raise issues between stadia owners and tenants. The attraction of expanding their wealth potential by penetrating new markets has seen professional clubs and franchises increasingly export their brand across continents (e.g., NFL in Wembley, London; UK Rugby Union matches in Dubai). The development of homogenized stadia throughout the world allows franchise and club owners to take their product to a large new customer base, overcoming the geographical barriers in their country of origin. Stadia development is potentially reaching saturation point with facility owners across the world consistently competing to secure lucrative visiting events. This oversupply again shifts the balance of power in favor of the powerful franchise and club owners who continue to demand partnerships that will maximize their profit.

Steven Osborne
Swansea Metropolitan University

See Also: Arena; Arena Funding—Public/Private; Mega Sports Events; Sponsorship; Venue Naming Rights.

Further Readings

Bale, J. *Sport, Space and the City*. London: Routledge, 1993.
Brown, M., M. Nagel, C. McEvoy, and D. Rascher. "Revenue and Wealth Maximization in the National Football League: The Impact of Stadia." *Sport Marketing Quarterly*, v.13 (2004).
Foster, W. M. and C. Hyatt. "I Despise Them! I Detest Them! Franchise Relocation and the Expanded Model of Organizational Identification." *Journal of Sport Management*, v.21 (2007).
Penny, S. and S. Redhead. "We're Not Really Here: Manchester City, Mobility and Placelessness." *Sport in Society*, v.12/6 (August 2009).

Arizona Cardinals

The Arizona Cardinals have played in three cities over more than a century of existence, but the one constant is that the club has had a losing record in all three locations.

The Cardinals began life in Chicago in 1898 as the Morgan Athletic Club. They were also known as the Racine Normals, after a park they played in on Racine Avenue. They became known as the Cardinals in 1901. After several suspensions of operation for lack of competition, World War I, and an outbreak of the Spanish flu pandemic, the team has operated since 1919, making it the oldest continuously operated professional football team in the United States.

Chicago was also home to another more popular NFL team, the Bears, so the Cardinals moved to St. Louis in 1960. St. Louis was already home to another Cardinals team, the popular and successful MLB team, which resulted in confusing references and joking comparisons, given the generally inept play of the football team compared to their baseball cousins. In search of a better and more lucrative stadium deal, owner Bill Bidwell agreed to move the team to Phoenix after the 1987 season when state and local officials there agreed to build him a new facility.

Unfortunately for Bidwell, the savings and loan industry collapsed shortly after his handshake deal with local officials, making it politically and financially impossible to finance a new facility. The team was forced to take up temporary residence at Arizona State University's (ASU's) Sun Devils Stadium in Tempe. At the urging of Phoenix politicians, Bidwell renamed the team the "Phoenix Cardinals." The team changed its name to "Arizona" in 1994 to better reflect fan interest, such as it was. During their 18 seasons as a tenant of ASU, the Cardinals' attendance was the lowest in the NFL, averaging around 35,000 in the university's 73,000-seat stadium.

ASU controlled all of the revenue streams at the stadium and kept most of the money for itself. It didn't help that Bidwell had a reputation for frugality, spending money only when absolutely necessary. The Cardinals had among the lowest payrolls and—thanks to the NFL's generous revenue sharing formula—the highest profits of any NFL team during their stay in Tempe. Despite their profitability, according to Forbes.com, they were also the league's least valuable franchise.

In 2000, Maricopa County (greater Phoenix) voters passed a bill to provide funding for, among other things, a new stadium for the Cardinals to be financed primarily from tourist-related taxes. The team selected a site in Glendale, a farming community west of Phoenix, which several years earlier had financed the construction of a new arena for the NHL's Phoenix Coyotes. The 73,000-seat, $455 million facility features a number of unique characteristics, including a retractable roof and a slide-out, real grass surface. The team began playing in its new facility in 2006. Two years later, the team went to the Super Bowl, losing to the Pittsburgh Steelers in the final seconds.

The Cardinals have found little overall success in any of the cities they have called home, with a winning percentage of .403 in Chicago, .481 in St. Louis, and .361 in Arizona (through games of December 21, 2008). The Cardinals were declared NFL Champions in 1925 when the team with the best record in the league (which is how the league champion was determined) had its franchise revoked for violating another team's territorial rights. The Cardinals also played in—and lost—the 1947 NFL Championship game.

Phoenix is a fickle market, with many residents having moved to the desert from other locales. Arizona fans support winners, which, until their Super Bowl run in 2008, rarely included the Cardinals. Of the four major league teams and owners in the Phoenix market, the Cardinals and Bidwell consistently finished fourth in popularity polls conducted

of the city's sports fans. After the Cardinals' surprising run to the Super Bowl, their popularity surged, nearly tying the Phoenix Suns for the top spot as the most popular professional team in Phoenix in a survey conducted in the spring of 2009.

In 2005, the Cardinals replaced their old cardinal-head team logo with an updated and more menacing looking bird. The team also added black as an additional color. Both changes proved popular with their fans, especially after the team's 2008 success. In Arizona, Cardinal merchandise outsold such nationally popular teams as the Cowboys and Steelers for the first time in team history.

Like other professional sports teams in Phoenix, the Cardinals have sought to build their brand and develop growth opportunities among the Hispanic community in greater Phoenix and in Mexico, less than three hours south of their stadium. In 2000, the team became the first NFL team to broadcast all its games in Spanish. The Cardinals also made history in 2005 by playing the NFL's first regular season game outside the United States, defeating the San Francisco 49ers in Mexico City before a crowd of more than 103,000 fans. That total nearly tripled the team's average attendance at Sun Devils Stadium.

The Cardinals partnered with the MBA program at the Thunderbird School of Global Management to develop a plan to build its brand south of the border. A group of six MBA students traveled with members of the Cardinals marketing staff to conduct interviews and surveys at youth football and cheerleading clinics sponsored by the Cardinals in Monterrey, Mexico. Based on an analysis of their data, the students presented detailed recommendations to the team designed to expand its footprint in Mexico.

Attendance at the Cardinals' new stadium, called University of Phoenix Stadium after the team signed a $154 million, 20-year naming rights deal with the online college, has been substantially greater than it was in Tempe. The team sold out every home game through the middle of the 2009 season, avoiding the stigma of NFL-mandated blackouts on local TV.

The Arizona Cardinals are now playing in a new stadium in Glendale, which cost about $455 million and can seat 73,000.

Jordan I. Kobritz
Eastern New Mexico University

See Also: Franchise; National Football League; St. Louis Cardinals; Super Bowl.

Further Readings

Arizona Cardinals News. http://www.azcentral
.com/sports/cardinals (Accessed December 2009).
Arizona Cardinals Official Site. http://www
.azcardinals.com (Accessed December 2009).
Forbes.com. "The Richest Game." http://www
.forbes.com/2008/09/10/nfl-team-valuations
-biz-sports-nfl08_cz_kb_mo_cs_0910intro.html
(Accessed December 2009).

Arizona Diamondbacks

The Arizona Diamondbacks were one of two expansion teams that began play in Major League Baseball beginning with the 1998 season. MLB awarded majority owner Jerry Colangelo and his group a franchise on March 9, 1995, for a fee of $130 million.

The ownership group had more than three full years prior to the first game to market the team, and market they did, starting with the team colors. The team originally chose turquoise, copper, black, and purple, the latter color because it had become a favorite of Arizona sports fans because of the success of the NBA Phoenix Suns, also owned by a group headed by Colangelo. The color combination proved successful and Diamondbacks merchandise was a hot seller long before the team took the field for its first regular season game. In 2007, the team updated their logo and colors to red, black, sand, and white.

Through the sale of team merchandise, and signing a host of multimillion-dollar marketing deals with major sponsors, including some in Mexico, the Diamondbacks became one of the five highest revenue-producing franchises in MLB before they played their first game. The team name was controversial, with politicians in Phoenix and Maricopa County (which funded a substantial portion of the cost to construct Bank One Ballpark, later known as Chase Field after the latter bank bought out Bank One) preferring "Phoenix" instead of "Arizona." Colangelo

knew he had to draw fans from around the state in order to be successful, and those fans preferred the prefix Arizona. Chase Field is a fan-friendly, retractable-roof stadium ideally situated in downtown Phoenix. With a capacity of 48,569, the facility is large by recent standards, as teams are downsizing in order to increase demand and ticket prices.

On the field, the Diamondbacks have been the most successful expansion team in MLB history, winning three National League West Division Championships in their first five years of existence and the World Series against the storied New York Yankees in 2001, their fourth season. In order to accomplish that feat, the team signed a number of free agents (including future Hall of Fame pitcher Randy Johnson) and made a number of shrewd trades (including one with the Philadelphia Phillies for one of the best big-game pitchers in baseball history, Curt Schilling). Johnson and Schilling were Co-MVPs of the 2001 World Series. By signing top talent to long-term deferred contracts—essentially mortgaging the future to win in the present—Colangelo was able to bring the first major professional sports team championship to the state of Arizona.

Colangelo was called a visionary by some, an irresponsible profligate by others. What is undeni-

The Diamondbacks owners are sensitive to the local economy, pricing tickets 46 percent below the MLB average.

able is that the sports entrepreneur paid dearly for his win-now management philosophy. When the deferred payments, totaling approximately $150 million, started to come due, many of the players who were cashing the checks were no longer with the team, having long since been traded or retired. The team's payroll budget was inflexible, the losses mounted on the field, and attendance was dropping, from a high of 3.6 million in the inaugural season of 1998, to barely over 2 million in 2005 and 2006. The toxic combination resulted in staggering financial losses, and Colangelo was forced out in 2006 by a group of minority investors led by Ken Kendrick. While no one could take away the team's World Series title, or Colangelo's ring, he lost the team he had nurtured from its inception.

New management kept a tight rein on the major league payroll, relying on an infusion of talent from its farm system, which was acknowledged by experts and the publication *Baseball America* as among the best in baseball in the first decade of the 21st century.

Phoenix has the lowest income per capita of any market in the country that is home to all four major league team sports. Competition for sports fan attention—and dollars—is fierce. Marketing the team has always presented unique challenges, and price sensitivity is a constant concern. In 2009, *Team Marketing Report* ranked the Diamondbacks as having the lowest priced tickets in MLB for the third consecutive year. The team's average ticket price of $14.31 was more than $12—or 46 percent—below the MLB average of $26.74.

Concession prices are also low, as evidenced by the team's Fan Cost index of $114.24, the lowest figure among the 30 MLB clubs for the 2009 season. The MLB average Fan Cost index is $197.17, which represents the cost for a family of four to attend an MLB game. The figure includes four average-priced tickets to a game, two beers, four soft drinks, four hot dogs, parking, two programs, and two adult-sized caps. Even with rock-bottom concession prices, the team is among a handful of MLB teams that allow fans to bring food into the stadium.

In addition to low ticket and concession prices, the team engages in marketing and promotional activities that more popular teams such as the Red Sox and Cubs would not consider. Car races, hot dog races, trivia challenges, giveaways, and non-stop pregame and between-innings entertainment enliven every Diamondbacks game. The team mascot, Baxter, and a bevy of cheerleaders (dubbed the "entertainment squad") also entertain the fans throughout the game.

In an attempt to stimulate merchandise sales, the team changed uniform colors prior to the 2007 season. Purple and turquoise were out and Sedona red, Sonoran sand, and black were in. Many fans complained about the change, but others felt the need to update their wardrobes. The change in colors accomplished the intended result, as merchandise sales increased.

Operating in the Phoenix market presents unique challenges for all professional sports teams. Fortunately, the Diamondbacks have shown a willingness to embrace an aggressive and varied marketing approach to putting fans in the seats, which should serve the team in good stead in future seasons.

Jordan I. Kobritz
Eastern New Mexico University

See Also: Concession Pricing; Expansion; Major League Baseball; Phoenix Suns; World Series.

Further Readings

Arizona Diamondbacks Official Site. http://www .azdiamondbacks.com (Accessed December 2009).
Arizona Republic. "Arizona Diamondbacks News." http://www.azcentral.com/sports/diamondbacks (Accessed December 2009).
BaseballAmerica.com. "Arizona Diamondbacks." http://www.baseballamerica.com/today/teams/ diamondbacks.html (Accessed December 2009).
Sherman, Len. *Big League, Big Time: The Birth of the Arizona Diamondbacks.* New York: Atria, 1998.

Assessing Event Risk

It is critical for sport organizations to implement an all-hazard risk management approach to prevent and protect against the threat of sport-related terrorism and respond to and recover from an incident. The biggest challenge for event managers is to determine the actual threats and which safety and security measures will reduce the risk to the event, staff, spectators, and athletes.

There are six categories of event risk: (1) organized-political terror (e.g., bomb threats), (2) organized-social terror (e.g., hooliganism), (3) spontaneous terror (e.g., crowd disorder), (4) natural threats (e.g., severe weather and fire emergencies), (5) medical hazards (e.g., H1N1 and anthrax), and (6) alcohol control (e.g., disorderly conduct). It has been recommended that sport organizations, event managers, and other key stakeholders establish a continuous improvement process for event risk management to include: (1) risk assessment, (2) training of personnel, (3) incident rehearsal, and (4) system auditing. The most critical step, risk assessment, will establish the threats to the event and vulnerabilities of the venue and aid in the development of risk reduction strategies.

Categorization of Event Risk

To properly assess, manage and control risk, event managers must have the ability to identify the hazards and possible impact of these threats. Most event managers in North America have established security measures to prevent sport-related terrorism, while managers in Europe and Asia-Pacific have implemented safety measures to protect against hooliganism and crowd disorder, respectively. Organized-political terror has been defined as politically motivated actions, involving preparation and rehearsal, to cause psychological and/or physical harm to a group of people. An example of this form of sport-related terrorism occurred during the 1996 Atlanta Olympic Games when a man detonated a bomb at Olympic Centennial Park, resulting in one death and 111 injured spectators. Organized-social terror has been described as socially motivated behavior, involving premeditated and impulsive acts, to damage an opposing team's reputation and/or harm its members. For example, a 2007 international match between Major League Soccer club Columbus Crew and English Premier League club West Ham United was marred by a melee between club supporters.

Spontaneous terror is often a form of crowd disorder characterized by disorganized individuals or groups impulsively reacting, out of disagreement, with violence against people (e.g., athlete, official and/or another spectator) or property (e.g., inside and outside the venue). This psychological and physical harm is often related to one of the following sport-related conditions: clash between traditional rivals; a team or athlete unexpectedly winning or losing a competition; or an athlete or spectator disagreeing with an official's decision. This form of sport-related terrorism typically involves the use of verbal assaults, throwing projectiles, disrupting play, fighting, vandalism, and/or rioting. One of the most infamous examples of spontaneous terror occurred at the end of the fourth quarter of a 2003 National Basketball Association (NBA) competition. It concluded with members of the Indiana Pacers team fighting on the court and in the stands with the opposing team and their supporters, respectively. This incident was fueled by their traditional rivalry with the Detroit Pistons, in addition to Detroit supporters throwing projectiles and verbally assaulting members of the Indiana team.

A natural disaster is the impact of a natural hazard on the event that results in the loss of financial, physical, and human assets. Event managers should be aware of the following natural threats to sport: severe weather (e.g., lighting storm, tornado, blizzard, and extreme heat), land hazards (e.g., earthquake and avalanche), water hazards (e.g., river flood and ruptured water main), and fire emergencies (e.g., electrical fire and brushfire). An example of a natural threat affecting sport was the 1989 San Francisco earthquake, which occurred while thousands of spectators were inside Candlestick Park. Following the earthquake, event staff evacuated over 60,000 spectators, athletes, and officials from the stadium with no injuries or casualties being reported. An example of a natural disaster impacting sport was the 1985 Bradford City stadium fire. The English football club was hosting a match when a small fire emerged at one end of the stadium and continued uncontrolled. The fire engulfed much of the stadium and resulted in 56 fatalities and hundreds of injured spectators.

A medical hazard is a threat to the health of the spectators, athletes, and event staff as a result of an infectious natural organism (e.g., SARS and H1N1) or manmade substance (e.g., anthrax). Because of the implications, it is important that event managers understand the threat, prevention practices, possible impact, and recovery procedures to minimize the effects of medical hazards. In the past 10 years, event managers of the English–Australian Ashes, Beijing Olympic Games, and Mexican First Division football matches had to prevent and protect against and respond to and recover from incidents related to anthrax, SARS, and H1N1, respectively. In 2004, there was an unsuccessful al Qaeda–planned attack on the English–Australian Ashes that involved event staff releasing anthrax into team locker rooms. In 2008, event organizers effectively safeguarded spectators and athletes from the SARS outbreak, which claimed almost 800 victims worldwide, during the Olympic Games. In 2009, officials of the Mexican Football Federation banned spectators from attending football matches until the spread of the H1N1 virus was contained.

Alcohol control is the ability of event organizers and staff to responsibly provide alcoholic beverages and spectators to consume them while abiding by a code of conduct. A recent study examining the association of alcohol consumption and spectator misbehavior at American football games indicated an increase in criminal behavior. There was an increase in liquor law violations by 76 percent on game day in addition to increases in disorderly conduct by 41 percent, physical assaults by 95 percent, and property vandalism by 18 percent. The Ohio State University (OSU) launched an investigation into alcohol control issues and countermeasures as a result of two post–football game riots. The riots followed the OSU football team's 2000 loss to and 2002 win over their traditional rival, the University of Michigan. The investigation found that alcohol-fueled spectators had disrupted play on the field, fought with opposing fans and spectators, and vandalized university and private property. As a result, sport organizations, such as OSU athletics, have implemented alcohol control strategies to reduce the risk to financial, physical, and human assets.

Most recently, sport organizations have developed and implemented a "Fan Code of Conduct," and in August 2008, the National Football League (NFL) put into practice such a code. From the Na-

tional Collegiate Athletic Association (NCAA) to Major League Baseball, their codes of conduct state the rules of behavior and penalties for violating these policies. The "Fan Code of Conduct" norms state that (1) spectators will refrain from unruly, disruptive, and illegal behavior, (2) the conditions for which a spectator is subject to ejection, (3) spectators who continue to violate these policies are subject to the loss of their season tickets, and (4) behavior considered to be unlawful is subject to prosecution. Additional organizational policies involve (1) clubs and concessionaires working in partnership with state alcohol control agencies and (2) clubs assembling and deploying alcohol management teams on event day. Other organizational practices include (1) event alcohol sales being discontinued no later than the end of the third quarter, (2) all alcoholic beverages being dispensed in plastic containers, and (3) an external review of concessionaire and security performance.

Process of Event Risk Management

High-profile sport venues and events are places of mass gathering and are at risk of bomb threats, hooliganism, crowd disorder, severe weather, fire emergencies, and biological hazards. For that reason, event managers must adopt an all-hazard approach to event risk management to protect their physical, human, and financial assets. Event risk management is the systematic process of assessing the impact of an incident on the infrastructure, assets and stakeholders and implementing countermeasures to reduce the risk and mitigate the impact of crowd control issues, sport-related terrorism, and natural/medical hazards. A problem for event managers is the ability (or inability) to determine the actual threat-causing sport organizations and venues to prepare for a range of possible incidents at their events. Both manmade and natural threats expose vulnerabilities, which are exploitable resources such as safety weaknesses, security limitations, venue deficiencies, and/or staff shortcomings. Therefore, in order to determine threats and vulnerabilities, each event (and venue) must perform a risk assessment.

Event managers must support and adopt a formal event risk management process (e.g., strategic analysis, choice, and implementation). The National Center for Spectator Sports Safety and Security

(NCS4) has developed a sport-specific seven-step risk management model based on government risk assessment principles. The NCS4 model highlights strategic analysis in steps 1–4 with the identification of security personnel, characterization of assets, threat assessment, and vulnerability assessment. These processes involve identifying all key personnel responsible for event safety and security to gather information on the existing infrastructure, resources, threats, and countermeasures. The focal point of steps 5 and 6 are strategic choice, the processes of consequence evaluation and countermeasure selection, which calculates the probable loss and determines which risk reduction strategies will minimize the impact of an incident (e.g., bomb threat, riot, and natural disaster), respectively. The final step involves strategic implementation through consequence reduction measures. These policies and procedures should produce a systematic yet adaptable protection plan that is supported by industry standards and/or government-based legislation.

The process of assessing event risk aids event managers' decision-making to accept, reduce, reassign, or transfer the risk and responsibility. According to the International Association of Assembly Managers (IAAM), there were five levels of risk (i.e., severe, high, elevated, guarded, and low), similar to the U.S. government alert system (which ended in April 2011). Severe risk (threat level 5) occurs less frequently, but it is associated with a high degree of loss (e.g., human, structural, and financial) and should be avoided altogether. Whereas high and elevated risk (threat levels 4 and 3) are associated with a moderate degree of loss and average frequency, and should be transferred to a third party willing to assume the responsibility. As for guarded and low risk (threat levels 2 and 1), these occur with greater frequency and are associated with minimal loss. Thus, event managers usually decide to accept these risks and assume financial responsibility. Regardless of the threat level, it is recommended that event managers reduce risk through staff training, preventive maintenance, and development of a formal event risk management plan to include standard operating procedures.

Standardization of Event Risk Management

Standardization refers to establishing a formal set of voluntary criteria, guidelines, and/or best practices.

These standards are utilized to improve services, consistency, performance, and quality of services, policies, procedures, and products, respectively. A variety of standards have been developed for venue managers to assist with assessing event risk and operational planning. To date, European event managers have had two options for match day security protocols to combat organized social and political terror. First, the British National Criminal Intelligence Service established the Football Intelligence Section (FIS) to effectively control hooliganism on both the national and international front. The FIS has a program to train football intelligence officers (FIOs) who are responsible for assessing event risk and developing offender profiles. Also, FIOs are attached to specific football clubs and continually analyze data and exchange information with other British and European police task forces to reduce and eliminate hooliganism. Most importantly, these practices are supported by British legislation (i.e., the Football Act of 1999 and Football Disorder Act of 2000), thus providing event managers with autonomy.

Second, the IAAM formed a Safety and Security Task Force that established a comprehensive guide highlighting best practices in stadium, arena, and amphitheatre security management. There are 13 security measures the Safety and Security Task Force (SSTF) considers necessary in order to develop a basic protection plan. The foundation of the protection plan is establishing a central command (e.g., inside the venue or proximal to the event) to coordinate all security responses. Additional countermeasures include: coordinating with local policing agencies; developing policies that establish formal risk management and evacuation plans; pre-event training programs for all staff; prohibiting deliveries 90 minutes before the event; installation of ventilation systems to block hazardous agents; restriction of unauthorized personnel in critical areas; use of clear trash bins and refuse bags for easy visual inspection; use of periodic broadcasts to inform spectators; having one crowd observer for every 250 spectators; banning carry-in baggage; and no re-entry for spectators. As a result, these countermeasures have produced consistency in safety and security policies and procedures and staff performance, especially for venues hosting high-profile sport events.

As for North American venue and event managers, American Society for Industrial Security (ASIS) International provides security management guidelines and recommendations; however, this organization is not specific to sport. ASIS International works in partnership with the International Organization for Standardization, a nongovernmental organization with no legal authority, developing voluntary standards recognized as industry best practice. While ASIS International has produced many standards and guidelines, the majority of sport organizations in North America have been establishing their own safety and security policies and practices. For example, the NCAA issued a Security Planning Options guide for university athletic programs while the NFL developed a Best Practices guide with recommended security measures for their 32 club members. In addition, it has been noted that the NBA follows strict emergency response procedures, while the National Hockey League conducts monthly security audits. Some organizations, such as the U.S. Olympic Committee and American Red Cross, have established a Sport Safety Training course to provide individuals with the knowledge and skills necessary to provide a safe environment for athletes.

Furthermore, members of the NCS4 have developed a standardized process of event risk management involving four key components: (1) risk assessment, (2) training of personnel, (3) incident rehearsal, and (4) system auditing. First, sport organizations, venue owners, event managers, and other stakeholders must be aware of risk assessment methodologies to establish threats and vulnerabilities and implement risk reduction strategies. Second, both pre- and post-event staff training are important components in protecting critical infrastructures. There should be adequate resources for the recruitment, training, and evaluation of personnel responsible for event security. Third, event managers should also conduct rehearsals to test their crisis management procedures and evacuation plans to identify procedural strengths and weaknesses. Fourth, allowing for an external audit of the organization's level of preparedness (system) to be conducted provides additional insight into event day operations. This four-step process provides a system of checks and balances to promote consistent

safety and security practices at all venues regardless of the event size and available resources.

Process of Assessing Event Risk

Based on U.S. government recommendations, assessing event risk should achieve four objectives (i.e., devalue, detect, deter, and defend) that will enhance safety and security plans, policies, and procedures. The Department of Homeland Security has identified high-profile events as vulnerable to the threat of sport-related terrorism because of the fact that these are places of mass gathering. From the local city marathon to an international competition, hundreds and thousands of athletes and spectators gather in one location, and are at risk if event managers do not properly assess the risk and implement countermeasures. The risk assessment should first identify event threats and venue vulnerabilities, followed by reviewing and updating safety and security policies and procedures. Next, there should be an evaluation of staff training programs and established countermeasures in addition to measuring the effectiveness of communication and emergency response. A comprehensive risk assessment should be conducted annually in addition to an event specific assessment prior to each event. These risk assessment methods are based on research conducted by NCS4 and should only serve as a blueprint.

The process of assessing event risk is not a simple solution of applying one checklist to all venues and events. It is a complicated process of analysis and application based on the level of threat. Event managers must assess the strengths and weaknesses to implement a variety of countermeasures to combat different threats to various areas of the venue that affect different event personnel and customers. Furthermore, sport organizations need reliable and skilled personnel who are flexible, not rigid, in the application of safety and security policies and procedures. The ability of the event manager to interpret the risk assessment and establish the appropriate level of preparedness is critical in providing a safe and secure environment for spectators, athletes, and officials. Safety and security personnel should use available guidelines to prioritize countermeasures, based on the size of the crowd, significance of the event, and known threats, assets, and vulnerabilities. In general, there are eight areas to be assessed: (1) perimeter control, (2) access control, (3) credential management, (4) physical security, (5) risk management, (6) communications, (7) security personnel, and (8) training programs.

Perimeter control refers to protecting the infrastructure to include an outer perimeter of 400 meters (437 yards) around the event. As it relates to perimeter control, the event risk assessment should examine the following policies, procedures, and countermeasures:

- Established central command to coordinate all crisis responses
- External (and internal) surveillance cameras (CCTV) to monitor perimeter
- Limited vehicle and pedestrian traffic around venue 12 hours before the event
- Prohibited deliveries 90 minutes before the event
- No-fly zones over and around the event

Access control refers to safeguarding spectators, athletes, and officials by controlling who (e.g., unruly spectators) and what (e.g., prohibited items) enters the event. As it relates to access control, the event risk assessment should examine the following policies, procedures, and countermeasures:

- Signage stating policies relating to inspections and prohibited items
- Search entering spectators for prohibited items
- Banning backpacks and large bags from the event
- Electronic scanning of tickets for ease of entry
- No re-entry to the event for any spectator

Credential management refers to limiting and controlling access to the event through restricting access to authorized employees and providing accountability of personnel entering the event. Implementing such a system will provide event staff with the ability to document information, track access attempts, and activate a secondary alarm. As it relates to credential management, all event personnel should be issued an identification card, following a security clearance, to include the following:

- Media personnel
- Athletes
- Administrative staff
- Food and beverage staff
- Maintenance personnel
- Internal and external security personnel

Physical security refers to securing the area immediately outside of and surrounding the event—an inner perimeter of 30 meters (100 feet). As it relates to physical security, the event risk assessment should examine these policies, procedures and countermeasures:

- Installation of one-meter-high barrier to form a 30-meter (100-foot) security perimeter
- Zone pass system to limit access to restricted areas
- Secure utility and mechanical rooms with locks and tamper-proof seals
- Establish venue lockdown prior to the event
- Use of bomb-sniffing dog patrols on event day

Risk management refers to the process of updating security plans, policies, and procedures, and continuing to improve awareness and performance. As it relates to risk management, the event risk assessment should examine these policies, procedures, and countermeasures:

- Establish formal crisis management plans
- Establish formal evacuation plans
- Mobile first aid/emergency personnel on stand-by
- Use of clear trash bins/refuse bags for easy visual inspection
- Ventilation system to block toxic/hazardous agents

Communications refers to the system of sharing information pre-event, during the event, and post-event between members of a sport event safety action team (SESAT). Establishing such a system will allow the event manager to coordinate with safety and security personnel (e.g., security coordinator, emergency management director, police commander, and emergency medical services). As it relates to communications, the event risk assessment should examine these policies, procedures, and counter-measures:

- Pre-event coordination with local policing agencies
- Periodic broadcasts detailing safety and security practices
- Surveillance teams equipped with radio communications
- Conduct formal post-event debriefing for all event personnel
- Post-event multiagency collaboration and coordination

Security personnel refers to the allocation of event personnel inside and outside the event in addition to enhancing their safety and security knowledge and skills. As it relates to security personnel, the event risk assessment should examine these policies, procedures, and countermeasures:

- Security personnel are provided by licensed and certified agencies
- Conduct background checks for all volunteers and part-time staff
- Personnel on location to provide 24-hour surveillance
- Security personnel located in all sections of the parking lot
- A ratio of one crowd observer to 250 spectators

Training programs refers to the providing a comprehensive employee training program to describe their roles and responsibilities within risk management, venue evacuation, and crisis management. Both internal and external training programs increase knowledge, skills, and awareness in addition to being invaluable the moment an incident occurs. As it relates to training programs, the event risk assessment should examine these policies, procedures, and countermeasures:

- Conduct pre-event training specific to the upcoming event
- Rehearsal of crisis management plans
- Rehearsal of evacuation plans

- Conduct post-event training based on previous incidents
- Required basic first aid and CPR certification for all event staff

In light of the six categories of risk identified, it is critical for sport organizations to institutionalize standardization of risk management and assessment. Regardless of the analysis conducted after an incident, the primary question will be whether or not reasonable steps were taken to protect the event. A movement to establish standard safety and security measures, policies and procedures, and training of event personnel will minimize the impact of an incident. Event managers must be proactive and implement effective risk assessment practices to prevent and mitigate the consequences of an emergency incident. Without standard risk

Officers from U.S. Customs and Border Protection watch over preparations for the 2005 Super Bowl in Jacksonville, Florida.

assessment practices, safety and security measures will vary across events. However, given the increasing likelihood of an incident and identification of major events being at risk of sport-related terrorism, sport organizations must impose standard risk management practices.

These measures should align with industry best practices to reduce the liability following an incident. In an ideal world, sport governing bodies would endorse standard risk management practices and require event managers to comply with these standards, thus ensuring consistent practices across all events.

Thomas J. Cieslak II
Eastern Michigan University

See Also: Acts of God; Contingency Planning; Control for Safety of Fans/Athletes/Volunteers; Crisis Management; Emergencies: Athletes/Fans/Volunteers; Event Risk Management Process; Insurance Against Risks; Legal Considerations in Sport; Murphy's Law; Negligence; Officials, Legal Responsibilities; Risk Management; Securing Sports Events.

Further Readings

Ammon, Robert, Richard M. Southall, and David A. Blair. *Sport Facility Management: Organizing Events and Mitigating Risks*. Morgantown, WV: Fitness Technology, 2004.

Cieslak, Thomas J. "Match Day Security at Australian Sport Stadia: A Case Study of Eight Venues." *Event Management: An International Journal*, v.13/1 (2009).

Frosdick, Steve and Lynne Walley. *Sport and Security Management*. Oxford, UK: Elsevier Butterworth Heinemann, 1999.

Hall, Stacey A., Thomas J. Cieslak, Lou Marciani, Walter E. Cooper, and James, A. McGee. "Protective Security Measures for Major Sport Events: Proposing a Baseline Standard." *Journal of Emergency Management*, v.8/1 (2010).

Hurst, Ron, Paul Zoubek, and Catherine Pratsinakis. "American Sports as a Target of Terrorism: The Duty of Care After September 11th." http://www.mmwr.com/publications/ AmericanTerrorism.pdf (Accessed September 2005).

International Association of Venue Managers. "Safety and Security Task Force Best Practices Planning Guide, 2002." http://www.iaam.org/ CVMS/cvms.htm (Accessed September 2008).

National Center for Spectator Sports Safety and Security. "Sport Event Security Aware Review." http://www.sporteventsecurity.com/sesa_seal.php (Accessed January 2010).

Ohio State University. "Task Force on Preventing Celebratory Riots. Final Report, 2003." http:// hec.osu.edu/taskforce/FinalReport.pdf (Accessed September 2006).

Rees, Daniel I. and Kevin T. Schnepel. "College Football Games and Crime." *Journal of Sport Economics*, v.10/1 (2009).

Wann, Daniel L., Merrill J. Melnick, Gordon W. Russell, and Dale G. Pease. *Sport Fans: The Psychology and Social Impact of Spectators*. New York: Routledge, 2001.

Athlete Representation

Endorsements are of great importance to athletes, not only because they can increase one's annual salary dramatically, but also because they can lead to postathletic career opportunities. Marketing client endorsements is a vital part of the athlete representation business. Whether it is a backup quarterback signing autographs at a local sporting goods store or a national television commercial involving a star wide receiver, successfully marketing athletes through endorsements can be instrumental in securing long-term relationships with them. Endorsements allow athletes to serve as spokespeople for companies, promote a specific brand, and even become part of the entertainment industry. In addition to receiving monetary compensation, athletes may also receive the endorsed product as payment. If the product is athletic equipment in the particular sport in which the athlete plays, it can be very beneficial to that athlete by aiding in his or her training and/or season.

Team Versus Individual Sports

Three out of the four major professional sports leagues have a salary cap in place, with Major League Baseball being the lone exception. As a result, teams can only spend so much money on players and, consequently, players are "capped" in terms of what they can make for their on-the-field athletic ability. Therefore, players and their advisors must look for other ways for the athlete to make money. This is where the importance of endorsements comes into play. Of the top 10 highest paid athletes in 2009, LeBron James (ranked third overall) made the most from endorsements for athletes involved in team sports. His earnings of $28 million through endorsements were nearly double his salary of $14.4 million for that year. Next on the endorsements earnings list was Shaquille O'Neal (ranked 5th overall) at $15 million, followed by Peyton Manning (ranked 10th overall) at $13 million. The top Major League Baseball players listed were Derek Jeter (ranked 9th overall) at $8.5 million and Alex Rodriguez (ranked 4th overall) at $6 million. Although the level of importance of endorsements may fluctuate depending on which league the player participates in (i.e., NBA versus NFL versus MLB), endorsements are nonetheless essential to an athlete's earnings.

When dealing with individual sports—such as golf and auto racing—endorsements can play an even bigger role in an athlete's annual compensation, because the athletes in these sports only make large amounts when they win a tournament/race, or at least finish near the top of the final standings. In the ranking list for 2009, the two highest-paid spots were taken by athletes who participate in individual sports. Tiger Woods's endorsement earnings were $92 million (ranked 1st overall), which far outweighed his 2009 winnings of $7.7 million. Right behind Woods was another golfer, Phil Mickelson (ranked 2nd overall), who earned $46.6 million through endorsements, compared to his tour winnings of $6.35 million. NASCAR driver Dale Earnhardt, Jr., who had not won a race since 2008, ranked 11th due, in large part, to his endorsement earnings of $22 million. Other athletes who participate in individual sports who made the top 50 highest paid list were NASCAR driver Jeff Gordon (ranked 21st overall) with $15 million in endorse-

ment earnings and PGA golfer Jim Furyk (ranked 41st overall) with $11 million earned through endorsements. Again, these rankings and numbers illustrate how the endorsement factor in individual sports, such as golf and NASCAR, may be more important to these athletes than athletes in football or basketball.

Although the degree to which an athlete depends on endorsements for annual income may depend on the sport and league in which one plays, it is extremely important to understand the crucial part that endorsements play in the professional athlete's life.

Fees

The representation fees for negotiating contracts on behalf of a professional athlete can range between 2 percent and 5 percent, with 5 percent being close to the maximum. Conversely, negotiating endorsement deals for that same athlete can earn the representative a fee of anywhere from 10 percent up to, and sometimes beyond, 30 percent. Accordingly, not only do endorsements play a crucial role in the lives of professional athletes, but being adept at finding, negotiating, and securing endorsement deals for these athletes can be very rewarding for their representatives as well.

Social Networking

Maintaining an online presence has become increasingly part of the professional athlete's daily repertoire and routine. Over the past few years athletes have begun "tweeting" on Twitter at halftime or on the sideline during a game, and often cultivate thousands of Facebook friends and fans. Social networking has become a major marketing tool for the representative and the athlete.

Endorsing companies are also looking for ways to get their name or product in the public eye as much as possible. As a result, the more friends or fans an athlete has on Facebook, the more often he or she "tweets," and, especially, the more elaborate his or her personal Website becomes, the more endorsement deals the athlete could receive.

Postathletic Career Opportunities

As an athlete's professional playing career is limited in duration, athletes must plan for careers after sports. Securing the right endorsements is one way for an athlete to find a niche in a new career. Through his endorsements, Peyton Manning found his way to hosting *Saturday Night Live*, among other ventures. Chad Ochocinco, a.k.a. Chad Johnson, has his own reality television show due, in part, to his "tweeting" and endorsement opportunities. Shaquille O'Neal has his own reality television show as well thanks to his numerous appearances through his endorsements. The entertainment industry is an obvious postcareer choice because many athletes have become comfortable in front of the television audience after long experience with endorsements and countless interviews.

Endorsements can lead to postcareer opportunities even for athletes who have not been star players. Whether it is as a spokesperson for local companies, as a motivational speaker for community groups, or in day-to-day business, a highly visible name and image helps attract attention to former athletes in many fields.

Insurance and the Economy

Over the past few years, athletes have become involved in off-the-field scandals or have had public image problems that have led their endorsing companies to take out insurance to protect themselves. When an athlete is viewed in a negative light it can cast a shadow on the company and its product as well. In addition to the off-the-field issues, the poor economy has companies taking a more precautionary approach as to which athlete they choose, how long the contract should be, and what specific terms should be included in the contract. Including a morals clause in a contract may allow a company to terminate the endorsement contract at will if the athlete develops a negative image through his or her actions.

The recent developments in this field not only put the athlete on notice in regard to how off-the-field behavior can affect endorsement deals, but also may put more emphasis on choosing the correct representation. The athlete wants to choose a representative who not only handles the contract negotiation well, but who also has a keen sense of knowing the right endorsement deal when it appears. Of course, if the athlete is a superstar in his or her sport, these deals may be easier to come by, but it does not mean that he or she is immune to scandal.

Conclusion

Endorsement deals have become more of a necessity than ever before. Representatives need to become skilled at maximizing athlete opportunities both on and off the field. The endorsement factor has become such an integral part of the athlete representation business that the study of endorsement may need to be introduced into sports management educational programs across the globe.

Gerik Jenco
University of Pittsburgh School of Law

See Also: Agent, Sports Brand Image; Endorsement; Facebook; MySpace; Twitter.

Further Readings

Belson, Ken and Richard Sandomir. "Insuring Endorsements Against Athletes' Scandals." http://www.nytimes.com/2010/02/01/sports/01insurance.html (Accessed September 2010).

Freedman, Jonah. "The 50 Highest Earning American Athletes." http://sportsillustrated.cnn.com/more/specials/fortunate50/2009/index.html (Accessed August 2010).

Isenberg, Marc. *Money Players: A Guide to Success in Sports, Business & Life for Current and Future Pro Athletes.* Los Angeles, CA: A-Game, LLC, 2008.

Rosner, Scott R. and Kenneth L. Shropshire. *The Business of Sports.* Sudbury, MA: Jones & Bartlett Publishers, 2004.

Sanders, Bill. "How Impact of 'Tiger Recession' Changed Athlete Marketability." http://www.sportsbusinessjournal.com/article/66409 (Accessed September 2010).

Athletes as Sponsors

Although there are numerous advantages to using athletes as product endorsers, there are also many negative aspects to such a marketing strategy. This article will explore the benefits and risks of using celebrity athletes as endorsers.

The benefits of working with a high-profile individual to promote a product or event can be substantial. Celebrity athlete appearances may enforce the recall and believability of an advertising message. When a consumer sees a well-known athlete's endorsement, he or she may be more likely to remember both the celebrity's face and the associated product. In addition to this benefit, consumers may be prone to look past the weaknesses of a product endorsed by a celebrity athlete because of their strong positive associations with that athlete, who is often seen as the epitome of greatness. In other words, consumers tend to feel that products endorsed by athletes are superior to competing products.

Numerous risks are associated with the use of a high-profile personality to endorse a product. Prudent sponsors need to evaluate the potential risks associated with the use of any athlete endorser. The number one challenge associated with the use of a celebrity athlete endorser is that of maintaining the desired image. When a high-profile individual is bound by contract with a sponsor, that sponsor is then identified with the athlete economically and morally simply by association. It is for this reason that veteran or retired athletes are often preferred when considering potential sponsors. The thinking is that these athletes have a more reliable image, as they have proven themselves both on and off the athletic fields over many years.

The Case of Tiger Woods

An analysis of the well-known case of professional golfer Tiger Woods illustrates the benefits and risks of athlete endorsement deals. Woods has had one of the most successful professional golf careers. He is one of the winningest players on the Professional Golf Association's (PGA) Tour, winning numerous major championships, and being the youngest to complete the career Grand Slam of professional major championships. Because Woods broke racial barriers in golf and also upheld a clean, family-man image, there is no question why he was selected by many companies to represent their brands. His face is known globally, and many who do not frequently show interest in golf have been apt to follow him at one time or another.

Woods's sponsors have included Accenture, Nike, Gillette, Electric Arts, and Gatorade. As a result of successful product and endorser matches, these brands gained exposure, respect, and recall, which helped to drive profits for both the companies and Woods. These endorsements ultimately contributed to making Woods the highest-paid athlete in the world. It is estimated that he earned between $80 and $90 million in annual income from his top five sponsors alone.

All of this changed on November 29, 2009, when coverage broke of a car accident involving Woods. As details of the accident emerged, the public came to know Woods in a completely different light than before. With Woods being a successful athlete and endorser, the public was eager to know the details of the accident. In fact, it was noted that 6 percent of the world's news was devoted to this story within the first week it broke. A swarm of local news stations, national news broadcasts, and sport journalists worked on the story. Initial reports claimed that Woods and his wife were involved in a domestic dispute. Later reports and investigations then uncovered Woods's affairs with several women outside of his marriage. Not only did his reputation suffer, but so did those of many of his sponsors. As a result of the situation, Woods took an indefinite leave from golf while sponsors evaluated the future of their product and endorser relationship. Most of these companies felt it was in their best interest to cancel existing endorsement deals with Woods.

Researchers set out to better understand the economic impact Tiger Woods's situation had on his sponsors by evaluating the market trends at the time for each associated corporation and attempting to link them to Woods. Daily market returns for Woods's endorsers, particularly their parent companies, were compared with that of the rest of the global stock market. The researchers reviewed reports dated back to 2005 and continued through to the date of the first trading day after the accident, November 30, 2009. They evaluated the reports for abnormal returns. Results indicated that for Woods's top five sponsors there was a 2.3 percent drop, worth approximately $12 billion. Other sports-related sponsors were found to have dropped 4.3 percent of their aggregate market share, worth about $5.5 billion. Therefore, though the sports-related sponsors were not worth as much as a whole, they and their shareholders absorbed a greater impact proportionately than the big five.

There have been many other high profile athlete endorsers who have found themselves in situations similar to that of Tiger Woods. For example, Nike established endorsement deals with Michael Irvin, Charles Barkley, Roberto Alomar, and John Rocker. Michael Irvin was brought up on drug charges. Charles Barkley was found to have been in a bar fight. Roberto Alomar infamously spit on an umpire. John Rocker made controversial racial comments. Randy Moss, also once a sponsor for Nike, was brought up on assault charges. In the end, all of them along with their sponsors felt financial impacts.

Conclusion

In conclusion, there are high-profile athlete endorsers who conduct themselves well and continue to benefit their sponsors at a pace that has been proven to beat the rest of the market. The benefits endorsers bring with them are many. However, the tarnishing of a celebrity's image can reflect on a company's image and may adversely affect its stock value.

Christina L. L. Martin
Rusty Cockrell
Troy University

See Also: Brand Image; Branding; Corporate Criteria for Sponsor Evaluation; Corporate Sponsorship Philosophy; Endorsement; Endorser Effectiveness; Image; Misbehavior by Athletes.

Further Readings

Agrawal, J. and W. A. Kamakura. "The Economic Worth of Celebrity Endorsers: An Event Study Analysis." *Journal of Marketing*, v.59 (July 1995).

Cooke, S. L. "Stop the Presses." http://www .thesportjournal.org/article/stop-presses (Accessed August 2010).

Drewniak, B., J. Mahar, and M. L. Russell. "An Examination of Stock Market Response to Publicity Surrounding Athletic Endorsers." http://www.financeprofessor.com/Jimspapers/

endorsement/Endorsement%20Paper%20 July%2020,%202004.pdf (Accessed August 2010).

Kahle, L. R. and P. M. Homer. "Physical Attractiveness of the Celebrity Endorser: A Social Adaptation Perspective." *The Journal of Consumer Research*, v.11/4 (March 1985).

Knittel, C. R. and V. Stango. "Shareholder Value Destruction Following the Tiger Woods Scandal." http://www.econ.ucdavis.edu/faculty/ knittel/papers/Tiger_latest.pdf (Accessed August 2010).

Rindova, V. P., G. T. Pollock, and M. L. Hayward. "Celebrity Firms: The Social Construction of Market Popularity." *Academy of Management Review*, v.31/1 (2006).

Stone, G., M. Joseph, and M. Jones. "An Exploratory Study on the Use of Sport Celebrities in Advertising: A Content Analysis." http://business.nmsu.edu/~mhyman/M454 _Articles/(Celebrity)%20Stone_SMQ_2003.pdf (Accessed August 2010).

Atlanta Braves

The Major League Baseball (MLB) club the Atlanta Braves has a storied history marked by franchise relocations, regional representation, long stretches of futility, and unprecedented championship runs, all the while paving the way to lay claim to the name *America's Team*.

History

The Braves are the longest continuously running professional franchise in the United States. The origins of the franchise can be traced back to 1871 when the team was christened the Boston Red Stockings (not to be confused with the modern-day Boston Red Sox franchise). From Boston, the team relocated to Milwaukee in 1953 and ultimately to Atlanta in 1966.

The move to Atlanta positioned the team as the regional MLB team for the southeast United

States. In later years, franchises were established in Florida, but Atlanta had a long run as the exclusive southern MLB team. Still today, throughout the southeast, the Braves are a source of pride, with fans traveling from North Carolina, South Carolina, Tennessee, and Alabama for games. The Braves' popularity spread across the nation because of Ted Turner's ownership of the team from 1976 until 1996. The association with Turner and his vast media empire provided the team with great visibility to a large and widespread viewing audience—particularly because of game broadcasts on the Turner Broadcasting System (TBS) Superstation, which fostered the nickname "America's Team." Turner made his presence known as a high-profile, visible face of the franchise. Under Turner's ownership the franchise's attendance woes, as well as its playing, improved. Turner's brash style, innovation, and prominently displayed dedication provided a strong identity for the organization. In 1996, Time Warner took over Turner Broadcasting Inc., and the Atlanta Braves franchise. Subsequently, Liberty Media Corporation, a subsidiary of Time Warner, assumed ownership of the franchise in 2007.

The Braves organization has achieved much success, as it was the first franchise to win championships in three different cities, winning in Boston, Milwaukee, and Atlanta. After the move to Milwaukee and Atlanta, the team suffered through years of lackluster performances. However, in the 1990s, under the leadership of manager Bobby Cox and General Manager John Schuerholz, the Braves established themselves as perennial division champions and postseason mainstays. Following a worst to first finish in 1991 that culminated with a World Series run, the Braves won 14 divisional championships in a row. As the "Team of the '90s," the Braves played in five World Series (1991, 1992, 1995, 1996, 1999), highlighted by their championship season in 1995.

Sponsorships and Marketing

Atlanta is home to many Fortune 500 companies, including Coca-Cola, Chick-fil-A, Delta, and Home Depot. These companies are loyal sponsors to the Braves and activate their sponsorships in unique ways. At Turner Field, a 49-foot Coca-Cola bottle

The Atlanta Braves name and logo, like those of the Cleveland Indians, continue to refer to Native American themes.

towers in left field. The bottle shoots fireworks after home runs and features high-resolution, programmable LED screens that display messages. Near the bottle stands a 40-foot Chick-fil-A cow that does the "Tomahawk Chop." Another crowd favorite is the Home Depot Tool Race, which features four tool-shaped mascots (screw, paintbrush, drill, and hammer) that dash across the outfield warning track during the middle of the 6th inning.

The 2010 season was the last for iconic team manager Bobby Cox, who coached in two different stints (1978–81; 1990–2010) and was the general manager (1986–90). The Braves utilized Cox's final season as a major marketing tool, specifically his uniform number 6. Tours at Turner Field had discounted "Bobby Cox $6 Days," where tickets were $6, rather than $12. Ticket plans were sold as "Bobby Cox 6 game ticket plans." Limited edition Bobby Cox programs were sold all season. A Bobby Cox "Appreciation Series" was planned for the final weeks of the season. Cox is well liked for leading the Braves to 14 straight division titles, but also holds the dubious record of most ejections in MLB history (158 to date).

Team Name and Logo

The Atlanta Braves are one of two MLB teams to utilize a Native American reference in their name. The use of a Native American team name has led to numerous protests by Native Americans, especially during the World Series in 1995 when the Braves played the Cleveland Indians. Fans at Turner Field can experience the "Tomahawk Chop," brought to the Braves by former Florida State Seminole Deion Sanders. The Braves are often called the "Bravos."

Jason W. Lee
University of North Florida
Beth Cianfrone
Georgia State University

See Also: Brand Image; Franchise; Identity; Mascots; Major League Baseball.

Further Readings

Brown, Kristine A. "Native American Teams and Mascots: Disparaging and Insensitive or Just Part of the Game?" *Sports Law Journal*, v.9 (2002).

Coca-Cola. "Coca-Cola to Unveil New Bottle at Turner Field." http://www.thecocacolacompany .com/presscenter/nr_20090713_turner_field.html (Accessed September 2010).

Collier, J. G. "Tomahawk-Chopping Chick-fil-A Cow Heads to Turner Field." http:// www.ajc.com/business/content/business/ stories/2008/06/11/turner_field_chick_fil_a.html (Accessed September 2010).

Green, Ron, Jr. *101 Reasons to Love the Braves*. New York: Stewart, Tabori & Chang, 2008.

Major League Baseball. "Braves Timeline." http:// atlanta.braves.mlb.com/atl/history/timeline.jsp (Accessed September 2010).

Major League Baseball. "The Official Site of the Atlanta Braves." http://atlanta.braves.mlb.com/ index.jsp?c_id=atl (Accessed September 2010).

Atlanta Falcons

Using the Atlanta Falcons as a case study, this entry will demonstrate how sport teams use franchise players and winning records as a marketing tool in attracting social, focused, and vested fans. Also,

After some success in 2004, the Falcons briefly became one of the top three teams for attendance in the NFL.

this entry will provide some historical information on the origination of the Falcons organization.

According to Daniel Wann and Paula Waddill, sport fans and spectators are motivated to attend sporting events by factors such as aesthetics, escapism, entertainment, and family affiliation. There is an interrelationship between the level of fan motivation/identification and spectatorship. William Sutton, Mark McDonald, George Milne, and John Cimperman indicate that attendance records are affected by the level of team or player identification. They classify fans into three categories: social (low fan identification), focused (medium fan identification), and vested fans (high fan identification). The more vested a fan is to a team, the more likely he or she is motivated to attend events.

On June 30, 1965, then NFL Commissioner Pete Rozelle approved ownership of the Atlanta Falcons for $8.5 million to Rankin M. Smith, Sr., making it the 15th franchise in the league. Smith was responsible for running the daily operations of the franchise until 1990, when he handed over control of the team to his son Taylor Smith. The team was later sold to current owner Arthur M. Blank in 2002 for the amount of $545 million. In 1991, the Falcons moved from the Atlanta-Fulton County

Stadium to the Georgia Dome. Organization personnel believed that it would be in the best interest of the fans to move to a bigger stadium. The Falcons played their first NFL game on September 11, 1966, at the Atlanta-Fulton County Stadium. Even after registering a loss, the fans saw the organization as a gift to the city of Atlanta. Residents showed their appreciation with a record-breaking season ticket sale.

Sporting organizations generate revenue through several sources, such as media and television, licensed goods, tickets sales, and stadium revenues. Franchise players' fame and status are utilized in selling memorabilia. For instance, the top 10 jerseys sold in the NFL are of players such as Brett Favre, Jay Cutler, and Adrian Peterson, all of whom are tagged franchise players. In addition, these players are utilized to bring in more fans and spectators to the games. Luxury suite and season ticket holders pay sizeable amounts of money to engage in sporting events. In the NFL some fans pay a seat license fee that guarantees the right to purchase a particular seat in a stadium. Several teams and leagues across the United States use this strategy as a means of generating additional revenue not shared by other teams.

Despite different marketing strategies employed, the selling of the Falcons as a sport franchise has not been easy. In the 2001–04 football seasons, the organization was not within the top 15 most populated stadiums. In the 2005 season, the Falcons jumped to the rank of third in attendance, averaging 72,032 per game. This was likely a result of a successful 2004 season. In addition, Michael Vick established himself as a franchise quarterback, leading the team to a division championship and an NFC Championship game.

As a result of a mediocre 2006 season, the Falcons' attendance dropped to 70,388. After Vick's suspension in 2007 following charges of dogfighting, the team played three different quarterbacks (Joey Harrington, Bryon Leftwich, and Chris Redman) averaging 67,520 spectators per game. In the 2008 season, the team drafted Matt Ryan, and average attendance dropped to 65,617. However, attendance increased to 70,416 the next year after establishing a franchise quarterback and a winning season.

Conclusion

Fan and spectator attendance are essential factors for generating revenue for sporting organizations. These individuals are dedicated to sports even when they are not directly engaged; however, they follow the activities of a sport team or team members. To sum up, sporting organizations will continue to utilize franchise players and winning records as a tool in generating greater revenue through tickets sales and stadium proceeds, because it has shown to be effective.

Emeka Anaza
University of Illinois, Urbana-Champaign

See Also: Attendance, Impact of Winning on; Fan Attendance, Reasons for; National Football League.

Further Readings

"NFL Attendance—2005 to 2009." http://espn
.go.com/nfl/attendance (Accessed July 2010).
Official Site of the Atlanta Falcons. http://www
.atlantafalcons.com (Accessed July 2010).
Sutton, W. A., M. A. McDonald, G. R. Milne, and J. Cimperman. "Creating and Fostering Fan Identification in Professional Sports." *Sport Marketing Quarterly*, v.6 (1997).
Wann, D. L. and P. J. Waddill. "Predicting Sport Fan Motivation Using Anatomical Sex and Gender Role Orientation." *North American Journal of Psychology*, v.5 (2003).

Atlanta Hawks

The Atlanta Hawks are a professional National Basketball Association (NBA) team owned by the investment group Atlanta Spirit, LLC. Corporate sponsorships include naming rights to the team's home, Philips Arena. Atlanta Spirit and the Hawks community development foundation as well as individual players participate in a variety of community marketing and service outreach programs to cultivate their fan base.

The Atlanta Hawks play in the Southeastern Division of the NBA's Eastern Conference. The franchise began in 1946 as the Buffalo Bisons and underwent several location and name changes before relocating to Atlanta in 1968. Atlanta Spirit, LLC, an investment group comprising five owners and three investors, purchased the Atlanta Hawks in 2004 for $208 million. Atlanta Spirit also owned the Atlanta Thrashers NHL hockey team (until its sale and move to Winnipeg in June 2011) and owns the operating rights to Philips Arena, where the Hawks play. The Hawks ownership group Atlanta Spirit, LLC has attracted a number of corporate sponsorship partners to the franchise. The major corporate sponsors of the Atlanta Hawks are Home Depot, Metro PCS, United Distributors, Anheuser-Busch InBev, Coca-Cola, Aaron's, and Philips Electronics, the latter of which holds the naming rights to Philips Arena.

The owners include Bruce Levenson, Michael Gearon, Steven Belkin, Ed Peskowitz, and Rutherford Seydel. The three investors are Todd Foreman, Michael Gearon, Sr., and Beau Turner. On the executive management side, the president of the Hawks is Bob Williams. The executive vice-president and general manager of the team is Rick Sund. Larry Drew is head coach of the Hawks, replacing Mike Woodson in the 2010 off-season. Local, regional, and national radio and television networks broadcast Hawks games. The team's radio and television broadcasters include Steve Holman, Bob Rathbun, Dominique Wilkins, and James Verrett.

The team's ownership uses a variety of game and community promotional tools to market the team and build a loyal fan base, including the mascots Skyhawk and Harry T. Hawk and the A-Town Dancers. Atlanta Spirit, LLC also funds and operates community development programs in the Atlanta area, providing educational programs and aiding community-service projects. The Hawks also have a designated driver booth inside Philips Arena to educate people about the dangers of drunk driving. The Hawks were one of the first professional sports teams to establish a community foundation for both community outreach and marketing purposes. The Hawks community foundation actively seeks to involve Atlanta's youth in community service initiatives, skills development, and cultural awareness.

The Hawks fund community initiatives through the distribution of charitable grants. Past initiatives receiving grants have included educating Georgia's youth, reducing childhood obesity, helping children live an active lifestyle, and helping youth get started in athletics and other physical programs. They also marketed a campaign called Dollars for Scholars, in which the Atlanta Hawks Foundation partnered with Project Grad of Atlanta to create scholarships for high school seniors.

The team has an annual fundraiser where fans can meet and greet the team and its coaches as well as legendary past players and team executives. In addition, the Hawks have an annual golf tournament benefiting the Hawks Foundation and its community projects and initiatives. The Hawks marketing department has established events such as College Media Day, where college students are given the opportunity to write a game story during one regular season game to be published on the team's official Website. The Hawks honored African American leaders during Black History Month and worked with United Way of Atlanta to celebrate Martin Luther King, Jr. Day through a writing contest for high school students. The top 15 finalists attended a poetry workshop, with the grand prize winner reciting his or her poetry during halftime of the Martin Luther King, Jr. Day game among other prizes.

Atlanta Hawks players assist the management in marketing the team, building the fan base, and performing community outreach services. Various players visit hospitals and local businesses, such as toy shops or sports stores, to meet with fans, especially around holidays such as Thanksgiving and Christmas. Some players also maintain their own community foundations. Many Hawks players participate in the Hawks' Player Assist Program, in which each player purchases a block of seats to every home game at Philips Arena. The tickets are then donated to youth groups and nonprofit organizations throughout Atlanta. Season ticket holders can also donate individual game tickets to Big Brothers and Big Sisters when they are unable to attend specific games.

David Trevino
Independent Scholar

See Also: Atlanta Thrashers; Community Relations; National Basketball Association; Venue Naming Rights.

Further Readings

Atlanta Hawks Foundation. http://www.nba .com/hawks/community/Atlanta_Hawks _Foundation-79913-33.html (Accessed September 2010).

Atlanta Hawks Official Website. http://www.nba .com/hawks (Accessed September 2010).

Atlanta Spirit, LLC. "Community Outreach." http://www.atlantaspirit.com/CommOutreach .htm (Accessed September 2010).

Falcous, Mark and Joseph Maguire. "Making It Local? National Basketball Association Expansion and English Basketball Subcultures." In Michael L. Silk and David L. Andrews, eds. *Sport and Corporate Nationalisms*. New York: Berg, 2005.

Atlanta Thrashers

The Atlanta Thrashers are a National Hockey League (NHL) team that came to Atlanta in 1997 and began play in 1999. The team was owned by Atlanta Spirit, LLC, but was sold in June 2011 to True North Sports and Entertainment, moving to Winnipeg, Manitoba, Canada, for the 2011–12 season. The team's management underwent key changes in the 2010 season. The team used a variety of marketing tools at games and within the community, such as cheerleaders and media coverage, to attract the fan base. The Thrashers maintained the Atlanta Thrasher Foundation to oversee the team's community development programs and grants, which emphasized children's issues such as education, physical activity, and an end to childhood cancer. The Thrashers also participated in NHL community outreach programs.

Atlanta was awarded an NHL franchise on June 25, 1997, to replace the departed Atlanta Flames, who relocated to the Canadian city of Calgary. The new franchise, named the Thrashers, played its first game during the 1999–2000 NHL season.

The Thrashers played in the Southeastern Division of the NHL's Eastern Conference. Atlanta Spirit, LLC, an ownership group comprising five owners and three investors, acquired the Thrashers in 2004. The owners include Bruce Levenson, Michael Gearon, Steven Belkin, Ed Peskowitz, and Rutherford Seydel. The three investors were Todd Foreman, Michael Gearon, Sr., and Beau Turner. Atlanta Spirit, LLC also owns the Atlanta Hawks, an NBA franchise, and owns the operating rights to Philips Arena, where the Hawks and Thrashers play.

Highlights of the team's early years included their first playoff appearance in the 2006–07 season, where they were eliminated by the New York Rangers in the quarterfinals, and the first NHL All-Star Game held at Philips Arena, which took place on January 27, 2008. Following several disappointing seasons after their first playoff appearance, Atlanta Spirit reorganized the team's management in 2010. General Manager Don Waddell became president of hockey operations and Rick Dudley took over as general manager, a position currently held by Scott Wilkinson. Craig Ramsey assumed head coaching duties that same year after John Anderson and his staff's contracts were not renewed.

Team management used a variety of methods to garner fan interest and loyalty both at games and within the community. The Thrashers featured a Brown Thrasher bird known as Thrash as mascot and cheerleaders known as the Blue Crew. The fan base as well as the team's home of Philips Arena was known as "Blueland." Team management also marketed the team through television and radio exposure. Television broadcasts of Thrashers games included Fox Sports South, SportSouth, VS, and NBC as well as paid subscription services such as NHL Center Ice. Darren Eliot was the team's television analyst and director of hockey programs while Matt McConnell provided television play-by-play commentary. A network of local and regional stations also carried Thrashers games, anchored by the flagship station WCNN-AM (680 The Fan). Dan Kamal provided the radio play-by-play commentary.

The Atlanta Thrashers organization performed much community work through their community development arm, the Atlanta Thrashers Foundation, founded in 1999. Their charitable programs serve as both community outreach and as a marketing tool. The mission statement of the Thrasher foundation included working toward improving the lives of children, creating charities and programs that will guide children toward living an active lifestyle, receiving an education, and becoming a well-rounded person. The foundation awarded over $4 million to over 2,000 state and local charities.

Thrashers Foundation grants were geared toward helping educate Georgia children, reducing obesity rates in youth by promoting an active lifestyle, and fighting cancer in children. The latter was a part of the NHL's Hockey Fights Cancer initiative. Some of the previous grant recipients have included the Boys and Girls Clubs of Atlanta, Special Olympics Georgia, the Muscular Dystrophy Association, and Prevent Blindness Georgia, among many others.

When the Thrashers move to Winnipeg, Atlanta will become the first city in modern years to lose two NHL teams; the Flames left Atlanta for Calgary, Alberta, Canada, in 1980. As of June 2011, a decision had not been reached on a new name for the team.

David Trevino
Independent Scholar

See Also: Atlanta Hawks; Calgary Flames; Charity Sports Events; Community Relations; National Hockey League.

Further Readings

Atlanta Thrashers Official Website. http://thrashers .nhl.com (Accessed September 2010).

Duhatschek, Eric. *Hockey Chronicles: An Insider History of the National Hockey League Teams.* New York: Checkmark Books, 2001.

Shaw, Warren. "Atlanta Thrashers to Winnipeg: Predictions for the Players on the Team." *Bleacher Report* (June 10, 2011). http:// bleacherreport.com/articles/728691-atlanta -thrashers-to-winnipeg-predictions-for-the -players-on-the-team (Accessed June 2011).

Whitson, David, and Richard S. Gruneau. *Artificial Ice: Hockey, Culture, and Commerce.* Toronto: Broadview Press, 2006.

Zirin, Dave. *Bad Sports: How Owners Are Ruining the Games We Love.* New York: Scribner, 2010.

Atmospherics

Spectators often reflect on how much they enjoyed a sporting event because of the smell of the popcorn, the roar of the crowd, a favorite song over the PA system, a mascot performing a funny antic, or the PA announcer introducing a favorite player. The emotional appeal of being part of the game day atmosphere is a strong motivating factor for many sport fans. Atmospherics is used within sport as a promotional tool, and sport marketers tap into a variety of strategies for creating cognitive and emotional effects in spectators. Atmospherics is a component of the promotional mix in sport and it is concerned with the "place" of purchase within the marketing mix.

Akin to producing a stage production, atmospherics is mostly concerned with the entertainment aspect of the sport experience. It may include elements of the physical setting or sensory elements. Within the context of a spectator event, elements of the physical setting may include factors such as the exterior structure or interior design of the stadium or arena, special displays, and in some cases the uniforms worn and actions of service personnel. Sensory elements may include cues such as music, scents, mascots, announcers, vendors, performers, athletes, fans, and other types of activities that enhance the experience for a spectator.

Music

Auditory effects such as music are commonly used by sport marketers to enhance the atmosphere of the stadium or arena. In many cases, music serves to motivate the team and excite the crowd for purposes of exploiting the home field/court advantage and filling downtime during intermissions or time-outs. Computer programs have given sport marketers access to a greater variety of songs in the press box than in the past.

Music evokes memories and incites spectator emotions. In many cases, spectators are drawn to their feet to participate in the experience as they sing along or dance. Songs from popular movies (e.g., *Rocky*), or television shows (e.g., *Jeopardy*) and a whole range of popular hits are played on a regular basis. Sporting events almost always begin with the national anthem, and often include school or team alma mater or fight songs (e.g., Ohio State or Michigan). Music is also commonly used to introduce a team as they enter the playing area. For example, Virginia Tech football players enter the playing field to "Enter Sandman," a song by the heavy metal band Metallica. The start of "Enter Sandman" is the cue for Virginia Tech spectators of all ages to jump up and down and cheer loudly.

Songs like "Let's Get It Started" by the Black Eyed Peas serve as a rallying cry to excite the home team to greater performance. A great defensive play by the home team may be followed by songs such as "We Will Rock You" by the music group Queen. In many cases music is used to highlight the fun and festival of sport or as a form of celebration. For example, Queen's popular song "We Are the Champions" is often blasted over the loudspeakers after a defining win, such as in a championship game.

While sport marketers in North America often use artificial means by playing previously recorded music, the music at many sporting events in overseas markets stems from crowd singing, anthems, and chants. For example, anthems such as the Arsenal FC chant or the Red Flag chant at Manchester United's Old Trafford are commonly sung by the fans.

Scents

Of all of the five senses, smell is the most strongly connected with an individual's emotions, and is increasingly used by sport marketers to create an immediate and lasting connection with fans. Thus, if used correctly, marketers of the fan experience can cater toward human emotion, which is an important aspect of sport marketing. Spectators often make the comment that they enjoy the atmosphere of a sporting event because of the smell of the ballpark, stadium, or arena. In some cases, scents may include natural elements such as that of an ice rink or freshly cut grass. Other times, scents may be less pleasant, such as spilled beer, sweat, or even garbage.

Most sport marketers seek to create a pleasant atmosphere by using artificial means. For example, concessionaires may use the scent of freshly popped popcorn, smoke from barbecue grills, hot dogs, and other food-related smells. Sport organizations such as the Tampa Bay Rays are even using sensory services such as those of DMX, Inc., which provides clients with environmental scents that provide "brand texture" for their customers. The Rays use an orange scent in the Tropicana Field rotunda and are considering using a cotton candy scent in the carnival area, a bubble gum scent in the Topps make-your-own baseball card alcove, and other scents such as freshly cut grass, suntan lotion, and sea spray. Fresh scents from cleaning supplies are also commonly used in fitness and recreational facilities to enhance participant experiences.

Mascots

Mascots are important performers that can greatly add value to the entertainment experience at a sporting event. In some cases, sport marketers utilize mascots because of expectations upon the part of many families that a sporting event should include a mascot who can entertain children. However, at the professional level, mascots may be very sophisticated. Mascots such as Ted Giannoulis (the "Famous Chicken") and Dave Raymond (the "Philly Phanatic") are highly skilled performers who mix athleticism with comedy.

The personality, costume, image, and actions of a mascot should be consistent with the promotional objectives of the team, and the mascot's behavior should be appropriate for the audience. Sport marketers should coordinate their efforts with the mascot and must also be prepared to handle inquiries for mascot appearances, provide security for the mascot, and handle complaints from fans. In 1995 the Philadelphia Phillies agreed to pay $128,000 plus $28,000 of interest to a plaintiff who sued the organization because of an injury that was caused by a fill-in Phanatic mascot who was performing at a church carnival in 1991. In their October 2006 game against New Mexico State, the University of Idaho unveiled the new "Joe Vandal" mascot because the older costume was frightening children and attracted rude comments from spectators.

Announcers

A good public address announcer can greatly enhance a spectator's experience at a sporting event. The public address announcer serves as the "master of ceremonies" for the sporting event and thus guides the audience through the performance that is happening on the field of play by introducing players and other supporting entertainers. In addition, the public address announcer keeps the audience abreast as to the latest happenings during the event. It is important that sport marketers work closely with the public address announcer by providing scripts and cues for announcing important information such as promotional sponsors, upcoming promotions, and ticketing information. Some public announcers are so much a part of the sport experience that they are better known than some of the players. For example, announcer Bob Sheppard of the New York Yankees was legendary for his authoritative voice that echoed throughout Yankee Stadium. Rex Barney, the longtime public address announcer for the Baltimore Orioles who always ended his announcements with his signature "thank youuuu," was also legendary.

Vendors

Food, beverage, and merchandise vendors are important supporting staff members in the production of a sporting event. Food and beverage vendors may sell a range of food and beverage items including hot dogs, cotton candy, pretzels, soft drinks, beer, and numerous other items. Merchandise vendors sell apparel and other items, such as t-shirts, caps, bumper stickers, glow sticks, seat cushions, and necklaces. Vendors are part of the entertainment experience for the fan, and some vendors can be very charismatic in delivering their sales pitches. Some dress in funny clothing, sing silly songs, or have a distinctive holler when they sell their product.

One of the issues facing sport marketers and concessionaires inside the sport venue is the increasing competition from food, beverage, and merchandise vendors outside the stadium. As spectators make their way to the stadium, food, beverage, and merchandise vendors are stationed at key areas, and often sell their products at a much lower price than the vendors inside the stadium. In some cases, fans are unaware that a merchandise vendor may be selling unlicensed merchandise.

Performers

The promotional schedule for many professional and collegiate sport organizations includes a number of invited performers who add entertainment value to events. Sport marketers are responsible for booking various acts that help to fill their promotional schedule, and often serve as an incentive for attracting spectators. Performers range from acts such as the Famous Chicken to the Blues Brothers, Zooperstars, Reggy the Purple Party Dude, Bird-Zerk, and Myron Noodleman. Other performers may be youth and former athletes, jugglers, animals, and musicians.

While some performers are booked as special acts, others (e.g., dance teams) are scheduled for most or all home events. For example, marketers of the NBA's Dallas Mavericks created a hip-hop dance troupe they call the "Mavs ManiAACS," which comprises beefy men who entertain fans during home games with their energetic, crowd-pleasing routines. Later, the Mavs GrannyAACs were born when a fan e-mailed Mavericks owner Mark Cuban with the idea of creating a squad of "Dancin' Grannies" to compete with the ManiAACs. In some cases, special performers will make personal contact, while others have an agent who schedules all of their appearances. Sport marketers must be careful to work with reputable acts and agents. In addition, it is important for the marketer to match the act with the target audience. Some performers are more tasteful than others, and some may not be suitable for children.

Athletes

Athletes are the primary actors who comprise the core product. While spectators attend sporting competitions to watch skilled athletes engage in their craft, sport marketers can integrate athletes into various promotions. For example, the Famous Chicken often has athletes tackle and pin him to the ground or he uses them as sidekicks in one of his acts. Athletes can also be used in other capacities such as signing autographs after a game, parading into the stadium or singing the alma mater (e.g., after Notre Dame football games). Athletes such as Rod Smart in the XFL (i.e., a football league founded by Vince McMahan and in existence for only one year in 2001) were entertaining because of the name on the back of his jersey that read "He Hate Me." Chad Ochocinco of the NFL's Cincinnati Bengals has used various antics to create a carnival atmosphere, such as attempting to bribe an official with a dollar bill and holding up a preprinted sign after scoring a touchdown that read "Dear NFL, please don't fine me again."

Fans

Fans are a key part of the act in any sporting event as they cheer, stomp, yell, sing, and make other various noises. Fans are more highly attached to a team than spectators, and some fans may paint their faces or dress in costumes or uniforms unique to their team. Fans can be used in various capacities to create a home field advantage. For example, announcers, cheerleaders, mascots, and special performers can spur the fans into action by asking them to make noise, start the wave, or other such antics. Some fans are more notorious than others. For example, a group of fans in Washington, D.C., dress up with hog noses and dresses for every NFL Redskins game and call themselves the "Hogettes." The Hogettes attend every game despite the fact that the original Hogs (i.e., the nickname for the Redskins offensive line) from the early 1980s no longer exist. In Portland, the NBA's Trail Blazers have a fan by the name of "Hippie Man" who dances and offers creative heckling. For many years, the most notorious fan of the MLB's Baltimore Orioles was "Wild Bill Hagy," who would stand atop the dugout and spell out O-R-I-O-L-E-S using his arms and legs.

David J. Shonk
James Madison University

See Also: Announcer; Anthems/Flag Raising; Baltimore Orioles; Event Hospitality; Experience Marketing; Fan Attendance, Reasons for; Fan Shops, Retail; Mascots; Promotion.

Further Readings

Curry, J. "Voice of Yankee Stadium May Be Done." *New York Times.* (April 2, 2009).

Dallas Mavericks. http://www.nba.com/mavericks/entertainment/Mavs_ManiAACs.html (Accessed November 2009).

Ginsburg, D. "O-R-I-O-L-E-S Fan 'Wild Bill' Hagy Dead at 68." http://www.usatoday.com/sports/baseball/al/orioles/2007-08-20-hagy-obit_N.htm (Accessed November 2009).

Irwin, R. L., W. A. Sutton, and L. M. McCarthy. *Sport Promotion and Sales Management.* Champaign, IL: Human Kinetics, 2002.

Seravalli, F. "A Day in the Busy Life of Comcast-Spectacor President Peter Luukko." http://www.philly.com/philly/sports/flyers/20090804_A_day_in_the_busy_life_of_Comcast-Spectacor_president_Peter_Luukko.html (Accessed November 2009).

"Tampa Bay Rays Score With Fans by Providing Scents From DMX." DMX, Inc. http://www.dmx.com/files/library/press-releases/103008tampaBay.pdf (Accessed November 2009).

Trail, G. T., M. J. Robinson, R. J. Dick, and A. J. Gillentine. "Motives and Points of Attachment: Fans Versus Spectators in Intercollegiate Athletics." *Sport Marketing Quarterly,* v.12/4 (2003).

Vecsey, G. "Sports of the Times: Liability Insurance for Mascots." *New York Times* (December 3, 1995).

Attendance, Impact of Winning on

For sports teams, winning has been found to lead to increases in fan interest, donations, merchandise revenue, media revenue and exposure, franchise value, college applications, and attendance. Winning is seen as a critical element in filling the stands and increasing revenue. Therefore, teams go to extraordinary lengths to obtain the best coaches and players, state-of-the-art facilities, and media exposure that can catapult them to the top of the standings.

A large encompassing study was conducted in 1999 on 10 Major League Baseball (MLB) teams. The teams were chosen because they had played in the same MLB location for over 100 years. All 10 teams showed that winning had a significant positive effect on attendance. However, winning had less of an effect on attendance for a few teams. The Cincinnati Reds and the New York Yankees were hypothesized to have less increase in attendance

A stadium packed with football fans wearing their team's colors. Teams that reach the playoffs can expect up to a 9.8 percent increase in merchandise and apparel sales, according to one study.

based on small city size for the Reds, and the high expectancy of winning in New York. Increased attendance did not necessarily mean that teams utilized increased resources to improve winning on the field. Overall, a boost in attendance did not lead to an increase on subsequent winning on the field. Winning percentage has also been found to be related to increased attendance in the National Basketball Association (NBA). Twenty-nine teams showed increases in attendance based on winning percentage from the 1993–99 seasons.

Winning has an effect on average capacity of a stadium, ticket cost, sales of luxury suites and personal seating licenses (PSLs), and ticket packages. Winning teams generally have stadiums that are 6–11 percent fuller than losing teams. They also maintain the ability to charge a higher cost for their tickets and are less likely to discount tickets to reach capacity. Corporations are attracted to winning teams for the positive association they pro-

vide. They buy luxury suites and use them to entertain and impress ongoing and potential clients. A fan can gain that association by purchasing a PSL. The PSL is the fan's own piece of real estate that attaches him or her to a winning franchise. Winning teams can restrict ticket sales to packages rather than single game purchases. Season ticket packages and multi-game opportunities assure more ticket sales for a winning organization.

Merchandise sales and franchise value can also be altered based on winning percentage. One study found that winning National Football League (NFL) teams showed a 2.8 percent increase in merchandise sales the following season. Conversely, losing teams demonstrated a 19.7 percent decrease in sales the next year. Reaching the playoffs has been found to have a similar effect. In the same study, teams that were playoff bound had a 9.8 percent increase in merchandise sales compared to a 21.3 percent decrease for the teams that failed to qualify for the postseason. Fans are motivated to wear apparel that sheds a positive light on themselves, and therefore they buy merchandise from a winning franchise to meet that goal. Franchise value is also affected by winning percentage. Winning teams were found to have a higher value than losing teams and demonstrated an elevated increase in worth the next year following a winning season. Some teams that have a long record of past achievement may be immune from the recent winning percentage effect based on their storied history.

Another aspect to examine is the impact of winning championships in big-time college sports and the subsequent effect on college applications at that winning institution. A significant effect was found for an increase in interest at schools that had recently won a men's football or basketball championship. Some schools in the study had an increase of applications of between 10 and 20 percent, and Miami demonstrated a 34 percent increase in applications after their 1987 NCAA football championship. It should also be noted that some schools showed a decrease in applications following a championship season.

Brian E. Pruegger
Independent Scholar

See Also: Avidity; Consumer Behavior; Fan Avidity; Fan Loyalty Continuum; Image; Luxury Boxes and Suites; Personal Seat License.

Further Readings

Branvold, S. E., D. W. Pan, and T. E. Gabert. "Effects of Winning Percentage and Market Size on Attendance in Minor League Baseball." *Sport Marketing Quarterly*, v.6/4 (1997).

Davis, M. C. "The Interaction Between Baseball Attendance and Winning Percentage: A VAR Analysis." *International Journal of Sport Finance*, v.3/1 (2008).

De Shriver, T. D. "Factors Affecting Spectator Attendance at NCAA Division II Football Contests." *International Sports Journal* (Summer 1999).

Hansen, H. and R. Gauthier. "Factors Affecting Attendance at Professional Sport Events."

Journal of Sport Management, v.3/1 (1989).

Jones, J. C. "Winners, Losers and Hosers: Demand and Survival in the National Hockey League." *Atlantic Economic Journal*, v.12/3 (1984).

Milne, G. R. and M. A. McDonald. *Sport Marketing: Managing the Exchange Process.* Sudbury, MA: Jones & Bartlett Publishers, 1999.

Nourayi, M. M. "Profitability in Professional Sports and Benchmarking: The Case of NBA Franchises." *Benchmarking*, v.13/3 (2006).

Toma, J. D. and M. E. Cross. "Intercollegiate Athletics and Student College Choice: Exploring the Impact of Championship Seasons on Undergraduate Applications." *Research in Higher Education*, v.39/6 (1998).

Wells, D. E., R. M. Southall, and H. H. Peng. "An Analysis of Factors Related to Attendance at Division II Football Games." *Sport Marketing Quarterly*, v.9/4 (2000).

Audience Measurement

Audience measurement is a key metric for the global sports industry. Media managers use audience size to set advertising rates. Marketers review these measures to determine how they will spend billions of advertising dollars. Clearly, marketers want to align with popular sports events, highly rated sports broadcasts, broadly circulated sports publications, and highly trafficked sports Websites. Brand marketers and media managers want measures that are timely and accurate. Brand marketers want to spend as little as possible to reach sports fans, while sports media managers want to set prices as high as audience figures will allow. This can lead to an adversarial relationship as media managers and brand marketers try to maximize scarce resources.

Key Broadcast Measurement Concepts

A program's rating refers to the percentage of households tuned to the program compared to the number of television homes that could be tuned to the program. Consider a local market with 1 million television homes. If a game is broadcast in that market and viewed in 200,000 homes, the broadcast rating is 20 ($(200,000/1,000,000) \times 100$). Of all the television homes in that market, 20 percent of them were tuned to the game. Substituting radio figures for television figures will provide the radio station's rating. Generally, the more highly rated the broadcast, the more expensive the ad time. Ratings can be calculated for local markets, marketing regions, or nationally. If the number of television and radio homes for each market is known, along with the number of homes viewing or listening to the broadcast, a rating can be calculated for any geographic area.

Every home in the market will not tune to the broadcast, so the station's share is compared to its rating. Share refers to the number of homes actually using television during the game's broadcast that are actually viewing the game. Consider the same market with its 1 million television homes. If only 500,000 of those homes are actually using television at the time of the broadcast, and 200,000 of those homes are viewing the broadcast, then the station's share is 40 ($(200,000/500,000) \times 100$). Of all the homes using television in the market at the time of the game, 40 percent of those homes were tuned to the game. Substituting radio figures for television figures will provide the radio station's share. Shares can be calculated for local markets, marketing regions, or nationally. If the number of television and radio homes in use is known for each market, along with the number of homes viewing or listening to the broadcast, a share can be calculated for any geographic area.

A high rating usually correlates with a high share, but it is possible to have a high share and a low rating. A baseball game broadcast at 2:00 P.M. on a weekday may have a low rating. Many of the team's fans are likely to be at work. Since few of the market's homes are tuned in, the rating is low. However, if many of the homes viewing at 2:00 P.M. on the weekday are tuned to the game, the share will be high.

A broadcast's accumulative audience, known as the cume in media jargon, is also key to evaluating a broadcast. With a 2:00 P.M. weekday baseball broadcast, the audience for the beginning of the game may be low. As fans return from work

throughout the afternoon, they may tune in to the broadcast. The audience accumulates during the afternoon. This is especially important for sports events, since many broadcasts last several hours. A closely contested Super Bowl is likely to retain its audience. If one team pulls ahead early and continues to dominate, viewers might tune away from the game. Lost viewership is certainly detrimental to those brands advertising during the fourth quarter.

Sports broadcasts face one peculiar problem: compared to other program types, sports broadcasts are much more likely to be enjoyed communally. Several fans may gather at a friend's home to enjoy the game. On a larger scale, hundreds, thousands, or even millions of fans go to sports bars or other venues for sports broadcasts. Traditional measurement methods do not account for this activity. This could result in sports broadcasts actually being underrated.

Television Broadcast Audience

The primary supplier of U.S. television audience data is the A.C. Nielsen Company. Nielsen divides the United States into 210 individual markets, also known as spot markets, ranked by the number of television homes in each market. The country's largest market is New York City with an estimated 7,515,330 television homes. The country's smallest television market, Glendive, Montana, is estimated at 4,040 television homes. Nielsen's national estimate is 115,905,450 television homes. Nielsen's television ratings data is sold to any person or company interested in television ratings, including sports leagues, television and radio broadcasters, advertising agencies, and brand marketers.

Nielsen conducts periodic market ratings analysis in these spot markets. The largest spot markets are continuously monitored. Many markets are assessed four times per year for one week during periods known as "sweeps weeks." The results of these weeks are used to set future ad rates for the station. Nielsen uses its peoplemeter technology in 25 U.S. markets to project ratings and demographic profiles. Other markets are digitally monitored to provide ratings data. Subscribers to this service will have daily access to the previous day's ratings. Smaller markets may be audited annually or less often, since local demand for the data, and the likelihood of generating many subscribers to the report, is likely to be low.

Nielsen uses a variety of methods to collect viewership data, including digital monitoring of televisions and self-reports of media activity. Nielsen randomly selects its participants to be representative of the market's demographic profile. Despite the care used to sample and assess viewership, many stakeholders still note a number of flaws, including nonrepresentative samples, especially where young people and ethnic minorities are concerned, and inconsistent self-reporting from participants. Most notably, Nielsen has not monitored commercials to provide ratings for the commercials broadcast during the programs. In response to these criticisms, Nielsen is developing better sampling and monitoring systems, including commercial ratings.

Radio Broadcast Audience

Arbitron is the primary supplier of radio audience data and sells the data to subscribers. Arbitron divides the United States into 291 spot radio markets ranked by population size of persons 12 years and older. Not all of Arbitron's radio markets correlate to Nielsen's television markets. The country's largest radio market, New York, has a metro population of 15,669,500. The smallest market, Casper, Wyoming, has 62,500 people 12 years old or older. Radio markets are monitored constantly or sporadically, depending upon market size and information demand. Many of the criticisms noted for television sampling and reporting methodologies can be leveled against Arbitron.

Print Media Audience

Print media are assessed by the vehicle's circulation defined as the number of copies printed and distributed or sold. Newspaper and magazine circulation includes subscribers to the publication along with those who may purchase single issues. Large circulation figures generally mean expensive advertising rates. Unlike broadcast media, there is no central source conducting this research and providing it to the industry. Often, print publications self-report circulation figures and demographic profiles based on independent research. These reports may be verified by the independent Audit Bureau of Circulation

(ABC). However, a publication is not required to submit to an ABC audit. The most reputable newspapers and magazines in the United States do supply data for ABC review.

Digital Media

Measures for broadcast and print vehicles have decades of history, but the new frontier of audience measurement is digital media. All major U.S. research organizations, including Nielsen, are developing technology and methods to assess digital media use. As of this writing, there are no firmly established criteria or market leaders in this area. On its face, it would appear easy to measure audience size, since it is easy to measure the number of visitors who clicked on a Web ad. The number of visitors clicking on a digital ad divided by the number of unique visitors to the site provides a measure called the click-through rate (CTR). Higher CTR levels will result in higher advertising charges for the site. As with print media, no centralized, independent firm has emerged to dominate the digital market the way Nielsen and Arbitron dominate the television and radio markets.

Another problem associated with digital media is capturing all the activity of the sampled population, short of the subject's willingness to have all of his or her digital devices monitored, including desktop computers, laptop computers, and handheld devices. This problem is compounded by the number of media companies that are active across a broad array of media platforms. For example, ESPN programs several cable television channels, syndicates radio shows, operates a national radio network, publishes a magazine, produces a national Website, and is moving into the local Website market. Even a very motivated subject would have trouble reporting all exposures to these varied platforms.

Lance Kinney
University of Alabama

See Also: Advertising Cost, Determination of; Advertising Media; Broadcast Rights; Click-Through Rate; Contracts, TV/Radio Network; Cost per Click; Cost per Thousand; E-Commerce; Frequency; Gross Ratings Points; Media Audience; Nielsen Rating; Reach.

Further Readings

Bernstein, A. and N. Blain. *Sport, Media, Culture: Global and Local Dimensions*. New York: Routledge, 2002.

Crawford, G. *Consuming Sport: Fans, Sport and Culture*. New York: Routledge, 2004.

Laudon, Kenneth and Carol G. Traver. *E-Commerce: Business, Technology, Society*. Upper Saddle River, NJ: Pearson Prentice Hall, 2010.

Surmanek, Jim. *Media Planning: A Practical Guide*. Chicago: NTC Business Books, 1995.

Avidity

In 2008, it was estimated that the sports industry was worth $213 billion, making it seven times larger than the movie industry. A key determinant of this figure derives from the revenue that sports fans generate by consuming sport and sport-related products. In fact, the sport industry is heavily dependent on loyal and committed (avid) sports fans for economic success. Fan avidity is defined as "the level of interest, involvement, passion, and loyalty a fan exhibits to a particular sports entity (i.e., a sport, league, team, and/or athlete)." Avid fans are unique in that they possess a deep emotional connection with sport, unlike regular sports observers. This passion and zeal for sports products transcends normal fan behavior. Not surprisingly, this type of fan is a marketer's dream because of their desire to purchase and consume all things associated with sport. ESPN/TNS Sports polls consistently show that avid fans allocate substantially more money, time, and effort for sports-related activities and goods, when compared to nonavid fans. Further, avid fans stay strongly committed to their teams, regardless of win-loss records.

The Center for Sports Business and Research at Penn State University has recently examined the issue of fan avidity. Specifically, the researchers explored behaviors associated with fan avidity, such as attending games, purchasing merchandise, watching games on television, reading about the team in newspapers, and playing fantasy sports. From their studies, the following four major dimensions of fan avidity were identified:

- Dimension I of fan avidity pertains to on-field participation. The activities can include trying out for the football team, dance team, cheerleading squad, marching band, or working at the stadium during the game.
- Dimension II includes all forms of passive engagement. This can be exhibited when a fan listens to the game on local radio, watches the game on television, reads about the game in the local newspaper, or follows the game on the Internet.
- Dimension III activities occur when a fan purchases a team's merchandise, such as clothing and memorabilia, and/or pays for a fan booster club membership.
- Dimension IV is the social dimension of fan avidity. This type of behavior can be seen when avid fans purchase season tickets, attend home and away games, tailgate, attend bowl games, and attend post-game parties.

Fans were surveyed to assess what types of fan avidity they participated in, based on the four dimensions, and were then classified into three market segments. The first is termed the *social butterflies* segment, who perform the social activities included in dimensions III and IV. A second market segment is termed *passive followers*, who share a similar interest level with social butterflies, but prefer to watch games on TV, follow the team in the newspapers, and other dimension II activities. The final market segment describes fans who do not regularly purchase tickets or merchandise, and thus do not generate revenue for the team.

Based on these findings, marketers should focus more attention on avid fans who are social butterflies and passive followers to ensure maximum revenue generation is achieved. By understanding the complexity associated with fan avidity, marketers will be better able to reap the economic benefits avid fans can bring a sports team.

E. Nicole Melton
Texas A&M University

See Also: Affiliation Activities; Fan Avidity; Fan Loyalty Continuum.

Further Readings

DeSarbo, W. S. "Examining the Heterogeneous Expressions of Sports Fan Avidity." *Journal of Quantitative Analysis in Sport*, v.6/2 (2010).

DeSarbo, W. S. "Measuring Fan Avidity Can Help Marketers Narrow Their Focus." http://www.sportsbusinessjournal.com/article/64438 (Accessed December 2009).

Wann, Daniel and Nyla Branscombe. "Die-Hard Fans and Fair-Weather Fans: Effects of Identification on BIRGing and CORFing Tendencies." *Journal of Sport and Social Issues*, v.14 (1990).

Award Ceremonies

Whether to recognize individual and team achievements at the end of the year, to celebrate lifetime accomplishments at annual events, or simply to "tip a cap" for a job well done, award ceremonies are a chance for organizations to gain some publicity while honoring employees and supporters. Awards ceremonies may be small, discrete affairs such as presenting a conference championship trophy to the women's soccer team at halftime of a men's basketball game or they can be full-blown extravaganzas, such as the Heisman Trophy presentation. They can recur repeatedly within one large event, as is the case with the Olympic medal ceremonies, or they can happen once a year (such as the ESPYs).

Big or small, one-time or annual, award ceremonies are an opportunity to honor coaches, athletes, staff members, supporters, volunteers, and teams who have performed exceptionally. Because they are meant to be a celebration, they are also a great way to gain interest from fans and the media. However, because they are so high profile, and because an award ceremony is generally expected to be special for the honorees, timing, planning, and producing are critical.

Ranking high among the reasons to hold award ceremonies is that they make people feel valued and appreciated. It is a gesture of goodwill between the organization and those being honored. It also demonstrates to fans and supporters that the organization is eager to share in the celebration the accomplishments of its personnel.

In addition, recognition motivates people. Highlighting the accomplishments of individuals encourages others to elevate their efforts. Student athletes in high schools and colleges who are named Athlete of the Year at their respective schools set a standard for others to follow. Countless young men and boys have watched the World Series and dreamt of one day hoisting the championship trophy.

An awards ceremony is also a chance for celebration and reflection. By their very nature, sports provide inspiring stories of individuals overcoming long odds and teams gelling to accomplish a goal. Providing fans and supporters an opportunity to share in these stories and to celebrate accomplishment is an excellent gesture of goodwill and an opportunity for sports organizations to show their appreciation.

Finally, because of the often-stressful nature of sports, awards ceremonies also afford individuals a chance to take a break and enjoy a social gathering. At the same time, they will have the opportunity to reflect upon the importance of their work and the achievements of those being awarded.

It is up to the organization how often and under which circumstances awards ceremonies should be sponsored. Of course, the easy answer is whenever a team or individual wins a championship. It is a given that a ceremony will be conducted on these occasions, though the organization may decide to offer a special celebration—a parade followed by a rally, for example—that is held in addition to the actual presentation of awards. Still, some organizations hold awards banquets annually to recognize the outstanding work of all teams and individuals at one time. Others present awards only occasionally, and only in response to truly outstanding achievements.

Award selections may be by committee or organizational leaders and ceremonies may be held for achievements ranging from team awards to national honors. In either case, it is important to note what kinds of awards will be presented—certificates, plaques, trophies, or the like.

U.S. Army Chief of Staff George W. Casey, Jr., presented silver medals to a wheelchair basketball team at the Warrior Games for wounded veterans in 2010.

It is also important to note that in athletics awards ceremonies need not be only for teams, athletes, and coaches. Professional sports teams are businesses with many entities not directly related to performance on the field. Marketing, accounting, human resources, community relations, and facilities management are only a few of the departments an organization may house. Recognizing employees of the month, years of service, exemplary innovation, or interdepartmental competition winners is a great way to maintain morale and to honor those who work behind the scenes.

The organizing process begins before the actual awards ceremony. Once the honorees have been selected, a budget should be developed for printing of tickets, sending mailings, and making lodging and travel reservations, though it should be determined if the host organization will actually make travel and lodging arrangements for award recipients and honored guests, or if individuals will be responsible for their own accommodations. Next it is time to select a date, time, and location for the event. Events may take place at the same location and time every year, which makes this step easier, but no less important. Tickets may then be produced and distributed and mailings may be sent to honorees and VIPs.

After all the preliminary arrangements have been made publicity efforts should begin. Biographical sketches of the award recipients should be written, photographs collected or taken, and a publicity plan developed. This begins with the development of a media list to whom materials may be sent. The plan may include production of news releases and videotaped highlights, scheduling of interviews, and promotional pieces such as posters, print, and broadcast ads, and registration brochures for guests.

Because the event will include introductions and the presentation of credentials, a well-spoken emcee is also important. This individual should be upbeat, entertaining, and able to pronounce names with little effort. He or she also is responsible for pacing the event well. The next phase is to determine the award format. Will the emcee introduce the award recipients or will a special guest provide background? Will a highlight film of the recipient's accomplishments be aired? Who will present the awards? Will the recipients speak, or simply receive their awards and pose for a photograph before being seated? Questions such as these must be considered if the event is to flow according to plan.

Joe Moore
University of Central Missouri

See Also: Employee Relations; Event Hospitality; Event Management; Event or Venue Location.

Further Readings

Helitzer, M. *The Dream Job: $port$ Publicity, Promotion and Public Relations.* Athens, OH: University Sports Press, 1992.
McGillivray, D. "Awards Ceremonies: The Last Impression." *Road Race Management*, v.318 (2010).

B2B, B2C

Marketing has been defined as "the management process responsible for identifying, anticipating, and satisfying customer requirements profitably." At the crux of this definition is the term *customer*, but to truly understand marketing, what a customer actually is needs to be defined, and it is this process that splits marketing into two segments:

1. Marketing by a business aimed at the general public or "consumers"
2. Marketing by a business aimed at other organizations or "businesses"

As a result, these areas are called business-to-consumer (B2C) and business-to-business (B2B) marketing. B2B may also be called industrial or business marketing. In many cases products destined for B2C sale have to be sold first to a retailer by the producer—a B2B sale. As such, B2C and B2B markets are often linked within an industry by concepts such as Porter's value chain. In other words, if there are no consumers to purchase a product, there is no reason for a business to exist in order to make it. If that business does not exist, it will obviously not need the products and ser-

vices offered by another business. This is termed the *chain of derived demand*.

B2B

Put very simply, B2B marketing is the marketing of goods and services by businesses to other businesses (they are still customers) in order to keep the customer companies operating. B2B marketing often involves heavy use of sports-related promotional strategies. Marketers use sport to advertise, and B2B companies become sport sponsors in order to communicate to their target audiences. B2B marketing also uses sport as a means to influence the decision making units (DMU) of its target audience. Corporate boxes at major sports stadiums and other hospitality events, such as golf days, are now a cornerstone of the profitability of many sports ventures and a key factor in their continued success and planning.

B2C

B2C marketing is the promotion of products and services to members of the public. B2C is aimed at individuals and promotes products directly to the end user rather than to intermediaries. B2C marketing often uses sports as a promotional vehicle for consumer products, via advertising at sports venues and sponsorship of sports teams, players, or events. For example, ING Group has sponsored a Formula 1 racing team.

Differences

A B2C sale is to an individual, and while a consumer may be influenced by other factors, such as family or friends, he or she ultimately makes the decision independently. As such, decision making about the sale is relatively uncomplicated and informal. A B2B sale is to an organization, and as such several complications overlay the purchase decision because of the organizational structure, procedures, and rules that govern most business purchasing decisions and the makeup of a DMU.

While B2C is aimed at large demographic groups through mass media and retailers, the negotiation process between the buyer and seller is more personal in B2B. B2B typically commits only a small part of its promotional budgets to advertising, and that is usually through direct mail efforts and trade journals. This is also aimed at supporting the personal sales team, which plays a much more prominent role in B2B compared to B2C.

B2B marketing is significantly more targeted than B2C. Even when marketing very specific products for a fairly small subset of individuals, the latter type of marketer has a far larger audience than the former.

The application of the marketing mix is affected by the contextual uniqueness of the product and market in relation to both B2C and B2B marketing. Factors to be considered by marketers in both cases are the complexity of products and services, diversity of demand and the differing nature of the sale itself (including fewer customers buying larger volumes). As a result, while B2B marketers do use advertising, it is predominantly print media, although the Internet has seen an increasing use of digital advertising.

For most B2B sales there is also a level of risk to the purchaser involved depending on the importance of the item being purchased to the continued operation of the business. Risk often increases the more expensive an item is, which results in a risk-value judgment in B2B sales that is much more significant than in B2C.

Andrew J. Whalley
Royal Holloway University of London

See Also: Advertising; Branding; Marketing Research Process; Marketing Through Sports; Relationship Marketing; Segmentation; Sponsorship.

Further Readings

Anderson, James C. and James A. Narus. *Business Market Management: Understanding, Creating, and Delivering Value*, 2nd Ed. Upper Saddle River, NJ: Pearson Education, 2004.

Brown, Duncan and Nick Hayes. *Influencer Marketing: Who Really Influences Your Customers?* Oxford, UK: Butterworth-Heinemann, 2008.

Dwyer, F. Robert and John F. Tanner. *Business Marketing: Connecting Strategy, Relationships, and Learning*, 3rd Ed. New York: McGraw-Hill/Irwin, 2006.

Greco, John A. Jr. "Past Indicates Promising Future for B-to-B Direct." *BtoB Magazine* (June 13, 2005).

Hutt, Michael D. and Thomas W. Speh. *Business Marketing Management: A Strategic View of Industrial and Organizational Markets*, 8th Ed. Mason, OH: Thomson/South-Western, 2004.

Morris, Michael H., Leyland F. Pitt, and Earl Dwight Honeycutt. *Business-to-Business Marketing: A Strategic Approach*. Thousand Oaks, CA: Sage, 2001.

Balance Sheet

A balance sheet may be defined as a statement prepared with a view to measure the exact financial position of a business on a certain date. The accounting balance sheet is one of the major financial statements used by accountants and business owners, the others being the income statement, statement of cash flows, and statement of stockholder equity. The balance sheet is also referred to as the statement of financial position. The balance sheet presents a company's financial position at the end of a specified date. Some describe the balance sheet as a "snapshot" of the company's financial position at a point (a moment or an instant) in time. For example, the amounts reported on a balance sheet dated December 31, 2008, reflect that instant when all transactions through December 31 have been recorded. While balance sheets usually represent all transactions in a 12-month period, some companies report half-yearly balance sheets, and a company undergoing a merger or acquisition may prepare a balance sheet at the time of the change in ownership.

A balance sheet has three parts: assets, liabilities, and ownership equity. The main categories of assets are usually listed first, then followed by the liabilities. The difference between the assets and the liabilities is known as equity, or the net assets, net worth, or capital of the company. According to the accounting equation, net worth must equal assets minus liabilities.

Another way to look at the same equation is that assets equal liabilities plus owner's equity. Looking at the equation in this way shows how assets were financed: either by borrowing money (liability) or by using the owner's money (owner's equity). Balance sheets are usually presented with assets in one section and liabilities and net worth in the other section, with the two sections "balancing"—hence the name.

Because the balance sheet informs the reader of a company's financial position at a moment in time, it allows other parties, such as creditors, to see what a company owns as well as what it owes to others as of the date indicated in the heading. This is valuable information to a banker who wants to determine whether or not a company qualifies for additional credit or loans. Others who would be interested in the balance sheet include current investors, potential investors, company management, suppliers, some customers, competitors, government agencies, and labor unions.

Assets are classified as follows:

- *Fixed assets*: the assets of a durable nature that are used in business and are acquired and intended to be retained permanently for the purpose of carrying on the business, such as land, building, machinery, and furniture. They are also sometimes called as capital assets, fixed capital expenditures, or long-lived assets. Fixed assets are collectively known as *block*.

- *Floating or circulation asset*: those temporarily held assets that are meant for resale or that frequently undergo change, such as cash, stock, stores, debtors, and bills receivable. Floating assets are again subdivided into two parts, liquid assets and nonliquid assets. Liquid assets are those that can be readily converted into cash without appreciable loss. Cash in hand and cash at bank are the examples of such assets. Other assets that cannot be readily converted into cash, or not without appreciable loss, are called nonliquid assets, such as, stock, or stores.

- *Intangible assets*: with the increasing attention paid to branding and its importance, many companies now include a valuation of their brand on a balance sheet, usually labeled as *intangible* or *goodwill*.

- *Fictitious assets*: those assets that are not represented by anything concrete or tangible. Preliminary expenses, debit balance of profit and loss account are the examples of such assets. These are also called *nominal* or *imaginary* assets. Note that these are usually distinguished from intangible assets despite their similarity.

Liabilities are classified as follows:

- *Fixed liabilities*: those liabilities that are to be redeemed after a long period of time. This includes long-term loans.

- *Current liabilities*: those liabilities that are to be redeemed in near future, usually within a year. Trade creditors, bank loans, bills payable, and so on, are examples of current liabilities.

- *Contingent liabilities*: not actual liabilities but their becoming actual liability is contingent on the happening of a certain event. In other words, they would become liabilities in the future provided the contemplated event occurs. If it does not occur, no liability is incurred. Since such a liability is not an actual liability, it is not shown in the balance sheet. Usually, it is mentioned in the form of a footnote.

Cost Conventions and Balance Sheets

In order to construct a balance sheet a convention for the recording of the value of assets and liabilities needs to be established. The historical cost accounting convention is an accounting technique that values an asset for balance sheet purposes at the price paid for the asset at the time of its acquisition; this is based on the stable measuring unit assumption. Historical cost is a generally accepted accounting principle requiring all financial statement items be based upon original cost. Historical cost means what it cost the company for the item; it is not fair market value. This means that if a company purchased a building, it is recorded on the balance sheet at its historical cost. It is not recorded at fair market value, which would be what the company could sell the building for in the open market.

The historical cost method has been subject to criticism, especially as it only considers the acquisition cost of an asset and does not recognize the current market value, a particular flaw in times of inflation or where an asset's value has appreciated significantly from its acquisition cost. Alternative measurement bases to the historical cost measurement system, which may be applied for some types of assets for which market values are readily available, require that the carrying value of an asset (or liability) be updated to the market price; mark-to-market valuation or some other estimate of value that better approximates the real value, that is, what it would cost to be replaced. The advantages of the historical cost method include the following:

- Historical cost accounts are straightforward to produce and do not require reference to market values.
- Historical cost accounts do not record revaluation gains until they are realized.
- Historical cost accounts are widely used and understood.

The disadvantages of the historical cost method include the following:

- Historical cost accounts give no indication of current values of the assets of a business.
- Historical cost accounts do not record the opportunity costs of the use of older assets, particularly property that may be recorded at a value based on costs incurred many years ago.
- Historical cost accounts do not measure the loss of value of monetary assets as a result of inflation.

Accounting standards in different countries vary in the different methods required or allowed considerably. Under the IFRS (International Financial Reporting Standards) rules, the revaluation of property, plant, and equipment is acceptable, but not required, to restate the values of property, plant, and equipment to fair value, but such a policy must be applied to all assets of a particular class. This principle of all or none applies in most international standards. The IFRS also specifically requires a separate method of accounting in currencies deemed to be hyperinflationary.

The Constant Item Purchasing Power Accounting model is an International Accounting Standards Board (IASB) approved alternative accounting model to the traditional Historical Cost Accounting model, so that values are recorded in units of constant purchasing power. However, the model is hardly ever chosen by those outside of hyperinflationary economies.

Form of a Balance Sheet

A balance sheet has two sides—the left-hand side and the right-hand side. These two sides, however, are not comparable with the debit side and credit side of a ledger account because the balance sheet is not an account. The words *to* or *by* are not used in the balance sheet. The left-hand side is the liabilities side and contains credit balances of all real and personal accounts. The right-hand side, which is the "assets" side, lists the debit balances of real and personal accounts.

All these assets and liabilities are displayed in the balance sheet according to the following principles:

- All real and personal accounts having debit balances should be shown on the assets side of the balance sheet, which is the right-hand side.
- All the real and personal accounts having credit balances should be shown on the liabilities side of the balance sheet, which is

the left-hand side. The excess of assets over liabilities represents the capital of the owner. This figure of capital must tally with the closing balance of the capital account in the ledger after the net profit or loss has been transferred therein.

Arrangement of Assets and Liabilities

The assets and liabilities are arranged according to rules called the "marshalling of assets and liabilities," of which two systems exist: (1) order of liquidity, and (2) order of permanence. In liquidity order, the most easily realizable assets are shown first and are followed by assets that are less easily resalable. So, the assets most difficult to realize will be shown last. In the case of liabilities, these will be shown in the order in which they are payable, with the most pressing liability being placed first.

Permanence order is where the assets are entered in the balance sheet in descending order of permanence, that is, land first, then buildings, then equipment. Liabilities would be entered in the order of their date of maturity, that is, those with the longest time to be paid back first, for example, long–term loans first, followed by debentures, then overdraft.

Common-Size Balance Sheet

One technique in financial statement analysis is known as vertical analysis. Vertical analysis results in common-size financial statements. A common-size balance sheet is a balance sheet where every monetary amount has been restated to be a percentage of total assets. The benefit of a common-size balance sheet is that an item can be compared to a similar item of another company regardless of the size of the companies.

A company can also compare its percentages to the industry's average percentages. For example, a company with inventory at 4 percent of total assets can look to industry statistics to see if its percentage is reasonable. A common-size balance sheet also allows two businesspeople to compare the magnitude of a balance sheet item without either one revealing the actual monetary amounts.

Andrew J. Whalley
Royal Holloway University of London

See Also: Break-Even Analysis; Information Systems, Kinds of; Management Decision-Making Process.

Further Readings

Horngren, C., G. Sundem, and W. Stratton. *Introduction to Management Accounting.* Upper Saddle River, NJ: Prentice Hall, 2002.

Robbins, Stephen P. and David A. DeCenzo. *Fundamentals of Management*, 5th Ed. Upper Saddle River, NJ: Prentice Hall, 2005.

Williams, Jan R., Susan F. Haka, Mark S. Bettner, and Joseph V. Carcello. *Financial & Managerial Accounting.* New York: McGraw-Hill, 2008.

Balanced Scorecard

The balanced scorecard (BSC) is a strategic planning and management system promoted by Robert Kaplan of Harvard Business School and David Norton as a performance measurement framework that adds strategic nonfinancial performance measures to traditional financial metrics. They recognized that previous approaches had inherent weaknesses, with a general lack of being able to translate strategy and planning into action and tangible results. With the BSC, they provided a clear prescription as to what companies should measure in order to "balance" the financial perspective.

The inclusion of customer and business processes perspectives make the BSC highly relevant to sports management, in that "fans" are much more connected to sports and teams. This requires a broader perspective to be taken in the management of sporting ventures. Otherwise, a disconnect between venture and fans may arise, such as with the Glazers and Manchester United fans. The approach gives a clear and detailed road map that helps an organization measure performance and is typically used to assist with short- and mid-term planning: one to five years to meet both near- and long-term objectives.

Art Schneiderman, an independent consultant, created the first BSC in 1987 while working at Analog Devices. The contemporary version now in use originated from Kaplan and Norton's 1992–96 *Harvard Business Review* articles. The BSC grew in popularity within commercial circles and among academics with a practical business focus. Graduates of MBA and accounting courses adopted the BSC within their commercial roles, with those in major U.S. sporting ventures being leading early proponents. As the approach gained momentum Kaplan and Norton authored two books: *The Balanced Scorecard: Translating Strategy Into Action* (1996) and *The Strategy-Focused Organization: How Balanced Scorecard Companies Thrive in the New Business Environment* (2001).

The BSC provides feedback on both internal business processes and external outcomes in order to improve strategic performance. It can give those responsible for managing business performance a more "balanced" view of organizational performance. This enables an organization's management to clarify their vision and strategy and translate them into action. Since its launch it has been widely adopted in both commercial and noncommercial businesses across the globe, especially where there is a need to align business activities to the vision and strategy of the organization, improve communications to stakeholders (a key issue in sports management), and monitor organizational performance against strategic goals. When fully deployed, the BSC transforms strategic planning from an academic exercise into the brain and nerves of an organization.

The BSC System

Under the BSC system, metrics are developed based on the priorities of the strategic plan. Processes to collect information relevant to these metrics are then designed so that the metrics are tracked continuously and can be assessed by both trend and variance analysis. The metrics chosen will either be lead or lag indicators of performance. A lead indicator is an in-process measure—it is predictive. A lag indicator is a measure of results, outputs, and outcomes—it provides an accurate snapshot in time.

The BSC suggests that an organization be viewed from four perspectives:

- *The learning and growth perspective.* This perspective includes employee training and corporate cultural attitudes related to both individual and corporate self-improvement. Metrics can be put into place to guide managers in focusing training funds where they can help the most. Kaplan and Norton emphasize that "learning" is more than "training"; it also includes things like mentors and tutors within the organization, as well as that ease of communication among workers that allows them to readily get help on a problem when it is needed. It also includes technological tools, what the Baldrige criteria call "high performance work systems." Given the rise and relative importance of "knowledge workers," and the management of knowledge within sporting organizations, for example, coaches and trainers, this has become a key facet of the BSC in sports management.

- *The business process perspective.* This perspective refers to internal business processes. Metrics based on this perspective allow the managers to know how well their business is running, and whether its products and services conform to customer requirements. These metrics have to be carefully designed by those who know these processes most intimately; the less familiarity someone has with the specific market segment being modeled via the BSC, the more likely inaccurate metrics will be developed. One can only manage what one measures, and if one measures inaccurately or wrongly, one will manage inaccurately or wrongly.

- *The customer perspective.* Recent management philosophy has shown an increasing realization of the importance of customer focus and customer satisfaction in any business. The sports environment makes this area a key consideration within a BSC. In developing metrics for satisfaction, customers should be analyzed in terms of kinds of customers and the kinds of processes for which a business is providing a product or service to those customer groups. In this regard, the BSC approach mirrors the marketing strategy process of segmentation, targeting, and positioning (STP), with its associated connections to branding and integrated marketing communications (IMC). These are leading indicators: if customers are not satisfied, they will eventually find other suppliers to meet their needs. It is vital that their feedback is gathered and used proactively, particularly when evidence shows that up to 90 percent of dissatisfied customers find another competitor to satisfy their needs, rather than complain. Poor performance from this perspective is thus a leading indicator of future decline, even though the current financial picture may look good. Considering this within sports, where the social identity of fans and supporters is likely to provide an extremely high contextual element, being able to measure, manage, and proactively engage them through the use of the BSC would seem to be necessary.

• *The financial perspective.* This includes traditional financial-related data, such as risk assessment and cost-benefit data. Timely and accurate financial data has always been a priority for those running an organization. As such, the majority of organizations have adequate systems to collect, analyze, and distribute such information.

These four perspectives are then combined to drive the strategic output of the BSC model.

Andrew J. Whalley
Royal Holloway University of London

See Also: Customer Satisfaction; Management by Objectives; Management Decision-Making Process; Strategic Management.

Further Readings

Baldrige Criteria. http://www.nist.gov/baldrige (Accessed January 2011).
Hubbard, Douglas W. *How to Measure Anything: Finding the Value of Intangibles in Business.* Hoboken, NJ: John Wiley & Sons, 2007.
Kaplan, Robert S. and David P. Norton. "The Balanced Scorecard: Measures That Drive Performance." *Harvard Business Review* (January–February 1992).
Kaplan, Robert S. and David P. Norton. *Balanced Scorecard: Translating Strategy Into Action.*

Cambridge, MA: Harvard Business School Press, 1996.
Kurtzman, J. "Is Your Company Off Course? Now You Can Find Out Why." *Fortune* (February 17, 1997).
Norreklit, H. "The Balance on the Balanced Scorecard—A Critical Analysis of Some of its Assumptions." *Management Accounting Research*, v.11 (2000).
Rohm, Howard. "A Balancing Act." *Perform Magazine*, v.2/2 (2004).
Voelper, S., M. Leibold, R. Eckhoff, and T. Davenport. "The Tyranny of the Balanced Scorecard in the Innovation Economy." *Journal of Intellectual Capital*, v.7/1 (2006).

Baltimore Orioles

Despite their successful history, the Baltimore Orioles have been a tough sell in recent years because of their on-field woes and frequent turnover in personnel. The Orioles began as the Milwaukee Brewers in 1894, eventually moving and becoming the St. Louis Browns in 1902. In 1951, legendary baseball promoter Bill Veeck bought the team. Perhaps his most notorious promotion was sending a pinch hitter to bat by the name of Eddie Gaedel, who was a three-foot, seven-inch midget who weighed only 65 pounds. Veeck sold the team in 1954 to Clarence Miles, and the club moved to Baltimore and was renamed the Orioles.

In 1979, Edward Bennett Williams became the majority owner of the team. The Orioles played their games at Memorial Stadium, which was home to both the Orioles of Major League Baseball (MLB) and the National Football League's Baltimore Colts. Baltimore residents have fond memories of watching Oriole greats such as manager Earl Weaver and players like Brooks Robinson, Jim Palmer, Boog Powell, Frank Robinson, Cal Ripken, and Eddie Murray in Memorial Stadium.

Baltimore was a mid-sized marke, and the team resembled the hardworking and blue-collar nature of its residents. Between 1966 and 1983, the Orioles went to six World Series, winning three times. During this time, average attendance at games ranged between 11,654 and 22,191. The Orioles became known for their great pitching, hard work, gracious play, impressive minor league system, and a focus on the fundamentals of baseball, which team officials referred to as the Oriole Way. Many fans were drawn to the ballpark to experience a game-winning walk-off home run or Earl Weaver's favorite, a three-run homer.

Tickets were relatively inexpensive, and the ballpark was known for great crab cakes, John Denver's version of *Thank God I'm a Country Boy* played during the 7th inning stretch, and their most famous fan, Wild Bill Hagy. The marketing slogan was "Orioles Magic." The accompanying song *Orioles Magic* was blasted over the PA system, and fans were able to buy recordings of it.

In 1993, Baltimore-based attorney Peter Angelos bought the team from Eli Jacobs for $173 million. Memorial Stadium gave way to Oriole Park at Camden Yards in 1992 and significant ticket increases in 1994. Although the site on which Camden Yards was built formerly served as a dilapidated railyard and warehouse district, the new stadium with its retro-style red brick exterior, green seats, and natural grass soon became a model for new stadium design. The new ballpark was easily accessible to downtown attractions, had a great view of the city skyline, excellent concessions, and easy access for motorists traveling on major interstate highways.

During the early years of Camden Yards, the Orioles' marketing efforts benefited from the popularity of the new stadium, Cal Ripken's record-breaking streak of playing in 2,632 straight games, and winning teams. The Orioles fan base drew not only from Maryland and the Baltimore area, but also from the Washington, D.C., market. Attendance at Camden Yards between 1992 and 2000 was consistently above 40,000 fans per game, and the Orioles went to the American League Championship Series twice during this time, only to lose to the New York Yankees in 1996 and the Cleveland Indians in 1997.

Recent Developments

More recently, the days of marketing "Orioles Magic" seem far removed. The Orioles have expe-

Despite difficulties with on-field performance and personnel, the Orioles have recently been valued at nearly $400 million.

rienced 12 years of losing seasons. Attendance has consistently declined since 2001, and in September 2006, almost 1,000 fans walked out of Camden Yards. Many have criticized Angelos for the team's poor performance over the past decade. Poor on-field performance has also had an effect on viewership of the Orioles Mid-Atlantic Sports Network.

Despite their problems, the Orioles are valued at almost $400 million. In addition, Angelos was able to strike a deal with MLB when the Expos moved from Montreal, Canada, to Washington, D.C., which guarantees him a minimum yearly gross of $130 million along with $360 million should he decide to sell the team. The Orioles have once again sought to restore the "Oriole Way" by building from the bottom up and trading their biggest stars for prospects. But until the winning seasons come back, team executives plan to market the enjoyment of baseball, the thrill of being at a major league game, the positive impact of Camden Yards on revitalization efforts, and community relations initiatives such as Orioles Reach, which provides children with a free afternoon at the ballpark.

David J. Shonk
James Madison University

See Also: Baltimore Ravens; Brand Image; Franchise; Major League Baseball.

Further Readings

Baltimore Orioles Website. http://baltimore.orioles .mlb.com (Accessed November 2009).

Baseball Almanac. "Baltimore Orioles Attendance Data." http://www.baseball-almanac.com/teams/ baltatte.shtml (Accessed November 2009).

Boswell, T. "Truth, Justice and the Oriole Way." *The Washington Post* (March 2, 2008).

"The Business of Baseball." *Forbes.* http://www .forbes.com/lists/2008/33/biz_baseball08 _Baltimore -Orioles_336064_print.html (Accessed November 2009).

Chapin, T. S. "Sports Facilities as Urban Redevelopment Catalysts: Baltimore's Camden Yards and Cleveland's Gateway." *Journal of the American Planning Association*, v.70/2 (2004).

Eisenberg, J. *From 33rd Street to Camden Yards.* New York: Contemporary Books, 2001.

Farmer, L. "Baltimore Orioles Marketing Department Has a Tough Job This Year." *The Baltimore Daily Record* (March 31, 2008).

Hawkins, J. C. *This Date in Baltimore Orioles & St. Louis Browns History.* Briarcliff Manor, NY: Stein & Day, 1983.

Baltimore Ravens

The Baltimore Ravens, one of the younger franchises in the National Football League (NFL), joined the league in 1996 when owner Art Modell (now a minority owner) moved the team from Cleveland to Baltimore. Baltimore is a city steeped in football history, with franchises dating back to the late 1940s. Baltimore's first team, the Colts, joined the NFL in 1950 after the All-American Football Conference merger, but are now in Indianapolis. Baltimore has a long history of strong franchise management that ultimately led to several championships. The city experienced four championships—with the Colts in 1958 (often referred to as "the greatest game ever played" featuring the Colts' Johnny Unitas and New York's Frank Gifford and Pat Summerall), 1959, and 1968—and again with the Ravens in Super Bowl XXXV.

Trade management and competent draft selections serve as evidence of the Ravens' recent managerial success. For example, the Super Bowl XXXV championship was due in large part to the acquisitions of veteran players like long-time Pittsburgh Steeler Rod Woodson and tight end Shannon Sharpe. The Ravens management and coaching staff were also adept at drafting and developing gifted young players like Chris McAlister, Duane Starks, Super Bowl MVP Ray Lewis, and running back Jamal Lewis, who set the single-season team rushing record in his first year in the league.

In its short history, the Ravens franchise has experienced several notable managerial and administrative changes. Like many other NFL franchises, the team appears committed to the model of bringing former players into prominent front office positions. For example, Hall of Famer Ozzie Newsome serves as the Ravens general manager and executive vice president. Newsome is often credited with building the team that won Super Bowl XXXV.

More recently, the Ravens hired former Cleveland Browns general manager George Kokinis. With the Ravens from 1996 to 2008, Kokinis held the post of director of pro personnel from 2003 to 2008 before departing for his short stint with the Browns. Kokinis said the Browns led him to believe he would have direct access to owner Randy Lerner and control over all player personnel matters. Access to Lerner and control over player personnel matters were inherent to Kokinis's managerial philosophy. When the Browns and Kokinis parted ways, he was hired by the Ravens in 2010 to serve as senior personnel assistant.

Marketing

The Ravens rely heavily on marketing efforts aimed at several groups cultivated by the franchise including the historic Marching Ravens, the kids club Ravens Rookies, the Ravens Tailgaters, and Purple, a group devoted to female fans.

The Marching Ravens is a unique marketing effort cultivated by the franchise. With a strong connection to the city, the all-volunteer marching band has more than 300 members and claims to be the largest musical group connected with an NFL team. With assistance from Ravens management, the band actively promotes the Ravens and Baltimore through various events and often performs during events in other cities.

Like many other professional sports franchises, the Ravens see value in the cultivation of young fans. With Ravens Rookies, members can attend special events such as autograph sessions with favorite players and training camp activities. Designed to welcome young fans up to age 14, the Ravens promote the Youth Football Challenge (i.e., skills games for various age groups), movie nights at the stadium, and several online games and activities.

Purple is an official Ravens club for female fans. Purple group members join a fan network that provides updates about the team, access to special events, and more. For example, female fans are treated to "Ladies Nights" at M&T Bank Stadium (The Ravens' home field), special access to training camp events, and a "Purple Evening" that provides group members access to coaches and players, an opportunity to meet other female fans, and a chance to get on the field to participate in drills. One offshoot of Purple is the Lavender Ladies, an elite group of female fans who receive exclusive invitations to events.

The franchise also devotes several marketing efforts aimed at tailgaters. On the Ravens Website, several pages are devoted to tailgating contests, tips for tailgating near M&T Bank stadium, game day weather reports, parking, directions, and special recipes for Ravens fans (cross-promoted with corporate sponsors such as the H.J. Heinz Company and Premio Foods).

Adam C. Earnheardt
Youngstown State University

See Also: Cleveland Browns; Moving a Franchise; National Football League; Pittsburgh Steelers; Super Bowl.

Further Readings

Baltimore Ravens Website. http://www.baltimore ravens.com (Accessed July 2010).

Matte, T. and J. Seidel. *Tom Matte's Tales From the Baltimore Ravens Sideline*. Champaign, IL: Sports Publishing, 2004.

Morgan, J. *Glory for Sale: Inside the Browns' Move to Baltimore and The New NFL*. Baltimore, MD: Bancroft Press, 1997.

Despite being one of the NFL's newer franchises, the Ravens won the Super Bowl 34–7 over the New York Giants in 2001.

Banner Ads

Banner ads, which are online graphic ads linked to the Website of an advertiser, are one of the oldest forms of displayed advertisement on the Internet. Total online advertising spending in 2009 was estimated at about $24.5 billion, of which display ads were $4.65 billion, or 19 percent. While this is a significant portion of ad spending, online display ads are estimated to be only 14.9 percent, or just $5.54 billion by 2013. According to the author Sam Fullerton, much of the anticipated growth in online ad spending is expected to be in search advertising and video ads.

Some estimates suggest that total advertising on sports-oriented sites is around $7 billion. Sports sites tend to be very content-driven, which often means advertising, and displays in particular, makes up a significant component of the site's revenue model. Content in sports typically incorporates a large base of information that users consult to find sports news, scores, and analysis. Many of these sites are associated with major television organizations, which may be local, national, or international in reach and scope (e.g., CNN, ESPN, or BBC). The largest of these sites tend to be broad in their coverage of sport.

However, organizations such as ESPN have recently attempted to localize content to cover specific geographic regions (e.g., ESPNChicago .com, ESPNLosAngeles.com). Localized sites attempt to customize the user experience to what is locally relevant, thus attracting more frequent users, while keeping them there for longer periods of time. This quality, known as the "stickiness" of a site, enhances the value of banner ad rates.

Banner ads are typically static in nature, and usually the graphics and copy remain the same across visitors. These ads may also feature Flash video and animation, thereby enabling a more engaging experience for users compared to still images. The Interactive Advertising Bureau (IAB) has established guidelines for banner ads in terms of required dimensions and image resolutions, thus ensuring consistency across sites.

Many sites such as ESPN.com and CBSSports. com provide much of their content for free; the main objective of their business model is to generate traffic and provide incentive for users to stay as long as possible. With this business model, the most common revenue source is advertising and sponsorship.

The amount charged by content providers (often referred to as "publishers" in the online advertising world) depends on the amount of traffic generated by each site. Banner ads usually command ad revenue based on a cost-per-thousand (CPM) approach. In some cases publishers may charge on a click-through rate (CTR). While this is a popular approach, the CPM approach is still more common.

Factors such as size, type, and location of the ad, and demographic audience reach, are all used to determine the amount to be paid for a display ad. Additionally, the general demand for the ad inventory relative to the supply also figures into ad pricing. During times of traffic spikes because of major sporting events (e.g., the Olympics or the Super Bowl) or popular sports news stories (e.g., player or team scandals) demand for advertising inventory on content sites may drive up the price paid for banner ads.

Banner ads continue to be a staple advertising form online. They are especially important and lucrative for content-heavy sites, which have compelling information that is updated very frequently.

Robert I. Roundtree
University of North Carolina, Charlotte

See Also: Advertising Media; Click-Through Rate; Cost per Click; Cost per Thousand; e-Commerce; Keyword Buys; Online Advertising; Pop-Up Ads.

Further Readings

Fullerton, Sam. *Sports Marketing*, 2nd Ed. New York: McGraw-Hill, 2010.
Hollis, Nigel. "Ten Years of Learning on How Online Advertising Build Brands." *Journal of Advertising Research* (June 2005).
Laudon, Kenneth and Carol Guercio Traver. *E-Commerce: Business, Technology, Society.* Upper Saddle River, NJ: Pearson Prentice Hall, 2010.

Barcoding

Barcoding (or bar codes) refers to patterns of black lines and white spaces—containing a variety of information such as price, quantities, printing sales receipts, and updating inventory records, among others—that can be read by scanning devices. The bar codes are decoded by measuring the distance from leading edge to leading edge of bars, trailing edge to trailing edge of bars, and leading edge to leading edge of characters. The symbols are designed for barcoding products and for printing on packages, so they can be scanned with any package orientation by omnidirectional scanners as long as a bar code faces the scanner. Bar codes can be printed using a variety of printing techniques; however, barcoding is

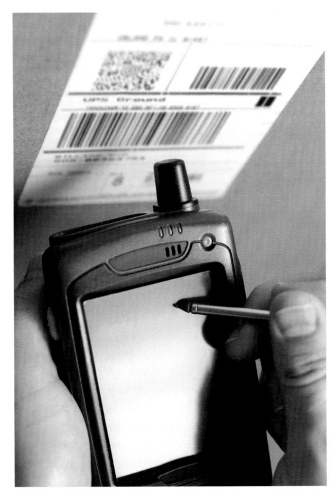

Barcode scanners can be up to 99.99 percent accurate. Barcoding has greatly improved distribution.

continuous with exacting tolerances, so it is difficult to print on any equipment.

Bar codes are fixed in length and can only encode numbers using four element widths. Bar code systems include the Universal Product Code (UPC), European Article Numbering (EAN), and Japanese JAN systems. UPC is a subset of the EAN code. Scanners equipped to read EAN symbols can read UPC symbols, but not necessarily vice versa.

UPC-A is a 12-digit symbol—11 data digits and one check digit—being used in retail applications. Usually the first digit represents the type of product being identified, followed by five digits that represent the manufacturer's code and the next five digits that identify a specific product. UPC-E is a smaller seven-digit UPC symbol, often used for small retail items. The six digits are specified and the barcoding

printing software calculates the seventh check digit. UPC-E is also known as zero suppressed UPC, as it suppresses a 12-digit UPC-A number into a six-digit code by suppressing the number system digit, trailing zeros in the manufacturer's code, and leading zeros in the product identification part of the bar code message. Thus, the main difference between a UPC-A symbol and a UPC-E symbol is the size.

EAN is a European version of UPC. EAN-8 encodes eight numeric digits consisting of two country code digits, five data digits, and one check digit. EAN-13 is the European version of UPC-A. The difference between EAN-13 and UPC-A is that EAN-13 encodes a 13th digit into the parity pattern of the left six digits of a UPC-A symbol.

Uses

Barcoding is useful in manufacturing and distribution. In distribution, firms can keep track of items in warehouses and en route to customers. Similarly, customers can also check the status of their orders without the need for calling the call center. Further, barcoding tracks the progress of jobs as they move through the production process when users scan bar codes of jobs before each operation. Specific processing instructions for the job at each operation can then be provided to operators. Thus, managers can update inventory records and monitor productivity.

Today, most shops and supermarkets have switched to computerized checkout systems using a laser scanner that reads a UPC or barcode printed on an item tag or on packaging. Barcoding represents a major change in the inventory systems of stores in that it is fast and accurate and gives managers continuous information on inventories. It reduces the need for periodic physical inventories and order size determinations, and improves the level of customer service by indicating the price and quantity of each item on the customer's receipt. These scanners have an accuracy rate of up to 99.99 percent.

Satyendra Singh
University of Winnipeg

See Also: Data Collection; Fan Shops, Retail; Inventory Control.

Further Readings

Abernathy, F. H., J. T. Dunlop, J. H. Hammond, and D. Weil. "Control Your Inventory in a World of Lean Retailing." *Harvard Business Review*, v.78/6 (2000).

Stevenson, W. and M. Hojati. *Production Operations Management*. Toronto: McGraw-Hill Ryerson, 2000.

Walker, M. L. and T. L. Seidler. *Sports Equipment Management*. Sudbury, MA: Jones & Bartlett Publishers, 1993.

Barriers to Entry

Entering a sports-related industry commonly involves overcoming challenges or problems referred to as industry entry barriers. A new professional football league, for example, would have to find ways to overcome the National Football League's (NFL's) brand awareness, size and scope, capital resources, extensive supply channel knowledge, effective distribution channels, fan loyalties, and many other characteristics that make it a formidable existing competitor. For those individuals or organizations trying to enter this or any other sports industry, entry barriers are generally viewed negatively as obstacles to progress. However, for organizations already in an industry, entry barriers serve as protection against new competition and may be supported, enhanced, or otherwise increased. As part of his Five Forces framework for analyzing industries, Michael Porter identified several major types of entry barriers; all can be factors in sports industries. When analyzing and assessing entry barriers, it is important for decision makers to accurately identify and understand the particular industry in question, because while the types of entry barriers described below may exist in every industry, they are not all present in the same degree or manner in each industry.

Economies of scale exist when the production of larger volumes of products or services results in lower per unit costs. For example, if a company produc-es football helmets, the more helmets it produces, the more units there are that can be used to cover overhead costs like rent, utilities, and payment of support personnel (e.g., accountants). Therefore, on a per unit basis, the cost of production of an individual helmet may be lower the more helmets a company produces, even though the overall expenses of the company may be higher. This allows the company to sell the helmets at a lower price than competitors that are not achieving significant economies of scale. Thus, if economies of scale are present in an industry, it can be more difficult for a potential new entrant to the industry because it will have to match the scale of other companies to be price competitive.

Product differentiation is another type of entry barrier. A product or service is said to be differentiated when it has characteristics that make buyers willing to pay a premium for it. For example, a student could go to a discount store and pay $20 or less for a pair of shoes. But that same student might be willing to pay 10 times that or more for the latest pair of Jordans. If an industry is dominated by buyers willing to pay premiums, it is more difficult for new entrants because they must be able to differentiate on par with existing firms in order to win business. However, if there are a significant number of price-sensitive customers (i.e., bargain shoppers), new entrants that can offer low prices on base-level merchandise without any bells and whistles may be able to carve out a niche for themselves.

Capital requirements for successful entry may serve as another barrier to entry. Some industries require very large sums of money for new entrants to be successful in the industry. This is a significant entry barrier for major professional sports leagues. For an organization to begin a new professional football league, for example, not only must the league be created, but each of the teams must be established as well (a league cannot exist without a number of teams for each other to play). This entry barrier is heavily dependent on larger economic factors such as availability of credit and economic cycles that have impacts on cash availability for potential new entrants.

Switching costs incurred by customers may also deter new entrants to an industry. Switching costs are those costs incurred by buyers when they change from one organization's product or service to another company's product or service. Switching costs do not have to be just monetary, they can also involve emotional ties (e.g., fan loyalty), intellectual effort (e.g., learning about a sport not previously followed), new procedures or systems (e.g., new safety equipment that requires new pregame routines), and other changes for buyers. If a new entrant into an industry has a product or service that will incur significant switching costs for customers, it is more difficult to be successful because the product or service will have to be better than existing products or services to such a degree that customers are willing to pay the switching costs, whatever form they may take. For example, many companies have membership benefits or offer prepaid discounts (e.g., a "season pass" option at a batting cage facility in which customers prepay for 100 sessions at a 25 percent discount). This is, in part, an attempt to create switching costs for customers and deter new entrants and new competition.

Access to distribution channels may be another source of entry barriers. Distribution channels are the means of getting the product or service of a company to its customers. For sporting goods retailers, the distribution channel is the real estate on which the stores are located; but for a baseball bat manufacturer, distribution channels may be those sporting goods retailers. New entrants must assess the possible ways of getting products or services to buyers. A significant shift regarding distribution channels has occurred as the information age has blossomed. Websites, PDAs, iPhones, etc., coupled with affordable and convenient shipping options, allow companies to bypass traditional distribution channels and connect with buyers directly. Some leagues and conferences have even developed their own television networks (e.g., NFL Network). This, however, still requires significant capital and is itself an entry barrier. There are still vital distribution channels with limited access, though. For a new league or sport, it can still be very difficult to get airtime on ESPN or other sports-related media outlets. Also, there are dozens, if not hundreds of individuals and organizations who would like to own a Major League Baseball (MLB) franchise, but a new team must have the approval of MLB owners and that is very difficult to procure. Thus, the entry barrier for new teams in most major leagues is extraordinarily high because access to the league distribution channel is tightly controlled.

Government policies can serve as entry barriers in some industries. Take for example many youth sport associations around the United States. The Anytown Youth Soccer Association may partner with a local municipality's parks and recreation department to fund the creation and maintenance of soccer fields in exchange for the exclusive or preferred right to play on those fields. A very significant entry barrier has been created. It would be very difficult for a new, rival youth soccer association to be successful given that it would have to arrange for non-government-owned land (not parks) to be used for its games and practices. Government policies such as this, or government regulations or requirements, can serve as significant barriers to entry in some industries.

Expected retaliation from existing competitors can also deter some new entrants. For example, the owner of a new sporting goods retailer opening a block away from an existing store should not be too surprised if the owner of the existing store is very aggressive in her advertising, promotional pricing, external sales, and supplier relations. However, in a city that has several recreation centers where a new, for-profit recreation center opens a few blocks from one of the existing recreation centers, it is quite possible the director of the existing center would welcome the new one because he may perceive the new center as serving the community better. The director may even assist the manager of the new center rather than try to put him out of business. The expected level of retaliation by existing organizations, then, can be a factor in whether or not potential new entrants decide to enter an industry.

Other Disadvantages

Other disadvantages not related to scale can also make entering an industry more challenging. Some of these include, but are not limited to the following:

1. Patents, trademarks, or other protected intellectual property (e.g., patents covering moisture-wicking fabrics may limit the number of new entrants into the athletic clothing industry)
2. Favorable access to raw materials (e.g., exclusive access to players from a minor

league system may make it more difficult for other teams or leagues to begin operations)

3. Favorable locations (e.g., having the best retail location in a town for a sporting goods store can inhibit new entrants because any new store will have an inferior location and ostensibly lower sales.

4. Government subsidies (e.g., in some countries, government bodies subsidize or fully fund athletic teams or organizations making it cost prohibitive for potential new entrants.

5. Experience (e.g., a sports organization that has been working with government officials on regulations and access to facilities has a significant advantage over new entrants without that experience and knowledge.

Michael E. Dobbs
Eastern Illinois University

See Also: Entrepreneurship; New Product; New Product Development Process; Sports Industry; SWOT Analysis.

Further Readings

Annacchino, Marc A. *New Product Development: From Initial Idea to Product Management.* Boston: Elsevier, 2003.

Porter, Michael E. *Cases in Competitive Strategy.* New York: Free Press, 1983.

Porter, Michael E. *Competitive Strategy: Techniques for Analyzing Industries and Competitors.* New York: Free Press, 1980.

Bartering for Sports Events/Vendors

Literally, bartering is exchanging one thing for another. More specifically, bartering is an exchange of goods or services for other goods or services instead of monetary payment. In sports events, bartering is one of the most effective ways of increasing projected income and minimizing financial exposure

as a method of obtaining necessary supplies. Also, bartering may reduce an organization's tax liability. However, some risks in event management will occur if it is undertaken without close scrutiny.

Why should an event organization and suppliers consider bartering? A bartering system equates to a corporate sponsorship. In other words, suppliers provide their products or services to the event organization, and at the same time, the event organization offers the suppliers the right to have their products or services advertised during the event. There are many promotional spots available for advertising. Opportunities include, but are not limited to, all marketing materials involved in a sporting event, such as advertising on tickets, program advertisements, giveaways, scoreboard space, banners, and arena signage. In return, the sponsoring organization can promote its products and services to the sports audience and gain public attention.

Peripheral exposure to the sponsoring organizations allows sponsors exposure they otherwise would not have. Through in-kind services or products, specialized but small-size vendors can have great opportunities to make profits as well as to transfer the goodwill toward the sport event to their businesses. The ultimate goal of bartering is a win-win strategy in which the event organization reduces or covers its expenses for the event, while the vendors have a chance to raise their brand awareness. Bartering allows both sides to reduce their expenses.

There are a variety of barter examples in sporting events. An event organization may contract with product or service suppliers in order to reduce costs. This can apply to refreshments, decorations, equipment, advertising, transportation, and other logistical aspects of an event. For example, in the case of a local sport event for a charity, an event organization may not have enough funds in its budget for the posters, banners, and signage it needs for advertising the event. If a printing company prints the event program free of charge, the event organization could provide the printing company with a free advertisement or exclusive sales in the event. Especially if the categories of goods or services are closely related to health and fitness, a supplier may effectively reach their target customers.

An event organization may need to contract with many types of suppliers for event management. It may make a barter agreement with, for example, a recycling company for waste management, a shopping mall or department store for satellite parking for a shuttle bus, a sport clothing manufacturer for T-shirts, a car dealership for transportation vehicles, and a grocery store or a local restaurant for food and beverages. All such materials help control and minimize event expenses.

Sports drinks are another example. A supplier may agree to provide bottled water for a marathon. The sponsor may then receive exhibit space and tables to promote its new product line of vitamin water in exchange for free bottled water for race participants. The event organization saves the cost of purchasing the bottled water for participants, and the supplier saves the cost of the promotion space. Each event employee and volunteer, as well as participants who drink the bottled water, becomes a prospective customer.

In a similar vein, a barter agreement also works for broadcasting. In this case, the event organization can provide the broadcasting rights free of charge in exchange for a share of advertising sales revenues. Organizations like IMG use this process to broadcast many events. The sponsoring organization and the media outlet then share the generated revenues.

Sang Uk Joo
University of Iowa
Seung Bum Son
Kang Won National University

See Also: Event Management; Sponsorship; Sponsorship Spending; Sponsorship Valuation; Value-in-Kind.

Further Readings

Graham, S., L. Neirotti, and J. Goldblatt. *The Ultimate Guide to Sports Marketing.* New York: McGraw-Hill, 2001.
Lynde, T. *Sponsorships 101: An Insider's Guide to Sponsorships in Corporate America.* Mableton, GA: Lynde & Associates, 2007.
Masteralexis, L. P., C. Barr, and M. Hums. *Principles and Practice of Sport Management.* Sudbury, MA: Jones & Bartlett Publishers, 2008.

Behavior

According to the Sporting Goods Manufacturers Association, sports makes up a nearly $70 billion industry in the United States. This means that it is critical for marketers to understand what motivates individuals to consume sports and sports-related products across a variety of levels including participation, sporting goods, and sports entertainment because of the size of the potential target markets for these activities. Motivation is the force that drives a consumer to take action, and it is an important consideration for both sporting organizations and the companies that spend their marketing dollars to reach sports fans. Marketers want to know how consumers will respond to their messages and activities as well as what inspires them to participate, appreciate, and purchase.

Fan identification is one trait that motivates fan behavior. It can be described as the intensity of a connection that an individual feels for a specific sport-related entity. Increasing the level of fan identification may motivate consumers to buy more, pay higher prices, and hold more positive attitudes overall.

Motivation

Motivation is the activation of behavior meant to generate a specific end and may be either intrinsic or extrinsic. Intrinsic motivation comes from the enjoyment of a specific activity and the rewards from achieving the task—for the love of playing the game. Extrinsic motivation comes from some outside force. In sports participation cheers from the crowd or accolades such as awards or trophies may motivate a participant to do well. In addition, competition is an extrinsic motivation because the reward is winning rather than the intrinsic enjoyment of the activity.

One of the most influential theories in understanding human motivation was developed by Abraham Maslow and is referred to as Maslow's Hierarchy of Needs. Maslow's Hierarchy consists of five levels of needs and requires that the lower-level needs be met before higher-level needs can be satisfied. The first level consists of the most basic needs for human existence. It is difficult for a human to survive if the basic needs of food, water, breathing, shelter, and clothing are not met.

Once the physical needs are relatively satisfied then safety becomes an important motivator for behavior. These needs relate to the desire for harmony and consistency and can revolve around a variety of things including personal safety, job security, health and well-being, and financial security. After physiological and safety needs are met, the third level of human needs is social. This piece of Maslow's Hierarchy involves emotional relationships such as the need for belonging and acceptance either in smaller groups like family or colleagues or in large social groups such as clubs or sports teams.

The next level of needs are those related to esteem. People long to be recognized and take part in activities that offer them a sense of contribution and self-worth in their personal lives, professions, or hobbies. Most people have a longing for self-esteem, and Maslow proposed two categories of esteem needs. At the lower level lies the need for respect from others in the form of status or recognition. The higher level consists of the need for self-confidence, competence, and mastery. After esteem needs are met, the highest level of needs in the hierarchy is self-actualization, which is displayed by the desire to realize one's own potential.

Maslow's Hierarchy is one of the most influential theories used by marketers to understand consumers' motives for action. Marketers historically look toward consumers' needs to outline their market plans because products that meet consumer needs should outperform in the market.

Participation

Individuals participate in sports activities for a variety of reasons including self-improvement, appreciation, and social reasons. People are often motivated toward sports participation to relieve stress or realize a level of accomplishment, but they may also choose to participate in sports simply for the love of the game or because friends or family members are active in the sport.

Sporting events allow participants to satisfy all five levels of needs, starting with the basic need of being active, safety needs associated with good health, belonging needs through being a member of a team or being associated with other individuals who participate in the sport, esteem needs of gaining status and recognition for accomplishments, and

self-actualization through achieving ultimate realized goals. With hundreds of millions of individuals participating in both organized and unorganized sports, it is critical for marketers to understand that these motivations can enhance participation in a variety of sporting entities from health clubs to triathlons.

Sporting Goods

In many sports, participation trends are clearly correlated with consumer purchases. For instance, individuals who play golf at least fairly regularly are likely to purchase goods related to this consumption activity including clubs, balls, tees, shoes, golf lessons, cart rentals, and any other related products.

On the other hand, some athletic categories may be fashion-driven. In categories such as apparel or footwear, the popularity of a specific team or athlete may have a stronger bearing on motivation to purchase than sports participation. For instance, Nike's exemplar in athletic footwear—the Air Jordan basketball shoe—was sought after as a fashion item by consumers who played basketball as well as by those who did not.

Motivation to purchase sporting goods may include the basic and safety needs of having appropriate equipment, belonging needs of purchasing goods that identify the individual as part of a specific group, and esteem and self-actualization needs associated with using goods that will help to achieve goals and showcase those achievements to others. Marketers who understand consumer motivations behind purchasing specific categories of sporting goods can design both products and appeals that will better meet consumer needs.

Sports Entertainment

A third outlet to consider for sports consumption motivation is sports entertainment. Sports entertainment includes things like event attendance, following sporting events on television as well as through newspapers and Websites, and overall appreciation of sport that is displayed through media consumption relating to sport in general.

When we look at motivations for sports entertainment consumption, we begin to consider what it means to be a fan. A sports fan, aficionado, or supporter is someone who has an intense interest in and enthusiasm for a specific athlete, team, sport, or all of sports in general. Motivations for fandom are usually associated with a sense of belonging to a group or esteem needs that are met when a beloved team is successful.

What drives people to be sports fans has been extensively studied by psychologists like Daniel Wann and his colleagues. They attribute people becoming fans to a variety of factors. For instance, sports is both entertainment and a form of leisure. It is also a form of escapism since being a fan allows individuals to yell or behave in other ways that may not normally be socially accepted. In addition, fan activities allow spectators to experience a combination of euphoria and stress referred to as *eustress*. Fans experience euphoria during moments when the outlook for their team is positive and stress when the team may lose. The tension between these two emotions generates heightened sensations.

Other fans are drawn to sports because they appreciate the precision or skill involved. From a social perspective, some fans are drawn to sports as a means of bonding. In addition, going to sports events can create a heightened sense of self-esteem through fan identification.

Again, for marketers, understanding what motivates fans to consume different forms of sports entertainment transforms into dollars for businesses associated with sport. A variety of media and other outlets including cable and satellite television, print magazines, satellite radio, pay-per-view events, the Internet, sports destination travel, and mobile media and applications prosper from individuals finding new and unique ways to follow their favorite athletes, teams, and sports.

In addition, fandom may serve to motivate consumers to purchase sporting goods. It is often the love for the team or the athlete that motivates purchases of items like apparel and footwear. Collegiate sports offers a great example with a wide array of officially licensed products, from more traditional items like t-shirts and jackets to items like throw pillows and shower curtains—a plethora of purchases motivated by enthusiasm for the team.

It is important to note that consumption of sports entertainment is not necessarily motivated by team performance. In a variety of markets, fans are fans because of some geographic or nostalgic connection (the team is in their city or in the city where they grew up) or some emotional connection (their alma mater). For example, the Chicago Cubs Major League Baseball club has not won a World Series since 1908 and has not won a National League pennant since 1945, yet the team still has a loyal fan base. On the other hand, the proliferation of media coverage for sporting events and teams may put more pressure on teams to win in order to keep fans. For instance, individuals can purchase television packages that allow them to watch any football team in the National Football League on any given week. For fans of losing teams like the Detroit Lions or the Oakland Raiders, this may allow them to move beyond geography and choose another favorite team based on history, records, or the specific athletes on the team.

Sponsorship and Fan Identification

Along with looking at the direct motivation to consume sports, it is also important for marketers to understand how consumers react to the specific marketing that is associated with sport. Worldwide sponsorship investment exceeds $37 billion annually. With a consistent rise in sponsorship spending, it has become increasingly important to understand how marketers motivate sports fans to purchase products and services that surround a favorite sporting activity. This makes it critical to understand fans' attitudes toward the persuasive appeals and the sponsoring brand as well as their motivations to purchase the sponsor's products.

One trait likely to influence the way consumers respond to sponsorship information is fan identification with an athlete, team, or event. Social identity is the part of the overall self-concept that is based on membership in a specific group. Individuals make social classifications as a means of defining others and locating themselves within a social environment and may possess many different categorizations of social identity including an identity derived from an attachment to, or interest in, a particular sports athlete, team, or event. Thus, fan identification can be viewed as the level or intensity of a connection that an individual feels for a specific sport-related entity. Highly identified sports fans begin to define themselves at least partly in terms of the organization and tend to equate team success or failure with their personal success or failure. A win for the team is a win for the individual ("we" won rather than "they" won). In addition, because of the strong level of emotional involvement, highly identified fans are more easily aroused while watching their favorite team and are more likely to remember a sponsor's name, think positively of the sponsor, and buy the sponsor's products. Therefore, by sponsoring consumer-favored teams and events and leveraging the relationship through related advertising and sales promotions, firms effectively connect their brands to consumer social identity.

This form of social identity most often manifests itself through identification with a favorite team, although specific cases in history like the saga played out with Brett Favre moving from the Green Bay Packers have highlighted the potential strength of identification with a specific athlete.

Increasing Fan Identification

There are a variety of factors that may potentially influence fan identification. For instance, although losing teams may be able to keep their fans, the level of fan identification may be influenced by a team's record. Individuals want to affiliate themselves with winning teams and publicize that affiliation to their peers. Thus fans may want to identify by saying "we won," but after repeated failure may resort to saying "they lost again." So, individuals may not want to embrace a losing team as an integral part of the self concept because of the consistent disappointment and repeated failure. Thus, merchandise sales are often related to team success since even relatively loyal fans are more inspired to publicly display their attachment to a winning team.

The image of the team off of the field may also influence fan identification. This includes perceptions of the decisions that are made by ownership and the image of the individuals on the team along with the team's commitment to the community. Thus, beyond winning percentage, image and a strong history may lead some fans to particularly pride themselves on the fact that they persevere with the team in good times and bad. On the other hand, when organizations continue to make decisions with which the fans do not agree, identification may decrease.

A third aspect that can influence fan identification is the strength of the community relationship with the team. This component can manifest both geographically when individuals use an attachment to the team to signify belonging to the community in general, and emotionally, when some experience with the organization or team fosters a strong commitment. Fans may feel that the sports organization is a vital part of the history of their community and has contributed to the overall growth of a place to which they are particularly attached. The Chicago Cubs are one of the two remaining charter members of the National League of Baseball, playing in Chicago since 1870. This long-standing tradition and link to the city leads fans to remain dedicated and loyal. This sense of community is also particularly apparent with college organizations where students and graduates alike see themselves as part of the same community as the particular sports team. Therefore, the emotional link to the collegiate community can lead to a very strong identification with the university sports teams.

The level of exposure can also impact the strength of fan identification. The proliferation of media outlets to follow a favorite team, the coaches, and the players allows individuals to form stronger attachments. These extensive outlets via television packages, the Internet, and mobile media allow individuals to stay connected to their favored team despite geographical boundaries. In addition, because fans are able to get more information about the individuals who make up the organization, they can incorporate more of that information into their social identity. Fans can make connections on a more personal level with the team.

From the marketer's perspective, increasing fan identification should have positive outcomes for both the team and its sponsors. For the athlete or team, finding ways to facilitate identification can make them less sensitive to ticket and merchandise prices and may reduce the link between performance and outcome variables, in turn reducing the pressure to win. For a specific event, finding a way to highlight the importance of identification may increase the overall appeal of the event. For example, the Olympics capitalize on patriotism and identification with the home team to increase the prestige of the event. For the sponsors, identified fans may see items that are linked to their favorite athletes, teams, or events as particularly desirable.

When something is central to a part of the social identity, then something related to that concept (e.g., a sponsoring brand) will also be perceived to reflect that identity. Sponsor-related offerings for highly identified individuals are largely in keeping with their personal interests and goals of connecting with the sports entity. This makes sports in general, and fan identification specifically, a very successful marketing vehicle for the sale of a variety of goods. This includes licensed items that capitalize on a fan's level of attachment by providing a wide array of goods for the home, office, vehicle, and individual that showcase identification, but it also includes products that are completely unrelated to sports—from retailers to vehicles to cable or financial services, these items are often purchased based on a sponsorship contract or specific endorsement by an athlete or team.

Conclusion

Understanding what sets consumers in action is important for marketers in general, but with the consumer dollars available and growth in the industry segment, the motivations behind sports participation, sporting goods purchases, and the consumption of sports entertainment looks to be a key outlet of the future. Along with fostering consumer relationships with their specific brands, companies may increasingly look to motivate fans by capitalizing on their commitment to their favorite athletes, teams, or events.

Susan Myers
University of Central Arkansas

See Also: Activation, Sponsorship; Attendance, Impact of Winning on; Brand Association; Brand Awareness; Fan Attendance, Reasons for; Fan Avidity; Identification of Sports Fans; Licensing; Maslow's Hierarchy of Needs; Sponsorship; Sports Industry.

Further Readings

Chicago Cubs Official Website. http://chicago.cubs .mlb.com (Accessed November 2009).
Deci, E. "Intrinsic Motivation, Extrinsic Reinforcement, and Inequity." *Journal of Personality and Social Psychology*, v.22/1 (1972).

Gwinner, K. and S. R. Swanson. "A Model of Fan Identification: Antecedents and Sponsorship Outcomes." *Journal of Services Marketing*, v.17 (2003).
Madrigal, Robert. "The Influence of Social Alliances With Sports Teams on Intentions to Purchase Corporate Sponsors' Products." *Journal of Advertising*, v.29 (2000).
Mael, F. A. and B. E. Ashforth. "Alumni and Their Alma Mater; A Partial Test of the Reformulated Model of Organizational Identification." *Journal of Organizational Behavior*, v.13 (1992).
Shank, Matthew D. *Sports Marketing: A Strategic Perspective*, 4th Ed. Upper Saddle River, NJ: Pearson Prentice Hall, 2009.
Sutton, William A., Mark A. McDonald, George R. Milne, and John Cimperman. "Creating and Fostering Fan Identification in Professional Sports." *Sport Marketing Quarterly*, v.6/1 (1997).
Tajfel, H. and J. C. Turner. "The Social Identity Theory of Intergroup Behavior." In S. Worchel and W. G. Austin, eds., *Psychology of Intergroup Relations*. Chicago: Nelson-Hall, 1985.
Wann, Daniel L. and Nyla R. Branacombe. "Influence of Identification With a Sports Team on Objective Knowledge and Subjective Beliefs." *International Journal of Sports Psychology*, v.26/4 (1995).
Wann, Daniel L., Katrina Koch, Tasha Knoth, David Fox, Aljubaily Hesham, and Christopher Lantz. "The Impact of Team Identification on Biased Predictions of Player Performance." *Psychological Record*, v.56 (2006).

Benchmarking

The term *benchmarking* was first used by cobblers when they measured feet for shoes. They would place someone's foot on a "bench" and mark its measurements out to make the pattern for the shoes. *Benchmarking* is now used to refer to measuring performance using a specific indicator (cost per unit of measure, productivity per unit of measure, cycle time of x per unit of measure, or defects per unit of measure) resulting in a metric of performance that is then compared to others.

Benchmarking is the process of systematically comparing an organization's products, services, and practices against those of similar organizations, particularly those that are superior performers. This then allows organizations to develop plans for how to make improvements or adapt specific best practices, usually with the aim of increasing some aspect of performance. Benchmarking is often treated as a continuous process in which organizations continually seek to improve their practices.

The Sports Industry

With the globalization of sport, benchmarking is commonly used by a wide range of sport organizations internationally. In 2008, the Global Benchmarking Network commissioned a study of benchmarking initiatives conducted by more than 450 organizations representing 40 countries. The study revealed that mission and vision statements and customer (client) surveys are the most used (by 77 percent of organizations) of 20 improvement tools, followed by SWOT analysis (72 percent), and informal benchmarking (68 percent). Performance benchmarking was used by 49 percent and best practice benchmarking by 39 percent.

Common types of benchmarking that occur in sport organizations includes process, financial, investment, performance, product, strategic, functional, and operational benchmarking. Organizations that institutionalize benchmarking into their daily procedures find it is useful to create and maintain a database of best practices and the companies currently associated with each best practice.

In collegiate sports, everything is benchmarked, from facilities to revenue generation to graduation rates. For example, in 2001 the Knight Commission called for a 50 percent graduation rate benchmark for postseason eligibility, and subsequently the National Collegiate Athletic Association has adopted policies that have moved toward that goal. Energy management is another area for which benchmarking is used as a cost saving strategy among collegiate and professional teams.

Benchmarking has been embraced by Major League Baseball (MLB), the National Basketball Association (NBA), and the National Football League (NFL). For example, in May 2010, several professional sports teams joined ENERGY STAR, demonstrating a growing interest in energy management and green activities among stadiums. In the area of energy benchmarking, more than a third of MLB teams participated in a portfolio manager benchmarking training Webinar.

In the NBA, benchmarking has been successfully used to increase productivity, improve arena designs, identify breakthrough techniques, and identify new opportunities. Additionally, among NBA and NFL franchises, benchmarking using measures such as recruiting, attendance, and profit maximizing objectives has proven useful in decision-making in human resources, public subsidies for new stadia and arenas, and maintaining a loyal base of fans.

Benchmarking inherently relies on the assumption of availability and use of information about competing organizations. More often than not, benchmarking is accomplished through cooperative efforts of benchmarking partners. Benchmarking with direct competitors requires a willing partner. It is important for the partners to share information and rely on such information gathered for benchmarking purposes. One of the primary barriers to the successful implementation of benchmarking initiatives is identifying partners willing to share information about their operations. It is unlikely that companies will share information that may be the source of their competitive advantage.

Alternatively, required information may be gathered in a "unilateral" approach by collecting information without the benefit of cooperation by a target partner. This approach relies on data published or available from sources such as trade associations or information clearinghouses. However, publicly available information is generally in summary form and sometimes lacks the detail and refinement that is required for a benchmarking project.

The Sport Executive Management Benchmarking Association (SEMBA) is an association of sport team management professionals who compare operating performance and identify the best business practices and performance gaps. Activity-based costing/activity-based management, balanced scorecard management, business process architecture, and capital asset management are several tools that organizations like SEMBA can create to help develop benchmarking programs.

In order for contemporary sport organizations to thrive they must maintain their competitive edge by staying abreast of best practices and addressing performance gaps that may become apparent through a well-constructed benchmarking program.

Steven N. Waller
University of Tennessee, Knoxville

See Also: Balanced Scorecard; Continuous Quality Improvement; Evaluation; Management by Objectives; Performance Standards.

Further Readings

Covell, David, Sharianne Walker, Julie Siciliano, and Peter Hess. *Managing Sports Organizations: Responsibility for Performance,* 2nd Ed. Oxford, UK: Butterworth-Heinemann, 2007.

Gilson, Clive, Mike Pratt, Kevin Roberts, and Ed Weymes. *Peak Performance: Inspirational Business Lessons From the World's Top Sports Organizations.* Mason, OH: Thompson, 2000.

John F. and James L. Knight Foundation. "Knight Commission Calls for College Sports Reform." http://www.knightfoundation.org/permalink/364379/225369 (Accessed July 2010).

Nourayi, Mahmoud M. "Profitability in Professional Sports and Benchmarking: The Case of NBA Franchises." *Benchmarking: An International Journal,* v.13/3 (2006).

Rosentraub, Mark S. *Major League Winners: Using Sports and Cultural Centers as Tools for Economic Development.* Boca Raton, FL: CRC Press, 2010.

Stadium Managers Association. "Several Pro Teams Now Benchmarking." http://www.stadiummanagers.org/images/stories/pdfs/energy.doc (Accessed July 2010).

Taylor, Tracey, Alison Doherty, and Peter McGraw. *Managing Sport Organizations: A Human Resource Management Perspective.* Oxford, UK: Butterworth-Heinemann, 2008.

Benefits for Sponsors

On a worldwide basis, spending on sponsorship reached $44 billion in 2009. Corporate investment in sponsorship in North America has grown from $850 million in 1985 to $16.51 billion in 2009, according to the IEG sponsorship report. Sponsorship is regarded as a marketing communications tool, such as advertising, public relations, and sales promotion, in that the basic goal is to achieve a company's marketing objectives. In other words, sponsorship is a strategic activity that helps accomplish a company's objectives.

In the early days, corporate sponsorship was viewed mainly as a form of patronage, but commercial sponsorship has increased tremendously in recent decades. Nowadays, sponsorship is viewed differently from patronage: Patronage is an altruistic activity where the patron holds little expectation of obtaining a benefit, while sponsoring companies expect some benefits from their financial deals. Thus, sponsorship is different from philanthropy in that the arrangement is a business relationship hoping to gain commercial advantage.

In successful arrangements, mutual benefits are exchanged between sponsors and a sporting event or organization. Sponsored entities get financial, in-kind, and media benefits from sponsors. Financial benefit is money received as a sponsorship fee, while in-kind benefits are different forms of product support (e.g., equipment, food, beverages), and personnel support (e.g., computer system support). Media benefit is the visibility provided by being associated with a sport event or organization. Often, media benefit is a critical attractor for potential sponsors. In exchange for providing financial, in-kind, and media benefits, sponsors receive the benefits of brand awareness, image enhancement, product trial/sales opportunities, hospitality opportunities, morale enhancement of employees, and a demonstration platform. Recently, more emphasis has been placed on the benefits of product trial/sales opportunities, demonstration platforms, and hospitality opportunities, since these benefits are more tangible and measurable compared to increases in awareness and image enhancement. A sponsor is likely to seek multiple benefits, or some selected benefits, depending on the company's marketing objectives.

Sponsor Benefits

One of most cited sponsorship benefits is increased brand and company awareness. If a sponsor is already well known and its products have high levels of awareness, the sponsor may not seek this benefit. However, if a sponsor is a new company, or is introducing a new product to markets, or taking its existing products to new markets, increasing awareness of the brand/company among target customers could be an important objective for the company. Sponsorship can increase brand/company awareness by effectively getting through communication clutters to reach consumers. Awareness is also fundamental for consumers to have a more favorable attitude toward a sponsor's brands, which possibly further results in purchase action (which equals an increase in sales). Increased awareness is made possible by exposing the company logo/product brand through on-site signage, printed promotional materials, and media coverage.

By associating with prestigious and well-established sport organizations or events, sponsors also might be able to enjoy an enhanced brand image transferred from the images of sponsored entities. Image is the sum of beliefs, ideas, and impression that a person has of an objective. Brand image is perceptions of a brand, which are reflected by a brand association. Since sponsorship creates an association between sponsors and a sport event or organization, the image can be transferred to each other. An enhanced image can bring more favorable attitudes toward the company and its brands in the consumer's mind. For example, if a company can afford to be a sponsor of Olympics, it signals to potential customers that the company is financially stable enough to be a sponsor of the mega event. In addition, the images such as "superiority" and "prestige" attached to the Olympic Games can be transferred to the associated sponsors. Because any images can be transferred, selecting the appropriate sponsor with the desired image is important in the selection of a sport organization or event. For example, tennis has a clean and preppy image, while auto racing has a dangerous and rugged image.

Sponsors can also try to change their current image by associating with a sporting event or organization that has the image a company is looking for. Sponsorship can be effectively used if a company had a recent scandal that resulted in a negative public perception about the company or when a company wants to form a new image.

Sponsorship also provides product trials or sales opportunities for participating sponsors. Increases in sales are often seen as the ultimate benefit of sponsorship. Increases in brand awareness and image enhancement are attractive, but sales increase is the most tangible ultimate benefit sought by sponsors. Especially for established companies, increased sales would be more attractive than brand awareness or image enhancement.

A consumer might have an interest in many products, but may have never had a chance to try those products. By providing an opportunity for product trial, sponsorship can effectively satisfy consumer needs for product evaluation prior to purchase. By encouraging those interested consumers to try their products on site, sponsorship can remove barriers (e.g., financial, social, or time) to consumer experience before the actual purchase. For example, Samsung distributed its new cell phones to media staff and Olympic officials at the Sydney Olympics, providing firsthand experience of its new products. If customers like the products they try, it is very likely that they will purchase the product in the future. Because on-site sales at sports events provide measurable numbers, rights for on-site sales are highly desirable for companies given a company's needs to justify sponsorship spending.

Sponsorship could bring various hospitality opportunities to participating sponsors to build and strengthen the relationship with potential or existing customers, distributors, and business partners by providing face-to-face interaction opportunities. Benefits such as free tickets and hospitality tents could be included as a part of a sponsorship package. Providing hospitality opportunities is important for relationship marketing in that it builds social bonds with a company's current and future stakeholders.

If a company sponsors an esteemed event, it could also enhance employee morale in the sense that they are a part of the company that sponsors a mega event. This notion could foster a sense of pride among employees, which could have a positive influence on employee retention and satisfaction with their company in the long term. Sponsors can also use sponsorship to develop various programs for employees engaged with the sponsored event to develop camaraderie among employees.

Sponsoring companies might be provided an opportunity to demonstrate the excellence of their products and services to the officials, spectators, and viewers of sponsored events. Especially for companies that provide technology, communication, and logistical services, sport events can be effectively used to demonstrate and introduce new services or products. For example, Seiko provided the official timers for the Salt Lake City Olympic Games. Given that the provided equipment meets the standards of Olympic Games with an accuracy of a hundredth or even thousandth of a second, it signals the excellence of Seiko watches to potential customers.

Conclusion

These received benefits by sponsors are possible because a sponsored event/activity provides exposure opportunities for sponsors and builds the association formed between sponsors and a sport event or organization. However, these various benefits received by sponsors are not automatically given to all sponsors. Various studies on sponsorship effectiveness suggest that many factors influence the extent to which sponsors get these benefits from their respective sponsorship arrangements. For example, factors such as how well sponsors activate or leverage their sponsorship rights and how well they integrate their sponsorships as a part of their marketing communications could influence the effectiveness of their sponsorship, which directly influences the resulting benefits.

Cindy Lee
West Virginia University

See Also: Olympics; Sponsorship Advantages and Disadvantages; Sponsorship Evaluation Considerations; Sponsorship Valuation.

Further Readings

"Behind the Numbers: Sponsorships Spending Decline." IEG. http://www.sponsorship.com/About-IEG/Sponsorship-Blogs/Jim-Andrews/January-2010/Behind-The-Numbers--Sponsorship-s-Spending-Decline.aspx (Accessed May 2011).

Cornwell, T. Bettina and Maignan Isabelle. "An International Review of Sponsorship Research." *Journal of Advertising*, v.27/1 (1998).
Cornwell, T. Bettina, Clinton S. Weeks, and Donald P. Roy. "Sponsorship-Linked Marketing: Opening the Black Box." *Journal of Advertising*, v.34/2 (2005).
Howard, Dennis R. and John L. Crompton. "Nature of Sponsorship Exchange." In *Financing Sport*, 2nd Ed. Morgantown, WV: Fitness Information Technology, 2004.
Meenaghan, Tony. "The Role of Sponsorship in the Marketing Communication Mix." *International Journal of Advertising*, v.10/1 (1991).

Bid Documents

While bidding processes and bid documents are relevant to many aspects of sport management, including bids to provide services or construction materials for sport franchises and facilities, it is bidding to secure events that is most relevant and the focus here. Formal bidding processes are used to determine where events such as the National Football League's (NFL) Super Bowl, National Collegiate Athletic Association (NCAA) competitions, continental multisport events, the Commonwealth Games, international and national sport federation events, and, most significantly, the Olympic Games are held. Bid documents include guidelines established by the event owner setting out specifications required to successfully host the event and often several levels of documentation provided by parties interested in hosting the event that are used to demonstrate that organizers from a host site have the capability of successfully hosting the event. Bidding to secure the right to host the Olympic Games is the most noteworthy example and will be the key reference point used here, as most cases of bidding to host an event follow the same basic structure.

The bid process usually begins with the event owner inviting interest from appropriate cities or venues. The NFL invites interest from the host cities of NFL teams, an international federation (IF) invites interest from among its national federations (NFs), and the International Olympic Committee (IOC) invites interest from the 203 national Olympic committees (NOCs). The process determining the host city for the Olympic Games formally begins approximately nine years prior, and the host city is selected approximately seven years prior to the scheduled games.

Often the governing bodies that are invited to identify potential bid cities will require a preliminary bidding process that includes additional bid documentation. For example, NOCs might establish preliminary bid specifications and bid books from cities that are vying to be put forth to the IOC. While the preliminary process helps the NOCs determine who they should nominate, it also helps the eventual nominee prepare a stronger bid package at the higher level.

Once potential hosts are identified, the event owner will distribute specifications, or a bid guide, to each group. The IOC provides a bid guide in the form of a questionnaire to all of the identified cities, which are classified as applicant cities at that point. For applicant cities interested in hosting the 2016 Games, the questionnaire consisted of 163 pages covering 17 themes as well as requirements to meet numerous guarantees. Applicant cities needed to show a commitment to the Olympic vision and values, political and public support, whether the city could provide adequate lodging, that scheduling of other major events would not conflict with the Olympic Games, adequate financial backing and financial guarantees, an adequate legal framework, and that they could guarantee the protection of the Olympic marks.

The next level of bid documentation is the potential host's response to the event owner's specifications or bid guide. For some events, the initial response to the bid guide is sufficient to determine the host. Larger events that generate more interest often use the initial response from the potential hosts to narrow down the number of sites under consideration to a group of finalists. The finalists are then required to submit further documentation. For the IOC process, the detailed responses and guarantees submitted in response to the applicant city questionnaire is evaluated by an IOC executive board consisting of the IOC president, four vice presidents, and 10 other IOC members elected by the general membership. The executive board's evaluation is used to eliminate some cities from consideration and to determine the remaining cities, which are then classified as candidate cities.

In cases where potential hosts are required to submit additional, more comprehensive documentation, it is often in conjunction with a formal site visit by an evaluation team commissioned by the event owners. In the IOC case, each candidate city submits a candidature file, informally known as a bid book, which includes an in-depth description of their Olympic plans. The bid book is a multimedia production that includes pictures, graphics, tables, and figures. It addresses in detail every aspect of a candidate city's vision for hosting the Games including preliminary financing plans, budgets, schedules of events, and venues. The candidature files/bid books are used by IOC members along with a written report from the IOC Evaluation Commission, based on a visit to each site and an assessment of each candidate city's bid documentation, for background information when voting on the eventual host city.

When the bidding to host an event is competitive, solid bid documentation is essential for a successful bid. In addition to the bid documentation, teams representing potential hosts are often given an opportunity to formally present their bid to the decision makers prior to the vote. In the case of the IOC selection process, the presentations involve music, video, and testimonials from renowned athletes, celebrities, and political dignitaries to include the appropriate heads of state. While stellar bid documentation is necessary to successfully secure the rights to host an event up for bid, it is not sufficient since it is often difficult to distinguish between bid documentation in the final stages of a competitive process.

Kevin Heisey
Liberty University

See Also: Commonwealth Games; Event or Venue Location; Governing Body; Mega Sports Events; Olympic Organization; Olympics; Sports Organizing Bodies.

Further Readings

Brighenti, Oliver, et al. *From Initial Idea to Success: A Guide to Bidding for Sports Events for Politicians and Administrators.* Chavannes-Lausanne: Sports Event Network for Tourism and Economic Development of the Alpine Space, 2005.

Commonwealth Games Federation. "2014 Commonwealth Games Bid Documents." http://www.thecgf.com/games/future/glasgow2014.asp?yr=2014 (Accessed September 2010).

Nickson, David. *The Bid Manager's Handbook.* Surrey: Gower, 2008.

Bill Davis Racing

Arkansas native and trucking business owner Bill Davis was the founder and owner of Bill Davis Racing. At its height, the team featured a successful engine-building business and multiple racing teams. Bill Davis Racing enjoyed a number of successful NASCAR seasons, including two NASCAR Craftsman Truck Series titles and five wins on the Sprint Cup series. Bill Davis Racing ran into financial difficulties associated with the loss of major corporate sponsors by 2008. Davis had sold his team and exited NASCAR racing by the end of that year, ending a more than 20-year career in the business.

Before he got involved in racing Bill Davis owned a very successful trucking business. Davis wanted to get involved in racing as a hobby and as an outlet for him to get away from the daily stress of owning a business. Eventually, however, racing became his passion and number-one priority. Bill Davis entered NASCAR in 1988 and teamed up with driver Mark Martin to run 13 Busch Series races.

From 1993 to 2008, Bill Davis Racing enjoyed some success in NASCAR, winning two truck titles and five Sprint Cup wins, including the 2002 Daytona 500 with driver Ward Burton. The team made 722 starts during that time period. Davis had been the owner of the NASCAR Winston Cup since 1993. That was the year Maxwell House sponsored

Caterpillar, Inc., which sponsored the #22 car shown here at Daytona International Speedway in Daytona Beach, Florida, in February 2008, was one of Bill Davis Racing's major sponsors. The loss of this sponsorship was a factor in the team's sale.

his #22 Pontiac driven by Bobby Labonte. In 1999, Caterpillar became the primary sponsor of the #22 Pontiac, while Polaris became a major associate sponsor in 2000. Siemens became a major associate sponsor of the #93 car and Amoco continued its major sponsorship of the same car. AT&T also sponsored the Bill Davis Racing full-time Busch Series racing team.

In the early 2000s, Bill Davis Racing had all the assets needed to succeed. It had a very good engine-building program, a multi-car team format, and a 130,000-square-foot motorsports facility. They had significant sponsors and the latest technology, too. In the early 2000s, Bill Davis Racing had four major sponsoring companies that ranked in the top 160 on *Fortune* magazine's Global 500. In later years, the team would make the switch to Dodge cars. Bill Davis Racing had also been racing Toyota trucks in the NASCAR Craftsman Truck Series since 2004.

The team was struggling in 2008, however, because of a lack of steady sponsorship, and Davis began to scale back and finally end his involvement in the auto racing industry. Davis's significant sponsor before he sold the team was Caterpillar, Inc., and Caterpillar left Bill Davis Racing for Richard Childress Racing. Davis had to drop his second racing team because of a lack of sponsorship. Davis also owned Bill Davis Trucking, which had already filed for Chapter 11 bankruptcy in 2007. Bill Davis Trucking is separate from his NASCAR operation.

Bill Davis Racing was a single-car team during this time and it had struggled to stay in the top 35 in the NASCAR standings. The bad state of the economy also factored into Davis's decision to leave the business. Bill Davis Racing first sold its Triad Racing Development, which is a major supplier of NASCAR engines and chassis, to Triad Racing Technologies. It then sold a major stake in its NASCAR teams to Triad Racing as well. Bill Davis had completely exited the racing business by late 2008. Mike Held and Marty Gaunt bought majority interest from Davis. When Davis sold his team he had been in NASCAR for over 20 years. He had owned the team with his wife, Gail, since 1983.

David Trevino
Independent Scholar

See Also: Economic Climate for Sports; National Association for Stock Car Auto Racing; Richard Childress Racing.

Further Readings

Clarke, Liz. *One Helluva Ride: How NASCAR Swept the Nation.* New York: Villard, 2008.
Hagstrom, Robert G. *The NASCAR Way: The Business That Drives the Sport.* New York: Wiley, 1998.
MacGregor, Jeff and Olya Evanitsky. *Sunday Money: Speed! Lust! Madness! Death!: A Hot Lap Around America With NASCAR.* New York: HarperCollins, 2005.
Menzer, Joe. *The Wildest Ride: A History of NASCAR (or, How a Bunch of Good Ol' Boys Built a Billion-Dollar Industry Out of Wrecking Cars).* New York: Simon & Schuster, 2001.
Miller, Timothy and Steve Milton. *NASCAR Now.* Buffalo, NY: Firefly Books, 2004.
NASCAR. "Bill Davis Racing." http://www.nascar.com/drivers/tps/bdavis/index.html (Accessed October 2010).

"Billboard" Rules

Outdoor advertising consists of short promotional messages on billboards, posters, and signs. Billboard advertising, which is relatively inexpensive, allows the marketer to focus on a particular area, and is directed toward a mobile audience. Billboards are particularly suitable for products that lend themselves to pictorial display. Like any other industry, the outdoor advertising industry is also governed by external laws and regulations. However, the Outdoor Advertising Association of America has adopted a set of voluntary industry principles/rules, and encourages its members to operate in conformance with the following principles:

- Observe the highest free speech standards
- Protect children
- Support worthy public causes

- Provide an effective, attractive medium for advertisers
- Respect the environment
- Provide effective and safe digital billboards
- Uphold billboard industry self-regulation
- Protect billboard industry rights

Several advantages and disadvantages of billboard advertising exist. Some of the advantages are: potential placement of the advertisement close to the point of sale; high frequency of exposure to regular commuters; high reach; 24-hour presence; geographic flexibility for local advertisers; economic efficiency in terms of low production costs and low cost per thousand exposures; visual impact from advertisement size and message creativity; and brand awareness. Disadvantages include: the need to limit the number of words in the message; short exposure to the advertisement; low demographic selectivity; and measurement problems.

Two factors—visibility and media efficiency—are closely tied to billboard advertising, and are equally applicable to sports outdoor advertising. Visibility refers to the ability of a billboard to make a strong visual impression, allowing it to break through the clutter. Media efficiency refers to broad and frequent exposure to the target audience, making the medium effective and cost-efficient as it is being noticed in a competitive environment. Based on Burton's *Advertising Copywriting* and the Traffic Audit Bureau's *Planning for Out-of-Home Media*, there are five main principles of effective billboard advertising: short copy (eight or fewer words in copy), simple background, product identification (billboard clearly identifies product or advertiser), simple message (single message communicated), and creative (use of clever phrases and/or illustrations). In fact, compared with other media, billboards were rated higher in terms of ability to communicate information affordably, attract new customers, and increase sales.

In recent years, the advancement in digital technology in billboards has provided countless benefits to diverse groups of consumers, as digital billboards can be updated electronically, operated remotely, and networked together to reach target customers quickly and efficiently. For example, the *Toledo Blade* newspaper in Toledo, Ohio, uses digital bill-boards to display daily headlines and deliver breaking news. Similarly, quite a few TV stations use the digital boards to advertise stories ahead of time. Indeed, the number of digital billboards in the United States is expected to grow by several hundred over the next few years.

Satyendra Singh
University of Winnipeg

See Also: Advertising Media; Marketing Concept, The; Media Choice; Publicity; Signage.

Further Readings

Blasko, V. J. "A Content Analysis of the Creative Characteristics of Outdoor Advertising: National vs. Regional Differences." In Nancy Stephens, ed., *Proceedings of the 1985 Conference of the American Academy of Advertising*. Tempe, AZ: American Academy of Advertising, 1985.

Burton, P. W. *Advertising Copywriting*, 5th Ed. Columbus, OH: Grid, 1983.

Charles, R. T., G. R. Franke, and H. K. Bang. "Use of Effectiveness of Billboards: Perspectives From Selective-Perception Theory and Retail-Gravity Models." *Journal of Advertising*, v.35/4 (2006).

Outdoor Advertising Association of America. http://www.oaaa.org (Accessed September 2010).

Taylor, C. R. and G. R. Franke. "Business Perceptions of the Role of Billboards in the U.S. Economy." *Journal of Advertising Research*, v.43 (June 2003).

Traffic Audit Bureau. *Planning for Out-of-Home Media*. New York: Malbridge, 1977.

Blackouts

The term *blackout* in sports is used to describe the convention by which the promoter or host team of a sporting event prohibits the broadcasting of that event either completely or by a certain type of broadcast medium or to a specific geography, most often the area where the event is being held. The primary purpose of blacking out sports events relates to maximizing live attendance at the event.

In the early days of television broadcasting of sport events, it was widely believed that local blackouts were necessary to preserve the sale of tickets for events. While the term *blackout* has been applied to radio broadcasting as well as to television, radio has never been perceived to be as significant a threat to event attendance and ticket sales as television.

It was the advent of television, with its potential to deliver both pictures and commentary rivaling the in-stadium experience, that seemed to threaten sports promoters, leagues, and teams. It encouraged the widespread and systematic use of blackouts to enhance live attendance, even though a negative link between televising a sporting event and its live gate has never been shown to exist.

In the 1950s, boxing and baseball were the two most popular television sports, with each beginning to adopt different types of blackout strategies. Boxing, which took place largely in reasonably small indoor arenas that made selling tickets easy, reserved the use of blackouts for its most significant events, ones that had been built up by prior televised fights. This use of the blackout strategy added a sense of exclusivity to championship fights, supporting higher ticket prices and allowing promoters to use larger venues, as there would be no other way for fans to see the event except in person. However, boxing promoters in the mid-1980s began to move an increasing number of events away from free broadcast and to pay-per-view broadcasts because of the financial incentives a pay-per-view audience offered. This included blacking out radio broadcasts, too, and by the early 21st century boxing had largely disappeared from the broadcast media.

Baseball teams, which were the first sports entities to partner with media companies to sell their broadcast rights, regularly blacked out a certain portion of their home games from broadcast entirely. They also reserved another portion of home game inventory exclusively for radio. Since baseball clubs have a very large number of games compared to other sports, it was believed that systematically blacking out a certain amount of inventory would help preserve ticket demand and attendance across a long season. Typically, two types of games would be subject to baseball blackouts. The games believed to have the least demand either because of day, timing, or attractiveness of the opponent were often totally blacked out. Games believed to have high in-person demand were often blacked out on television to enhance radio broadcast listenership and rights values. Baseball would slowly abandon these strategies as the revenue from broadcast rights fees from radio and sports-specific cable television rose in importance in the 1990s. Today, it is common that all of a team's baseball games are available in the team's local market both on radio and television.

However, the North American sport most directly associated with blackouts is professional football. The NFL has long maintained some form of institutional local market blackout of the home team's games to support local ticket sales. This ban was absolute, even after the league signed its national broadcast deal in 1961, and applied even to the pre–Super Bowl era league championship games. This policy was liberalized in the 1970s, permitting the local broadcast of the local team's home games if the game was sold out 72 hours before kickoff.

The ticket sales success of NFL teams, in part buoyed by the interest created by broadcasts, made local blackouts rare from the 1990s onward. But the economic downturn of 2008, coupled with rising ticket prices, has returned the blackout to being a more regular occurrence. While the NFL has created more flexible rules allowing teams to avoid blackouts, a number of commentators have urged that the league consider ending the rule, especially as blacking out the home games of a struggling franchise may actually injure rather than bolster that team's future ticket sales. The continued existence of the blackout is now more of a tool to move fans to pay-per-view or subscription platforms where blacked out or embargoed content is available for purchase.

Robert A. Boland
New York University

See Also: Broadcast Rights; Contracts, TV/Radio Network; Distribution (Spectator); Media Contracts With Sports Teams/Events; NarrowcastingVersus Broadcasting; Pay-per-View Sports; Piracy; Sports Networks; Sports Networks, Regional; Sports Radio; Subscription-Based Broadcasting; Televised Sports; Territorial Rights; TV Rights/Contracts.

Further Readings

Fecteau, Alan. "NFL Network Blackouts: Old Law Meets New Technology With the Advent of the Satellite Dish." *Marquette Sports Law Journal,* v.5/22 (Spring 1995).

Igel, Lee. "Time to Abandon the Blackout Rule, Pro Football's Sacred Cow." http://blogs.forbes .com/sportsmoney/2010/09/13/time-to-abandon -the-blackout-rule-pro-footballs-sacred-cow (Accessed October 2010).

Leahy, Sean. "Blackout Blues? NFL Ticket Sales Slumping in Some Areas." *USA Today.* http:// www.usatoday.com/sports/football/nfl/2009-08 -31-nfl-tickets_N.htm (Accessed October 2010).

Boston Bruins

The Boston Bruins are one of the "original six" National Hockey League (NHL) franchises and were the first NHL franchise in the United States (1924). The team began when Charles Adams, owner of the First National Stores (a large grocery store chain) convinced NHL President Frank Calder to grant him an expansion team in the United States. He named Art Ross general manager (a post he would hold until 1954), and arranged for the team to play in the Boston Arena, a 4,500-seat arena.

After two unsuccessful seasons, Ross purchased the Western Hockey League for $300,000, acquiring a number of key players, including Eddie Shore. The Bruins started the 1928–29 season by moving into the new Boston Garden, built by Adams for $500,000. They finished the 1929 season by winning their first Stanley Cup.

Early Years

The team would be strong throughout the 1930s and early 1940s, winning the Stanley Cup again in 1939 and 1941, with players such as Shore, Babe Siebert, Goalie Tiny Thompson, Cooney Weiland, Goalie Frank Brimsek (who replaced Thompson after he was injured), Bill Cowley, and the members of the "Kraut Line": Milt Schmidt, Bobby Bauer,

and Woody Dumart. The Bruins did not win another Stanley Cup for 29 years, and would have only four winning seasons between 1947 and 1967 (they would make it to the cup finals three times during this period: 1953, 1957, and 1958).

In 1951, the Adams family relinquished control of the Bruins and the Garden to Walter A. Brown, the owner of the Celtics. Three years later, the Bruins became the first NHL team to purchase a Zamboni, an ice resurfacing machine. On January 18, 1958, the first black person ever to play in the NHL stepped onto the ice for the Bruins—left wing Willie O'Ree. He played in 45 games for the Bruins between 1957 and 1961, scoring six goals and 10 assists.

Weston Adams, who had sold the team in 1951, re-purchased the Bruins in 1964 after Brown's death. Adams signed Bobby Orr, a defenseman, who entered the league in 1966–67 and revolutionized the game with his speed and playmaking ability from the blue line. A trade with the Blackhawks brought Phil Esposito, Ken Hodge, and Fred Stanfield. These players, along with John Bucyk, John McKenzie, Derek Sanderson, and goaltender Gerry Cheevers helped create the "Big Bad Bruins," one of the NHL's elite teams from the late 1960s into the 1980s.

Recent History

In 1970, the Bruins won their first Stanley Cup in 29 years. After losing in the quarterfinals in 1971 to Montreal, the Bruins won the Cup again in 1972. The team lost a number of stars to the World Hockey Association (WHA), notably Cheevers, McKenzie, and Sanderson, but remained a Stanley Cup contender, making it to the finals in 1974, 1977, and 1978. Don Cherry, who would later gain fame as a commentator on *Hockey Night in Canada,* coached the team from 1974–75 until 1978–79. Under Cherry, the Bruins became more of a "blue-collar team," the so-called "Lunch Pail A.C."

Esposito was traded to the Rangers in 1975 for Jean Ratelle and Brad Park (both of whom, like Esposito, ended up in the Hockey Hall of Fame) and Orr left for the Blackhawks in 1976. In 1975, the team was purchased by Jeremy Jacobs.

In 1979, Ray Bourque joined the team. He would win the Calder Trophy as the NHL Rookie of the Year and be named a First-team All Star. Bourque would spend 21 years in Boston, becoming the face of the franchise. In 1986, he was joined by Cam Neely (who arrived in a trade from Vancouver), who would spend 10 seasons in Boston (like Bourque, he would be elected to the Hockey Hall of Fame). The team would reach the Stanley Cup Finals in 1988 and 1990. The 1994–95 season would be the Bruins' last at the venerable Boston Garden. The team moved into the Fleet Center (now known as the TD Garden) at the beginning of the 1995–96 season. In 1996–97, the Bruins missed the playoffs for the first time in 30 years; their streak had set the record for the most consecutive postseason appearances by a North American professional sports team.

On January 1, 2010, the Bruins won the 2010 NHL Winter Classic, defeating the Philadelphia Flyers in overtime, 2–1, at Fenway Park.

Until the 2010–11 season, the Bruins failed to qualify for the playoffs in five of the previous 12 seasons. During the last four seasons, the team has returned to the playoffs, but only made it past the conference semifinals in 2010–11, when they faced the Vancouver Canucks in the Stanley Cup Final. Boston beat the Canucks 4–0 in Game 7, winning the Stanley Cup for the first time in 39 years.

Outreach and Marketing

As for their work in the community, the Boston Bruins Foundation is a 501(c)(3) nonprofit foundation whose mission is to assist charitable organizations that work with children in New England. Since its inception in July 2003 by the Jacobs family, the foundation has raised more than $5 million through a series of fundraising events. Through its grants to organizations that meet the standards of its mission, the foundation aids athletic, academic, health, and community outreach programs that enrich the lives of children throughout the New England region.

Bruins games are telecast on NESN, which airs approximately 70 games per season. The Bruins own 20 percent of NESN, which is a regional sports network covering New England; the Boston Red Sox own the remaining 80 percent. Bruins coverage includes *Bruins Face-Off Live* (pre-game) and *Bruins Overtime Live* (post-game) shows. There is also a weekly magazine show (*The Instigators*) and a highlights show (*The Buzz*). Radio telecasts are heard on 98.5, the Sports Hub. The team mascot is

Blades the Bear, who wears a Bruins jersey with the number "00." In addition to entertaining at games, Blades makes personal appearances, including at birthday parties.

In 2009–10, the team drew an average of 17,388 spectators (99 percent capacity). This reflects growth since attendance bottomed out in 2006–07, when the team averaged 14,764. The team's improved attendance reflects their improved performance on the ice. In 2009, *Forbes* assessed the team's value at $271 million, making it the sixth most valuable franchise in the NHL. Major corporate sponsors are Anheuser-Busch InBev, Coca-Cola, Verizon Wireless, McDonald's, General Motors, Chipotle, and the Toronto Dominion Bank.

Jeffrey Kraus
Wagner College

See Also: Boston Celtics; Boston Red Sox; Franchise; National Hockey League.

Further Readings

Cusick, Fred. *Fred Cusick: Voice of the Bruins (60 Years of Boston Sports).* Champaign, IL: Sports Publications, 2006.
McFarlane, Brian. *The Bruins.* Toronto: Stoddart Publishing, 1999.
Simpson, Rob. *Black and Gold: Four Decades of the Boston Bruins in Photographs.* Mississauga, Canada: John Wiley & Sons Canada, 2008.

Boston Celtics

The Boston Celtics are a charter National Basketball Association (NBA) franchise, and the team that has won more titles (17) than any other in the NBA. Known for its parquet floor, the team dominated the league from the mid-1950s to the mid-1980s (winning 16 of its titles during this period). The team then fell into a period of decline, which ended in 2007 when key acquisitions restored the Celtics to elite status within the NBA.

Beginnings

The Celtics began as a franchise in the Basketball Association of America (BAA) in 1946 and became part of the NBA when the BAA merged with the National Basketball League in 1949. The team was owned by Walter A. Brown, the manager of the Boston Garden (where the team played its home games) and president of the Boston Athletic Association, the group that organized the Boston Marathon. The team played its first home game at the Boston Arena and continued to play some games there, when the Boston Garden was not available, until 1955. From that point (except for the games the team played at the Hartford Civic Center between 1975 and 1995), the Boston Garden would be home to the team until the facility closed in 1995.

In 1950, Brown hired Arnold "Red" Auerbach to be the coach. Auerbach began building the Celtic dynasty, picking up Bob Cousy when the Chicago Stags (the team that held Cousy's draft rights) folded in 1951, and drafting Tom Heinsohn and Bill Russell in 1956. He would later add players like K. C. Jones, Sam Jones, and John Havlicek, strengthening his dynastic team.

The Celtics won their first NBA championship in 1957. After losing in the 1958 NBA finals, the Celtics would win eight consecutive NBA titles. After the 1965–66 season, Auerbach turned over the coaching duties to Russell (who served as player-coach) while remaining general manager. The Celtics won two more championships in 1968 and 1969 (giving the 11 in 13 seasons).

Ownership Changes

After two decades of ownership stability, the team went through a period of 10 different ownership groups during an 18-year period. In June 1965, the team was sold by Brown's estate to Marvin Kratter, who bought the team to serve as a promotion vehicle in New England for Knickerbocker Beer, which he owned. Kratter sold to P. Ballantine and Sons Brewery in 1968. Ballantine then sold the team for $6 million in 1969 (the highest price paid for an NBA franchise up to that time) to Trans National Communications.

When Trans National defaulted on a payment in 1971, the franchise reverted to Ballantine. Robert Schmertz bought the Celtics in 1972 and sold 50 percent of the team in 1975 to Harold Lipton and Irving Levin. Following Schmertz's death, Lipton and Levin took control of the franchise in November 1975. In 1978, ownership of the team was swapped with the owners of the Buffalo Braves, John Y. Brown, Jr., and Harry Mangurian (allowing Levin to then move the Braves to San Diego, where he lived). Brown sold out to Mangurian the following year, and he later sold the team in 1983 to a partnership of Don Gaston, Alan N. Cohen, and Paul Dupee, bringing stability to ownership.

Russell retired after the 1968–69 season. Tom Heinsohn, Russell's teammate, replaced him as coach, and the team failed to make the playoffs for the first time in 20 years. Auerbach would draft Jo Jo White (1969) and Dave Cowens (1970), and trade for Paul Silas, creating the nucleus of a team that would win NBA titles in 1974 and 1976.

Larry Bird

Larry Bird was drafted by Auerbach with the sixth pick in the 1978 NBA draft. Bird remained in school for his senior year, leading Indiana State to the NCAA finals where they lost to Magic Johnson and Michigan State. Bird joined the Celtics for the 1979–80 season. Auerbach traded for M. L. Carr and signed Gerald Henderson from the Continental Basketball Association (joining Dave Cowens, who had helped lead the team to championships in 1974 and 1976), turning the team around. The team had won 29 games in 1977–78; in Bird's first year, the team won 61 games in the regular season before losing to Philadelphia in the Eastern Conference Finals.

Before the 1980–81 season, Auerbach traded for Robert Parish (who replaced Cowens as center after his retirement) and drafted Kevin McHale. The Celtics won the 1981 NBA Championship, and again became one of the top teams in the league. The team won again in 1984 and 1986.

In 1986 the Celtics drafted Len Bias out of the University of Maryland with the second pick in the NBA draft. Bias was seen as a likely NBA superstar who would keep the Celtics among the NBA's elite as Bird, Parish, and McHale reached the end of their careers. However, Bias died 48 hours after he was drafted, after using cocaine at a party and overdosing. While remaining competitive into the early

1990s, injuries to Bird and others often resulted in early playoff exits for the Celtics.

The End of an Era

Bird retired in the summer of 1992 (after playing for the "Dream Team" in the Olympics), McHale retired a year later, and Parish signed with the Charlotte Hornets in 1994. Reggie Lewis, seen as a successor to Bird, died of a heart attack during the summer of 1993 while shooting baskets at Brandeis University. The 1994–95 season would be the Celtics' last at the venerable Boston Garden. The team moved into the Fleet Center (now known as the TD Garden) at the beginning of the 1995–96 season. The team finished 33–49 in its new home, and did worse the following year (15–67). Paul Gaston (who had taken control of the team from his father) hired Rick Pitino in 1997 as team president, director of basketball operations, and head coach, forcing Auerbach out of the presidency. However, despite drafting Paul Pierce (1998), Pitino failed to lead the Celtics back to dominance and resigned in 2001.

In 2003, the Celtics were sold by owner Paul Gaston to Boston Basketball Partners LLC, led by H. Irving Grousbeck, Wycliffe Grousbeck, Steve Pagliuca, Robert Epstein, David Epstein, and John Svenson. The partnership hired Danny Ainge (who had played on the 1984 and 1986 championship teams) as general manager.

In 2007, Ainge acquired Ray Allen from Seattle and Kevin Garnett from Minnesota. The team, which had won 24 games in 2006–07, had the best record in the NBA during the regular season (66–16). They defeated the Los Angeles Lakers in six games. In 2009 the Celtics lost to Orlando in the Eastern Conference Finals. In 2010, despite injuries to key players, the Celtics were able to make it back to the finals, losing in seven games to the Lakers.

Marketing the Celtics

The Celtics' success on the parquet floor has led to an increase in attendance, as the team is again playing to sold-out houses as was the case during the Larry Bird era. As the team's CEO Rich Gotham said in a 2007 interview, "Winning is the best marketing, and the second-best marketing is the hope of winning." Therefore, their marketing has focused on engaging fans beyond those in the seats, while

many other programs (mainly ticket discount programs) have been eliminated.

Like other teams, the primary goal of the Celtic's online efforts is to drive people to their Website. Celtics.com features GameTime Live, an application that features real-time scores, tweets, and blogging with supporters throughout the world. There is also a Celtics YouTube Channel, a Facebook fan page, and a Twitter feed.

As for their work in the community and for charity, the Boston Celtics Shamrock Foundation is a 501(c)(3) nonprofit foundation that supports nonprofit organizations providing healthcare, shelter, and other vital services for New England children.

Celtics games are telecast on Comcast SportsNet New England, which airs approximately 70 games per season. Radio broadcasts are heard on WEEI (850 AM). The team mascot is Lucky the Leprechaun. Lucky provides in-game entertainment and makes appearances throughout New England.

In 2009–10, the team drew an average of 18,169 spectators (97.6 percent capacity). This reflects a slight decline from the two previous seasons (18,624) when the team sold out all 41 home games. In 2000–01, the team drew an average of 15,346 spectators. That season, the Celtics were 36–46 and failed to make the playoffs. In 2009, *Forbes* assessed the team's value at $433 million, the eighth most valuable franchise in the NBA. Major corporate sponsors are Comcast, Anheuser-Busch InBev, PepsiCo, Lexus, adidas, and Ford.

Jeffrey Kraus
Wagner College

See Also: Boston Bruins; Boston Red Sox; Draft System; National Basketball Association.

Further Readings

Araton, Harvey and Filip Bondy. *The Selling of the Green: The Financial Rise and Moral Decline of the Boston Celtics.* New York: HarperCollins, 1992.
Greenfield, Jeff. *The World's Greatest Team: A Portrait of the Boston Celtics, 1957–1969.* New York: Random House, 1976.

Hilton, Jodi. "Celtics Chief Sees Winning as the Best Marketing Tool." http://www.boston.com/business/articles/2007/10/28/celtics_chief_sees_winning_as_the_best_marketing_tool (Accessed September 2010).

May, Peter. *The Last Banner: The Story of the 1985–86 Celtics, the NBA's Greatest Team of All Time.* New York: Simon & Schuster, 1996.

May, Peter. *Top of the World: The Inside Story of the Boston Celtics' Amazing One-Year Turnaround to Become NBA Champions.* New York: Da Capo Press, 2008.

Russell, Bill. *Red and Me: My Coach, My Lifelong Friend.* New York: Harper Collins, 2009.

Whalen, Thomas J. *Dynasty's End: Bill Russell and the 1968–69 Boston Celtics.* Lebanon, NH: Northeastern University Press, 2004.

Boston Red Sox

The Boston Red Sox are one of the oldest franchises in Major League Baseball (MLB). They play their home games in Fenway Park, which is the oldest venue utilized by a professional sport franchise in the United States. The club was founded in 1901 as part of the newly established American League. The franchise has a rich history, having won the first contested World Series in 1903 and numerous other championships in its first 18 years of existence.

However, despite their early success and the presence of numerous Hall of Fame players on most of their teams, the franchise would fail to win a championship from 1919 to 2004. During those years, many fans became worried that they might never witness a Red Sox World Series victory, especially since many of their critical games were lost because of unusual and agonizing occurrences.

Once the 2004 team was improbably able to overcome a 3–0 deficit in the American League Championship Series, the team crushed the St. Louis Cardinals in the World Series. After waiting decades for the 2004 championship, the Red Sox rewarded their fans with another World Series victory in 2007.

Curse of the Bambino

During the 1910s, the Boston Red Sox were the most successful MLB team. Led by star pitcher/outfielder Babe Ruth, the team dominated the 1916 and 1918 seasons while winning the World Series both seasons. Though Ruth's talents were obvious, Red Sox owner Harry Frazee sold Ruth to the New York Yankees to address some financial issues and also to finance what would eventually become the Broadway play *No, No, Nanette.* The immediate effect of the Ruth sale was the shift of power in the American League. Behind Ruth's tremendous home runs, the Yankees became the dominant team of the 1920s, while the Red Sox's performance floundered.

The sale of the greatest player in baseball history was believed by many to have "cursed" the Red Sox. Despite their poor performance in the 1920s and early 1930s, the arrival of star outfielder Ted Williams and other prominent players energized the Red Sox and their fans. Williams was able to lead the Red Sox to many successful seasons, but each of them fell short of a World Series championship—often directly because the team could not beat the Yankees. Though Ted Williams retired in 1960, the team was optimistic that young outfielder Carl Yastrzemski could overcome the "curse" and lead the team to a title. During Yastrzemski's career, the Red Sox continued to fail to win a World Series, while the Yankees continued to win championships. In 1978, the Red Sox fielded one of their best teams, but lost a 14-game lead in the standings that resulted in a regular season tie with the Yankees. In the one-game playoff, light-hitting Yankee shortstop Bucky Dent blasted a three-run 7th inning homer to lead the Yankees to a 5–4 victory.

The Red Sox continued to struggle in their quest for a championship. They lost the 1986 World Series to the New York Mets when they surrendered a two-run 10th inning lead as Ray Knight scored the winning run when Mookie Wilson's slow grounder rolled through first baseman Bill Buckner's legs. In 2003, it appeared the Red Sox might finally end the Ruth curse, but the Yankees tied the game after trailing 5–2 in the 8th inning of Game 7 of the American League Championship Series. With the

The Boston Red Sox, a storied MLB franchise dating to 1901, plays in the oldest venue used in U.S. professional sports.

memory of Bucky Dent in the mind of every Yankee and Red Sox fan, third baseman Aaron Boone hit an 11th-inning game-winning homer.

World Series Championship—Finally

After the crushing loss in 2003, the 2004 Red Sox had a successful regular season, but they quickly fell behind the Yankees 3–0 in the American League Championship Series. In Game 4, the Yankees entered the 9th inning with a 4–3 lead and the majority of observers thinking once again the Red Sox would fall short. However, the Red Sox were able to mount an improbable comeback to win. They repeated their late inning heroics in Game 5 and then dominated the Yankees in Games 6 and 7 to become the first team in MLB history to overcome a 3–0 playoff deficit. The 2004 World Series was anticlimactic as the Red Sox easily swept the St. Louis Cardinals 4–0. The championship triggered huge celebrations among "Red Sox Nation" as many fans were in disbelief that they had won the World Series, and with a playoff victory over the hated Yankees as an added bonus.

The Red Sox have continued to build upon their 2004 championship, both on the field and in the front office. The team won the World Series again in

2007, and tickets to Red Sox games in Fenway Park are among the most difficult to procure in sports. The franchise has also been aggressive in its marketing efforts both in New England and the rest of the world. When the Red Sox play a road game, there are typically thousands of Red Sox fans in attendance, and broadcasts of the team's games in the United States and in foreign countries like Japan are among the most popular in Major League Baseball.

Mark S. Nagel
University of South Carolina

See Also: Attendance, Impact of Winning on; Major League Baseball; New York Yankees; World Series.

Further Readings

Boston Red Sox Official Website. http://boston.redsox.mlb.com (Accessed February 2010).
Golenbock, Peter. *Red Sox Nation.* Chicago: Triumph Books, 2005.
Mnookin, Seth. *Feeding the Monster.* New York: Simon & Schuster, 2006.

Bowl Championship Series

For those interested in pursuing careers in college sport administration, working in sport media, or developing marketing plans for intercollegiate athletic programs, having a fundamental understanding of the Bowl Championship Series (BCS) is essential. This entry introduces the Bowl Championship Series, offers an overview of the relationship between the BCS and the National Collegiate Athletic Association (NCAA), and covers the controversy over the lack of a playoff system for the nation's elite college football programs.

According to BCS materials, it is not an entity but an event. Further, the BCS is an arrangement that manages five of the most high-profile and lucrative college football postseason bowl games or properties, including the Tostitos Fiesta Bowl, FedEx Orange Bowl, Rose Bowl, Allstate Sugar Bowl, and the

National Championship Game. The stated purpose of the BCS is twofold: to match up the two highest ranking teams to compete in the national championship game while also creating competitive and exciting pairings in the remaining bowls featuring highly ranked teams.

As a business venture, the BCS is managed by the commissioners of the 11 conferences that make up the NCAA Football Bowl Subdivision (FBS), the athletic director at the University of Notre Dame (which remains an independent in the sport of football), and representatives from each of the bowl organizations. The FBS conferences, which represent 120 of the nation's elite college football programs, include the Atlantic Coast, Big East, Big Ten, Big 12, Conference USA, Mid-American, Mountain West, Sun Belt, Pacific-10, Southeastern, and Western Athletic. Decisions made by the BCS management team are done in consultation with an advisory board comprising FBS directors of athletics and are subject to the approval of a presidential oversight committee.

The BCS's preference for the term *arrangement* alludes to its contractual agreements, which form the basis for its authority and relationships. Those include:

- The actual BCS agreement with its member conferences, the University of Notre Dame, and three bowl games (the Fiesta, Orange, and Sugar)
- A contract between the Big Ten, Pac-10, and the Rose Bowl
- A contract between the Rose Bowl and ABC
- Multiple contracts between the BCS conferences and Notre Dame and their television partners, Fox Sports and ESPN/ABC

The value of the BCS can be assessed in several ways. Estimates indicate that the total economic impact of the five games in the host cities for 2009 was more than $1.2 billion, while revenue available for distribution to BCS conference schools amounted to just under $150 million. A new four-year television deal with ESPN starting in January 2011 guarantees $125 million per year, marking the first time that BCS games will be covered by a cable network instead of a major network. Other aspects of the deal give ESPN rights to rebroadcast past BCS games on ESPNU and ESPN Classic, while also awarding the network exclusive radio, digital, international, and marketing rights to the games.

The BCS and the NCAA

Outside observers often wonder what the relationship is between the BCS and the NCAA. Although the NCAA is clear that no revenues from the BCS are shared with the association, nevertheless there is a shared interlocking power base between the two organizations, as seen in the fact that the FBS conferences and institutions that make up the BCS also dominate the decision-making structure within the NCAA. Despite the ties that bind the two organizations, the BCS exists as a result of a dispute between the football powers and the NCAA dating back to the 1970s.

Signaling an escalation in pressures to win and a need to better control the athletes producing on the field, the effects of the television age were being revealed during this decade in the rule-making structure of the NCAA. Two of the most significant changes included alterations to rules governing athletic scholarships where four-year awards were converted to one-year awards renewable at the discretion of the coach. It was also during this time that the association reorganized its membership, leading to the three-tier divisional structure the NCAA has today, with Division I representing the institutions with the highest reliance on external sources of revenue, more media exposure, and a commitment to a spectator-oriented college sport product compared to Divisions II and III, which are more committed to student-centered models of college sport and a reliance on revenue coming from institutional sources. NCAA Division I is further split into the Football Bowl Subdivision (FBS) and the Football Championship Subdivision (FCS).

Frustrated by limits placed on the number of times the best teams would be televised under the existing contract the NCAA had negotiated with ABC, and receiving little satisfaction to appeals to expand those opportunities, the top football programs set out to challenge the NCAA, alleging it was operating as a monopoly in violation of antitrust laws. In the end, the football powers won out, setting the stage for the emergence of the BCS and the consolidation of access to decision making, power, and money among a smaller and smaller group of football playing institutions over time.

BCS Controversy

The BCS has been roundly criticized over the years for establishing a system of selecting the teams to play in the national championship game without a playoff. It has further been the source of controversy because of the method of automatic qualification through which top teams gain access to the coveted BCS bowl berths, which leaves little opportunity for at-large teams to be considered, regardless of their records. FBS officials argue that this system is necessary because, unlike professional sports, college football does not have one league but is a constellation of many leagues. Because of the historic relationships these leagues have had with established postseason bowls, combined with the magnitude of regular season media coverage, FBS leaders have shied away from establishing a playoff system.

Regardless of the BCS defense of the system in place, there are yearly disputes over the fairness of the selection process and the potential bias that exists favoring the power elites. Calls to remedy the situation have been made at times by prominent government leaders, most famously newly elected U.S. President Barack Obama in 2009, in response to schools with undefeated seasons being passed over for the prestige postseason bowls by teams in more powerful conferences with lower rankings and lower winning percentages. Concerns abound that the BCS violates the Sherman Antitrust Act by reducing competition and unfairly allocating the revenue generated by the BCS.

Ellen J. Staurowsky
Ithaca College

See Also: Bowl Games; National Collegiate Athletic Association; Rose Bowl.

Further Readings

Bowl Championship Series Official Website. http://www.bcsfootball.org (Accessed November 2009).

Dunnavant, Keith. *The 50 Year Seduction: How Television Manipulated College Football.* New York: St. Martin's Press, 2004.
"ESPN Official Signs Deal for BCS Games Beginning In 2011." *SportsBusiness Daily* http://www.sportsbusinessdaily.com/Daily/Issues/2008/11/Issue-46/Sports-Media/ESPN-Officially-Signs-Deal-For-BCS-Games-Beginning-In-2011.aspx (Accessed April 2011).
Hatch, Orrin. "Leveling the Playing Field." *Sports Illustrated* (July 6, 2009).
Oriard, M. *Bowled Over: Big-Time College Football From the Sixties to the BCS ERA.* Chapel Hill: University of North Carolina Press, 2009.

Bowl Games

Festive, fun, and filled with anticipation, the tradition of bowl games in the sport of college football has been around for over a century. The expression *bowl* derives from the shape of football stadiums, the template for which was created at Yale University and emulated by others over time. Dating back to 1902, powerhouse Michigan stepped to the scrimmage line opposite Stanford in a game held on New Year's Day, hosted by the Tournament of Roses in Pasadena, California. Michigan handily won that day by a score of 49–0, claiming title as the National Champions. Pictures of the game show spectators either crowding around the ropes that cordoned off the field or sitting in horse-drawn carriages just a few feet further removed from the venue. Out of that memorable east versus west contest arose the game now famously nicknamed "The Granddaddy of Them All"—the Rose Bowl.

Bowl games epitomize high-stakes contests that occur at any point in the college football calendar year. The Wheat Bowl, for example, is a pre-season event sanctioned by the National Association of Intercollegiate Athletics (NAIA). In comparison, the Amos Alonzo Stagg Bowl serves as the site for the National Collegiate Athletic Association (NCAA) Division III football title game, while the Victory

Bowl is the championship for teams that are members of the National Christian College Athletic Association (NCCAA). Canadian universities, as members of either NCAA Division II or Interuniversity Sport (CIS) (the governing body for college sport in Canada), also participate in bowl games, with CIS sponsoring a semi-final round of games between the top four teams with the championship decided at the Vanier Cup Game.

While team bragging rights and good television serve as the basis for most bowl games, the bowl game formula has also been applied to events that showcase senior talent. As a prelude to the National Football League (NFL) draft, professional football prospects are featured in events such as the East-West Shrine Game, the Senior Bowl, and the Texas vs. the Nation Bowl. The best NCAA Division III players are selected to play in the Aztec Bowl, which is held in Mexico.

Regular season rivalries have also been marketed as bowl games in an effort to capture the regional politics represented in particular games and capitalize on the economic potential they represent. Thus, fierce loyalists of the Auburn Tigers and the Alabama Crimson Tide gather to witness the confrontation that takes place in the Iron Bowl the day after Thanksgiving. The Bayou Classic, known as Black America's biggest football game, similarly provides a national showcase for Grambling and Southern universities, replete with its pageantry and Battle of the Bands.

As a business model, postseason bowl games serve as a point around which local host communities, corporate sponsors, national media, and major athletic conferences converge. The college bowl structure is unique in sport. Whereas teams vying for national championships in the NCAA Football Championship Subdivision (formerly Division I-AA), Division II, and Division III participate in single-elimination tournaments leading to a final winner, teams in the most competitive division within the NCAA, the Football Bowl Subdivision (FBS), studiously avoid a playoff system, opting instead for a ranking system that is used to determine bowl eligibility, and ultimately, the winner.

The Bowl Championship Series, managed by commissioners from the 11 conferences that comprise the Football Bowl Subdivision along with the independent University of Notre Dame, represents an arrangement between the conferences and five bowls—the Fiesta Bowl, the Orange Bowl, the Rose Bowl, and the Sugar Bowl—and the BCS National Championship Game. Six of the 11 BCS conferences receive automatic bids for the winners of their conferences, while one automatic bid is reserved for a team from one of the other five remaining FBS conferences that meets additional eligibility criteria. In order for Notre Dame to receive an automatic qualification, it must be among the top eight teams in the BCS rankings.

Although the BCS controls access to the national championship game and the economic benefits associated with it, creating considerable debate about fairness and potential restraint of trade, there has been a proliferation of postseason bowl games during the past 20 years. In 2009–10, 68 teams representing over half of all FBS institutions were awarded berths to 34 bowls. Regardless of whether the method of determining bowl-eligible teams is based on merit or conference alignments, the value of participating in a postseason bowl for competing schools, conferences, and host cities is considerable.

Financial Benefits

While coaches and higher education officials argue that the experience of playing in a bowl game is an excellent learning opportunity for athletes and one that hardworking teams deserve, the financial benefit is clearly a key consideration. Reports indicate that over $228 million from bowl games was distributed to BCS and non-BCS institutions through conference revenue sharing plans for 2008–09.

Conferences and athletic departments are not the only ones that reap the financial rewards of bowl games. The appeal for host cities resides in the capacity of the games to draw a guaranteed number of travelers from outside of the city or region during a time of year when business is slow. Given the demographic, which is well-educated and middle to upper class, a bowl game can mean significant revenue in the form of direct visitor spending (for example, money spent at the game, in nearby restaurants and bars) and indirect visitor spending (for example, money spent by local businesses to support visitors when they are in town). For those who argue that sport events can serve as an important aspect of an economic development plan for a city, the value of an event goes beyond the immediate economic impact through greater exposure to more visitors and positive word-of-mouth marketing, media coverage for the city on national television and in multimedia platforms, and a source of civic pride. It has been estimated that college bowls generate $1.3 billion worth of economic impact annually for host cities.

Ellen J. Staurowsky
Ithaca College

See Also: Bowl Championship Series; National Collegiate Athletic Association; Rose Bowl.

Further Readings

"The BCS Is . . . ." Fox Sports. (July 13, 2009). http://www.bcsfootball.org (Accessed June 2009).

Davis, Kimberly. "The Bayou Classic: Black America's Biggest Football Game: Grambling State and Southern Continue a 30-Year Tradition." *Ebony* (November 2003).

Hawkins, Nicole. "State Farm Bayou Classic— More Than A Game: A Full Slate of Events Scheduled Beginning November 27, 2009." Press Release. (November 9, 2009).

"Local Bowl Games Produce Economic Impact For Region." Poinsettia Bowl.com (May 9, 2008). http://www.poinsettiabowl.com/news/local-bowl -games-produce-economic-impact-for-region .html (Accessed November 2009).

National Collegiate Athletic Association. "Behind the Blue Disk—Football: Bowl Championship Series." (November 8, 2008). http://www.ncaa .org (Accessed November 2009).

National Collegiate Athletic Association. "Financial Review of 2008–2009 Postseason Bowls: 5-Year Summary of Gross Receipts." http://www.ncaa .org (Accessed November 2009).

Outback Bowl. "College Bowl Games . . . Where Everybody Wins." http://www.outbackbowl .com/facts/collegegames.html (Accessed November 2009).

Tournament of Roses. "Tournament of Roses History." http://www.tournamentofroses.com/ history (Accessed November 2009).

Brand Association

For sport management and marketing professionals, understanding brand associations is important, as they represent what individuals think of, or have stored in their memory, for a particular brand. Typically, brand associations are also the first thoughts that come to someone's mind when they see the brand logo or name. For example, if an individual were to see the New York Yankees logo, the first things that might come to mind may include items such as the current or former players on the team, the history of the team, images of the city of New York, or how well the team is performing. These thoughts are what form the image that person has for the team.

Brand associations are a vital component of brand equity, are often used when making purchase decisions, and are the basis of a consumer's formation of loyalty toward a brand. Because of the important role brand associations play in consumer behavior, it is necessary to understand what types of brand associations exist both in and outside of sport management and marketing.

Brand associations can take on a number of different forms, each playing an important role in determining whether a consumer or fan will have a positive or negative evaluation of the brand. The first are called attributes and relate to items necessary for the product or service to function, or associations that consumers might have that related to the purchase of the particular product. Some examples might include the packaging or product appearance, what type of people typically use the product, in what type of situations the product is used, country of origin, or the price of a particular product. For example, if someone were deciding on which brand of golf clubs to purchase, clubs with a higher price may be associated with high quality. He or she may also choose one whose club head is bigger, which could be an example of a product appearance association, as he or she may associate the larger club head with a club that is easier to use and hit the ball with.

Another category is benefit associations, which are simply what value an individual places on what the product or service provides to him or her. These associations could serve a variety of purposes. They could be functional benefits, as the brand allows the individual to meet his or her basic needs. For example, those that engage in some sort of sports activity typically will need to rehydrate themselves. There are a number of different brands of sport drinks that have built functional associations by claiming to have the ability to quench an athlete's thirst and provide energy. Benefit associations could also take the form of experiential benefits, which are what needs are met by actually experiencing the product or brand. For example, experiencing a live sporting event may provide entertainment, excitement, a stress release, or any number of other benefits to those in attendance. Finally, benefit associations may also be symbolic. One such example may be expensive luxury seating at sporting events. Sitting in this section could be seen as a way to demonstrate one's wealth because of the high-end associations that are typically attached to this type of seating at sporting events.

While many associations will develop based on the attributes of a particular product or service as discussed above, associations may also derive from the organization itself. In professional sport, many teams will develop associations based on how the organization operates. For example, a team that spends a lot of money on player salaries may be considered to be associated with being high-class and committed to winning by some. However, some may also then associate this same team with being greedy or overspending on players. Brand associations may also take the form of human characteristics. It is possible that sport brands will have associations and be described in a similar fashion to how one might describe an individual's personality. For example, extreme sport brands might be described as being young, flashy, hip, or anti-establishment. Often, teams are also described in this way. For example, some associations used to describe team brands might be tough, hard-nosed, winners, or losers.

While there are a number of different types of brand associations outlined above, there has been some effort to identify categories of brand associations as they relate to team sport brands. In general, the following are the different items that have been identified as types of brand associations that individuals may hold for sport teams: the quality, success, or performance of the team and players; the history of the team; the commitment the team shows toward the fans; the organizational attributes not associated with the team itself (e.g., ownership, coaches, etc.); the facility the team plays in; the city or surrounding area where the team plays; the style of play and personality the team exhibits; the team's logo and colors and what they stand for; the ability to socialize with friends during the team's games; the team's fan base and how loyal they are in following the team; and the team's competitors.

No matter what the category of association, it is important that organizations attempt to create brand associations that are strong, favorable, and unique. Creating these positive brand associations will allow an organization to develop positive brand equity, which for a consumer-based sport brand could influence purchase and brand loyalty. For a team sport brand these positive associations could ultimately influence

Sports drinks are an example of a product that often accrues brand associations related to functional benefits.

items such as media exposure, team loyalty, and the team's overall ability to generate revenue through the sale of items such as tickets, corporate sponsorship, and team merchandise.

Patrick Walsh
Indiana University

See Also: Brand Awareness; Brand Equity; Brand Image; Brand Personality; Brand Preference; Branding; Image.

Further Readings

Aaker, David. *Building Strong Brands.* New York: Free Press, 1996.

Gladden, James and Daniel Funk. "Developing an Understanding of Brand Associations in Team Sport: Empirical Evidence From Consumers of Professional Sport." *Journal of Sport Management,* v.16 (2002).

Keller, Kevin. "Conceptualizing, Measuring, and Managing Customer-Based Brand Equity." *Journal of Marketing,* v.57/1 (1993).

Ross, Stephen, et al. "Development of a Scale to Measure Team Brand Associations in Professional Sport." *Journal of Sport Management,* v.20/2 (2006).

Brand Awareness

As defined by the *Business Dictionary*, brand awareness is the ability for potential consumers to correctly associate a brand and product. In other words, brand awareness refers to the consumer's awareness of the company, brand, and product. Without company, brand, or product recognition, potential consumers will not have much information about where to go to satisfy needs or wants. Thus, without brand awareness, the primary goal of any business entity, which is to drive profits, cannot be achieved.

Many sport marketers see the brand awareness process as the initial point in developing brand eq-

uity. Brand equity refers to the recognition a brand earns through time. As brand equity becomes established, businesses often see increases in revenues. Of course, this is simply explained, as the likelihood of a consumer purchasing a product increases as he or she becomes more aware of the company, brand, or product. Upon the establishment of a recognizable brand, marketers strive to move consumers to a higher level of company, product, or brand commitment. In other words, the marketers want to position their products in a manner so that consumers will prefer a single brand over others when given the opportunity. This is known as brand preference. A marketer ultimately strives to establish brand insistence or a level of consumer involvement in which a consumer only buys one brand.

How do marketers go about creating a brand? Nearly all successful brands begin with researching and understanding the four Cs of marketing: company, consumer, competitor, and climate. It is crucial that clear mission, goals, and objectives are formulated early in the marketing plan. This will guide marketers in establishing the message that they would like to portray in their company, brand, or product. Equally important is the ability to understand the needs and desires of a clearly defined target audience, or the intended product consumer population. By conducting thorough market research on the company, consumers, competitors and climate, marketers can then begin developing the sport marketing mix (product, place, price, promotion, and public relations) specific to the company, brand, and product. This includes but is not limited to establishing names, logos, slogans, distribution points, advertising campaigns, packaging plans, sales plans, and media and community relations campaigns.

Once brand awareness has been achieved, the marketer's concerns should be aimed at maintaining or enhancing the recognition. A fundamental concept in achieving and maintaining brand awareness is consistency of the company, brand, and product. In addition to consistency, marketers need to continuously evaluate their plans so that positive points can be further accentuated while negative aspects can be eliminated. Evaluations should be tailored to the company, product, and brand, and new methods to generate awareness should be produced. Boosting awareness may be done via numerous methods; however, some tips for boosting awareness include: focusing on attributes that will gain media attention, becoming skilled at e-mail campaigns, incorporating technologies such as social networking and text messaging, and winning and incorporating awards into press releases.

Conclusion

In a marketplace that is vast and growing, it is critical to examine the sport product and differentiate it from other competitors. Brand awareness is an initial step in establishing a niche in the marketplace. However, marketers cannot begin to create a brand awareness campaign without first researching and understanding the company, consumer, competitor, and climate. Over time, brand awareness will lead to brand equity. Ideally, after establishing brand equity, consumers will have a positive image of a company, product, or brand. As a result, the likelihood of product purchases increases.

Christina L. L. Martin
Troy University

See Also: Brand Association; Brand Equity; Brand Image; Brand Insistence; Brand Personality; Brand Preference; Branding; Image.

Further Readings

Carmichael, Evan. "Effectively Using PR Tactics: Seven Tips to Boost Brand Awareness." http://www.evancarmichael.com/Public-Relations/239/Effectively-Using-PR-Tactics--Seven-Tips-To-Boost-Brand-Awareness.html (Accessed September 2010).

Gustafson, Tara and Brian Chaot. "The Cornell Maple Program." http://www.nnyagdev.org/maplefactsheets/CMB%20105%20Brand%20Awareness.pdf (Accessed September 2010).

Mullin, Bernard J., Stephen Hardy, and William A. Sutton. *Sport Marketing*, 3rd Ed. Champaign, IL: Human Kinetics, 2007.

Pitts, Brenda and David Stotlar. *Fundamentals of Sport Marketing*, 3rd ed. Morgantown, WV: Fitness Information Technology, 2007.

Brand Equity

Brand equity is the concept in marketing that refers to the added value endowed to a product or service. Brand equity and related research began to gain attention in the late 1980s in general business management. Gradually, many sport managers saw that brand equity can be essential in achieving organizational goals; it is now applied widely in the sport business industry. Establishing and strengthening brand equity have become a marketing priority in many businesses. When product differentiation is no longer the key profit margin generator to the company, developing the brand and brand differentiation is the primary solution. In this entry, the key theories of brand equity in general business and in sport industry will be introduced.

Marketers and researchers use various perspectives to explore brand equity. David Aaker is one of the most familiar names in the field of brand management. In his 1991 managing brand equity model, he views brand equity as a set of five categories of assets and liabilities linked to brand that add or subtract from the value provided by the product or service to the firm and/or to the firm's customers. The five categories are: brand awareness, brand associations, perceived quality, brand loyalty, and other proprietary brand assets.

Brand awareness is the degree to which consumers automatically think of a brand when a given category is mentioned. Brand associations are anything in a consumer's memory linked to a specific brand. Perceived quality is the customer's perception of the overall quality or superiority of a product or service with respect to its intended purpose, relative to alternatives. Brand loyalty consists of a consumer's commitment to repurchase or continue using the brand. It can be displayed by repeated purchasing of a product or service or other positive behaviors such as word-of-mouth advocacy. Other proprietary brand assets are patents, trademarks, and channel relationships. Brand assets will be most valuable if they inhibit or prevent competitors from diluting the customer base and customer loyalty. These assets can perform in several ways. For example, a trademark will protect brand equity from competitors who might want to confuse customers by using a similar name, symbol, or package. If a patent is strong and relevant to customer choice, it can prevent direct competition.

Aaker states that brands are a company's key assets. Building a strong brand requires careful planning and great deal of long-term investment. At the heart of a successful brand is a great product or service, backed by a creatively designed and executed marketing campaign. Consequently, brand equity provides value to customers by enhancing their confidence in their purchase decision. On the other hand, it provides value to organizations by enhancing the efficiency and effectiveness of marketing programs and improving brand loyalty, margins, trade leverage, and competitive advantage.

Customer-based brand equity can be defined as the different effect that brand knowledge has on a customer's response to marketing of the brand. Kevin Lane Keller includes three key points in his definition of customer-based brand equity. First, the "differential effect" must be implemented or the brand is little more than a generic version of the product. Next, the "brand knowledge" that creates the differential effect is influenced by the brand's marketing. However, it settles in the minds of consumers. Third, "consumer response" is the behavior a consumer might display such as repeated purchasing or willingness to pay a price premium, as well as favorable associations related to a given brand.

The differences between Aaker's model and Keller's are that perceived quality and brand loyalty are absent from Keller's framework. Keller sees perceived quality as a product-related association, and brand loyalty as a manifestation of brand equity. He also emphasizes brand associations, suggesting that the type, favorability, strength, and uniqueness of the associations contribute to brand knowledge.

The three major categories of brand associations based on their level of abstraction are attributes, benefits, and attitudes. Attributes are the features of a specific brand. Benefits are the meaning and value consumers attach to the product. Attitudes are the most abstract form of brand associations. The term *attitudes* is defined as a consumer's overall evaluation of the brand, and often depends on the strength and favorability of the attributes and benefits provided by the brand.

From a firm's financial perspective, brand equity is the incremental cash flow resulting from a product with a brand name versus the cash flow that would result without the brand name. Favorable brand equity increases the probability of brand choice, customer retention, higher profit margins, willingness to pay premium prices, marketing communication effectiveness, positive word-of-mouth, brand licensing opportunities, and brand extensions. Overall, studies continually suggest that strong brand equity is important for the organization and product.

Sport Product and Brand Equity

Sport product is unique in many ways. Sport product can be intangible, ephemeral, experiential, and subjective in nature. It can simultaneously be production and consumption, and may depend on social facilitation, leading to inconsistency and unpredictability. The results for some core sport products are beyond marketer control. Therefore, some researchers have utilized brand equity models in the sport management field.

Professional sport is a type of entertainment based on the uncertainty of the results, surrounding promotional activities, and providing an emotional escape for fans, especially when the fans seek social identification among their peers. Teams should utilize brand equity management to satisfy the needs of their fans. It can also help decrease the effects of uncontrollable factors, such as team losses. When franchises build brand equity, managers need to consider the uniqueness of sporting events and match a team's attributes to increase brand equity effectively, ultimately bringing benefits to the organization.

James M. Gladden, George R. Milne, and William A. Sutton have proposed that brand equity be utilized in collegiate sport and professional sport, and they connect their brand equity in the team sport setting framework with David Aaker's brand equity model. They describe four major categories. First, antecedents of equity (team related: success, head coach, star player; organization related: tradition, conference/schedule, product delivery, logo design, stadium/arena; market related: local/regional media coverage, geographic location, competitive forces, team support/following). Second, brand equity dimensions of David Aaker's model (brand awareness, brand associations, perceived quality, and brand loyalty). Third, consequences of equity, including national media exposure, merchandise sales, corporate support, atmosphere, ticket sales, and additional revenues. Finally, marketplace perception will be generated from the previous three categories. The term *marketplace perception* refers to consumer's perception and evaluation of sport product. The four categories in this framework form a continuous feedback loop that can assist franchise managers to understand the foundation of brand management, develop antecedents of equity and process, and consequently to predict benefits.

For understanding spectator-based brand equity, Stephen D. Ross proposed a model modified from a service brand equity study and Gladden et al.'s structure. There are three categories in his framework. The first category is the antecedents, which include organization-induced marketing mix—seven P's, market-induced word-of-mouth, and experience-induced actual consumer experience. The second category uses Keller's brand awareness and brand association. The last category is the consequences that consist of team loyalty, media exposure, merchandise sales, ticket sales, and revenue solicitation.

Another study that also focuses on sport team brands connects brand equity with internationalization. In their framework, André Richelieu, Sten Söderman, and Frank Pons use the brand equity pipeline to illustrate the internationalization of a brand. Along the pipeline, the level of brand equity is on the Y axis and the geographic scale is the X axis. From the low level of brand equity as local brand, teams can move along the pipeline to that of regional brand, national brand, and international brand (continental brand first, then global brand as ultimate level). The team managers realize that an international brand must be strong at home before it considers expanding abroad, which is supported by other studies.

André Richelieu et al. also identify that a successful international sport team will understand the importance of positioning, differentiation, and brand community strategies. The team can take several initiatives to leverage the brand internationally and trigger an emotional connection with its fans.

In summary, the brand equity concept has been discussed and utilized in sport settings and the brand equity model has been developed from several different perspectives. Currently, most studies focus on spectator sport, but the application of the brand equity concept can be seen in a wide range of sport industries.

Doris Lu-Anderson
California State University, Long Beach

See Also: Brand Association; Brand Awareness; Brand Extension; Brand Image; Brand Preference; Branding, Global Sport; Branding; Customer Equity.

Further Readings

Aaker, D. A. "Brand Extension: The Good, the Bad, and the Ugly." *Sloan Management Review,* v.31 (1990).

Aaker, D. A. *Managing Brand Equity: Capitalizing on the Value of a Brand Name.* New York: The Free Press, 1991.

Gladden, J. M. *Evaluating Brand Equity in the Team Sport Setting.* Doctoral Dissertation. Amherst: University of Massachusetts, Amherst, 1997.

Gladden, J. M. and D. C. Funk. "Developing an Understanding of Brand Associations in Team Sport: Empirical Evidence From Consumers of Professional Sport." *Journal of Sport Management,* v.16 (2002).

Gladden, J. M. and G. R. Milne. "Examining the Importance of Brand Equity in Professional Sport." *Sport Marketing Quarterly,* v.8/1 (1999).

Keller, K. L. *Strategic Brand Management: Building, Measuring, and Managing Brand Equity.* Upper Saddle River, NJ: Prentice Hall, 1998.

Mullin, B. J., S. Hardy, and W. A. Sutton. *Sport Marketing,* 3rd ed. Champaign, IL: Human Kinetics, 2008.

Pitts, B. G. and D. K. Stotlar. *Fundamentals of Sport Marketing,* 3rd Ed. Morgantown, WV: Fitness Information Technology, 2008.

Richelieu, A., S. Söderman, and F. Pon. *The Internationalization of a Sports Team Brand: The Case of Football Club Barcelona.* Paper presented at the Sports Marketing Association Annual Conference, Pittsburg, PA: 2007.

Ross, S. "A Conceptual Framework for Understanding Spectator-Based Brand Equity." *Journal of Sport Management,* v.20 (2006).

Brand Extension

When a company uses its brand name and develops a new product or service that exists in a new product category, this is known as a brand extension. For example, a professional sports team's product category could be considered to be sport and entertainment. If a team then opens up a team merchandise store, for example, the Buffalo Bills Pro Shop, this would be considered a brand extension, as the team is extending its brand name from the sport and entertainment product category to the retail product category. The original brand, in this instance the Buffalo Bills, is often called the parent brand. The team in this example is using its pre-existing parent brand name and image to its advantage. The use of brand extensions in sport has increased significantly, particularly within the past decade. There are a number of pros and cons associated with brand extensions, as well as conditions for success. Some examples of brand extensions in team sport include merchandise stores, restaurants, team Websites, television shows, and team publications (e.g., newsletters, team magazines).

There are a number of reasons why a sport organization would introduce brand extensions. First, as costs to operate these organizations continue to rise, brand extensions offer a way to potentially generate additional revenue. They may also enhance the image of the overall brand name, and provide an avenue for fans/consumers of the organization to interact with the brand. This is a positive outcome in particular for teams as consumers previously could only interact with the brand during the team's events. Brand extensions offer significantly more ways for brands to communicate and reach their consumers. However, there are some potential negatives associated with brand extensions, particularly if they fail.

A failed brand extension could negatively impact overall brand equity. For example, if a fan/consumer has a negative experience with the brand extension he or she could develop negative attitudes toward the parent brand. This resulting damage to brand equity could ultimately decrease a fan/consumer's overall behavior and attitudes toward the brand, in turn negatively impacting the brand's ability to generate revenue. In addition, introducing new brand extensions can be costly if they fail. In February 2006 ESPN introduced a new cell phone service (Mobile ESPN) that provided sport content to its subscribers. It was estimated that ESPN spent an estimated $150 million to develop and introduce the extension. Consumers were relatively unresponsive to the new product, purchasing an estimated 5,000–20,000 subscriptions, which was well below ESPN's projections of 250,000 subscribers. However, ESPN has had some successful brand extensions as well, such as its publication *ESPN the Magazine*.

Pros and Cons of Brand Extension

As there are a number of pros and cons associated with brand extensions, it is important for any organization to have a good understanding of how a fan/consumer evaluates a brand extension. Their evaluations are highly related to the attitudes they have for the parent brand. In general, if a fan/consumer has favorable attitudes toward the brand that introduces the extension, the fan will then have favorable attitudes toward the brand extension. For example, if someone thinks highly of the New York Yankees and they introduce a new restaurant, this individual may also tend to think highly of the restaurant. Also, if an individual thinks the parent brand is of high quality, he or she will tend to think that the brand extension is also of high quality. However, this transfer of attitudes and feelings toward the extension may not take place in all instances. For this transfer to take place it is generally supported that the image of the product category of the extension should fit with the image of the product category of the parent brand. For instance, if a football team were to introduce an extension of football equipment this might be considered to be a fit. However, if this same team introduces a line of cologne this may not be considered a fit. Generally, consumers would form more favorable attitudes toward the football extension equipment in this example. Finally, when considering sport team's related extensions it is important to understand how loyal the team's fan base is.

Fans who are very loyal to the team will tend to support a team's brand extension regardless of the items mentioned above, and it would be unlikely that a failed extension would harm the attitudes and purchasing behaviors of these very loyal fans.

Patrick Walsh
Indiana University

See Also: Brand Equity; Brand Image; Brand Insistence; Brand Rejection; Branding.

Further Readings

Aaker, David. *Managing Brand Equity.* New York: Free Press, 1991.

Apostolopoulou, Artemisia. "Brand Extensions by U.S. Professional Sport Teams: Motivations and Keys to Success." *Sport Marketing Quarterly,* v.11/4 (2002).

Bhat, Sobodh and Srinivas Reddy. "The Impact of Parent Brand Attribute Associations and Affect on Brand Extension Evaluation." *Journal of Business Research,* v.53/3 (2001).

Broniarczyk, Susan and Joseph Alba. "The Importance of the Brand in the Brand Extension." *Journal of Marketing Research,* v.31 (1994).

Fisher, Eric and John Ourand. "Flop Hangs an 'L' on ESPN." *Street and Smiths SportsBusiness Journal,* v.9/22 (October 2–8, 2006).

Loken, Barbara and Deborah John. "Diluting Brand Beliefs: When Do Brand Extensions Have a Negative Impact?" *Journal of Marketing,* v.57 (1993).

Brand Image

To fully comprehend the meaning of brand image, one must understand the branding process. First, marketers create awareness of their company's products and services through publicity and promotional efforts. Before even buying a company's products and services, consumers begin to develop opinions and attitudes; in other words, they start to develop a brand image. Second, once the public begins to buy and use a company's unique products and services, the consumer's previous opinions and attitudes are either reinforced or changed. It is consumer opinions and attitudes that set the stage for a positive or negative brand image. Third, if marketers are able to shape a positive brand image, this will eventually lead to creating brand equity. In simple terms, brand equity is the reputation of a company's products and services that consumers hold in comparison to their competitors. Fourth, a positive reputation ultimately leads to consumer brand loyalty.

Brand image can be viewed as traits and qualities. In essence, brand image is the character of products and services. This character can be described as a set of beliefs consumers hold about a brand. These beliefs in turn shape consumer attitudes toward brands. In the end, marketers hope to have created strong, positive attitudes through brand associations. Since brand associations help influence brand image, marketers need to ensure that the messages behind all brand associations are both strong and flattering. To illustrate this point, let's consider a single brand: Mossy Oak.

Mossy Oak is first and foremost a camouflage brand. Through its popular camouflage patterns, it has grown into a multifaceted outdoors icon. The following are some of the associations connected with Mossy Oak that have enhanced its brand image over time:

- *Logo*: A mature, flourishing oak tree
- *Slogan*: "It's Not a Passion. It's An Obsession"
- *Core values*: Spending time with family and friends in the outdoors, being stewards of the land, and supporting conservation initiatives
- *People*: Owner, management team, staff personnel, ProStaff
- *Camouflage patterns*: Break-Up, Break-Up Infinity, Brush, Duck Blind, Obsession, and Treestand
- *Licensees*: Some notable partners are Browning, Leupold, PSE Bows, Polaris, Rocky, Ram Trucks, and Under Amour
- *Biologic wild game products*: Wild game forage seeds for deer, turkey, fish and waterfowl
- *"MOOSE Media"*: Mossy Oak Outdoor Sport and Entertainment that serves as the sales and marketing arm for both Mossy Oak Productions and the Pursuit Channel networks
- *Mossy Oak Productions*: Some production titles include *Hunting the Country, Fist Full of Dirt, Turkey Thugs, Deer Thugs,* and *Ted Nugent Tooth Fang and Claw*

- *Mossy Oak Properties*: Consist of real estate professionals who are dedicated to land stewardship
- *Mossy Oak Land Enhancement Services*: Consist of land management professionals who serve clients in their habitat management goals
- *"Nativ Nurseries"*: Offering a variety of trees that allow landowners and managers the ability to provide natural food for wildlife in their natural habitats
- *Online store*: Just about anything for the outdoors enthusiast
- *ProStaff*: Approximately 900 individuals who attend outdoor events across the country to promote Mossy Oak, hunting, and spending time in the outdoors

Through all these associations, the Mossy Oak brand has become a household name. Mossy Oak continually exposes its brand through consistent press releases, outdoor media CDs, outdoor writer hunts, newsletters, supporting conservation organizations, and being a presence at all national outdoor trade shows. As a result of these marketing efforts, Mossy Oak has achieved a strong, recognized brand name. Its consistent marketing strategies have resulted in consumer loyalty and a positive reputation. The brand is an example of how brand image can be developed over time through carefully managed positive experiences and associations, and significant ongoing efforts to maintain that brand's visibility in the marketplace.

Eric Forsyth
Bemidji State University

See Also: Brand Association; Brand Awareness; Brand Equity; Brand Personality; Brand Preference; Branding.

Further Readings

Forsyth, E. "Mossy Oak." In Lee, J., ed. *Branded: Branding in Sport Business*. Durham, NC: Carolina Academic Press, 2010.
Fullerton, S. *Sports Marketing*. New York: McGraw-Hill/Irwin, 2007.
Gladden, J. "Managing Sport Brands." In Mullin B., S. Hardy, and W. Sutton, eds., *Sport Marketing*, 3rd Ed. Champaign, IL: Human Kinetics, 2007.
Miloch, K. "Introduction to Branding." In Lee, J., ed., *Branded: Branding in Sport Business*. Durham, NC: Carolina Academic Press, 2010.
Shanks, M. *Sports Marketing*, 4th Ed. Upper Saddle River, NJ: Prentice Hall, 2009.

Brand Insistence

For years, sport marketers have strived for brand insistence, otherwise known as brand loyalty, in hope of achieving greater brand value and profitability. Research has shown that, in addition to being less sensitive to prices changes, consumers who are insistent upon a certain brand are less likely to move toward a competing product or service than are others who merely prefer the brand to the competition. Further, it has been found that it is much more cost effective trying to keep brand-insistent consumers than it is to convert new consumers. Whereas brand preference is concerned with the partiality consumers have for certain brands, brand insistence refers to the behavior whereby consumers become emphatic in their demands that a particular brand be made available.

Brand insistence involves an overt action on the part of the consumer to demand a certain brand of product or service. For example, a sports consumer who is insistent upon watching a favorite NFL football team play on television every week is likely to seek out and purchase an exclusive NFL package from a network provider that broadcasts each game. Whereas a more passive consumer would be more likely to go without watching any games altogether (brand preference), the behaviors of the brand-insistent consumer are active in getting what is perceived as needed. Such behavior explains why some MLB baseball franchises that have remarkably insistent sports fans, such as the New York Yankees, Boston Red Sox, and

New York Mets, have formed their own television networks (YES, NESN, and SNY, respectively) to broadcast all team games and provide comprehensive press coverage.

Sport marketers wanting to create sustainable brand insistence must understand the factors that generate loyalty among consumers to a product or service and the brand that represents it. There are various factors affecting the different levels of attachment or affinity consumers have with relation to brands. The first level sport marketers must be concerned with involves creating brand awareness and recognition. Research has found a correlation between first recall (a form of brand awareness and recognition) and brand preference and loyalty. While this might seem obvious, it is interesting to understand that without brand awareness and recognition, brand insistence cannot be achieved. The second level consists of factors that move consumers beyond awareness and recognition to what is known as brand preference. As the term implies, consumers with this type of brand affinity show

a consistent preference for a certain brand. While brand preference is certainly more valuable than brand awareness, it is insufficient to result in brand insistence and does not necessarily imply consumer loyalty to the brand.

As discussed prior, brand insistence involves the loyalty consumers have toward a brand, which is highly desired by sport marketers. However, measuring brand insistence in terms of understanding its effects on brand profitability can be difficult. The extant literature on the topic suggests the determinants of brand insistence are based on a brand's personality and whether the consumer's personality is reflected in the brand. The more effective a brand is at emphasizing such aspects of brand personality as relevance, distinction, value, and consistency, the higher likelihood that consumers will adopt attitudes and behaviors of brand insistence. In addition, the brand must also stand for something that is important to the consumer. Consider, for example, what the Pittsburgh Steelers mean to people in the city of Pittsburgh, Pennsylvania. While the core

Fans in Pittsburgh, Pennsylvania, await the Pittsburgh Steelers after their 2009 Super Bowl victory. The distinct personality of the Steelers' brand has resonated with fans on many levels, making the team an example of brand insistence.

product is relatively the same as any other NFL team, the hardnosed playing style of the Steelers has become an integral part of the Steelers' personality over the years and has come to epitomize the personality of the industrial city. Because the Steelers' brand is able to connect with consumers on multiple levels, consumers insist upon supporting the team regardless of how the core product may vary (wins/losses).

However, for all of its benefits, there are some important considerations that must be taken into account regarding brand insistence. Research shows that a higher level of brand affinity (brand insistence) can lead to a greater likelihood that a consumer will disapprove of changes made to product or service attributes. For example, loyal fans in Boston and Chicago have voiced their overwhelming opposition to the proposal that the respective baseball teams in each city move into new stadiums and tear down the older, deteriorating venues.

Similarly, loyal sports fans have long since voiced their opinions about various team and league management decisions affecting the sport product. Whereas more passive consumers are less likely to have an opinion concerning matters involving the image and value of the brand, loyal consumers are passionate about their voices being heard. Thus, sport marketers must be resolute of the value trade-off between various courses of action.

Ultimately, brand insistence can be achieved over time through providing consumers with consistent, positive shared experiences built around the brand. With regard to traditional marketing of goods and services, the most persuasive brands typically bond with consumers on an emotional level. In relation to marketing the sport product, the tradeoffs for consumer loyalty are highly influential, and can include experiential, social, and self-expressive benefits. Given the uncontrollable and intangible aspects of the sport product, however, the challenge for sport marketers is to ensure that the brand personality of the sport team or business is perceived as both highly relevant and esteemed by target consumers.

Khalid Ballouli
Texas A&M University

See Also: Brand Awareness; Brand Equity; Brand Image; Brand Personality; Brand Preference; Brand Rejection; Fan Loyalty Continuum; Levels of Brand Familiarity.

Further Readings

Aaker, David A. *Building Strong Brands.* New York: Simon & Schuster, 1995.

Gobe, Marc. *Emotional Branding: The New Paradigm for Connecting Brands to People.* New York: Allworth Press, 2010.

Griffin, Jill. *Taming the Search-and-Switch Customer: Earning Loyalty in a Compulsion-to-Compare World.* Hoboken, NJ: John Wiley & Sons, 2009.

McEwen, William J. *Married to the Brand: Why Consumers Bond With Some Brands for Life.* New York: Gallup Press, 2005.

Oliver, Richard L. "Whence Consumer Loyalty?" *Journal of Marketing*, v.63 (1999).

Brand Personality

Brand personality is in essence a personification of a brand. It occurs when brand image or brand identity is expressed in terms of human traits. The concepts of brand personality and brand image are different and should be distinguished. Brand image denotes the tangible attributes and benefits of a brand, while brand personality refers to the emotional associations of the brand. Establishing and maintaining a specific brand personality represents a significant component and step in sport brand management. The unique and ever-changing nature of sport provides sport brands with numerous opportunities to create and maintain brand personality. The consumer's emotional attachments to sport entities may also prove advantageous when establishing and maintaining brand personality.

Brand personality involves attributing human personality traits to a brand. In essence, brand personality embodies the humanistic characteristics or traits of a brand. Examples of such traits could include seriousness, warmth, competitiveness, being hardworking, or being antagonistic. These traits are intended to differentiate the brand from its competitors. By assigning human personality traits or characteristics to a brand, differentiation can be achieved by encouraging consumers to see the brand as a friend rather than a logo or object.

Brand personality can be demonstrated in a variety of advertising and promotional forms. It can be illustrated through traditional advertising methods such as radio and television advertisements and through nontraditional mediums such as online communications and social networking. Regardless of the medium selected to deliver the message, the goal is to emotionally connect with consumers. For example, many brands use sport to help create and maintain brand personality. In fact, some of the most memorable commercials in advertising history have centered on sport. Global brands such as Coca-Cola and McDonalds strategically reinforce their respective brand personalities via sport sponsorships, athlete endorsers, and direct communications with consumers. Brand personality also assists in positioning the brand through symbolic use of logos and slogans.

Brand personality helps develop brand equity as it sets the attitude of the brand. As such, the brand personality is fundamental to the overall marketing and communication strategies. Brand personality not only includes personality features and characteristics, but it also considers demographic aspects like age, gender, and socioeconomic class, and psychographic and lifestyle characteristics. The concepts of brand personality and celebrity can be used to complement each other. The trustworthiness of celebrity endorsers can transmit awareness and acceptability for a brand. This can be seen in numerous relationships between brands and athlete endorsers including Brett Favre and companies such as Wrangler Jeans or Snapper mowers, and Michael Jordan and companies such as Hanes and Nike.

Brand personality dimensions can include a variety of considerations. A popular brand personality framework identifies five core dimensions: sincerity (e.g., down-to-earth, wholesome), excitement (e.g., daring, imaginative), competence (e.g., reliable, successful), sophistication (e.g., upper class, charming), and ruggedness (e.g., outdoorsy, tough). Each dimension assists in establishing an emotional connection with different consumers. Such connections

form the essence of the brand personality and serve as the foundation for brand equity.

Conclusion

In establishing and maintaining a brand personality, marketers should strategically position the brand to align with human characteristics and differentiate the brand from competitors. This strategy plays a central role in establishing brand equity. Through such identification and differentiation, sport brands can be more visible in the competitive and cluttered sport marketplace. Effective brand personality strategies can be extremely valuable in assisting organizations in guiding marketing campaigns and strategies and attaining marketing goals.

Jason W. Lee
University of North Florida
Kimberly Miloch
Texas Woman's University

See Also: Brand Image; Branding; Endorsement; Endorser Effectiveness; Logo; Slogan; Sport Celebrities.

Further Readings

Aaker, Jennifer. "Dimensions of Brand Personality." *Journal of Marketing Research*, v.34 (August 1997).

Aaker, Jennifer and Susan Fournier. "A Brand as a Character, a Partner, and a Person: Three Perspectives on the Question of Brand Personality." *Advances in Consumer Research*, v.232 (1995).

Braunstein, Jessica R. and Stephen D. Ross. "Brand Personality in Sport: Dimension Analysis and General Scale Development." *Sport Marketing Quarterly*, v.19/1 (2010).

Heere, Bob. "A New Approach to Measure Perceived Brand Personality Associations Among Consumers." *Sport Marketing Quarterly*, v.19/1 (2010).

Voeth, Markus and Uta Herbst. "The Concept of Brand Personality as an Instrument for Advanced Non-Profit Branding: An Empirical Analysis." *Journal of Non-Profit & Public Sector Marketing*, v.19/1 (2008).

Brand Preference

The main objective for any marketer is to gain favorable attitudes from consumers to increase the overall profitability of the brand. However, this is difficult to achieve because consumers invariably approach the marketplace with a predetermined set of likes and preferences. As research shows, it is well known that people begin to develop preferences for certain brands at a very early age. However, these preferences begin to change as consumers form positive and negative opinions about brands because of previous experiences with a variety of products and services. Dependent upon these experiences is brand preference, which is the degree to which consumers express in their buying behavior a personal liking for a certain brand in the presence of competing brands.

Brand preference works as a scale on which brands can move up or down (and sometimes even off) depending on the branding strategies and marketing tactics implemented by a company. While the competition is constantly trying to find ways in which to vie for the same share of market interest, the advertising, promotions, and pricing of a company all have a significant impact on the association a brand has in the minds of consumers. Put simply, brand preference exists when a given brand becomes more relevant to consumers than competing brands. Thus, brands that can develop and continually reinforce their perceived quality in the minds of consumers will remain relevant to the consumer.

Research on Brand Preferences

In marketing research, a plethora of studies have been conducted to determine the awareness specific brands and companies have among target audiences and the degree to which the same target audience prefers (or does not prefer) to purchase a specific product over other products. Further, sport marketing researchers have shown that preference for a sports brand is improved when consumers perceive the brand personality of the sport brand as being reflective of their own personality. For example, when a distance runner makes a judgment about which brand of running shoe to purchase, the decision-making process will consist of more information than just the physical attributes of the product. The process will also consist of additional information regarding the attributes of the brand, such as attitude, image, and reputation. Studies also indicate that these components have significant influence on consumer attitudes toward brand purchase and usage.

Much of our understanding pertaining to consumer behavior and brand preference comes from the concepts and hypotheses used in experiential psychology research, in particular from studies conducted on learning theory. Whereas motivation theory concerns a certain force or driving agent as a means to changing behavior, learning theory provides direction through choices of action one can assume that might lead to one course of action over various other actions. According to research, repeated experience is a key form of human learning behavior. As such, researchers have found that learning can be very relevant in explaining conceptually the notion of brand preference.

A key component to building brand preference is appropriate and effective brand advertising designed with the specific purpose of changing consumer attitudes toward the brand. This style of brand advertising consists of a strong emphasis on the company brand logo and name, and is designed in such a way as to influence target consumers to consider the advantages of purchasing the product and placing their trust in the brand. Many brands do not necessarily need to commit to this type of advertising, as their brand reputation has been long established and their name in the industry has developed steadfast loyalty from their target audience. However, for brands that do not have the same history with consumers, certain measures are often needed to change the existing climate surrounding the brand's image. One such measure brands can take to ensure brand preference would be to create their own social media presence on the Internet. Consider, for example, two pro sports teams both competing for the loyalty of a target audience. Fans of one team might be swayed by the social media promotions for the other. In this instance, it is likely that fans start to develop a stronger affinity for the latter because of the relationship they aspire to have with a sports team in general. If the competition is developing relationships with the tipping-point fans, then brand preference will be lost on the company without a presence on the Internet. However, if a brand can capitalize on the affinity people have to social media content and promotions, then consumers will choose the brand over others in the same category.

Khalid Ballouli
Texas A&M University

See Also: Brand Awareness; Brand Equity; Brand Image; Brand Insistence; Brand Personality; Brand Rejection; Fan Loyalty Continuum; Levels of Brand Familiarity.

Further Readings

"Achieving Brand Preference." UpMarket. http://www.smithandjones.com/content485 (Accessed May 2010).

Gobe, Marc. *Emotional Branding: The New Paradigm for Connecting Brands to People.* New York: Allworth Press, 2010.

Griffin, Jill. *Taming the Search-and-Switch Customer: Earning Loyalty in a Compulsion-to-Compare World.* Hoboken, NJ: John Wiley & Sons, 2009.

McEwen, William J. *Married to the Brand: Why Consumers Bond With Some Brands for Life.* New York: Gallup Press, 2005.

Oliver, Richard L. "Whence Consumer Loyalty?" *Journal of Marketing,* v.63 (1999).

Brand Protection

Brand protection refers to the programs and processes implemented by an organization to proactively and strategically combat infringement of the company's trademark and other intellectual property rights. Organizations in the sport industry must safeguard intellectual property rights to protect brand value and prevent consumer confusion. Social media platforms such as Twitter and Facebook create opportunities for sports marketers and sponsors to inexpensively and effectively boost brand awareness and increase customer loyalty. However, the constantly evolving digital marketplace also creates corresponding business challenges and legal concerns.

The Chief Marketing Officer (CMO) Council, a group of over 5,000 senior corporate marketing leaders, recently launched the Doing Away With Foul Play in Sports Marketing initiative to help sports sponsors and franchises deal with trademark trespassing, property rights violations, and online fraud. The CMO Council surveyed over 200 senior-level sports marketers and found that sponsors, as well as sport leagues, teams, and professional athletes, often fail to protect their brand image and assets because they either ignore or inadequately invest in brand protection programs.

Historically, ambush marketing and counterfeit merchandise have posed the greatest threat to sport-related brands from a brand protection perspective. However, in recent years new technology has led to additional issues such as online scams, cyber fraud, and digital trademark infringement.

Ambush marketing is a controversial (and arguably unethical and illegal) business tactic in which companies attempt to capitalize on the goodwill and media exposure associated with a sport-related event without forming an official association with the company that holds the rights to the event. A classic example of ambush marketing occurred during the Atlanta Summer Olympic Games in 1996. Nike did not pay to be an official sponsor of the Olympic Games. Nonetheless, Nike purchased billboard space near event venues, created a "Nike Village" next to the athletes' Olympic Village, and distributed Nike flags to fans. When television audiences who watched the Olympic Games were asked to name the official sponsors of the Olympic Games, over 20 percent of the viewers erroneously thought that Nike was an official sponsor. Although Reebok paid a large fee to be an official sponsor of the 1996 Olympic Games, only about 15 percent of the viewers correctly identified Reebok as an official sponsor. Companies that pay millions of dollars each year for sports sponsorships must develop strategies to prevent unauthorized associations by competitor organizations that dilute their sponsorship investment.

The Consumer News and Business Channel (CNBC), a major satellite and cable television business news channel, recently produced a documentary called *Crime Inc.*, in which CNBC investigated counterfeit goods. CNBC labeled the business of counterfeit goods as the largest underground industry in the world. Many sport organizations continue to aggressively pursue producers of counterfeit merchandise in order to protect profits and improve brand security. And companies continue to produce T-shirts and other apparel with the logo of sport teams without paying for and receiving the required license to lawfully make those products.

In addition to physically tracking down producers of counterfeit apparel and merchandise, those involved in the sport industry need to be aware of online threats to brand integrity. For example, sport enthusiasts have many options when it comes to purchasing tickets to sporting events. A core problem is that some tickets purchased by fans through the secondary market turn out to be counterfeit. A fan of a particular sport team likely loses confidence in that team if he or she is denied entry to a game because the purchased ticket is counterfeit. The sport team may not only lose a customer, but it may also lose revenue, because of the sale of counterfeit tickets.

Another example of online threats to brand integrity is "cybersquatting." Cybersquatting occurs when a person wrongfully appropriates an Internet domain name to profit from the trademarks or goodwill associated with an individual or a company. A cybersquatter typically registers a domain name (for example, chrisbosh.com) and then attempts to sell that domain name to the individual or company who has trademark or other legal rights in that domain name (for example, Chris Bosh or the NBA). It is imperative to deter others from creating and managing Websites with domain names similar to the name of athletes or sport organizations, as this could negatively impact consumer perception. Sport marketers, sponsors, and franchises should also routinely monitor and track the online use of their trademarked logos and other marks to ensure that the individuals and companies who are using those marks for online advertisements are official sponsors who pay for that right.

Conclusion

It is essential for sports marketing agencies, sponsors, league executives, team owners, and professional athletes to systematically monitor the use of their brands and to proactively enforce their intellectual property rights. As new technologies develop and new business opportunities emerge, brand pro-

tection strategies must be implemented to directly address opportunities for unscrupulous individuals and unprincipled companies to infect a brand. Hiring a knowledgeable intellectual property attorney with experience representing sports organizations is an important first step for companies interested in protecting the integrity of their brand. Legal counsel can assist companies in registering trademarks with the U.S. Patent and Trademark Office and in prosecuting intellectual property rights violations. Sport business executives must also play a key role in managing risks associated with the unauthorized use of brand assets (which directly and adversely impacts brand reputation, revenue generation, and consumer trust).

Scott J. Bukstein
University of Central Florida

See Also: Ambush Marketing; Intellectual Property; Risk Management; Trademark, Registered/Infringement/Protection.

Further Readings

Chief Marketing Officer Council. "Doing Away With Foul Play in Sports Marketing." http://www.sportsbrandprotect.org (Accessed October 2010).
Oriard, Michael. *Brand NFL: Making and Selling America's Favorite Sport.* Chapel Hill: University of North Carolina Press, 2010.
Post, Richard S. and Penelope N. Post. *Global Brand Integrity Management: How to Protect Your Product in Today's Competitive Environment.* New York: McGraw-Hill, 2007.
Sharp, Linda A., Anita M. Moorman, and Cathryn L. Claussen. *Sport Law: A Managerial Approach,* 2nd Ed. Scottsdale, AZ: Holcomb Hathaway, 2010.

Brand Rejection

Brand managers spend considerable time and resources attempting to understand the factors that influence consumer purchase decisions. The primary objective of such efforts is to increase the perceived value of a product offering and thereby increase brand preference among target consumers. However, while it is important to know the reasons why certain brands are preferred, it is also necessary to understand why it is certain brands come to be rejected.

Brand rejection is a form of consumer behavior that involves the refusal of the consumer to purchase the brand unless its image or product attributes are changed in some way. Whereas positive associations can lead to an increase in brand preference and product purchase, negative associations with a brand can lead to brand rejection and consumers purposely avoiding brand products altogether.

Brand rejection can occur prior to purchasing a product or following its consumption, the differences in which constitute various fallouts. Pre-purchase brand rejection is typically the result of consumers being predisposed to making negative judgments about a brand sans any personal evaluation of its product offering. That is, consumers will perceive a product within an evoked set to be inept because of being unfavorably disposed to the brand prior, resulting in summary rejection of the product entirely. Consider, for example, a consumer who relies heavily on product reviews or word of mouth for information regarding product quality. A consumer such as this will often reject a brand based on the negative evaluations of others without evaluating the product for him- or herself. In the context of sports, consumers will often make judgments about a brand based on its endorsement of athletes with whom the consumer does not wish to identify. For example, when Nike ended its endorsement deal with NFL star quarterback Michael Vick after allegations of his involvement in animal cruelty surfaced in the media, the company was able to remove any semblance of association consumers might have perceived. In doing so, Nike was able to maintain a favorable position among its target consumers, thus avoiding any potential damage to its brand image that might otherwise have resulted.

With regard to post-purchase behavior, it is commonly known that consumers are more likely to reject a brand based on a single negative experience.

Converse to pre-purchase behavior, post-purchase rejections stem from a consumer's negative evaluation of an experience with a brand product. If the perceived value of the product does not meet consumer expectations, it is likely he or she will eliminate the brand from consideration for not only the same, but also other related product categories. For example, if a consumer has an unpleasant experience with a certain brand of baseball glove, because of any number of factors, the consumer is likely not to consider the brand again when purchasing that and other future baseball equipment.

For a sport business to sustain longevity, it must understand not only the importance of brand rejection, but also the strategies that can be employed to overcome such an obstacle. In order to eliminate pre-purchase rejection, companies often communicate with target consumers through strategic advertising in attempts to persuade them into thinking a certain way about their brand. To avoid post-purchase rejection, a company must attempt to change the consumption-based judgments consumers make about the brand by implementing better value delivery and following through on its brand promise.

Khalid Ballouli
Texas A&M University

See Also: Brand Association; Brand Image; Brand Personality; Brand Preference; Branding.

Further Readings

Aaker, David A. *Building Strong Brands*. New York: Simon & Schuster, 1995.
Cromie, John G. and Mike T. Ewing. "The Rejection of Brand Hegemony." *Journal of Business Research*, v.62/2 (2009).
Gobe, Marc. *Emotional Branding: The New Paradigm for Connecting Brands to People*. New York: Allworth Press, 2010.
Klein, Naomi. *No Logo*. London: Picador, 2009.
Lamb, Charles W., Joseph F. Hair, and Carl McDaniel. *Essentials of Marketing*, 6th Ed. Mason, OH: South-Western/Cengage Learning, 2008.

Branding

Branding is a strategy used to differentiate products and companies, and to build economic value for both the consumer and the brand owner. Brands have become an integral part of contemporary society and have invaded many areas of consumer lives: social, economic, sporting, religious, and cultural. The word *brand* comes from the Old Norse word *brandr,* which means "to burn" and refers to the means livestock owners use to mark their animals to recognize them.

The American Marketing Association defines *brand* as "a name, term, sign, symbol or design or a combination of them, intended to identify the goods and services of one seller or group of sellers and to differentiate them from those of competition." A brand consists of elements such as a name, logo, symbol, and packaging design that identify a product and differentiate it from others. Brands provide several functions to consumers, such as identification of the source or manufacturer of a product, reduction of time in product-related information processing, risk and search cost reduction, signal of quality, and facilitation of product decisions because of previous knowledge and experiences. Brands have meaning to the consumers and are taken into consideration before a purchase decision is made. Thus, when a brand perceived as having benefits in the mind of the consumer is recognized, it acts as a shortcut to elude large amounts of information. In situations where consumers search for a product or service but are not familiar with a brand, they need to conduct an extensive information search. However, when a brand is recognized, it functions as a cue that assists consumers in reaching a purchase decision more easily and conveniently.

Today, consumers are confronted with a variety of products/services to choose from, so a strong brand can play a catalytic role in their purchase decisions. While it is often possible to imitate manufacturing processes, the beliefs, attitudes, and associations established in the consumer's mind cannot simply be imitated. Therefore, a large number of businesses recognize that the brand name associated with their products or services is one of the most valuable assets they own. Brands provide several benefits to contemporary businesses. Brands play a substantial role in differentiating products from those of competitors, in increasing customer loyalty, in establishing credibility for a new product, in charging a price premium, and in emphasizing a characteristic or element of differentiation. Moreover, brands constitute a means of identification to simplify handling and/or tracing—of legally protecting unique features, of competitive advantage, of financial outcomes—and a signal of quality to satisfied customers.

Each of the brand functions helps potential customers in remembering, understanding, and selecting a company and its products from other competitive offerings. To businesses, branding is a long-term commitment. Brands are built over time by regularly meeting and exceeding the expectations of customers and investors, and by consistently representing the brand in ever-changing market conditions. Over time, a well-managed portfolio of brands can assist in developing long-term growth and profitability. To accomplish longitudinal outcomes, brand managers need to understand how day-to-day actions will impact the long-term benefits of branding, and to have the discipline to withstand short-term pressures that will ultimately do harm to both the brand and the business.

Brand Equity

One of the most important concepts linked to branding is brand equity. Brand equity refers to the added value with which a brand endows a product and to the addition of the brand's attributes including reputation, symbols, associations, and names. The author David Aaker defines brand equity as "a set of brand assets and liabilities linked to a brand, its name and symbol that add or subtract from the value provided to a firm and/or to that firm's customers." The brand value is the financial expression of the elements of brand equity. Brand equity increases the importance of the brand in marketing strategy and provides a common denominator for decoding marketing strategies and measuring the value of a brand.

Two main approaches to brand equity can be found in the literature: customer-based brand equity (CBBE) and financial-based brand equity. Customer-based brand equity refers to the differential effect brand knowledge has on consumer response to the marketing of that brand. Thus, brand equity takes place when consumers are familiar with a brand and have formed strong, favorable, and unique associations in their memory. Brand awareness and brand image are considered the two main sources of brand equity that can influence consumer response. The dimensions of brand equity are brand loyalty, name awareness, perceived quality, brand associations, and other proprietary brand assets.

Financial-based brand equity refers to the financial value of the brand that can be estimated either by the market value of the brand (present value of the future economic benefits to be derived by the brand owner), or by the cost of the brand (amount of money required to replace a brand, including the costs of product development and marketing of the brand) and by the income produced by the brand (net income derived from the brand).

High brand equity results in enhanced performance (e.g., increased market share) and/or marketing efficiency (e.g., reduced advertising and promotional expenditures) in relation to the brand, in long-term effects because of increased customer loyalty distribution relationships, and in carryover effects (e.g., brand extensions) to other brands and markets.

Strategic brand management involves planning and execution of marketing activities to develop, assess, and manage brand equity. The strategic brand management process involves four steps: (1) identifying and establishing brand positioning, (2) planning and implementing brand marketing campaigns, (3) measuring and interpreting brand performance, and (4) growing and sustaining brand equity.

Branding Strategies

Two well known branding strategies are brand extensions and co-branding. Brand extension refers to using the leverage of a well known brand name in one category to launch a new product in a different category or market. Brand extensions can be classified into line extensions and category extensions. Line extension takes place when the parent brand is used for a product that targets a new market segment within a product category served by the parent. Category extension takes place when the parent brand is used to enter a different product category from that of the parent brand.

Brand extensions provide several benefits. The main advantage of a brand extension is that you take the equity/goodwill from an existing brand and use it in another context. If successful, this can save a lot of money because you do not have to invest the standard $1 million in developing a new brand. Brands with well-known quality perceptions and associations can be introduced into a new product category. Thus, the extended brand can capitalize on brand awareness and leverage the associations consumers have about the parent brand. Moreover, consumers who favorably evaluate a parent brand are more willing to try and adopt the brand extension than an unfamiliar brand in the same category. However, brand extensions might also have some disadvantages. They might fail in the new product/service or market because the brand is not compelling in that area. They might result in losing the tight focus of the parent brand, and therefore its intimacy (differentiation and relevance). Moreover, they might damage the parent brand by introducing new conflicting/confusing attributes.

Co-branding is considered a type of brand extension, a source of brand equity, and a long-term brand alliance strategy in which two or more brands are combined to form a new brand. Co-branding refers to any pairing of two brands in a marketing context such as advertisements, products, product placements, and distribution outlets. Brand equity is directly related to co-branding because high brand equity of partner brands improves the perceived brand equity of the co-branded product and generates positive direct effects.

Co-branding can be seen at both a product level and corporate level. At a product level co-branding is a popular strategy to introduce new products in the market place. It is an effective marketing development strategy, since there are multiple benefits associated with it. First of all, co-branded products can acquire the attributes of both parent brands; furthermore, perceptions of a co-branded product can have spillover effects on the parent brands. Finally, it is a favorable situation for increasing an existing customer base or attracting new target groups, since the partner in the co-branding arrangement brings its own customer base, which is potentially available to the other partner. Corporate co-branding refers to partnerships between corporate brands and other corporate, product, or service brands in order to establish a co-branded identity. This strategic alliance enables the parties involved to expand and reinforce their existing set of corporate brand values without diminishing their corporate brand equity. Corporate brands differ from product brands in their strategic management, communication, and culture.

Branding in Sports

The marketing of sports has become highly sophisticated over the years, utilizing marketing management principles. Sport teams (e.g., Manchester United, Dallas Cowboys), sport leagues (e.g., NBA, NFL), and sport events (e.g., Olympic Games, Formula 1) have built strong brands that are recognized and supported by millions of sport consumers globally.

In 1985, ISL Marketing conducted a survey in the United States, West Germany, Portugal, and Singapore to explore the visibility of several brands. The study showed that the Olympic Rings are one of the most widely recognized symbols in the world, with nearly 80 percent of all respondents being able to immediately recognize and identify them. The only other corporate logos that achieved similar identification levels were McDonald's and Shell. The Olympic Rings were adopted and shown for the first time during the Antwerp Games in 1920 and became the most recognizable Olympic trademark in the world. Five different color rings (red, blue, green, yellow, and black) on a white field were selected so that each participating nation would have at least one of the colors in their national flag, with the rings representing each of the five inhabited continents, with America considered as one continent alone.

In addition, sport teams are considered brands with their own name, logo, and symbols differentiating them from similar product offerings. Sport teams often represent unique brands of a sport product category/activity based on their promotional activities, their style of play, the personality

These banners and logos helped reinforce the New York Yankees brand inside the new Yankee Stadium in 2009.

of the players, and their logos, slogans, and other brand markers. Like with any other brand, sport consumers make their purchase decisions based on their awareness, perception, and attachment to their favorite sport teams. Because winning is not under the control of marketing, sport teams are also being marketed like any other product or service. Sport marketers aim to increase fan awareness, positive images, and loyalty to the team in order to increase ticket sales independently of team performance. Today, brand logos and symbols contribute to the financial performance of professional sport teams via licensing agreements and merchandising sales. There are strong sport team brands all over the world such as Manchester United, Real Madrid, the Dallas Cowboys, and the New York Yankees.

The NFL is the most popular U.S. sports league, with strong television ratings and annual league revenue topping $7 billion. While TV ratings have slipped over the past decade, NFL games still boast the strongest ratings among sports leagues. In 2008, the average team in the National Football League was worth more than $1 billion, marking the first time any sports league has surpassed that level. According to *Forbes* magazine, the 2008 average valuation for the 32 NFL teams was $1.04 billion, up 8.7 percent from the previous year's $957 million because of the sport's popularity and cash-generating new stadiums. Ten years ago, when *Forbes* first valued NFL teams, the average franchise was worth $288 million. The top three teams in the *Forbes* list are: the Dallas Cowboys ($1.612 billion), the Washington Redskins ($1.538 billion), and the New England Patriots ($1.324 billion). The Redskins have the highest estimated revenue and operating income at $327 million and $58.1 million, respectively.

Recently, sport sponsorship has become recognized as either brand extension or as corporate co-branding that can be used for strategic purposes. Sport sponsorship is considered either a brand extension or a co-branding partnership situation because it enables values to be extracted from the sponsorship relationship at a variety of levels, and can be a significant driver of brand strategy that leverages the value of the sponsor brand.

Rodoula H. Tsiotsou
University of Macedonia

See Also: Brand Association; Brand Awareness; Brand Equity; Brand Extension; Brand Image; Brand Insistence; Brand Personality; Brand Preference; Brand Protection; Brand Rejection; Branding, Global Sport.

Further Readings

Aaker, David A. *Managing Brand Equity*. New York: The Free Press, 1991.
Beech, J. and S. Chadwick. *The Marketing of Sport*. Upper Saddle River, NJ: Prentice Hall, 2007.
Chernatony, Leslie de and Malcolm McDonald. *Creating Powerful Brands in Consumer Service and Industrial Markets*, 3rd Ed. Oxford: Butterworth Heinemann, 2003.
Chernatony, Leslie de and S. Segal-Horn. "The Criteria for Successful Services Brands." *European Journal of Marketing*, v.37/7–8 (2003).
Cliffe, Simon J. and Judy Motion. "Building Contemporary Brands: A Sponsorship-Based Strategy." *Journal of Business Research*, v.58 (2005).
Farrelly, Francis J., Pascale Quester, and Stephen A. Greyser. "Defending the Co-Branding Benefits of Sponsorship B2B Partnerships: The Case of Ambush Marketing." *Journal of Advertising Research* (September 2005).
Fullerton, Sam. *Sports Marketing*. New York: McGraw-Hill, 2007.
Gwinner, K. P. and J. Eaton. "Building Brand Image Through Event Sponsorship: The Role of Image Transfer." *Journal of Advertising*, v.28/4 (1999).
Kahuni, Abel T., Jennifer Rowley, and Arnaz Binsardi. "Guilty by Association: Image 'Spill-Over' in Corporate Co-Branding." *Corporate Reputation Review*, v.12/1 (2009).
Keller, Kevin L. *Strategic Brand Management*, 2nd Ed. Upper Saddle River, NJ: Prentice Hall, 2003.
Motion, Judy, Shirley Leitch, and Roderick J. Brodie. "Equity in Corporate Co-Branding: The Case of Adidas and the All Blacks." *European Journal of Marketing*, v.37/7–8 (2003).
Winters, Lewis C. "Brand Equity Measures: Some Recent Advances." *Marketing Research*, v.3/4 (1991).

Branding, Global Sport

In recent years, intense globalization has influenced the marketing of brands in the sports business and has become a key factor in marketing decisions. The advent of globalization has changed the manner in which sport is produced, marketed, delivered, and consumed. This is the case when franchises try to promote their brands through tournaments overseas (for example, a European soccer team in Asia or NBA franchises around the world), or when suppliers open shops worldwide or try to create campaigns to attract new markets.

Branding globally is of course a much more complex activity than operating in a local market. In order to be successful, global sports marketing strategists need to take into consideration differences in the local consumer culture in comparison with the original market. In the sports business the situation may be more complex, because most of the brands (such as clubs and franchises) are supported by local identification. In order to avoid the risk of losing local support for the brand in exchange for global support, most teams have decided to brand their clubs at different types of levels: locally, nationally, and globally.

A successful marketing plan should be customized for each specific area. For example, because of the significant differences between Asia and Europe, marketing plans need to be very different in the two areas. In order to promote a brand in multiple areas it is important to take into account all of the steps of the process. The pricing may need to be different because the perceived value of a product or a brand may not be the same in dissimilar markets. Targeting might be uncommon in certain areas, and the target of a brand may not be similar all around the world. Moreover, the distribution and logistics of a brand need to be tailored to different areas. Of course, one of the most important operations in the globalization process of a brand is advertising. Different campaigns need to be formulated in order to attract new consumers overseas; to be effective this process needs to consider different cultures and values.

Media and Other Promotion

New media have played a key role in the global branding process. New technologies have made it easier to market sport brands and products globally. It has become easier and cheaper to promote a brand utilizing new technologies. For example, one may now promote a brand on Websites or spread information about a brand through other online operations, such as broadcast, narrowcast, or podcast.

Using these new opportunities, brand managers have been able to reduce dependency on traditional advertising. They also have the opportunity to use multiple channels such as product placement, sponsorship, and events marketing to attract new consumers and sustain interest in the brand.

The promotion of sports events may help in promoting a brand worldwide. For example, according to FIFA (the football international governing body, Fédération Internationale de Football Association) statistics, the FIFA World Cup Korea/Japan set a new record for a sports event of 49.2 billion viewer hours worldwide. The 2002 final between Brazil and Germany was the most viewed match in FIFA World Cup history, with 1.1 billion individuals watching the game, which was broadcast in 213 countries. This event was an opportunity for European clubs to expand their notoriety in Asia and increase their consumer base.

Marketing via Sports

As an indirect consequence of globalization and the increase of trade in different countries, several new opportunities for sponsors have arisen. For example, there is the possibility of reaching a vast number of sports consumers around the world, even in places where a certain sport may have no tradition or heritage. At the same time, foreign sponsors may start to appear for local leagues. Overall, global sponsorship can be used as a sustainable competitive advantage.

Conclusion

The promotion of a brand worldwide is an important operation that involves many variables. In order to succeed, marketers need to account for a wide variety of cultural and social aspects. However, the presence of new technologies has assisted greatly in the branding of new products and the spread of brand awareness all over the world.

Alessandro Da Re
State University of New York College at Cortland

See Also: Brand Image; Global Market Expansion; Global Sport; Global Sports Expansion: Baseball, Basketball, NASCAR, Football; Globalization of Sports; Global-Local Paradox; Integration of Sport, Globalization, Commercialization; Olympics; World Cup.

Further Readings

Amis, J. and T. B. Cornwell. *Global Sport Sponsorship*. Oxford: Berg Publishers, 2005.

Dolles, H. and S. Söderman. "Globalization of Sports—The Case of Professional Football and Its International Management Challenges." Deutsches Institut Für Japanstudien Working Paper 05/1 (2005).

Douglas, S. P. and Y. Wind. "The Myth of Globalization." *Columbia Journal of World Business*, v.22/4 (1987).

Fédération Internationale de Football Association. "2006 FIFA World Cup Broadcast Wider, Longer and Farther Than Ever Before." http://www.fifa .com/aboutfifa/marketing/factsfigures/tvdata .html (Accessed October 2010).

Santomier, J. "New Media, Branding and Global Sports Sponsorship." *International Journal of Sports Marketing & Sponsorship* (October 1, 2008).

Shobe, H. "Place, Sport and Globalization: Making Sense of La Marca Barça." *Treballs de la Societat Catalana de Geografia*, v.61 (2006).

Breach of Contract

Breach of contract is a concept within contract law that occurs when one or more parties fail to perform their duties as specified within a legal contract. In other words, breach occurs when a party to the contract does not "live up to their end of the bargain." The breach itself may either be termed a minor breach or material breach. A minor breach can be viewed as a partial breach and does not fundamentally destroy the value of the contract. A material breach, on the other hand, is the breach of an essential (i.e., material) term of the contract. Both minor and material breach of contract entitle the nonbreaching party to sue the breaching party for damages, but only a material breach of contract excuses the nonbreaching party from performance of its contractual duties. Thus, when one party engages in action constituting a material breach, the other party is let out of the contract without penalty. When one party breaches a contract, the nonbreaching party is entitled to one or more legal or equitable remedies. Before examining the types of remedies that may be awarded, the role of the court in such a dispute must be addressed.

Under the American legal system, a contract is simply an agreement between two or more parties that has binding legal force. The idea that people are free to engage in the exchange of promises with one another and enter into contracts is a fundamental aspect of American legal history. The whole basis of contracting, however, is predicated upon consensual exchange and the idea that the parties will keep their word. When they do not, courts are used to either force compulsion or award damages. Thus, the role of the court when hearing a dispute (i.e., case) regarding a breach of contract claim is to first decide whether (1) there was a legally enforceable contract that existed and (2) how to award damages so as to appropriately compensate the nonbreaching party.

Breach of contract is remedied by awarding damages to the nonbreaching party so as to place it in the position it would have held had the contract been performed by the other party. There are two basic types of damages that may be awarded in such a case:

- *Compensatory damages.* These damages are meant to compensate the nonbreaching party for losses suffered as a result of the nonperformance of the breaching party. These damages only relate to damages actually sustained and proved to have arisen directly from the breach. These are typically calculated by comparing the difference between the value of the performance of the breaching party to the promised performance under the contract for the breaching party (i.e., what a party did versus what it promised to do). These damages are limited, however, to the extent that the nonbreaching party can recover some of the loss from the breach. For example, a client agrees to purchase 100 tickets at $10 per ticket for a baseball game, totaling $1,000, from a sport organization. The client fails to pay for the tickets at the last minute, and the sport organization is only able to sell 25 of the tickets and is thus out the cost of the remaining 75 tickets. The sport organization has only sustained damages relating to the 75 tickets, and thus the compensatory damages would be $750.

- *Consequential damages.* These damages relate to foreseeable damages suffered by a nonbreaching party that are caused by special circumstances beyond the contract itself. For example, a sport organization fails to deliver on a contract to provide posters signed by players to a sports memorabilia store. The sport organization knows the memorabilia store was planning on reselling the posters immediately for a profit. Compensatory damages would be awarded relating to the actual costs of the posters, and consequential damages would be awarded for the loss of profit. A breaching party is only liable for consequential damages if it knew, or should have known (i.e., it was foreseeable), that additional loss would be sustained by the nonbreaching party as a result of the breach.

In certain circumstances, monetary damages are not a sufficient remedy for a breach of contract. In such instances, a court may order a different remedy called specific performance, which is an equitable remedy in which the breaching party is made to actually perform the promised act in the contract (i.e., they are made to do what they agreed to do). Consider a contract to purchase an extremely rare, signed baseball card. The buyer pays his or her money, but the seller changes his or her mind and decides not to sell, thus breaching the contract. Although the compensatory damages would equal the amount of the card and could be awarded back to the buyer, the unique nature of the item being sold makes it such that the buyer may not be able to obtain a substantially similar item in the market. To simply refund the buyer's money is an insufficient remedy, and thus a court may order the seller to follow through with the sale. Specific performance is a remedy not appropriate to all circumstances and is generally awarded when damages are insufficient.

Michael S. Carroll
University of Southern Mississippi

See Also: Contract, Key Factors in a; Contracts, Athlete; Contracts, Venue.

Further Readings

Cross, F. B. and R. L. Miller. *West's Legal Environment of Business,* 6th Ed. New York: Thomson West, 2007.

Niland, B. "Contract Essentials." In D. J. Cotten and J. T. Wolohan, eds., *Law for Recreation and Sport Managers,* 5th Ed. Dubuque, IA: Kendall Hunt, 2010.

Sharp, L. A., A. M. Moorman, and C. L. Claussen. *Sport Law: A Managerial Approach.* Scottsdale, AZ: Holcomb Hathaway, 2007.

Break-Even Analysis

Break-even analysis (BEA) is a technique based on categorizing all costs associated with the production of the product/event between those that are variable (costs that change when the production output changes), and those that are fixed (costs not directly related to the volume of production). Total variable and fixed costs are compared with sales revenue in order to determine the level of sales volume, sales value, or production at which the business makes neither a profit nor a loss; this is called the "break-even point" (BEP).

The BEP can be calculated in either units (volume) or revenue. If you can accurately forecast your costs and sales, conducting a break-even analysis is a matter of simple math. A company has broken even when its total sales or revenues equal its total expenses. At the BEP, no profit has been made, nor have any losses been incurred. If the product can be sold in a larger quantity than occurs at the BEP, then the firm will make a profit; below this point, the firm will make a loss. This calculation is critical for any business owner, because the BEP is the lower limit of profit when determining margins. The BEP is then compared with forecasted demand to determine if proceeding is economically viable. The BEP can be calculated using a simple equation or can be plotted graphically as a break-even chart (BEC).

Fixed, Variable, and Semi-Variable Costs

To understand BEA requires an understanding of the nature of costs. Fixed costs are those business costs that are not directly related to the level of production or output. In other words, even if the business has a zero output or high output, the level of fixed costs will remain broadly the same. In the long term, fixed costs can alter, perhaps as a result of investment in production capacity, for example, adding a new factory unit, or through the growth in overhead required to support a larger, more complex business.

Variable costs are those costs that vary directly with the level of output. They represent payment for output-related inputs such as raw materials, direct labor, and fuel, and revenue-related costs such as commissions. A distinction is often made between direct variable costs and indirect" variable costs. Direct variable costs are those that can be directly attributable to the production of a particular product or service and allocated to a particular cost center. Raw materials and the wages of those working on the production line are good examples. Indirect variable costs cannot be directly attributable to production but they do vary with output. These include depreciation (where it is calculated related to output—e.g., machine hours), maintenance, and certain labor costs.

While the distinction between fixed and variable costs is a convenient categorization of business costs, in reality some costs that are fixed in nature actually increase when output reaches certain levels. In these circumstances, we say that part of the cost is variable and part fixed. For example, for every 20 factory workers a foreman is needed, so when you employ the 21st worker you need a foreman too, but you will not need another until you employ the 41st worker, and then another at the 61st. The associated cost is therefore a "step" increase and is treated as a fixed cost for BEP purposes.

Calculating the BEP

The BEP for a product is the point where total revenue received equals the total costs associated with the sale of the product (TR = TC). A BEP is typically calculated in order for businesses to determine if it would be profitable to sell a proposed product, as opposed to attempting to modify an existing product instead so it can be made lucrative. BEA can also be used to analyze the potential profitability of an expenditure in a sales-based business. There are a number of ways BEP can be calculated:

Break-even point (for output) = fixed cost / contribution per unit

Contribution (p.u) = selling price (p.u) – variable cost (p.u)

Break-even point (for sales) = fixed cost / contribution (pu) × selling price (pu)

Break-even Point = Total fixed costs / (selling price – average variable costs)

The last equation is less widely used and requires some explanation. In the denominator, "price minus average variable cost" is the variable profit per unit, or contribution margin of each unit that is sold. This relationship is derived from the profit equation:

Profit = Revenues - Costs where Revenues = (selling price × quantity of product) and Costs = (average variable costs × quantity) + total fixed costs

Therefore,

Profit = (selling price × quantity) – (average variable costs × quantity + total fixed costs)

Solving for quantity of product at the break-even point when profit equals zero, the quantity of product at break even is:

Total fixed costs / (selling price – average variable costs)

Margin of Safety and Sensitivity Analysis

Margin of safety (MOS) is the excess of budgeted or actual sales over the BEP of sales. It states the amount by which sales can drop before losses begin to be incurred. The higher the margin of safety, the lower the risk of not breaking even.

Margin of Safety (Money or Units) = Total budgeted or actual sales − Break-even sales

Or as a ratio:

Margin of Safety Ratio = (expected sales − break-even sales) / break-even sales

By performing multiple calculations using different prices a range of BEPs can be calculated as part of a Sensitivity analysis. Comparing this with pricing perception points (PPP) from research aids in final price decisions.

Limitations

Among the limitations of break-even analysis is that it is only a supply side (i.e., costs only) analysis, as does not address what sales are actually likely to be for the product at these various prices. It also assumes that fixed costs (FC) are constant, and that average variable costs are constant per unit of output, at least in the range of likely quantities of sales (i.e., linearity). BEA assumes that the quantity of goods produced is equal to the quantity of goods sold (i.e., there is no change in the quantity of goods held in inventory at the beginning of the period and the quantity held in inventory at the end of the period). In multiproduct companies, it also assumes that the relative proportions of each product sold and produced are constant (i.e., the sales mix is constant).

Andrew J. Whalley
Royal Holloway University of London

See Also: Balance Sheet; Information Systems, Kinds of; Management Decision-Making Process.

Further Readings

Camp, R. "Multidimensional Break-Even Analysis." *Journal of Accountancy* (January 1987).
Chan, K. "Break-Even Analysis: A Unit Cost Model." *CGA Magazine* (March 1985).
Dayananda, D., R. Irons, S. Harrison, J. Herbohn, and P. Rowland. *Capital Budgeting: Financial Appraisal of Investment Projects.* Cambridge, UK: Cambridge University Press, 2002.
Horngren, C., G. Sundem, and W. Stratton. *Introduction to Management Accounting.* Upper Saddle River, NJ: Prentice Hall, 2002.
Rickey, K. R. "To Market, to Market." *N.A.A. Bulletin* (December 1958).

Broadcast Rights

Broadcasting is a very dynamic field in the sport industry driven by escalating viewer demand for sport content, technological advancements, and innovations. Over the past decade, broadcasting has experienced a rapid evolution with several developments in its technology. Advancements in content acquisition, production, and delivery technologies have enabled traditional broadcasters to increase the quality and quantity of sport content. New companies marketing highly innovative products or services have also appeared.

Sport broadcasting evolved into a multibillion-dollar business and a major source of revenue for sport organizations (leagues, federations, associations, and clubs) because of increasing viewership demand and value. In 2008, the Fédération Internationale de Football Association (FIFA) generated $556 million in revenues from selling broadcasting rights for its competitions. That year, the Union of European Football Associations (UEFA), the governing body of European football (soccer), received 800 million euros from selling the 2008 European Football Championship media rights. According to UEFA, each of the 31 EURO 2008 games was watched live by at least 155 million TV viewers, whereas the final round of the tournament was broadcasted in 231 countries. Because of their large viewership, sports have become an integral programming content for broadcasters. The sporting events with the largest worldwide audience are the Summer Olympic Games, FIFA World Cup, Tour de France, Cricket World Cup, Rugby Union World Cup, Super Bowl, and the FIA Formula 1 World Championship.

The competition for the acquisition of sports broadcasting rights, along with the large sums of money spent on them, demonstrate the dominant position of sports in television programming. In 2003, the International Olympic Committee (IOC) signed a $155 million contract with the Japanese broadcasting consortium NHK for the television rights of the Athens 2004 Olympic Games. In June 2003, the IOC concluded a $2.1 billion renewal deal with NBC for the U.S. TV rights to the 2010 and 2012 Olympic Games. The European Broadcasting Union bought the rights for the same Olympic events for $800 million. Both deals include all television, radio, mobile, video-on-demand, Internet, broadband, and audio rights. More than 840 million people in China tuned in to the opening ceremony of the 2008 Beijing Olympic Games, perhaps the largest television audience in history for a single event. China Central TV paid about $17 million for exclusive broadcast rights in China and raised approximately $394 million in Olympic advertising revenue. By comparison, NBC paid $894 million for broadcast rights in the United States and was expected to garner more than $1 billion in ad revenue.

Escalating viewer demand for sport content continues to drive many of the technological advances in broadcasting, resulting in changes not only in the way sports are watched but also in how they are delivered. Sport broadcasting constitutes a dynamic business area with rapid developments in the creation and use of new media and technologies that provide numerous business opportunities.

Main Sport Rights Holders

Broadcasting is the live or recorded transmission of a sport event via analog or digital methods using ground receivers, satellite, or cable networks by a form of media. There are various ways and different distribution channels that are used to broadcast a sporting event. In any case, when discussing broadcasting rights in sports and regardless of the medium used, there are three main parties involved: the sports rights holders, the licensed broadcasters that bought the rights to broadcast the event, and the viewers of the event.

Sports rights holders may be either main holders or secondary holders. Event organizers such as sport federations (e.g., national sport federations), leagues (e.g., Major League Baseball), committees

(e.g., the IOC), associations (e.g., FIFA), unions (e.g., the Union of European Football Associations), school teams, and sport clubs (e.g., Juventus, Chelsea) constitute the main sports rights holders. Marketing or sport marketing agencies (e.g., Octagon, Sportfive Group, Dentsu Group, Infront Sports and Media, CSI Sports, and Sports Marketing Australia) are considered secondary holders because they buy the rights from the main holders in order to sell them to broadcasters.

The main rights holder is usually the organizer of a sport event. It controls the broadcasting because it owns or controls access to the facilities where the event takes place. Thus, only the broadcaster that has bought the rights is allowed admission to the premises of the events and production of the television signal. The right to broadcast a sport event is granted usually for a given territory (e.g., per country) on an exclusive basis. Exclusivity is the main element of the value of a sport program. The number of viewers and the amount of advertising money a sporting event attracts indicate the broadcasting value of a sport program.

Broadcasting rights constitute a major source of revenues for the main sports rights holders. In 2008, FIFA generated $957 million in revenues. The lion's share of its revenues was attributable to the sale of broadcasting rights ($556 million, or 58 percent of revenues). Similarly, 60 percent of UEFA's EURO 2008 revenues came from selling its broadcasting rights.

The main sport rights holders either sell the broadcasting rights of their events to broadcasters, sell them to secondary holders, or combine the above strategies either by broadcasting medium or by territory. For example, the IOC has recently changed its marketing strategy for the broadcasting rights for the Olympic Games. For the 2010 and 2012 Olympic Games, IOC sold its European broadcasting rights to the European Broadcasting Union (EBU) for $800 million. However, more recently the IOC awarded Sportfive the broadcasting rights for all media platforms—including free and subscription television, Internet, and mobile phones—across 40 countries in Europe for the 2014 Winter Games and 2016 Summer Olympics in a deal worth $316 million. The IOC excluded broadcast rights in France, Germany, Italy, Spain,

Turkey, and Britain from this agreement because it already had deals with broadcasters in Italy (Sky Italia) and Turkey (Fox Turkey), and will directly negotiate in the other four countries. This strategy will provide IOC an expected 30 percent increase in its revenues from broadcasting rights, reaching $1 billion.

Today, it is very common to split broadcasting rights and sell them to two or more media platforms and broadcasters. From the rights holder's standpoint, this is done in part to increase revenues and comply with regulations (e.g., the European Union competition law), but mostly to secure revenues. The collapse of many digital platforms such as Kirch's Media Group in Germany and Alpha Digital in Greece in the past years has made event organizers more cautious in selling broadcasting rights to only one broadcaster. Leagues and clubs have lost significant amounts of money, and in many cases their continued existence was in question. Championship and professional club operations reached a critical point since broadcasting rights are one of the main revenue sources for most sport organizations. As a result, many sport organizers have changed their strategy in selling broadcasting rights, split them into two or more packages, and are selling them to different broadcasters. For example, UEFA developed 10 different broadcasting rights packages for the Champions League tournament, while the German football league split its broadcasting rights into nine packages, four for TV broadcasting, two for Internet, and two for mobile phone streaming.

Secondary Sport Rights Holders

Marketing and sports marketing agencies also have emerged as main intermediaries in the broadcasting rights process. In many cases, a sports event organizer sells broadcasting rights to an agency that is authorized to sell those rights to broadcasters. In this case, the event organizers maximize revenues and avoid separate negotiations with individual broadcasters. It is a recommended approach especially when the event organizer does not employ experienced people or does not have the capacity to directly negotiate and sell its broadcasting rights.

In line with this reasoning, Dentsu Group, a Japan-based marketing company, has been awarded the job of selling broadcasting rights for several international sport events. Thus, Dentsu sold the broadcasting rights in Japan for the 2006 FIFA World Cup, the exclusive worldwide marketing and broadcasting rights (excluding Europe and Africa) of the IAAF World Athletics Series, and the exclusive broadcasting rights in Japan (2004–09) of Major League Baseball.

Sportfive Group, a network of companies based in Europe and controlled by the French media giant Lagardere, marketed and sold the broadcasting rights of Euro Cup 2008 for UEFA. Several television channels across the globe acquired the telecasting rights of Euro 2008. The Sportfive Group took a market-to-market strategy of selling the Euro 2008 broadcasting rights. Thus, it sold the rights to telecast the Euro 2008 soccer matches to more than 60 television channels in 55 countries all over the world.

Over the past decade, colleges and universities in the United States have been changing their strategy from making direct deals with broadcasters to outsourcing most or all of their media rights sales to sports marketing firms. This approach provides athletic departments more revenues, and at the same time lets them focus on ticket sales and fundraising activities. For example, Louisiana State University signed a 10-year, $74.5 million deal in 2005 to consolidate media rights with CBS Collegiate Sports Properties. In this vein, the universities of Texas, Arizona, Tennessee, and Kentucky have signed multiyear multimillion-dollar contracts with IMG College (formerly Host Communications) for their media rights.

Licensed Broadcasters

Broadcasters (television, radio, Internet, broadband, and mobile telecommunications) buy the rights to broadcast a sporting event to viewers. Broadcasters may be sellers of broadcasting rights as well as buyers. They may sell (sublicense) all or part of their broadcasting rights to another media platform or they may sell advertising time for the event they have the right to broadcast.

Broadcasters are usually interested in securing broadcasting of sport events in order to increase their market share and value, and to test new technologies. For example, in 1995, Unity/Arena bought the rights to broadcast the Bundesliga's (Germany's top-level soccer league) games and attracted more than 900,000 subscribers in a few months. At the same time, Premiere, a pay-TV group and the previous owner of these rights, lost 42 percent of its market value and some of its subscribers.

Until recently, television was the dominant medium in airing sports events, followed by radio. However, broadband, Internet, and mobile have emerged as new platforms for broadcasting sport content all over the world. This shift to new media channels is the result of the changing needs of consumers, as several recent studies have reported.

Although when they first appeared, new media rights were only partially exploited by sports rights holders, there is increasing interest in developing and selling these rights. These new broadcasting platforms are expected to change the landscape of sports broadcasting in the coming years by taking a niche marketing approach, reaching global audiences, and dealing with new issues (e.g., online piracy). Moreover, Internet broadcasting will change the way broadcasting rights are sold from a territorial to a worldwide base.

Current Trends

New digital media such as digital terrestrial television, digital cable, digital radio, Internet TV, and mobile TV have significantly changed the way sport content is delivered and watched. With the introduction of new broadcasting platforms (e.g., Internet and mobile phones), new media rights are being developing and more fully exploited by rights holders. Thus, new media are gaining additional value in the media sector and compete against other broadcasting media for larger market shares.

The proliferation of new media and broadcasting technologies has enabled sport rights holders to generate substantial new revenue streams. Recently, sport rights holders are facing a new challenge that is threatening the value of broadcasting rights: broadcasting piracy. Broadcasting piracy refers to the illegal live broadcasting of sports events over various media such as TV, radio, mobile devices, and the Internet.

Broadcast piracy causes serious harm to both sport rights holders and broadcasters, requiring content monitoring services and substantial legal protection. Because sport broadcasting rights are usually sold on an exclusive basis, the illegal copying and/or retransmission of sport content, either live or deferred, devalue broadcasters' costly investments and prevent their further exploitation (e.g., increased advertising revenue and sublicensing). Furthermore, when value is diminished by piracy, sport rights holders can no longer secure large revenues from broadcasting rights because they cannot guarantee exclusivity, a significant part of the value of the rights.

Rodoula H. Tsiotsou
University of Macedonia

See Also: Media Content Rights Fees; Media Contracts With Sports Teams/Events; Media Rights; Media Suppliers; Mobile Technology; Narrowcasting Versus Broadcasting; New Media; On-Site Distribution Rights; Pay-per-View Sports; Piracy; Rights Fees; Sports Networks; Sports Networks, Regional; Sports Radio; Subscription-Based Broadcasting; Televised Sports; Territorial Rights; TV Rights/Contracts; Webcasts.

Further Readings

Barboza, David. "Olympics Are Ratings Bonanza for Chinese TV." *New York Times*, http://www.nytimes.com/2008/08/22/sports/olympics/22cctv.html?_r=1 (Accessed August 2010).

Euro2008. "TV Channels Broadcasting EURO 2008." http://www.euro2008info.net/tv-channels-broadcasting-euro-2008.html (Accessed June 2010).

Kepreotes, Peter. "The Revolution of Sports Broadcasting." http://www.broadcastaustralia.com.au/assets/files/White%20Papers/2007%2003%20-%20The%20Revolution%20of%20Sports%20Broadcasting.pdf (Accessed March 2010).

McCarthy, Michael. "Schools, Coaches Cash in on Lucrative Media Deals." *USA Today.* http://www.usatoday.com/sports/college/football/2006-11-16-cover-coaches-media_x.htm (Accessed March 2010).

Sessa, Danielle and Scott Soshnick. "New York Yankees TV Network Might Fetch $2 Billion." http://www.bloomberg.com/apps/news?pid=2

0601079&refer=home&sid=aTcfoWsgk6Yg (Accessed March 2010).

Sport Business. "Real Madrid TV Kicks Off in the UK Via Satellite, 2006." http://www .sportbusiness.com/news/160897/real-madrid -tv-kicks-off-in-the-uk-via-satellite (Accessed March 2010).

Sport Business. "XFMedia Wins Europa League Rights." http://www.sportbusiness.com/ news/168153/xfmedia-wins-europa-league-rights (Accessed March 2010).

Tsiotsou, Rodoula. "The Effect of European Union Regulations on Marketing Practices." *Journal of Euro-Marketing*, v.15/1 (2005).

Worldtvpc.com. "Massive Growth Shows USA Is Loving Online TV." http://www.worldtvpc.com/ blog/massive-growth-shows-usa-is-loving-online -tv (Accessed March 2010).

Buffalo Bills

The Buffalo Bills, a charter franchise of the American Football League (AFL), became part of the National Football League (NFL) after the merger of the two leagues in 1970. Owned by Ralph Wilson since their inception, the Bills began life in 1959 as one of the eight original franchises in the AFL. The AFL was a rival league established by Lamar Hunt after he had been turned down by the NFL for an expansion franchise for Dallas, Texas. Wilson, a minority owner of the Detroit Lions, had sought to place an AFL franchise in Miami, but was turned down. The team started play during the League's inaugural season in 1960, playing its home games in War Memorial Stadium (built in 1937), ending the season in last place in the AFL Eastern Division. The first head coach was Buster Ramsey, who was fired after the 1961 season.

As part of an effort to prove its legitimacy, the AFL challenged the Canadian Football League (CFL) to an exhibition game. The Bills were chosen to play the Hamilton Tiger-Cats because the two cities were geographically close to one another. On August 8, 1961, the game was played at Hamilton's Ivor Wynne Stadium, and the Ticats defeated the Bills 38–21. This was the first and only game between teams from the two leagues.

Lou Saban became the head coach in 1962 and picked up Jack Kemp on waivers from the San Diego Chargers. Kemp led the Bills to two consecutive AFL Championships (1964, 1965), and the Eastern Division Championship in 1966. In 10 years in the AFL, the Bills were 67–71–6. Notable players during the AFL era included Kemp (who retired after the 1969 season to run for Congress); Fullback Cookie Gilchrist (1960–64); wide receiver Elbert Dubenion (1960–68); safety George Saimes (1963–69); linebacker Mike Stratton (1962–72); guard Billy Shaw (1961–69); defensive tackle Tom Sestak, and O. J. Simpson (1969–77), who joined the team during their last season in the AFL.

The NFL

War Memorial Stadium, the Bills' home since the team's inception, had a capacity of 46,500, which was below the 50,000-seat minimum required of NFL stadia. After considering the relocation of the team to Seattle, Wilson decided to move to a new stadium in suburban Orchard Park. The 80,000-seat facility opened in 1973. The stadium was named Rich Stadium, as Rich Products agreed to pay $1.5 million over 25 years for the naming rights to the stadium. In 1998, the stadium was renovated and the seating capacity was reduced to 74,000. The stadium was refitted with larger seats and more luxury and club seating at that time. In summer 2007, a new HD Mitsubishi LED board measuring 88.8 feet by 32.5 feet, and ribbon boards were installed.

During the 1990s, the team captured four consecutive American Football Conference (AFC) championships (1990–93), but failed to win the Super Bowl. The Bills last appeared in the playoffs in 1999. Marv Levy coached the teams of the late 1980s and early 1990s. He was 112–70 as head coach between 1986 and 1997, when he retired (Levy came out of retirement to serve as general manager during the 2006 and 2007 seasons). During Levy's tenure (1986–97), the Bills made the playoffs eight times. A trio of Pro Football Hall of Famers led the team during the Levy era: Jim Kelly, who quarterbacked the Bills from 1986 to 1996;

The Buffalo Bills, an original AFL franchise, have recently sought greater identification with the region beyond Buffalo.

Argonauts). The team was also paid $78 million (Canadian dollars) by Rogers Communications, the owner of the Rogers Center, which owns the CFL team and has expressed interest in securing an NFL franchise for Toronto.

The 2008 games (one regular season and one pre-season game) averaged 50,284 spectators, who paid an average of $183 Canadian per seat (compared to an average ticket price of $51 Canadian for tickets at Ralph Wilson Stadium). In 2009, Rogers Communications reduced ticket prices by 17 percent.

Jeffrey Kraus
Wagner College

See Also: Buffalo Sabres; Economic Climate for Sports; Fan Avidity; Fan Loyalty Continuum; National Football League.

Further Readings

Gehman, Jim. *Then Levy Said to Kelly—The Best Buffalo Bills Stories Ever Told*. Chicago: Triumph Books, 2008.

Miller, Jeffrey J. *Rockin' the Rockpile: the Buffalo Bills of the American Football League*. Toronto: ECW Press, 2007.

Pitoniak, Scott. *The Good, the Bad, and the Ugly Buffalo Bills: Heart-Pounding, Jaw-Dropping, and Gut-Wrenching Moments From Buffalo Bills History*. Chicago: Triumph Books, 2007.

Tasker, Steve. *Steve Tasker's Tales From the Buffalo Bills*. Champaign, IL: Sports Publishers, LLC, 2006.

Thurman Thomas, who rushed for 11,938 yards in 12 seasons (1986–99) with Buffalo; and defensive end Bruce Smith. Other stars included Andre Reed, who caught 941 passes for the Bills between 1985 and 1999; offensive linemen Kent Hull and Jim Richter; linebacker Darryl Talley; and special teams star Steve Tasker. Another Pro Football Hall of Famer, James Lofton, played four seasons (1989–92) during his career with the Bills.

Regionalization of the Franchise

Maintaining the Bills as a viable franchise in the Buffalo market has become a challenge. When the Bills entered the AFL in 1960, the city's population was 532,759; in 2008, the city's estimated population was 270,919. The area has also experienced a loss of jobs and large corporations, making it difficult for the Bills to effectively market the franchise.

In response to the population decline of its market, the Bills have attempted to "regionalize" the franchise. The team has held its training camp in Rochester, New York, since 1999. In 2008, they entered into an agreement that will have the team playing eight games at Toronto's Rogers Center between 2008 and 2012.

The "Bills Toronto Series" is an effort by the team to attract more fans from southwest Ontario (which is home to two Canadian Football League Franchises: the Hamilton Tiger-Cats and the Toronto

Buffalo Sabres

The Buffalo Sabres are a National Hockey League (NHL) franchise. They are assigned to the Northeast Division of the Eastern Conference of the NHL. The team entered the NHL as an expansion team for the 1970–71 season. The original owners were Seymour Knox III and Northrup Knox. The Knox brothers had sought an expansion franchise when the NHL expanded from the "original six" to 12 in 1967–68, but were not awarded a franchise. They also had negotiated a deal to move the Oakland Seals, which was blocked by the NHL because the Los Angeles Kings did not want to be the only West Coast–based team in the league. In June 1969, the Knox brothers purchased a 20 percent stake in the Seals, which they sold when they were awarded the Buffalo franchise.

The Sabres played their home games at the Buffalo Memorial Auditorium, a facility constructed in 1940 and expanded for the Sabres and the Buffalo Braves, a National Basketball Association team that also started play in 1970–71. George "Punch" Imlach, who had won four Stanley Cups as coach of the Toronto Maple Leafs during the 1960s, was the team's first coach.

The Sabres' first draft choice was center Gilbert Perreault, who scored 38 goals in 1970–71. The following season, the Sabres drafted Richard Martin and traded for Rene Robert. They joined Perreault on the "French Connection" line, which played together until Robert was traded at the beginning of the 1979–80 season. The Sabres were a playoff contender throughout the 1970s and made the finals in 1975 (their fifth season in the League) and had the best regular season record in 1979–80. For the next 30 years, the team was a playoff fixture, appearing in 22 playoffs. However, the team did not go deep into the playoffs, making it to the finals once (1998–99).

In 1995–96, the Knox brothers sold the team to John Rigas, owner of Adelphia Communications, the cable systems operator that also owned the Empire Sports Network, which carried Sabres games. A new general manager (Darcy Regier) and head coach (Lindy Ruff) were hired; both remain with the team in those capacities. Timothy Rigas, son of the new owner, was named the team's president. In 1996–97, the team moved into a new arena, Marine Midland Arena (now HSBC Arena), after 25 years at the "Aud." During the first season, the jumbotron crashed to the ice surface shortly after a Sabres practice.

In 2002, John Rigas and his sons were indicted for bank, wire, and securities fraud for embezzling more than $2 billion from Adelphia Communications. The NHL took control of the team. There were concerns that the team would move or fold,

and the Sabres' average attendance during 2002–03 was 13,776, down from 17,206 the season before.

In March 2003, B. Thomas Golisano, the founder of Paychex (a payroll processing company) and a three-time candidate for governor of New York, took control of the Sabres, purchasing the team for $92 million. One of his partners was Larry Quinn, who had been president of the club before the Rigas family takeover. Quinn became managing partner and he and Golisano lowered ticket prices. Average attendance increased to 15,290 in 2003–04.

Over the past five seasons, the team made the playoffs three times (2006, 2007, and 2010), losing in the Conference Finals (2006 and 2007). The team won the President's Trophy for the Best Regular Season Record in 2006–07.

Community Outreach

As for their work in the community, the Buffalo Sabres Foundation is a 501(c)(3) nonprofit foundation established in 1995 and reinvigorated in 2004 following the acquisition of the Buffalo Sabres by Golisano.

The Buffalo Sabres Foundation aims to enhance the quality of life in the western New York and southern Ontario region, making its primary focus to (1) assist youth hockey initiatives, (2) support children's health and wellness initiatives, specifically those that serve the underprivileged and handicapped, and (3) provide support to nonprofit organizations that provide vital services to those in need in the community.

The Buffalo Sabres Foundation has been involved in a number of fundraising and community activities since 2004, most notably its annual Corporate Challenge Hockey Tournament, Golf Tournament, and Aces and Blades Gala. Since 2004 the Buffalo Sabres Foundation has raised over $250,000 through these and other activities. Since 2004, the Buffalo Sabres Foundation has made numerous grants, totaling over $200,000, to western New York organizations. These included a $100,000 gift to Buffalo's Women's and Children's Hospital in 2005 and, in 2006, a $30,000 grant to Hasek's Heroes, and a $15,000 grant to SABAH.

The Buffalo Sabres Street HockeyFest, presented by Dick's Sporting Goods, is an annual street hockey tournament held on the streets outside HSBC

Arena. The event has grown to be the largest street hockey tournament in western New York.

Television, Radio, and Mascot

The Sabres Hockey Network is a joint venture of the Sabres and Entercom Communications, a company that owns radio stations around the country and is headquartered in Bala Cynwyd, Pennsylvania. Rick Jeanneret has been the play-by-play voice of the Sabres since 1971, their second season in the NHL, and has the longest tenure of any NHL announcer. Harry Neale, a former NHL and WHA coach, has been the color commentator since 2007–08. The between period and post-game (known as *Shootout)* shows on television are hosted by former Sabres Mike Robitaille and Rob Ray, and Kevin Sylvester from a studio at the HSBC Arena. In the 2009–10 season, the Sabres did not send their television broadcast crew on the western road trip and instead aired the local broadcasts of the Phoenix Coyotes, Anaheim Ducks, Los Angeles Kings, and Vancouver Canucks. The radio network's post-game show is hosted by Brian Koziol. The pregame show, which airs on the flagship station WGR (550 AM), is hosted by Mike Schopp and Chris "Bulldog" Parker. The radio network, in addition to all-sports WGR, includes WCMF (96.5 FM), Rochester; WROC (950 AM), Rochester; WKSN (1340 AM), Jamestown; WMXO (101.5 FM), Olean; WBTA (1490 AM), Batavia; and WDOE (1410 AM), Dunkirk.

Since the collapse of Adelphia Communications, Sabres games have been aired on the MSG Network throughout upstate New York. MSG airs approximately 70 games a year, with the remaining games airing on Versus or NBC. The radio broadcast has been simulcast as the audio on the Sabres television broadcasts since 1997. In 2010–11, 69 of the 70 games aired on MSG will be available in high definition television (HDTV).

The team mascot is Sabretooth, the saber-toothed tiger. From 1992 to 1998, he was also the mascot of the Buffalo Bandits indoor lacrosse team of the National Lacrosse League. He has a house in HSBC Arena. Before games, he rappels from the ceiling to the ice while rock music plays, and has also been known to ride a four-wheeler on the ice while followed by a spotlight. He has a t-shirt bazooka, which he uses to shoot shirts into the crowd.

Marketing the Sabres

When Golisano purchased the Sabres he reduced ticket prices and introduced variable pricing, basing ticket prices on opponent and weekday or weekend scheduling. The number of season tickets is capped at 14,800, a gain of 9,000, generating capacity crowds at prices near the bottom of the league average (the average ticket price in 2009–10 was $33). The team has a season ticket waiting list that now has 6,000 names. While a logo change introduced after the lockout initially generated criticism, sales of team merchandise increased. Labatt USA extended its marketing effort to the Sabres' alumni group and a pond hockey tournament.

During 2003–04 and 2005–06, the Sabres played a regular season game in Rochester at the 11,215-seat Blue Cross Arena at the War Memorial. (Golisano is from Rochester, New York, and the Rochester Americans were the team's American Hockey League affiliate at the time.) In 2009–10, the team drew an average of 18,529 spectators (99.1 percent capacity).

In 2009, *Forbes* assessed the team's value at $170 million, making it the 23rd most valuable franchise in the NHL. Major corporate sponsors are Anheuser-Busch InBev, Coca-Cola, Labatt Breweries, and Chevrolet.

Jeffrey Kraus
Wagner College

See Also: Buffalo Bills; National Hockey League; Ticket Price, Variable.

Further Readings

Brewitt, Ross, ed. *Sabres: Twenty-Six Seasons in Buffalo's Memorial Auditorium.* Dallas, TX: Taylor Publishing, 1996.

Maiorano, Sal. *Thank You Sabres: Memories of the 1972–1973 Season.* Coal Valley, IL: Quality Sports Publications, 1997.

Swados, Robert O. *Counsel in the Crease: A Big League Player in the Hockey Wars.* Amherst, NY: Prometheus Books, 2006.

Wieland, Paul. *"Then Perreault Said to Rico": The Best Buffalo Sabres Stories Ever Told.* Chicago: Triumph Books, 2008.

Calgary Flames

The Calgary Flames are a National Hockey League (NHL) franchise located in Calgary, Alberta's largest city and the business center of western Canada. After being based in the city for 30 years, the Flames are now entrenched as a local institution. The Flames arrived in Calgary in 1980 after eight years in Atlanta, Georgia (where the club was also known as the Flames). As Atlanta, the club had been the first NHL expansion team in the southern United States. They were added, in part, to meet a need for tenants along with the Atlanta Hawks of the National Basketball Association in the newly built Omni—and also to balance the expanded NHL schedule because of the addition of the New York Islanders that same year. During their eight years in Atlanta, the Flames made the playoffs all but two years, although they did not advance beyond the first round. Like many other southern-based NHL franchises in the 1970s, the team encountered financial difficulties and was then purchased by a group of Alberta businessmen in 1980.

The Flames, upon arriving in Calgary, first played in the Stampede Corral, a small rink in the same venue as the Calgary Stampede, the world renowned rodeo. In 1983, the team moved into the

Saddledome, which was built nearby on the Stampede Grounds in preparation for Calgary hosting the 1988 Olympic Winter Games. Today, the Saddledome remains the home of the Flames; it is one of the oldest arenas in the NHL and is an iconic image of the city of Calgary. In 2010, talk of a new arena in the city had begun.

In their first season in Calgary, the Flames lost in the semi-finals to the Minnesota North Stars, followed by a 15-year run up until 1996 where the Flames made the playoffs every year except one. Following the 1988–89 season, the Flames defeated the Montreal Canadiens four games to two, to win their first and only Stanley Cup. From 1997 to 2004, the Flames' on-ice performance slumped, coinciding with a downturn in the Canadian dollar compared to the American one—which when combined with Calgary's comparatively small market size (approximately 1 million) made it difficult to keep or attract marquee players.

With star players being traded away and financial losses mounting, the fans also began to lose their passion, and attendance sagged. By 1999, the ownership group issued an ultimatum that more season tickets were required or the Flames would follow the exodus to the U.S. following other Canadian teams such as the Winnipeg Jets (to Phoenix, Arizona) and the Quebec Nordiques (to Denver, Colorado). Nearly 2,000 fans responded to this plea, and the club remained in Calgary.

The Flaming C

The club's momentum changed drastically in 2002 when the team made a surprise run to the Stanley Cup finals, where they lost to the Tampa Bay Lightning in the seventh game, by one goal. During this series, the now-famous Red Mile and C of Red were born: Flames fans wearing the newly christened red jerseys with the Flaming C as the logo would swarm 17th Avenue just outside the Saddledome after the games, for a festival-like atmosphere. The Red Mile is estimated to have attracted as many as 35,000 fans into the streets during those playoffs, peaking at over 60,000 in the finals. The red jersey was the top-selling launch in NHL history, and was in high demand nationwide during those playoffs. Fan support has continued at a high level since 2002.

Recently, the Flames have expanded their operations. The ownership group jointly controls operations for the Calgary Flames, the Pengrowth Saddledome, and the Western Hockey League's Calgary Hitmen; the group also holds a small stake in the Calgary Stampeders of the Canadian Football League. The purchase of the Hitmen was done, in part, to help fill dates in the Saddledome, which had been purchased by the Flames in 1994 with a 20–year lease. Originally called the Canadian Airlines Saddledome, the building was renamed the Pengrowth Saddledome following a new naming rights deal.

More recently, the Flames opened a sports bar and entertainment center called Flames Central, located in the downtown core. The Flames recognize that hockey is still their core business, but have been entrepreneurial in encouraging their fan base to continue supporting the team when away or during sellouts. To help celebrate 30 years in Calgary, the Flames in 2010 launched their retro jersey, which was worn for five home games against the other Canadian teams.

David Legg
Mount Royal College
Norm O'Reilly
University of Ottawa

See Also: Arena; Expansion; Fan Avidity; National Hockey League.

Further Readings

Duhatschek, Eric, et al. *Hockey Chronicles*. New York: Facts on File, 2001.
Norman, Darcy. *HockeyNomics*. Edmonton, Canada: Folklore Publishers, 2009.

Capital Investment

Typically, a capital investment made by a professional sports team, a college athletic department, or a manufacturer of sports products refers to money spent on fixed assets like stadiums, arenas, land, machinery, or buildings. This investment on the part of the sports business is used to bring in revenue for that business, but can be distinguished from operating expenses like the phone bill or the heating bill. The cost of facilities is one of the two major expenses for professional sports franchises around the world; the other major cost being player salaries. The capital asset is expected to be used for quite some time and is usually depreciated on a company's balance sheet. The ability to depreciate this capital investment is a tax advantage that was enacted to make these types of outlays more palatable to the bottom line of a business. Rather than expense that item when it has been constructed, the cost of this capital facility will be expensed over time, as that asset is being used in the business.

A stadium for a National Football League (NFL) franchise is used by that team to play football. This capital investment permits them to charge an entry fee to fans. The teams can earn rights fees by televising games played in that stadium, and these facilities offer opportunities for companies to buy ad space on signs within the stadium. Stadiums around the league usually have retail space where teams will sell products like T-shirts, hats, and other team trademarked merchandise to their fans. NFL franchises will offer sponsorship opportunities for companies to place their names on the stadium; for example, FedEx Field in the Washington, D.C., area, Lucas Oil Stadium in Indianapolis, and University of Phoenix Stadium in Arizona. Teams also will invest money in the building of concession stands, restaurants, and bars in the stadium to sell food and drink during the course of the football game.

Many sports teams and athletic departments will choose to upgrade their facilities in order to build luxury boxes or suites, or club level seating with added amenities, or to add television screens, new digital video display boards, state-of-the-art scoreboards, or more comfortable seating for their highest-priced seats. All of these improvements in fixed assets represent capital investments. Upgrades or stadium renovations are usually not as costly as the building of new facilities, but these "capital improvements" can still involve large sums of money for the team, the school, or the local jurisdiction. The renovation of legendary Arrowhead Stadium in Kansas City, home to the NFL's Kansas City Chiefs, cost a cool $375 million.

Planning

A sports business will make a cost–benefit analysis when capital investments are contemplated. Can the cost of this improvement be justified by the revenue projections? For example, if we add a state-of-the-art computerized scoreboard and sign display package to our arena, will this expense be covered by the ability to offer more advertising opportunities for our clients? Will the new locker room the football coach wants actually attract more top-tier high school recruits to the football team? If we add luxury boxes to our baseball stadium, can we sell them to local season ticket holders and businesses? Will a downturn in the economy make this capital investment a very bad decision? Are there energy savings and tax breaks if we make this capital investment? Are interest rates so low that we should borrow the money and make a substantial capital improvement now?

Many of these capital investment decisions relate to the competition. Is our stadium bigger than theirs? Does our arena have nicer luxury boxes? Do our locker rooms have bigger TVs than the other teams in our league? The bar for capital investment in stadium upgrades and new construction has been raised exponentially. The Dallas Cowboys (NFL), New

York Yankees (Major League Baseball), the New York Jets/Giants (Meadowlands Stadium/NFL), and the New Jersey Nets (Barclays Center in Brooklyn/National Basketball Association) will build or have built facilities that will cost over $1 billion.

Because capital investments are typically for large amounts of money and because they are also more permanent than, for example, the purchase of new phones or a new rug in your office, a greater amount of planning and research must go into these decisions. A decision to spend $20 million on the construction of club level seating will be scrutinized much more closely, as it should be, than a decision to change the color of the carpet in the executive suite.

The National Basketball Association (NBA) and NHL, both major sports leagues in the United States, use large indoor arenas to play hockey and basketball as part of their businesses. Many of these arenas are shared by teams in the same city. The NHL's Los Angeles Kings play in the same arena as the NBA Lakers and Clippers. The Washington Capitals use the Verizon Center with the Washington Wizards. The New York Knicks share Madison Square Garden with the New York Rangers. The building of these arenas and their renovations represent a substantial capital investment by owners. All of these arenas are also concert sites. They are used when the circus comes to town and for other entertainment purposes, bringing valuable revenue to their owners.

The capital investment in stadiums, arenas, gymnasiums, and race tracks can be paid for by the owner of the sports franchise or, in many cases, the taxpayer in that locale will be asked to foot the bill. A bond might be floated by local politicians, taxes might be raised on local businesses, or a sales tax levied on consumers to pay for the project. When capital investment in a new facility is approved, additional infrastructure spending is usually required. Roads have to be built, traffic lights installed, pipes and utility lines moved or upgraded. All of these costs fall under the heading of capital investments.

Mega Sports Events

Mega sports events like the Olympics and the World Cup require substantial capital investment. The Beijing Olympics in 2008 required stadiums for baseball competition, softball games, swimming events, and volleyball matches. A new facility was built to house the opening and closing ceremonies as well as the track and field events. There was an Aquatics Park built for rowing events, a gymnastics arena, weightlifting facility, and boxing venue. An Olympic Village was constructed to house the athletes and coaches from the more than 200 countries that participated in the Games. It has been estimated that the Chinese spent well over $30 billion to host the 2008 Summer Olympics; a large part of that expense was the aforementioned capital projects.

The 2010 World Cup in South Africa saw a substantial capital investment in new facilities, practice facilities, and the renovation of older facilities across the country. South Africa also made substantial infrastructure investments to enhance spectator, team, and media travel between stadiums. This capital outlay is there for all to see now, after the World Cup has ended. South Africa and the sports ministry must now find ways to generate revenue and also provide sports events to make use of these facilities. The Chinese Sports Ministry and the Beijing government will also face these same issues with their large capital investment in sports facilities and infrastructure in the hosting of the Olympics.

Craig Esherick
George Mason University

See Also: Arena; Arena Funding—Public/Private; Cost–Benefit Analysis; Facilities Financing; Kansas City Chiefs; Signage; Venue Naming Rights.

Further Readings

Gratton, Chris and Ian Henry. *Sport in the City: the Role of Sport in Economic and Social Regeneration*. London: Routledge, 2001.
Humphreys, B. and Dennis Howard, eds. *The Business of Sports*. Westport, CT: Praeger Publishers, 2006.
Russo, F. E., L. A. Esckilsen, and R. J. Stewart. *Public Assembly Facility Management: Principles and Practices*, 2nd Ed. Coppell, TX: IAAM, 2009.
Zimbalist, Andrew. *The Economics of Sport: Volume I and II*. Northampton, MA: Edward Edgar Publishing, 2001.

Carnegie Reports

In the early 1920s, college football was extremely popular as commercial radio began to broadcast games across the nation. In 1927, the first coast-to-coast broadcast was done at the Rose Bowl. Therefore, with all the attention and money at stake, universities were recruiting heavily, breaking rules, and many players and coaches were "on the take." The corruption and commercialization of college football was threatening the climate and integrity of the higher education experience and existence.

In 1929, the Carnegie Reports, a 350-page research finding, was produced by the Carnegie Foundation after three and a half years of investigation into 112 colleges and universities. The report appeared, among other places, on the front page of the *New York Times* and was titled "American College Athletics." Alarming discoveries were presented: the report focused on college football and found academic abuses, as well as recruiting violations, and payments to student athletes. The main issue that was validated through the report was that college football was completely commercialized. The issue of commercialism in college athletics is in existence today, even after further reports by the American Council on Education in the 1950s and the Knight Commission in 1980s. Even before the Carnegie Reports, a Harvard president, Charles Eliot, called these commercial interests in higher education a "great evil."

The Carnegie Reports exposed the amount of subsidies that universities and colleges were using to recruit and sustain their student athletes. These subsidies included scholarships, loans, payment for jobs that were never done or done to a minimum, favors of all kinds, and arrangements where students were "taken care of." The reports estimated that one in seven athletes received some kind of subsidy. In as much it was athletic officers who committed most of the acts of subsidizing, their proportion was about 50 percent. Another 30 percent was done by alumni, and 8 percent by college administrative officers. This information points to the argument that athletic officials feel student athletes are poorer than the typical student, which is an exaggerated statement. However, the report holds the university president and faculty, the ones with authority, to blame. They are the ones who hold the intellectual integrity of the university.

Recommendations

The recommendations brought forth by the report included to do away with the paid coach, the gate receipts, costly sweaters, and recruiting at high schools. They wanted to do away with the publicity that was given, or gifts "showered" on these athletes, and with journeys in nice cars. They argued for sports in which a large number of students could participate, and where there was not a large expenditure of time and money that would take away from the academic integrity of the student or university.

In essence, these reports changed the National Collegiate Athletic Association (NCAA). Prior to these reports, the NCAA was primarily a rule creator and competition developer, but now it evolved into an organization that oversaw academic standards for student athletes, monitored the recruiting activities of coaches and universities, and established sound principles for governing amateurism. This was done in hopes of alleviating the now common manner of paying student athletes by alumni and boosters.

Despite all of these reform efforts, coaches have the highest paid salaries ever. For example, in 2007 the football coaches earned three times the salaries of the university president at over 45 public institutions. Even worse, the football coaches earned 20 times more than the salary of the professors. To afford these coaches, colleges and universities are building massive luxury suites, auctioning off opportunities to meet the team or run on the field; and television has turned the regular football coach into a movie star. Commercialism in college athletics is here again, even after 80 years of reform efforts and the NCAA handing down a mountain of penalties and violations for recruiting, academic compromises, and financial favors.

Therefore, now more than ever people are calling for those outside of athletics to come and regulate. For years, the university itself has been called upon to regulate its athletics programs; however, it does not seem to be working. Commercialism in athletics is at an all-time high. Are student athletes students who are in college to receive an education and go on to a career—or are they professional athletes who are a part of big-time business in college athletics?

Some have called on the colleges to just admit that they are in the entertainment business, as they do not expect schools to suddenly stop exploiting the commercial opportunities they have. Instead, they must admit what is going on, so that it does not hurt the academic integrity of the institution.

Conclusion

Currently, most athletic departments at big-time institutions are run separately. They do their own fundraising, pay their own salaries, and do their own marketing. Therefore, they are their own entity, separate from the institution of higher learning. This creates a separation that is not only known by professors, staff, and administrators—but also students, alumni, and fans. The mission of a school is not to win and make money. There is a place for athletics and competition, but it should not be commercialized to the point where it upsets the mission and goals of the institution as a whole. Athletic departments should join forces with the institution and become reintegrated into the collegiate system.

Shane Hudson
Texas A&M University

See Also: Ethics in Sport; Knight Commission; Marketing Through Sports; National Collegiate Athletic Association; Student Athlete.

Further Readings

Duderstadt, James. *Intercollegiate Athletics and the American University. A University President's Perspective.* Ann Arbor: University of Michigan Press, 2003.

Friday, William C. and Theodore M. Hesburgh. *Report of the Knight Foundation Commission on Intercollegiate Athletics, March 1991–1993.* Miami, FL: John S. and James L. Knight Foundation, 1993.

Sailor, R. W., ed. "Study of College Athletics" and "Carnegie Athletic Research." *Cornell Alumni News,* v.32/6 (October 31, 1929).

Smith, Ronald A. *Sports and Freedom: The Rise of Big-Time College Athletics.* New York: Oxford University Press, 1990.

Carolina Hurricanes

Since 1997 the Carolina Hurricanes have been the key National Hockey League (NHL) franchise in the mid-south region, specifically the Research Triangle area of North Carolina. Carolina is in the Southeast Division of the Eastern Conference of the NHL. The team is headquartered in Raleigh, the North Carolina capital, and plays its home games at the 18,680-seat RBC Center.

The Hurricanes' most outstanding moment has been winning the 2006 Stanley Cup over the Edmonton Oilers, four games to three. The seventh game was won 3–1. Hurricanes Cam Ward and Rod Brind'Amour took individual honors; the former won the Conn Smythe Trophy as most valuable player and the latter won the Frank J. Selke Trophy as best defensive forward. This championship was the first major league professional sports title won in North Carolina. The other two professional franchises in North Carolina—the NFL Carolina Panthers and the NBA Charlotte Bobcats—are both headquartered in the state's largest city, Charlotte.

The Hurricanes were selected to host the 2011 NHL All-Star Game at the RBC Center. Fans of the franchise have originated some NHL firsts: they meet the team at the airport after every road trip and host tailgate parties prior to home games; both are common practices in college and professional football. These fan fests date from the 2002 season. The team's mascot is Stormy, the fan-pleasing ice hog. The team's colors are red and black; its logo is an oval figure that depicts a hockey puck in the eye of a hurricane. The 2009–10 season record was 35–37 with a total of 80 points.

The Hurricanes played an exhibition game in St. Petersburg, Russia, on October 4, 2010, against SKA St. Petersburg of the KHL. It was the first NHL interaction with Russia in 20 years. The regular season began with games against the Minnesota Wild in Helsinki, Finland, on October 6 and 7.

Origins and Moves

Understanding the present-day Carolina Hurricanes requires knowledge of the team's origins in the northeastern United States and the World Hockey Association (WHA). In 1971 the WHA, looking to establish an alternative to the NHL, awarded a franchise to New England; the team was named the Whalers. In 1972, Larry Pleau was selected as the first Whaler; he later coached the team. Jack Kelley, Boston University hockey coach, was selected as first coach and general manager. The team won its first game, at home in the Boston Garden, defeating the Philadelphia Blazers 4–3 and overcoming a 2–0 deficit. At the end of its first season, the Whalers beat the Winnipeg Jets 9–6 on a national CBS broadcast to claim the World Trophy as the league's top team. Jack Kelley was named coach of the year.

In January 1975, the Whalers moved their home ice to the new Hartford, Connecticut, Civic Center (HCC). Pressure from the Boston Bruins had made that market problematic. The Hartford Whalers won their first game against San Diego 4–3 in overtime. In 1977, the Whalers outmaneuvered the NHL and signed the entire Howe family—Gordie, Mark, and Marty—to long-term contracts. In January 1978, the roof of the HCC collapsed, and the team relocated its home games to Springfield, Massachusetts for two years. They asked fans to be loyal, and fewer than 300 season ticket holders cancelled. On February 6, 1980, the Whalers returned to HCC to beat the Los Angeles Kings before 14,000, including 4,200 season ticket holders.

In 1979, the Whalers and three other WHA teams were incorporated into an expanded NHL. In the same year, the Entertainment Sports Programming Network (ESPN) began; it was headquartered in Bristol, Connecticut, only 15 miles from Hartford. Even with the relocation to North Carolina, ESPN continues its affection for the Whalers and their latter-day incarnation, the Carolina Hurricanes.

In June 1980, Gordie Howe retired; his number 9 jersey was officially retired in February 1981. The team eventually faced market challenges due to being between the Boston Bruins and the New York Islanders. Owner Peter Karmanos announced in May 1997 that the team would relocate to Raleigh, North Carolina. Since the Raleigh facility was not finished, the team was to play at the Greensboro Coliseum, 90 miles west, for the first two seasons. That two-year interval failed to build fan enthusiasm or brand enthusiasm.

John Todd Llewellyn
Wake Forest University

See Also: Arena; Moving a Franchise; National Hockey League.

Further Readings

Norman, Darcy. *HockeyNomics*. Edmonton, Canada: Folklore Publishers, 2009.

Pincus, Arthur, Dave Rosner, Len Hochberg, and Malcolm, Chris. *The Official Illustrated NHL History: From the Original Six to a Global Game*. Chicago: Triumph Books, 1999.

Carolina Panthers

The Carolina Panthers are only the second National Football League (NFL) team to be owned by a former player. In this regard, Panthers owner Jerry Richardson follows in the footsteps of the legendary George Halas, sole owner of the Chicago Bears from 1932 until his death in 1983. The Panthers play and practice at Bank of American Stadium, a 77,778-seat facility in Charlotte, North Carolina. The team draws fan loyalty from both North and South Carolina; Charlotte abuts the border of the two states.

Charlotte was awarded the 29th NFL franchise in October 1993; this action was the league's first expansion since 1976. The path to the bid began in 1987 as Richardson and a small group of civic leaders investigated and then developed an expansion franchise proposal. The centerpiece of their effort was the plan for a stadium to be built entirely with private funds; in an era of stadium projects underwritten by government entities, this approach in itself was notable. The mechanism for this process is the permanent seat license (PSL), through which ticket holders purchase both the seat and the right to purchase tickets.

On the first day of availability, June 3, 1993, all 8,314 club seats sold, all 104 luxury boxes were reserved, and 41,832 PSLs were purchased. The depth of community support for the franchise was clear. In 1996, the stadium was dubbed Ericsson Stadium; in 2002, it became Bank of America Stadium; it is an open-air, natural grass facility.

The team played its first game in 1995 in the Hall of Fame Game in Canton, Ohio, against that year's other expansion entry, the Jacksonville Jaguars. The Panthers prevailed 20–14 and became the first NFL expansion team since the 1961 Minnesota Vikings to win its first game. In its inaugural season the team had a 7–9 win-loss record, three victories better than the previous expansion team mark. The first player taken by the Panthers in the 1995 college draft was Pennsylvania State University quarterback Kerry Collins.

Record and Marketing

In their tenure, the Panthers have shown stability; the three head coaches have been Dom Capers (1995–98), George Seifert (1999–2001), and John Fox (2002–10). The 2010 season, with a 2–14 record, was the second time the Panthers held the NFL's worst season record; they had notched a 1–15 record in 2001. The Panthers announced in December 2010 that the team would search for a new coach for the 2011 season, and former Chicago Bears linebacker Ron Rivera was selected.

The team's colors are black, silver, and Panthers blue. The mascot is Sir Purr, a costumed cat in black and blue that walks upright and entertains fans with hugs and antics and does community relations work in schools and hospitals. The team enjoys solid business-to-business relationships as illustrated by the 2007 action of US Airways in outfitting an Airbus A319 in Carolina Panthers colors and logo. The airline flies out of Charlotte Douglas International Airport. US Airways had similar relationships with the Pittsburgh Steelers, the Arizona Cardinals, and the Philadelphia Eagles. The team is also connected to the community with events like cooperation with Operation Wounded Warrior; through this program in 2007 nine veterans injured during their service in Iraq were guests of the team. Some of the veterans accompanied Panthers players onto the field for the pregame coin toss while others led the team out onto the field. The veterans also relaxed with the players in a pregame visit by joining them in the popular locker-room game of "bin ball," where contestants compete for accuracy by throwing footballs into laundry bins.

In 2002, the Panthers were assigned to the NFL South along with the Atlanta Falcons, the New

The Panthers' unusual privately funded stadium was largely supported by the sale of 41,832 permanent seat licenses.

Orleans Saints, and the Tampa Bay Buccaneers. This change repaired the earlier alignment that had this East Coast team situated as part of the NFL West. The high point of the team's history to date is its 2004 appearance in Super Bowl XXX-VIII against the New England Patriots. After just a decade in the league, the Panthers qualified for the ultimate game and came back to tie the score at 29 with a minute to go. A 41-yard field goal by the Patriots' Adam Vinatieri ended the Panthers dreams. The fact remains that an upstart franchise had put itself on the NFL map in a definitive way.

John Todd Llewellyn
Wake Forest University

See Also: Arena Funding—Public/Private; National Football League; Ownership, Professional Teams.

Further Readings

MacCambridge, Michael. *America's Game: The Epic Story of How Pro Football Captured a Nation.* New York: Anchor Books, 2004.

McDonough, Will, Peter King, Joe Gergen, Harold Rosenthal, and Ed Bouchette. *The History of the NFL: The Complete Story of the National Football League, 1920–2000.* New York: Smithmark, 1999.

Cartel

A cartel is typically defined as a formal or explicit agreement among a group of competitor firms to control or manage prices, available output, labor costs, market shares, or customer allocation. The traditional acts of a cartel or acts of cartel behavior include price fixing, agreements not to compete, and collusion against external forces including labor. Antitrust laws around the world have sought to ban private cartel formation and explicit cartel behavior by powerful firms as expressly anticompetitive and injurious to the marketplace.

Sports Leagues as Cartels

Most major sports leagues fit the definition of a cartel, described above, nearly perfectly. They are created by explicit agreement, by a fixed number of competitors, who have elected to limit competition to increase profits and control labor costs. Types of cartel behavior common in sports include: price fixing in the form of group licensing fees and the collective sale of broadcast rights; collusion in having roster limits, salary caps, free agency limitations, ticket prices, revenue pooling or sharing, restricting the number of franchises, and issues of general league governance; and blacklisting in the form of player drafts or suspended lists—all of which can have negative effect on the relevant markets for fans, potential league business partners, and league labor.

Practically speaking, nearly every major sports league in North America operates as a natural monopoly, existing in a marketplace where costs of operation and barriers to entry are significant enough to prevent the existence or entry of competitors. As monopolistic collectives, the leagues therefore act as cartels in virtually every common task they undertake. This interpretation of sports leagues as cartels is reinforced by both the historic and currently prevailing legal view of sports leagues as a collection of competitors requiring some type of antitrust exemption for all concerted acts.

In June 2010, the U.S. Supreme Court in the case of *American Needle v. National Football League,* in an extremely rare unanimous decision for a politically divided Court, reaffirmed this long-held view of sports leagues as monopolistic cartels, requiring a form of antitrust immunity to permit any course of conduct agreed to by two or more clubs.

Sources of Immunity

There are several primary sources of the antitrust immunity that protect even the most basic sports league activity that would otherwise be deemed cartel behavior.

The statutory labor exception, found in the Clayton Antitrust Act of 1914, is perhaps the most comprehensive antitrust exception. The statutory labor exception expressly allows unions and employers to enter into agreements regarding wages, hours, and working conditions that might restrain interstate commerce. When the antitrust laws were first seriously applied to the sports context by courts, beginning in the 1970s, the statutory labor exception became a key layer of antitrust protection for leagues and also dramatically increased the leverage of player's unions.

The nonstatutory labor exception is a judge-made doctrine that reflects a policy preference for collective bargaining, and prevents antitrust challenge to the agreed-upon outcome of union and employer agreement. The nonstatutory labor exception extends broader protection to the result of arms-length bargaining, even if it is not perfectly memorialized in a collective bargaining agreement or a collective bargaining agreement has expired. Player drafts, for example, have been upheld because of the application of non-statutory labor exception.

Sports leagues also get direct antitrust protection with regard to the collective sale of media rights, by virtue of an act of Congress called the Sports Broadcasting Act of 1961. Leagues, like all other entities, may also immunize cartel activities by arguing that such antitrust violations are actually pro-competitive—but such immunity is narrowly construed by courts.

Finally, Major League Baseball, by virtue of a 1922 U.S. Supreme Court decision, has had blanket antitrust immunity, but the Court never extended that protection to any other sport or league.

Cartels in Other Settings

European sports leagues largely function as cartels, but most enjoy strong governmental exception from European Union antitrust laws. Pro sports leagues are not the only sports entities that have been subject to antitrust lawsuits. College and amateur sports entities also function as cartels and have faced similar legal challenges. If anything, such amateur entities—including the National Collegiate Athletic Association, national governing bodies, and athletic associations—have less immunity for their cartel-like concerted activities than do professional leagues, which have the benefit of labor exceptions.

Recognizing sports entities are in need of broad antitrust immunity, two recent trends have developed. The first is the single entity theory, which essentially says the league and its teams are a single entity incapable of competing against one another. The second is that certain affiliated activities of sports leagues maybe viewed as joint ventures between the competitively owned teams, their league, and perhaps another outside party. These structures had received reasonably favorable treatment from courts and economists—however, the Supreme Court's holding in *American Needle* casts some doubt on the future of both doctrines.

Robert A. Boland
New York University

See Also: Antitrust Laws and Sports; Collective Bargaining Agreement; Free Agents; Labor Law; League Structure; Monopoly Power; Monopsony; Sports Broadcasting Act (1961).

Further Readings

Katz, H. C. and T. A. Kochan. *An Introduction to Collective Bargaining and Industrial Relations,* 2nd Ed. New York: McGraw-Hill, 2000.

Ross, Stephen F. and Stefan Szymanski. "Antitrust and Inefficient Joint Ventures: Why Sports Leagues Should Look More Like McDonald's and Less Like the United Nations." *Marquette Sports Law Review*, v.16/2 (2006).

Zimbalist, Andrew. *May the Best Team Win: Baseball Economics and Public Policy*. Washington, DC: Brookings Institute, 2004.

Categorizing Sport

Sport participation can be categorized based on the level of participation for athletes. The categories of sport are professional, intercollegiate, interscholastic, and youth—as well as amateur and grassroots sport categories. The highest level of competition is professional. Professional athletes receive payment for their athletic services and accomplishments. This is the only level of sports that receives money outright for performance.

The second highest level of participation is intercollegiate athletics. This category comprises student athletes enrolled in colleges who participate in their respective varsity athletics programs. These participants do not receive money directly for their performance—but in many cases they do receive money in the form of athletic scholarships and stipends.

The next category is the level of interscholastic sport. Similar to intercollegiate sport, interscholastic sport comprises student athletes. However, these student athletes are participating in sport at the high school level. There are many more high school athletes than college athletes. High school student athletes do not receive money for performance or scholarships. They also do not receive any type of stipend for participation. However, some schools may have booster clubs that use money to pay for meals, trips, or athletic apparel.

The final category of sport participation is youth sport. Youth sport is present in numerous communities across the United States and has the greatest amount of participants. These athletes often pay to play their respective sport. The youth sport category may also include recreational adult leagues for a given sport. Every other category of sport has some sort of tryout system that makes participation in their level more exclusive.

Amateur and grassroots sport are used as grouping terms for other categories of sport. Amateur sport encompasses the intercollegiate, interscholastic, and youth categories of sport. Amateur sport simply refers to the fact that participants in these categories do not receive money for their performance in a given sport.

Grassroots sport refers to the local levels of sport participation, and the funding comes largely from the participants. Interscholastic and youth sport make up this category of sport. Interscholastic sports are often funded by booster clubs made up of parents of the athletes. They raise and contribute money to the program. Youth sport participants pay an entry fee and provide their own uniforms for participation.

These levels within the categories of sport can also be based on skill level, prestige, or exclusivity, as well as other definitive terms.

The Professionals

In sports, a professional is someone who participates for money. The term *professional* is at times used incorrectly when referring to sports, as the distinction simply refers to how the athlete is funded, and not necessarily competitions or achievements. However, professional athletes and coaches are widely regarded as the highest-skilled participants in their respective sport.

Professional team sport athletes have contracts that stipulate their salary and their behavior. Individual sport professionals, such as golfers and tennis players, do not have such contracts. They are paid with prize money based on their performance.

Professional athleticism has come to the fore through a combination of developments. Mass media and increased leisure have brought larger audiences, so that sports organizations or teams generate large amounts of revenue. As a result, more people can afford to make sport their primary career, devoting the training time necessary to increase skills, physical condition, and experience to modern levels of achievement. A good example of a professional athlete or professional team would be Tiger Woods or the New York Yankees, respectively.

Intercollegiate Level

College athletics refers primarily to sports and athletic competition organized and funded by institutions of tertiary education (colleges or universities). In the United States, college athletics can be divided into two categories. The first includes the sports that are sanctioned by one of the collegiate sport governing bodies. The major sanctioning organizations include the National Collegiate Athletic Association (NCAA), the National Association of Intercollegiate Athletics (NAIA), and the National Junior College Athletic Association (NJCAA). Additionally, the first tier is characterized by selective participation, since only the elite athletes in their sport are able to participate. The second includes all intramural and recreational sports clubs, which are available to a larger portion of the student body.

In the United States today, many college sports are extremely popular on both regional and national scales, in many cases competing with professional championships for prime broadcast and print coverage. The average university will offer at least 20 different varsity sports and a wide variety of intramural sports as well.

Intercollegiate athletics exist in numerous countries around the world; however, nowhere does it have the impact and popularity that it does in the United States. This can be explained partly by the extent of participation and competition that results from these organizations. This is measured by the great number of universities that participate, the number of both male and female athletes that participate, and the number of sports being played. Another reason for the importance of college athletics in the United States is the important role it plays in the hierarchy of sport organizations. In many respects, the intercollegiate sports level serves as a feeder system to the professional level, as many of the elite college athletes are chosen to compete at the next level.

College athletes help to generate a large amount of revenue for their school, but are not personally rewarded for their contribution. Instead, this money is distributed among administrators, coaches, media outlets, and other parties. On the other hand, college athletes are given rewards such as a full scholarship to their respective college, and benefit from perks that the general student body does not receive.

Interscholastic

Sports teams commonly exist at the high school level. Students who participate, commonly referred to as student athletes, do so during their course of study. Occasionally, sports success in high school sports may lead to a professional career in the field. There are different levels of high school competition. Generally, each sport has a ninth-grade team, a junior varsity team, and a varsity team. If there is not enough interest and student participation, one or more of these levels may not exist for a sport. The varsity level is the highest level of competition and comprises higher-skilled student athletes. There are also classifications of high schools based on their student population. Since there are more students to choose from, the schools with a higher population tend to have better teams than those schools that are much smaller. In general, schools will compete against other schools of approximately the same size.

High school student athletes are not paid to play, but their transportation and uniforms tend to be provided for them from funds allocated in the school budget. There tend to be booster clubs for each sport made up of parents that help contribute to the funds needed for that team. Fundraisers are frequently held in order to build up funds to use for such things as team meals, trophies, and facility upkeep.

A student athlete is a participant in an organized competitive sport sponsored by the educational institution in which he or she is enrolled. The term *student athlete* is used to describe the direct balance of a full-time student and a full-time athlete, and can be either a high school or college participant. Student athletes in high school (and junior high or middle school) are expected to meet or exceed the academic requirements in order to play sports in high school. Many states enforce strict rules for their student athletes, which are sometimes called "no pass, no play."

Youth Sports

Youth sports have the largest number of participants when compared to any other category. There

This varsity college crew team is in the second highest category of sports participation.

Different regions of the United States offer different sports to the children and youth in that community. While some sports, like baseball, football, and basketball, are offered in most areas, specialized sports are more prominent in different regions. Hockey, for example, is offered more in the north than the south. Lacrosse, another example, is offered more in the mid-Atlantic region than in most other regions in the United States.

Youth sport has historically been used as a means of social development and recreation for children around the world. Recently, especially in the United States, the main effect that youth sports has had on the participant has been shifted in many areas from social development goals such as hard work and cooperation, to a more of a competitive spirit. Parents and coaches tend to put a lot emphasis on the outcome of youth league games, instead of the actual participation of their children. This emphasis dichotomy has become a main topic of discussion in the area of youth sports.

Some youth leagues offer teams that are more competitive and structured more like a high school or college team. These teams travel for their competition and are focused more on the outcome than the process of the game. One of the ultimate competitive youth sport events in the United States is the Little League World Series. This event has emphasized cooperation and good sportsmanship, but the ultimate goal is still being the champion.

Amateur

Most sports played professionally have amateur players outnumbering the professionals. Amateur sports, as opposed to professional, are sports in which participants engage largely or entirely without being paid money for their athletic performance. By the early 21st century, the Olympic Games and all major team sports accepted professional competitors.

However, there are still some sports that maintain a distinction between amateur and professional status with separate competitive leagues. Problems can arise for amateur athletes when sponsors offer to help with an amateur's playing expenses in the hope of striking lucrative endorsement deals with him or her in case he or she becomes a professional at a later date.

are several reasons for this. First, youth sport does not have a definitive age limit or eligibility period, as intercollegiate and interscholastic sports do. Leagues may comprise children as young as 5 years old, and they can participate until high school levels. High school and college generally have a four-year eligibility period, whereas youth has about a 10-year window for participants.

Second, most communities offer community-based youth sports that are available to both boys and girls. Where there might be three or four high schools in a select area, that same area may have multiple youth leagues comprising numerous teams in each league. A third reason is that any child is allowed to participate in youth league sports. Youth sport is not selective of the participant, as other categories are.

Amateur sport includes all sport that does not pay their players based on performance. Some amateur leagues, such as semi-pro football, pay their players per diem, money paid to each player in order to pay for their daily food and expenses. This is not the same as paying a salary based on performance, since each player and coach is paid the same amount regardless of his or her performance.

Other amateur leagues have the teams that make up the league pay for their spot to play. For example, recreational league softball, a popular league across the country, requires an entry fee to be paid by each team in order to pay for the umpires and other staff as well as the upkeep of the facilities.

Grassroots

Grassroots sport refers to sport organizations played locally without extensive travel. It usually refers to younger sport participants, but not exclusively. High school and youth leagues are considered grassroots sport categories, since they are played locally and include younger teams compared to most professional status sports. Recreational community teams may include adult leagues, but these are still considered grassroots. Local club teams are also included in this category. The term *grassroots* refers more to the teams being local and the competition being local, than the age or skill level of the participants.

Professional and intercollegiate teams are frequently made of athletes not necessarily from the same city where their team plays. They also sometimes travel great distances in order to participate in a competition.

Grassroots tends to refer to British sport leagues and is used more internationally then in the United States. It also tends to refer to soccer more than any other sport. The United States commonly refers to these types of leagues as *recreational* or *club* categories.

Joey Gawrysiak
University of Georgia

See Also: Amateur Athlete; Amateur Athletic Union; Grassroots Sponsorship; National Collegiate Athletic Association; Participants in Sports; Student Athlete; Youth Sports.

Further Readings

Hogshead-Maker, Nancy and Andrew Zimbalist, eds. *Equal Play: Title IX and Social Change.* Philadelphia: Temple University Press, 2007.

Miloch, Kimberly and Keith Lambrecht. "Consumer Awareness of Sponsorship at Grassroots Sports Events." *Sports Marketing Quarterly*, v.15/3 (2006).

Sporting Goods Manufacturing Association. *Sports Participation in America: Participation Trends in 103 Fitness, Sports, Outdoor and Recreational Activities.* Washington, DC: Sporting Goods Manufacturing Association International, 2005.

Category Exclusivity

The concept of category exclusivity is relevant to sport sponsorships and refers to the right of a sponsor to be the only representative of its product category associated with the sports property. Therefore, awarding category exclusivity to a sponsor would preclude any of the sponsor's competitors to associate with the same property. Category exclusivity is a quite special benefit for sponsors. Given that such exclusivity limits the number of potential sponsors available to the sports property, it increases the appeal and value of a sponsorship to a sponsor.

Sponsorship surveys often find that sponsors consider category exclusivity as the most important benefit in a sponsorship package. On the other hand, because it comes at a higher price, sponsors may decide to do without it in order to receive a more affordable deal.

A key issue in understanding the concept of category exclusivity pertains to how broadly or narrowly a product category is defined. For example, if Ford was a sponsor of a major sporting event, defining the product category as "vehicles" (very broadly defined) would mean that no other automobile or truck manufacturer could be associated with that event at all. From the standpoint of a sponsor, that would be the desired scenario. However, that would likely make the sponsorship prohibitively expensive; what often happens is that a category is more thinly defined, to allow for several similar companies to all be sponsors while still maintaining exclusivity in their respective categories. In that case, Ford could be the "official truck" of the sporting event, while Toyota could be the "official automobile," and so on. Similarly, product categories like telecommunications or nonalcoholic beverages can include multiple sub-categories within them.

It is also important to keep in mind that, while a sponsor may have category exclusivity directly with the sponsored property, such exclusivity usually does not extend to third parties also associated with the property. This is especially likely in cases where companies have exclusive rights with a league but no exclusivity with the league's broadcast partners that televise the games.

Coors is the official beer of the National Football League (NFL) but the deal does not also entail sponsorship (exclusive or not) of individual NFL teams or broadcasts of NFL games on television. In fact, Anheuser-Busch, a Coors competitor, has exclusive rights to TV advertising during the Super Bowl, a marquee event of the NFL.

Conclusion

Category exclusivity can be beneficial to a sponsor by facilitating fans and consumers to make a clear connection between the sponsor and the sponsored property; presence of competing companies would make it harder for such a connection to be established. Given the positive benefits associated with sponsorship, being the only company from a product category associated with a desired sports property can thus become a competitive advantage.

While obtaining category exclusivity can strengthen a sponsor's sponsorship, it may become a pointless benefit if the sponsor fails to be deliberate about activation of the sponsorship. Such activation is necessary in order to maximize the impact of the sponsorship and reduce ambush marketing attempts by competitors.

Vassilis Dalakas
California State University, San Marcos

See Also: Activation, Sponsorship; Ambush Marketing; Sponsorship Advantages and Disadvantages; Sponsorship Valuation.

Further Readings

Mullin, Bernard J., Stephen Hardy, and William A. Sutton. *Sport Marketing*. Champaign, IL: Human Kinetics, 2007.
Pitts, Brenda and David Stotlar. *Fundamentals of Sport Marketing*. Morgantown, WV: Fitness Information Technology, 2007.

Cause Marketing/Branding

Corporate social responsibility is a method of self-regulation that firms integrate into their business model. It has become more imperative that corporations practice social responsibility, because many consumers are basing purchase decisions on the socially responsible activities of corporations.

There are a variety of benefits that businesses can receive if they choose to demonstrate some degree of responsibility for things that occur in everyday society.

However, a business can also suffer if its managers are unable to properly incorporate this practice into their system. Demonstrating concern for the environment, human rights, community development, and the welfare of their employees both in the United States and abroad can be a strategy for differentiating a brand in the marketplace. This will allow firms to gain a competitive advantage to consumers by being able to appeal to the growing numbers of socially and environmentally oriented individuals in the company's internal and external audiences.

There are many approaches a corporation can consider when engaging in social responsibility. One in particular, cause marketing, refers to the partnership of a for-profit business and a non–profit organization. Corporations have long been involved in supporting community, but when the first cause marketing programs were successfully implemented, it signaled a dramatic shift in the relationship between for-profit and nonprofit organizations. This method distinguishes itself from other forms of social responsibility in that corporate contribution levels are frequently dependent on consumer action. Also, they are often more formal agreements with the nonprofit entity and typically involve more promotion.

Cause marketing appeals to both the public and stakeholders because it provides a firm a means for demonstrating social responsibility. Cause marketing is a tactic that is mutually beneficial to the for-profit sponsor and the nonprofit beneficiary. The sponsor enjoys image enhancement from supporting a worthy cause, and it can experience incremental sales gains generated by the cause promotion. The nonprofit organization sponsored in the cause promotion benefits from the exposure provided by its sponsor, as well as being the beneficiary of donations raised by the sponsor through its cause marketing campaign.

Launching With Lady Liberty

The term *cause marketing* was coined in the 1980s. Between 1981 and 1984, American Express used this approach to support more than 45 local causes. The company believed that card members would use its American Express card more with local purchases if a local cause was attached to it. The most recognized of the causes that American Express supported was the Statue of Liberty restoration project. With this program, one cent for each use of the American Express card, and one dollar for each new card issued, was given to the Statue of Liberty renovation program. Over a short period of time, $2 million was raised for the Statue of Liberty, and transaction activity of American Express cardholders jumped 28 percent. The term *cause marketing* continued to be used with projects such as this, and is frequently used to describe a broader range of initiatives.

Many companies attempt to develop and implement a cause marketing initiative, but not all are successful. Those that are most likely to succeed produce products with a large market, have well-established and wide distribution channels, and would benefit from offering their consumers a chance to make a charitable contribution. It can

also be successful if a company has an existing relationship with a cause or charity, and adds the initiative. Cause marketing should be considered if a company desires to increase sales, co-brand with a cause, or seeks image enhancement.

Typically, cause marketing can be implemented through three different forms of corporate sponsorship: media support, media support plus conditional donations, and media support plus dual incentive donations. Media support is the most common form of cause marketing. Conceptually, a jointly sponsored media plan focuses on a charitable cause and the company's products or services. An example of this is a telethon, where the telethon or cause and the company products are promoted. The second form, media support plus conditional donations, is when media advertising promotes the cause, and the sponsoring corporation's contributions are dependent on consumer response to the company's product or service. American Express's partnership with the restoration of the Statue of Liberty is an example of this. The final form of cause marketing is media support plus dual incentive donations. Under this, two forms of incentive are used to gain support for the charitable organization.

Cause marketing is designed to provide corporate and cause-related benefits. If successfully implemented, these initiatives have the potential to attract new customers, raise funds for a cause, increase product sales, reach niche markets, increase product sales, and build positive brand identity. As a result of all of these benefits, cause marketing is essentially a combination of philanthropic benefits, support for a cause, and tangible business benefits focused on driving profitability.

Cautionary Issues

Just as there are many supporters of cause marketing, there are those who pose potential concerns with the idea. Some of the concerns are related specifically to cause marketing, and there are also some that are common issues to arise with social initiatives. Problems could stem from: the contractual agreements that have to be written between the company and charity, legal restrictions, consumer levels of interest, skepticism with the validity of the charity, and with the media channels that will be needed. Also, consumers may question the motives or sincerity of a cause sponsor. Such questioning can occur if it is perceived that the donation by the sponsor is relatively small (e.g., a $1 donation for a $100 purchase). Another example of how cause sponsor sincerity can be questioned is if advertising and other promotional messages for the cause place too much focus on the sponsor.

For a cause marketing initiative to succeed, certain selection and implementation factors should be considered. Managers should be sure to select a cause that is perceived to be a good match with the company and its consumers. For example, Major League Baseball (MLB) sponsors the Reviving Baseball in Inner Cities (RBI) program. Such a cause sponsorship would be perceived to be a good match for MLB, given that it benefits a cause related to its core product. Cause sponsors should choose a charity or nonprofit that has relationships that will benefit them, target an offer that is connected to the cause, perform adequate research, make efforts that will also be beneficial to the cause, and accept that there might be a reason to make changes to their initial plan.

It can be advantageous for a firm to practice cause marketing, but it is essential that it understands how to develop a cause marketing initiative plan. The steps to do so are somewhat similar to traditional marketing plans. The company should being with a situation assessment, set objectives and goals, select target audiences, determine marketing mix, allocate a budget, and implement and evaluate its plans.

In early cause marketing efforts, the nonprofit organizations were considered to be apprehensive. They questioned whether over time cause marketing would cause nonprofit organizations to lose their focus and whether individuals would cut back from making contributions to the organization. However, after it was proven that the mission of the charities was never forgotten and there was an increase in donations, the nonprofit organizations became more open to establishing these agreements with companies.

Cause marketing support has experienced tremendous growth since the 1980s. In 2009, sponsorship spending in North America on causes was projected to reach $1.57 billion. Companies and nonprofit organizations continue to collaborate and receive significant benefits. This growth is not just restricted to North America. Cause marketing is now recognized as a global phenomenon. Britain, Europe, and Australia are all creating cause marketing campaigns.

Conclusion

The concept of cause marketing is a very distinct form of corporate social responsibility. A company's contribution to a cause is directly affected by the involvement of the consumer. Cause marketing can prove to be beneficial to both parties; however, if necessary, each organization should properly eliminate concerns. Overall, cause marketing is a valuable strategy that corporations and charities should consider when attempting to exhibit social responsibility.

Donald P. Roy
Amia Steele
Middle Tennessee State University

See Also: Charity Sports Events; Social Responsibility; Sponsorship Evaluation Considerations.

Further Readings

Kotler, Phillip and Nancy Lee. *Corporate Social Responsibility: Doing the Most Good for Your Company and Your Cause.* Hoboken, NJ: John Wiley & Sons, 2005.
Smith, Scott M. and David S. Alcorn. "Cause Marketing: A New Direction in the Marketing of Corporate Responsibility." *Journal of Consumer Marketing*, v.8/3 (1991).

Centralization Versus Decentralization of Authority

Centralization refers to authority and decision making by a central body such as top management. Decentralization refers to authority and decision making being delegated to lower-level management or frontline employees. If one were to place the two concepts on opposite ends of a continuum, he or she could begin to judge how centralized the decision making and authority were of an organization; most organizations will fall somewhere in between the two concepts. To judge what is best for an individual organization, it must examine the system, the structure, the environment, and the type of decisions that are needed for success.

Authority and power are important considerations regarding organizational decision making, along with structure and strategy. The concepts of centralization and decentralization may generate discussion regarding the realm of authority and determining the when, where, and who of making decisions. In an organization, one may be given authority to have the power to make decisions affecting others. Further, authority refers to the power an individual has to make decisions affecting others; generally there is a superior and subordinate.

In most organizational settings, authority is granted based on the position one holds in the company. A basic understanding of power is the possession of controlling influence over another. Or, power is the ability to influence a subordinate to work toward the goals and objectives of the organization.

Centralization

The more centralized an organization, the more authority and decision making is made by top executives. The strengths of centralization would be the speed of decision making, experienced decision makers, standardized control, and repetition of tasks.

When making decisions for the entire organization, sometimes the speed of a decision may be crucial. A general manager or owner of a National Football League (NFL) franchise may need to make a decision regarding a draft choice under time constraints. He or she must make a snap judgment and make the choice. In these situations, centralizing the decision could be useful. It requires the manager be an experienced decision maker; it also helps that he or she is informed.

In environments that are predictable, centralization of authority makes a lot of sense. Standardized control will allow an organization in this type of en-

vironment to reduce risks. Policies and procedures can be developed with a proactive approach to decision making; thus, top management can make decisions ahead of time for lower-level personnel. Further, in such predicable environments, an organization can reduce the number of tasks that are repeated, by having control of the decisions and the assignment of tasks.

Structure will have an impact on whether an organization has centralized authority. Taller structured companies will, generally, be more centralized. At the same time, flatter structured companies will, generally, be more decentralized. However, smaller companies are flat by nature but are usually centralized.

Decentralization

On the opposite end of a continuum from centralization is decentralization. Basically, decentralization is when decision making and authority have been delegated downward away from top executives or top management. The general thought process behind decentralization is to allow those closest to the customer the responsibility to make prudent decisions. Advantages of this delegation would be speed of decision making, innovation, employee satisfaction, and growth.

In the centralization section, we discussed how the speed of decision making was an advantage for a central authority. It can also be an advantage for decentralization as well. For example, position coaches in the NFL might need to make some snap decisions regarding their players. If a player is injured, the coach must make a substitution before a penalty is received. It would be his responsibility to be aware of his players' needs and adjust quickly during the course of the game. Thus, adaptability in erratic environments might require decentralization for some decision making, to stay competitive.

Successful organizations that operate in ever-changing and uncertain environments have displayed decentralized structures. This allows for decisions to be made closer to the customer that can have an impact on the sale. Contributing factors to the environment are the numerous avenues for social networking and technology. In order to stay ahead of the competition, an organization would need to explore the advantages of decentralization for their situation.

People who take part in decentralized organizational decision making are more inclined to contribute to new strategic initiatives or innovation. Creativity within the organization has been shown to increase when employees are allowed to have input with thoughts and ideas. As new and innovative ways are established, tasks may be introduced that reduce costs and increase revenues. Employees who are allowed to take part in problem solving show increased satisfaction in their jobs. Decentralized decision making allows and encourages this to take place, hopefully leading to a more contented employee.

Paul Keiper
Texas A&M University

See Also: Management Decision-Making Process; Performance Motivation; Strategic Management; Structure and Strategy.

Further Readings

Lussier, Robert N. and David C. Kimball. *Applied Sport Management Skills*. Champaign, IL: Human Kinetics, 2009.
Slack, Trevor and Milena M. Parent. *Understanding Sport Organizations: The Application of Organization Theory*. Champaign, IL: Human Kinetics, 2006.
Taylor, Tracy, Alison Doherty, and Peter McGraw. *Managing People in Sport Organizations: a Strategic Human Resource Management Perspective*. Oxford, UK: Butterworth-Heinemann, 2008.

Change and Sports Management

Change has been a recurring theme in the more than a century that sports have been considered a business, and the field of sports management emerged to study them. On many levels, the modern history of sports has been marked by dramatic social, technological, and global changes, and sports is regarded by many as the most current reflection of any movement for societal change because its fair and level playing field allows for faster recognition and inclusion than do most other, more exclusionary social institutions.

Both Reflective of and Driven by Social Factors

The constant pressure for change in sports has been mirrored by the changes and shifts in the method of study sports and the purposes this academic inquiry serves. Sports are as ancient as human history. They represented a social ideal to ancient Greeks, and an economic and political forum for Romans. They endured centuries of struggle just to survive in Europe. Sport as a business begins in earnest at the end of 19th and beginning of the 20th century as three forces combined to create a confluence of wide spread and increasing public interest.

The first of these changes involved the assimilation of many shifts wrought by the Industrial Revolution, including the creation of large urban populations that would become a potential consuming base for sport and the advent of free time caused by increased wealth, industrial reform, and unionization that gave sport both potential participants and consumers. Next the growth of media—first newspapers and then motion picture and finally broadcasting—found sports an important and critical form of content, and in turn allowed significant larger populations to both know of and maintain a constant interest in sports and events. Finally, dramatic societal and political change sparked in part by immigration and changing populations (particularly in the United Kingdom, the United States, and Canada) made sports a forum for significant social integration, and the support of athletic teams and events became an important hallmark of racial or ethnic identity or societal class.

This confluence of events, growing populations, and interest in sports gave rise first to professional coaches—experts who trained largely amateur athletes—but this in fairly short order led to the rise of professional athletics, especially in the United States where no entrenched aristocracy perpetuated potentially exclusionary amateurism rules. Once sports became commercial, it would not be long before professionals in all areas surrounding the event would enter the field, and the compilation of a broader specialized field of knowledge would evolve.

Shaped by Physical Education Models

A number of religious and utopian movements, including the Young Men's Christian Association (YMCA), founded in England in the middle of the 19th century and Baron DeCoubertain's Olympism movement founded after the French defeat in the Franco-Prussian War in 1871, also brought attention to sports as a new societal ideal and as a method of solving urban and social problems created by industrialization. Accordingly, much of the early study of sport surrounded its potential for producing greater character and enhancing values of its participants. With the pursuit of excellence physically and ethically at the core of early sports study, the field of physical education, with its emphasis on teaching and values development, soon grew. The study of physical education and social and psychological nature leisure would dominate until sports reached a new broader plateau of popularity and significance after World War II, which stands as a line of demarcation for change in most societal practices.

Even after the conclusion of World War II sparked a dramatic surge in the popularity of professional sports enterprises, they remained nominally small organizations and jobs surrounding them were comparatively few. There also was a significant and increasingly widening disconnect between the academic study of sports in physical education and the business of sport as it was developing professionally and commercially. The advent of significant media rights fees, larger stadia, and more complex business practices necessitated by increasingly contentious labor relations and the growth of professional leagues as significant economic forces in the 1960s and 1970s made the evolution of new areas of sports study a necessity.

New Models Emerge

Medical and human performance scholars flocked to sports both out of passion and interest and the developing fields of kinesiology and sports science

emerged. On the opposite flank of historic physical education and recreation study, a new, more business-oriented field emerged in the form of sports administration or sports management, drawing more from the fields of business administration, law, and communication.

Behavioral change theory, including the work of B. F. Skinner and others, demonstrated that human change is the result of a slow process of small learned behaviors, thoughts, and cognition; the embrace of new fields of study by the academy is a slow process as well. However, radical developments in the interest, consumption, and societal importance of sports in the past several decades have spurred rapid changes in how the field of sports management views itself, is viewed and is understood externally, and what content and preparation is entailed in the field.

The field of sports management and trends in sports management now include an examination of sociological trends; globalization; politics and governance issues; antitrust, communications, contract, intellectual property, labor and employment law; risk management; finance; facility construction; macro- and microeconomics, and the management of sports specific ventures, including professional franchises and leagues.

Circa 2011 Changes in the Discipline

In the second decade of the 21st century, sport appears to be poised as a business of increasing complexity and global importance. The study of sports management, while not yet contained in a single institution or setting, has grown tremendously to match the expansion of the field.

American schools of sports management now offer courses both true to the physical education roots, but also in the sociology and history of sport and the structures and key issues facing the field as a business.

One of the exemplars of this transformational change is exemplified by the curriculum at New York University's Preston Robert Tisch Center for Hospitality Tourism and Sports Management. The Tisch Center and Ohio University were among the first institutions in the United States to offer master's of science degrees in Sports Business, although Ohio's program was not titled as such from the onset.

Most traditional M.B.A. programs were reluctant to consider sports an area worthy of a major, but interest in the field both from employers and potential students demanded the more specialized degree. Columbia, Georgetown, and Northwestern universities launched similar programs in succeeding years.

Robert Boland
New York University

See Also: History of Sports Event Marketing; Marketing of Sports; Sport Marketing Differences.

Further Readings

Lussier, Robert and David Kimball. *Applied Sport Management Skills.* Champaign, IL: Human Kinetics, 2009.

Maraniss, David. *Rome 1960:The Olympics That Changed The World.* New York: Simon & Schuster, 2008.

Masteralexis, Lisa P., Carol A. Barr, and Mary Hums. *Principles And Practice Of Sport Management.* Sudbury, MA: Jones & Bartlett, 2008.

Mullin, Bernard, Stephen Hardy, and William Sutton. *Sport Marketing*, 3rd Ed. Champaign, IL: Human Kinetics, 2007.

Rosner, Scott and Kenneth L. Shropshire. *The Business of Sports*, 2nd Ed. Sudbury, MA: Jones & Bartlett, 2010.

Zimbalist, Andrew. *In the Best Interests of Baseball: The Revolutionary Reign of Bud Selig.* Hoboken, NJ: Wiley, 2007.

Charity Sports Events

Worldwide, charitable giving has increased in recent years, exceeding the $300 billion mark in 2007 from contributions by individuals, foundations, and corporations. Charity sporting events have been growing in the past decade as a means for an organization to generate funds. One of the reasons for the increased popularity of these events is the enormous sports and recreation participant base from which events can draw. There has been a distinctive shift in consumer attitudes toward involvement in experiences that provide meaning. These charity sporting events include individuals participating in physical activities including basketball, running, golf, cycling, walking, and hockey, with most, if not all, of the proceeds going to the benefit of some charity.

Today, charity sporting events are supported by athletes, sport organizations, sport leagues, conferences, and individuals with a keen interest in contributing to some social good. These events, athletes, and sport organizations have developed foundations for the purpose of supporting charitable organizations though sport. The Susan B. Komen Breast Cancer Foundation, which founded the Race for the Cure, formerly relied on other philanthropic events to raise money for its organization, before starting its highly profitable race series. The American Cancer Society's Relay for Life is reported as being among the most successful charity sport events in the world, generating over $350 million in 2006.

The first charity walkathon, the March of Dimes Walkathon, was created in 1970. Today, there are a multitude of charitable sports and recreational events that function in various ways. Events vary from sponsored bike rides to polar bear plunges, but all share one defining attribute: the participant or attendee gains some private benefit, be it a sense of personal achievement, an opportunity to show his or her generosity, or simply having fun. The fact that the participants are supporting the charity may come secondary to the private benefit they gain from attending the event. Fundraising events therefore provide a means for charities to broaden their donor bases beyond those people whose primary motivation to support the charity is their fundamental belief in the particular charity's cause.

Choosing the Cause

Essentially, the affiliation with charitable organizations improves both the reputation and credibility of the sport event by adding to the perception of social responsibility—but also improving the potential to raise funds and generate revenue. This concept of *super community* is accomplished in a number of ways. The event that aligns itself with a charity has the potential to attract both sport participants and corporate sponsors who are interested in a relationship with that charitable organization. Building relationships with consumers and corporate partners requires investment of both time and money. Corporations seek to reach target consumers and also opportunities to align with charitable organizations that will enhance their reputation and perception of corporate responsibility. Therefore, sponsors who align themselves with your organization have the potential to access consumers and to "buy in" to the already established relationship with the charitable cause.

Typically, organizations seek to align themselves with various types of charitable causes, so that they have the potential to reach a wider range of target audiences whether they are broad health issues such as health and medical research, educational issues, youth involvement, drug abuse, or violence prevention. All of these social issues create opportunities for organizations to contribute to social change and to impact both individuals and communities. The Race for the Cure and other charity events find that personal meaning is critical to the success of a charitable organization. Meaning is derived from camaraderie with other participants in a common cause and through a single activity (walking, running, cycling, etc.), the inspiration that is provided by other participants, and by the opportunity for self-expression through physical activity and attachment to the cause. Additionally, the challenge that is presented to participants and to those afflicted with health challenges who are also affiliated with the event is heightened through the training and completion of these physical endurance events.

The overarching purpose of charitable events can be narrowed to very specific organizational objectives. Sport charity events can serve many different objectives which can include: to extract extra income from a current set of donors, to thank a current supporter base, contributing to social or community based occasions, acquisition of new support (especially young people who will contribute to future support), networking for attendees from a business-to-business perspective, or maintaining and developing brand name, particularly for large household-name charities. The fees for participation in charitable sport events will typically exceed the actual cost of participation.

The motivation for consumer participants to pay these fees is based on the private enjoyment of the event itself and also the desire of the individual to support a charitable cause.

The reasons for supporting charitable causes can be philanthropic. That is, the donor participant believes in the charitable cause. Another reason for donors to contribute is for some other private reason, such as the opportunity to meet a celebrity athlete. Donors also contribute money to charities because of the prestige associated with giving. Often their friends and other social networks also give to charitable causes, or the giving is a sign of personal wealth. In some cases, such as with charitable foundations of professional athletes, the giving is a form of generosity that encourages others to also give. Often, the donor may have some personal relationship with the charity, a result of direct experience, or the donation may provide a sense of enjoyment from contribution to altruistic causes. Finally, participation and donations may occur as a result of peer pressure from friends or others involved with the race with whom the donor is related. These motivations of donor behavior are important for event leaders to understand in order to effectively communicate with donors.

Event organizers must understand the essential elements of sport event production in order to create a successful brand and to establish the credibility of both the event and all the corporate partners associated with that event. Money generated from the event, economic impact on the host community, and money raised for the charity are all critical aspects to track. One of the important aspects of reputation is financial performance. Another important element of reputation is the management of the event. The leadership for the event should have a perspective on both directing the event and directing the organization toward its vision and mission. The quality of the leadership will affect the relationship with employees and volunteers, relationships in the financial community, and ultimately be a reflection of the overall quality of the event.

Keys to Success

The key aspects of organizing a successful charity sport event include some of the following points. First, choosing the sport or recreational platform:

This "polar bear plunge" into Lake Calhoun in Minneapolis, Minnesota, in March 2008, was organized as a charity fundraiser for Special Olympics. Similar events have drawn as many as 25,000 people in support of Special Olympics.

the sport should be popular and have the potential to attract the attention of people from both a participant and a spectator perspective. In turn, this consumer appeal will attract corporate partners, which can help to increase revenue and improve the image and brand of an event. Sports such as basketball or golf that have a large participant base would contribute to long-term success. One of the reasons that walking and running events are so popular is that runners and walkers can participate in the same event. Walking is the number one most participated sport in the United States, with 86.0 percent of the total population participating in exercise walking, according to the National Sporting Goods Association.

Alternatively, some events have had great success choosing a more niche sport, such as cycling. Cycling attracts both serious and recreational cyclists, as well as crossover athletes who participate

in triathlons and want opportunities to compete in cycling–alone events. Bike MS, for example, is the nation's largest organized charity cycling event, drawing 100,000 participants each year to 100 unique rides benefiting the National Multiple Sclerosis Society.

These niche sports also tend to have highly loyal participant bases that are likely to pay attention to both the cause and to patronize corporate sponsors that support these events. Golf events are one of the most popular types of sport event fundraisers in part because golf targets some of the most affluent consumers who are capable of paying large entry fees and contributing to other related fundraising activities, such as auctions.

One of the reasons that breast cancer awareness is such a popular charitable cause with which sports organizations affiliate is because of the large numbers of people who are affected by breast cancer. In choosing a charitable organization, sports organizations should follow guidelines for selection of a target market. These guidelines include being sizeable, reachable, measurable, and having behavioral variation. The size of the population that is affected by breast cancer is significant, making this a desirable and also very emotional issue with which both individuals (consumers) and corporations (sponsors) will be highly attracted. The Race for the Cure targets the largest group of people who could potentially participate, as opposed to other sports platforms like golf, basketball, rowing, and so on.

Reachability refers to the ability of a marketer to reach a group of targeted consumers. In the past, mass media such as magazines, newspapers, and television, and more recently, the Internet, have been the preferred channels for organizations to communicate with the markets. However, as the promotional market has become increasingly cluttered and the sheer amount of advertising that individuals are exposed increases, it has become more important for organizations to seek alternate channels to reach out and deliver messages about their products. This need for attention and differentiation is in large part responsible for the increase in sport sponsorship activity over the past 20 years.

Another consideration for the selection of a particular target market is its measurability, from the perspective of the characteristics of that market including demographics and geodemographics. Understanding your consumer and the potential of that group of consumers to be compatible with organizational objectives is paramount to the success of charitable sport events. Breast cancer affects a wide variety of individuals and families and therefore is a heterogeneous group of consumers who vary among age, income, and education. However, this target group will have some similar behaviors and attitudes with respect to a common experience related to breast cancer.

Golf, walking, running, and cycling are popular recreational activities and likely to draw participants—yet more creative ventures have also been used. The *Shape* magazine Pilates for Pink event has raised $400,000 in three years from a single-day event created when it partnered with Pilates studios throughout the country that encouraged people to take a 45-minute Pilates class and to donate money

to the cause. This event was leveraged with a variety of other activities to bring attention to the cause and also to promote its sponsors. *Shape Magazine* created a breast cancer handbook that was a part of a special issue that attracted a number of new advertisers.

Another form of creative activity that raises money is the so-called polar bear plunge, in which participants dive into some body of water in the middle of the winter to raise money and bring attention to a charitable cause. In Maryland, the Criminal Justice Association raised money for Special Olympics in an event they called the Plungapalooza.

The potential for large numbers of participants for events such as these that are fun, exciting, and create memorable experiences is huge. The Maryland Plungapalooza started its fundraising event with 350 participants in 1997, and has involved over 25,000 people since that time.

The venue is also a critical aspect of a successful event because paying to rent a venue detracts from the profit. Most charity events get venues donated or at a discounted price. The availability and suitability of a venue will also impact the decision to choose a certain sport platform for the event.

New and Evolving Methods

The amount of money that will be raised from the event from potential participants, spectators, and corporate partnerships can be estimated, in addition to funds from activities such as silent auctions and direct donations.

Next, finding celebrity athletes who are relevant to the event participants and also popular enough to draw a crowd should be considered. The presence of a celebrity will enhance the overall participation and also add credibility if the event is seeking participants to donate to the cause. If trying to schedule a sports or entertainment celebrity to appear at an event, it is important to understand that the demand for appearance of celebrities is high, and it may require six to 24 months of advance notice for a commitment; the professionalism of the event management will have a bearing on whether the celebrity will consider you. Additionally, the best way to decide on which celebrities to invite is to research the types of events and causes that a celebrity usually attends, to determine if there is a good fit between your event and the celebrity. Celebrities will usually focus their efforts toward certain types of causes.

Auctions are an effective way of fundraising for charitable organizations because items to be auctioned can be donated. Autographed memorabilia in particular can bring in a considerable sum, based on the increased value of the item from a having the signature of a sports celebrity. The PGA Tour raised a record $124 million for charity in 2008, and the largest income from a single event was $8.6 million. Non–sports organizations that produce golf events also have the potential to generate significant revenue. Bi-Lo, the southern food store chain, raised more than $4.5 million at its 2005 annual charity event, which represented an $800,000 increase from the previous year.

One method by which charitable giving is conducted is through donation with each purchase that the consumer makes. The pledge for some completed feat (number of miles or other specific challenge) has become so common that the mycharity.ie Website was set up to help charitable organizations to collect donations from pledges and also help participants to locate and identify events they would like to participate in. The Ireland-based site administers a total of 162 charities for events such as sponsoring a dog sled, skydiving, or climbing Mount Kilimanjaro, and experienced a 70 percent growth in 2008.

Charity events involve large numbers of volunteers who produce and participate in the events to help bring awareness and raise money for a cause. Recruiting a sufficient number of personnel to effectively work the event and create an overall excellent experience for all involved is crucial. Event coordinators should overestimate the number of people that will be needed for an event, in case people back out at the last minute for illness or emergencies. Since volunteers are such a critical component of the success of charity events, event managers must create entertainment and fun for everybody involved, guests and volunteers alike.

Charity events strive to include key components of education, awareness, auction, and a lot of interactive activities, a real party atmosphere in which people are going to be in a good mood and willing to give, or at least to create an emotional connection with everyone involved. All aspects of event and hospitality management should be considered, including providing music and creating a festival atmosphere, providing food and beverages, and medical and other safety personnel on staff for a given day.

Some nonprofits are utilizing sport in a different manner; Team for Training is one such charity. This organization raises funds for the Leukemia & Lymphoma Society, but does not run athletic events. Instead, Team for Training is focused on training experienced athletes and first-time athletes to participate in marathons, half-marathons, and other endurance events. The participants seek donations in exchange for training support and entry into popular races.

Three Leading Examples

There are many different athlete foundations and sporting organizations that utilize the qualities expressed for running a successful sporting event; among some of the more compelling are The Jimmy V Foundation, Livestrong, and AIDS Walk Atlanta & 5K Run.

The Jimmy V Foundation, which supports cancer research, was started by ESPN in honor of the late Jim Valvano, the former coach of the North Carolina State University basketball team and an award-winning ESPN broadcaster. Livestrong is a foundation developed by Tour de France cyclist champion Lance Armstrong for the purpose of providing support for people affected by cancer and for cancer research. The AIDS Walk Atlanta & 5K Run has been going on for two decades for the purpose of HIV primary healthcare, case management, HIV testing and counseling, and supports AID Atlanta's education program.

The Jimmy V Foundation fundraises for cancer research through many different sporting events ranging from basketball and football to golf outings. One of the events is the annual ESPY Celebrity Golf Classic, which raised $950,000 for cancer research in a single event. It is hosted in warm golfing communities such as southern California. In 2009, the event touted professional athletes such as Evander Holyfield, Bruce Jenner, Joe Mantegna, Willis McGahee, Salli Richardson-Whitfield, and Ben Roethlisberger. Since the development of the charity in

1993, it has raised over $90 million. With the success of the ESPY event and others that the Jimmy V Foundation has established, the Charity Navigator auditing service has awarded it the four star rating for seven consecutive years, through 2010.

The Lance Armstrong Foundation, or Livestrong, was developed in 1997, and has committed more than $15 million toward cancer research projects. The funds are generated through the Livestrong Challenge, a combination of team events in cycling, running, swimming, and walking. Participants compete in 17 major athletic events across the United States and around the world, including triathlons, marathons, half-marathons, and bicycle classics.

The AIDS Walk Atlanta & 5K Run is a local charity event, but one that has broad recognition and enormous support from corporations, foundations, local businesses, and community organizations. Funding such programs as HIV primary healthcare, case management, HIV testing and counseling, and an education program that provides more than 80,000 prevention contacts annually, the charity serves over 25,000 clients. In 2009, the AIDS Walk Atlanta & 5K Run raised over $850,000. The organization also hosts other events to support HIV and AIDS research, such as a One Mile Run and a 5K Challenge. AIDS Walk Atlanta & 5K Run has also had city support from the park and recreation department, law enforcement, fire department, volunteer medical personnel, and local celebrities lending a hand with the singing of the national anthem and donating time and raising money. These are all elements that a good charity event should incorporate.

Conclusion

Charity sport events represent an effective means for a charitable organization to provide a meaningful event experience while communicating the mission of the organization. While charity events serve the dual purpose of being a fundraising and community-building prospect, a broader goal is to spread appreciation and effect change. In order to effect change, engagement, and empowerment, event managers can work to increase attachment among participants. Sport events provide an inherent sense of community, which can be leveraged to effect change in a community's programs and expand the reasons that athletes get involved.

When considering the greater goal of charity sport events, a desirable outcome may be to create an empowering event with an established outcome and social engagement among participants. The societal impact of the event may be enhanced if participants, through their attachment to the event, become socially engaged and empowered; this can be one of the most important parts of a charity sporting event. This commitment and empowerment may be manifested by participants through increased effort toward advancing the cause. Socially engaged and empowered participants can act as advocates of the charitable cause. Finally, charity sport events can facilitate the sense of community among participants, and increase attachment through enabling sociability, creating event-related social events, facilitating informal social opportunities, producing ancillary events, and creating independent themes. This type of engagement and involvement by all stakeholders demonstrates what motivates participants to take part in charity sport events, as they seek to satisfy a variety of needs and motives, social, physical, and educational.

Andrea Pent
Neumann University
Charles Crowley
California University of Pennsylvania

See Also: Affinity Programs; Cause Marketing/Branding; Corporate Sponsorship Philosophy; Social Marketing.

Further Readings

Filo, Kevin, Daniel Funk, and Danny O'Brien. "The Meaning Behind Attachment: Exploring Camaraderie, Cause, and Competency at a Charity Sport Event." *Journal of Sport Management*, v.23/3 (2009).

Sachs, Jane and Melinda Grenier. "Maryland Corrections Chapter Takes the Plunge." *Corrections Today*, v.71/2 (2009).

Shank, Matthew. *Sports Marketing: A Strategic Perspective.* Upper Saddle River, NJ: Pearson Education, 2009.

Stoldt, G. Clayton, Stephen Dittmore, and Scott Branvold. *Sport Public Relations: Managing Organizational Communication.* Champaign, IL: Human Kinetics, 2006.

Taylor, Chris. "Will You Play My Charity Event?" *Canadian Musician,* v.31/3 (2009).

Charlotte Bobcats

Marketing a National Basketball Association (NBA) franchise in Charlotte, North Carolina, has been a historically rocky road. From 1988 to 2002, the Charlotte Hornets were hosted by the city. However, the Hornets moved to New Orleans in 2002, leaving behind bitter fans; yet the road was paved for a second franchise, the Charlotte Bobcats. In December 2002, the NBA approved an expansion franchise in Charlotte, to be owned and operated by Robert L. Johnson, founder and CEO of Black Entertainment Television. Johnson was challenged with creating a successful new brand in Charlotte amidst a negative climate.

The new Charlotte franchise began its branding and marketing efforts in 2003. In June, the franchise selected Bobcats as the nickname, and unveiled a logo and team colors, orange and blue. Ground-breaking on a new arena (completed for the 2005–06 season) began in July, and in August the Bobcats began to strategize regarding ticket sales for the inaugural 2004–05 season. The Bobcats introduced a season ticket program whereby former Charlotte Hornets season ticket holders had first priority to purchase Bobcats season tickets and could reclaim their exact seat locations in the Charlotte Coliseum for the 2004–05 season. Also in August, the Bobcats announced that individuals who purchased season tickets for the first five years would receive a free seat license for each seat, thus avoiding personal seat license fees.

Season tickets for the inaugural season went on sale to the general public in November, the same month the Bobcats announced the team mascot, Rufus the Bobcat. Lastly, in November, the Bobcats participated in multiple community service events, in attempt to create goodwill with city of Charlotte. Given the lengthy tenure of the Charlotte Hornets, the majority of 2003 was spent creating the new team and strategizing ways to successfully build the new Bobcats brand.

The departure of the Hornets left the NBA fans in Charlotte disillusioned. Many in Charlotte advised Johnson that he needed to be wary of both this attitude and a saturated corporate sponsorship market. Johnson quickly realized that his marketing strategy needed to focus on the Bobcats' newness, rather than deal with prior fan concerns. As such, the positioning strategy for the Bobcats aimed to create a positive public image, and to make a fresh start, leaving behind the negative associations with the Hornets. In multiple interviews, Johnson was quoted as saying that he didn't intend to deal with negative perceptions of the past franchise; he believed Charlotte was receiving a brand-new franchise and planned to market it as such.

While the strategy was well intentioned, figures from the inaugural 2004–05 season did not indicate success. Of the 23,000 available seats in the Charlotte Coliseum, only 9,000 season tickets were sold. Further, attendance averaged 14,000 per game, or 63 percent of capacity, ranking third worst in NBA attendance that season. The 2005–06 season was not much better; the Bobcats were one of the lowest teams in the NBA for season ticket sales.

Turnaround Point

Another indicator of limited early success was the inability to secure a naming-rights partner for the new facility. Although an agreement was reached with Time Warner Cable in April 2008, the facility went "unnamed" for the first three seasons it was occupied by the Bobcats. The 2006–08 seasons did not show improvement; the franchise did not improve ticket sales, and had difficulty attracting and retaining sponsors. The team's win-loss record resulted in a declining franchise after only six years of existence. However, a winning 2009 season, coupled with the team's first-ever playoff appearance, has produced a positive outlook for 2010 and beyond. Most significantly, in March 2010, superstar Michael Jordan bought his ownership share for $275 million, replacing Johnson with a homegrown basketball legend.

Due in part to the change of ownership and organization culture, 2010 showed indications of success. The Bobcats increased the number of team sponsors to 90 from 50, including a pair of new sponsorships worth an estimated $300,000 to $500,000 per year. Sponsorship renewals are also seeing marked improvement over past seasons. By August 2010, the Bobcats had renewed 85 percent of expiring sponsorships. Further, season ticket sales and renewals dramatically increased, ranking among the top 10 off-season performances in the NBA.

Kristi L. Schoepfer
Winthrop University

See Also: Brand Image; Franchise; National Basketball Association; Positioning.

Further Readings

Branch, Dallas. "Charlotte Bobcats: (Re) Launching a New (Old) NBA Franchise." *Sports Marketing Quarterly,* v.17/1 (2008).
Lombardo, John. "New Owner Must Rebuild Charlotte Market" and "Q&A: Johnson Touts his Vision." *Sports Business Journal,* v.5/35 (2002).
Spanberg, Erik. "Charlotte Bobcats Win Business, Fan Dollars." *Charlotte Business Journal.* (August 16, 2010) http://www.bizjournals .com/charlotte/stories/2010/08/16/story3.html (Accessed January 2011).

Chat Rooms

A chat room is a Website, part of a Website, or part of an online service that provides a venue for communities of users with a common interest to communicate live, in real time. The controversy about when chat rooms actually started is an ongoing debate. E-mail started in 1972, and e-mail-based "bulletin boards" started in 1979. The first widely regarded real-time chat room was created by CompuServe CB in 1980. Using CompuServe, members could exchange real-time messages on 40 different channels, which later evolved into the concept of chat rooms.

Chat rooms started in 1980 for the purpose of making communication on the job easier. Workers desired a way to talk to fellow employees instantly, instead of posting a bulletin and waiting for a response. Once the idea of real-time chat emerged from the business world, it exploded into a social phenomenon.

Chat rooms can work in a variety of ways, but they all have similar basic characteristics. Before entering a chat room you must first make a user name and password; this can usually be done on the Website providing the chat room. Next, you can pick among chat rooms; it is common for Websites to have a variety of topics defining each chat room. Examples might be sports, singles, business, entertainment, and even specific topics like presidential debates and political party discussions. Once you have entered a chat room, you can see a list of everyone else in the chat room and their comments. There are very few, if any, rules for chat rooms, which can make them a dangerous place for some.

All types of advertising appear in chat rooms, and people may unknowingly be exposed to marketing of certain products and companies. Chat rooms have the potential to be hugely beneficial to sport marketers if used correctly. Chat rooms can provide limitless advertisement for teams, products, and even players. The screens on chat rooms stay very consistent, so an advertisement on the side of a chat would be seen countless times during a steady conversation. It would also be beneficial for marketers to pay Websites to open chat rooms on predetermined topics. If a marketer was trying to market Gatorade as the official sponsor for college basketball, he or she could pay a Website to open a chat room discussing the topic. This way, not only can the company advertise its product, but it can get specific feedback from consumers on the idea.

There is an older form of chat room that is becoming popular again: forum or message boards. Websites such as TMZ and Deadspin that post breaking news stories about celebrities and popular news events allow members (memberships are free) to make their own comments, and comment on other member comments about the news stories and celebrities at any time.

There has been related controversy concerning Deadspin and then New York Jets football player Bret Favre. According to reports, Bret Favre sent inappropriate text messages and naked pictures to an in-house sideline reporter. Deadspin was the first Website to break this controversial story, and nearly doubled its online traffic within its Website.

Conclusion

Chat rooms have developed from work-only services, to social networking, to a replacement for television and radio news. Chat rooms allow for instant communication, and have increased accessibility to people from all around the world. Chat rooms have unlimited possibilities for social networking, and may represent a largely untapped market for the world of sport marketing.

Samantha Gilpin
State University of New York College at Cortland

See Also: Facebook; Internet/Online; MySpace; Online Communities; Twitter; Virtual Communities.

Further Readings

Disabled World. "Chat Room History of IRC MUD and Voice Chat." http://www.disabled-world .com/communication/chat-history.php (Accessed December 2010).

Harrison, Hayley. "The History of Chat Rooms." http://www.ehow.com/about_5038841_history -chat-rooms.html (Accessed December 2010).

HistoryKing.com. "The History of Chat Rooms." http://www.historyking.com/ miscellaneous/2010/7/History-of-Chat-Rooms .html (Accessed December 2010).

Cheerleaders

As one explores the evolution of sport, particularly American football, it is nearly impossible to discount cheerleading and its impact on athletics. Its history is closely aligned with that of collegiate football, as just 11 years after the first intercollegiate football game was played in 1869, the first-ever cheer squad was formed at Princeton University. This squad comprised all males; it was not until 1923 that women were allowed to participate.

Fast forward to today's athletics, and cheerleaders are ever present at most junior high schools, high schools, colleges, universities, and professional sporting events. It is even likely to see cheerleading as part of recreational sporting activities or as a stand-alone activity. It was recently reported by *Varsity* that 3.7 million youth participate in some form of cheerleading. For most of these programs, the roots of cheerleading remain; that is, most cheerleading squads operate to promote school or community spirit—but all operate to enhance spirit and leadership qualities.

That most cheerleading squads function to promote school or community spirit is evident by attending most professional, college, high school, or junior high athletic events where cheerleaders have a likely presence. It is their responsibility to get the crowd involved in the game. In other words, from a marketer's perspective, cheerleaders are fundamental in creating game atmosphere. They can truly make or break an environment. Cheerleaders are charged with keeping an environment positive when the game might not be going as hoped, or further exciting a crowd when a team is making great plays. As such, cheerleaders should have a fundamental understanding of the sport for which they are rooting.

These traditional cheer squads practice nearly year round. Many cheerleaders travel throughout several sport seasons and uphold obligations to not only cheer on their teams, but also maintain grades and perform in school or community service roles. In addition to these expectations, most interscholastic cheer groups will attend summer camps. These camps assist the groups in preparing for their upcoming sport seasons, and also serve as preliminary qualifying competitions. At these camps, squads can compete for bids to regional and national competitions. In addition to squad competitions, individual cheerleaders have the opportunity to compete for all-star positions.

During these tryouts, cheerleaders showcase a variety of skills including a cheer, chant, dance, jumps, tumbling, and stunts. If selected as an all-star, the individual cheerleader has the opportunity to represent his or her program and school at a variety of events including international events, national parades, bowl games, etc. The most notable organizations that host these camps include: the Universal Cheerleaders Association, the National Cheerleaders Association, the United Spirit Association, the American Cheerleaders Association, Spirit Xpress, American Cheer Power, and V!ROC Choreography.

Cheerleading has developed beyond its original roots, where some individuals and squads strive to be in a competitive role as opposed to a supportive role for sports. For example, in the late 1980s all-star cheerleading programs that focused on competition, as opposed to support, made initial appearances (such a program is different from the above-noted all-star camp tryout). Today, all-star cheerleading has grown tremendously and has helped to create an international cheer industry.

The Sport Question

With the rise in popularity of cheerleading, and the ever-increasing athleticism required to cheer, many have asked the question, "Is cheerleading a sport?" A 2010 federal court responded to this great debate and ruled that cheerleading is not a sport. Specific points of consideration included that a sport must have coaches, practices, competitions during a defined season, and a governing organization. Though many traditional cheer squads, along with the all-star squads, do compete, and recently the formation of cheer governing bodies has emerged, there has been no defined season for competitive cheer. Consequently, cheer cannot be defined as a sport.

Though cheerleading has not yet been recognized as a sport, most of the participants are recognized as athletes, as it takes a variety of skill sets to cheer at elite levels. It is for this reason that some within cheerleading would like to have it formally recognized as a sport. As mentioned, to gain sport classification, cheerleading will need a governing body and a sport season. USA Cheer, the recently established governing body for all forms of cheerleading in the United States, has set out to define cheer, or at least some form of cheer, as a sport. Specifically, USA Cheer recently announced *Stunt* as an emerging National Collegiate Athletic Asso-

ciation (NCAA) sport. Stunting has traditionally been a part of many programs (with the exception of programs that are ground-bound, or not allowed to stunt); however, USA Cheer is announcing Stunt as an NCAA emerging sport initiative in which it will be a new sport, separate from traditional cheerleading. USA Cheer is proposing that Stunt be implemented as a spring sport with a required eight regulation competitions during its first season and a final tournament to be held in April 2011. During this inaugural year, 15 collegiate teams have committed to the new sport, and several more are considering its addition.

Those close to cheerleading are familiar not only with its reputation in the United States, but also with its global attractiveness. In 2003 the United States All Star Federation (USASF) and the International All Star Federation (IASF) were formed to support international club cheerleading and competitions. Additionally, the International Cheer Union (ICU) was developed to act as the international federation for the sport of cheer. Collectively, these organizing bodies helped to host the first World Cheerleading Championship in 2004. This championship included 14 of the top selected world teams. ESPN followed the competition and taped a global broadcast of the event. In 2010, the IASF and ICU hosted the 7th World Cheerleading Championship, in which 60 countries and five continents were represented.

Conclusion

Though cheerleading may not be classified as a sport, it definitely has a home in the sport industry, as it is estimated to generate millions of dollars. The *Christian Science Monitor* reported that on average, a cheer program can cost its participants around $400 to $3,500 annually. (The range is because of the inclusion of all-star programs). Cheerleading is an activity that promotes fitness, athleticism, team, school, and community. Further, cheerleading has been known to foster leadership abilities. In fact, several public figures were once cheerleaders, including presidents Franklin Roosevelt, Dwight Eisenhower, Ronald Reagan, and George W. Bush. Though the future of cheerleading as a sport is uncertain, the popularity is not. Cheerleading has shown dynamic growth throughout the years; future sport managers should not underestimate the value of cheerleading and its impact on the global sport industry.

Christina L. L. Martin
Troy University

See Also: Amateur Athlete; Avidity; Mascots; National Collegiate Athletic Association; Sports Organizing Bodies.

Further Readings

Boyce, Rebecca. "Cheerleading in the Context of Title IX and Gendering in Sport." *The Sport Journal.* http://www.thesportjournal.org/article/ cheerleading-context-title-ix-and-gendering-sport (Accessed September 2010).

Figueroa, Alissa. "Cheerleading May Not Be a Sport, but It Is an Industry." *The Christian Science Monitor.* (July 22, 2010) http://www .csmonitor.com/Business/new-economy/ 2010/0722/Cheerleading-may-not-be-a-sport -but-it-is-an-industry (Accessed September 2010).

USA Federation for Sport Cheerleading. "2011 Team USA Tryouts." http://usacheer.net/Content .aspx/News/2011%20Team%20USA%20 Cheer%20Tryouts.xml (Accessed September 2010).

Varsity Brands, Inc. "Being a Cheerleader—History of Cheerleading." http://www.varsity.com/ event/1261/being-a-cheerleader-history.aspx (Accessed September 2010).

Chicago Bears

The Chicago Bears are one of the mainstays of the National Football League (NFL) and an iconic franchise in a sports-loving city. The team has a blue-collar reputation and a blue-collar flavor to its constituency. It is one of the most long-lived sports franchises, one that has enjoyed on-field success and a great fan following across many decades. The Bears have more NFL Hall of Fame enshrinees—26—than any other team.

The Bears' Soldier Field was renovated in a $587 million scheme that helped the team stay in Chicago proper.

The franchise began as the Decatur Staleys in 1920. The pivotal character in the story of the Chicago Bears is George Halas. In 1921, the team was relocated to Chicago and in 1922 it was renamed; "Bears" was chosen to complement the popular Chicago professional baseball franchise of the Cubs. The collective enterprise was redefined as well; the APFA (American Professional Football Association) became the National Football League. The Bears and the Arizona Cardinals (formerly of Chicago) are the two remaining founding NFL franchises.

Upstarts and Stalwarts
The upstart league, and football in general, benefitted from baseball's 1919 "Black Sox" scandal. Halas, known as Papa Bear, played for and coached the team, as well as owning the Bears from 1922 until his death in 1983. Halas was an innovator of the first order: he named the new league, made its first player trade, and hired its first public relations representative. The team ownership remains in his family.

The stadium itself is a character in the drama that is the Chicago Bears. The team began playing at Wrigley Field (then known as Cubs Park) in 1921 and remained there for 49 years. Soldier Field, which would become identified with the Bears, was built in 1924 but not used for the professional football team until 1970. The field was not designed for football; the seating had shallow banking, creating poor sight lines, and the facility was dubbed "the mistake by the lake." Despite some flirtations and threats about taking the team to a suburban stadium, the Bears stayed in Chicago proper. In 2000, a $587 million plan for renovating Soldier Field was announced, and the new venue opened in 2003.

The Chicago Bears have had a bumper crop of remarkable players through the decades: Harold "Red" Grange, Sid Luckman, Gayle Sayers, Mike Ditka, Mike Singletary, William "Refrigerator" Perry, and Walter Payton, among others. The highlight of the franchise would have to be the 1986 win in Super Bowl XX. They bested the New England Patriots 46–10, the greatest Super Bowl margin of victory to that date and the second largest on record. In addition, the Bears have won the NFL championship nine times.

Team colors are dark navy, orange, and white. Nicknames include "Da Bears" and "The Monsters of the Midway." The mascot is Staley Da Bear. Prior to game time, the team makes its entrance to Soldier Field through a giant bear head. Since 1941, the team has embraced its fight song, *Bear Down, Chicago Bears*. It is sung after every score in home games.

The Bears play in the NFC North Division along with the Detroit Lions, the Green Bay Packers, and the Minnesota Vikings. The team has several charitable projects as part of its community relations efforts including a program, Heroes in the Classroom, for recognizing and rewarding outstanding teachers in the Chicago area; and the Bears Care Gala, which raises research funds for breast and ovarian cancer.

John Todd Llewellyn
Wake Forest University

See Also: National Football League; Ownership, Professional Teams; Sport Celebrities.

Further Readings

Davis, Jeff. *Papa Bear: The Life and Legacy of George Halas*. New York: McGraw-Hill, 2005.

MacCambridge, Michael. *America's Game: The Epic Story of How Pro Football Captured a Nation*. New York: Anchor Books, 2004.
McDonough, Will, Peter King, Joe Gergen, Harold Rosenthal, and Ed Bouchette. *The History of the NFL: The Complete Story of the National Football League, 1920–2000*. New York: Smithmark, 1999.

Chicago Blackhawks

The peculiar ownership tactics of the Chicago Blackhawks National Hockey League (NHL) franchise, which led the once-proud team to being named the worst franchise in all of sports in 2004, have suddenly turned a major corner and renewed a passionate fan base surrounding one of the NHL's most historic franchises. A successful and important Chicago staple through the 1960s, the Blackhawks quickly became infamous locally on account of their stingy owner, "Dollar" Bill Wirtz, who was named team president 12 years after his father purchased the team in 1954. Among a number of unpopular ownership strategies, including high ticket prices and frugality in signing and retaining top players, Wirtz refused to allow home games to be broadcast locally in Chicago. Still, for decades the team continued to draw large crowds in their original facility, Chicago Stadium, and beginning in 1994, the 20,000-seat capacity United Center.

After the team's long run of playoff appearances ended in 1998, Wirtz steadfastly refused to participate in the trend of escalating player salaries, a trend that would eventually lead to the 2004 NHL lockout and the cancellation of the 2004–05 season. As a result, the Blackhawks suffered through an entire decade of losing, hitting rock bottom in February 2004 when ESPN named the team the worst franchise in all of sports. In the two seasons following the lockout, home attendance figures for the Blackhawks placed them 29th out of 30 NHL teams.

Big Turnaround

The team began to turn around after a series of successful personnel moves from 2006 to 2008. Under the leadership of Bill Wirtz's son, Rocky, and a host of former Chicago Cubs executives, the team began televising home games and reconnecting with a passionate but disenchanted fan base. During the 2008–09 season, in which the Blackhawks returned to the playoffs for the first time since 2002, the team hosted the NHL Winter Classic in Wrigley Field, an outdoor hockey extravaganza that not only helped Chicagoans re-embrace the youthful 'Hawks, but earned the highest national television ratings for a regular season NHL game in 34 years. This historic event was followed in 2009–10 with a Stanley Cup victory, the team's first NHL championship in 49 years. The subsequent celebratory parade drew over 2 million fans to the city streets to celebrate Chicago's first championship since the Chicago White Sox 2005 World Series victory.

Because of the historically turbulent relationship between ownership and fans, the marketing of the Blackhawks had, until recently, been difficult even for such a passionate sports city. The team's renaissance since 2008, however, has helped to unleash the team's true marketing potential as an historic hockey franchise with a dedicated fan base. Merchandise sales have steadily increased, with a flurry of activity around the team's nostalgia-inspired third jersey, first worn during the 2009 Winter Classic and as an alternate during the 2009–10 season. Consequently, Blackhawks players Patrick Kane and Jonathan Toews have been among the top 10 (#6 and #8, respectively) in the NHL in individual jersey sales during the past two seasons. Attendance has also skyrocketed. In 2008–09, the team set a franchise record and led the league in average attendance. The follow-up season produced similar numbers as the team's consecutive sellout streak, which began three years prior, reached the century mark. As a result, just five years removed from having less than 4,000 season ticket holders and despite a 20 percent price increase for the 2010–11 season, there is now a waiting list for season tickets. A non-factor before Bill Wirtz's death in 2007, the Blackhawks' local television ratings on Comcast Sports Net Chicago

have surged. The 2009–10 regular season average was up 287 percent from the average rating just two seasons prior. The Blackhawks also regularly feature on the NHL's national broadcast and cable channels.

While the team's improvement on the ice is certainly playing a part, several off-ice developments have established the franchise as one of the most fan-friendly in all of the NHL.

Beginning in 2008, the team began hosting an annual weekend-long convention for its fans, complete with exhibits, Q&A sessions, and numerous autograph signings and player appearances at the downtown Chicago Hilton. That same year, the Blackhawks also held their first annual Training Camp Festival. Coinciding with the first day of Blackhawks training camp, the event features various fan activities, as well as the chance to listen to head coach Joel Quenneville run the team through on-ice drills in the United Center.

Stephen Andon
Florida State University

See Also: Fan Attendance, Reasons for; Fan Avidity; National Hockey League; Ownership, Professional Teams.

Further Readings

Duhatschek, Eric. *Hockey Chronicles*. New York City: Checkmark Books, 2001.

Johnson, George. "Worst Franchise: Blackhawks." *ESPN.com*. http://sports.espn.go.com/espn/page2/story?page=johnson/060417_blackhawks (Accessed August 2010).

NHL.com Network. "Stanley Cup Playoffs Attract Largest Audience Ever." (June 14, 2010) http://blackhawks.nhl.com/club/news.htm?id=531636 (Accessed August 2010).

Norman, Darcy. *HockeyNomics: What the Stats Really Reveal*. Folklore Pub., 2009.

Schaper, David. "Blackhawks vs. Flyers for the Stanley Cup? Really?" NPR.org. (May 29, 2010) http://www.npr.org/templates/story/story.php?storyId=127257170&ft=1&f=1001 (Accessed August 2010).

Chicago Bulls

When one thinks of the Chicago Bulls and sports marketing, the name that epitomizes each is Michael Jordan. From 1984 until he left the Bulls for good in 1998, Jordan's time with the Bulls coincided with six National Basketball Association (NBA) championships, the beginning of an attendance sellout streak that eventually reached 610 straight games over 14 years, and the building of a new arena (United Center) with three levels of luxury suites, various fan and athlete amenities, and a seating capacity of 20,917. Not only was Jordan, a Hall of Fame inductee in 2009, synonymous with the Chicago Bulls, but also with the marketing revolution of the NBA and the Nike brand of athletic merchandise.

The Chicago Bulls franchise began in much more humble circumstances in 1966. As with any new sports franchise, the team struggled both on the floor and in attendance. Playing at the International Amphitheater for one year, then moving to spacious Chicago Stadium, the team averaged about 4,000 fans per game. Although they won their inaugural game and their coach, Johnny "Red" Kerr, who played high school basketball in Chicago and college hoops at the University of Illinois, won coach of the year honors, the team finished 34–48.

The 1970s resulted in a gradual turnaround for the team, both on the court and in the stands. Average attendance per game jumped above 10,000 for most of the decade. This growth in popularity can be attributed both to an improved team and the arrival of Pat Williams as general manager. Williams was a protégé of Bill Veeck, the ultimate showman of professional baseball. Williams brought many of the zany promotions and entertainment from Veeck into Bulls games. He introduced a mascot, Benny the Bull, to interact with the crowd and toss gifts to the children, and provided halftime entertainment, including world-famous Victor the wrestling bear. A 2010 *Forbes* magazine poll found Benny to be one of America's favorite mascots.

Marketing of the Bulls in the 1960s and '70s was handled by a staff of no more than four, whose primary task was to handle ticket orders. Little effort was made to sell tickets to individuals or groups. That changed in 1985, when Jerry Reinsdorf, a suc-

cess in real estate, led an ownership group to buy the team. Season ticket holders went from 4,800 at that time to 10,800 by 1987. The marketing staff continued to grow as well, reaching a size of over 50 people today.

Enter Jordan

The 1980s marked the arrival of Jordan, who was drafted in 1984. Attendance almost doubled from the previous year, as Chicago and the rest of the NBA experienced what was arguably the best player in basketball history. By 1987, the Bulls began to experience sellout crowds that would last an astounding 610 consecutive games, finally ending in 2001. However, it took Jordan and the Bulls until 1991 to put it all together and win their first championship. Once started, this championship machine couldn't be stopped, winning championships again the following two years to produce a threepeat before record crowds, and sponsorship dollars to go with it. In the summer of 1993, Jordan shocked the world by announcing his retirement, citing grief over the murder of his father and eventually pursuing his dream to play professional baseball. His pro baseball career was short-lived; he returned to the Bulls in March 1995.

The United Center, named after the Chicago-based airline and opened in 1994, was half-owned by the Bulls ownership group and shared with the ownership of the other primary tenant, the Chicago Blackhawks, a National Hockey League franchise. Concession and parking revenues unavailable to this ownership duo in the previous building were now a part of the two teams' revenue streams. And with the Bulls concluding the second of a three-year string of world championships in 1998, attendance and sponsorship dollars were at astronomical levels. However, Jordan and coach Phil Jackson retired, other star players like Scottie Pippen and Dennis Rodman signed elsewhere, and team performance declined. Nonetheless the sellout streak continued for another three years; both fans and sponsors continued to value the entertainment at a Bulls game.

This entertainment currently includes frequent game appearances by the Luvabulls cheerleading squad, alternate spirit squads of various shapes and sizes, Benny the Bull, and others. The Bulls outreach to the community is also strong, with the Charita-Bulls, a program started in 1987 with the mission to enhance the lives of youths by supporting education, recreation, and social programs around the Chicago area. Each year over $1 million is funneled into these programs.

It is not surprising then, that *Forbes* magazine's estimate of the franchise's value is over $500 million. Not bad for an initial investment of $1.6 million, in 1966.

James Pokrywczynski
Marquette University

See Also: Brand Personality; Franchise; Licensed Goods; National Basketball Association; Sport Celebrities.

Further Readings

Nichols, John. *The History of the Chicago Bulls.* Mankato, MN: Creative Education, 2002.
Sachare, Alex. *Chicago Bulls Encyclopedia.* Lincolnwood, IL: Contemporary Books, 1999.

Chicago Cubs

The Chicago Cubs, a Major League Baseball (MLB) team in the National League (NL), underwent a major management change in 2009, when Tom Ricketts's family became the eighth owners of the team, purchasing it from the Tribune Company for $845 million. The team has a storied history, beginning in 1876 when it was referred to as the White Stockings. Other nicknames of the team included the Orphans and the Colts, and by 1907 the team was officially named the Cubs.

Prior to Ricketts's ownership of the Cubs, the team was owned by the Tribune Company from 1981 to 2009, the William Wrigley family from 1919 to 1981, and a host of other owners prior to 1919, such as William A. Hulbert, Albert Spalding, Charles Murphy, Charles Taft, and Charles Weeghman.

Although the Ricketts family's purchase of the team occurred in October 2009, the family wasted no time in making management and marketing changes throughout the organization. In late October, the family announced that it would begin renovating areas of Wrigley Field, the Cubs ballpark since 1916 and the second-oldest MLB ballpark behind Fenway Park, home of the Boston Red Sox. Renovations will include improving restrooms, making the concourses wider, adding seats to the stadium, improving the ballpark food, and adding a restaurant and gift shop. Additionally, in November 2009, the Cubs installed billboards in the back of the left-field bleachers, blocking a famous rooftop advertisement on a house across the street from the stadium. Because the advertisement was prominently seen by most fans during games, as well as clearly visible on television broadcasts, Ricketts chose to block the rooftop in order to showcase sponsors of the Cubs.

Another change instituted by the Ricketts family has been the addition of Wally Hayward as the chief sales and marketing officer for the Cubs. The position is newly created, and Hayward was hired with the intent of enhancing the game experience for Cubs fans, as well as improving corporate partnerships.

The Cubs ranked third in the MLB in attendance in 2009, filling their ballpark to 96.20 percent capacity on average.

The Cubs have earned the moniker "loveable losers" because of the team's failure to win the MLB World Series since 1908 and its failure to make an appearance in the World Series since 1945. Several stories of curses have circulated through the team's iconic ballpark, such as the curse of the goat, which stems from an incident in 1945 in which William "Billy Goat" Sianis tried to bring his pet goat into the ballpark and was asked to leave. More recently, fans have spoken of the curse of Steve Bartman, a Cubs fan who was blamed for the team's collapse in the 2003 NL Divisional Series against the Florida Marlins, when he reached over the left field wall to grab a foul ball that would have otherwise likely been caught by Cubs outfielder Moises Alou. The Cubs were one game away from advancing to the World Series, and eventually lost the Division Series to the Marlins.

Despite the team's postseason failures and rumored curses, Cubs fans are extremely loyal consumers and continually pack the ballpark for each game. In 2009, the Cubs averaged 96.20 percent capacity for the team's 80 home games, ranking third in the MLB in attendance behind the Boston Red Sox and Philadelphia Phillies. This is especially impressive considering the Cubs had the third highest average ticket price per game, at $47.75.

Wrigley Field itself has been one reason for fans' continued support of the Cubs despite the team's lackluster on-field performance. As the second-oldest ballpark in the league, many fans view Wrigley as an historical monument. It is affectionately nicknamed "The Friendly Confines," and is decidedly no-frills, with very few of the luxury amenities prevalent in modern-day ballparks such as playgrounds, fountains, giant sculptures, or jumbotrons. The scoreboard at Wrigley Field is the original one installed in the park in 1937, and is hand operated. Additionally, Wrigley Field does not have a great deal of sponsor signage or advertisements on the outfield walls, giving the ballpark an old-time feel. While most MLB teams' bleacher tickets are among the least expensive ones sold, bleacher tickets for Cubs games are among the most expensive, as fans flock to the select-your-own-seat bleachers.

Andrea N. Eagleman
Indiana University

See Also: Fan Attendance, Reasons for; Franchise; Major League Baseball; Stadium Operations.

Further Readings

Brown, Maury. "Average Ticket Price Up 5.4 Percent in MLB." *The Biz of Baseball*. (April 2, 2009) http://www.bizofbaseball.com/index .php?option=com_content&view=article&id=31 47:average-ticket-price-up-54-percent-in -mlb-yankeesmets-skew-total&catid=56:ticket -watch&Itemid=136 (Accessed November 2009).

Lefton, Terry. "Cubs Hire Hayward as Top Sales and Marketing Executive." *Street & Smith's SportsBusiness Journal* (November 23, 2009).

Sandomir, Richard. "New Owner to Improve Wrigley, and Maybe the Cubs." *New York Times*. (October 30, 2009) http://www.nytimes .com/2009/10/31/sports/baseball/31cubs.html (Accessed January 2011).

Stout, Glenn. *The Cubs: The Complete Story of Chicago Cubs Baseball*. New York: Houghton Mifflin, 2007.

Chicago Fire

The Chicago Fire Soccer Club is a professional Major League Soccer (MLS) team owned by Andell Holdings. The Chicago Fire was established in 1997 and played its inaugural game in 1998. The Fire is located within the MLS Eastern Conference. The team's community development outreach arm, the Chicago Fire Foundation, provides grants to local charities and holds numerous public events throughout the year to raise funds and allow fans to meet and greet team players and staff.

Winning Tradition

Team highlights include winning the MLS Cup in 1998, with second-place finishes in 2002 and 2003, and winning the U.S. Open Cup in 1998, 2000, 2003, and 2006, with a second-place finish in 2004. The team finished third in the Confederation of North, Central American and Caribbean

Association Football (CONCACAF) Champions Cup in 1999 and 2004.

Fire games were initially held at Soldier Field, but the team relocated to its own stadium, Toyota Park, in 2006; it is located in the Chicago suburb of Bridgeview, Illinois. The team's developmental leagues include the Chicago Fire Premier, the Chicago Fire NPSL, the Chicago Fire Development Academy, and the Chicago Fire Juniors youth teams. The team has sponsored the Ring of Fire along with the Chicago Fire Alumni Association since 2003, in order to honor key contributors to the team's success.

Andell Holdings is a Los Angeles–based private company with global investment interests; the company purchased the Fire in 2007 for $35 million. Andrew Hauptman and his wife, Ellen, own Andell Holdings. The president of the Fire is Dave Greeley and the chief operating officer is Mike Humes. Emigdio Gamboa is the director of multicultural marketing and business development. The technical director for the team is Frank Klopas; the head coach is Carlos de los Cobos, who assumed the role from Denis Hamlett in 2010.

Key corporate sponsors include adidas, the team's kit manufacturer since 2006; Best Buy, the team's jersey sponsor since 2008; and Toyota, which holds the naming rights to Toyota Park.

The Chicago Fire organization established the Chicago Fire Foundation (formerly FireWorks for Kids) in 1998 in order to improve the quality of life for the communities that support them. They have primarily worked with Chicago's disadvantaged youth. The Fire's marketing strategies are geared toward health, education, wellness, and the environment within its community and the supported charities. The foundation awards contributions and grants, and also teams up with local charities in creating fun runs to raise money. The Chicago Fire's charity partners include the Boys and Girls Clubs of Chicago, Children's Memorial Hospital, and the YMCA, among others.

The Fire markets itself and fundraises through various public events, including celebrity golf outings and an annual kickoff luncheon before each season begins. These events provide fans an opportunity to interact with the team and its staff.

The team also has a stadium jersey auction and autographed memorabilia are auctioned off at ev-ery Fire home game, with the proceeds benefitting the foundation. The foundation and local charities conduct 50/50 raffles during every home game; the winning ticket gets 50 percent of the profit, with the charities getting the other 50 percent. The Fire also partners with local businesses to offer fans discounts at those establishments, with the proceeds benefiting the foundation. Other events include the Fire Goes Green environmental awareness program, Kicks for Kids, and a sponsored Chicago Marathon team.

The Chicago Fire team management uses a variety of promotional and community outreach initiatives to build its fan base, sometimes a difficult task in a sport that has not achieved the popularity within the United States that it has achieved elsewhere. Fan-based initiatives include the dog mascot Sparky, a kids club, and designated Official Fire Pubs where fans can gather to watch games. Team fans also sit together in what is known as Section 8 at Toyota Park.

The Fire's outreach initiatives to its diverse Chicago fan base include the acquisition of international players, and games broadcast in both Spanish and English. Local media outlets that provide game coverage include Comcast SportsNet Chicago and WP-WR-TV. English announcers include Dan Kelly and Chris Doran, while Spanish announcers include Oscar Guzman and Enrique Fernandez.

David Trevino
Independent Scholar

See Also: Community Relations; Fan Avidity; Major League Soccer; Promotion.

Further Readings

Fizel, John. *Handbook of Sports Economics Research.* Armonk, NY: M. E. Sharpe, 2006.
Wangerin, David. *Soccer in a Football World: The Story of America's Forgotten Game.* Philadelphia: Temple University Press, 2008.
Zimbalist, Andrew S. *The Bottom Line: Observations and Arguments on the Sports Business.* Philadelphia: Temple University Press, 2006.

Chicago White Sox

The Chicago White Sox professional baseball franchise has constantly battled for respect and attention since arriving in Chicago in 1901. Some of the lack of respect has been self-inflicted, coming from stunts such as uniforms with short pants, or a disco record demolition promotion that resulted in a forfeiture of a ballgame, one of the few in baseball history. The other source of disrespect comes from being in the same market with the Chicago Cubs, which has developed an elite and special image in the minds of many despite having the longest championship drought in professional sports history. The past 20 years have featured an uptick in the franchise's reputation, with the opening of a new ballpark (called U.S. Cellular Field since 2003) that seats 40,000 plus, and a World Series championship in 2005.

The franchise began in 1901 when Charles Comiskey moved his team, the St. Paul Saints, to Chicago to compete in a larger market. Comiskey soon built a ballpark on the south side of town, named it after himself, and won two championships, the last under his ownership in 1917. After that, the franchise has been volatile, reaching the depths during the Black Sox scandal of 1919, when eight players were accused of conspiring with gamblers to affect game scores to win bets. Although the players were found not guilty in court, they received lifetime bans from baseball.

Showmanship and Winning
The highlights of the franchise include the Bill Veeck years, with the controversial and promotion-happy owner introducing uniforms with short pants, an exploding scoreboard when the Sox hit home runs, a shower in the outfield stands to cool patrons during hot summer games, and other unusual promotions. The man who once found a 3'7" pinch hitter to bat against the St. Louis Browns, to draw attention away from the rival local team the Cardinals, brought bizarre events to the field in Chicago, convincing White Sox Hall of Famer Minnie Minoso to return for a brief stint in 1980 just to achieve the unusual record of a player competing in five different decades, four with the Sox.

Attempts to change the image of Sox game attendees as rowdy drunks using foul language to

When the White Sox won the World Series against the Houston Astros in 2005, it was their first championship since 1917.

more family-oriented has had some hiccups along the way. Disco Demolition Night was one of the ugliest nights in White Sox baseball history. A local radio station promoting the anti-disco music movement held an event in between games of a double header that included blowing up all the disco records fans brought to the game that night. The huge fireball that accompanied the explosion damaged so much center field grass that the field was unplayable and the Sox had to forfeit the second game.

Change occurred in 1981, when Jerry Reinsdorf, a success in real estate, led an ownership group to buy the team. Reinsdorf soon recognized the need to build a new stadium to replace aging Comiskey Park and threatened to move the team to Florida unless a new ballpark was built. After a lot of political wrangling and a last-minute deal, the state of Illinois built the ballpark. It opened in 1991, the first sports facility to be built in Chicago since 1929. In 2003, a 23-year, $68 million naming rights deal was struck with a midwest cellular phone company. Two years later, U.S. Cellular Field was the site for the World Series against the Houston Astros. The White Sox championship in 2005, the first for the franchise since 1917, came with the added satisfaction that their bitter crosstown rival, the Cubs, now stand alone with a streak without championships that has surpassed 100 years.

Current promotions include an Elvis look-alike night, mullet night, and ethnic nights for Asian, Greek, Hispanic, and Polish populations that are significant in Chicago. In 2006, the White Sox changed the starting time of night games to 7:11 P.M. to lure a sponsorship from convenience store chain 7-Eleven. An innovative, interactive Website allows potential sponsors to see how their sponsorship signage would look in different areas of the ballpark. Camelback Ranch, opened in 2009 in Glendale, Arizona, is a state-of-the art spring training facility that is a joint venture with the Los Angeles Dodgers.

James Pokrywczynski
Marquette University

See Also: Franchise; Major League Baseball; Promotion; Sponsorship.

Further Readings

Lindberg, Rich. *Total White Sox: The Definitive Encyclopedia of the World Champion Franchise.* Chicago: Triumph Books, 2006.
Veeck, Bill. *Veeck as in Wreck: The Autobiography of Bill Veeck.* Chicago: University of Chicago Press, 2001.
Vorwald, Robert. *What It Means to Be a White Sox: The Greatest Players Talk About White Sox Baseball.* Chicago: Triumph Books, 2010.

Chivas USA

Club Deportivo Chivas USA, or Chivas USA as they are more commonly referred to, is an expansion franchise in Major League Soccer (MLS) that joined the league in 2004. Chivas USA is based in the Los Angeles area, and shares the Home Depot Center, the home stadium for the Los Angeles Galaxy, a rival MLS franchise. What makes Chivas USA unique among MLS clubs is its connections with Club Deportivo of Guadalajara of the Primera División de México, the highest-level professional soccer league in Mexico. Both C. D. Guadalajara, which is known as Chivas, and Chivas USA are owned and operated by Omnilife, an organization that also is in control of Deportivo Saprissa, a club in top-flight soccer in Costa Rica. Omnilife's president, Jorge Vergara, a successful businessman and movie producer, is the main driving force behind the expansion of Omnilife and the Chivas brand, leading to the creation of Chivas USA.

In 2002, Vergara managed to get ownership of C. D. Guadalajara, which at the time, while being one of the most popular clubs in Mexican soccer, was in severe financial trouble. Vergara bought the club because of his belief of being able to turn around the club's finances, as well as expand the Chivas brand into new markets. It was thus, while attending the 2003 MLS All-Star Game at the Home Depot Center, that Vergara announced that he would expand Chivas into the MLS through an expansion franchise.

The public reaction to this announcement was quite varied, with fans from both Mexico and the United States worried about the quality of club teams in both countries, as well as the issue of whether the two Chivas clubs would be moving players back and forth, with one serving as a farm system for the other. Furthermore, Vergara famously alienated a large number of fans when negotiating a television contract for C. D. Guadalajara in Mexico. Wanting a large contract, he refused to allow Chivas matches to be broadcast on television for two weeks, until the networks capitulated and signed a $200 million deal with the club.

It was for these and other reasons that fans, officials, and the media were somewhat wary of Vergara and the Chivas brand coming to the United States. While Vergara has continually been criticized as an owner by fans and the media, his ownership of the Chivas brand has lead to the success of Chivas USA in the MLS.

Fueling Fan Passion

The placement of Chivas USA in Los Angeles is no accident, but is rather smart planning by both Vergara and the MLS to take advantage of the large Mexican and Hispanic population in the Los Angeles area. As Chivas is one of the most popular clubs among Mexican soccer fans, having a team directly related to the Chivas brand in the MLS was seen as a great way for the league to bring fans to matches, who had usually stayed at home to watch the Primera División de México on cable or satellite television. In this manner, much of Chivas USA's marketing and branding strategy has been specifically targeting Chivas fans and those with Latino heritage to a franchise that is friendly and responsive to their needs and wants. The Chivas popularity with the large Mexican population of the Los Angeles area is very influential in helping the club have one of the top average attendances among franchises in the MLS, despite being a young expansion team. Much of this success can be directly attributed to the fan clubs of the main Chivas squad, known as Legión 1908. Legión 1908 is probably one of the most broad-based support groups for soccer clubs in North America, and also has chapters all over the world, making them it of a few international support groups for soccer clubs in North America. The Los Angeles Legión 1908 group is one of the largest in the world, with well over 1,000 members, and has been a primary reason for the rather high attendance numbers evidenced at Chivas USA matches.

While this strategy has been successful, it has also created a dichotomous relationship in Los Angeles soccer, with Chivas USA seen as a team for Latinos, and the Galaxy as a team for Caucasians. While this division is not something that MLS wants as a league on a whole, the division and creation of a rivalry in the same city has been successful for both of the Los Angeles clubs in terms of attendance and revenue. For the time being, it seems Vergara's expansion of the Chivas brand into the MLS has been very successful. It will be interesting to see in the future whether Chivas USA is able to expand further into other markets in America, and gain popularity among the general population of soccer fans in the United States.

Nicholas M. Watanabe
University of Missouri

See Also: "Color"; Los Angeles Galaxy; Major League Soccer; Marketing of Sports; Ownership, Professional Teams.

Further Readings

Buckheit, Mary "Chivas USA Holding Its Own in Southern California Market." *ESPN.* (October 15, 2008). http://sports.espn.go.com/espn/hispanicheritage2008/news/story?id=3642048 (Accessed November 2009).
Major League Soccer, LLC. "Chivas USA Official Website." http://chivas.usa.mlsnet.com/t120 (Accessed September 2009).

Cincinnati Bengals

The Cincinnati Bengals are a National Football League (NFL) franchise that currently plays in the American Football Conference (AFC) North Division. The Bengals are one of two NFL franchises in the state of Ohio; they play in the same division with the Cleveland Browns. The Bengals team recently has been noted for both underachieving and player troubles. In past years, their off-the-field legal troubles have been more newsworthy than their play.

Origins and Struggles

The Bengals originally joined the struggling American Football League in 1937. The AFL folded after the Bengals' inaugural season, but the Bengals continued as an independent team in 1938 before joining the new AFL the following year. This pattern continued until 1941, when the league again folded indefinitely.

The Bengals returned to Cincinnati in 1967 when an ownership group, led by Hall of Fame coach Paul Brown, acquired an expansion franchise in the AFL. Brown is considered the "father of the modern offense," and one of the most successful and storied coaches in history. He coached the team until 1976, but remained as the team's general manager and president until his death in 1991. Upon his father's

The name Bengals *was selected by founder Paul Brown in reference to historic Cincinnati teams of the 1930s.*

death, Mike Brown took over team operations, and the Bengals remain a family-run organization today. Under Mike Brown's ownership, his decision making has readily been an area of fan concern.

The 1970s took the Bengals to three winless playoff appearances. The 1980s proved successful for the team, however, with two trips to the Super Bowl. Still, the Bengals were unable to clinch wins both times against the San Francisco 49ers. The 1990s and into the early years of the new millennium brought despair to the franchise, with 14 consecutive nonwinning seasons. The team moved into the newly built, publicly funded Paul Brown Stadium in 2000. In 2003, the Bengals drafted quarterback Carson Palmer, and they returned to the playoffs in 2005 for the first time since 1990. The present-day Bengals have been inconsistent from year to year; they did win the AFC North Divisional title in 2005 and 2009, but in each case then lost out to the Wild Card team the following week.

Like some other small-market teams, the Cincinnati Bengals for the first time since the opening of Paul Brown Stadium in 2000 faced potential television blackouts and diminishing tickets sales in the 2009 and 2010 seasons. This is in part to the Bengals' poor performance in the 2008 season and in-

consistency in seasons past. Additionally, declining ticket sales and season ticket renewals plagued the franchise, due in part to the current economic state of the nation but also in part to the disapproval of the team's management style by the local fans and community. Cincinnati remains one of only four NFL franchises without a general manager.

Second Chances

While the Bengals in many ways signify the long-standing football history and tradition of the state of Ohio, they have made national headlines for being a "troubled" franchise throughout the league with a number of players finding themselves in legal trouble over past seasons. Most notably, former wide receiver the late Chris Henry, who was arrested numerous times in his five–year career, and suspended for eight games in 2007 by NFL commissioner Roger Goodell for violations under the league's personal conduct policy. During a 13-month span between 2006 and January 2007, the Bengals had nine players arrested and two players suspended from the league. The Bengals, some would say, were strong contributors to the commissioner's newly adopted personal conduct policy.

As of 2009, the team was noted for being a team of "second chance" players, with the likes of running backs Cedric Benson and Larry Johnson and defensive tackle Tank Johnson.

The team, even given their first-place divisional standing throughout their 10–6 campaign in the 2009 season, did face potential television blackouts. With league-granted extensions the team managed to avoid all blackouts, with community partners, sponsors, and players actually purchasing the remaining blocks of tickets. With this, the team sold out all home games for its sixth straight season. However, in 2010, a season that ended with a disappointing 5–11 record, several blackout dates did come to pass.

Paul Brown chose the name Bengals as a nod to the historic Cincinnati teams of the 1930s. The team is known for their black and orange color scheme and tiger stripes. The logo has changed over time from a leaping tiger to plain block type to the current tiger-striped "B" logo.

The franchise's most legendary football star remains coach and founder Paul Brown. Otherwise, only tackle Anthony Munoz has been inducted into the Football Hall of Fame. Other notables with Hall of Fame potential include Bengals alumni Boomer Esiason and Corey Dillon, and current stars Carson Palmer and Chad Ochocinco.

Kristi Sweeney
University of North Florida

See Also: Blackouts; Franchise; National Football League; Ownership, Professional Teams.

Further Readings

Merrill, Elizabeth. "Bengals Mired in Mediocrity." *ESPN.com.* (August 24, 2009) http://sports .espn.go.com/nfl/trainingcamp09/news/ story?id=4417295 (Accessed December 2009).
Perry, Kimball. "Brown Got 'GM Bonus,' Records Show." *Cincinnati Enquirer.* (April 24, 2009) http://news.cincinnati.com/article/20090424/ SPT02/304250001/Brown-got-GM-bonus -records-show (Accessed January 2011).

Cincinnati Reds

Originally known as the Cincinnati Red Stockings, the Reds have been in existence since 1869. They are one of the first franchises in Major League Baseball (MLB)'s National League, and the only one to still compete in the league from the original eight teams. Through the years, the Cincinnati Reds have changed their name from the Red Stockings to the Reds, and then during the 1950s changed their name to Redlegs to avoid any association with communism. Once the anti-communist fervor of those years subsided, they returned to their name the Cincinnati Reds.

Steeped in History

Relatively speaking, the Cincinnati Reds have had a significant amount of success, compiling five World Series championships and one American Association (AA) championship. However, each successful season was followed with numerous seasons of mediocrity. In 1882, they won their first championship in the AA league, and it was not until the Chicago "Black Sox" scandal that they won their first World Series title.

The 1920s and 1930s were not the greatest for Cincinnati; however, the period culminated with a World Series appearance in 1939 and a title in 1940. Following this championship, the Reds remained at the basement of the standings, with the exception of one World Series appearance in 1956, until the era of the "Big Red Machine" in the 1970s. During this span, 1970–76, the Reds won an astonishing six National League pennants and two World Series titles (1975 and 1976). Numerous players from these teams have been awarded a spot in the Hall of Fame.

In 1981, the Big Red Machine was no longer in existence, and it was demonstrated on the field when the team lost 101 games. Not long after, in 1984 Marge Schott, the second woman to own a major league franchise and first to buy one, purchased controlling interest in the Reds for $11 million. In the first six seasons of her ownership, the Reds finished second in the division four times, missing the playoffs. However, in 1990, Cincinnati not only won the division, they went on to win

From 1970 to 1976, the Reds won six National League pennants and two World Series titles.

their fifth World Series title, tying them for sixth most at that time.

Even with this success, Schott's lasting impact would be the inept minor league system she developed, which dramatically impacted the Reds' performance in the 1990s. In addition, Schott's tenure was marred throughout her ownership with racist, homophobic, and anti-Semitic remarks, and she was thus barred from managing team operations in 1996.

Since 1995, the Cincinnati Reds failed to return to playoff contention until the 2010 season—when they were swept by the Philadelphia Phillies for the National League Division Series in three games. In 1999, the Reds won 99 games, but lost a one-game playoff versus the New York Mets. Given their woes on the field, attendance began to decline as well. In 1994, the Reds averaged just more than 33,000 per home game at Riverfront Stadium. This marked a high point in the 1990s, with almost 1.9 million fans for the season. In 1997, Riverfront stadium was renamed Cinergy Field when Cinergy Corporation, the greater Cincinnati electric company, purchased the stadium naming rights for an undisclosed amount. During the last nine years of Cinergy Field, the Reds broke the 2 million fans barrier twice; once in 1999 and again in 2000.

New Digs and Managers

Like many franchises in the late 1990s and early 2000s, Cincinnati was able to fund a new stadium: Great American Ballpark. Voters in 1996 passed an increase in sales tax of 0.5 percent to fund stadiums for both the Reds and the Bengals, Cincinnati's National Football League team. This would mark the first time since the 1937 the two teams did not share a stadium.

The Reds immediately saw an increase in attendance, amassing more than 2.2 million fans for each of the next two seasons. However, as the team continued to perform poorly, attendance rapidly declined to its lowest level since 1986, with only 1.7 million fans in attendance during the 2009 season. Even with their success in the 2010 season, the Reds continued to struggle in the box office.

The current Reds owner, Robert Castellini, led a group that purchased the Cincinnati Reds for $277 million. With a strong emphasis on tradition, Castel-

lini has attempted to capture some of the great history of the franchise. Making numerous changes in the front office, including two general managers and three team managers in his brief time in control, Castellini hired veteran manager Dusty Baker and Walt Jocketty to head the front office—viewed as his two best decisions to date. Castellini has also placed an emphasis of developing young talent, and has done well drafting promising talent and trading for young players, which is promising for the future.

Thomas J. Aicher
Northern Illinois University

See Also: Franchise; Leagues, Major; Strategic Management.

Further Readings

Covatta, Anthony. "The Wallflower." *Cincinnati*, v.32/5 (1999).

Sheldon, Mark. "Reds Hire Jocketty as Special Advisor." MLB.com. (January 11, 2008) http://cincinnati.reds.mlb.com/news/article.jsp?ymd=20080111&content_id=2343896&vkey=news_cin&fext=.jsp&c_id=cin (Accessed January 2011).

Stupp, Dann. *Opening Day at Great American Ballpark*. Champaign, IL: Sports Publishing, 2003.

Cleveland Browns

The Cleveland Browns began play in 1946 as part of the All-America Football Conference (AAFC). The original owner, Arthur "Mickey" McBride, was a wealthy real estate mogul. He aggressively promoted his team and went after then Ohio State University coach Paul Brown, a legend in Ohio football, to direct football operations. Under their direction, the Browns won the AAFC championship in the first four years of their existence, from 1946 through 1949. In 1950, the AAFC merged with the National Football League (NFL) and the Browns continued to win championships in 1950, 1954, and 1955. McBride ultimately sold the team to a group headed by David Jones, yet the team continued to find success, due in large part to Brown's direction as a football coach.

Art Modell Era

In 1961, Art Modell purchased the team. One year later, word of tensions based on philosophical and ideological differences between Modell and Brown surfaced. After the season, Modell fired Brown. Under Modell's direction, the team won one championship in 1964. Modell's tenure as owner was marred by mediocre teams and playoff disappointments.

Iconic names such as "Red Right 88," "The Drive," and "The Fumble" are legendary plays in Cleveland Browns history that signify the team's frustration under Modell's leadership. When Modell had a successful team, one that went to the playoffs consistently, he would interfere with the coach, ultimately leading to the coach's dismissal. For example, Marty Schottenheimer coached the Browns from 1984 to 1988, taking them to the playoffs each year. But he left the team by mutual agreement with Modell, citing the owner's interference in coaching decisions and personnel choices.

On November 6, 1995, Modell announced that he had signed a deal to relocate the Browns to Baltimore. This move lead to unprecedented hostility directed at Modell and his family, forcing him to flee the city for his safety. Fans of the Pittsburgh Steelers, longtime rival of the Browns, joined Cleveland fans in a rare gesture of solidarity to protest the move. Several lawsuits led to the NFL allowing Cleveland to keep the namesake "Browns" and its history, and also promising to field a team in the city following a three-year "deactivation." (Modell's team, once in Baltimore, became the Baltimore Ravens.)

The Lerner Era

In 1998, Al Lerner, CEO of a credit card company, was awarded ownership of the "new" Cleveland Browns. Although Lerner loved football, he was immensely private and preferred to stay out of the limelight. He died of brain cancer in 2002, passing the team on to his son, Randy. Al and Randy never hired a coach with a proven track record, and never experienced consistent success. Further-

more, like his father, Randy was also very private, preferring to have someone else run the day-to-day operations of the organization. Many fans believe this management style is one of the main reasons why the Cleveland Browns have been a disappointing team since their return in 1999. The Browns have posted a losing record in nearly every season since then. In late 2009, the Browns hired a proven winner and leader, Mike Holmgren, as president. With this hire came renewed optimism among the Browns fan base—but at the end of the 2010 season, Holmgren's staff announced the firing of head coach Eric Mangini, whose two seasons ended with a combined 10–22 record.

The Cleveland Browns' long and proud history has nonetheless resulted in 21 former players and coaches being honored in the NFL Hall of Fame. They include Jim Brown (considered by many to be the greatest running back of all time), Otto Graham, Paul Brown, Marion Motley, Lou Groza, Dante Lavelli, Len Ford, Bill Willis, Willie Davis, Doug Atkins, Bobby Mitchell, Paul Warfield, Mike McCormack, Frank Gatski, Len Dawson, Leroy Kelly, Henry Jordan, Tommy McDonald, Ozzie Newsome, Joe DeLamielleure, and Gene Hickerson.

The Browns have honored a former player, Ernie Davis, by retiring his number 45 despite his never

Browns fans wear orange and brown clothing and dog-related accessories such as collars and dog ears to games.

playing a game. The subject of the recent motion picture *The Express*, Davis won the Heisman Trophy with Syracuse University, was drafted by the Washington Redskins, and immediately traded to the Cleveland Browns. Tragically, Davis contracted and died of leukemia without ever playing a down in the NFL.

Fans Worldwide

Marketing of the Browns relies heavily on two distinct groups in its worldwide fan base: (1) the Dawg Pound, and (2) the Browns Backers. The Browns home field, Cleveland Browns Stadium, is situated on the banks of Lake Erie. One notable seating area preserved by the new ownership sits behind the east end zone, a bleacher section referred to as the Dawg Pound. This term was coined by former cornerback Hanford Dixon, referring to the 1985 defensive team. Dixon and fellow cornerback Frank Minnifield used the metaphor of the pound suggesting a dog-and-cat relationship between the defense and offense (most often the quarterback position). One of the more famous Dawg Pound members is John "Big Dawg" Thompson, who was instrumental as a spokesperson for Browns fans fighting Modell's move to Baltimore. Among his public appearances, Thompson testified before a U.S. House Committee about moving the team.

Members of the Dawg Pound and other fans of the Browns don orange and brown clothing with black highlights. On game days, fans can be seen wearing hard hats (symbolizing the city's historic connection to the steel industry) and dog-related paraphernalia (i.e., bones, collars, dog masks, and dog ears).

With more than 300 chapters and over 90,000 members, the Browns Backers Worldwide (BBW) is considered one of the largest organized fan clubs in professional sports. BBW Clubs have been established in all 50 states and throughout the world, including active chapters in Australia, Canada, England, Germany, and Taiwan. The Cleveland Browns actively market to the BBW and nurture development of new chapters as well as new members of the Dawg Pound.

Adam C. Earnheardt
Jeff Tyus
Youngstown State University

See Also: Baltimore Ravens; Fan Avidity; Moving a Franchise; National Football League; Ownership, Professional Teams; Pittsburgh Steelers.

Further Readings

Heaton, Chuck. *Browns Scrapbook: A Fond Look Back at Five Decades of Football, From a Legendary Cleveland Sportswriter*. Cleveland, OH: Gray & Co., 2007.

Knight, Jonathan. *Kardiac Kids: The Story of the 1980 Cleveland Browns*. Kent, OH: Kent State University Press, 2003.

Pluto, Terry. *When All the World Was Browns Town*. New York: Simon & Schuster, 1993.

Smith, Ron. *The Cleveland Browns: The Official Illustrated History*. New York: McGraw-Hill, 1999.

Cleveland Cavaliers

Since the founding of the franchise, the Cleveland Cavaliers of the National Basketball Association (NBA) have had an inconsistent history in terms of the organization's marketing efforts and on-court play. The Cavaliers teams from 1970–2000 saw a lack of substantive interactive marketing or relationship building with fans, and relied strictly upon the success of the team to generate interest and revenue. The arrival of new owner Dan Gilbert and the drafting of superstar LeBron James helped the Cavaliers franchise revitalize their on-court performance, off-court marketing activities, and engagement with fans.

Inconsistent History

Beginning play during the 1970–71 season under the guidance of owner Nick Mileti, the Cavaliers saw many difficult seasons throughout the 1970s. After a brief ownership change, the team was again sold, to advertising executive Ted Stepien in 1980. To increase the team's brand value, Stepien considered changing the team's name to the Ohio Cavaliers to reach a larger fan base. This plan also included playing home games outside of Ohio and a much-despised polka-derived team theme song. During 1980–83, the Cavaliers experienced a lack of on-court success and a fading fan base.

New life was injected into the team in 1983 when George and Gordon Gund took over ownership. The Gunds changed the team colors from wine and gold to blue, orange, and white. The fan base was reignited by the acquisitions of a new core of talented, marketable, and successful players (e.g., Mark Price, Brad Daugherty) and head coach Lenny Wilkens, a former player and NBA champion. With several 50–plus win seasons, the team was a consistent playoff contender in the late 1980s and early 1990s, but after this, the team entered another period of losing, declining attendance, and fan apathy. The Cavaliers moved from Richfield, Ohio, to downtown Cleveland and the newly built Gund Arena, with little improvement in fan excitement.

LeBron James

The selection of LeBron James as the first pick in the 2003 NBA draft rapidly altered the business and basketball operations of the franchise. Born and raised in Akron, Ohio, James quickly became the face of the franchise and began appearing nationwide in advertisements and being regularly featured on sports news programming. New owner (since 2005) Dan Gilbert refurbished the renamed Quicken Loans Arena, returned to original team colors, and began to take proactive steps to reach out the Cavaliers fan base.

The team has regular national televised appearances, expanded corporate relationships, and high numbers of season ticket sales. The team averaged over 20,000 fans per game during the 2008–09 season, an increase from around 18,000 in 2003–04 (James's rookie year), and up from around 11,500 in 2002–03.

The team provides an enhanced game experience with a live band in the arena concourse before games, a live DJ, and a massive scoreboard that shoots flames as part of the player introductions. Family nights and packages, faith-based nights, and the Scream Team/CAVS Crew further developed and diversified the offerings to the Cavaliers fan base. In-arena events include contests and activities before, during, and after games. The Cavaliers were

also industry leaders in the ticket market, as they introduced Flash Seats as a way for ticketholders to buy, sell, or transfer their tickets to others.

The team also maintains an online presence with an innovative Website and a popular fan site at www.cavfanatic.com. They utilize multiple platforms to communicate with fans (e.g., Twitter) and have created successful partnerships with Cub Cadet, Time Warner, Fathead, and the Cleveland Clinic (for practice facility name rights). The Cavaliers routinely schedule sponsored giveaway items (e.g., posters, bobbleheads), theme nights (e.g., Veteran's Day game), and family nights (sponsored by MDonalds). Activities for younger fans include making signs (sponsored by Office Max) and face painting, as well as group nights (e.g., Scouts Night), Kids Days (sponsored by Nesquik), and free post-game free throws (sponsored by KeyBank). Charitable nights (e.g., toy, eyeglass collections) are also held. The economic difficulties of 2008–09 affected the Cavaliers less than expected, as the team saw strong ticket and merchandise sales and expect the trend to continue.

Adjusting Again

On June 8, 2010, LeBron James announced his departure from the Cavs to the Miami Heat. Superstars have changed teams before, but the franchise player on a championship-contending team leaving was unusual. The impact of James's departure on the Cavaliers is difficult to predict. Short-term predictions had the team struggling to win games and no fan support in the stands. Significant economic impacts to the local economy were predicted (e.g., restaurant and hotel losses).

It is reputed the franchise lost as much as $100 million in value because of the move. However, the Cavaliers season ticket base had to renew their tickets in order to get 2009–10 playoff seats, allowing the team to continue to generate revenue for the 2010–11 season. The fans even showed a renewed dedication to the team as they felt spurned by James and wanted to show the team they still supported them. Over time, the team's performance under coach Byron Scott will help determine the sustainability of the Cavaliers recent success.

Michael E. Pfahl
Ohio University

See Also: Brand Identity; Marketing Mix; National Basketball Association; Sport Celebrities.

Further Readings

Gordon, Roger. *Tales From the Cleveland Cavaliers: LeBron James's Rookie Season.* Champaign, IL: Sports Publishing, 2004.

Menzer, Joe and Burt Graeff. *From Fitch to Fratello: The Sometimes Miraculous, Often Hilarious Wild Ride of the Cleveland Cavaliers.* Champaign, IL: Sagamore Publishing, 1994.

Windhorst, Brian and Terry Pluto. *The Franchise: LeBron James and the Remaking of the Cleveland Cavaliers.* Cleveland, OH: Gray & Co. Publishers, 2007.

Cleveland Indians

The Cleveland Indians began as a minor league team, called the Cleveland Lake Shores, in 1900. The team received major league status when the American League (also known as the American League of Professional Baseball Clubs) joined the Major League in 1901, which before that time, consisted only of National League teams.

The first owners were coal mogul Charles Somers and tailor Jack Kilfoyl. One of the major issues these owners addressed was the name of the club. Initially named the Bluebirds, many players voiced displeasure with the name, and writers often shortened it to the Blues. The Blues were a financial disaster their first two seasons. The arrival of star second baseman Napoleon "Nap" Lajoie, however, led to an attendance increase. Nearly 10,000 fans attended League Park nightly to watch Lajoie and the Blues. By 1905, Lajoie was named manager and the team's name was changed to the Naps. Lajoie's success as manager was short-lived, though, and by 1909 he was removed as manager and assumed player-only duties.

By 1915, Lajoie was sent to Philadelphia; the Cleveland Naps were once again in need of a new nickname. Although it is unclear how Cleveland adopted its current name, one story suggests that Somers asked local newspapers to establish a new name—and they chose Indians.

In 1916, Somers sold the team to a consortium headed by Chicago railroad contractor James C. Dunn. Cleveland went on to defeat the Brooklyn Robins 5–2 in the 1920 World Series for their first major league title.

Continuing Changes

The team did not reach the World Series for another 28 years. In fact, the Indians spent much of this time in the bottom of their division. In 1922, Dunn died ,and his widow sold the team in 1927 to a group headed by Alva Bradley. After several mediocre years, the team was purchased in 1946 by Bill Veeck. He soon abandoned League Park and moved the team to the cavernous Cleveland Municipal Stadium in 1947.

Under Veeck's leadership, one of Cleveland's most significant achievements was breaking the color barrier in the American League by signing Larry Doby, a player with the Newark Eagles of the Negro Leagues. In 1948, they also turned to the Negro Leagues to find the first black pitcher, Satchel Paige. Players signed from the Negro Leagues were instrumental in the Indians winning their second World Series, in 1948.

During 1960–93, the Indians were the epitome of underachievers, finishing no higher than third in their division. The team hired numerous general managers and had several owners over this period, but to no avail.

In 1994, the Indians experienced a rebirth. The team opened Jacobs Field (now Progressive Field) with the intent of fielding a high-quality team befitting the new high-quality stadium. Owner Richard Jacobs and general manager John Hart excelled at acquiring talented players. New players and a new ballpark eventually led to the Indians posting a Major League Baseball (MLB) record for consecutive sellouts at 455 that began June 12, 1995, and ended April 4, 2001. Although the team reached the playoffs in several years and made appearances in the World Series in 1995 and 1997, they were still unable to bring home the championship.

In 2000, Larry Dolan purchased the Indians, and as the quality of the team diminished, so did atten-

This controversial logo of Cleveland mascot Chief Wahoo has been in use since the mid-1940s.

dance. From a management and marketing perspective, it became clear that fans would support the team if they perceived ownership was invested in the success of the team (i.e., acquiring talented players). However, Dolan's management style has been characterized by the number of top players traded in exchange for inexperienced players, in an effort to reduce salary costs.

Mascot and Marketing

For many Native Americans, the team name, Indians, and the cartoon logo of Cleveland mascot Chief Wahoo, are insensitive and reinforce negative stereotypes. Since the mid-1940s, the team has used the logo in various marketing materials and paraphernalia. Several protests have been waged over the years, including demonstrations at the opening of Jacobs Field in 1994 and at the 1997 World Series, which resulted in several arrests.

Recently, the team introduced new hats without the Chief Wahoo logo and a new, kid-friendly,

fuzzy, fuchsia-colored mascot named Slider, in an effort to distance the franchise from the controversy. However, the logo still exists in much of the Cleveland Indians' marketing efforts (e.g., the Chief Wahoo logo is prominently displayed on the team's official Website). In fact, the Cleveland Indians play on the Indians metaphor using terms such as "The Tribe" and "The Wahoos" to reference the team and fan club.

During the dry spell from 1960 to 1993, the Cleveland Indians tried several marketing tactics to bring fans to the stadium. One such promotion was a Ten Cent Beer Night in 1974 that ended in a fan riot and Indians forfeiture. Another unlikely marketing opportunity involved the making of the motion picture *Major League*. Released in 1989, the movie was a comedy that explored a fictional Cleveland Indians team. The movie prompted marketing opportunities for the real franchise, including visits to home games by some of the fictional players, and the playing of *Wild Thing* when relief pitchers would enter the field. The Indians were selected as the team for the movie in part because of their history of losing seasons. However, in the wake of the film's success, the Cleveland Indians found success of their own, including five winning seasons 1995–99.

Adam C. Earnheardt
Jeff Tyus
Youngstown State University

See Also: Major League Baseball; Mascots; Ownership, Professional Teams; World Series.

Further Readings

Eckhouse, Morris. *Legends of the Tribe: An Illustrated History of the Cleveland Indians.* Lanham, MD: Taylor Trade, 2000.

Knight, Jonathan. *Classic Tribe: The 50 Greatest Games in Cleveland Indians History.* Kent, OH: Kent State University Press, 2009.

Pluto, Terry. *Dealing: The Cleveland Indians' New Ballgame.* Cleveland, OH: Gray & Co., 2008.

Schneider, R. *The Cleveland Indians Encyclopedia.* Philadelphia: Temple University Press, 1996.

Click-Through Rate

Click-through rate (CTR) measures the percentage of people exposed to an online advertisement who actually click on the advertisement. CTR is a fluid—although at times misleading—measure of advertising effectiveness. Since many online ads do not lead to an immediate response (i.e., a click), the online advertising industry has created a new term to measure long term hits: view-through rate (VTR). VTR is intended to measure the 30-day response rate to an ad, and not just the immediate effect. While CTR does measure the percentage of people who click on an online ad, it does not however measure the percentage that eventually make it to the site's landing page (i.e., they may get there later as a result of the ad's influence).

Stickiness and Pricing

Advertising has historically been a longer-term strategy for marketers as compared to promotions' shorter-term strategic effects. It is because of the Internet's current capabilities that marketers are now able to more accurately measure the long term impact of a single message. Whichever measure is used, these are very important concepts because they may be used to determine advertising rates that Websites may charge their advertisers. This concept is especially important to many sports-related Websites where advertising is a significant component of their revenue generation strategy (e.g., ESPN.com or CBSsports.com). Many of these sports sites thrive on content being king; sites such as CBSSports.com use content (e.g., video highlights, game footage, box scores) to generate traffic and increase time spent on their site. The more traffic and the "stickier" the site is, the more value the banner ads have, thus justifying higher CTR charges.

CTR is also important in determining the cost of placing an ad on a search engine site such as Google. E-commerce sites, like StubHub.com or DicksSportingGoods.com, often drive traffic to their sites by bidding on keywords that allow StubHub or Dick's Sporting Goods to appear as a sponsored link on Google when a fan types in terms such as "World Series Tickets" or "Under Armor Gear." In these examples, a CTR would be determined based on the percentage of Google users who click on StubHub or Dick's Sporting Goods ads when they appear after receiving Google's search results. This is especially important when a sports related site uses search engines as the primary means to drive traffic to their sites.

Another example of CTR's importance as an ad effectiveness measure is when targeted ads (usually the same text and wording as the sponsored link ads) are placed on content sites through advertising networks such as Google's AdSense. These ads usually are labeled as Ads by Google and are selected based on a match between the ad and the content of the site. In turn, users of these sites should be consistent with the targeted market for the product or service being advertised.

For example, a site dedicated to mountain climbing enthusiasts would likely serve up product/service ads (e.g., climbing gear, related apparel, or mountain lodging) that either relate to the users' shared activity (mountain climbing) or demographic variables (e.g., age, gender, etc.). More likely, it will be a combination of demographic descriptors and various lifestyles and value attributes The key point is, it will likely be a noteworthy match between the advertised products/services and the needs of the site's users. In this scenario, a Website may generate revenue based on exposing product/service ads to as many users as possible (i.e., impressions); the more relevant the ad is to the site's users, the greater percentage of "click through" to the advertiser sites.

It often takes hundreds of impressions to generate a single click through. CTRs have declined since the 1990s, to less that 3 percent currently, and it is therefore imperative that sites have a proper match between context and their corresponding ads in order to keep the CTR as high as possible. While clicking through does not always lead to sales conversion (i.e., consumers making a purchase as a example), a high CTR is typically desirable.

A case when a high CTR is a negative occurrence is when sites experience click fraud. Click fraud occurs when a person—or more usually an automated script, or computer program—clicks on an ad to generate per click charges, without a genuine interest in opening the link.

Conclusion

CTR continues to be an important and valued measurement of online advertising effectiveness. The continued evolution of the Internet and marketer interest in and ability to track online behavior will make this concept even more relevant in the years to come.

Robert I. Roundtree
University of North Carolina, Charlotte

See Also: Advertising Cost, Determination of; Audience Measurement; Internet/Online; Marketing Through Sports.

Further Readings

Laudon, Kenneth and Carol Guercio Traver. *E-Commerce: Business, Technology, Society.* Upper Saddle River, NJ: Pearson Prentice Hall, 2010.
Wertime, Kent and Ian Fenwick. *DigiMarketing: The Essential Guide to New Media & Digital Marketing.* Singapore: John Wiley & Sons Asia, 2008.

Club Seats

Club seats are a preferred seating section commonly found in most professional athletic venues constructed throughout the past two decades. Club seats are priced at a higher investment level compared to nonpriority ticket options, and may also require an additional membership fee before tickets can be purchased. Club seats typically provide the ticket bearer added benefits, amenities, access, and comfort. This preferred seating option offers sports properties a highly sought after revenue generating opportunity to market to fans and corporations as part of season ticket packages or sponsorship agreements.

The location of the Club seating section is usually found on the lower level of a sports facility or arena, either below or adjacent to the Suite level. The Club seating section will normally connect to a private concourse, party suite, or other hospitality area. Access into the Club seating section is restricted to only those who have tickets or passes. Seats may be found to be slightly larger in size and offer fans additional leg room compared to other locations in the venue.

Club seats may also offer the member or ticket bearer access to one or more private dining options found only in the Club seating section of the facility. Club sections will typically feature an expanded concession menu selection, with private wait staff assigned to guests sitting in this premium seating area. Club seats will also provide fans with access to their own merchandise stands and restrooms. Other additional perks may include: food vouchers to be used each game, reserved VIP parking, first right of refusal to purchase concert and other entertainment event tickets inside the facility, exclusive meet-and-greet opportunities with players and coaches, and access to golf or other entertainment options outside of the game season.

Major Revenue Booster

Sport teams offer Club seating options to fans and corporations as a way to increase ticket revenues for their organization. As one example, the Minnesota Twins of Major League Baseball (MLB) constructed a new stadium, opening Target Field for the 2010 season, with an increased number of premium seating options to offer consumers compared to their previous venue. Target Field contains 3,000 Club seats, with an average price of $52 per ticket resulting in a potential yield of $12.4 million for the Twins from Club seating alone. Twins fans interested in purchasing Club seats at Target Field will not only pay a premium per game for access into the Club level, but will also be required to pay a fee or personal seat license of $1,000 to $2,000 per seat before the transaction can occur.

The added benefit of Club seating as a priority seat location to National Football League (NFL) ownership is the partial exclusion of Club seat and Luxury Box revenues under the current NFL revenue sharing agreement. Thus, organizations have added more such preferred locations in recent years to boost team revenues and help pay off debt for new stadium construction. The Dallas

Cowboys have taken advantage of this exclusion with the addition of 15,000 Club seats in their new stadium, which may generate up to $50 million additional for the Cowboys ownership in new ticket revenue.

Club seating sections of arenas or stadiums may also be named after companies, donors (intercollegiate athletics), or former athletes and coaches, in exchange for cash or honorary recognition by the teams or colleges and universities. Some organizations may also refer to their Club section for marketing purposes with such monikers as the "Hall of Fame Club" (Philadelphia Phillies) or "Dugout Club" (Tampa Bay Rays).

Brett M. Burchette
Drexel University

See Also: Luxury Boxes and Suites; Premium Seating; Stadium Operations; Ticket Price, Tiers.

Further Readings

Jacobson, Gary. "Analysis: Cowboys Stadium Could Generate Extra $90 Million." *The Dallas Morning News*. (June 4, 2009) http://www.dallas news.com/sharedcontent/dws/spt/stories/0604 09dnspocowrevenue.445fb39.html (Accessed January 2011).
Roberts, Johnnie L. "If You Build It, Will They Pay?" *Newsweek*. (October 10, 2008) http://www.newsweek.com/2008/10/09/if-you-build-it -will-they-pay.html (Accessed January 2011).

Club System in Other Countries

Perhaps the simplest way to explain a club-based sport system to the U.S. reader is to demonstrate how it is different from the school-based sport system generally employed and recognized in the United States. In the United States, young athletes often develop their skills in a particular sport by participating in school-sponsored sports teams.

In many sports popular in the United States, young men and women who want to participate at a competitive level will play for their junior high school and senior high school teams. Athletes excelling at this level, and who are academically qualified, are frequently recruited to play at the collegiate level, where they represent a university and its athletic department. This school-based system has a long history and is predicated on the principle that sport participation plays an important role in one's education and personal development. Nearly all school-based sport requires participants to comply with certain eligibility requirements, which include maintaining certain academic standards.

While many other sport participation options do exist in the United States that are not linked to schools, such as recreational leagues, church-sponsored activities, and sport clubs (such as a swimming club), most elite sport development and training begins with high school and collegiate teams. Many of the top athletes in the United States, such as Michael Jordan (University of North Carolina), Tiger Woods (Stanford University), and Peyton Manning (University of Tennessee), honed their talents while playing for a university team.

Inclusive Structure

In most other nations throughout the world, this close link between elite sport development and the education system does not exist. Instead, young athletes, regardless of talent level, participate at sport clubs, which have no affiliation with schools. Sport clubs vary considerably in size and the number of sports sponsored. A small single-sport club may have as few as 20 members, while large, multisport clubs may have thousands of members.

Sport clubs typically cater to many ages and ability levels. Clubs are voluntary organizations and are primarily nonprofit entities. In many countries, sport clubs are heavily subsidized by the government. In addition, participants typically pay a yearly membership fee to join. Many clubs also seek sponsorships and may generate revenue from concession and ticket sales and fundraising measures. Club coaches range from volunteers to highly paid professionals, but are often trained and administered through the club. Club administrators also manage their own facilities or lease existing facilities for competition.

While school-based sport is typically divided by the grade level of participants or by varsity/junior varsity status, clubs adhere to an age division classification. For example, children ages 12 and 13 would play in an under-14 (U14) division. Children might begin sport participation at a club when they are as young as 5 or 6, and often continue participation in that same club well into adulthood.

As stated above, some clubs are oriented toward a single sport, while others feature many sports. For example, Manchester United Football Club in Manchester, England, sponsors only soccer teams; and Kilsyth Basketball Club in Melbourne, Australia, is dedicated strictly to basketball. On the other end of the spectrum, Olympiacos in Athens, Greece, sponsors 17 different sports including soccer, volleyball, basketball, and swimming; and Israel's Maccabi Tel Aviv sponsors 13 sports, including soccer, basketball, handball, swimming, and volleyball. A few other well-known multisport clubs include CSKA Moscow in Russia; Spain's Futbol Club (FC) Barcelona; Portugal's Futebol Clube do (FC) Porto; and Cardiff Athletic Club in Wales.

As a side note, while the school-based sport system is strongly entrenched in the United States, not all elite U.S. athletes develop through that system. For example, swimmer Michael Phelps credits much of his development through the North Baltimore Aquatic Club, while many top U.S. tennis and golf stars (such as Andre Agassi, Serena and Venus Williams, and Paula Creamer) trained extensively at the IMG Academy, in lieu of playing for high school or college teams.

The Elite Level

The sport club structure can be traced to England sometime during the 18th century. The earliest clubs organized competitions or annual events and provided social opportunities for members. Administrators in these clubs were typically wealthy aristocrats who also participated in competitions. These athletic contests were not revenue driven, but rather served as symbols of prestige and status for participants.

The earliest sport clubs were dedicated to the sports of thoroughbred racing, cricket, soccer, boxing, and rugby union. Many of these clubs are still running today. For example, the Royal Ascot Racing Club can trace its history back to its first race in 1711; the British Jockey Club in Newmarket has functioned as a sport club since 1750. The Marylebone Cricket Club, home of the historic Lord's Grounds, was founded in 1787. Popular soccer clubs like Manchester United (founded in 1878), Arsenal (1886), Celtic (1888), and Liverpool (1892) formed well over a century ago, and are among the premier sport clubs in the world today.

Many sport clubs oversee the management of elite-level teams that often comprise professional or semiprofessional athletes. In fact, for some clubs the elite teams have become the primary focus of the organization, while youth and recreational teams are no longer a part of the club's structure. In some cases, clubs with high-profile professional teams will create academies that serve as junior development feeder programs for the parent team.

Elite-level club teams compete in regional, national, and international competitions. Some of the more notable international club competitions include the United European Football Association (UEFA) Champions League for soccer, and the Euroleague for basketball. Many sporting bodies also sponsor international club tournaments, such as the FIFA Club World Cup.

One unique feature of the club sport structure is that in many countries, the regional and national club leagues operate under a system of promotion and relegation. Under this system, league officials determine how many teams will play in the top league, frequently referred to as the first division. Elite club teams that are not part of the first division will play in a lower-level league, such as second division or third division. However, at the end of each competitive season, a predetermined number of teams at the bottom of the standings in the first division will be relegated to the second division for the following year. Meanwhile, the same number of teams from the top of the standings in the second division will be promoted to first division. Thus any club team has the opportunity to work its way up to first division.

For example, in Brazil, the bottom four teams in the 20-team Campeonato Brasileiro Serie A exchange places with the top four teams in the Campeonato Brasileiro Serie B after each season.

This system of relegation and promotion is meant to serve as motivation for clubs to put their best team and effort forward throughout a season, even if they are not in contention for the league championship. The process of relegation and promotion does not play a role in every club sport system, however. Australia and Canada are two countries that have not adopted this practice.

An aspect of the elite club sport system that is unique to the European Union is the procedure for the transfer of elite players from one club to another. While club teams develop most of their talent through their junior levels and academies, they will also attempt to acquire the services of players from other clubs by offering those players attractive salaries. If a player is under contract with one club but is sought after by a second club, the two clubs can negotiate a transfer fee. This fee is paid directly to the original club (not the athlete) as compensation for the loss of the player. The second club would also negotiate a contract with the player.

Until relatively recently, European sport clubs had the ability to prevent an elite-level club player from leaving their club at the end of his or her contract, by charging excessively high transfer fees. This policy was found to be in violation of European Union (EU) law, as it prevented Union citizens from "freedom of movement" within the EU to find employment. Belgium soccer player Jean-Marc Bosman tested this rule in the legal system, and in 1995 the European Court of Justice found in his favor. As a result, when Bosman's contract with his Belgium club, RFC Liege, was complete, he was allowed to transfer to a French club, Dunkerque, without Dunkerque paying a transfer fee to RFC Liege. The Bosman case has effectively created a situation among European Union clubs similar to free agency in U.S. professional sports. As a result of this decision, elite EU club players have gained significant negotiating power and have seen their contracts grow in both value and longevity.

Prior to the Bosman case, many clubs also enforced quotas limiting the number of non-nationals participating on club teams. For example, teams in the United European Football Association (UEFA) allowed only three foreign-born players per team prior to the Bosman ruling, but now UEFA teams can contract an unlimited number of players from EU nations. Quotas limiting the number of players

from non-EU countries are still enforced in many club-based sport systems, however. Thus a soccer club team in Spain can have an unlimited number of players from Portugal or France, but may be restricted in the number of players it can bring in from Brazil or Australia.

One major difference between sport clubs with elite-level teams and pro sports franchises in the United States is the concept of club membership for supporters. In most clubs that feature an elite-level team or teams, the large majority of members for that club will be supporters, not participants. Membership requires supporters to pay yearly dues, which grants them benefits such as entrance to social clubs and perhaps season tickets to follow the team. As an example, the popular Greek multisport club Olympiacos has approximately 3,800 participant members, but has a paid club membership of over 80,000. In 2006, the *Guinness Book of World Records* verified the multisport club Sport Lisboa e Benfica in Portugal as having the world's largest paid club membership. At the time, the club boasted over 160,000 paid club members, a number the club states has since grown to over 200,000.

Lower-Level Club Sport

While a few of the high-profile clubs that sponsor elite-level teams tend to get the most media attention, the large majority of sport clubs are oriented toward grassroots and mass participation opportunities. For example, in the high-profile German Bundesliga soccer league, there are only 36 clubs; 18 in first division and 18 in second division. While these 36 clubs are some of the most popular in the country, there are roughly 88,000 other sport clubs throughout Germany, many operating only at a local level.

In fact, one criticism that has been leveled at some clubs is their emphasis on elite sport development, particularly when those clubs are funded in large part by the government. In certain countries, national sport policies are developed to emphasize the "sport for all" movement, which encourages mass sport participation by people of all abilities, races, genders, and socioeconomic status. However, in other countries, national sport policy may place an emphasis on elite sport development and success in international competitions, such as the Olympic Games. Under such policies, clubs that develop elite athletes may receive more resources than clubs that do not.

While many sport clubs do provide mass participation opportunities, many of their members may join strictly for social reasons. In fact, many clubs will operate non-sport-related operations such as restaurants, pubs, or small casinos in addition to their sport facilities. Club members have exclusive access to these non-sport facilities, and revenue generated through them funds sport operations. Outside of the largest clubs, most club administrators and staff are volunteers or part-time employees.

International Student Athletes
The differences between a club-based sport system and a school-based system have created a hot-button issue for the National Collegiate Athletic Association (NCAA) and its member schools. Over the past few decades, U.S. college coaches have been recruiting international athletes in increasingly high numbers, most of whom were first noticed playing for their club team. As of 2010, there were over 16,000 international student athletes competing at NCAA schools. Many of these international student athletes have been very successful, and a few have gone on to notable professional careers. Examples include basketball players Andrew Bogut, Dikembe Mutombo, Steve Nash, and Hakeem Olajuwon; hockey players Martin St. Louis, Jonathan Toews, and Thomas Vanek; baseball players Alex and Joey Cora; and golfers Rory Sabbatini and Annika Sorenstam.

One current issue regarding international student athletes is their amateur status. Under NCAA rules, individuals are not eligible to compete collegiately if they have been paid to play that same sport prior to enrolling in school. While this rule is commonly understood among American high school athletes and coaches, it is not as well known in international circles.

Many sport clubs outside of the United States pay their elite young players stipends, although it is often a relatively meager amount, to assist them with training expenses and to discourage them from leaving for another club. Such payments could cost a young international athlete his or her amateur status, which could prevent the athlete from playing for an NCAA school. Determining what sort of compensa-

tion would shift an athlete from amateur to professional status is one dilemma facing NCAA officials. Tracking such payments is another problem, particularly when the athlete or college coach involved may not want the NCAA to find out about such compensation. Complicating matters is the fact most such transactions are conducted in a foreign country.

While the NCAA and its member schools are grappling with the issue of amateur status for international student athletes, many club officials are dealing with another problem: losing their top prospects to NCAA schools. Because clubs typically cannot afford to pay for a top prospect's university education, and rarely are universities outside of the United States willing to accommodate their academic schedules with an elite athlete's training regime, many of these top prospects elect to accept U.S. scholarship opportunities. This can create a "brawn drain," a situation in which top athletes leave their home nation and club to train and compete in the U.S. college system.

Nels Popp
Illinois State University

See Also: Global Sport; Globalization of Sports; Integration of Sport, Globalization, and Commercialization; Sports Organizing Bodies; Student Athlete.

Further Readings
Bale, John. *The Brawn Drain: Foreign Student-Athletes in American Universities.* Champaign: University of Illinois Press, 1991.
Chalip, Laurence, Arthur Johnson, and Lisa Stachura. *National Sport Policies: An International Handbook.* Westport, CT: Greenwood Press, 1996.
Masteralexis, Lisa P., Carol A. Barr, and Mary A. Hums. *Principles and Practice of Sport Management.* Sudbury, MA: Jones & Bartlett Publishers, 2009.
Noll, Roger G. "The Economics of Promotion and Relegation in Sports Leagues: The Case of English Football." *Journal of Sport Economics,* v.3/12 (2002).

Clutter Sponsorship

Corporations often use sport as a medium for promoting their brand; this action is known as marketing through sport. Each of these corporations develops a marketing campaign for their brand that can include a wide array of promotional strategies. A couple of the more popular and frequently used strategies are sponsorships and advertising. Across all sports, it has been estimated that sponsorship spending increased 11.9 percent in 2007. In addition, advertising saw an increase of 5.4 percent in that same year. Accompanying this spending is an increase in the number of brands being marketed to consumers through sport. This, in turn, leads to clutter.

Clutter in sport sponsorship and advertising is the increased number of brands within a single marketing medium. The term *clutter* refers to this saturation of brands causing consumer confusion by having too many marketing messages in one vehicle. Ultimately, marketers are searching for marketing media where they receive a return on investment (ROI). This ROI is often measured by how much brand equity the sponsoring brand has in the minds of consumers.

Many sport marketing practitioners and researchers suggest that cluttered marketing environments lead to reduced recognition and identification of individual brands, and decreased memory of sponsors and advertisers. This increases avoidance of these marketing strategies by consumers. This in turn presents a significant problem for marketers of these brands. If their brand equity is reduced by clutter, they must figure out how to cut through the clutter. For example, if a brand is sponsoring an event that many other brands are also sponsoring, the marketers for that brand must develop a message that is applicable to the event and align their message with all other marketing efforts outside the event. In order to do this, marketers must develop and implement creative tactics that grab consumers' attention.

Not only do brand managers need to be aware of sponsorship and advertising clutter, marketers of the sport entity (i.e. event, venue, team) need to be attentive. One of the negative effects of excessive sponsorship and advertising that sport marketers must be

A sign full of sponsor names on the new Citi Field ballpark in Queens, New York. Clutter sponsorship can cause confusion among consumers who are bombarded by multiple messages in one medium.

aware of is consumers avoiding the marketing effort. A primary example of this would be the increased popularity of digital video recorders (DVR). Studies have shown that when there is excessive advertising during a televised event, consumers attempt to avoid these brands, often through prerecording an event and skipping the broadcasted commercial messages. A second negative effect of clutter is that consumers often remember less about a brand when there is excessive advertising and sponsorship than if there are fewer advertisements and sponsors.

Conclusion

An example of effective sponsorship clutter management can be seen when examining the National Association for Stock Car Auto Racing (NASCAR) sponsorships directly targeting consumers with high levels of loyalty. Dedicated NASCAR fans seem to look beyond the mass quantity of sponsors, and become very loyal to the brands associated with their favorite driver. Issues arise when examining non-loyal fans of NASCAR; the message may be diluted and the sponsorship value may decrease. Fan avidity and loyalty toward a brand is most commonly affected by sponsorship clutter.

Jason Daniel Reese
Texas A&M University

See Also: Marketing Through Sports; National Association for Stock Car Auto Racing; Return on Investment; Sponsorship Advantages and Disadvantages.

Further Readings

Green, Ethan. "NASCAR's Sponsorship Challenge." *Sport Business Journal* (July 21, 2003).
Green, Mark, et al. "Are Brands Standing Out From the Crowd in the World-Cup Advertising Clutter?" *B&T Magazine* (June 11, 2010).
Hammer, Peter, Erica Riebe, and Rachel Kennedy. "How Clutter Affects Advertising Effectiveness." *Journal of Advertising Research*, v.49/2 (2009).
Mullin, Bernard J., Stephen Hardy, and William A. Sutton. *Sport Marketing*. Champaign, IL: Human Kinetics, 2000.

Cold Call

A cold call is routinely part of the personal selling process. A cold call involves a salesperson attempting to make a sale by telephoning a potential client or dropping in to see a potential client in person, without the potential client having met or interacted with the salesperson previously, and without the potential client having expressed an interest in the salesperson's product or service. In short, the potential client does not know the salesperson, has no connection to the salesperson, and is not expecting contact from the salesperson. A warm call is similar, but in the case of a warm call, the salesperson has had prior contact with the potential client, or has been referred to the potential client by a third party, or knows the potential client has expressed an interest in the salesperson's product or service.

Most sport organizations have a significant amount of inventory that needs to be sold, ranging from tickets (season tickets, flex packs, mini-plans, and so on), to advertising opportunities (stadium signage, game program advertisements, and so on), to sponsorships, to luxury box rentals and group outing packages. Many entry-level positions in the sport management industry involve sales of some sort.

To ensure efficiency and customer courtesy, sport organizations will go to great lengths to ensure that potential clients are not haphazardly contacted by multiple salespeople from the organization. To do this, known potential clients (commonly referred to as leads) are organized in a document commonly called a lead list. Each salesperson is then assigned a section of the lead list that he or she—and no one else—is to contact in hopes of making a sale. In many cases, the lead list contains merely the name of a business or organization the sport property hopes to have as a client. The salesperson then must do some rudimentary research to find contact information, and hopefully the name of the appropriate contact person, before placing a cold call.

When calling potential clients, the warmer the call, the better. Ideally, the person being called has expressed some interest in doing business with the sport organization. Even without an expression of interest, some previous personal contact or a referral from a trusted third party can help a salesperson build some rapport with the potential client in that first phone call. Otherwise, salespeople making cold calls can frequently be seen by the busy potential clients as nuisances who are interrupting their day. As such, salespeople making cold calls must make every effort to gain trust and generate interest in the first few seconds of the conversation. This may involve suggesting a way that the sport property may be able to help the potential client's business, such as driving traffic into a retail establishment via a coupon promotion, boosting employee morale with a group outing, or helping to build name recognition with stadium signage.

Conclusion

If the potential client believes that the sport organization has the potential to help satisfy a want or need, there is a greater chance that the salesperson will make a sale, than if the potential client fails to see any value in doing business with the sport organization.

Craig G. Hyatt
Brock University

See Also: Eduselling; Personal Selling; Up-Selling.

Further Readings

Burton, Rick and Robert Y. Cornilles. "Emerging Theory in Team Sport Sales: Selling Tickets in a More Competitive Arena." *Sport Marketing Quarterly*, v.7/1 (1998).
Irwin, Richard L., William A. Sutton, and Larry M. McCarthy. *Sport Promotion and Sales Management*. Champaign, IL: Human Kinetics, 2008.

Collective Bargaining Agreement

In most of the developed world, a relationship exists between employers and those they employ. The term *labor relations* encompasses this relationship, with the employer or management team acting as one party to the relationship and the labor force acting as a second party. Historically, there have been concerns by both labor and management in the fair and efficient treatment of each party's interests, which has led to the governmental regulation of the relationship. The terms of agreement between these parties are called collective bargaining agreements. Collective bargaining applies to professional sports because professional leagues engage in interstate commerce and the players union and owners have a formal employee/employer relationship. These two parties negotiate agreements through a number of subprocesses, specifically distributive bargaining, integrative bargaining, attitudinal structuring, and intra–organizational bargaining.

Collective bargaining in the United States is governed by the National Labor Relations Act (NLRA). The NLRA instituted procedures for the selection of a labor organization to represent a unit of employees in collective bargaining. The act prohibits employers from interfering with this selection. The NLRA requires the employer to bargain with the appointed representative of its employees. It does not require either side to agree to a proposal or make concessions, but does establish procedural guidelines on good faith bargaining. Proposals that would violate the NLRA or other laws may not be subject to collective bargaining.

The NLRA also establishes regulations on what tactics (e.g., strikes, lockouts, picketing) each side may employ to further their bargaining objectives. State laws further regulate collective bargaining, and make collective agreements enforceable under state law. They may also provide guidelines for those employers and employees not covered by the NLRA, such as agricultural laborers. The federal NLRA guides collective bargaining in professional leagues because they engage in interstate commerce.

In sports, the owners and player unions are required by the NLRA to bargain over "wages, hours, and other terms and conditions of employment." This usually includes wages (salary caps, player drafts, size of roster) and fringe benefits, grievance procedures (injury and noninjury), arbitration, health and safety (drug testing), length of contracts, management/commissioner rights, and discipline procedures.

Basic Structure

In most instances of collective bargaining, a specific labor force unites to act as a single entity, called a trade or labor union, to ensure consistent, fair, and equitable treatment of all members of the union. As the labor union works with management to ensure such treatment, they agree to terms and conditions that are acceptable to both parties. This occurs in a collective bargaining agreement (CBA). A CBA is a document that outlines the terms of employment and working conditions between a group of employees, usually a union, and an employer for a specified amount of time. Collective bargaining accomplishes numerous goals for both management and employees; specifically, it offers protection and parameters for both management and the union within their interrelationship, ideally to the benefit of both groups.

Labor relations and collective bargaining occur in the sport and recreation industry in a number of ways. The most recognizable labor relationship happens in professional sports, where negotiations and disputes are a focal point for media outlets and fans. Lockouts and work stoppages are remembered by fans in infamy (i.e., 1994 MLB World Series and 2004–05 NHL season cancellations). The NLRA applies to professional sports both because professional leagues engage in interstate commerce and because they utilize a formal employee/employer relationship.

In professional team sports in the United States, the structure of the business relationship between management and players takes on one of two forms. The first is a single-entity structure that has gained popularity in second-tier sports, such as Major League Soccer and arena football. The second structure type, which is defined by competitive team owners, includes all of the other major leagues. While both structures involve some collective bargaining, the second structure type incorporates a stronger players union because of the inherent nature of the league management structure

The structure of collective bargaining in professional sports is generally consistent. Almost all of the active players are members of the players union and bargain as a single group. The owners, as representatives of their clubs, join together to bargain with the players union, therefore the negotiated contract applies to all the teams in the league. Collective bargaining in sports has some unique elements that are less likely to be observed in other American industries. Specifically, clubs and players unions bargain over certain aspects of collective wage caps, schedules, work conditions, and player behavior—but individual salaries are negotiated between the club and individual players. These salaries do not necessarily account for length of service or job type, but are calculated by numerous factors such as potential, signing bonuses, roster spot bonuses, and other factors. This creates a dynamic and unique collective bargaining structure that is not witnessed in most other areas of American industry.

Four Types of Bargaining

Bargaining in and of itself has a number of subprocesses and strategies in which both sides participate. There are four main subprocesses of labor negotiations: distributive bargaining, integrative bargaining, attitudinal structuring, and intra–organizational bargaining. Distributive bargaining is generally used to resolve conflicts of interest by distributing the shares of a fixed profit or operational income. Distributive bargaining is really a feature of a zero-sum game, as defined by one side winning a point and the other side losing the point. This type of bargaining is generally viewed as the classic vision of collective bargaining, with two parties sitting at the table haggling over every item of interest.

Integrative bargaining focuses on solving joint problems and seeking to unify the common interests of both the union and management so that all can profit. Integrative bargaining seeks to expand the profit margins and operational income so that both groups make economic gains. This type of bargaining is considerably less adversarial; it focuses on each party's position and leverage over the whole negotiation.

Attitudinal structuring is a third subprocess and is focused around trust building. The focus of attitudinal structuring is to increase the quality of the relationship between the players union and management. This subprocess is focused more on the social contract than on the written contract or transaction.

Within collective bargaining there is a fourth subprocess, intra–organizational bargaining. This occurs when the negotiating teams return to their constituency and present various options. Within each organization, decisions must be negotiated and made with the intention of bringing back the decision to the collective bargaining negotiation table. This can be a very complex subprocess, as the interests of players union members may be very diverse. In many cases, the veteran players and rookies have differing goals and interests. This may also be true for league owners and management, as the market size may dictate preferences for certain types of benefits.

Conclusion

Collective bargaining between players unions and the league management is a very important facet in the health of professional sports. Collective bargaining is a major factor in the three elements of the labor relationship: efficiency, equity, and voice.

Craig Paiement
Ithaca College

See Also: Labor Law; Monopoly Power; Monopsony; Player Mobility; Reserve Clause; Reserve System.

Further Readings

Goldberg, Jonathan. "Player Mobility in Professional Sports: From the Reserve System to Free Agency." *Sports Lawyers Journal*, v.15/1 (2008).
Katz, Harry C. and Thomas A. Kochan. *An Introduction to Collective Bargaining and Industrial Relations*, 2nd Ed. New York: McGraw-Hill, 2000.
Rosner, Scott and Kenneth Shropshire, eds. *The Business of Sports*. Sudbury, MA: Jones & Bartlett Publishers, 2004.

Collusion

Collusion is two or more entities acting to limit open competition through deception, fraud, illegal price setting, wage fixing, or production curtailment. In professional sports, players expect that each owner will act independently and in his or her team's best interest, which should result in free agent players receiving multiple offers for their services and potential compensation offerings to be realistically related to their on-field abilities and likely production. If owners were to secretly agree to limit salary offers to players, the overall profits of team owners would increase as the compensation provided to players would be artificially depressed below natural equilibrium points. Though every professional sport's players union is concerned about potential owner malfeasance in regard to player compensation, Major League Baseball (MLB) players are particularly mindful of the actions of owners, because during the 1980s owners illegally conspired to limit player compensation.

MLB Collusion

In 1966, Los Angeles Dodgers pitchers Don Drysdale and Sandy Koufax negotiated their contracts in tandem, in the hopes that their unified stance would improve the compensation provided in their next contract. Though Drysdale and Koufax did not receive the compensation they initially desired, their team effort at the negotiating table yielded higher salaries than they likely would have received if they had bargained individually. With the Drysdale/Koufax negotiation still fresh in some of their minds, during the 1977 collective bargaining negotiations the MLB owners insisted that language preventing players from acting in concert with other players be included in the upcoming labor agreement. MLB Players Association (MLBPA) Executive Director Marvin Miller agreed to the request, but insisted that the requirement also apply to individual teams.

After MLB players earned the right to become free agents because of arbitrator Peter Seitz's 1975 ruling in the Andy Messersmith/Dave McNally case, player compensation steadily increased over the next nine years. As salaries increased, many owners expressed concern. In 1985, under the direction of commissioner Peter Ueberroth, MLB owners did not offer contracts to prominent free agents. When only four of 35 free agents changed teams, the MLBPA filed a grievance, with the language prohibiting the cooperation of individual teams as a key component.

As the 1986 season ended, owners continued to not offer free agents contracts to play for other teams. All-Star Andre Dawson was one of the few players who changed teams, and he had to sign a one-year deal with the Chicago Cubs for considerably less money than he would have received on the open market, given his prodigious talents. The MLB-PA once again filed a grievance against the owners.

Late in the 1987 season, the MLB players won their initial arbitration case against the owners, with arbitrator Thomas Roberts eventually awarding the players $10.5 million. Despite the ruling, the MLB owners created an "information bank" after the 1987 season to help teams restrict player movement. The players once again filed a grievance against the owners. Arbitrator George Nicolau eventually ruled for the players in the second and third collusion complaints. Nicolau awarded the players $38 million for actions following the 1986 season, and $64.5 million for actions following the 1987 season. In addition to the initial payments, the owners were required to compensate the players for additional ancillary financial losses. In 1991, the players agreed to settle all of the collusion claims in exchange for $280 million, with the money eventually being divided among affected players through a complex process.

Recent Concerns

Despite the large financial settlement the owners paid to the players in the 1980s collusion cases, MLB owners continued to provide players with reasons to be concerned about potential collusion. In 2006, the owners and players settled a collusion dispute that occurred after the 2002 and 2003 seasons. As part of the settlement, MLB owners agreed to pay $12 million to the players, but admitted to no illegal behavior having occurred.

After the 2007 season, the MLBPA expressed some concerns regarding the sharing of information among teams, pertaining to All-Star Alex Rodriguez. Despite the MLBPA's concerns, Rodriguez re-signed with the New York Yankees and earned $28 million in 2008.

After breaking the all-time career home run record in 2007, Barry Bonds did not receive any contract offers for the 2008 season. At age 43, Bonds was certainly far from his physical peak, but he was still a productive player. Some MLBPA officials worried that the owners had colluded to prevent Bonds from playing. Other observers noted the controversial Bonds would likely attract extensive media attention that could disrupt a clubhouse. Those disruptions were tolerable for the San Francisco Giants when Bonds was one of the top players in the game, but as his skills eroded, many teams likely felt that signing Bonds was not worth the investment.

After the 2008 and 2009 MLB seasons, some player agents complained that their clients received nearly identical offers from different teams. The MLBPA has threatened to file a grievance if these actions are further substantiated or if similar actions occur in future years.

Mark S. Nagel
University of South Carolina

See Also: Antitrust Laws and Sports; Collective Bargaining Agreement; Free Agents; Major League Baseball.

Further Readings

Helyar, John. *Lords of the Realm*. New York: Random House, 1994.
Zimbalist, Andrew. *May the Best Team Win: Baseball Economics and Public Policy*. Washington, DC: Brookings Institute, 2004.

"Color"

Color is defined as the general appearance of the skin, complexion, or the skin pigmentation. When we think of color in relation to sports, we are inclined to think of the hues used to represent a team, or on a more profound level, race. An early mention of the word *color* as used to describe a group of people, took place on February 9, 1864. The *Milwaukee Daily Sentinel* described its Protestant Hospital as having fair treatment by stating that patients are received without distinction of country, color, or religion. Since that time, the word *color* has been used to describe groups of people, evident in terms such as *people of color* and *man or woman of color.*

With regard to sport, the term *color* has defined a generation of athletes and has been pertinent in many media reports. For example, baseball legend Jackie Robinson was often referred to as the first African American to break the *color line* in the sport. Until his presence, the color line prevented players of black African descent from the major leagues. Jesse Owens, an African American track and field athlete, rose to fame during the 1936 Summer Olympics in Berlin, Germany, by winning gold medals in the 100 meters, 200 meters, long jump, and as a member of the 4x100 meter relay team—only to be referred to by Adolf Hitler as a colored American runner with primitive jungle ancestors.

Color was not only used to describe African American athletes, but was used to portray Latino, Native American, and Asian American athletes as well. In more recent times, analysis of Title IX legislation has led to the study of the impact of color on female athletes. The following information has been discovered:

1. Since the passage of Title IX, female college athletes of color have experienced a dramatic increase in National Collegiate Athletic Association (NCAA) sports participation opportunities.
2. Female college athletes of color have also experienced a substantial increase in scholarship assistance.
3. Sex discrimination negatively impacts all female athletes, including female athletes of color.
4. Unlike female athletes of color, male athletes of color in NCAA varsity sports (22.1 percent of male athletes) were proportionally represented compared to their presence in the student body (22 percent of male students).
5. There is a pattern of racial inequality in most NCAA sports.
6. Sports help to advance opportunities for some students of color in higher education.
7. Scholarship opportunities for male and female athletes of color are greater than their proportion within the athlete population.
8. Female scholarship athletes graduated at higher rates than the general female student body.
9. Graduation rates of both female and male athletes of color were significantly lower than the corresponding rates for white athletes.
10. Title IX has not decreased the participation opportunities for male athletes of color.

In essence, the use of the term *color* has gone from a derogatory term to one that is valued and used to describe a multitude of individuals. The word is now accepted as a descriptive term to describe those of nonwhite ancestry, and can include individuals from many races and ethnic backgrounds.

Ananka Allen
Texas Woman's University

See Also: Gender Equity; National Collegiate Athletic Association; Olympics; Student Athlete; Title IX.

Further Readings

Butler, Jennifer and Donna Lopiano. "The Women's Sports Foundation Report: Title IX and Race in Intercollegiate Sport." East Meadow, NY: Women's Sport Foundation, 2003.
Jordan, David M., Larry R. Gerlach, and John P. Rossi. "A Baseball Myth Exploded: The Truth About Bill Veeck and the '43 Phillies." *The National Pastime*, v.18/1 (1998).
Speer, Albert. *Inside the Third Reich*. New York and Toronto: Macmillan, 1970.

Colorado Avalanche

The Colorado Avalanche is a professional ice hockey team that currently plays in the National Hockey League's (NHL) Northwest Division. The team was founded in 1975 as the Quebec Nordiques, and moved to Colorado in 1995. The franchise left Quebec after the provincial government of Quebec refused to fund a new arena for the team.

The team name was decided through a poll conducted by COMSAT in 1995. The team colors are burgundy, steel blue, black, silver, and white. The team's primary logo is a burgundy letter "A" surrounded by snow falling around it, in the form of an avalanche, which forms the letter "C." The team's alternate logo is the foot of a Sasquatch. The Avalanche is the second NHL franchise based in Colorado. From 1976 to 1982, the Colorado Rockies played in the NHL before moving to New Jersey at the end of the 1982 season. That original Colorado Rockies franchise was owned by John McMullen.

Going into the 2010–11 season, the Avalanche's all-time regular-season record is 595 wins, 376 losses, 101 ties, and 57 overtime losses. During that same period, the team's all-time playoff record is 130–113. In 1996, the Avalanche won their first NHL Championship (the Stanley Cup playoffs) when they defeated the Florida Panthers in a four-game sweep. In that series, Joe Sakic was named the playoff's Most Valuable Player. In Game 4, defenseman Uwe Krupp scored a goal in the third overtime to give the Avalanche a 1–0 victory and the Stanley Cup. Notably, in winning that 1996 Stanley Cup, the franchise became the first to win the championship just one year after the team had been moved to a new city. That team was coached by Marc Crawford.

In 2001, the club was coached by Bob Hartley. That team won the franchise's second Stanley Cup when the Avalanche defeated the New Jersey Devils in a grueling seven-game series. Colorado won the deciding game by a score of 3–1. In that series-clinching victory, Alex Tanguay scored two goals and an assist as Colorado raced to a 3–0 lead in that game. Goalie Patrick Roy was named the Most Valuable Player of the 2001 Stanley Cup Finals.

Some of the most famous hockey players who played for the team include Hall of Fame goaltender Patrick Roy (voted into the Hockey Hall of Fame in 2006), defenseman Raymond Bourque (voted into the Hockey Hall of Fame in 2004), forward Peter Forsberg, forward Joe Sakic, and forward Paul Stastny. In fact, the club has retired

the jersey numbers of Sakic (19), Roy (33) and Bourque (77). In addition to its Stanley Cup championships, the Avalanche have qualified for the NHL playoffs 20 times. They played in the Western Conference finals in 1997, 1999, 2000, and 2002. The Avalanche are currently coached by Joe Sacco. Previous Avalanche head coaches include Tony Granato and Joel Quenneville.

Since the 1999–2000 season, the team has played its home games at the Pepsi Center, which can be configured to seat 18,007 fans for a hockey game. The Pepsi Center, located in downtown Denver, was built for a cost of more than $161 million. The Pepsi Center also serves as the home to the Denver Nuggets of the National Basketball Association and regularly hosts NCAA tournament games as well as concerts and other entertainment events. During the 2009–10 season, the club averaged 13,947 fans per game. Previously, their home games were played at the McNichols Sports Arena.

The Avalanche are currently owned by business entrepreneur and Walmart heir Stan Kroenke, who bought the team in 2000 for more than $200 million. Kroenke also owns the St. Louis Rams of the National Football League and the Denver Nuggets of the National Basketball Association. In 2008, *Forbes* magazine estimated the value of the club at more than $231 million. The club is engaged in several marketing and public relations efforts to engage fans, including the use of high-tech devices that fans can use during games to vote on the best player of the game and send messages to one another.

Outreach

The franchise has also developed many programs to interact with the community, including Av for a Day, which provides public recognition to children who have done outstanding civic work; Team Fit, which provides education and support to encourage physical fitness among children and adults; and the Qwest Leadership Challenge Program, which honors high school student athletes in the region. Other community programs sponsored by the team include Break the Ice, which provides free hockey instruction to elementary school students who are inexperienced skaters; and Quality Time, which provides schoolchildren and community groups the chance to spend extra time with the team on game days and to buy game tickets at reduced prices.

Ricard W. Jensen
University of South Dakota

See Also: Denver Nuggets; Moving a Franchise; National Hockey League; St. Louis Rams.

Further Readings

Farber, M. "Hoo-Roy!" *Sports Illustrated*, v.94/25 (June 18, 2001).

Farber, M. "Show Stoppers." *Sports Illustrated*, v.89/24 (June 17, 1996).

Greene, M. *Peter Forsberg*. New York: Chelsea House Publishers, 1999.

McAuliffe, B. *The Story of the Colorado Avalanche*. Mankato, MN: Creative Education, 2008.

Ozanian, M. and K. Badenhausen. "The Business of Hockey." *Forbes.* http://www.forbes.com/2007 /11/08/nhl-team-values-biz-07nhl_cx_mo_kb _1108nhlintro.html (Accessed October 2010).

Colorado Rapids

The Colorado Rapids is a professional soccer team that is a member of Major League Soccer (MLS). The club was one of many MLS franchises owned and operated by the Anschutz Entertainment Group, a sport management company started by Denver billionaire Philip Anschutz. The Rapids were one of the 10 original MLS member teams upon the league's formation in 1995.

In its history, the club played for the league championship (the MLS Cup) in 1997, where it lost to 2–1 to DC United. The Rapids reached the semifinals of the MLS Cup in 2002 (when they lost to the Los Angeles Galaxy), in 2005 (another loss to Los Angeles Galaxy), and in 2006 (when they fell to the Houston Dynamo). The franchise also played in the championship for the U.S. Open Cup in 1999.

In the 2003 MLS season, the Rapids set a new MLS record for the lowest home field goals-against average over a season (0.53 goals allowed), in 15 matches at Invesco Field. During that stretch, the club went undefeated in 16 consecutive home games and never allowed more than one goal in a single game. Despite those successes, the club fell to Kansas City in the MLS playoffs that year.

The club has had many head coaches, including Bob Houghton (1996), Glenn Myernick (1997–2000), Tim Hankinson (2001–04), Fernando Clavijo (2005–08), and Gary Smith (2008–present).

New Owner, New Arena

In 2004, Kroenke Sports Enterprises purchased the club. Kroenke Sports also owns and operates the Denver Nuggets of the National Basketball Association and the Colorado Avalanche of the National Hockey League, and it purchased the St. Louis Rams of the National Football League in 2010.

The Rapids now play their home matches at Dick's Sporting Goods Park, a soccer-specific venue that opened in 2007. The park can seat more than 18,000 fans and is located in Commerce City, Colorado, just north of Denver. Dick's Sporting Goods Park is one of the world's most state-of-the-art soccer stadiums. The stadium and its adjoining set of 24 practice fields were designed with cooperation from such prestigious international football clubs as Arsenal FC of the English Premier League and C. F. Pachuca of Mexico Premeira Division. Previously, the club played its home games at Mile High Stadium from 1996 to 2001 and at Invesco Field at Mile High from 2002 to 2006.

One of the club's main rivals is Real Salt Lake, based in the neighboring state of Utah. Since Real Salt Lake joined the league in 2005, the two clubs have played for the Rocky Mountain Cup, which is awarded to the winner of head-to-head games between the teams during that season. The Rapids have won the cup twice, while Real Salt Lake has captured the cup three times.

The Rapids have been known for developing innovative promotions to attract fans and create a fun atmosphere, including such efforts as having a team of Elvis impersonators parachute over the stadium to bring the game ball to the field.

Throughout its history, the Rapids have averaged more than 14,195 fans per game. They led the league in attendance in 2002 when they attracted more than

20,600 fans for each home match. The Rapids fans include two supporters groups organized by fans: the Bulldog Supporter's Group and Pid Army. Dick's Sporting Goods Park is uniquely designed to create areas where supporters groups can stand and cheer throughout home games.

Team Colors

The Colorado Rapids team colors are currently burgundy and blue, and they share the same color scheme used by the Kroenke-owned Colorado Avalanche of the NHL. Previous versions of the team colors included green, and black and blue. The current Rapids logo is a soccer ball set against the backdrop of the Rocky Mountains. Previous logos have featured a rapidly flowing mountain river. The Rapids are one of only four MLS franchises that do not have a shirt sponsorship, which is a large advertisement across the front of the jersey that displays the name and/or logo of a corporate sponsor.

Ricard W. Jensen
University of South Dakota

See Also: Arena; Fan Avidity; Major League Soccer; Ownership, Professional Teams.

Further Readings

Edward, James. "Real Salt Lake, Rapids to Resume Heated Quest for the Cup." *Deseret News.* (May 2, 2009) http://www.deseretnews.com/mobile/article/705300963/Real-Salt-Lake-RSL-Rapids-to-resume-heated-quest-for-the-Cup.html (Accessed October 2010).
Lefton, Terry. "Commerce City to Be New Home for Rapids." *The Denver Business Journal.* (July 27, 2004) http://denver.bizjournals.com/denver/stories/2004/07/26/daily21.html (Accessed October 2010).
Wallace, Sam. "Rich, Reclusive and Relentless: the Man Who Would Be King (of North London)." *The (UK) Independent.* (July 25, 2007) http://www.independent.co.uk/sport/football/premier-league/rich-reclusive-and-relentless-the-man-who-would-be-king-of-north-london-458560.html (Accessed October 2010).

Colorado Rockies

The Colorado Rockies have seen their share of ownership and management issues since they entered the National League along with the Florida Marlins as a Major League Baseball (MLB) expansion franchise in 1993. After an ownership group recruited by Colorado governor Roy Romer submitted a successful bid to MLB to bring baseball to the state, two members of that ownership group were involved in a major accounting and embezzlement scandal with a company they separately owned. One of their replacements was Jerry McMorris, who was regularly involved in disputes and disagreements with other members of the ownership group. In 1999, McMorris's trucking business went bankrupt, and in 2005 his interest in the club was purchased by others in the franchise's syndicate.

Aside from the myriad of front office issues that the club has had to contend with, the team has been subject to a different set of related controversies. In 2006, a *USA Today* article appeared in which it was written that Rockies management had instituted a Christian-based code of conduct for players that included such restrictions as prohibiting men's magazines such as *Playboy* and *Maxim*, and barring sexually explicit music from being played in the clubhouse. Team management was quoted in the article as saying that they believed that this approach would

The Rockies set an all-time attendance record of 4,483,350 in their first year in Mile High Stadium.

help the team focus and ensure the franchise's future success, although they claimed that such a strategy was not meant to impose their beliefs on anyone. After the article was published, several Rockies players were quoted as saying that the article included factual inaccuracies such as the team's alleged prohibition of men's magazines and the claim that Bibles could be found in the clubhouse.

Meanwhile, in 2007, the Rockies and its ticketing partner Paciolan were involved in a federal investigation regarding World Series tickets. Despite announcing previously that tickets would be available at retail outlets in the local Denver area, the Rockies later stated that World Series tickets could only be purchased online, via Paciolan. In the first 90 minutes of the tickets being made available for sale, the computer servers were inundated and overwhelmed with 8.5 million hits, preventing thousands of fans from being able to purchase tickets. As a result, an FBI investigation was launched, involving the alleged hacking of the servers—but found no proof of any wrongdoing by the Rockies, Paciolan, or any other party.

Mile High Performance

Despite the club's history of ownership problems, the decision by MLB to grant Colorado an expansion franchise has proven to be a wise one. In their first year of play in cavernous Mile High Stadium, the Rockies managed to set an all-time attendance record of 4,483,350 and the record for most first-season victories by an expansion franchise, with 67. After a 1994 season in which attendance remained high, the Rockies moved into the new Coors Field, where their first 203 home games were sellouts. Furthermore, the club christened the new stadium with its first postseason appearance, becoming the fastest expansion team to make it to the playoffs.

In September 2007, the red-hot Rockies compiled a 20–8 record for the month, including 11 wins in a row, leading them into the playoffs, where they succeeded in making their first World Series appearance, against the Boston Red Sox. After a dismal 2008 campaign that saw them finish with a losing record, the Rockies found themselves back in the playoffs in 2009, but lost to the Philadelphia Phillies in the National League Division Series, three games to one.

The Rockies should remain a viable franchise in the Colorado area for many years to come, as the team continues to enjoy above-average attendance figures and relatively consistent success on the field. Furthermore, the club has been very involved in the RBI program, an organization dedicated to reviving interest in baseball in the inner city. Recently, the Rockies decided to store game balls during home games in a humidor, which retains moisture in the baseball, in part to compensate for Colorado's thin, dry air that allows baseballs to travel further than in other major league parks. However, the use of the humidor has been controversial, and the team has been accused of manipulating baseballs by using non-humidor baseballs (which travel farther) in situations in which the team needs to score late-inning runs. However, there has been no proof that any of these allegations are true.

Cory Hillman
Bowling Green State University

See Also: Expansion; Major League Baseball; Ownership, Professional Teams; Ticketing.

Further Readings

Boeck, Scott. "Broadcaster Jon Miller Says Rockies Need to Be Watched for Cheating." *USA Today.* (July 12, 2010) http://content.usatoday.com/communities/dailypitch/post/2010/07/broadcaster-jon-miller-says-rockies-need-to-be-watched-for-cheating/1 (Accessed September 2010).

Josza, Frank P. Jr. *Major League Baseball Expansions and Relocations: A History, 1876–2008.* Jefferson, NC: McFarland & Company, 2009.

Nightengale, Bob. "Baseball's Rockies Seek Revival on Two Levels." *USA Today.com.* (June 1, 2006) http://www.usatoday.com/sports/baseball/nl/rockies/2006-05-30-rockies-cover_x.htm (Accessed September 2010).

Slater, Jane. "FBI Looking Into 'Malicious Attack' During Ticket Sales." (October 25, 2007) http://www.thedenverchannel.com/sports/14425776/detail.html (Accessed September 2010).

Columbus Blue Jackets

The Columbus Blue Jackets are a professional National Hockey League (NHL) franchise with an individual owner, John P. McConnell. The team plays within the Central Division of the NHL's Eastern Conference. Management emphasizes marketing and community development as well as building a successful franchise. The Columbus Blue Jackets Foundation funds a number of initiatives and hosts fundraisers that emphasize child safety and wellness within the community. Events include an annual golf outing, Hockey Fights Cancer Night, and Hockey Fest Carnival and Auction.

The Jackets were founded as an expansion team and played their first game in 2000. Their home is Nationwide Arena; their mascot is a green bug named Stinger. Traditions include the firing of a replica cannon at the start of the game as well as for Jackets goals and victories. The team reached their first playoffs in 2009. Games are covered locally on FSN Ohio and various radio affiliates. Television and radio announcers include Jeff Rimer, Bill Davidge, George Matthews, Bob McElligott, Mark Wyant, Jeff Hogan, and John Michael.

Under the leadership of owner McConnell, the Blue Jackets president is Mike Priest; T. J. LaMendola is the chief financial officer. The head coach is Scott Arniel, who was given the job in 2010. On the business operations side, Karen Davis is the director of business communications, Kimberly Kershaw is the director of event presentation/production, and J. D. Kershaw is the director of marketing and fan development. Equally important, Wendy Bradshaw is the director of community development. Corporate sponsors include IGS Energy, whose name appears on a blimp at home games, Tim Horton's, and Nationwide Insurance.

Like many other professional sports teams, the Blue Jackets have a foundation—the Columbus Blue Jackets Foundation. The foundation markets itself within the community through involvement in four key areas: education, pediatric cancer, children's health and safety, and youth and amateur hockey development. With regard to education, the Blue Jackets sponsor programs in central Ohio that promote elementary and middle schoolchildren's healthy eating and noneating choices in and out of the classroom. The team also helps pay for the costs of providing newspapers to students and teachers in the classroom. The Blue Jackets Foundation donates 25 percent of its proceeds to the growth and support of youth hockey, and annually awards an educational scholarship to a graduating high school senior who has shown commitment to both hockey and his or her education.

The Blue Jackets promote involvement in the Boy Scouts and recognize new Boy Scouts at a home game each year. Team players spend time visiting children with cancer, including such activities as horseback riding and dinner as well as hospital visits. Children also drop the puck before a home game or model on the runway with the players during the annual Black Tie Blue Jackets Style show, one of the most significant marketing events of the year in terms of raising proceeds and promoting cancer awareness.

The Blue Jackets host numerous marketing fundraisers to help their foundation raise money and to meet and instill goodwill with their fan base. At the beginning of each season, the team holds a golf outing or classic for their fans to meet and play with their favorite players. They also have Hockey Fights Cancer Night during one home game to raise awareness among fans. The annual Hockey Fest Carnival and Auction, an all-day event featuring a variety of activities, ends with a team auction. All these activities benefit not only the Blue Jackets Foundation, but help support the people and charities that they work with and garner the team positive name recognition within the Columbus community.

David Trevino
Independent Scholar

See Also: Community Relations; Expansion; National Hockey League; Ownership, Professional Teams.

Further Readings

Duhatschek, Eric. *Hockey Chronicles: An Insider History of National Hockey League Teams.* New York: Checkmark Books, 2001.

Whitson, David, and Richard S. Gruneau. *Artificial Ice: Hockey, Culture, and Commerce.* Toronto: Broadview Press, 2006.

Columbus Crew

The Columbus Crew is one of the original 10 Major League Soccer (MLS) franchises, and is currently owned by Clark Hunt, son of former owner Lamar Hunt. Clark Hunt took over operation of his father's sport franchises when Lamar Hunt passed away in 2006. Before his death, Lamar Hunt along with Phil Anschutz virtually controlled the majority of franchises within the MLS; both were considered to be major benefactors to the growth of soccer in the United States. This is further evidenced by the fact that the premier knockout soccer competition in the United States, the U.S. Open Cup, named the trophy for Lamar Hunt long before his passing.

The Columbus Crew are notable in MLS for many reasons, including being the first franchise to construct its own soccer-specific stadium, as well as being one of the most successful teams in the league, despite playing in one of the smallest media markets.

Like many teams in MLS, the Crew has been quite aware of the local market and regional history, and has made special considerations when naming the team and creating logos. While the name was selected through a contest among local fans, the team's logo and colors, a gold and black shield featuring three men in hard hats, is considered to be reflective of the working-class blue-collar roots of the Rust Belt. This mentality is further reflected in one of the nicknames the team was given, "America's hardest-working team." The team's fans have embraced the franchise's use of these motifs to represent the team, and have additionally paid tribute to the large population of German heritage in the region, by naming the supporter group that sits in the north side of the stadium *Nordecke,* literally German for "north corner." From all of this, the Crew has managed to tie well into the blue color and working class roots of the Rust Belt region in which they are located, and through paying homage to this regional background has managed to garner a solid fan base among fans in Ohio.

Soccer-Specific Stadium

While the Crew remained rather similar to other MLS franchises in its marketing, promotion, and outreach to fans, another factor that distinguished the franchise was its gamble to be the first team in the league to build its own soccer-specific stadium to play in. From 1996 to 1998 the Crew played at Ohio Stadium, on the campus of The Ohio State University, which seats around 100,000. Because this stadium was clearly too big for the Crew, and also made them the secondary tenant at Ohio Stadium, the Crew felt the urgent need to have their own stadium. Thus it was that Crew Stadium was planned and built, and the Crew became the first MLS franchise to play in their own stadium in 1999.

Crew Stadium, which seats just over 20,000, is an important milestone in the history of the MLS, not only because it was the first soccer-specific stadium, but because it showed how popular and successful such a stadium could be in terms of fan attendance, as well as from a financial and marketing standpoint. The Los Angeles Galaxy, which were quick to follow the model set by the Crew by building their own stadium, would find similar success, and become the top draw in terms of attendance in the MLS, as well as the first team in league history to turn a profit in a single season.

In this sense, the Crew is considered to be the franchise that took the risk, and helped prove to the league that building a soccer-specific stadium wasn't a liability, but rather something that proved to be beneficial. It is important to note that this stadium was the vision of the Crew's owner Lamar Hunt, who helped to finance a great deal of the cost for the project. The expansion and construction of soccer stadiums within the league is still booming; currently eight franchises play in seven soccer-specific stadiums (the Los Angeles franchises share the Home Depot Center), and five more clubs have broken ground or are planning the construction of their own soccer-specific stadiums.

The success of Crew Stadium and franchise's fan base has been so great that the United States Soccer Federation (USSF) has started to use the stadium as a hosting site for national team games for both men's and women's international soccer. From all of this, it can be seen that Lamar Hunt's vision of soccer-specific stadiums has indeed paid off, not just for the Crew, but for MLS and soccer in general in the United States.

Nicholas M. Watanabe
University of Missouri

See Also: Expansion; Major League Soccer; Ownership, Professional Teams; Stadium Operations.

Further Readings

Dell'Apa, Frank. "Hunt a Quiet Pioneer of U.S. Soccer." ESPN.com. (December 13, 2006) http://soccernet.espn.go.com/columns/story?id=394199&root=us25&cc=5901 (Accessed September 2009).

Major League Soccer, LLC. "Columbus Crew Official Website." http://columbus.crew.mlsnet.com/t102/index.jsp (Accessed September 2009).

Noll, Roger. "The Economics of Promotion and Relegation in Sports Leagues: The Case of English Football." *Journal of Sports Economics,* v.3/2 (2002).

Commissioner System

The commissioner of a professional sports league is the highest ranking executive in the league. He or she have many responsibilities leading the business operations. The commissioner also generally holds the authority to act in the best interests of the league. That power is manifested in various ways, most commonly in the form of disciplining players or club owners who engage in inappropriate behavior.

Landis Sets the Tone
The concept of a commissionership took hold in U.S. professional sports in 1920, when Major League Baseball (MLB) owners hired former judge Kenesaw Mountain Landis to serve in the role. The owners were befuddled following a scandal the previous baseball season in which eight players of the Chicago White Sox were alleged to have been paid by gamblers to intentionally lose the World Series to the Cincinnati Reds.

From this first hiring, it was clear that the powers of the commissioner would be all but absolute. In fact, when a November 1920 meeting of baseball owners produced a recommendation that Landis's powers be tempered, the judge flatly refused to ac-

cept the job. According to Landis, the key to the proper performance of the job was objectivity, requiring the commissioner to be entirely apart from the owners or the players. Landis said that the commissionership must be "an authority outside of [the owners'] business, and that a part of that authority would be a control over whatever and whoever had to do with baseball."

When owners and Landis finally reached a contract—memorialized, in part, as the "National Agreement"—the functions of the commissioner were stated as "to investigate, either upon complaint or upon his own initiative, any act, transaction, or practice charged, alleged, or suspected to be detrimental to the best interests of the national game of baseball, with authority to summon persons and to order the production of documents, and, in a case of refusal to appear or produce, to impose such penalties as are hereinafter provided."

As the first commissioner in professional sports, Landis used his "best interests" powers to rule over baseball with an iron fist. He suspended players and coaches alike for the mere suspicion of gambling; he even suspended the legendary Babe Ruth for 40 days in 1922 when Ruth ignored Landis's prohibition against participating in out-of-town barnstorming tours. Landis proclaimed that the Ruth case "resolves itself into a question of who is the biggest man in baseball, the commissioner or the player who makes the most home runs." It was clear that the former carried the greater power.

Commissioners since Landis have utilized this power in a variety of ways. Other baseball commissioners have used the power to justify prohibiting trades and player sales, as Bowie Kuhn did in blocking the Oakland A's trades of three key players in 1976. Baseball commissioners also have used the power to move franchises, as Bud Selig did in moving the Milwaukee Brewers from the American to the National League. Others have used the authority to suspend owners entirely, as Kuhn did to George Steinbrenner in 1974 after the Yankees owner was indicted for participating in illegal contributions to Richard Nixon's presidential campaign.

Other Leagues
Other commissioners in professional sports have seen their positions as neutral arbitrators. Former

National Football League (NFL) commissioner Pete Rozelle famously assisted the players and the owners throughout his tenure as head of the league, helping the two sides in labor negotiations and instituting hiring equity rules. National Basketball Association commissioner David Stern has worked in a similar way to head off labor disputes in that league.

Team sports commissioners today often find their primary responsibility being that of a sort of player-conduct hall monitor, fining and suspending players for inappropriate conduct. To be sure, much of this discipline is handed out as a result of on-field actions, such as NFL commissioner Roger Goodell's five-game suspension of Tennessee Titan Albert Haynesworth for kicking another player in the face during a 2006 game. However, with the seemingly increased degree of inappropriate activity by players off the field, commissioners have found themselves responsible for monitoring such out-of-workplace activities as well. For example, Goodell often finds himself referring back to the league's Player Conduct Policy, as he did in 2008, when he suspended Denver Broncos player Brandon Marshall for three games following arrests for domestic violence and drunk driving.

The concept of the separation of the commissionership from team ownership was tested in 1992, when Milwaukee Brewers owner Bud Selig also was named chairman of MLB's executive committee, a body that took the place of ousted commissioner Fay Vincent. Selig held this position atop baseball's management structure at the same time as his family owned a controlling share of the Brewers. Some critics point to this lack of centralized and independent leadership as a reason for MLB's governance, labor, and drug culture problems of the 1990s.

Tour Sports Commissioners

The role of the commissioner at the individual-sport level—such as on the golf and tennis tours—is quite different. As these tours are governed by committees comprising executives and players—in contrast to professional team sports leagues, which are governed by a commissioner overseeing a collective bargaining agreement—the tour sports commissioners' jobs more often involve marketing, public relations, sponsorships, and broadcasting relations. To

be sure, commissioners of individual-sport tours are not above criticism and rebuke. When Carolyn Bivens, commissioner of the Ladies Professional Golf Association (LPGA) announced a policy requiring players to speak in English, she was besieged by criticism that eventually led to her ouster in 2009.

Theodore Curtis
Lynn University

See Also: Ethics in Sport; Ownership, Professional Teams; Professional Tournament Sports; Sports Organizing Bodies.

Further Readings

Quirk, Charles. *Sports and the Law.* New York: Garland Publishers, 1996.

Seymour, Harold, et al. *Baseball: The Golden Age.* New York: Oxford University Press, 1971.

Standen, Jeffrey. "Pete Rose and Baseball's Rule 21." *Nine: A Journal of Baseball History and Culture,* v.18/2 (2010).

Commonwealth Games

The Commonwealth Games, known as the "Friendly Games," is an international multisport event that involves athletes from member countries of the Commonwealth of Nations, an association of 54 independent countries, most of which are former British colonies, or their dependencies. Consequently, an unique characteristic is that all participating nations speak English. The Games are envisioned as a way to develop sport for the benefit of people, nations, and territories in the Commonwealth, thereby strengthening that body. The Games motto is "Humanity, Destiny, Equality." From small beginnings of 450 athletes and officials, 11 countries and six sports, this is now a significant sporting event, with the 2006 Melbourne Games involving 5,700 athletes and officials, 71 countries, and 16 sports.

The first Games, held in 1930, in Hamilton, Canada, were organized by a group of Canadians rather than by a group representing Commonwealth countries. Subsequently in 1932, the British Empire Games Federation, now Commonwealth Games Federation, was formed; it is the organization responsible for direction and control. Commonwealth nations have their own Commonwealth Games Associations, made up of representatives who vote at the Commonwealth Games Federation's General Assembly, which ultimately makes decisions on all matters concerning the Games.

The Games are held in a quadrennial cycle in between the Olympic Games, but were not held in 1942 and 1946 because of World War II. Initially known as the British Empire Games (1930, Hamilton, Canada; 1934, London, England; 1938, Sydney, Australia; 1950, Auckland, New Zealand), the Games have had several name changes reflecting political changes within the Commonwealth. Subsequently they were known as the British Empire and Commonwealth Games (1954, Vancouver, Canada; 1958, Cardiff, Wales; 1962, Perth, Australia; 1966, Kingston, Jamaica), the British Commonwealth Games (1970, Edinburgh, Scotland; 1974, Christchurch, New Zealand), and since 1978 the Commonwealth Games (1978, Edmonton, Canada; 1982, Brisbane, Australia; 1986, Edinburgh, Scotland; 1990, Auckland, New Zealand; 1994, Victoria, Canada; 1998, Kuala Lumpur, Malaysia; 2002, Manchester, England; 2006, Melbourne, Australia; 2010, New Delhi, India; with the next Games set for 2014 in Glasgow, Scotland; followed by 2018 in either Gold Coast, Queensland, Australia or Hambantota, Sri Lanka). A bidding process decides which country will next host the Games.

Format and Categories

The format of the Games is similar to the Olympic Games. There is an opening ceremony with a march by athletes and an athlete's oath declaring participation in the "spirit of good sportsmanship." The Queen's Baton Relay is one of the great traditions of the Games, and begins with a ceremony at Buckingham Palace, London, where the baton containing Queen Elizabeth II's message to athletes is handed to the first relay runner. The baton travels throughout the Commonwealth by relay, until it arrives to be read by Her Majesty or a representative at the opening ceremony. Sporting events are held at a number of venues throughout the host city, and accommodation for competitors is provided in an athlete's village. A closing ceremony is the last event of the Games.

Initially, the games comprised only individual sports, with athletics arguably being the key event, central to its popular appeal and commercial viability. From 1998, partially to ensure the event remained vibrant and relevant, team sports were included. The constitution of the Games Federation requires 10 core sports to be included in each Games: athletics, aquatics (swimming), badminton, boxing, hockey (men and women), lawn bowls, netball (women), rugby sevens (men), squash, and weightlifting. Additional sports may be included by a host city, up to a maximum overall total of 17 sports, including no more than four team sports. Some of the sports, such as lawn bowls, netball, and rugby sevens, are played predominantly in Commonwealth countries. Events are held over a maximum 11-day period.

While women originally participated in only a few events, there is now extensive participation by women across the sports program, reflecting increased gender parity in many countries. In Manchester, for the first time at any multisport event, a fully inclusive sports program was provided that included elite male and female athletes with disabilities; they came from 20 countries competing in five different para-sports: athletics, lawn bowls, swimming, table tennis, and weightlifting.

Economic Factors

The Games are a hallmark sporting event across the Commonwealth; making them commercially successful and sustainable is a goal of the Federation. Given that the Commonwealth comprises around one third of the world's population, the Games provide considerable economic and business opportunities to generate income through television rights, sponsorship, advertising, and merchandising. This is balanced by the requirement that the Games be staged in a dignified manner and without excessive commercialization. High-quality event marketing is required to ensure the Games remain popular and attract commercial support, and also to attract spectators and volunteers. Volunteers are key to the success of any Commonwealth Games and provide an opportunity for people from all walks

Marathon runners from several different countries at the Commonwealth Games in Melbourne, Australia, in 2006.

of life to be involved across a variety of levels and in a number of roles.

The Games offer many economic benefits. These include a heightened profile for the host city and country including tourism opportunities; impetus for the development of new sporting facilities and associated commercial developments; job creation; establishing new trade links; and immediate economic benefits through spending on items such as accommodation, hospitality, retail, tourist attractions, and the use of training facilities. Social benefits to the host city arise from increased national pride, as well as through cultural and educational initiatives that typically accompany the Games.

Jeffery Adams
Massey University
Lynette Adams
Sport Waitakere

See Also: Amateur Athlete; Mega Sports Events; Olympic Organization; Recurring Versus Hallmark Events.

Further Readings

Commonwealth Games Federation. "Uniting the Commonwealth Through Sport." http://www .thecgf.com (Accessed November 2009).
Maguire, Joseph. *Global Sport: Identities, Societies, Civilizations.* Hoboken, NJ: Polity, 1999.
Van Bottenburg, Maarten. *Global Games.* Chicago: University of Illinois Press, 2001.

Community Relations

Community relations is the processes by which an organization interacts and builds relationships with people in order to improve the quality of life in the community. It is not only a communications strategy, but also a management approach designed for mutual benefit by contributing to local, regional, national, and global community. Sport organizations operate in and draw resources from their communities. As part of an organization's civic responsibility, it may take an active interest in the well-being of its community. Community relations is one branch of the broader concept of public relations intended to establish and maintain positive lines of communications between an organization and its publics. Overall, the main function of public relations is managing reputation in order to influence opinion and behavior. Other branches include product public relations (e.g., promoting a new or existing product or service), employee relations (e.g., keeping employees informed and providing them with channels of communication to upper levels of management), financial relations (e.g., building a positive reputation among stockholders, potential investors, and financial analysts), and government relations (e.g., representing an organization to elected officials and regulatory bodies).

Community relations provides a unique opportunity for sport organizations to enhance their dealings with outside groups and individuals while contributing to society in a meaningful way. For example, they may target crime prevention, children and youth, urban renewal, employment, environmental issues, performing arts, or other social and educational programs.

Community relations in the corporate context is also closely tied to a growing movement called corporate social responsibility (CSR). CSR views corporations as citizens with a responsibility for shaping the social contexts in which they operate. In particular, CSR seeks to raise awareness of the environmental and human rights impacts of business practices, and to enhance socially driven principles to guide corporate activity. Both concepts highlight that an organization can gain reputation value when it demonstrates that it is a good neighbor and deserves the support and loyalty of the community, even if reputation was not the original purpose for getting involved. However, while both strategies focus on corporate citizenship and require a certain level of awareness and engagement in community issues, the purpose of community relations (as a branch of public relations) is more directly related to marketing, whereas the roots of CSR are ethical, philanthropic, legal, and economic responsibilities.

Purpose and Benefits

A comprehensive, ongoing community relations program serves to benefit both the organization and the wider community by developing mutual understanding and trust. Organizations can enhance their visibility and reputation through supporting programs that improve the lives of those in their communities. This may further translate into larger market share, long-term customer loyalty, and the ability to attract highly qualified employees. Community relations activities may also help a company generate new business contacts through the partnerships that various programs facilitate. Such contacts may be willing to provide support and references for expansion, new facilities, or tax credits.

Community involvement may also promote morale and teamwork among an organization's employees as they take pride in their employer's commitment to civic responsibility. This is beneficial for organizations as it can result in greater effort, job satisfaction, and organizational commitment,

which can ultimately improve the bottom line for the organization. Strong community relations are also beneficial in times of crisis for an organization. For example, an organization may survive an economic downturn or environmental disaster because of the goodwill that has previously been generated. There are also significant benefits for communities when organizations take an active interest and get involved. Different forms of support that a community can receive include financial resources, help with recruiting volunteers, employee participation, and greater media coverage.

In the sport sector, community relations strategies have been shown to provide reliable benefits and opportunities. Regardless of the type and level of sport, local businesses, community associations, schools, and other clubs will appreciate the investment and care they receive and cast their own support in return. As an example, arranging for players to visit sick children in the hospital has been shown to be a valuable opportunity for connecting with the community, and may supplement or even surpass other strategies such as multimedia advertising campaigns or the allure of star athletes.

Programs in Sport

Some larger and professional sport organizations may have a director of community relations whose primary role is to propose, coordinate, and evaluate the implementation of a community relations strategy. In some organizations, this role may be done by a general public relations manager. Community relations programs may also be the responsibility of a marketing associate who creates and executes the marketing strategy for the community and drives the sales process.

Although the specific job titles may vary, responsibilities generally include meeting with community partners, building relationships with business partners, planning and hosting marketing events and awareness campaigns, coordinating speaking engagements, developing a marketing budget plan for the fiscal year, and managing subordinates in the community relations department (e.g., coordinators, interns).

In smaller sport organizations such as small businesses or clubs, the most visible representative of the organization often handles the community relations function. This may be advantageous, as the person may already be well-known in the community. However, some caution must be exercised as these individuals already have a variety of responsibilities, and need to ensure that they are qualified and able to give this function the time and attention it requires. If not, it may be wise to hire a consultant, or strike up a community relations committee among the organization's volunteers. All organizations, and especially smaller or nonprofit sport organizations, should keep in mind that the conduct and activities of everyone involved with the organization contribute to the relationship that the organization develops with the community.

Examples

The leadership of the organization (i.e., senior executives) may decide to connect with a specialized group, or may choose a diversified strategy that targets a wider population. There are many examples of organizations from various sport sectors being connected to the community. Most teams in the "big four" leagues (MLB, NFL, NBA, and NHL) are involved in their communities through local groups, schools and businesses. For example, the Toronto Raptors NBA team is similar to other professional sport franchises in that it has several staff members and a section of its Website devoted to community relations. The Website describes the various ways that the team is involved in the community, outlining an in-school program devoted to promoting literacy, player appearances, community partnerships, merchandise donations, and stories about events where Raptors players, coaches, and management have taken an active role in community causes.

The New York Yankees provides another exemplary case of community relations, through their HOPE Week initiative (Helping Others Persevere & Excel). This is a unique weeklong program created and coordinated by the director of media relations and other staff, intended to provide hope and encouragement while inspiring individuals into action in their own communities. For one week each year, each Yankees player, coach, the manager, general manager, and team executive devotes time to people who are in need or have made a tremendous impact on their community and gives them a unique experience they'll never forget. For many major league

teams, community relations awards, or "community MVPs," are used to recognize players or coaches for outstanding work in the community and commitment to being a positive representative of the team while off the court or field.

One of the more sensitive areas of community relations in professional sport involves team relocations. Understanding community responsiveness is an important factor in determining how successful a franchise can be in a new city. However, a well-planned community relations campaign, offering special programs, and controlling rumors through direct communication with employees and the community can help to minimize the tensions that such upheaval can cause.

Many intercollegiate athletics programs foster positive change by promoting education, health, wellness, and physical fitness, and engaging at-risk and challenged youth. Intercollegiate programs also give back to their communities by offering access to athletic events and facilities, and by providing student athletes as mentors to youth in the community. Each of these activities serves to benefit the wider community in some way, while engaging student athletes in local causes, and creating opportunities for ongoing, long-term partnerships between the university or college and community-based organizations. As an example, Ohio State University Athletics promotes their student athletes as community leaders who make an impact, not just on the local landscape, but on a global scale as well. Each varsity team is involved in a different initiative, such as raising money for breast cancer research at a soccer tournament, or hosting an after-school volleyball program for youth.

Expectations for small sport-related businesses to give back to their communities are often very high and as a result, an organization's community involvement should go beyond just an annual contribution to a charitable fund. Organizational leaders often can focus community relations efforts on causes that are of particular interest to them, and encourage their employees to do the same. Managing community relations in this context also involves ensuring that employees and volunteers represent the organization well in all their interactions. Other effective community relations strategies might involve implementing a charity auction where the proceeds go to local amateur sports clubs, allowing community groups to use office space or other facilities, or getting involved in community advocacy and adding an influential voice on municipal affairs.

Conclusion
Sport governing bodies at the national, state/provincial, or community levels can also demonstrate commitment to their communities through engaging in community relations programs. For example, they may achieve community visibility by connecting local businesses with sport teams and tournaments. They may also offer free trial or drop-in programs to promote sport in the community. Further, many nonprofit sport organizations are now realizing that their role in the community goes beyond providing basic sport services. Instead, they are taking a role as community leaders by integrating concerns and action on wider social issues into their programs, operations, and plans.

Katie Misener
Ryerson University

See Also: Corporate Public Relations, Marketing Public Relations; Growth Strategies; Social Responsibility.

Further Readings
Coalter, Fred. *A Wider Social Role for Sport: Who's Keeping the Score?* New York: Routledge, 2007.
Godfrey, Paul. "Corporate Social Responsibility in Sport: An Overview and Key Issues." *Journal of Sport Management*, v.23/6 (2009).
Hall, Margarete. "Corporate Philanthropy and Corporate Community Relations: Measuring Relationship-Building Results." *Journal of Public Relations Research*, v.18/1 (2006).
Hall, Michael, Steven Ayer, Fataneh Zarinpoush, and David Lasby. *Corporate Community Investment Practices, Motivations and Challenges: Findings From the Canada Survey of Business Contributions to Community.* Toronto: Imagine Canada, 2008. Hopwood, Maria, James Skinner, and Paul Kitchin. *Sport Public Relations and Communication.* Oxford, UK: Butterworth-Heinemann, 2010.

Community Sports

Community sports can exist as organized and sanctioned (amateur) competitions that are delivered through a recognized provider, such as a sport club or association, which is part of a state and national sport governing body and resulting delivery structure. Community sports can also exist as less organized amateur or social competitions that are delivered through providers such as a for-profit leisure centers, local government associations, or schools. Further community sports can exist as "pick up" or "corner-lot" competitive games between groups in a community, at a local park or recreation public space. Community sports are provided by many different types of organizations, and these form the basis of sport development. Community sports typically reside in the public sector, and facilities used for sports at the community level are typically developed and funded by local government authorities or partnerships between public and private sector organizations.

National sport organizations have paid increasing attention to community sports. After all, attracting participants into their sports at the level of the community, and then retaining them by providing adequate pathways and processes for their development, is at the core of their business. Of course, the sport development process relies on the organizations that deliver sport at the level of the community. There has also been increasing emphasis on providing community sports by governments as they strive to tackle issues of obesity, heart disease, and other "lifestyle" illnesses that are costly and resource-intensive to healthcare systems. In the United States, such preventable illnesses cost in excess of $100 billion per year. Community sports have been considered an important tool in preventing such illnesses, and therefore to lessen the burden on healthcare systems.

Focus on Facilities
At the core of the existence of community sports, regardless of how they are delivered, are facilities. Without appropriate facilities, community sports would not exist—and this would have an impact on whether sport opportunities are delivered in communities or not, and the types of sport opportunities that are offered. Urban planning methods

have determined what facilities are included in communities—and why. Facilities are more likely to be provided in communities for sports that are considered to be popular.

Sport facility planning at community level has not often been driven by governing bodies of sports themselves—it is rather driven by urban planning within local government areas, where local governments will decide what facilities are included in their communities, and why. Traditional planning for recreation and leisure facilities drew on the standards approach, where the number of facilities provided in a community was based on population. More recently, however, planning has included community consultation, and urban planning policies now require communities to include facilities for sport and recreation participation opportunities.

Facilities for community sports have an impact on sport development. Facilities are the "store-front" for sports. At the community level of sport, facilities are where consumers gain their first experience of sports. Participants make their decisions about continuing in sports in part because of their experiences at such facilities. Therefore, community sports facilities are an important consideration for sport organizations that wish to recruit and retain participants. The sport facility at community level is a very important part of business strategy and planning—for sport development and ultimately the sustainability of sport. After all, the facility will determine if a sport can be played in a particular community, and the quality and size of the facility will determine the types of sport programming that can be delivered there. A good example of facility-driven strategic development programming for community sport is that of tennis in Australia.

Tennis Australia, the national governing body for the sport in Australia, has employed a strategic approach to the development of facilities for tennis. To develop it national facility framework, the organization needed to know more about existing facilities in Australian communities. In 2004, it recognized that it had little knowledge of the number of tennis facilities that existed in Australia, or any information about the quality of the facilities or their attributes (such as the type of court surface, number of courts, or information about the adjoining clubrooms). This lack of knowledge was partly because of the fact that the development of tennis courts at the level of the community has always been under the jurisdiction of urban planners in local government authorities, rather than that of the national governing body for the sport.

Tennis Australia recognized that in order to develop participation programming for community-level sport, it first needed to know where it could deliver new programs, and the quality of facilities in which programming could be delivered. It commissioned a study to audit tennis facilities around the nation and to build a database, so that tennis facilities and their attributes could be geographically mapped and strategic planning for participation could be matched to population data.

Conclusion

As a result of the study, Tennis Australia is better able to provide for the sport at the level of the community. For example, by mapping tennis facilities, Tennis Australia was able to identify clusters of facilities with specific attributes for different programming opportunities. Using the mapping tool, officials can readily identify facilities that are most appropriate, for instance, to conduct junior tournaments (with appropriate numbers of courts, court surface type, clubrooms, with appropriate amenities etc). As the mapping tool is also linked to community population data, Tennis Australia is now able to strategically plan which facilities are most appropriate for the delivery of targeted programs, and assist their coaches to build their businesses accordingly.

Using the mapping tool, they can understand the demographics of communities surrounding tennis facilities and plan appropriately for the delivery of targeted programs; they also can plan for coaches to deliver seniors tennis in communities where the population profile shows a large percentage of individuals in that age group. They can furthermore plan to deliver their modified programs in areas where there are young families.

Pamm Kellett
Deakin University

See Also: Amateur Athlete; Facilities Planning, Sports; Sports Organizing Bodies.

Further Readings

Green, Mick and Shane Collins. "Policy, Politics and Path Dependency: Sport Development in Australia and Finland." *Sport Management Review*, v.11/3 (2008).

Henderson, Karla A. "A Paradox of Sport Management and Physical Activity Interventions." *Sport Management Review*, v.12/2 (2009).

Shilbury, David and Pamm Kellett. *Sport Management in Australia: An Overview.* London: Allen & Unwin, 2010.

Vail, Susan. Community Development and Sport Participation. *Journal of Sport Management*, v.21/4 (2007).

Compensation

Even though most fans consider professional sports as entertainment, the players, managers, owners, and others who fuel the sports industry generally consider it a business, and they are determined to make as much money as possible. Players, particularly those who play football, must also consider that their careers may be relatively short because of the toll the sport takes on their bodies. Players in all sports venues are also well aware that sudden injuries can end a career; therefore, it is to the athletes' advantage to draw salaries that are big enough to provide them with nest eggs to fall back on if their careers do not go the way they planned.

On average, the National Football League (NFL), Major League Baseball (MLB), the National Basketball Association (NBA), and the National Hockey League (NHL), collectively known as the Big Four, earn approximately $17 billion in annual revenue. The teams of the NFL, which is the highest money-maker in the group, had an average value of $1.04 billion in the final quarter of 2008. The most valuable franchises within the NFL are the Dallas Cowboys, with a worth of $1.6 billion, and the Washington Redskins, with a worth of $1.5 billion.

The various leagues and team owners have hammered out agreements with players and their unions that establish various forms of salary control; however, all the different actors involved in the various franchises want as big a piece of the pie as possible. As a result, it is a foregone conclusion that battles over fair compensation are ongoing. Many of those battles involve increasing the salaries of players who make only minimum salaries, even if it means taxing high-end salaries to do so. Revenue sharing is now being used throughout the Big Four to level the playing field and make all teams competitive with one another.

The battle over what players see as fair compensation and management sees as greed has led to four strikes and three lockouts since 1983. The MLB started the trend in 1983 when the players went on strike for 50 days. During that period, 712 games were canceled. The following year, the NFL followed suit, holding out for 57 days and 98 games. The 1987 NFL strike was shorter, lasting only 24 days and 56 games.

It was not until 1994 when tensions again erupted. In that year, NHL management initiated a lockout that lasted for 103 days and 442 games, and MLB players went on strike for 232 days. Baseball fans were outraged that they lost the opportunity to see 920 games for the season, and many people were convinced that America's love affair with baseball had come to an end. For the first time in its history, the NBA was involved in a lockout during the 1998–99 season, lasting for 191 days and 424 games. In 2004, NHL management initiated a lockout that endured for 310 days and 1,230 games.

National Football League

The NFL first instituted a salary cap in 1993 as part of a collective bargaining agreement with the players union. Since 1990, player salaries had grown at a rate of approximately 9 percent. During that same period, the salaries of players in the other three leagues grew between 12 and 16 percent. In 2008, the NFL salary cap was equal to 65 percent of a particular team's revenue. Bonuses, unlike salaries, were prorated throughout the life of a contract.

Team owners agreed to increase the salary cap in 2009, raising it from $116 million to $128 million for each franchise. Team owners also voted to discard the old collective bargaining agreement and announced that it would be abandoned entirely if a new agreement were not reached by the time the old one expired.

In addition to the salary cap, the NFL has established revenue sharing among all teams within the league, allowing them all to benefit from profitable activities such as broadcast rights and the sale of NFL-licensed merchandise. Revenue sharing is intended to balance out inequities among the various teams so that they are competitive when drafting players and when playing one another. Revenue generated at the local level is retained by individual teams.

Major League Baseball

Battles over player rights have been a part of the business of professional baseball in the United States for over a century. In 1879, the Reserve Clause was first initiated at the end of the National League season. Its purpose was simply to control baseball players. While owners could trade, sell, or release any member of the team, a player himself could not choose to leave under any circumstances. The players spent the next several decades battling to overturn the Reserve Clause, and they finally succeeded in establishing a union that could viably fight their battles.

In 1969, the challenge of Curt Flood of the St. Louis Cardinals made it all the way to the Supreme Court, but the justices refused to overturn the clause. The right to salary arbitration was instituted in 1974, providing for binding arbitration in the case of salary disputes. This paved the way for the abolition of the Reserve Clause in 1975 as part of a binding arbitration decision. By the following year, the mandated Reserve Clause had been removed from all player contracts.

The MLB has engaged in revenue sharing since 2002. In 2007, the league reported gross income of $6 billion. By the following year, that income had increased by half a billion. During that same period, average team worth rose to $482 million. The fact that less-wealthy teams have won the World Series since the practice was instituted is cited as proof that revenue sharing has indeed reduced inequities in the MLB.

National Basketball Association

The NBA has had salary caps of some sort since its first season during 1946–47, when the average player earned $4,000 to $5,000. Revenues increased once television changed the nature of sports, and player salary demands grew accordingly. In 1995, the owners and the players union hammered out a collective bargaining agreement that provided for free agency, allowing any player not under a current contract to choose to sign with any team in the NBA. The agreement also allowed the owners to opt out if salaries exceeded 51.8 percent of projected revenue. When this happened during the 1997–98 season, the owners followed through on the opt-out. They also attempted to enforce tighter salary restrictions.

Although three of the Big Four had been involved in strikes or lockouts, in was not until this time that NBA management initiated its own lockout amid mounting tensions over their attempt at tighter salary restrictions. A last-minute compromise saved the season from being cancelled. Subsequently, players were collectively guaranteed 57 percent of team revenue. That agreement was set to expire on June 30, 2011.

While professional basketball has had its share of superstars over the years, no one has generated the kind of attention and adulation given to Michael Jordan. During the 1995–96 season, Jordan led the Chicago Bulls to 72 wins. He was paid well for his efforts, earning an annual salary of $3.85 million.

The previous year, the Milwaukee Bucks seized on Glen Robinson, the top draft pick of the year. A salary dispute followed, with Robinson eventually signing a 10-year contract for $68 million, an unprecedented amount for a rookie. He also won the right to automatic raises each year. To prevent Robinson's salary from setting a precedent, the NBA placed a cap on rookie salaries the following season.

National Hockey League

Historically, the NHL has not imposed salary limits on its players. There was considerable discussion about instituting one in the Great Depression, but the league continued to go its own way. It also refused to engage in revenue sharing as other members of the Big Four were doing. In the 1970s, the NHL Players Association appeared on the scene, giving professional hockey players a greater voice in salary negotiations. Things came to a head during the 1994–95 season over the issue of salary caps. A lockout ensued, but an agreement was ultimately negotiated. That agreement expired in 2004, and the subsequent refusal to negotiate a new agreement led to a second lockout and the cancellation of the entire season. This was the first time that had ever happened in professional sports in the United States.

The agreement that resulted from that fiasco instituted both a salary cap and revenue sharing. In 2005, the salary cap was 54 percent. The NHL salary cap varies each year, according to annual revenues. During the 2009–10 season, it amounted to $56.8 million, but rose to $59.4 for the following season.

Elizabeth Rholetter Purdy
Independent Scholar

See Also: Agent, Sports; Free Agents; Reserve Clause; Salary Cap; Salary Escalation.

Further Readings

Berri, David J., et al. *The Wages of Wins: Taking Measure of the Many Myths in Modern Sports.* Stanford, CA: Stanford Business Books, 2007.

Pedersen, Paul Mark, et al. *Contemporary Sports Management.* Champaign, IL: Human Kinetics, 2010.

Plunkett, Jack W. *Plunkett's Sports Industry Almanac 2010.* Houston, TX: Plunkett Research, Ltd., 2010.

Shropshire, Kenneth L. and Timothy Davis. *The Business of Sports Agents.* Philadelphia: University of Pennsylvania Press, 2008.

Szymanski, Stefan. *Playbooks and Checkbooks: An Introduction to the Economics of Modern Sports.* Princeton, NJ: Princeton University Press, 2009.

Thornley, Stew. "The Demise of the Reserve Clause: The Players' Path to Freedom." http://milkeespress.com/reserveclause.html (Accessed October 2010).

Competencies

A competency in sport management and sport marketing is a characteristic of an individual that is related to effective or superior performance in a job situation. Competencies in sport management and sport marketing are able to be developed. The examination of competencies is important to help determine the content of academic programs, on-the-job training, and continuing education. These competencies may span managerial, cognitive, personal effectiveness, theoretical, impact, and helping dimensions.

Different competencies are needed for different positions in sport management and sport marketing. Competencies are helpful distinctions for recruiting, placement, retention, and promotion in sport management and sport marketing positions. Human resource managers for sport organizations may utilize competencies for performance management, succession planning, employee development, and pay scales. Specific competencies needed for a job will be based on assigned tasks, type of organization, and size of the organization.

Value in Sports

Increased importance has been given to knowledge, skills, and abilities in communication, technology, multiculturalism, and social media. These require both basic and advanced training in these areas. Many sport management tasks and projects require computer skills; the most common computer skills needed in sport organizations involve word processing, using spreadsheets, and communicating through Internet means.

Other traditional competencies for sport management on the information management side include advertising, developing publications, fundraising, interviewing, promoting, selling, tracking game statistics, and writing. Higher-level information management skills may be needed in sport marketing, sport media, sport writing, and social media in sport.

Many of these competencies are not just specific to sport management and sport marketing. These could be transferable skills to other jobs and other professions. Competencies more specific to the organizational management side of sport include accounting, budgeting, coordinating, directing, evaluating, leading, public speaking, and record keeping. The required competencies will depend on the responsibilities of a particular position in sport management and sport marketing.

Manager Competencies

Several research studies have examined competencies in various sport management positions utilizing surveys and interviews. Some research studies have found competencies differed by upper-level and entry-level employees. The upper-level employees needed competencies in budgeting, communication, delegation, goal setting, problem solving, legal understanding, and personnel evaluation. Entry-level competencies included communication skills, recognizing hazards, problem solving, decision making, computer knowledge, time management, and risk management. Despite some differences by levels, a broad base of competencies was needed in sport management. One study on sport leaders also included the competencies of adapting to change, commitment to the sport organization, and professional integrity. Other research indicated the need for competencies in directing boards of volunteers and community relations. Sport management competencies span a wide range of qualities for success.

In recent sport management work regarding competencies, the topic of personal development has increased. Individuals also possess personal and professional qualities that support effectiveness. These may include work ethic, flexibility, open-mindedness, creativity, and intellectual curiosity. Individuals should be focused on goals, and be able to work independently and as part of a team. The Commission on Sport Management Accreditation included personal development as one of five assessment areas that need to be addressed in the outcomes assessment plan of sport management programs applying for accreditation.

Different approaches exist regarding development of personal competencies. Some academic programs concentrate personal development competencies in sport ethics or sport leadership courses. Other academic programs believe personal development should spread throughout the curriculum and student experience. Empirically validated measurements do exist for validating the development of personal competencies.

Conclusion

Regardless of the specific competencies needed for specific sport organizations and for specific sport management jobs, a strategic approach and extensive planning are also important in the process. The program culture as a whole may be shifted by changes in plans to develop certain competencies. This shift could influence a wide array of people, from students, to faculty, to job trainers. Both academic sport management programs and sport organizations could implement a framework for training and developing sport management and sport marketing competencies.

Lisa M. Miller
Ohio Dominican University

See Also: Employee Development; Human Resources Management; Management by Objectives.

Further Readings

Ball, James, Steven Simpson, Patricia Ardovino, and Karen Skemp-Arlt. "Leadership Competencies of University Recreation Directors in Wisconsin." *Recreation Sports Journal*, v.32/1, 2008.

Chia-Chen, Yu. "Important Computer Competencies for Sport Management Professionals." *International Journal of Applied Sport Sciences*, v.19/1, 2007.

Hurd, Amy and Tracy Buschbom. "Competency Development of Chief Executive Officers of YMCAs." *Managing Leisure*, v.12/1 (2010).

Parks, Janet, Jerome Quarterman, and Lucie Thibault. *Contemporary Sport Management*. Champaign, IL: Human Kinetics, 2007.

Competitive Balance

Competitive balance is a concern for amateur and professional sports leagues because the empirical evidence suggests that fans, both avid and casual, appreciate more rather than fewer competitive events and seasons. This concept has been formalized in what is called the Uncertainty of Outcome Hypothesis (UOH), which posits that sports consumers have a preference for increased competition, that is, uncertainty in outcome, and are willing to pay a premium, either with time, money, or both, to witness more rather than fewer competitive events. The UOH has been shown to hold at the game level in professional baseball, basketball, football, rugby, Australian rules football, cricket, soccer, college football, and stock car racing.

How exactly does the UOH work? Fans derive utility from a sporting event in at least two dimensions: whether their favored team wins, and how their favored team plays relative to their opponent. While fans might also derive utility from interacting with others who attend or watch the game, from discussing the game after the fact, or from consuming concessions during the event, these are not the focus of the UOH. Avid fans for a team likely put greater emphasis and value on whether their team wins or loses, and less emphasis and value on how their team wins or loses. Avid fans likely gain a lot of utility from their team winning, even if all of the wins are lopsided. In contrast, the casual fan likely places more emphasis and value on how any two teams play the game, and less on which team actually wins. These fans gain more utility from closely contested matches where the outcome is uncertain—and are put off by lopsided victories.

Team and League Priorities

The connection between competitive balance and fan utility has practical consequences for teams and leagues. Generally speaking, the more utility derived from a product, the more an individual is willing to spend in the process of consuming, everything else being equal. Avid fans, who like lopsided wins, and casual fans, who like close competition, contribute offsetting pressures on teams through their impact on revenues. Avid fans provide incentive for teams to increase quality, even at the expense of their opponents, that is, avid fans encourage divergence in quality. Casual fans, on the other hand, encourage convergence in team quality and improved competitive balance.

Which influence dominates is important for how leagues operate and, ultimately, how competitive balance can change over time. Individual teams likely garner more net benefit from seeking divergence in quality, that is, satisfying avid fans at the expense of casual fans, than from seeking convergence in quality and satisfying casual fans at the expense of avid fans. The incentive to seek divergence in quality and the limited supply of high-quality players motivates teams to bid for players, either through salaries or in-kind payments. Many express concern that the bidding process will lead to competitive imbalance because only a few very wealthy (and likely popular) teams will obtain the best players.

For these reasons, sports leagues often justify intervention in the sports market for labor either through salary caps, luxury taxes, limiting the number of players on a team, limiting how many players can be paid by a team, or mandating minimum salaries, all to help ensure competitive balance. Leagues also manipulate schedules from year to year, as in the National Football League or the English Premier League, so as to match teams of more similar expected quality, and thereby increasing the uncertainty of which team will win a particular game.

Background and Metrics

The background of why competitive balance might be important in league sports is useful to guiding how competitive balance should be measured. If game-level uncertainty is more important than season-over-season uncertainty, this suggests one way of measuring competitive balance. On the other hand, if there is more concern about the distribution of league championships or postseason appearances rather than game-by-game uncertainty, this suggests that competitive balance should be measured differently. Once a competitive balance measure has been chosen, it is helpful to calculate the measure for a long period of time, to help determine if there are any trends in competitive balance and whether league-wide decisions, such as labor market restrictions or deregulation, rules changes, expansion, contraction, firm relocation, or venue construction (to name a few possibilities) have a noticeable impact on competitive balance.

As the background concerning the uncertainty of outcome hypothesis suggests, there are at least three ways to measure competitive balance: at the game level, at the season level, or across seasons. The first focuses on how likely it is for a team to win any particular game. The second would investigate the distribution of wins across a league at the end of the season, placing less emphasis on the outcome of individual matchups. The third approach investigates long-term competitiveness in the distribution of championships, or participation in postseason play.

The majority of competitive balance measures that have been developed look at the distribution of wins and losses at the season level, including the Gini coefficient, entropy, the relative standard deviation, and the Herfindahl-Hirschman Index. One reason for the extensive focus on season-level outcomes is that the vagaries of weather, officiating, and player mistakes might be "averaged out" over the course of the season. Therefore, many researchers look at the season-level distributions of wins and losses as a better measure of competitive balance because of its broader view. Competitive balance measures looking at inter-season competitiveness include the Herfindahl-Hirschman Index of playoff appearances or championships, variance decompositions, and the recently suggested Adjusted Churn (discussed here).

Because of the large number of competitive balance measures that have been generated, only a select few are outlined here.

Relative Standard Deviation

The Relative Standard Deviation (RSD) of winning percentage is the ratio of the actual standard deviation in winning percentage and the standard deviation in winning percentage that would prevail in a perfectly balanced league wherein each team had a 50–50 chance of winning each game it plays. The actual standard deviation of winning percentage is calculated as $\text{ASD} = \left(\Sigma(\text{winpct}_i - 0.5)^2/N\right)^{0.5}$, where N = number of teams in the league and the Σ notation indicates the sum over all the teams in the league. The ideal standard deviation is calculated as $\text{ISD} = 0.5/(G)^{0.5}$, where G is the number of games played by each team. The RSD is therefore calculated as ASD/ISD. This measure is relative easy to calculate, has been used in many studies, and is sensitive to the number of teams in the league. One downside to this measure is that it does not capture

year-to-year changes in the rank-order finish of the teams in the league.

Relative Herfindahl-Hirschman Index

The Relative Herfindahl-Hirschman Index (RHHI) is the difference between the Herfindahl-Hirschman index (HHI) of wins and the HHI of a perfectly balanced league. The HHI is the sum of the squared market shares of wins in a league, and falls in a range of $10,000/N$ to $10,000$. The ideal HHI equals $10,000/N$. Therefore the RHHI falls between 0 and $10,000(N-1)/N$. The HHI is relatively easy to compute and is more sensitive to changes in rank-order finish of teams from year to year.

The Adjusted Churn

The Adjusted Churn is an inter-year measure of competitive balance and is calculated as follows. Let $f_{i,t}$ be the finishing position of team i in year t and $f_{i,t-1}$ be the finishing position of team i in year $t-1$. Let $\text{absdiff}_i = |f_{i,t} - f_{i,t-1}|$ be the absolute value of the difference in finishing position for team i. The total churn is calculated as the average of the absolute difference in finishing position for all the teams in the league, i.e., churn = $\Sigma\text{absdiff}_i/N$, where N is the number of teams in the league. The adjusted churn is the actual churn normalized by the maximum possible churn. If the number of teams is even (odd) then the maximum churn is calculated as $N/2\left((N^2-1)/2N\right)$. The adjusted churn is in the range of zero to one, with zero being least competitive and one being most competitive.

MLB

Over time both balance measures suggest that both Major League Baseball (MLB) leagues have become considerably more competitive, perhaps counter to conventional wisdom. The adjusted churn measures suggest that both leagues enjoyed an upward trend in the turnover in rank-order finishes during the post–World War II period, which coincided with expansion, specialization, integration, free agency, and improvements in sports medicine and training. The late 1990s through the early 2000s witnessed a reduction in the adjusted churn, primarily caused by the unprecedented 14 consecutive division titles by the Atlanta Braves and the dominance of the New York Yankees and the Boston Red Sox in the

American League's Eastern Division. Both leagues have shown more turnover in rank-order finishes in the latter part of the 2000s.

The improved competitive balance in MLB has been the focus of a tremendous amount of research, both in trying to explain why the improvements have occurred and what, if anything, MLB (and other sports) can learn to promote competitive balance in the future. Research has identified two primary reasons for competitive balance to have been improving over the past several decades: integration, which happened in 1947; and free agency, which was introduced in 1976. To a lesser extent, the various periods of expansion and franchise relocation (in the 1950s, the 1960s, the 1970s, and the 1990s) have also seemed to contribute to an improvement in competitive balance.

The NBA Differences

In contrast to MLB, the National Basketball Association (NBA) is known to be a league with one of the lowest levels of competitive balance. The relative standard deviation in the NBA has increased over time, suggesting that the dispersion of wins has increased rather than decreased over time, that is, in a given season, there are more wins by fewer teams and more losses by more teams. This is rather different than the situation in MLB, where the relative standard deviation has been falling over time. Likewise, the relative HHI measure did not fall as quickly in the early history of the NBA as it did in the early history of the MLB. Moreover, when the relative HHI settled to a fairly stable level in the NBA during the early 1980s, it did so at a higher level than it did in the MLB. Finally, the adjusted churn in the NBA has been a bit more volatile over its history, with about the same mean as in the MLB, but the NBA has had much lower adjusted churns during its history, indicative of less turnover in rank-order finish from season to season.

Conclusion

It is easy to read too much into any competitive balance measure, but it should be noted that competitive balance is not an end in and of itself. Rather, competitive balance is a contributing factor to the television and in-arena demand for, and interest in, the sport. To the extent that fans are interested in

competition rather than any particular team, league policies that promote parity will have a greater impact on league and team revenues.

It is perhaps better to consider competitive balance the result of a complex interaction of influences arising from the labor market, from individual team markets, and from oversight by the league. Thus, in the case of baseball, integration was shown to quickly improve competitive balance, arguably because integration increased the pool of high-quality players, whereas free-agency has had almost no impact on competitive balance in MLB despite repeated claims that free-agency would lead to monopolization of talent. On the other hand, the unique structure of the free-agent market, salary caps, dictated salaries attributed to seniority, and other restrictions on the market for basketball players has limited the beneficial impact of free-agency on competitive balance in that league. It is commonly claimed that the amateur draft helps bad teams become better and that amateur drafts should improve competitive balance. It has not proven to be the case in the NBA—and the extensive amateur draft, coupled with an extensive minor league system, causes the draft to have little impact in the MLB as well.

League officials often point to competitive balance to justify changes to the rules, revenue sharing policies, and other actions that seem to sacrifice an individual team's interests to those of the league. However, many of these claims have gone unfounded in the literature focusing on competitive balance and how it is impacted by league policies. This suggests that leagues may play less of a beneficial role toward competitive balance than generally believed.

Craig A. Depken II
University of North Carolina, Charlotte

See Also: Data Collection; Fan Avidity; League Structure; Monopoly Power; Player Mobility.

Further Readings

Bradley, N. *Marketing Research*. New York: Oxford University Press, 2007.
Burns, Alvin and Ronald Bush. *Marketing Research*. Upper Saddle River, NJ: Prentice Hall, 2009.

Scully, Gerald W. "Pay and Performance in Major League Baseball." *The American Economic Review*, v.64/6 (1974).

Complementary Advertising

Synonyms for complementary are harmonizing, balancing, and matching. In economics, the definition of a complementary good, or product, is defined as a material or good whose use is interrelated with the use of an associated or paired good such that a demand for one (peanut butter, for example) generates demand for the other (jelly, for example). Other examples include burgers and fries, balls and bats (or gloves), gasoline and automobile tires, and winter coats and gloves. Note that sometimes the products are purchased simultaneously, sometimes not. If the price of one good falls and people buy more of it, they will usually buy more of the complementary good also, whether or not its price also falls. Similarly, if the price of one good rises and reduces its demand, it may reduce the demand for the paired good as well. A perfect complement is a good that has to be consumed with another good, such as right shoes and left shoes, or pencils and erasers.

Complementary marketing is recognized as agreements between two or more marketers with complementary products (such as cosmetics and toiletries) or different seasonal sales cycles (such as raincoats and winter coats, or football, baseball, and basketball teams in the same city) to promote or sell each other's products with their own. Complementary marketing can and does occur throughout the components of the marketing mix:

- *Product*: fast food operations and their beverage suppliers.
- *Price*: shared discounts based on membership in groups. Lodging businesses partner with other components of the travel business such as airlines and rental car companies.
- *Place*: common location for the provision of the product/service. Walmart has developed marketing partnerships into its business model, incorporating food, personal services, and banking into its retail locations.
- *Promotion*: coupons and the sharing of their expense by retailers and producers.

Advertising is only one component of the promotion function, and there are numerous examples of where companies are partnering to do complementary advertising.

- *Strategic alliances*: companies cooperate to market the same product in different market segments or to market different but complementary products in common market segments. Airlines, telecommunications industries, and professional sports leagues are areas where it is a viable strategy to market the same product in different market segments. Wedding support services (catering, photography, florists, musicians/performers, and so on) can cooperate to market their individual products/services to a common customer.
- *Affiliate marketing*: revenue sharing between online advertisers/merchants and online publishers/salespeople, where compensation is based on performance measures, typically in the form of sales, clicks, registrations, or a hybrid model. Individual travel industry providers (airlines, hotels, etc.) have begun linking to the sites of the other functional providers, in order to establish the convenience of one stop shopping.
- *Branded differentiator*: an actively managed, branded feature, ingredient or technology, service, or program that creates a meaningful, impactful point of differentiation for a branded offering over an extended period of time. Examples include Westin Hotels advertising the "Heavenly Bed," and workout rooms "powered by Reebok," as well as automobile manufacturers promoting an exclusive interior design line for their vehicles, such as Ford partnering with Eddie Bauer.
- *Branded energizers*: a brand or sub-brand that energizes and enhances a parent brand.

Energizers could be products, promotion, endorsers, or any source of energy attached to the brand

Common examples are sub-brands such as Ronald McDonald House; corporate sponsorship of music festivals and sporting events—NASCAR, almost by definition, has sponsors integrated into the car and driver public image; brand symbols such as Tony the Tiger and the Nike "Swoosh"; branded social programs like Breast Cancer Awareness linking themselves with likely (Avon) and unlikely partners (NFL and its players); and endorsement by recognized athletes of footwear and other athletic gear.

Charles W. Richardson Jr.
Clark Atlanta University

See Also: Advertising; Branding; Complimentary Advertising; Differentiation.

Further Readings

Aaker, David A., *Brand Portfolio Strategy: Creating Relevance, Differentiation, Energy.* New York: The Free Press, 2004.
Aaker, David A. *Building Strong Brands.* New York: The Free Press, 1996.
Aaker, David A. *Strategic Market Management.* Hoboken, NJ: John Wiley & Sons, 2011.
Ferrell, O. C. and Michael D. Hartline. *Marketing Strategy.* Mason, OH: Thomson, 2008.
Samuelson, Paul and William D. Nordhaus. *Economics.* New York: McGraw-Hill, 2001.

Compliance

The enterprise of college sport bears more than a passing resemblance to corporate America in the way in which business is done. Consider this parallel. The U.S. Securities and Exchange Commission, otherwise known as the SEC, is the regulatory agency that ensures investment firms and financial institutions abide by federal laws designed to foster fair dealing and public accountability. The "other" SEC, the Southeastern Conference, serves much the same purpose in facilitating competition among member university athletics programs, while providing a rules mechanism to create common understandings regarding how programs run.

Institutional Control

In effect, where there are rules, there is an accompanying system of checks and balances to make sure that those rules are followed. The checks and balances system in college sport has two key components—a process called compliance and another called enforcement. The term *compliance* refers to the extent to which people working in intercollegiate athletics understand, are informed about, and adhere to existing rules. Critical to the management of any college or university athletic program, compliance efforts are focused on educating anyone with a stake in the program, whether they be administrators, athletes, boosters or fans, coaches, gamblers, media, parents, or sponsors, about what the rules are to protect their interests, the integrity of the games themselves, and to avoid potential violations.

Compliance is often thought of as an indicator of what is called institutional control, meaning that the people in charge of overseeing how an athletics department runs, ultimately presidents or chancellors, have made concerted efforts to convey an expectation that programs will be run with a high degree of integrity.

While it would seem like a fairly straightforward exercise to know what the rules are and to live by them, rules compliance is not nearly so simple. Sometimes a bylaw may be passed that appears to make sense to those who wrote it, but isn't as clear to those who have to implement it in their own work. Sometimes rules are clear but people find loopholes to subvert the impact of what those rules were designed to do. And in still other circumstances, people will intentionally disregard rules, believing that whatever can be gained by doing so is a risk worth taking. In a highly competitive atmosphere where winning games is important and the pressure to win can mean the difference between a coach keeping her or his job or an athlete being ranked higher in a professional draft, the temptation to break rules is part of the calculation of running a modern collegiate athletic program.

As a consequence, every college and university athletic program in the country has a designated compliance officer who is entrusted to take positive and persistent steps to remind interested parties of their obligations under the rules, and to monitor behavior to ensure that programs are running in accordance with rules requirements. To that end, compliance entails ongoing educational outreach to inform constituencies of what the rules are and what they mean. This is done through in-person and online training sessions, dissemination of information in the form of handbooks and brochures, and regular updates regarding rules changes and interpretations through newsletters and e-mails. Efforts are also made to maintain extensive records documenting relevant behavior (e.g., how many phone calls a coach makes to a recruit, when those calls occur within the recruitment cycle, whether athletes are meeting academic standards and are eligible to play, financial aid information for athletes, amount of hours teams practice per week, number of weeks of pre-season, and number of practices within that span of time).

Enforcement

It is at the point where there is a failure in the compliance mechanism that enforcement takes over. Built into the rules structure are penalties for rules violations or what are called infractions. Enforcement is the process of determining the extent to which compliance has not occurred, what motivated or contributed to the failure, and what an appropriate penalty is for breaking a rule. The National Collegiate Athletic Association (NCAA), which is the largest college sport governing association in the United States, has determined that institutions found to be in violation of rules may be subject to one of two types of penalties depending on the type of violation.

A secondary violation, which recognizes that a rule may be broken inadvertently because the rule is so complex that an error is understandable or where the violation is isolated with minimal effect on recruiting, competitive, or other advantage; and did not create a significant recruiting inducement or extra benefit.

A major violation, which reflects a disregard for the rules, carelessness in implementing the rules, or multiple secondary rules violations that demonstrate a lack of control over the program.

Schools can sometimes minimize the impact of an infraction by identifying the problem themselves, doing what is called a self-report (meaning that school officials contact the NCAA to inform them of the problem), and meting out their own penalties. In circumstances where a secondary violation yields no benefit to the institution or harm elsewhere, the NCAA may opt not to punish an institution at all. Still at other times, the NCAA may levy fines and punishments in accordance with the *NCAA Manual*.

The severest form of punishment bears the ominous name of the *death penalty*, reserved for institutions that ignore the rules with impunity. Designed to punish repeat offenders, institutions may be barred from competing in certain sports for one or two seasons. As of this writing, the NCAA has imposed this sanction on five institutions—the University of Kentucky Basketball (1952–53), Southwestern Louisiana Basketball (1973–75), Southern Methodist University Football (1986–88), Morehouse College Men's Soccer (2003), and MacMurray College Men's Tennis (2005).

Ellen J. Staurowsky
Ithaca College

See Also: Ethical Conduct; National Collegiate Athletic Association; Student Athlete.

Further Readings

Associated Press. "NCAA Investigates University of Tennessee for Possible Violations Under Lane Kiffin." http://www.nj.com/sports/njsports/index.ssf/2010/08/ncaa_investigates_university_o.html (Accessed January 2011).
Covell, Daniel and Carol A. Barr. *Managing Intercollegiate Athletics*. Scottsdale, AZ: Holcomb Hathaway, 2010.
National Collegiate Athletic Association (NCAA) Staff. *NCAA Division I Manual*. Indianapolis, IN: NCAA, 2011.

Complimentary Advertising

Complimentary advertising includes all unpaid advertising activities that are offered by an organization. The format of this kind of advertising can be a combination of text, pictures, animation, video and sound. Complimentary advertising can be used in traditional media such as television, radio, newspapers, magazines, billboards and direct mail or new media such as text messaging and Websites.

The idea is to provide advertising free of charge that makes it very attractive for potential customers to use. Complimentary advertising is normally provided by an organization to its business customers. It distinguishes itself from other forms of unpaid advertising such as word-of-mouth by being exclusively designed and structured for organizational customers. Complimentary advertising is typically offered in addition to something else being purchased.

For example, soccer stadiums sell contracts for executive corporate boxes. The price for even the smallest boxes typically starts at $100,000 per year. Companies that buy into these contracts are often provided with complimentary advertising. For example, during breaks in the game, the display in the stadium could be used to advertise these companies. Complimentary advertising could also be offered to exhibitors at a sports conference. The exhibitors pay their usual fees and receive complimentary advertising in the form of free advertising space in the conference program or regular newsletter; or they may be allowed to put their own advertising material in the delegate bags for free. Complimentary advertising can also be given away as a prize in a competition to encourage companies to enter and provide information about the consumer. This information could be retained and used later in approaching these companies to become major advertisers.

Complimentary advertising can be used for sponsorship as well as conventional advertising. The power of traditional advertising lies in its ability to convey a direct and specific message while sponsorship, on the other hand, provides a chance to indirectly deliver a message. The distinctive assets of the two media present opportunities for synergy that are not available when used independently. Any organization that provides complimentary advertising must examine both the additional expenditure and the positive outcomes.

In the short-term, it may be costly to provide complimentary advertising to customers. However in doing so, an organization can gain certain advantages. Often an organization's motives for complimentary advertising are altruistic, such as creating goodwill, which increases its reputation or establishing long-term business relationships with its clients. If complimentary advertising is offered to companies, it is important to identify a good fit between the provider of this free advertising and the company that takes up the offer. When there is a good fit between the two organizations then complimentary advertising will be far more successful.

Sven Kuenzel
University of Greenwich

See Also: Advertising; Marketing of Sports; Sponsorship; Word-of-Mouth.

Further Readings

Belch, George and Michael Belch. *Advertising and Promotion: An Integrated Marketing Communications Perspective.* New York: McGraw-Hill/Irwin, 2011.

Fruchter, Gila E., Eitan Gerstner, and Paul W. Dobson. "Fee or Free? How Much to Add On for an Add-On." *Marketing Letters,* v.22 (2011).

Pickton, David and Amanda Broderick. *Integrated Marketing Communications,* 3rd Ed. Upper Saddle River, NJ: Prentice Hall, 2011.

Ridout, Travis N. and Glen R. Smith. "Free Advertising—How the Media Amplify Campaign Messages." *Political Research Quarterly,* v.61/4 (2008).

Yeshin, Tony. *Advertising.* London: Thomson Learning, 2006.

Yu, Chia-Chen and Richard. P Mikat. Corporation's Objectives for Web Sponsorship and Advertising on Professional Sport Team Web Sites." *International Journal of Sport Management,* v.5/4 (2004).

Concession Pricing

Concessions are a major element of fan enjoyment at sporting venues, and they also tend to be major sources of profits. As early as 1981, overall concession sales topped $3.5 billion. The revenue realized from concessions drops proportionately according to the size of the sporting venue at issue. Long considered a traditional revenue source for sporting venues, concessions are particularly important in intercollegiate sports, generating some $2.3 billion in 2008 alone. The Hartford Civic Center's concession revenues were reported at $21.1 million, or 36 percent of its total operations, in that same year.

Raw Numbers and Branding

Some concession managers believe that profits from concessions are a major determinant in overall financial success. Since the majority of season ticket holders who frequent concessions at sporting venues tend to be economically comfortable, prices tend to be high when compared to the same food obtained from outside sources. It is generally understood that price is less important than quality and variety. Nevertheless, pricing structures must be reasonable, and the various offerings need to consume minimal preparation time and offer a low average cost per unit.

Overall, average per capita investments at professional sporting events and shows amount to $4 to $7.50, and there are concentrated efforts to increase that per capita amount. As an added attraction, concession owners/managers often specialize in items that cannot be found elsewhere. Because decisions concerning the advisability of choosing between in-house and leased concessions are so important, professional organizations such as the International Association of Auditorium Managers and the National Association of Concessionaires provide assistance in the matter.

The largest venues are now investing in a variety of concession services designed to appeal to fans on every level. For instance, Invesco Field, which hosts the Denver Broncos, has a seating capacity of more than 76,000. In order to service that clientele at a ratio of one point of sale for each 135 customers, there are 15,000 employees and volunteers working each game at 79 permanent concession stands and 101 portable kiosks. Invesco Field also offers catering services for parties of up to 2,500 guests, and has 20 merchandise locations.

A typical menu at concessions includes hot dogs with a fat content of more than 82.9 percent, French fries with a fat content of more than 46 percent, hamburgers with a fat content of more than 52 percent, and beer with variable fat content. In order to convince fans to frequent concessions, most owner/managers concentrate on signature items that customers associate with particular concessions and for which they are willing to pay accordingly. For example, AutoZone Park in Memphis, Tennessee, is known for its BBQ Rendezvous Nachos. At Busch Stadium in St. Louis, Missouri, Pretzelry specializes in hand-rolled pretzels. A

Professional sports concession managers are trying to increase average per capita spending, which ranges from $4 to $7.50, by adding unique or brand-name foods.

main attraction at Fenway Park in Boston is their famous clam chowder.

Other ways of attracting fans and increasing profits include partnering with companies that already have a strong fan base. Qualcomm Park in San Diego, for instance, has a partnership with doughnut chain Krispy Kreme. PNC Park in Pittsburgh partners with Outback Steakhouse, and Los Angeles' Dodger Stadium has developed close ties with restauranteur Wolfgang Puck. Brand names are also used to enforce customer confidence in concession offerings and encourage monetary outlays.

Operating Options

Technology is increasingly being employed at sporting venue concessions. With television monitors constantly flashing menus, most concession stands have done away with the menu boards of the past. At Portland's Rose Garden, Internet access allows suite holders to order food and drink before an event takes place. To keep fans happy by getting food and drink to them in a reasonable amount of time and preventing them from missing important events taking place in sporting arenas, companies such as FanGo have partnered with concession managers to provide free branded mobile apps that allow customers to order and pay for items without leaving their seats. Those orders are delivered directly to designated seats.

Traditional methods also continue to be employed as a means of attracting customers, and concession managers depend on impulse buying that results from the wafting smell of a hot dog being grilled or a billboard suggestively displaying attractive foods. Employee training is extremely important to increased profits, and concession employees are trained to encourage customers to forego the traditional small-size product for costlier large-size products by convincing them that larger sizes are higher-value buys.

Revenue potential from concessions is integral to financial planning, and managers of each venue have to decide whether concessions should be handled on site or whether they should be leased to professional concessionaires. In-house management provides greater control over operations and allows for immediate responses and decisions. It also gives managers complete control over pricing, which can be compared to competitor prices and adjusted to mirror fair market prices whenever needed. Quality

control is also much easier for in-house operators, and there is greater potential for increasing revenue derived from the operations. However, leasing also has its advantages, chiefly because volume buying results in lower prices for consumers. Because of the vast experience of professional concessionaires, there is great potential for increased profits at the same time the cost of equipment is reduced. Leasing concession operations also transfers the responsibility for staffing, purchasing, inventory, storage, and vendor relations to outside sources.

Elizabeth Rholetter Purdy
Independent Scholar

See Also: Customer Satisfaction; Point-of-Sale, Point-of-Purchase Display; Pricing Strategies; Stadium Operations.

Further Readings

Depken, Craig A. "New Stadiums and Concession." http://www.belkcollege.uncc.edu/cdepken/P/novelty.pdf (Accessed October 2010).
Plunkett, Jack W. *Plunkett's Sports Industry Almanac 2010*. Houston, TX: Plunkett Research, 2010.
Wakefield, Kirk L. *Team Sports Marketing*. Oxford, UK: Butterworth Heinemann, 2007.

Conferences, Collegiate Athletic

Sports fans usually feel primary loyalties to specific universities and rivalries. They may also pay close attention to conference championships and national playoffs. However, the athletic life cycle of games, seasons, and championships requires an organizing presence, which occurs through athletic conferences and the National Collegiate Athletic Association (NCAA). To understand how the world of college sports works, it is important to grasp this organizational hierarchy and the interrelationships within it.

The first college football game was played between Rutgers University and Princeton University on November 6, 1869, in New Brunswick, New Jersey. Rutgers then played Columbia University in 1870. The form of the game was more like rugby, but these were the forerunners of American college football. As the popularity of the game grew, so did the risks; plays like the flying wedge produced injuries and death. This prompted President Theodore Roosevelt in 1905 to threaten to ban the sport. Roosevelt's actions led to the formation of the Intercollegiate Athletic Association of the United States (IAAUS) in 1906. In 1910, the IAAUS changed its name to the National Collegiate Athletic Association (NCAA); this body was a discussion and rule-making entity in its early years.

While college athletics were being discussed on the national level, there were also regional organizational efforts underway with the formation of athletic conferences. These groupings of schools compete together in a variety of sports. To understand the development of athletic conferences, knowledge of the tripartite structure of the modern NCAA is important: Divisions 1, 2, and 3, or D1, D2, and D3.

NCAA Divisions

D1 has three parts: the football bowl subdivision (FBS), the football championship subdivision (FCS), and the balance of the division (97 schools) that do not participate in football. D1 comprises schools that award athletic scholarships and field teams in a minimum of 14 sports (FBS schools must field 16 teams). When 14 sports are offered, seven or eight are required to be women's teams. The football championship subdivision schools are also members of D1 and are often more regionally focused institutions. D2 schools operate on a model of partial athletic scholarships (full athletic scholarships are very rare) and field teams in a minimum of 10 sports of which five or six are women's teams. In D2, the emphasis is on striking a balance between athletics and other aspects of college life; the competitive arena has a regional focus with benefits for students' time and university travel costs. D3 schools do not offer athletic scholarships.

This administrative framework of U.S. athletic conferences dates back to 1888 with the Michigan Intercollegiate Athletic Association; in 1896 the Big Ten Conference took shape; the Ohio Athletic Conference was created in 1902; and the Rocky Mountain Athletic Conference arose in 1909. Conferences are voluntary associations of schools that set schedules and administer seasons and championships.

At first, conference memberships were based on proximity; schools near one another were more likely to have the communication and transportation resources necessary to sustain competition. Advances in communication and transportation, as well as modern media consumption habits fed by cable television and all-sports channels, have produced conference realignments designed to consolidate athletic prowess and enhance revenue. Proximity has taken a backseat to national visibility and the pursuit of market share. For example, the Atlantic Coast Conference (ACC) was formed with seven teams in 1953; it covered 400 miles of the mid-Atlantic coast from South Carolina to Maryland. The league expanded slowly until 2005 when it added three teams, including the University of Miami and Boston College, to bring total membership to 12 and enlarged its footprint and media markets to reach from Miami to Boston—a distance of 1,500 miles.

Among the newest conferences are the Great West in 2004 (D1), the Great Lakes Football Conference in 2006 (D2) and the Eastern Collegiate Football Conference in 2009 (D3). Between 1892 and 1995, 23 athletic conferences either disbanded or were absorbed into newer conferences. Over time, the conferences themselves have become distinct institutions with publicly recognized identities; conference loyalties promote rivalries among member schools and with competing conferences. Conference realignment highlights the tension between maintaining the collective identity of a group of schools and pursuing the ambition of outstanding conference members. These members long to "move up" to a more prestigious grouping with the prospect of greater fame and reward. In conference realignments, the "team spirit" of the conference is often jeopardized when a school makes a decision in its own interest.

Conferences are creations of the aggregated universities that compose them. College presidents function as the board of directors for the conference and select the commissioner, who is charged with administering programs to serve the best interests of member schools. In turn, conference commissioners form coalitions with other conferences in order to advance their communal interests. Policy and reform proposals can be brought before the NCAA convention by member institutions by university or conference officials. While fans focus on individual schools and rivalries, the framework for college athletics resides in the conferences and the NCAA.

Atlantic Coast Conference (1953)
The Atlantic Coast Conference (ACC) comprises 12 schools from Florida to Massachusetts. The ACC is famous as a basketball conference; four of the schools have won the men's championship (Duke, Maryland, North Carolina, and NC State). Since 1953, conference members have won 105 national championships (56 women's, 49 men's), and 225 individual championships (86 women's, 139 men's).

Big East Conference (1979)
The Big East, with 17 schools from Texas and Florida to Wisconsin and Rhode Island, has been a power basketball conference. Men's teams have won the national championship 11 times (Cincinnati [2], Connecticut [3], Georgetown, Louisville [2], Marquette, Syracuse, and Villanova). Since 1979, the conference has won 28 national team championships in six different sports and 128 individual championships. The Big East is the largest D1 conference and includes nine of the 35 largest media markets.

Big Ten Conference (1896)
The Big Ten has 12 schools from Nebraska and Minnesota to Pennsylvania. It is a famous football conference with storied rivalries: Michigan/Ohio State and Purdue/Indiana. Schools in this conference have claimed the men's national football championship 41 times since 1869; in the absence of definitive championship format their public claims speak for themselves. The schools and championships are: Illinois (5), Iowa (1), Michigan (11), Michigan State (6), Nebraska (5), and Ohio State (7). Men's national basketball championships have also been won by four member schools: Indiana University (5), Michigan State (2), Michigan (1), and Wisconsin (1).

Big Twelve Conference (1996)
The Big Twelve Conference comprises 10 schools from Iowa to Texas. Member schools have won 38 team championships and 459 individual championships. Conference schools have made seven appearances in BCS title games, more than any other

conference. The conference has had four Heisman Award winners (Sam Bradford, OU, 2008; Jason White, OU, 2003; Eric Crouch, UN, 2001; Ricky Williams, UT, 1998) in the last 13 years.

Conference USA (1995)
Conference USA (C-USA) comprises 12 schools from Florida to West Virginia to Texas. Member schools have made 53 bowl appearances and 114 appearances in the NCAA men's basketball tournament. One national championship, three national championship game appearances and 10 Final Four appearances have been earned by C-USA teams. The conference has won 28 championships in track and field and cross-country.

Mid-American Conference (1946)
The Mid-American Conference includes 13 schools from Illinois to Michigan to New York. In 2008, five member schools participated in bowl games. Four teams defeated Big Ten schools in football. Three teams made the NCAA volleyball tournament; one advanced to the Sweet 16.

Mountain West Conference (1999)
The Mountain West Conference includes schools from Hawaii to Idaho and New Mexico. Boise State University joined in 2011 and the University of Hawaii in 2012 for football. Fresno State University and the University of Nevada also joined. In 2011, BYU left for the West Coast Conference in 2011, and Utah left for the PAC-10. Conference members have won three team championships; 595 athletes have won All-America honors in 19 sports. UNLV won the men's basketball championship in 1990.

Pacific Pac-10 Conference (1915)
The Pacific Pac-10 Conference comprises 12 schools from Washington to Arizona to Colorado. The University of Utah joined in 2011 and the University of Colorado in 2012. Member schools have won 171 national team titles in the past 20 years; eight of them in 2009–10. There have been 390 individual titles (123 women's, 207 men's) as well. Seven of the top 10 Division 1 programs are in the PAC-10. UCLA's success in the men's basketball championships is unrivaled: they have won 11 championships.

Southeastern Conference (1932)

The 12 Southeastern Conference (SEC) schools, from Florida to Kentucky to Louisiana, won four national team titles in 2009–10, and were runners-up in four other championships. There were also 41 individual championships and 440 first-team All Americans. Since 1990, SEC schools have won 135 national team titles.

Sun Belt Conference (1976)

The Sun Belt Conference, with 12 schools from Florida to Kentucky to Colorado, instituted football in 2001 and became a BCS conference. The conference secured appearances for member schools in the New Orleans Bowl and the GMAC Bowl. Member schools made the College World Series in baseball and softball. In 2008, two men's teams made the NCAA men's basketball tournament, one advancing to the Sweet 16.

Western Athletic Conference (1962)

The Western Athletic Conference (WAC) comprises eight schools from Louisiana to Idaho to California. Denver, Texas-San Antonio and Texas State are slated to join in 2012. Member schools have participated in bowl games 31 times since 2001. Two men's teams have made the NCAA basketball tournament in 24 of the last 27 years. Member schools have won two NCAA baseball championships since 2003.

John Llewellyn
Wake Forest University

See Also: Amateur Athlete; Blackouts; Bowl Games; Commissioner System; Final Four; Image; Knight Commission; March Madness; NCAA.

Further Readings

Crowley, Joseph N. *In the Arena: The NCAA's First Century*. Indianapolis, IN: National Collegiate Athletic Association (NCAA), 2006.

Feinstein, John. *The Last Amateurs: Playing for Glory and Honor in Division I College Basketball*. Boston: Little, Brown, 2000.

Jacobs, Barry. *Golden Glory: The First 50 Years of the ACC*. Greensboro, NC: Mann Media, 2002.

Congruency of Product and Target Market

A strategic sport marketing process includes a calculated manipulation of the sport product, price, distribution, and promotion activities geared to best capture the intended target market in order to fully satisfy consumer needs or wants. All aspects of the sport marketing mix are important, as sport consumers rarely make a purchase decision based on one element alone. These elements work together to produce an intersecting impact on the consumer.

The Sport Product

The sport product, however, is unique and at the heart of this mix. In order to obtain congruency between the target market and the sport product, market research must be conducted and the sport consumer population properly segmented. Then, effective sport marketers can establish the best combination of the tangible and intangible elements of the sport product for their intended target market.

The sport product comprises both goods and services. Sporting goods are physical and tangible (e.g., a golf ball) while sport services are non-physical and intangible (e.g., game atmosphere). Most sport products cannot be delineated as purely tangible or intangible; most have characteristics of each. For example, a participant in a golf tournament pays for the experience of competing in the tournament (intangible) as well as some tangible items such as a sleeve of golf balls, tees, and lunch.

Thus, any definition of a sport product must include goods and services. Further, the sport product can be delineated by its core elements (including such things as players, game, and venue) or by sport product extensions (including such things as concessions, music, mascots, and programs). As a result, sport products are often referred to as a "bundle of benefits" that is designed to satisfy consumer needs.

Sport products are unique from others in that they are very experiential, typically involve some sort of social process, and often elicit strong personal devotion and passion. Further, sport marketers typically have very little control over the core product. For example, a sport marketer would have no control over how well a golfer in a tournament plays, how the golfer gets along with his or her playing partners, or the weather on the day of the tournament. And yet, these become part of the sport product experience for the consumer. Thus, in order to satisfy the sport consumer, the effective sport marketer also focuses on product extensions and bundling the various elements of the sport product to best meet the needs and wants of the intended target market.

Segmented Market

Not all sport consumers possess the same wants and needs. Therefore, the sport consumer market must be segmented. The large, heterogeneous sport consumer market must be broken down into more similar groups of people who have comparable wants and needs. This is done so that the sport marketer is better able to establish the best mix of tangible and intangible elements for each targeted segment.

Sport consumer markets are often segmented by demographics (e.g., sex, age, socioeconomic status, and so on), psychographics (e.g., personality traits, level of team attachment), product benefits (e.g., fashion, durability, enhanced performance), and product usage (e.g., season ticket holders, single game purchasers) or some combination of these. Sport marketing research is necessary to provide information relative to the most salient segments for a particular sport product. Additionally, quality sport marketing research provides the sport marketer with an idea of the most important features of the sport product for each consumer segment. Armed with good market research, a sport marketer can determine the most viable target markets, and the best way to provide congruency between their sport product and those target markets.

Such congruency between the sport product and the target market is essential to the success of the sport organization. When the individual consumer feels that his/her wants and desires are being met by the sport organization, he or she is more satisfied and more likely to make a purchase, or repeat purchase. The National Football League (NFL) recognized that female fans might want slightly different merchandise options than their male counterparts. Rather than offer merchandise suited only to men in cut and style, they partnered with

Victoria's Secret to offer T-shirts, sweats, hoodies, and tank tops that are a part of the popular Pink Collection. Thus, the NFL segmented its current market by gender, and produced a new product extension (merchandise) geared precisely for the female NFL fan.

The NFL, with this effort, attempted to produce greater congruency between a product extension (i.e., merchandise) and a target market (i.e., female fans). As a result, women's apparel has become the league's fastest-growing business. This is just one example of the NFL's attempts to make its product more congruent with its target market of female NFL fans. NFL stores also offer NFL 101 Workshops for Women, which cover the rules and history of the game; they established a girls flag football program; and they encourage girls to participate in the NFL Pepsi Pass Punt & Kick contest. In 2006, the NFL fan base was 43 percent female; in 2010, that percentage had risen to nearly 50 percent. It appears that congruency between the target market and these NFL extensions are paying off.

Janet S. Fink
University of Connecticut

See Also: Brand Personality; Marketing Research Process; Total Product Concept.

Further Readings

Mullin, Bernard J., Stephen Hardy, and William A. Sutton. *Sport Marketing*, 3rd Ed. Champaign, IL: Human Kinetics, 2007.

Shank, Matthew D. *Sports Marketing: A Strategic Perspective*, 4th Ed. Upper Saddle River, NJ: Pearson Prentice Hall, 2009.

Wakefield, Kirk L. *Team Sports Marketing*. Oxford, UK: Butterworth-Heinemann, 2007.

Consumer Behavior

Studying influential factors is vital to sport marketing success, because marketers gain insight on which aspects of the sport package are being focused on heavily and which aspects need to be enhanced. To put into context the significance of modern sport consumer behavior studies, prehistoric sport consumer behavior origins began with the exchange of sports between different countries and cultures. The Greek games contained elements that are still exhibited in modern-day sports. In another example, basketball has been widely accepted into many different nations and cultures. Basketball had a solid foundation in China long before David Stern started to market the National Basketball Association (NBA). In the years after James Naismith drew up the rules of basketball in 1891 at the YMCA Training School in Springfield, Massachusetts, YMCA missionaries showcased the game worldwide as a physical gospel wherever they went. Basketball's flexibility—it had few requirements for equipment and facilities—its obvious contributions to fitness, and its special blend of individual skill and team play helped its popularity.

Sporting Industry Today

The sport industry currently generates revenues of between $213 billion and $441 billion annually, according to various researchers. Consumers show no signs of giving up the opportunity to play or watch their favorite sport activities. Therefore it is very important to better understand why consumers behave certain ways toward sports and their related products. Before consumer behavior can be examined, it is vital to examine the overall sport product package. The complete modern sport package contains benefits related to health (stress and stimulation seeking), entertainment, sociability, and achievement.

While sport consumers can receive the benefits of the package through direct and indirect participation, they must first be made aware of the products and services that sport offers, through a variety of marketing techniques. Throughout the history of sport, many marketing tools have affected consumer behavior in different ways. For most segments in the sport industry, 70 percent of all customers are referred by word-of-mouth from existing customers, according to research published in 2007 by Mullin et al. This example shows that officials with government authority, sport creators and their af-

filiates, and players have an active role in "selling" various sports to countries and cultures.

Returning to the prehistoric promotion of sports, travel also aided in the marketing of different types of sports: the belief that sports unified people from diverse backgrounds was significant to its implementation. Successful integration of sport within a nation assists in the attempt to eliminate internal conflicts such as racial, ethnic, regional, and class diversity. Whether or not sport has been successfully integrated remains a focus of sport sociologists. Before integration of schools and communities and the development of Title IX, many consumers and players were limited to the sport activities readily available to them. However, as sports modernized, the attitudes of citizens toward different sports led them to become active participants or spectators.

Attitudes include affective, cognitive, and behavioral components; people are innately motivated to harmonize all three attitude components, and will alter their overall attitudes to achieve consistency. Consistency in participation and consumption of sport can be observed and recorded to track trends in the behaviors of sport consumers.

All parties involved in sport have not kept consistent attitudes about who shall consume what activities. Although sport may have spread in part to eliminate a nation's internal conflicts, its earliest consumer behavior studies depicted sport as a segregated institution. Some sport motivation studies reveal that sport motives have "generally" been ascertained from white/European cultural points of view, with the assumption that such motives will equally or generally apply to all sport consumers.

Researchers Harrolle et al have stated that a need exists for a more comprehensive understanding of the Latino consumer, for instance, and whether consumption behavior predictors differ between Latinos and non-Latinos, especially as it relates to sport consumption behavior. In response to the few studies that mentioned the consumption behaviors of sport and its by-products by people of different races, these researchers respectively created the Black Consumers' Sport Motivation Scale (BCSMS) and the Model of Sport Spectator Conative Loyalty (MSSCL, based on Model B). Both models were surveys developed from previous studies, with certain factors being loaded to fit the needs of the researchers.

Harrolle et al in a 2010 work revealed that some racial groups, such as Latinos and African Americans, react similarly to certain motivators and stimuli (e.g., television and Internet advertisements featuring high-profile athletes), in comparison to other racial groups such as Asians and white European Americans. It is important to discuss how corporate sponsors have become major consumers of sport and influenced the involvement of sport celebrities in advertising. Sponsors typically spend more money endorsing athletes when big or high-profile events are being held in a particular area. Further, with the emergence of college athletes as celebrities, recent number one draft picks can be seen in lucrative commercials promoting athletic apparel, such as those by Nike.

Consumers also purchase nonsport products—such as high-definition televisions, satellite radios, and barbeque grills—to enhance their sport experience. Whatever causes consumers to buy these sport-related products can be classified as influential factors and placed into categories for questionnaires. Many such questionnaires place influential factors for sport consumption in groups that show how they relate to either external or internal influence.

Influential Factors

Several factors influence the behavior of sport consumers, and these can be classified as being external (or environmental) or internal. A number of direct and indirect influences on behavioral outcomes cause emotional reactions and personal predispositions of spectators. Environmental factors may include significant others, such as family, peers, and coaches, as well as social norms. Cultural and social class structures including race, gender relations, climatic, and geographic conditions also create influences on sport consumers. Further examples include self-concept, family cycle, physical characteristics, learning, perceptions, and the complex process of consumer decision making itself.

Each factor listed can positively or negatively affect sport consumer behavior, but new research shows that these internal and external factors only explain part of consumer behavior related to sport, in particular as they relate to attending sport venues rather than other alternatives. In their 2001 research, Trail and James administered and collected the Motivation Scale for Sport Consumption at a Women's NBA (WNBA) game. Their goal was to determine why people chose to attend the live sport event (motivators) instead of watching the event at home or attending a nonsport event occurring in the same location at that time (constraints). They found that women attend live sport events more for the social aspect, while men attend them more for entertainment and achievement; most fans watch from home when work or other scheduled priorities conflict.

External and Internal Factors

One example of an external factor is technology, which plays a major role in the way sports participants consume sport product. Particularly for indirect users, media consumption and its related products provide a seemingly endless amount of entertainment options. As technology has evolved, companies have found and invested millions in sporting events through live broadcast, webcasting, and other streamlining avenues. For example, National Football League (NFL) players Chad Ochocinco and Terrell Owens hosted network TV reality shows that have led to immense popularity. They have been Facebooked, Tweeted, and texted about enough to carry many fans to Cincinnati with them for the 2010–11 NFL season. The number of such fans activated enough to purchase Cincinnati Bengals tickets, attend games, or otherwise show more interest in Ochocinco and Owens merchandise, points to consumer behavior that can easily be associated with the external factor of technology.

The terms *Facebooked*, *Tweeted*, and *texting* are used to describe a new, technology-enhanced version of word-of-mouth, collectively termed *buzz marketing*. "Facebooked" relates to the social networking Website Facebook, where people post personal status updates and create fan pages for their favorite celebrities, including sports teams and athletes. With millions of users, Facebook recently added sidebars that allow participants to click on links and share them with others who may share similar interests. "Tweeted" relates to the newly developed Twitter online function, which people use to follow their favorite celebrities and find out about popular events and where to get deals on promotional items. "Texted" refers to the sending of text messages from cellular phones and other messaging devices.

The invention of the Apple iPhone and other smartphones has made it easier to participate in these forms of buzz marketing. Being able to access multiple media applications simultaneously has created a better media flow for sport consumers to receive their products, thus increasing their likelihood of being a fan or participant of sport activities and moving consumers up the "sport escalator." Researchers O'Cass and Carlson recently applied the concept of flow to professional sport Websites, to discover if online marketing tools lead to overall consumer satisfaction and the desire for consumers to experience the process again. Their main focal points were Website satisfaction, Website-aroused feelings, Website loyalty, and Website word-of mouth behavior. After loading and distributing a questionnaire related to consumer interactions while using a sport Website, all factors were found to have a significant positive influence on consumer behavior.

Internal factors that influence consumer behavior stem primarily from the classic five P's in the sport marketing mix: product, price, place, promotion, and people. The product, the particular item being sold and marketed to the sport consumer, is the pivot of the marketing mix because it drives attitude toward participation in any event. The price of the sporting event dictates at what level fans will commit to the product. If the price of the product is set at a point where fans cannot afford to attend, they will always remain near the ground level of the sport escalator. Pricing is often influenced by the quality of the product. Place connotes a direct effect on the organization's ability to distribute the product, which affects consumer accessibility to the sporting event. How the product is promoted is heavily influenced by a person's ability to sell and advertise the product. The people factor is often driven by public relations directly associated with the product and its image—the foundation for the brand. Consumer behavior is influenced by each of these factors, which work together to develop fan loyalty.

The Escalator Effect

The sport consumer escalator is a graphic representation of consumer movement to higher levels of involvement in a sport, as a participant or fan.

Developed by researcher Mullin in 1978, the escalator suggests that sport organizations should find innovative ways to nurture their existing customers to higher levels of involvement while enticing nonconsumers to become active users of a sport product. The flow of the escalator is upward and shows a continuum of non-consumers, indirect consumers, light consumers, medium consumers, and eventually heavy consumers. Factors—either external or internal—influencing consumer behavior affect consumer movement on the escalator.

The escalator effect has a direct impact on consumer behavior; it is a concept that has been supported by participants and audiences alike. The idea of consumer escalation is based on the "positioning frequency" of sport participants and attendees at sporting events. One of the major principles in activating the escalator is to cater to (or "position") existing consumers rather than spending a lot of time creating new patrons. Sport organizations would like to move the sport consumer from the ground level of consumption eventually up the scale to heavy users.

The nonconsumers are described those consumers who are misinformed and are considered to be low-level, isolated consumers. The indirect consumers generally consume sporting events through the media and other outlets. Light consumers are patrons who attend sports events such as special or marquee match-ups; they purchase single game tickets and attend mostly single games. An example of a medium sport consumer would be football fans that purchase a season mini-pack consisting of three to four games per season, which may or may not be renewable. The heavy users are the die-hard season ticket holders. They are typically alumni, boosters, or even investors. The heavy users are the group that sport organizations nurture; they are the most loyal consumers. The escalator provides a very good example of how consumer behavior is developed and sustained; it provides a framework for understanding consumer behavior.

Trends

With the rapid growth of sport into a multibillion-dollar industry, there is a greater need to study the sport consumer. With increasing sport event choices, sport managers can no longer depend on the size and population of the crowd that shows up for a game. Marketers must look at the intangibles surrounding sporting events in their effort to continue the growth of the industry. Experiencing the special atmosphere of a sports event is one of the pivotal value-creating elements of live sport consumption. Both theoretical considerations and empirical findings show that an emotionally appealing atmosphere is one of the most important motives for spectators attending an event. This provides support to the growing notion that the need to market sporting events has taken on a much greater theme than just advertising ticket sales.

The atmosphere is some cases is the primary product. This can be especially true in the case of major sports events. In cases where we see the atmosphere as a primary product of the sports event, it satisfies some experiential needs of the consumer. This is in direct contrast with findings of many earlier consumer behavior studies, in which atmosphere was considered to be promoted as a secondary product. Emotional reactions to event atmosphere do not only affect long-term behavioral reactions, but also the immediate experiential value of sports events. The behavioral reactions of spectators are of great importance, since they affect economic variables. As with consumer behavior in retail stores, the short-term reactions of spectators may generate longer stays at venues and increased spending while there.

As fan loyalty increases, so does the value of the product brand, which is tied to its uniqueness and its intangible qualities. Regarding the uniqueness of the social setting in sport consumption, it is postulated that event spectators enrich their social psychological lives through the sociable, quasi-intimate relationships available. Researchers Hewitt and Coakley refer to these forms of psychological enrichments in terms of symbolic interactionism, a theory that helps to illuminate how human beings define their experiences and give meaning to their identities, behaviors, realities, and social interactions. Symbolic interactionism seeks to examine the symbolic meanings associated with the individual's experiences in relation to his or her self-identity as created by and based on interactions with others.

Since affiliation gives meaning to their identities, behaviors, realities, and social interactions, a sense of empowerment is developed from fan loyalty: the fan at this point moves up the consumer escalator. This is manifested in consumer behavior in the form of symbolic consumption, that is, purchasing behavior. Symbolic purchases are only as effective as the meanings that consumers attach to them. The influence that a symbolic purchase opportunity has on an individual's perception of self may be a more pervasive influence on consumption of that product than the actual property of the product.

Aaron Livingston
West Virginia University
Quindarien Price
Grambling State University

See Also: Avidity; Fan Loyalty Continuum; Marketing Concept, The; Sport Buyer Behavior.

Further Readings

Carlson, Brad D., D. Todd Donavan, and Kevin J. Cumiskey. "Consumer-Brand Relationships in Sport: Brand Personality and Identification." *International Journal of Retail & Distribution Management*, v.37/4 (2009).

Harrolle, Michelle, Galen Trail, Ariel Rodriguez, and Jeremy Jordan. "Conative Loyalty of Latino and Non-Latino Professional Baseball Fans." *Journal of Sport Management*, v.24/4 (2010)

Kim, Yu Kyoum and Galen Trail. "Constraints and Motivators: a New Model to Explain Sport Consumer Behavior." *Journal of Sport Management*, v.24/2 (2010).

O'Cass, Aron and Jamie Carlson. "Examining the Effects of Website-Induced Flow in Professional Sporting Team Websites." *Internet Research*, v.20/2 (2010).

Consumer Satisfaction, Facility

There are many factors that motivate consumers to return to a facility, or conversely, to have a bad experience and never revisit in the future. The overall venue experience can include accessibility, seating area, concessions, customer service, fan interaction, parking, excitement of the game, and facility cleanliness. Dirty restrooms and eating areas can alter perceptions negatively and cause health concerns. Negative perceptions are associated with less motivation for consumers and subsequent lower turnout at a sport facility. The financial considerations stemming from a lack of cleanliness can include lower attendance, loss of revenue, and potential liability for illness and transmission of disease.

From Arenas to Clubs

Bill Veeck, the legendary owner of the Chicago White Sox, recognized how important cleanliness was in attracting female consumers and families. He determined that customers prefer a clean stadium, which ultimately leads to repeat patronage. George Steinbrenner, the owner of the New York Yankees, also recognized the importance of a clean venue. Steinbrenner viewed the fans as guests in his home. Therefore, spectators at Yankee Stadium were treated to spotless conditions right down to a floor clean enough to serve a gourmet dinner. He believed that cleanliness led to a better experience in the stadium, which would motivate customers to come back for future games. In both examples, a clean facility was deemed to be a step in the right direction toward repeat customers, whereas dirty, neglected facilities could cause people to go elsewhere.

A worker cleans a stadium in Bournemouth, England. Dirty sports facilities can result in fewer repeat customers.

The cleanliness philosophy involves addressing perceptions by those who utilize and manage sport-based facilities. For example, cleanliness of a fitness facility is essential and is ranked second only to convenience when a consumer is factoring the value of fitness club membership. Surveys conducted with club members show cleanliness to be a significant factor in likability of their workout environment. Clean locker rooms and bathrooms, sparkling floors and mirrors, equipment in pristine condition, a pleasant smell in the air, and freshly laundered towels are all open to evaluation and perception.

Amenities in a fitness center that add to personal hygiene can also attract a potential buyer. Good quality soaps, shampoo, deodorant, body lotion, and towels can positively alter the perception of the user. Cleanliness can be prioritized in a facility by training employees to attend to these consumer needs. Simple checklists and adding a few quality inventory items can assist in positively changing patron views. Cleanliness is a customer priority, but if neglected by management it can also become a risk management and health issue.

Of all sport facilities, the aquatic center may be the most susceptible to the safety and hygiene perceptions of consumers. Potential users are especially turned off by a dirty restroom, and are apt to swiftly exit a dirty facility. Pool water that is not tested regularly is a potential health hazard for the customer. Aquatic center cleanliness is the responsibility of the entire staff, and even customers can be involved by providing venue managers with their input. Comment cards can be made to be easily accessible; feedback from members should be actively encouraged. Cleaning is an everyday pursuit, and neglect of those duties can lead customers to look for a more pleasing environment.

Conclusion

Safety of the customer should be the number one concern of a facility manager. A clean sport setting may be a crucial step in attaining that goal by keeping the patron's health protected. Secondarily, the consumer's viewpoint is vital when determining repeat business. Therefore, an immaculate sport venue can provide safe conditions, promote a positive experience, and subsequently induce a return visit.

Brian E. Pruegger
Independent Scholar

See Also: Consumer Behavior; Fan Attendance, Reasons for; Risk Management.

Further Readings

Canfield, Owen. "Sweeping Success in Stands." *Hartford Courant.* (August 3, 2008) http://articles.courant.com/2008-08-03/features/owensun0803.art_1_rock-cats-yankee-stadium-new-hampshire (Accessed January 2011).
Fawcett, Paul. *Aquatic Facility Management.* Champaign, IL: Human Kinetics, 2005.
Grantham, William C., Robert W. Patton, Tracy D. York, and Mitchel L. Winick. *Health Fitness Management.* Champaign, IL: Human Kinetics, 1998.
Mullin, Bernard J., Stephen Hardy, and William A. Sutton. *Sport Marketing.* Champaign, IL: Human Kinetics, 2007.

Consumer Shows

A consumer show, trade show, or expo is an exhibition held for companies in a particular industry to demonstrate, preview, and showcase their latest products and services. Those that call themselves consumer shows are generally open to the public; other shows may be "trade only," or reserved for professionals in the industry and relevant members of the press. Over 2,500 consumer shows are held each year, in various industries. Virtually every industry has a consumer show; it has become a part of the way business is conducted. Many industries have more than one show—a show may be geared toward a specific region, or a specific aspect of an industry. The larger ones, those expected to attract attendees from all over the country, are often held in destination cities like New Orleans, Las Vegas, New York, and Los Angeles.

Trade shows involve a good deal of expense. The space must be rented, trade show displays must be constructed (and often designed with input from marketing consultants and other experts), telecommunications and travel arrangements must be made, and once at the show, costs are incurred for booth maintenance (cleaning, Internet, electricity, and drayage). Cities will often subsidize the building of a convention center for exactly this reason, to attract that economic activity.

A trade show display is set up in a booth at a trade show, and varies in cost, complexity, and goals. It typically consists of banners and physical screens, and now will often include computer monitors displaying presentations from a laptop. The display both lures attendees to the exhibit booth and serves as a passive way to distribute information, to complement the active components of the booth workers and the take-home components of any materials provided to attendees, like brochures, DVDs, and samples. The purpose of a trade show display can be to increase or reinforce market share (it is a phenomenon of consumer shows that the best-known, most dominant brands—the ones least in need of exposure—often have the most prestigious booths, and expensive giveaways for attendees), to encourage existing customers to buy more or to expand their purchases to other products from the company, to introduce new products, or to position or reposition the brand identity.

Bill Kte'pi
Independent Scholar

See Also: B2B,B2C; Brand Awareness; Trade, Marketing to the.

Further Readings

Jozsa, Frank P. *Sports Capitalism*. London: Ashgate Publishing, 2004.

Milne, George R. and Mark A. McDonald. *Sport Marketing*. Sudbury, MA: Jones & Bartlett Learning, 1999.

Contest Fraud/Losses

Running a contest is a good way for an organization to raise awareness of its business, draw attendance, or build relations with the public. A contest is a game of skill, whereas a sweepstakes is a game of chance. In other words, a contest requires a participant to actively complete some kind of task in order to receive a premium item. While most warnings about contest fraud deal with fraudulent contests seeking to scam contestants, an unfortunate fact is that sometimes the organizer of a legitimate contest will himself be the victim of fraud.

Early examples of fraudulent contestants in sports included ringers: competitors used illicitly in a competition in order to gain an unfair advantage. The term is thought to have possibly come from "dead ringer" and the illegal practice in horse racing of establishing an inferior horse as a perennial loser and then replacing it with a superior look-alike horse—a dead ringer for the first horse—in order to win or place in races once the odds have been raised substantially against the horse. Ringers are a problem in amateur athletics such as company softball leagues, in which an employee may be hired purely for his athletic ability.

The allegation has been made that college sports at the most competitive levels have essentially become a competition among ringers, as many of the players were recruited by the school not because of their academic abilities but purely for their athletic prowess, and cannot be considered to be a real representation of the student body, as would have been the case in the earlier, less profitable days of college athletics and remains the case now at schools that focus less on sports competitiveness.

Ringers can also be a problem in fan contests. The fan competing in a shooting competition at halftime at a basketball game may turn out to be a former development league or college player, or a street ball trick-shooter. There is no real protection against this. It goes against the spirit of the contest, which is to provide an "everyman" with the opportunity to make a lucky shot, but there is no way to guarantee that the fan won't be in possession of unusual skills. What can be protected against in contests is the participation of employees or the relatives of employees, whether of the sports organization or of closely related companies. Such restrictions are commonplace in order to guard against the possibility of tampering.

Bill Kte'pi
Independent Scholar

See Also: Counterfeit Detection Program; Insurance Against Risks; Promotional Contests.

Further Readings

Crawford, Garry. *Consuming Sport: Fans, Sport and Culture*. New York: Routledge, 2004.

Zimbalist, Andrew S. *The Bottom Line: Observations and Arguments on the Sports Business*. Philadelphia: Temple University Press, 2006.

Contingency Planning

College, university, or professional teams and the operators of arenas and stadiums are responsible for the safety of athletes, spectators, and other employees and volunteers who use their premises. Emergencies may arise at sporting events with little or no warning, and it is the responsibility of the venue to provide for spectator, athlete, and staff safety. In exercising this responsibility, management needs to identify any potential hazards that might imperil the safety of athletes, spectators, or others. Contingency planning is way of dealing with the types of incidents identified by risk management procedures that might pose a threat to athletes or the public. Operators of arenas or stadiums, often in conjunction with team management, draw up contingency plans to ensure the safety of those at the venue.

When planning a sporting event, arena or stadium managers need to plan how they will respond to any incident that might endanger public safety or disrupt normal operations. This plan must be made in advance, and must consider any such incident that might cause injury to athletes, spectators, or others. As failure to prepare adequate contingency plans may result in civil or criminal liability, such planning should be a priority to individuals and organizations alike. Before contingency plans may be addressed, a thorough and comprehensive safety audit and risk assessment must be conducted. The safety audit and risk assessment must identify any hazards to which athletes and spectators might be exposed, determine the potential risk from these hazards, and assess whether existing safety management procedures are sufficient to eliminate the hazard or to minimize its risk. Hazards that are typically assessed include fire, bomb threats, weather, damage to structures, power failure, gas or chemical leaks, crowd disorder, or safety equipment failure. Once the safety audit and risk assessment is complete, contingency plans may be drawn up to address potential remaining risks.

Contingency plans vary by organization and venue, but most contain several common elements. First, contingency plans should set forth a structured and graduated response to certain incidents, including clear guidelines to be adopted should particular circumstances arise. For example, in the event of lightning, the contingency plan should set forth what actions should be taken by ground crews and other safety personnel. Second, contingency plans should clearly define a command and control structure, one that considers the configuration of the venue and available means of communication. While considering the facility and its setup, the contingency plan should assess possible communication upgrades and backup systems needed in the event of a system failure. Third, contingency plans should result in a written spectator safety policy statement, which includes the assignment of specific tasks to identified individuals. Those individuals identified must have a clear awareness of their designated responsibilities,

as well as the skills and willingness to carry them out. Fourth, specific and timely training related to the contingency plan must take place, and the results of practices must be thoroughly assessed. Following each practice, a detailed debriefing of all safety personnel must take place and adjustments to the contingency plan must be made as needed.

Those preparing contingency plans must not assume that police officers, firefighters, or other first responders will be available in the event of an emergency. Management of an arena or stadium must be prepared to coordinate with first responders beforehand to ascertain what support might be expected in particular situations. To the extent possible, a venue must be prepared to contain or resolve an incident using its own personnel and resources. Arrangements must also be made to hand over and retake control of a situation to local police officers and firefighters. Whenever possible, this arrangement should be put in writing and agreed to by all interested parties.

For a contingency plan to be effective, various documents must be attached to it indicating certain information. This information would include plans of the facility, including the location of important safety elements such as the ground control room, access routes for emergency services, entrances and exits, fire alarms and firefighting equipment, first aid points, casualty handling areas, key safety management personnel, gas and water shutoffs, parking areas, and a telephone list of key personnel. Contingency plans should also consider post-incident recovery processes, so that normal operations can be resumed with a minimum of disruptions and delays. Some post-incident recovery processes that might be considered include contacting any insurance carriers, procuring plans and design drawings, defining the roles of surveyors and engineers, obtaining temporary security for the site, operating a salvage team, keeping the public informed of progress, running the business while repairs are made, and determining when the venue will again be safe. Although contingency plans cannot prevent crises or disasters, they can minimize injuries and deaths and make the recovery process more speedy and efficient.

Stephen T. Schroth
Brian E. Paul
Knox College

See Also: Continuity Possibilities; Corporate Public Relations, Marketing Public Relations; Foreseeability; Management Decision-Making Process; Risk Management; Stadium Operations.

Further Readings

Graham, S., L. D. Neirotti, and J. J. Goldblatt. *The Ultimate Guide to Sport Event Management and Marketing*, 2nd Ed. New York: McGraw-Hill, 2001.

Jordan, J. S., A. Kent, and M. B. Walker. "Management and Leadership in the Sport Industry." In A. Gillentine and R. B. Crow, eds., *Foundations of Sport Management*, 2nd Ed. Morgantown, WV: Fitness Information Technology, 2009.

Continuity Possibilities

Major professional sports teams and college athletics in the United States center around a variety of competing interests, including competition, marketing, economic considerations, and operations. Continuity possibilities touch upon each aspect of a professional or amateur team's existence, as competition for consumer entertainment spending and the relatively short competitive life of athletes makes such preparation especially important. Most sports teams and athletic organizations face a continuity situation at some point, and those that have considered continuity possibilities, and developed a plan to deal with these, ensure themselves a higher likelihood of success. Sports teams and organizations may use models regarding continuity management from the business community, although these must often be adapted to address their specific needs and requirements.

Continuity Management

Continuity management requires planning and preparation to consider the possibilities that must be faced and addressed. Standard continuity management plans focus on the following:

- Formulating a framework for project management
- Identifying assumptions and conditions for continuity planning
- Introducing action plans
- Testing, reviewing, and modifying
- Addressing other items.

Within the context of sports, project management often centers on selecting the team that will take the field, but also considers stadium or arena administration, scouting, marketing, and ticket sales. Identifying assumptions and conditions involves identifying critical operations—such as coaching, scouting, and sales—and then contemplating certain scenarios and determining objectives and plans for how to respond to these in real time. This might include developing practical manuals, developing decision-making procedures and communication strategies, ensuring that backup data exist, and thinking seriously about continuity measures. Once action plans have been formed, these must be subjected to testing, reviewing, and modifying so that the organization or team is continually prepared for change. Finally, teams and organizations must address other items, such as selecting third-party vendors to provide certain services, such as data backup and storage, and precluding or mitigating disaster damage.

For sports teams and athletic organizations, continuity possibilities must consider a variety of disaster scenarios, including natural disasters, human actions, economic crises, and personnel matters. Natural disasters refer to such incidents as floods, earthquakes, blizzards, and other conditions that might prevent a team or event from occurring as planned or scheduled. Human actions include terrorist threats, cyberattacks, labor unrest, and industrial espionage. Economic crises consist of economic downturns and recessions, as well as those factors that might affect only an individual team or organization, such as a bank failure or embezzlement. Personnel matters involve recruiting, drafting, or otherwise procuring players to take the field, but also ensuring that adequate management, coaches, scouts, trainers, and other workers are available to perform duties for the team or organization. Although often seen as preparation for disaster, careful consideration of continuity possibilities can have many benefits for a team or organization, and can result in on-field and box office success.

Effects of Continuity Plans

All of the major professional sports leagues in the United States, such as the National Hockey League (NHL), the National Basketball Association (NBA), Major League Baseball (MLB), and the National Football League (NFL) face a variety of continuity considerations. In any sport, teams from larger markets have a potential competitive advantage over smaller market teams because they can draw potential fans from a greater geographic area. In a sport such as baseball, with only limited revenue sharing, player recruitment is easier for large-market teams as they typically have more revenue to spend on player salaries. However, this does not necessarily mean that small-market teams cannot win. Several small-market MLB teams have been very successful because of careful planning and implementation of continuity possibilities. Teams such as the Cincinnati Reds, the Minnesota Twins, and the Oakland A's have developed tactics of continuity plans with their organization to help build and continue success on the field. After Billy Beane became the General Manager of the A's in 1998, he revamped the A's minor league teams, or farm system, to assure a steady stream of young talent. Although by 2005 many of the A's best prospects were sought after by other MLB teams and eventually lost to free agency, the A's were able to continue to field a winning ball club. Through strong scouting and procuring new talent through the amateur draft, many smaller-market MLB teams are able to compete with richer teams. Certainly the superior financial resources of a team such as the New York Yankees have allowed them to have continued success on the field, but this is done through paying for free agent talent on the open market. Considering continuity possibilities allows smaller-market teams to compete.

Failure to develop ways to deal with crises can also harm a team, organization, or league. Although all amateur and professional sports were affected by steroids, MLB's failure to consider continuity possibilities caused criticism related to the integrity of the game. MLB's failure to consider the ramifications of player use of steroids resulted in pressure from fans, the media, the players, and ultimately the U.S. Congress for change. MLB Commissioner Allan "Bud" Selig appointed George Mitchell, the former U.S. Senate majority leader, to investigate the use of steroids in baseball. This investigation found that at least one member of each of the 30 MLB teams had tested positive for a performance enhancing drug (PED). As a result of the investigation, and indeed before the final report was issued, Selig implemented a testing program to assure PED use was discouraged. While this program has reduced criticism of MLB, fallout from player PED use continues to have ramifications, and better consideration of continuity possibilities might have permitted earlier intervention.

Stephen T. Schroth
Jonathan R. Fletcher
Knox College

See Also: Acts of God; Contingency Planning; Information System Security; Stadium Operations.

Further Readings

Graham, S., L. D. Neirotti, and J. J. Goldblatt. *The Ultimate Guide to Sport Event Management and Marketing*, 2nd Ed. New York: McGraw-Hill, 2001.

Hiles, A., ed. *The Definitive Handbook of Business Continuity Management*. Hoboken, NJ: John Wiley & Sons, 2011.

Continuous Quality Improvement

Until the last decade or so of the 20th century, sports organizations could be seen as unique in their structure, organization, and management concerns. Today, however, they are likely to resemble typical organizations of the same size. If they were ever arguably immune, sports organizations are now increasingly affected by changes in demographics and economics, relationships between management and various constituencies, and requirements for successful operation.

A main reason for this rapid change has been the influx of investments and resources by businesspeople who first found success in other industries. This is a significant transformation, in part because they have gradually introduced and applied business management practices to sports organizations. One of the most popular of these has been the movement toward continuous quality improvement, though it has attracted little notice.

Perhaps one reason for the scant attention to continuous quality improvement is that there is not yet complete acceptance and integration of modern management practices in all sports organizations. Another reason may be that continuous quality improvement is a seemingly obvious, if self-explanatory concept. It concerns quality—a comparative standard—and continuous improvement—an ongoing effort to enhance the present state of a product, service, or process. Still, there is plenty of confusion about what constitutes both quality and continuous improvement, no less about what the concept is and how to incorporate it.

The Underpinnings

Most people believe that distinguishing between levels of quality can be reduced to "you know it when you see it." This logic is a manner of reducing information overload that has developed from a world in which consumers are asked to choose between nearly identical products and services offered by competing brands. But while convenient, it is not a practical way for consumers to make decisions; it is too gross a measurement and therefore unwieldy to manage. Measurements that are too ambiguous also complicate things for manufacturers and sellers, who are tasked with orienting their marketing and operations toward satisfying the needs of their customers.

Even though they are often temporarily unaware of it, customers do inevitably go about assigning a value to a product, service, or process. They do so depending on their needs and what is available to them under the circumstances. In this way, they necessarily determine what constitutes quality, and what they are willing to pay in exchange for it. Understanding this mind-set is how manufacturers and sellers determine what it is they will offer, its price, its distribution channels, and its promotion in the marketplace.

The central challenge faced by manufacturers and sellers is that customer needs and demands are constantly growing and changing, even if in slight ways and over long periods of time. This means the various external and internal areas of an enterprise need systematic and continuous improvement. One way of accomplishing this is to organize work on improvement of a product, service, or process and with specific goals and deadlines. For instance, the goal could be a certain percentage reduction in cost over a certain span of time. Or, in another instance, it could be a certain percentage improvement in reliability or performance characteristics during a specific period. Such a regimen is intended to lead to innovation, the introduction of new methods and means that change an enterprise and keep it relevant. Without it, an enterprise will at some point experience stagnation—and, eventually, demise—of its products, services, processes, technologies, operations, and human resources.

Management Systems

To achieve any standards as outlined above requires investment in a formal system that is at once rigid and flexible. There has to be harmony between productivity needs, costs, human resources, and the decisions that lead to preserving or phasing out particular operations—a realization that has become increasingly fashionable for the better part of the past 50 years. This has led companies to develop and use methodologies that emphasize systematic, ongoing efforts to assess and improve the quality of existing products, services, and processes.

At present, there is a range of programs and tools available to managements of organizations that seek to improve quality in and of everything they do: Total Quality Management, Zero-Defects Management, and Six Sigma are among the more popular programs in this vein. Each has its own specific features and jargon. Yet they are often mistakenly put under the banner of "continuous improvement," which is itself a stand-alone program rather than an umbrella term.

Overall, continuous improvement owes its origins in business management to a few late-19th and early-20th century American companies that purposefully defined and set annual improvement goals for performance, quality, and cost of their activities. Its theoretical underpinnings stem from the studies about manual worker productivity that Fredrick Winslow Taylor conducted in the late 19th century, which over a span of 20 years were refined and developed into what came to be known as "scientific management."

Despite its origins, continuous improvement became lost on many American and other Western companies over time, until around the early 1980s. It was then that they began to examine why their Japanese counterparts were surpassing them, especially in highly visible industries such as consumer electronics and automobile manufacturing. Western companies had settled into a period of malaise, a condition reinforced by double-digit rates of inflation and unemployment. One of the assumptions as to what made Japanese companies and the broader economy so successful was their particular approach to management. Specifically, the focus fell on quality control techniques grounded in processes of continuous improvement, which the Japanese call *kaizen*.

What encouraged Japanese companies to develop policies of continuous improvement is attributed to its roots in Japanese tradition and culture. That is, decision makers and employees throughout organizations were receptive to continuous improvement because it is a manner of applying to work the basic elements of Japanese society. Part and parcel of this approach to work and working is that employees are dedicated to their tasks, responsibilities, and company over the long term. There is also respect for a decision-making process that involves several cycles of understanding, review, and comment by managers at various levels. These features, on top of a regard for management as an organ of the enterprise and not master of it, imply why Japanese companies were able to take a leading position in applying continuous improvement to quality control processes.

Japanese businesses began to seriously involve themselves with continuous improvement during the American occupation following World War II, when Western experts were dispatched to Japan to assist in an economic and social recovery effort led by General Douglas MacArthur. One of the experts who took an early part in the post-war rebuilding activity was W. Edwards Deming, a professor of statistics at New York University. Deming was invited to teach Japanese business executives in a series of courses about quality and productivity in manufacturing. His overarching message was oriented toward designing processes for improved results. To accomplish better results, there would have to be measurements for performance and the variations that deviated from what the customer values in the end product; assessments of operations so that decision makers could have the right information; and management for changes in areas that needed improvement.

Although not the sole factor, the principles and method Deming taught are considered to have played a major role in transforming Japanese exported products from objects known for their poor quality in the 1950s, to objects of envy, within 20 years. Since that achievement, however, Japanese companies and others throughout the world that subscribe to a philosophy of continuous quality improvement have moved more toward programs that attempt to achieve zero defects in the output of a product or service, such as mentioned earlier. Ironically, this shift may have caused a resistance to introduce enough change into organizational systems—and could help explain rashes of recent failures in the areas of quality output and performance.

Conclusion

Continuous quality improvement remains largely ignored in sports organizations, though perhaps more in name than in practice. Just as with any other accepted system of analysis used to make decisions, an organization would have to first experience success and then attribute it to continuous quality improvement, before the policy would be so much as recognized by the majority of professionals. Even then, its implementation would require that organizations change their strategies, practices, and vocabularies, as well as reconsider—and probably abandon—a number of policies that have been successful for so many years and regarded as sacred. It would also require that organizations and their divisions, subsidiaries, and affiliates define objectives for performance, quality, and costs. And they would therefore equally need to define the results that they hope to produce.

Above all, however, it is important to realize that continuous quality improvement is not a be-all, end-all, though many organizations treat it as such. Rather, it is a tool for determining that which defines the organization in the present, and creates its future.

Lee H. Igel
New York University

See Also: Customer Relationship Marketing; Customer Satisfaction; Management by Objectives; Performance Standards; Price Determination.

Further Readings

Aguayo, Rafael. *Dr. Deming: The American Who Taught the Japanese About Quality*. New York: Fireside, 1990.

Drucker, Peter F. and Joseph A. Maciariello. *Management*. New York: HarperCollins, 2008.

Ohmae, Kenichi. *The Mind of the Strategist: The Art of Japanese Business*. New York: McGraw-Hill, 1982.

Pascale, Richard Tanner and Anthony G. Athos. *The Art of Japanese Management: Applications for American Executives*. New York: Simon & Schuster, 1981.

Schwartz, Barry. *The Paradox of Choice*. New York: HarperCollins, 2004.

Contract, Key Factors in a

Contracts are used to define most business relationships and transactions, even those in the sport industry. A contract is a promise or set of promises that can be enforced by courts of law. Legal enforceability is what separates contracts from other agreements or promises. There are three factors that must be present in every legally enforceable contract. The required factors are (1) offer, (2) acceptance, and (3) consideration. The absence of any one of these three factors may prevent the formation of a contract.

The Offer

An offer is a conditional promise made by one party—the offeror—to do or refrain from doing something specified in the future for another party—the offeree—in exchange for something from that party. Offers can be distinguished from other statements in negotiations in that offers present the offeree with a power of acceptance. Power of acceptance is the contractual authority that an offer vests in the offeree to accept the offer and create a binding contract.

Offers, once made, have limited lifetimes. There are three ways in which an offer may cease to exist: lapse, revocation, and rejection. An offer lapses if its time limit runs out before acceptance. If the offer specifies a time frame for acceptance, the offer will lapse when the time frame tolls. For example, if an offer to purchase tickets to Game 1 of the World Series gives the offeree three days to accept, then the offer will lapse at the end of the third day. If no time frame is provided in the offer, the offer will lapse at the expiration of a reasonable amount of time, as determined by the court. Lastly, an offer will lapse if either the offeror or the offeree dies or loses mental capacity before the offer is accepted.

Revocation is the second method in which an offer may cease to exist. The general rule is that the offeror has the power to revoke an offer anytime before acceptance. After an offer has been accepted, the power of revocation no longer exists. Rejection is the third and final way in which an offer can cease to exist. Offers can be rejected outright by the offeree or through counteroffers made by the offeree. A counteroffer acts as a rejection of the original offer.

Acceptance

Acceptance is only valid when it comes from the person to whom the offer was directed. Once acceptance occurs, the offer cannot be revoked. As a general rule, acceptance will not be presumed and requires some positive action on the part of the accepting party, either through words or conduct. Acceptance has no legal effect until it is communicated to the offeror.

Notification of acceptance can be performed through any reasonable means of communication, unless the offer directs the communicative method for notification of acceptance. Reasonable means of notification can include instantaneous communication like fax or e-mail. Below is an example taken from a Major League Baseball Properties, Inc. license agreement. The offeror has control over the terms of the offer, and also has control over the method and means of notification for acceptance. The example below demonstrates how a party to a sport licensing contract may dictate the means for acceptance:

ACCEPTANCE BY LICENSOR: This instrument, when signed by Licensee or a duly authorized officer of Licensee if Licensee is a corporation, shall be deemed an application for a license and not a binding agreement unless and until signed by a duly authorized officer of Licensor. The receipt and/or deposit by Licensor of any check or other consideration given by Licensee and/or the delivery of any material by Licensor to Licensee shall not be deemed an acceptance by Licensor of this application. The foregoing shall also apply to any documents relating to renewals or modifications hereof.

As a general rule, acceptance must be made on the exact terms of the offer, and may neither add nor omit terms. An exception to this "mirror image" rule can be found for merchants in Uniform Commercial Code *Article § 2-207*. A purported acceptance that varies to any material degree from the terms of the offer will act as a rejection of the offer, but may provide the terms for a valid counteroffer.

For example, the owner of a sport boat may present an offer to a potential buyer to purchase the boat for $130,000. The buyer responds by saying, "I accept your offer to purchase the sport boat, but I'll only pay $125,000." Because the buyer's attempted acceptance does not mirror the terms of the offer, it acts as a rejection of that offer. However, that rejection may also be deemed a counteroffer. After all, the buyer has set new terms for purchasing the boat that are very specific. A reviewing court may find that the owner of the boat now has the power to accept a counteroffer made by the buyer. If so, then the owner could agree to the terms and bind the potential buyer to a contract. However, the owner

would be deemed the offeror and the potential buyer—the original offeror—would be the offeree.

Consideration

Consideration is the term used to describe the bargain-for-exchange element of a contract. Each party to a contract must exchange something of value in order for to create a legally binding agreement. For this reason, gifts do not serve as legal consideration for contracts, because there is no bilateral exchange.

Similarly, past performance does not provide a basis for consideration because the services were already rendered and remuneration (payment) for those services was already provided. In the last example involving the sport boat, the owner's consideration from the buyer is $125,000, and the buyer's consideration from the owner is the boat. Consideration will only be valid if it is legal, so the exchange of money for illegal services will not provide a basis for consideration in contract.

Good Faith

Good faith is not one of the three factors required for contract formation. However, good faith is a covenant that is implied as a matter of law into every contract. The implication of contractual good faith comes from both common law and the Uniform Commercial Code. Specifically, all parties entering into a contractual agreement must do so in good faith, and execute the contract with good-faith performance of contractual obligations. A want of good faith on the part of one party could excuse the other from performance or result in a breach of contract that requires compensation from the party who acted in bad faith.

Thomas A. Baker III
University of Georgia

See Also: Breach of Contract; Contracts, Athletes; Contracts; Venue; Legal Considerations in Sport.

Further Readings

Farnsworth, E. Allan. *Farnsworth on Contracts*, 3rd ed. New York: Aspen Publishing, 2003.

Gabriel, Henry D. and Linda J. Rusch. *ABCs of the UCC, Article 2: Revised: Sales*. Chicago: American Bar Association, 2005.

Lewis, Adam and Jonathan Taylor. *Sport: Law and Practice*. Haywards Heath, UK: Tottel Publishing, 2008.

Spengler, John, Paul Anderson, Daniel Connaughton, and Thomas Baker. *Introduction to Sport Law*. Champaign, IL: Human Kinetics, 2010.

Contracts, Athletes

Contracts for professional athletes have evolved dramatically since the development of professional leagues. Initially, athletes were powerless in contract negotiations. Because of the reserve clause, owners wielded so much power over the sports that athletes were presented with a "take it or leave it" option in contract negotiations. Since the creation of unions in the four major leagues, player contracts have become more equitable for athletes, who have also acquired more bargaining power in their individual contracts. Athlete contracts must still meet the requirements of a contract to be enforceable, but aside from the standard components of contracts, athlete contracts have evolved tremendously, moving from the reserve system to a free agency system.

The American common law Restatement (Second) of Contracts defines a contract in section 1 as "a promise or a set of promises for the breach of which the law gives a remedy, or the performance of which the law in some way recognizes as a duty." Although most contracts, especially contracts for professional athletes, are complex and intricate, a valid contract must consist of at least three things: offer, acceptance, and consideration. The offer is a promise to do something. Acceptance is agreement to that promise and an understanding of that agreement (mutual assent). Finally, consideration is the exchange element of the contract.

While these basic components of a contract are usually present, the terms that embody each component are what incite most of the legal challenges of athlete contracts. Courts will not require a party to perform in an employment contract. This means that an athlete who refuses to play for a team and holds out cannot be forced to play. Nonetheless, a negative injunction prohibits the athlete from signing with another team and sometimes another league. Also, players cannot transfer their contracts to other athletes—but teams can assign or trade their contract rights to other teams.

Collective and Individual Factors

Athlete contracts are usually based on a standard league contract called the Uniform Player Contract or Standard Player Contract, which all players in a league must sign. Unlike most employment contracts that are drafted exclusively by the employer, player contracts must fit within the framework established by the collective bargaining agreement (CBA) between the players union and the league. The terms and conditions of employment are codified in the player contract. Collective bargaining establishes minimum and maximum salaries, and in some leagues (e.g., the National Basketball Association) the maximum length of contracts for athletes. However, specific amounts and contract lengths, along with other terms including bonuses are negotiated by individual players with agents.

The CBA also determines the negotiation status of the player. Players who have reached a determined level of seniority are given free agent status and allowed to market their services to the club making the best offer.

Players with less seniority are subject to a reserve clause and may negotiate only with their current employer. In some leagues, there is an intermediate status of "restricted free agency"; this designation permits a player to negotiate with other teams, but the current employer must be compensated if the player transfers.

Historically, all player contracts included reserve clauses that tied a player to a team indefinitely or until the team decided to trade him. Player mobility was entirely at the discretion of the team because these clauses allowed teams to perpetually renew player contracts. Also, owners were able to suppress salaries because there was no competition among the teams for players. Through unions and collective bargaining, free agency, which gave athletes more mobility, was implemented in the leagues and increased the competition for their services among the teams. As a result of these developments, player contracts have become much more lucrative.

In addition to more lucrative salaries, free agency has also given rise to the long-term, or multiyear, contract. Free agency implies that teams risk losing a player to another club or paying the player a considerably higher salary at the expiration of his or her contract. This market risk for the team creates the incentive to offer players long-term contracts that guarantee a predetermined salary for multiple years. The reserve clause established what could be described as a one-way, long-term contract—as the clubs faced no market risk, long-term contracts were unnecessary.

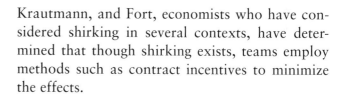
While contracts may be based on the Uniform Player Contract or Standard Player Contract, contract length, pay, and other terms are negotiated by players and agents.

Economist Joel Maxcy has described the market conditions that determine the likelihood a long-term agreement will be entered into by a player and team. Teams offering a player a long-term contract must balance market risk against the performance risk that the player will not perform as expected in future periods. Thus offers of guaranteed long-term contracts are typically reserved for only the highest level and most consistently performing players. The National Football League, where injury rates are high, has rare instances of guaranteed long-term contracts.

A latent side effect of long-term contracts is that the incentive to "shirk" is increased. Since income is guaranteed and thus not directly tied to performance, players have less incentive to provide their maximum performance effort. Several economic studies have been conducted to determine the incidence of shirking, given guaranteed contracts. The results are generally mixed. However, Maxcy, Krautmann, and Fort, economists who have considered shirking in several contexts, have determined that though shirking exists, teams employ methods such as contract incentives to minimize the effects.

Cyntrice Thomas
Joel Maxcy
University of Georgia

See Also: Athlete Representation; Collective Bargaining Agreement; Free Agents; Player Mobility; Reserve Clause.

Further Readings

Goldberg, Jonathan. "Player Mobility in Professional Sports: From the Reserve System to Free Agency." *Sports Lawyers Journal*, v.15/1 (2008).

Hale, Darryl. "Step Up to the Scale: Wages and Unions in the Sports Industry." *Marquette Sports Law Review*, v.5/1 (1994).

Maxcy, Joel. "Motivating Long-Term Employment Contracts: Risk Management in Major League Baseball." *Managerial and Decision Economics,* v.25/2 (2004).

Maxcy, Joel, et al. "The Effectiveness of Incentive Mechanisms in Major League Baseball." *Journal of Sports Economics,* v.3/3 (2002).

Rapp, Geoffery Christopher. "Affirmative Injunctions in Athletic Employment Contracts: Rethinking the Place of the Lumley Rule in American Sports Law." *Marquette Sports Law Review,* v.16/1 (2006).

Contracts, Coaches

The employment contracts of coaches follow the laws and regulations that govern all employment relationships. Unlike players, coaches are not members of unions, and there are not standard or uniform coach contracts across leagues. Coaching contracts are negotiated individually and often contain clauses to define the resolutions to a variety of possibilities if the contract is not completed. In professional team sports compensation for head coaches is lucrative, but is generally substantially less than the annual salaries of star players. The head coaches in the highest revenue-generating college sport programs, primarily football and men's basketball, have contracts authorizing compensation similar to their professional sports counterparts.

In contrast to player contracts, coaching agreements are noteworthy because, although often long-term or multiyear agreements, they are commonly terminated before having run their complete term. Contract termination is a double edged sword. It is very common for the employer to dismiss a coach under contract when the coach's team is performing below expectation. Likewise it is not unusual for a successful coach to accept a more lucrative offer while under contract. The latter situation is most common in intercollegiate (NCAA) sports. Public contract law specifies the legal framework for dealing with the breach or nonperformance of contracts. However private law, as dictated by the contingencies laid out in the contract itself, is increasingly more likely to determine the settlement of prematurely terminated contracts.

When a coach is terminated by his employer before the term of the contract is complete (club or university athletic department) the termination is specified as being "with cause" or "without cause." Coaches who are fired simply because the employer is not satisfied with their performance are deemed as terminated without cause, and unless otherwise specified by the contract, are entitled to the compensation due them for the remainder of their contract. Such terminations are routine in professional and college sports as many coaches are fired, even in mid-season, when their teams fail to perform to expectations. A coach fired with cause means that a violation of the contract has occurred, and no further compensation is due. Coaching contracts typically have a clause that specifies that conduct, comportment, compliance with league or NCAA rules, etc. must be maintained or the coach is subject to termination with cause. The firing of a coach because of a NCAA rules violation or for personal misconduct, such as in the case of University of South Florida football coach Jim Leavitt in 2010 for striking a player, is an example of a "with cause" termination. (Leavitt filed a wrongful termination suit that was settled out of court in January 2011.)

Coaches who leave their contracts early to take a more lucrative position may be sued by their employer for breach of contract. This is a more frequent occurrence in college sports as professional leagues have "no tampering" rules, which discourage teams from negotiating with a coach under contract with a competitor. Courts will not enforce "specific performance" for personal service or employment contracts, meaning the coach cannot be forced to remain with, or go back to, his current employer. A court-ordered injunction, however, can proscribe the coach from performing his duties for any other employer other than the current holder of his contract. Injunctive relief thus offers the same result, in that if the coach desires to stay employed he must honor the remainder of his contract. Notwithstanding, and although injunctive relief is often sought, a monetary settlement is viewed as the most efficient choice as it allows the coach to migrate to the employer that most values his services, while at once allowing the aggrieved party economic compensation to offset his or her loss.

Because termination is commonplace and reliance on third-party settlement through the court system is expensive, compensation given for early termination is often specifically detailed in the contract. For example, if a coach desires to leave his current contract for a more lucrative offer the exact terms of the "buyout" are specified in the contract and are actually part of the negotiation process. Likewise the payment amounts and schedule for a coach who may be fired without cause are determined in advance through negotiation and are included in the contract.

Joel Maxcy
University of Georgia

See Also: Compensation; Contracts, Athletes; National Collegiate Athletic Association.

Further Readings

Sander, L. and P. Fain. "Coaches' Contracts Are Fertile Ground for Conflict." *The Chronicle of Higher Education.* http://chronicle.com/article/Coaches-Contracts-Are-Fert/44424 (Accessed October 2010).

Upton, J. and S. Wieberg. "Contracts for College Coaches Cover More Than Salaries." http://www.usatoday.com/sports/college/football/2006-11-16-coaches-salaries-cover_x.htm (Accessed October 2010).

Weiler, Paul C. and Gary R. Roberts. *Sports and the Law: Cases and Problems.* St. Paul, MN: West Publishing, 2004.

Contracts, Contest Participants

It is fundamental for sport marketers to recognize the legal consequences of their actions, to protect themselves and their organization from liability resulting from contests. A contest is a competition of intellect or skill that offers participants the opportunity to receive or compete for gifts or prizes. It requires that specific rules and predetermined criteria be used to fairly judge contestants. Regardless of the weight of the event or the magnitude of the prizes, the sport marketer must identify and manage risks accordingly.

Clarity Reduces Risk

One way to alleviate risk is to draft a clear and complete formal contract. For a contract to be legally enforceable there must be mutual consent, offer and acceptance, the mutual exchange of something of value, and performance or delivery. Depending on the situation, a contract can be oral, informal, or formal. However, it can be very difficult to prove that an oral contract exists.

The trend in sport is to draft formal written contracts to avoid ambiguities. Contracts are especially critical for sport marketers issuing contests involved with incentives. For difficult contests like half-court shots, hole-in-one contests, or field goals, the prizes are usually large. If a sport marketer is drafting a contract involving large incentives, the contract must be exceedingly clear about how the contest will be run. The contract language should be definite and unmistakable. With substantial prizes like $1 million or a new car, the sport marketer will usually take out an insurance policy to pay the prize money if someone wins. An insurance company can refuse to pay if there is confusion about how the contest is run, or if the contract is indistinct.

The sport marketer should be familiar with contract law when drafting a contract. Contract law is a part of civil law that covers mutual promises and their enforcement. There are several legal principles of contract law to consider. Some of the principles are offer and acceptance, capacity, consideration, and legality.

Offer and acceptance involves an offer or a promise to a person, and the agreement of both parties to the terms of the contract.

Capacity concerns a person's ability to enter into a contractual agreement. For example, a contract agreement should not be entered by someone who does not have the capacity to take on legal responsibility such as a minor, a person who is mentally incompetent, or someone incapacitated from the use of drugs or alcohol.

Consideration is anything of value used to induce one person to enter into an agreement with another. There is no incentive to enter into a contract without consideration.

Legality is the principle that a contract cannot violate public policy or break any laws. When drafting a contract for a contest with large incentives, the marketer should also insert an exclusion clause that states that participants cannot enter a contest if they have a professional advantage. For example, an ex–Major League pitcher should be excluded from a pitching contest to win $50,000.

Another major element that the sport marketer must be familiar with is tort law. Tort is wrongful conduct by one individual that results in injury or the civil wronging of another. Certain legal principles associated with tort law are negligence, assumption of risk, waivers and release of liability, and vicarious liability. Negligence is a type of tort where a person's actions create a foreseeable risk that results in another person being injured. Assumption of risk demonstrates that a person has given consent to take on a risk of damage, injury, or loss as a result of his or her participation in a contest. Waivers and release of liability are types of contracts that release one party from liability if the other displays negligence. Vicarious liability is when one person is liable for the actions of another person, based on their relationship. As a sport marketer you can be liable for the actions of your employees and volunteers assisting with a promotional activity or contest.

Conclusion

Issuing contests is a great way to entertain crowds and increase attendance, but the sport marketer must have an effective risk management plan in place. The sport marketer should make sure his or her organization has insurance. Otherwise, in order to reduce liability the sport marketer should purchase event insurance.

Insurance is a major part of the risk management plan, but it is not the be-all, end-all. The sport marketer should set up a risk management group to identify risks. Safety checks should be made on the contest equipment, as well as the surrounding area where the contest will be held. The risk manage-ment plan should list emergency procedures and emergency contacts, schedule regular safety checks, and contain official waivers and release forms. The risk management plan should be available to all staff members. Staff members should also be trained to safely administer a contest involving physical activity.

Shawn Bailey
State University of New York College at Cortland

See Also: Breach of Contract; Contract, Key Factors in a; Event Risk Management Process; Negligence; Tort Issues in Sports.

Further Readings

Irwin, Richard L., William A. Sutton, and Larry M. McCarthy. *Sport Promotion and Sales Management.* Champaign, IL: Human Kinetics, 2002.
McQuillan, Lawrence J. and Hovannes Abramyan. *U.S. Tort Liability Index: 2010 Report.* San Francisco, CA: Pacific Research Institute, 2010.

Contracts, Insurance Brokers

Colleges and universities that field athletic teams, professional sports organizations, arena and stadium operators, and others must manage the risk they face concerning potential liability for injuries or other harm suffered by players, fans, employees, or others. Certainly well-run operations and organizations formalize risk management plans to minimize potential harm. Part of any risk management plan is the purchase of insurance to help shift some of the potential risks to a third party, in this case an insurance company.

While many insurance companies sell their product through their own agents, insurance brokers also work with many colleges and universities, teams, and arenas and stadiums to assist them in independently procuring insurance products.

Contract law relating to insurance broker contracts is interpreted differently than that of other commercial agreements, making it important for all parties to carefully review paperwork and to be forthcoming with regard to disclosure and other communications.

Insurance Brokers

In the United States, insurance brokerage is a regulated industry. Most states have an insurance commissioner or other executive officer who organizes the regulatory or supervisory efforts for that state. Insurance brokers find "brokes," or sources for, insurance contracts on behalf of their customers. Insurance is a form of risk management that is used by individuals and organizations to minimize exposure to unwanted risks. Insurance can also be described as an equitable transfer of the risk of a loss, from one individual to another, in exchange for the payment of a premium.

An insurer is the company that sells the insurance, while an insured, or policyholder, is the individual or organization that purchases the insurance. A great deal of insurance is sold by insurance agents. An agent is a representative of the insurance company, and his or her primary responsibility lies with the insurance company, not with the insurance buyer. A broker, in contrast, has no contractual agreements with the insurance company, and is paid by the insurance buyer, a relationship that can have significant benefits for the buyer with regard to rates and other negotiations with the insurance company. Major American insurance brokers include Aon Corporation, Marsh & McLennan Companies, and Willis Group Holdings.

Many colleges and universities, professional sports teams, and arena and stadium operators often use insurance brokers, who are sometimes known as insurance consultants. Whereas insurance agents are paid by the insurance company, insurance brokers are usually paid a fee by the customer, and in theory will thus procure the best insurance policy from many companies. In recent years, however, more insurance brokers have been allowed to accept fees from insurance companies, which in the eyes of some critics creates a conflict of interest. Insurance brokers assist clients in a broad range of risk management advice. Insurance brokers assist clients with the purchase of a broad range of insurance products, including property and casualty insurance, but also health, dental, and other coverage.

Insurance Contracts

In most contract law, when a dispute arises, a court generally resolves the dispute by determining the mutual assent of the parties. Mutual assent is based upon the intentions of the parties forming the contract, and occurs only once there has been a meeting of the minds. In cases involving insurance, however, courts often disregard the actual intent of the parties and instead resolve disputes through interpretation of the contract. This approach is followed because if a court were to find that a meeting of the minds did not exist, the contract would be invalidated, which would leave the insured without coverage. By treating the case as one of contract interpretation, courts are able to preserve the insured party's coverage.

Insurance contracts are almost always drafted by the insurance company. There are several reasons for this. First, the insurance company has broad experience in preparing such agreements, while the insured usually is involved in such a transaction at most only a very few times per year. Second, since the insurance industry is regulated by state officials, certain language must be contained in agreements related to a policy's issuance. The insurance company is in a far better position to ensure that such language is contained in the contract. Which party draws up the agreement is important because courts tend to determine disputes regarding insurance contracts by interpreting disputes in the favor of the nondrafting party. Although the insurance contract is interpreted relying upon information within the four corners of the agreement, any ambiguities are resolved against the interests of the drafter, which is usually the insurance company. Thus when a contract is open to two or more reasonable interpretations, the one that benefits the insured is taken, as this works in the public interest of protecting the insured. Disputed insurance policies are often also resolved in favor of the reasonable expectations of the insured. This allows a court to consider the insured public's best interests, in addition to a case at issue before it.

Although colleges and universities, individual sports teams, and other organizations that obtain insurance policies often are wealthy, the companies that insure them have still greater resources. The courts wish to encourage the purchase of insurance, because such decisions ultimately protect athletes who participate in games or the people who attend sporting events. As a result, disputes relating to insurance contracts often are resolved in the favor of the insured.

Stephen T. Schroth
Melvin E. Taylor Jr.
Knox College

See Also: Agency Law; Arena Owner/Operator/Tenant Balance; Contracts, Vendors; Event Risk Management Process; Insurance Against Risks; Risk Management; Stadium Operations.

Further Readings

Irwin, Richard L., William A. Sutton, and Larry M. McCarthy. *Sport Promotion and Sales Management.* Champaign, IL: Human Kinetics, 2002.
McQuillan, Lawrence J. and Hovannes Abramyan. *U.S. Tort Liability Index: 2010 Report.* San Francisco, CA: Pacific Research Institute, 2010.
Schwartz, D. "Interpretation and Disclosure in Insurance Contracts." *Loyola Consumer Law Review,* v.21/2 (2008).

Contracts, Management

One of the largest industries in the United States, sports generates greater revenues than such well-established fields as banking, healthcare, real estate, and transportation. As with any enterprise, managers are involved in directing the activities of a sports organization's employees, with an eye toward accomplishing established goals and objectives. Sports management contracts are, like all agreements, affected by agency law, whereby a relationship exists between an agent, or employee, and a principal, an individual or organization providing employment. All areas of the sports industry use contracts, and management uses them for employing front office officials, players, and other staff. Many involved in management utilize lawyers to assist them in drafting contracts and other documents. All management personnel, however, must have a basic understanding of contracts to limit their organization's liability and to help control risk.

Agency/principal relationships are formed when an individual or organization hires someone to work in any capacity. Agency law establishes the duties the principal, or employer, and the agent, or employee, owe to each other. The principal and agent often have entered into an agreement that defines the relationship's parameters, but certain fiduciary duties exist between the two parties regardless of contractual obligations. Agency law is important in sports because it binds the principal in certain relations with third parties to uphold actions of the agent, providing the agent is acting pursuant to the authority granted him or her by the principal. Pursuant to agency law, the principal owes the agent the following three obligations:

- Complying with an employment contract if one exists
- Compensating the agent for his or her services
- Reimbursing the agent for expenses incurred while acting on the principal's behalf

In return, the agent owes the principal a level of fiduciary responsibility. A fiduciary duty is the legal and ethical responsibility of the agent to act in the principal's best interests. The five primary fiduciary duties the agent owes the principal are as follows:

- Obeying the principal's direct instructions and complying with organizational policies and procedures
- Remaining loyal to the principal's best interests
- Exercising reasonable care in pursuit of the agent's duties
- Notifying the principal of significant developments, opportunities, or problems

- Accounting for and reporting information and financial results on a timely basis

These duties are very important, as the acts of an agent may incur liability for the principal, either through contracts entered into by the agent on behalf of the principal or as a result of negligence on behalf of the agent.

Parties who feel they have been aggrieved as a result of some negligent action on the part of a sports team's or other organization's management may sue the team or organization pursuant to the theory of vicarious liability. Lawsuits frequently arise when an agent commits a tort, and a plaintiff seeks redress from the agent's principal, who generally has "deeper pockets," that is, more money and a greater ability to pay damages. Employers might also be found liable for employing an unqualified individual or not providing proper supervision for that employee.

When faced with a vicarious liability lawsuit, a principal has three possible defenses to the claim. First, the principal may assert that the agent was not negligent in his or her behavior, thus negating the plaintiff's claim. Second, the principal may argue that the agent was acting outside the scope of his or her employment, which eliminates the employer's liability since the employee was acting on his or her own behalf. Third, the principal may assert that the agent is an independent contractor, that is, an employee who is not under the employer's direct supervision and control. Although many services, such as team doctors, photographers, and trainers, may be provided by independent contractors, courts have increasingly taken a hard-line approach in denying such claims by principals.

Employment contracts for managers are written or oral agreements that create a legal obligation to fulfill the conditions arranged between the parties. A valid contract requires an offer by one party and an acceptance by the other. Contracts also require that both parties provide consideration to the other. Within the context of an employment contract, consideration usually amounts to payment on the part of the employer and services rendered on the part of the employee.

Once an agreement is made, the breaking of any of the promises or conditions it contains is con-

sidered a breach. For management employment contracts, an award of monetary damages to compensate the injured party is usually considered adequate, as this will allow an aggrieved employee to find other employment, or a wronged employer to find another employee. In some cases involving very senior management, an injunction may be used to prevent a former employee from working for a competitor, although this is generally only allowed when a noncompete clause is contained in the employment agreement.

Managers in sports organizations also negotiate other contracts for other employees, always seeking to further organizational goals and objectives. All management contracts, at whatever level, must comply with state and federal laws regarding hiring and discrimination.

Stephen T. Schroth
Sara S. Patterson
Knox College

See Also: Contract, Key Factors in a; Contracts, Coaches; Employee Benefits; Facilities Management; Organizational Design; Wage and Human Capital.

Further Readings

Graham, S., L. D. Neirotti, and J. J. Goldblatt. *The Ultimate Guide to Sport Event Management and Marketing.* New York: McGraw-Hill, 2001.
Jordan, J. S., A. Kent, and M. B. Walker. "Management and Leadership in the Sport Industry." In A. Gillentine and R. B. Crow, eds., *Foundations of Sport Management.* Morgantown, WV: Fitness Information Technology, 2009.

Contracts, Officials

Generally amateur sport officials are considered independent contractors and not employees of the schools, recreational leagues, or conferences that pay them to officiate at sport contests. Sport officials

Unlike officials in other major league sports, National Football League (NFL) officials (above) are part-time and usually work other jobs because of the league's short season.

are also considered members instead of employees of their own officials associations even though these associations may train and have responsibility for assigning them to games. This impacts sport officials in several ways. First, officials are generally excluded from worker's compensation coverage and unemployment benefits. Second, officials cannot obtain liability insurance from youth sport programs, schools, and leagues.

Most amateur sport officials officiate on a part-time basis and have other full-time employment. Since amateur sport officials are generally considered independent contractors they are paid on a per game or per season basis. Depending on their experience and level of certification officials can work games at various levels (youth, high school, collegiate, recreational) and advance to the upper levels (collegiate, elite amateur, and professional) of a particular sport.

Sport officials at the upper levels of sport, those who officiate collegiate and professional games, are generally paid employees of college conferences and professional leagues. Sport officials employed by professional leagues are full-time and belong to unions. The exception is the National Football League (NFL): its officials are part time and most have full-time jobs, although NFL officials do belong to a union. Compared to the other professional leagues (MLB, NHL, NBA, WNBA), the NFL season is relatively short, and most NFL games are played on the weekends.

Elements

The game or season contract is an important document to sport officials. Although legally contracts can be oral or written, game contracts should be in writing, signed, with copies distributed to the parties involved in the contract. Further, contracts must include four important aspects to be valid. The first important element of a contact is the agreement. The agreement, in this case, involves an offer on the part of the sport organization, a conditional promise to pay for the services of the official, and acceptance. If the official agrees to the terms of the contract by signing the contract he or she has agreed to accept the contract in its entirety. Officials should carefully review the terms and conditions of the game contract before signing the contract.

The second important element is consideration, which involves an exchange of value. In other words, the sport official exchanges her or his services as an official in return for a specific fee. These game fees are based on the official's level of certification and regular season versus tournament games. More experienced sport officials with higher levels of certification are paid more per game than less experienced officials. Additionally, sport officials are generally paid more for tournament and championship games than for regular season games.

The third important element is capacity, which means that both parties to the agreement have the legal capability of entering into a contractual relationship. Generally, minors are considered not to have the legal competence to enter into a contract. Thus, a contract signed by a minor may be voidable. Finally, the content and terms of the contract must not violate state or federal laws. In other words, in order for the contract to be enforceable it must not compel either party of the agreement to engage in an illegal act.

As previously mentioned, a contract includes the terms and conditions of an arrangement between two parties. Typically a game contract details the contest date, time, place, and fee to be paid to the official by the recreational league, high school, or college team that is hosting the game. Standard game fees are generally set by the state high school athletic associations, recreational leagues, or college conferences to which the athletic team is a member. Conversely, sport officials who are selected to work postseason tournaments are generally paid by state high school associations, instead of the individual schools, and receive greater pay per game than for regular season contests. Generally, certified assigners are responsible for assigning

and contracting with sport officials for regular season games. They are given this authority to assign officials and issue regular season game contracts by state high school athletic associations, schools, and leagues.

Other Terms

In some cases, an official's contract will explicitly state that the official is an independent contractor and must have personal liability insurance. As independent contractors sport officials have a contractual duty of care to the participants involved in the contest. This contractual duty of care means that an official must first and foremost ensure the safety of the game participants. In addition, the terms of the contract may require that officials maintain a certain level of physical fitness and conditioning as well as adhere to a code of conduct. Oftentimes, when signing a contract, officials are required to certify that they have an official's permit or license. Further, officials can be penalized as well as sanctioned for a breach of contract in which they fail to fulfill the essential terms and conditions of their game contract. For example, if an official fails to show up to officiate a contest he or she will likely face sanctions by the state high school association or college conference. These sanctions may involve the temporary suspension or loss of his or her officiating license.

Corinne M. Daprano
University of Dayton

See Also: Breach of Contract; Contract, Key Factors in a; Independent Contractors; Legal Considerations in Sport; Officials, Associations.

Further Readings

Collins, Donald. *Officials and Independent Contractors.* Franksville, WI: Referee Enterprises, 1999.
Goldberger, Alan S. *Sports Officiating: A Legal Guide.* Franksville, WI: Referee Books, 2007.
Weiler, Paul C. and Gary R. Roberts. *Sports and the Law: Cases and Problems.* St. Paul, MN: West Publishing, 2004.

Contracts, Premium Seating

Contracts, such as permanent seat licenses (PSLs) that provide up-front revenues and multiyear premium seating deals that provide contractually obligated revenue, play a crucial role in a sport franchise's ability to raise capital for new facility construction. PSLs consist of an up-front payment that guarantees the license holder access to a seat under contractually defined terms that address, among other things, the length of the contract, transfer rights of the holder, and conditions that must be met for the license holder to retain his or her rights. Premium seating inventory is often sold in multiyear, staggered contracts that provide financial advantages for the organization.

In order to secure the private debt that is often required to finance a new facility, large amounts of cash and/or multiyear, contractually guaranteed revenue is usually needed as collateral. The PSLs and premium seating not only bring increased revenues to sport franchises, the structure of their contracts also provides an important foundation for a franchise's long-term financial well-being.

Evolution of Financing

Seat bonds that resemble what are referred to today as PSLs were used to help finance Texas Stadium, the home of the National Football League's (NFL's) Dallas Cowboys from 1971 to 2009. PSLs were introduced more recently as the primary source of financing for Bank of America Stadium, formerly known as Ericsson Stadium, the home of the NFL's Carolina Panthers since 1996. During the stadium building boom that began in the 1990s, using some sort of seat licensing plan became a common practice in the financing of new stadiums in the NFL and Major League Baseball (MLB).

PSLs give the license holder the right to purchase tickets for a specific seat or seats for contractually specified amounts of time, for events identified in the contract. A PSL contract also addresses the rights and conditions under which the license holder is permitted to transfer the PSL, as well as conditions that must be met to retain the license. Behavior clauses are often included that cover the PSL holder and anyone else who might use the seat under license.

For the sport franchise, PSLs are a significant one-time revenue generator that can be used directly to help finance a franchise's share of a new stadium or as collateral to secure private loans for stadium financing. For example, the San Francisco Giants used seat licenses they call charter seat licenses to generate revenue that, along with a naming rights contract, was used to secure private loans that paid for the construction of their stadium, which opened in 2000.

The addition of premium seating inventory is one of the primary reasons behind the explosion of new sport facilities across prominent professional and college sports leagues in the United States over the past several decades.

Facilities with premium seating generate significant increased stadium revenues compared to the stadiums of previous eras. The total seating inventory of the old MLB facilities in New York—Yankee Stadium and Shea Stadium—was approximately 115,000. With the 2009 opening of the new stadiums, new Yankee Stadium and Citi Field, total MLB seating inventory was reduced in New York to approximately 100,000. During the 2008 season, the Mets and Yankees together had an average attendance of over 52,000 per game. Even if they sell out every game in their new stadiums, overall attendance would be approximately 2,000 fans per game lower than it was in the last year of the old stadiums. This clearly illustrates that the new stadiums were not constructed to generate more revenue by selling more tickets and accommodating more fans. They were constructed to accommodate increased premium seating inventory, along with more retail and dining facilities.

Premium seating contracts require the purchaser to pay for the premium area, but do not include tickets for the event. Contracts stipulate which events and when purchasers have access to the area. In most cases, the contract entitles the holder to all events at the arena—and can even include use of the premium area during nonevent times. Premium seat contracts are often marketed and priced in a way that encourages the purchase of multiyear contracts. If the stadium owner can sell premium seating for staggered five-, seven-, or 10-year terms, he or she can show a stable stream of contractually obligated revenue that can be used for long-term planning or collateral on loans. The staggered contract terms ensure that only a minority of contracts expire in any given year, and result in a more stable revenue stream.

Conclusion

Many of the revenue sources normally associated with sports, such as ticket sales, parking, and concessions, are by themselves considered inherently risky by lenders of large sums of money that is paid back over the long term. Bad weather, poor play, safety threats, and a weak economy can have dramatic effects on these revenue streams from year to year or even month to month. Contracts like PSLs, that lead to a significant amount of cash on hand, and premium seating contracts, that provide a stable, relatively secure source of revenue, allow sport franchises to secure the financing it takes to build the modern facilities deemed essential to maintaining economic competitiveness.

Kevin Heisey
Liberty University

See Also: Facilities Financing; Permanent Seat License; Premium Seating; Pricing of Tickets.

Further Readings

Crawford, Garry. *Consuming Sport: Fans, Sport and Culture*. New York: Routledge, 2004.
Mullin, Bernard J., Stephen Hardy, and William A. Sutton. *Sport Marketing*. Champaign, IL: Human Kinetics, 2007.
Shilbury, David, Hans Westerbeek, Shayne Quick, and Daniel Funk. *Strategic Sport Marketing*, 3rd Ed. London: Allen & Unwin, 2009.

Contracts, TV/Radio Network

The right to broadcast the games of a team, league, or sports entity has become for many of these organizations their single most valuable revenue stream, exceeding even revenue from ticket sales or live attendance at games or events.

How the broadcast rights contract most commonly exists today is that a media company, a television network, cable television channel, or radio station or network pays the originating entity a fee for the right to air the game or event for a specific fee. The broadcaster bears the cost of producing the broadcast and sells advertising on the broadcast presentation of the event. If the advertising time available on the broadcast sells for more than the fee paid to the sports team or event creator combined with the costs of production, this represents the profit left for the broadcaster.

Exclusivity

The broadcast right is also usually an exclusive right, by which the broadcaster is the only media outlet where the game or event can be seen or heard. This was not the case in the early stages of development of broadcast media. In fact, it was not media entities that first purchased broadcast rights, but rather sponsors who in turn offered the broadcast of the game or event to radio and later television outlets to broadcast, while reserving all the commercial time. General Mills and its cereal Wheaties were among the very earliest purchasers of broadcast rights, beginning in the early 1930s; the Wheaties association with sports remains strong even today.

However, the broadcasts of games were hardly exclusive to local radio broadcasters in the early days of the medium. A number of radio outlets would observe and report on early games, and even more would re-create games from teletype descriptions. Many of these early broadcasters cited First Amendment Rights to describe newsworthy events in support of their right to broadcast games. These claims came to a head in the case of *Pittsburgh Athletic Club v. KQV* in 1934.

KQV radio observed Pittsburgh Pirates games from the windows of their offices overlooking Forbes Field in Pittsburgh and broadcast the games. However, the Pirates had just for the first time sold the rights to broadcast their games to General Mills for $2,000, and General Mills had contracted with another radio station to air the Pirates games and its commercials. An appeals court's ultimate rejection of KQV's First Amendment or newsworthiness claims helped firmly establish the origins of broadcast rights as beginning with the team or creator of an event, and ensured that it remained a right that could be traded or sold exclusively to a single media outlet. It is this concept of exclusivity that helped make media rights contracts the most valuable revenue stream in sports, because it made the purchase of broadcast rights a zero sum game where only one outlet would win.

NFL Expands Rights

The National Football League (NFL) is the league most associated with development of league broadcasting contracts, beginning with its first league-negotiated agreement with CBS in 1961. While baseball innovator Branch Rickey first pioneered the concept of selling league-wide broadcast rights to television with his Continental Baseball League (which never played a game), and the American Football League actually sold its broadcast rights to ABC prior to the NFL's deal with CBS, the NFL gained two tremendous advantages in selling its broadcast rights collectively to one network.

First, CBS agreed to air NFL games in all the markets it served, not just markets with an NFL team. This kind of distribution was rivaled only by events like the World Series—and absolutely unprecedented for regular season games. Second, the sale of all rights prevented media outlets from competing only for the most valuable league games, or for rights to a few of the most attractive teams. While the NFL and the other leagues that adopted a league-wide model for selling media rights ultimately would need an antitrust exemption to do this, which they received in the Sports Broadcasting Act of 1961, the pooling of media rights brought new levels of exposure and revenue to teams that had previously been poor performers. The on-field success of the Pittsburgh Steelers, Buffalo Bills, and Green Bay Packers in the television era were all aided by revenue from the sale of league-wide broadcast rights.

ABC Leverages Sports

The success of the NFL with CBS established sports as valuable television programming. Rival network ABC took note, and capitalized perhaps more than any other broadcast entity in the 1970s. Long the distant third network among the broadcast networks, ABC nevertheless had built an enviable collection of sports broadcast properties with relatively low or no rights fees. These included the Olympics in 1964 and 1968, college football, and events for its signature *Wide World of Sports* franchise. ABC found that sports events both provided a platform for promoting its prime time broadcasts and actually drew better ratings than its entertainment programming.

Under the leadership of Roone Arledge, ABC began paying high broadcast rights fees for more and more events, including the Olympic Games, Major League Baseball and the World Series, National Basketball Association games, and Monday night NFL games. This set off a bidding war among all the networks that continues relatively unabated for many years, as ABC used the ratings generated by its sports broadcasts, and the ability to promote its other programming during sports events, to become number one in the ratings for the first time, by the late 1970s. In the late 1980s and early 1990s, just as it appeared the growth of broadcast rights was unsustainable and sports leagues would have to accept retrenchment, Rupert Murdoch and Fox enter the scene, dramatically winning the rights to the NFL's National Football Conference (NFC) games package by over-bidding—but in doing so, Fox emerged as the fourth major network.

Significance Today

Today, the NFL receives nearly $5 billion in annual revenue from broadcasters. It has split its content five ways. Its American Football Conference (AFC) games are aired by CBS, and its NFC games by Fox, which has yet to earn a profit on its carrying of football. NBC owns the rights to air a single Sunday evening game, while ESPN, the cable network, airs *Monday Night Football*. Yet it is the subscriber-driven Direct TV, a satellite television company, that pays the most, an estimated $1 billion to air all out-of-market NFL games for a fee, under a program called *NFL Sunday Ticket*. Revenue from the sale of broadcast rights accounts for about 60 percent of the NFL's total annual revenue. While the NFL is uniquely television- or broadcast-centric, most other leagues have broadcast rights fees running around the 50 percent mark of all revenue.

Deregulation of cable and television in the 1980s allowed for greater use of the time buy concept, where a sponsor or league produces the event and sells the advertising time on the broadcast, and ultimately offers the broadcast to a network for little or no fee, sometimes merely a split of ad revenue for reserved spots, just to get the event on the air. Presently, time buys seem the dominant mechanism by which smaller or less popular events get on the air.

The rise of the time buy, and the consolidation of interest in few sports properties that draw big ratings, have also driven a number of sports away from free-to-air television and to cable, where networks have two revenue sources to offset high rights fees, subscription fees and advertising revenue. Now fewer properties than ever appear exclusively on free-to-air television, and they are almost always proven ratings winners like the NFL and the Olympics, where top dollar continues to be paid for broadcast rights.

Robert A. Boland
New York University

See Also: Advertising; Broadcast Rights; Exclusivity; Media Content Rights Fees; National Football League.

Further Readings

Arledge, Roone. *Roone: A Memoir.* New York: HarperCollins, 2003.

Lattinville, Robert H., Robert A. Boland, and Bennett Speyer. "Labor Pains: The Effect of a Work Stoppage in the NFL on Its Coaches." *Marquette Sports Law Review,* v.20/1 (2010).

MacCambridge, Michael. *America's Game.* New York: Anchor, 2005.

Sugar, Bert Randolph. *The Thrill of Victory: The Inside Story of ABC Sports.* New York: Hawthorn Books, 1978.

Contracts, Vendors

Although sports teams, arenas, stadiums, and others receive the bulk of attention, a bevy of vendors and suppliers provide a host of goods and services that permit sports teams and venues to operate. Vendors agree to provide these services through a variety of contracts, which assure both parties a level of certainty with regard to price, markets, and supply. Depending upon the type of transaction, both formal and informal vendor contracts are used. Certain agreements, such as those regarding pouring rights, are carefully negotiated and result in a formal executed contract. Other transactions, involving smaller amounts, often are conducted using purchase orders or other commercial paper. Regardless of the form, vendor contracts play an important role in the management of sports teams, arenas, stadiums, and other sports-affiliated businesses.

Contract Formation

Law governing vendor contracts is determined by a variety of sources, including case law and statutes. Case law is that developed within the court system, and is an important part of the Anglo-American common law system, whereby courts announce a rule of law that applies to the facts of a particular case. This holding is then considered precedent for other courts to follow. Statutes are laws passed by the U.S. Congress or individual state legislatures. Statutes regulate, command, or prohibit certain conduct, and require individuals and corporations to act in certain ways when engaged in specific situations. Since most contracts are controlled by state law, disputes regarding agreements are controlled by local law. Exceptions where federal law affects vendor contracts include federal statutes and policies such as the Americans with Disabilities Act, the Sherman and Clayton Antitrust Acts, and the Bankruptcy Act.

Although the specifics of contract formation may vary from jurisdiction to jurisdiction, certain commonalities exist across the United States. Contracts are agreements that constitute an exchange of promises between two or more parties. Contracts create legally enforceable duties and obligations that bind the parties with regard to a specific transaction or series of transactions. Although some contracts can be verbal in form, most agreements are written as this provides reliable evidence of the terms of the contract, as well as establishes proof of the agreement. In order for a valid contract to be formed, four elements must be present.

These elements include legal capacity, agreement, consideration, and legality.

Legal capacity is the first element required, and involves the relative strength of bargaining power between the parties. To ensure fairness, courts will disallow contracts if one of the parties was a minor (a person under 18) or had significant mental disabilities. Agreement refers to the very essence of a contract, and requires a process where an offer and acceptance occur. Generally the parties to a contract make a series of proposals for the exchange of goods, services, or money that leads to a meeting of the minds on the part of all parties.

Consideration is concerned with the parties exchanging something of value as part of the contract. Consideration may relate to the payment of money for goods or services, or some other exchange where the promise is made to provide something of value.

Legality involves society's concern that contracts not require performance of an illegal act. In the interest of public policy, courts will not enforce agreements concerning illegal narcotics, gambling, prostitution, or other unlawful activities. If all four elements are present, a contract is legally binding on the parties and can be enforced by a court or other dispute resolution process.

Vendor Agreements

Sports vendor agreements often involve procurement of equipment, professional services, and food and drink. Many stadiums, arenas, and teams have entered into vendor agreements with large corporations such as the Coca-Cola Company, PepsiCo, Inc., Anheuser-Busch InBev N. V., and MillerCoors. These vendors sign pouring rights agreements with stadiums, arenas, and teams that permit them market dominance within sports venues. Vendor contracts concerning equipment can cover a wide range of products, from jerseys, shoes, helmets, and socks to chairs coaches sit upon. Vendor contracts for equipment are often in the form of purchase orders. A purchase order (PO) is a form of commercial paper that is issued from a buyer to a vendor. POs specify the type, quantities, and agreed-upon prices for products or services that vendors will supply to buyers. The management of a stadium, arena, or sports team sends a PO to a vendor, constituting an offer. Acceptance of the PO by the vendor is gener-

ally indicated by provision of services or delivery of goods. Agreements regarding professional services constitute another major type of sports-related vendor agreements. Examples of professional services procured by vendor agreements vary greatly, but include cleaning services for everything from restrooms to bleachers, announcers, or halftime or post-game entertainment. Vendor agreements may also cover legal, accounting, or medical services used by a team or venue.

Dispute Resolution

In addition to terms related to quantity, category of goods or services, price, delivery, and the like, vendor contracts sometimes contain specific language regarding dispute resolution and choice of forum for resolving such disagreements. When disputes arise between the buyer and vendor, contract law will resolve the dispute in the court system unless the parties agree to do otherwise. Dispute resolution language in vendor contracts can allow the parties to elect arbitration rather than going to court. Arbitration resolves disputes between parties by an impartial third party. When complete, an arbitrator's decision is legally binding to the two parties involved within the dispute. Arbitration is frequently used to resolve commercial disputes as it is perceived as less expensive and faster than resorting to the courts.

Stephen T. Schroth
Jason A. Helfer
Evan M. Massey
Knox College

See Also: Benefits for Sponsors; Concession Pricing; In-Arena/Stadium Sales Promotions; Marketing Partner; Pouring Rights; Stadium Operations.

Further Readings

Mitten, M., T. Davis, R. Smith, and R. Berry. *Sports Law and Regulation: Cases, Materials, and Problems.* Riverwoods, IL: Aspen, 2009.
Schmitz, J. K. "Ambush Marketing: The Off-Field Competition at the Olympic Games." *Northwestern Journal of Technology and Intellectual Property,* v.3/2 (2005).

Contracts, Venue

Organizations that enter into contracts for events and venues include vendors, concessionaires, game officials, sponsors, insurance agents, mascots, entertainment, promotional activities, essential personnel, and media (specifically television and radio). There are four main types of contracts that facility and event managers should be familiar with. The type of contract will determine the specific consideration of the contract. These types of contracts are the following:

- Game contracts
- Event contracts
- Venue and Facility contracts
- Sponsorship contracts

A venue or facility contract is essentially a rental agreement for use of a venue/facility. The agreement must be in writing, and it should include the specific terms of the lease to include time, length of event, how much rent, maintenance, custodial, grounds, security, medical support, etc. In addition, individuals or groups renting and using a venue for an event usually must present evidence of a certificate of insurance with minimum policy limits (typically $1 million of coverage or more). Even though venue/facility contracts can be specific to the event, many venues use a basic boilerplate contract for almost every group coming in a venue.

Contract Basics

It is important when discussing contracts specific to facility management, or anything regarding contracts, to define what a contract is and how it is used. By simple definition, a contract is a legally binding agreement or a way to enforce a promise made as a bargained exchange. Sport administrators must have a working knowledge of contracts and how they fit into the overall scheme of managing a sport or entertainment event. In addition, penalties associated with noncompletion of the terms of a contract should be understood. The failure of any party (i.e. event manager, vendor, auxiliary entity) to meet the terms of the contract can have a major impact on the execution of an event as well as the possibility of causing financial hardship to all involved.

The principles of contracts and the process of entering into a contract in venue management are similar to those of other contracts. Typically, negotiations between parties occur and revisions are made prior to a contract being finalized. The goal of any negotiation is to protect all involved through ensuring each party involved will get what they expect, within the time frame needed, at the anticipated cost. It is highly recommended that a lawyer is consulted when a contract is involved. During the process of drafting the contract, negotiating the terms, understanding ramifications of penalties, and final signature of the contract, a lawyer is essential.

Components of a Valid Contract

Although there is room for creativity with respect to areas of performance indicated in the contract, there is less room for creativity when dealing with the contract components and structure. Specifically, all contracts are subject to four standard elements that ensure validity of a contact. The four elements are as follows:

- *Offer*: the proposal that forms the contract
- *Acceptance*: accepting the terms and provisions
- *Consideration*: details of the contract
- *Capacity*: parties must be legally able to enter into contract

All four of these must be present for a legally binding contractual arrangement to exist. If one of these is missing, there is not a legally binding contract that will hold up against the scrutiny of the legal system.

Contracts in Facility Management

The reason contracts are used in facility management is to protect all of those involved. For any sporting or entertainment event, there will be a multitude of groups and individuals that need to be under contract with the host organization or venue. Misunderstandings and miscommunications are avoided though the use of a well-drafted, legally binding contract. Events at facilities can involve large sums of money, thousands of people, and safety concerns, and have many potential pitfalls so protection through contracts is important. If event managers are in charge of an event bringing in thousands of people, they have needs in the area of customer service, security, food and beverage service, logistics, parking, sponsorship, and merchandise. The massive list of what needs to be done, which people need to do it, how it needs to be done, and when it needs to be done can be daunting for an event manager. The use of contracts is one way to ensure that all involved understand their roles and responsibilities.

Besides the who, what, when, and where aspects of contracts related to events, contracts also commonly contain language that provides for legal liability protection for individuals and groups working the event at any facility. Individuals working events should also demand that they receive a contract in writing specifying their formal working relationship with the sport organization and the expectations of the organization. In rare circumstances, breach of contract may occur and the contract will be primary documentation used by the legal system to determine if there was nonfulfillment of any aspect of the contract and what the remedy should be.

Conclusion

Basic contract knowledge is essential in that contracts are a set of promises made in some type of a bargained exchange. A basic contract has four parts: the offer, acceptance, consideration, and capacity. These basic tenets of a contract are also applied in event management through venue, event, sponsorship, and game contracts. These four types of contracts are the primary types used in event management. In all contract dealings it is recommended to use legal counsel to make sure the contract passes legal standards and provides for adequate insurance coverage in the event of unforeseen circumstances. Well-written contracts are essential to successful venue planning and management.

B. David Ridpath
Ohio University

See Also: Contract, Key Factors in a; Contracts, Management; Contracts, Vendors; Legal Considerations in Sport; Negligence.

Further Readings

Epstien, A. *Sports Law.* Clifton Park, NY: Thomson Delmar Learning, 2003.
McMillen, J. D. "Game, Event, and Sponsorship Contracts." In D. Cotten and J. Wolohan, eds., *Law for Recreation and Sport Managers.* Dubuque, IA: Kendall Hunt, 2003.
Ridpath, B. "Event and Facility Contracts." In H. Lawrence and M. Wells, eds., *Event Management Blueprint.* Dubuque, IA: Kendall Hunt, 2009.
Schraber, G. and C. Rohwer. *Contracts.* St. Paul, MN: West Nutshell Series, 1984.

Control for Safety of Fans/Athletes/Volunteers

Sporting events are susceptible to risks that can negatively affect event operations and key stakeholders, including spectators, athletes, venue staff, and sponsoring agencies. Examples of risks associated with sporting events include crowd disorder, logistical failure, counterfeit tickets, theft, inclement weather, and terrorism. Given the multitude of risks and the possible legal and economic implications, venue and event managers implement processes and control measures to prevent, prepare for, respond to, and recover from consequences of potential incidents.

An effective safety and security management system requires venue and event managers to establish a working group (or working partnership) with multiple individuals, responding agencies, and outsourced contractors, such as: law enforcement, emergency management, emergency medical services, fire department, public utilities, government security agencies, contractors, vendors, and media/public relations. The working group will assess risks, train staff, and exercise their plans, procedures, and control measures.

Plans and Policies

Planning is critical to the overall safety and security management system. In order to effectively

A U.S. Customs and Border Protection Blackhawk helicopter pilot surveys the area surrounding the University of Phoenix stadium in Glendale, Arizona, before the 2008 Super Bowl.

plan, the venue and event manager and representatives of the working group identify venue and event risks, threats, and vulnerabilities. Addressing specific risks ensures appropriate planning measures are implemented, such as relevant policies, procedures, and safety control measures. Venue safety and security policies may include an alcohol policy, fan conduct policy, search policy, credential policy, ticket policy, prohibited items policy, and parking policy. In addition, an emergency response plan is developed with annexes for evacuation procedures, all-hazard incident response, and business continuity and recovery.

Safety control measures are enforced to devalue, detect, deter, and defend the venue or event from disruption. Management aims to lower the value of a venue to terrorists, criminal activity, or crowd management issues, thereby making the venue less attractive as a target for illegal or unruly behavior.

Identifying the presence of suspicious people or unruly fan behavior in advance helps provide responders with information needed to execute an effective response. The goal is to respond effectively to an incident, protect the venue and its assets (human and physical), and mitigate any consequences of an incident. Safety and security control measures being utilized at sporting and entertainment venues address venue design, physical protection systems, perimeter control, access control and credentialing, staffing, and training and exercise. Control measures vary across venues, depending on stadium size and structure, event type, and available resources.

Venue design and safety features are guided to an extent by legal regulations, such as occupational safety and health administration rules, transportation and zoning, life safety codes, environmental codes, fire codes, and seismic safety codes. In the 21st century, sport venue architects and engineers work in collaboration with security professionals and first responders during the design process. Most stadiums built today include a modern command center (command post) with communication capabilities for security and emergency management forces to monitor events inside and outside of the venue. The sport organization normally has an interoperable communication system in place with access to the stadium's command center. This enables responding agencies to communicate with each other on the same network to coordinate security management, response, and recovery efforts. Cameras are also utilized to monitor the venue, surrounding perimeter, playing field, and concession areas.

Establishing perimeter controls helps prevent illegal entry (person or vehicle) into the venue or restricted areas of the venue. Access control and credentialing measures have utilized technological security solutions in recent years. For example, electronic scanning of tickets (or contact cards) helps the organization capture ticket holder information. Furthermore, innovative technological security systems in the command center are capable of identifying unruly fans and criminal behavior by running database searches of spectator photos through facial recognition technology. Basic credentialing considerations include an employee background screening program for all venue personnel and contracted staff. Credential systems for an event can be simplified by indicating zone access and color code by game function.

Staff and Volunteers

An effective security plan requires a qualified and trained venue staff. Venue staff includes parking attendants, gate security, ticket takers, ushers, concessions/maintenance, field staff, and security forces. All personnel and contracted staff working events are trained in standard operating procedures (SOPs) for emergency response and security awareness (e.g., suspicious persons and packages).

The hiring and training of security personnel is conducted in accordance with local or state regulations, as some states require security personnel to be certified or licensed. Additionally, managers must ensure they have an adequate number of staff working the sporting event. Managers do not want to be understaffed (which may present a legal concern) or overstaffed (which may be a financial concern to the venue owner/operator). There are several factors to considered when determining the number of staff required for an event; these include anticipated attendance, number of events (single event versus multiple events), level of expertise required for each specific role, scheduling of shifts for personnel, and potential venue and event threats/risks.

When managers determine staff roles and numbers for a specific event, they develop a recruitment strategy. Sport organizations can choose to utilize outsourcing services through an independent contractor or operate using in-house safety and security personnel. Many venues have chosen to develop and maintain their own in-house security response teams that are familiar with the venue. Training is conducted annually, semiannually, or as needed if plans, policies, or measures change within the system. Some organizations outsource because of the difficulty in recruiting and training part-time staff, temporary staff, and volunteers.

Volunteers are an essential addition to event staff for major sporting events. The integration of full-time staff, part-time staff, temporary workers, and volunteers is critical to the success of the event. Volunteers do not receive financial compensation for their time and are motivated by other factors, such as uniforms and official event merchandise, travel, accommodation and meals, social events and activities, and rewards and incentives (e.g., promotional gifts and experiences).

Once measures and plans are determined, and the venue staff is trained, venue and event managers conduct exercises to evaluate operations and plans, and identify gaps in capabilities. Exercises help venue managers to clarify roles and responsibilities, improve multi-agency coordination and communication, reveal resource gaps, develop individual performance, and identify opportunities for improvement. There are several types of exercises that can be defined as either discussion-based or operations-based. Discussion-based exercises familiarize participants with current plans and policies, or may be used to develop new plans and policies. Types of discussion based exercises include seminars, workshops, tabletop exercises, and game simulations. Operations-based exercises are more complex than discussion-based exercises; operation-based exercises validate plans and policies, clarify roles, and identify resource gaps in security operations. Operations-based exercises normally involve the deployment of resources and personnel in real time. Types of operations-based exercises include drills, functional exercises, and full-scale exercises.

Conclusion

Sporting events are susceptible to various risks; however, management may take a proactive approach by establishing a working group with safety and security entities (i.e., law enforcement, emergency management, emergency medical services). The working group identifies venue and event risks/threats in order to develop and implement appropriate policies, procedures, and control measures. Once these standards are developed, personnel are trained in necessary protocols and eventually tested through an exercise format to identify gaps in capabilities and areas of need for improvement. The continuous cycle of analyzing risk, developing plans and control measures, training staff, and exercising is critical to the overall success of a sport event safety and security system—and to protect key stakeholders such as spectators, fans, players, and sponsoring agencies.

Stacey A. Hall
University of Southern Mississippi

See Also: Assessing Event Risk; Crowd Management/Control; Event Risk Management Process.

Further Readings

Hall, Stacey, et al. "Protective Security Measures for Major Sporting Events." *Journal of Emergency Management*, v.8/1 (2010).

Marciani, Lou, et al. *Sport Event Risk Management.* Washington, DC: U.S. Department of Homeland Security, 2009.

Stevens, Andy. "Sports Security and Safety: Evolving Strategies for a Changing World." London: Sport Business Group, 2007.

Convention and Visitors Bureaus

The involvement of the convention and visitors bureau (CVB) in the promotion of sports is as American as the old ball game. The mission of the CVB is to bring visitors to town, and they do that in part by marketing, advertising, and selling their community's sports and sporting facilities. Travel and tourism is big business and makes the work of the CVB very significant to sports in the community. Although many CVBs are part of chambers of commerce, their goals and methods are different. Their funding is strictly regulated, and they are usually evaluated by how many people they help bring into local hotels or motels.

Definition and Impact

CVBs are sometimes called destination marketing organizations (DMOs) or tourism boards. Some cities call them visitors and convention bureaus, or VCBs. Whatever they are called, they promote the long-term development and marketing of a destination, focusing on convention sales, tourism marketing, and service. CVB employees may put together campaigns marketing an entire destination to meeting professionals, business travelers, tour operators, and individual visitors. They represent the hotels, facilities, attractions, restaurants, and other providers serving travelers.

Primarily, convention and visitors bureaus are predicated on the assumption that travel and tourism enhance the quality of life for a local community by providing jobs, bringing in tax dollars for improvement of services and infrastructure, and attracting facilities like restaurants, shops, festivals, and cultural and sporting venues that cater to both visitors and locals.

Travel and tourism is one of the world's largest service exports and largest employers. In the United States, travel and tourism is the third biggest retail sales sector. In 2009, the U.S. travel industry received $704.4 billion from domestic and international travelers, not including international passenger fares. These travel expenditures directly generated more than 7.4 million jobs with $186.3 billion in payroll income for Americans, as well as $113 billion in tax revenue for federal, state, and local governments. International visitors spent $121.1 billion traveling in the United States in 2009, including international passenger fares.

CVB Services

Typically, a convention and visitors bureau provides information about a destination's lodging, dining, attractions, events, museums, arts and culture, history, and recreation.

Some even provide bus services, insider tips, top-10 attraction and activity lists, blogs, photos, forums, free things to do, season-specific activity suggestions, and more. The CVB works with tourists and meeting planners to provide valuable information on their local area.

Their goal is to help make a visitor's trip or a conference attendee's meeting a much more enjoyable and rewarding experience. In many locations, the CVB works closely with a convention center that will offer spaces for larger meetings, trade shows, and conventions than can be accommodated in a single hotel. Usually, these organizations also have a local office where one can find maps, brochures, travel professionals, local insight, visitors guides, souvenirs, and more. The CVB can provide the following:

- Assist in creating collateral material
- Assist with on-site logistics and registration
- Provide housing bureau services
- Develop pre- and post-conference activities, spouse tours, and special events
- Assist with site inspections and familiarization tours, as well as site selection
- Provide speakers and local educational opportunities
- Help secure special venues
- Assist in coordinating local transportation

Chamber of Commerce

Although some chambers of commerce and CVBs share office space or staff, they are not the same. There are approximately 7,000 chambers of commerce and 4,000 CVBs listed in the U.S. Directory of Chambers and Visitors Bureaus. The larger the city, the more likely the CVB is separate from the chamber and has its own staff, board, and volunteers.

The U.S. Chamber of Commerce is the world's largest business federation, representing the interests of more than 3 million businesses of all sizes, sectors, and regions, as well as state and local chambers, and industry associations. Chambers represent the interests of local businesses that may or may not include tourism. CVBs focus primarily on events or activities that bring people into town. The job of the CVB is generating "heads in beds," or people sleeping in hotel rooms. The CVBs are primarily funded by a percentage of their community's hotel-motel tax. This local tax is often in addition to a state hotel occupancy tax.

In Texas, for example, there is a 6 percent state hotel-motel occupancy tax on the amount visitors pay for a hotel room. The Texas comptroller of public accounts reported that in 2008 tourism in the state generated more than $60 billion in direct spending, $2.9 billion in state revenue, and employed more than 544,000 Texans. The sports industry helps put those heads in beds, fueling state hotel occupancy tax collections, which pumped $371 million into the state's general revenue fund in 2008. Another $548 million was generated in local hotel tax receipts that helped communities promote tourism, build facilities, and generate economic development.

Cities and counties also can each levy taxes of up to 7 percent of the cost of a hotel room, meaning some hotels will have a state, a county, and a city tax added to the cost of a room. Local voters must approve each city tax; more than 500 Texas cities levy a city hotel occupancy tax. The rules are different for counties. Typically, the legislature must pass a law allowing a county to collect the tax. Once the legislation is in place, county commissioners must approve the tax; voter approval is not required.

In Texas, a two-step process governs how hotel tax revenues may be used to promote a local area. First, funded projects, whether for convention centers, sporting arenas, or drag-boat races, must bring in overnight visitors. Next, projects must fit into one of the six following categories

- Site acquisition for convention and/or visitor centers
- Convention registration
- Advertising the city or county

- Promotion of the arts
- Historical preservation and restoration projects
- Sporting events in a county with a population of less than 1 million

Other Regions

In 2010, Wisconsin Gov. Jim Doyle said that tourism was Wisconsin's third largest industry. Paul Upchurch, president and CEO of VISIT Milwaukee, and a member of the Governor's Council on Tourism, said, "Tourism makes a significant impact on the quality of life we enjoy here. It brings billions of dollars into our state and supports tens of thousands of jobs statewide." The Council on Tourism consists of 20 members representing the diversity of Wisconsin's tourism industry. The board advises the Department of Tourism on how to best promote Wisconsin's various attractions and grow the state's economy.

VISIT Milwaukee markets greater Milwaukee to tourists and convention and meeting planners nationally and internationally; it has more than 600 members, including hotels/motels, restaurants, attractions, services, and area businesses. Tourism generated $2.3 billion in spending in greater Milwaukee in 2009, and supported about 58,000 local jobs.

Tucson, Arizona's sports staff is a good example of how CVBs work with sports management and marketing. Two staff people are dedicated to providing information about Tucson's sports facilities and figuring out how Tucson relates to specific competition needs. They provide the assistance to help find a facility that meets the needs of the tournament or competition, and they provide site inspection itineraries for sports event planners. Their free planning services include a sports facility selection counsel, marketing and publicity counsel, and itineraries for exploring Tucson. They will supply people searching for a sports event, tournament, or conference a free Tucson destination planning guide, a presentation video, an interactive CD, an event planning notebook, promotional materials, a media kit, local contact list, official Tucson lure brochures, postcards, brochure shells, downloadable Tucson images, Tucson logo merchandise, and on-site services and literature.

A promotion by the St. Louis Convention & Visitor's Commission (CVC), which operates the region's largest venue, America's Center, illustrates how the organization markets sports. Two promotions linked to Major League Baseball's All-Star Game were designed to lure business from around the country. Qualifying meeting planners who submitted requests for meeting proposals to the CVC were registered for a VIP trip for two to St. Louis, including tickets to the All-Star Game. Separately, the CVC identified key customers whose meetings and events it wanted to host, and invited them to St. Louis for the weekend leading up to the game.

The St. Louis Busch Stadium has a total of 14 venues available to the public, and plans to add features such as fantasy batting practice with a live pitcher, and dinner at home plate or on the warning track.

In Iowa, the Des Moines Area Sports Commission is under the umbrella of the Greater Des Moines Convention and Visitors Bureau. Tiffany Tauscheck, vice president of marketing, said the CVB has a budget of $3 million and spends 25 percent of it on sports marketing. Three full-time employees are dedicated to selling sports events. The CVB's marketing team, made up of six full-time individuals, assists the sports team whenever needed. When sports groups want media/PR support and assistance, the marketing team steps in and offers media contact lists, press release assistance, media pitching assistance, and guidance on how to best work with the media.

The Lexington, Kentucky, CVB has a budget of $5 million. One employee is assigned to work on sports marketing and uses the budget for bid fees, sports facilities, and sporting events. The criteria for CVB involvement is strictly return-on-investment and how many hotel-motel nights will be used.

In Rochester, Minnesota, the CVB and the Amateur Sports Commission are separate entities but share office space, some board members, and a commitment to promoting the city. The sports commission gets approximately 20 percent of the CVB's $1.75 million budget. Brad Jones, executive director of the CVB, said that six years ago the sports commission was unfunded. He said, "When they wanted to do something, they had to go find sponsors, sell ads, or find other ways to raise money to bring in tournaments. It was very difficult. We said to the community, folks, this is tourism. They're bringing in tourism and successful events. We decided to fully fund them. Their production has gone through the roof in terms of room nights, so they have proven how important sports are to Rochester."

Ed Hruska, executive director of the sports commission, said that having many different sports facilities helps market Rochester. The complex at the university includes a sports bubble that is filled from November to May with groups that are generating hotel-motel money. He said the sports commission helps fill girls soccer camps, wrestling, the softball complex, soccer field, baseball fields, and a huge national volleyball center. His group is applying to the city to get a portion of the local sales tax to help build a venue for national lacrosse, which he said is the second-fastest-growing sport in the country. In addition, he said, the commission helps with approximately 50 events a year "from the time we get the bid until they leave town."

On the Battlefront

A battle is beginning at CVBs across the United States as they face off against online travel companies (OTCs) over hotel tax collections they believe are being shortchanged. The Texas comptroller's office said that battle stems from the OTC practice of buying hotel rooms at negotiated discounts from hotel companies, then reselling them at a higher price to the public. Some of the biggest companies in the online travel industry, such as Expedia, Orbitz, and Travelocity, are involved in disputes with taxing authorities and litigation in courts across the country, asserting they are merely providing a nontaxable service and not liable for collecting state or local hotel taxes on the difference between their negotiated price with the hotels and the retail price their customers pay.

Sports is a major factor in putting heads in beds all over the United States, and CVBs are a strong force in maximizing the impact on their communities. Tauscheck expressed what seems to be the feeling of CVB employees across the country when she said, "Sporting events are very important to our community. They boost the local economy, engage locals, and garner strong media coverage—sometimes equating to national media coverage. Sports

bookings account for approximately 45 percent of the business booked by the CVB. Since the Des Moines Area Sports Commission is under the umbrella of the CVB, both work in tandem, creating a stronger, more cohesive effort and voice for Greater Des Moines to visiting groups."

Linda Thorsen Bond
Stephen F. Austin State University

See Also: Community Sports; Creating a Strong Event, Keys to; Economic Climate for Sports; Hospitality, Sport; Marketing of Sports; Sports Tourism.

Further Readings

Desloge, Rick. "St. Louis Venues Willing to Cut Deals to Make Bookings." *St. Louis Business Journal.* http://www.bizjournals.com/stlouis/stories/2009/04/06/focus6.html (Accessed January 2011).

Destination Marketing Association International. "About the Industry." http://www.destinationmarketing.org/page.asp?pid=21 (Accessed January 2011).

Gratton, Chris and Ian Henry. *Sport in the City: the Role of Sport in Economic and Social Regeneration.* London: Routledge, 2001.

Vail, Susan. "Community Development and Sport Participation." *Journal of Sport Management,* v.21/4 (2007).

Cookies

Computer cookies are small files that are placed on computers by Websites; these files store information about the user and his or her site usage. There are two common types of cookies created by Websites. Temporary cookies are bits of information that are stored on your computer and only last the duration of your session; these are erased once you log off the site. On the other hand, permanent cookies are files that have the potential to recognize a user on a site forever. These cookies are what enable you to place an order for tickets on StubHub and not have to re-key needed information to place an order.

Because cookies and the management of cookies can be a strategic tool for many sites, it is important that the most relevant information to the user experience is accumulated. Cookies may help you bookmark a place of your favorite player on NBA.com, or remember your size or style preference when you purchase licensed merchandise from Major League Baseball. Cookies give Website marketers an opportunity to customize the user experience and better target users, thereby increasing the chance that they will return for another visit and stay on the site.

Marketing messages have the potential to be more relevant and timely than they otherwise might be without the information stored in cookie files. Cookies have also been credited with injecting life into the seemingly untargeted display banner ads of the early days of the Internet. There is, however, a potential drawback to cookies; many perceive a fine line between enhanced user experience and invasion of a user's privacy. For this reason, marketers face the challenge created by user controlled cookie functionality. Most modern Web browsers give users the ability to easily disable cookies on their computer or merely erase them on a periodic basis. These challenges may be overcome with transparent privacy policies and incentives for users who at least allow session cookies on their computers.

A very practical application of cookies is in the area of dynamic pricing. Sports memorabilia auction sites (e.g., sportsmemorabilia.com) rely heavily on the ability to dynamically price sports merchandise and collectibles. Other Websites, such as eBay, have for years used cookies to dynamically price items based on their bidding system. Cookies also help to enhance user experiences on e–commerce sites, fantasy sports leagues, and rich media content distribution sites (e.g., MLB.tv). Cookies will continue to play a vital role in enabling marketers to customize user experiences and better target their product and services messages. This is extremely important for sports-related sites, since there is a heavy reliance on content such as sports news and information and game content.

Robert I. Roundtree
University of North Carolina, Charlotte

See Also: Audience Measurement; Internet/Online; Marketing Through Sports.

Further Readings

Laudon, Kenneth and Carol Guercio Traver. *E-Commerce: Business, Technology, Society.* Upper Saddle River, NJ: Pearson Prentice Hall, 2010.
Wertime, Kent and Ian Fenwick. *DigiMarketing: The Essential Guide to New Media & Digital Marketing.* Singapore: John Wiley & Sons Asia, 2008.

Cooperative Advertising

Cooperative advertising, also known as co-op or advertising allowance, is a form of integrated marketing communication where two or more parties support a single advertising effort.

Support can include providing complete ads that can be customized by local retailers, or reimbursing a local advertiser for a portion of the cost of advertising time or space. The primary objective of co-op advertising is to stimulate short-term sales for local suppliers.

Projecting the Brand

Co-op is commonly observed as one of three types. The first type, vertical or upstream co-op, involves a manufacturer or retailer supporting a downstream retailer. A manufacturer of sports apparel, for example, may offer advertising material or financial support to retailers stocking the manufacturer's merchandise. Horizontal co-op is businesses of similar types or with similar objectives pooling advertising funds to support common efforts. Several golf resorts close to one another might create advertising to encourage area golf tourism. Each course will contribute funds to underwrite the expenses of ad production, as well as the advertising time or space costs. Each resort will be featured in the ads.

A third major form of co-op, ingredient producer, is when a supplier of goods or services supports the efforts of retailers or brands using the goods or services. The manufacturer of a fiber used in sports apparel may support the advertising efforts of any sports apparel brands using the fiber.

Co-op advertising offers advantages to the manufacturers and distributors of sports industry goods and services. The manufacturer or distributor is able to control the consistency of the brand's advertising messages. If thousands of local suppliers were producing independent advertising messages for each brand or service, the quality and content of the advertising could vary, or perhaps undermine the brand's national efforts. Preparing completed print advertisements that can be customized for local markets, called ad slicks, protects the brand's image and ensures message consistency.

Brands can also produce and provide broadcast-ready radio and television ads. Brands can provide silent video with suggested scripts that can be customized for local use. Radio scripts can be provided and produced at local stations. Co-op advertising also generates brand support in the distribution channel. When vendors are considering how to allocate limited advertising funds and sales efforts, brands offering generous co-op allowances are likely to receive more effort at retail.

Going Local

Local vendors rely on co-op advertising to support their efforts. Many vendors are small businesses with limited advertising budgets and no expertise at creating or placing advertising. Supplying local vendors with advertising material ready for local media provides many retailers with their only means for media advertising. A golf club manufacturer may provide a local retailer with completed newspaper, radio, and television ads.

The local vendor provides the ads to local media that can customize the ad with phone number, address, vendor names(s), etc. The ad then appears in local media. The local vendor does not need an ad agency or any media expertise to advertise locally. Often, local media will customize the ad at no charge. As part of the co-op agreement, the upstream manufacturer will likely underwrite some portion of the media costs. The local vendor benefits from professional advertisements that might not otherwise be available, as well as stretching the local retailer's

advertising budget. Local media also benefit from co-op programs. Local media often offer different rates to national and local advertisers, with local advertisers receiving lower rates.

A golf club manufacturer advertising directly in a local newspaper may pay the more expensive national rate. If the same manufacturer places the same advertisement in the same paper through a local retailer, less expensive local rates are applied. This advertising arrangement serves the local media, the local vendor, and the national brand. Many media have a co-op manager on staff to help local vendors find co-op support.

Negative Aspects

While cooperative advertising serves all parties in the distribution channel, there are several negative aspects to consider. Many national brands provide ad material to protect the brand's image and ensure consistent presentation. Even when completed ads are provided from the national level, the brand is still subject to local production standards. Print media may not be able reproduce the ad as the brand intends. Local announcers may not deliver the provided script as intended. Local vendors may be required to provide other considerations in return for the co-op support, such as featuring the brand prominently at the retail outlet or merchandising the store with brand posters. A national brand representative may need to visit the vendor to certify compliance.

Co-op providers must provide an equitable system for dispersing co-op benefits. Co-op arrangements should be available to all vendors, unless the brand can prove the support is not being used as intended. Co-op support can be distributed based on the vendor's provable contribution to the brand's efforts and success.

Local vendors using co-op support should expect to prove that the ads appeared as intended. Print media can provide tear sheets, physical copies of the printed advertisement as it appeared, as proof. Broadcast media should provide notarized affidavits along with the media invoice for broadcast time. Tear sheets and affidavits are forwarded to the co-op partner prior to reimbursement.

Lance Kinney
University of Alabama

See Also: Advertising Media; Brand Image; Integrated Marketing Communication; Media Choice.

Further Readings

Mullin, Bernard J., Stephen Hardy, and William A. Sutton. *Sport Marketing.* Champaign, IL: Human Kinetics, 2000.

Pitts, Brenda and David Stotlar. *Fundamentals of Sport Marketing.* Morgantown, WV: Fitness Information Technology, 2007.

Shank, Matthew D. *Sports Marketing: A Strategic Perspective.* Upper Saddle River, NJ: Prentice Hall, 2009.

Copyright Law and Sports

Copyright ownership is an important financial asset in the sports business. Such rights generate billions of dollars in revenues each year—in the United States and around the world. Copyright ownership grants exclusive rights to the author or creator of an original work. These exclusive rights include the right to copy, distribute, and adapt the protected work. There are few exceptions to copyright, such as fair use that does not require permission from the copyright owner. All other uses require permission from the copyright owners, who can license, permanently transfer, or assign their exclusive rights to others. Four major areas of copyright assets in sport are original music, trading cards, broadcasts, and media guides.

Original Music

Music is a pervasive part of sports. Whenever fans enter a sports arena or stadium, they hear music—during warm-ups, during time-outs, or when a baseball player goes to bat. Music is played to get both the fans and the players energized. When the home team is down, music is played to rally the crowd. Each time music is played, the copyright holder receives a royalty.

Broadcast Music Inc. (BMI) tracks performances of songs at National Football League (NFL), National Hockey League (NHL), and Major League Baseball (MLB) events, collects fees from the teams, and distributes royalties to songwriters and composers. One of the most popular rock songs played at sports venues across the country is *We Will Rock You* by British rock group Queen. According to BMI, the NHL's Minnesota Wild and the NFL's Dallas Cowboys played the song the most during one recent season. ESPN devoted an entire series of articles to stadium music, including an article listing the best and worst stadium songs. Among the best are *Celebration* by Kool and the Gang, *Welcome to the Jungle* by Guns N' Roses, and *Glory Days* by Bruce Springsteen.

Trading Cards

Sports trading cards, typically with player statistics and photos, have been around for more than 100 years. Today, although many sports cards are still collected and swapped by young people, they are also a big part of the commercial market for collectibles. The Honus Wagner T206 trading card is the most valuable and the most famous baseball card in existence; in late 2007, a private collector acquired one of the existing cards for nearly $3 million.

In the legal case *Cardtoons, L.C. v. Major League Baseball Players Assoc.*, the plaintiffs had contracted with a sports artist, a sports author, and a political cartoonist to create a set of baseball trading cards. The cards featured recognizable caricatures and narratives about individual players, leaving no doubt as to the identity of the players. The Tenth Circuit noted that the presence of celebrities and athletes in the media was pervasive and was an important part of public vocabulary. Cardtoons had added a significant creative component to its cards and created an entirely new product.

An athlete's statistics are not deemed to be an original creative compilation. The numbers are readily found in newspapers, on the Internet, and on television. The statistics in a box score are not copyrightable facts.

Broadcast Rights

The telecasts and broadcasts of sporting events are presented under agreements among television and radio networks, Internet companies, and other parties whereby video and/or audio are presented to an audience. During each event, one of the announcers reads a copyright statement asserting the rights of the holders. For many sports leagues, especially the National Football League, broadcast rights generate an impressive stream of revenue. The NFL's television partners include CBS, Fox, NBC, and ESPN. Given its powerful position, the NFL imposes significant restrictions on the terms of broadcasts, and has often pitted networks against one another in bidding.

In the NFL, each of the 32 teams gets an equal share of the broadcast revenue that is generated through the national contracts; these contracts generate the vast majority of broadcast revenues for teams. Local radio rights are owned by the football teams. On the other hand, even though Major League Baseball has national television contracts with Fox, ESPN, and TBS, these contracts account for a much smaller share of broadcast revenues. This is because of teams owning the rights to televise the games not shown nationally, through a local contract or their own networks. The most lucrative team network is the Yankee Entertainment and Sports (YES) Network.

As a result of his golfing accomplishments, Tiger Woods has global endorsement deals with Nike and many other firms. Nike could not have asked for better publicity than his shot at the 2005 Masters Tournament. As Woods's ball rolled within inches of the 16th hole, it slowed down and essentially gave Nike a free 17-second advertisement that reached 15 million viewers. Woods went on to win the Masters, leading to a new Nike advertising campaign. Since the Masters owned the rights to the video, Nike had to negotiate to show the clip in subsequent commercials.

A video highlighting an Alex Rodriguez home run would be copyrightable material. But the fact that Rodriguez hit a home run is just that—a fact. Similarly, a video showing Peyton Manning throwing a touchdown pass may be copyrighted by the NFL. But the fact that Manning threw the touchdown with 7:32 left in the fourth quarter to make the score 35–17 is not a statistic for which the NFL may claim ownership.

In *Motorola v. NBA*, the National Basketball Association (NBA) sued Motorola for its statistics service that transmitted live NBA scores to paid subscribers of a special Motorola pager. Motorola created a handheld pager called SportsTrax for the purpose of transmitting real-time information of professional basketball games. At the district court level, Motorola was enjoined from being able to transmit the data from games in progress. The pagers provided the following information to Motorola subscribers: teams playing, team in possession of ball, score changes, free throws, what quarter the game was in, and how much time remained in each quarter. The information was keyed into a computer by SportsTrax workers who watched the game on television or listened to it on the radio, meaning the information was not quite real time. The NBA claimed Motorola infringed on its copyright in the transmission of NBA data. The appellate court, however, said that the underlying basketball games do not fall within the subject matter of federal copyright because they do not constitute original works of authorship. Further, the Second Circuit held that Motorola did not infringe any NBA copyright because it was only the facts of the games, not the broadcasts, that were reproduced.

Media Guides

Sports leagues and teams typically print a variety of materials: media guides, scorecards, yearbooks, and player photos. In the past, media guides were prepared mostly to help market the leagues and teams by including a history of the team or league, team rosters, team and player statistics, human interest stories, community relations activities, and photos. The guides were freely distributed to reporters and others who covered the sport. Today, even media guides are a big business, and they are sold to fans in a glossy format. As with any publication, the look and design of the media guides, scorecards, etc., and the stories and photos in them are protected by copyright. Individual facts gleaned from these works are not.

At sporting venues across the country, fans follow games on scorecards sold at the stadium. Any fan in attendance at a game can record statistics. The same is true for a fan watching the game from home. The manner in which fantasy sports companies use player names and statistics involves purely factual information that any patron of a baseball game could acquire from watching or reading the newspaper. These sites are not duplicating a copyrighted game broadcast but instead utilizing the facts that result from playing baseball (or football).

Copyright and the Web

Because Websites such as YouTube are still relatively new, the courts have yet to address most issues regarding the misappropriation of copyrights on the Internet. However, as the United States and other countries around the world continue moving toward greater reliance on the Internet as a mode of communication, it will not be too long before the courts are asked to address the issue of imposter profiles and illegally uploaded, copyrighted videos—among many other intellectual property issues.

It will be up to the media, sports firms, and celebrities themselves to decide if they will fight the "Internet monster" or embrace it. From a practical point of view, it would often make sense to go the route of the NBA, NHL, and others to together control the content available to the public. Additionally, with the global reach of the Internet, it will be nearly impossible to legally regulate every Website that comes out. The jurisdiction of the U.S. courts only reaches so far—there is not much the courts can do to prosecute foreign defendants.

Stacey B. Evans
American Conference Institute
Joel R. Evans
Hofstra University

See Also: Broadcast Rights; Intellectual Property; Fantasy Sports; Legal Considerations in Sport; Links to Other Websites.

Further Readings

Gardiner, Simon, Richard Parrish, and Robert Siekmann. *EU, Sport, Law and Policy*. The Hague, Netherlands: Asser Press, 2009.

Neel, Eric. "Sweet (and Sour) Stadium Songs." ESPN.com. (July 28, 2004) http://sports.espn.go.com/espn/page3/story?page=neel/040727. (Accessed January 2011).

Spengler, John, Paul Anderson, Daniel Connaughton, and Thomas Baker. *Introduction to Sport Law*. Champaign, IL: Human Kinetics, 2010.

Copyright Versus Trademark

A copyright is a form of intellectual property that gives the author of an original work an exclusive right for a certain time period. Works not fixed in a tangible form of expression are ineligible for copyright protection. A copyright does not last indefinitely, with its term varying by state. There are also federal rules.

A copyright grants its owner several exclusive rights: (1) to import or export the work, (2) to produce copies or reproductions of the work and sell those copies for profit, (3) to create derivative works, (4) to display the work publicly, (5) to license or sell the rights to others, and (6) to broadcast the creation.

Exceptions to copyright law are made when a new work is of a transformative nature or uses only a small portion of the copyrighted work. In other instances, the limitation takes the form of a "compulsory license," under which certain limited uses of copyrighted works are permitted upon payment of specified royalties and compliance with statutory conditions.

A trademark protects words, phrases, symbols, or designs identifying the source of the goods or services of one party and distinguishing them from those of others. Trademark infringement involves a violation of the exclusive rights attaching to a trademark without authorization by the owner. Infringement may occur when one party uses a trademark that is identical or confusingly similar to one owned by another party in relation to goods or services that are identical or similar to those that the registration covers. Trademark use is likely fair when a product cannot be effectively identified without use of the trademark or when there is no other effective way to compare, criticize, refer to or identify it.

Copyrights and Sports

The Internet is rapidly advancing sports technology, while simultaneously sparking copyright infringement issues. Websites such as Yahoo!, CBS Sportsline, and ESPN have used real-time gamecasts to transmit copyrighted information (and profit from it) without a license. Las Vegas hotels broadcasting the Super Bowl in 7,000-seat venues were found to be in violation of the NFL's telecast copyright. Sports videogames have used popular music without the permission of the copyright holder. A search on the popular video sharing site YouTube can direct a fan to numerous video and photo montages on virtually any sport or athlete. Each video receives a few thousand to a few million views.

In 1998, Congress passed the Digital Millennium Copyright Act. As long as Internet service providers comply with procedures for removing copyrighted content posted by users, providers do not suffer monetary penalties for infringement. The National Basketball Association (NBA) was the first professional sports league to partner with YouTube, in creating the NBA channel.

Professional sports leagues and teams, as well as individual athletes, have logos and other images to protect. Marks such as the NBA silhouette of Jerry West, the blue color used by the University of North Carolina Tarheels, and the National Football League (NFL) logo are trademarked. Popular micro blogging site Twitter was the source of a lawsuit by St. Louis Cardinals manager Tony LaRussa. A fake Twitter page was created under his name and he sued the site for trademark infringement, trademark dilution, and misappropriation of name and likeness over unauthorized statements made under his name. LaRussa later settled the suit.

Stacey B. Evans
American Conference Institute
Joel R. Evans
Hofstra University

See Also: Brand Protection; Copyright Law and Sports; Intellectual Property; Strategic Brand Communications.

Further Readings

Associated Press. "LaRussa Drops Suit Against Twitter." ESPN.com. (July 7, 2009) http://sports .espn.go.com/mlb/news/story?id=4311197 (Accessed January 2011).
Lynch, Matt. "What's Mine Isn't Yours: Sports, Copyright and YouTube." *Medill Reports* (July 9, 2007) http://news.medill.northwestern .edu/chicago/news.aspx?id=40539 (Accessed January 2011).
Spengler, John, Paul Anderson, Daniel Connaughton, and Thomas Baker. *Introduction to Sport Law.* Champaign, IL: Human Kinetics, 2010.
United States Copyright Office. "Copyright Basics." http://www.copyright.gov/circs/circ1.pdf (Accessed January 2011).

Core Product

Marketers must first define what the core benefits the product will provide the customer; these core benefits are also often called the core product. A product's main reason for existence is called its core benefit. It is the simplest possible answer to an expressed need: the benefit the customer receives from using the product. In some cases these core benefits are offered by the product itself, for example, liquid soap, while in others the benefit is offered by other attributes of the product, for example, the bottle of liquid soap has a measure for portions. At the very root of product development are decisions to determine what core benefits a product will provide. From this decision, the rest of the product offering can be developed.

Development of the Theory

In the 1960s, the economist Philip Kotler changed the perception of marketing. He was the first to describe marketing in terms of what it is, rather than what marketers do. This began to change the perception of marketing from a departmental specialization into a corporate doctrine, namely that the customer is central to the success of a firm and that marketing is charged with understanding customers and communicating what this means internally to an organization.

Kotler was among the first to see marketing as a "social process by which individuals and groups obtain what they need and want through creating and exchanging products and value with others."

This attitude is important, as it led to thoughts on products and what a product really is.

Kotler was instrumental in the evolution of marketing thought, in viewing a product as more than just its physicality. A product is anything that can be offered to a market for attention, acquisition, or use, or something that can satisfy a need or want. Therefore, a product can be a physical good, a service, a retail store, a person, an organization, a place, or even an idea. Products are the means to an end wherein the end is the satisfaction of customer needs or wants. Kotler distinguished the following three components:

- *Need.* A lack of a basic requirement
- *Want.* A specific requirement for products or services to match a need
- *Demand.* A set of wants plus the desire and ability to pay for the exchange.

Customers will choose a product based on their perceived value of it. Satisfaction is the degree to which the actual use of a product matches the perceived value at the time of the purchase. A customer is satisfied only if the actual value is the same or exceeds the perceived value. Kotler defined five levels to a product:

- *Core benefit.* The fundamental need or want that consumers satisfy by consuming the product or service
- *Generic product.* A version of the product containing only those attributes or characteristics absolutely necessary for it to function
- *Expected product.* The set of attributes or characteristics that buyers normally expect and agree to when they purchase a product
- *Augmented product.* Inclusion of additional features, benefits, attributes, or related services that serve to differentiate the product from its competitors
- *Potential product.* All the augmentations and transformations a product might undergo in the future

Kotler noted that much competition takes place at the Augmented Product level rather than at the Core Benefit level or, as Levitt put it: "New competition is not between what companies produce in their factories, but between what they add to their factory output in the form of packaging, services, advertising, customer advice, financing, delivery arrangements, warehousing, and other things that people value."

Kotler's model provides a tool to assess how the organization and its customers view their relationship, and which aspects create value. This development is sometimes called Total Product Concept.

Alternative Definition

Within the model known as Resource-Based View of the Firm, Core Products are a company's products that are most directly related to their core competencies. These products are then integrated into a variety of end products, either by the company holding the core product or by a second company to which the core product is sold, and the end products are sold to users.

Such products are also termed Flagship Products in some texts. In general, these products sustain the cash flow and profitability of the organization, and in some cases may be the products the organization was originally founded around. Some conglomerates are now said to have several Core Products and refer to them as a Core Product Portfolio (CPP); this clearly has overlap to portfolio management in product marketing concepts.

Andrew J. Whalley
Royal Holloway University of London

See Also: Congruency of Product and Target Market; Marketing Objective; Product Line; Total Product Concept.

Further Readings

Baines, Paul, Chris Fill, and Kelly Page. *Marketing.* Oxford, UK: Oxford University Press, 2008.
Kotler, Philip. *Marketing Management—Analysis, Planning, Implementation, and Control.* Upper Saddle River, NJ: Prentice Hall International, 1997.
McDonald, Malcolm. *Marketing Plans—How to Prepare Them, How to Use Them.* Oxford, UK: Elsevier Limited, 2007.

Corporate Criteria for Sponsor Evaluation

Increased numbers of sport teams and events have increased the competition for sponsors. On top of this, the economic downturn in recent years has made the solicitation of sponsors even more competitive. From a potential sponsor's perspective, the increased number of received sponsorship proposals calls for some kind of evaluation criteria to select the best sponsorship opportunity that can help achieve a company's marketing objectives, fits its budget, and can possibly yield the highest return on investment.

Having sponsorship evaluation criteria and screening processes helps in selecting appropriate proposals from among the many received proposals. The evaluation criteria should be company-specific, reflecting a company's vision and goals, future direction, and representing its product/services in a good manner. In summary, screening criteria for sponsorship should help weed out many inadequate proposals and select the best sponsorship opportunity that can fulfill a company's marketing objectives and deliver maximum benefits. A few criteria that can be used in sponsorship evaluation follow:

- *Market fit.* In selecting sponsorship, target market fit between the company's target consumers and the audience of the potential sport organization/event/activity is very important. Sponsorship provides an opportunity for the sponsor to be exposed to its audience, and ideally the exposure to the audience eventually should result in increased sales of the company's goods or services in the future. If there is no fit between the target markets, there will be no tangible benefits derived from the sponsorship. In that sense, market fit is the most important consideration point in sponsorship evaluation. The target market fit could range from demographic to lifestyle of the target audience. In addition, geographic market fit should also be considered. Companies should decide whether they want to sponsor a sport event or organization that has international, national, regional, or local coverage, depending on the distribution scope of their products or services.

- *Image fit.* Sponsoring companies and sponsored entities have their unique images, and companies want to see a certain kind of image fit in evaluating the potential sponsorship opportunities. For example, high-end product companies like Mercedes-Benz or Rolex sponsoring tennis, golf, or high-brow art is considered more appropriate than sponsoring X-Games, because the projected images are congruent. Image congruency is also an important determinant in sponsorship effectiveness. Unless a company wants to change to a new image from an existing image, companies should look for a sport entity that carries a congruent image.

- *Higher return on investment (ROI).* As the expenditure on sponsorship keeps increasing, justifying the expenditure on sponsorship is getting more important. Potential sponsors should select a sponsorship opportunity that can yield higher ROI compared to other sponsorships when other conditions are same. Although there is no definite measurement of sponsorship effectiveness and ROI, information such as increase in sales could serve as an indicator for ROI. Because every company operates with a limited amount of resources, using company resources effectively and efficiently is an important issue.

- *Media coverage of target audience.* The ability to provide exposure to sponsors is an important determinant in a sponsorship evaluation. There are two kinds of exposure: exposure to on-site people including participants and fans onsite, and exposure to audience via media coverage. Therefore, whether a potential sport event has a sizable number participants or fans is something to be considered. However, whether a potential event/game has good media coverage or not is often the more important factor in sponsorship selection. Media coverage makes it possible for sponsors to reach millions of people around the world, in the case of mega events. For example, a record 4.7 billion viewers are reported to have watched the 2008 Beijing

Exposure to an audience via media coverage can be an important determinant in a sponsorship evaluation. Sponsors of the 2008 Beijing Summer Olympics gained access to a record 4.7 billion viewers of the TV broadcasts.

Olympics on TV; Olympics sponsors enjoyed extensive exposure to this audience. Granted that the viewers can be potential buyers of a company's products or services, the media coverage has a significant meaning for sponsors. Sometimes, companies calculate the cost per number of people that can be reached via media exposure. If a company can reach more people per dollar, the sponsorship opportunity might be considered more attractive.

• *Sponsorship cost.* If a company can find a potential sponsorship proposal that could fit all of the evaluation criteria mentioned above, that would be outstanding. However, if the rights fee attached to sponsorship is too high for a company's budget, it would be monetarily impossible for that company to be a sponsor of that particular event. The bigger and more prestigious the event, the higher the price tag for sponsorship rights fees. When it comes to budget, a company should consider not only

sponsorship rights fee it need to pay but also activation fees, to leverage the sponsorship rights once the company becomes a sponsor. Since a company cannot reap sponsorship benefits without activating the purchased sponsorship rights, reserving enough funds to activate sponsorship is fundamental for the success of sponsorship. The overall sponsorship involvement cost should fit a company's budget.

Conclusion

Other than the sponsorship evaluation criteria mentioned above, companies should also look into the potential sport organization and event to determine whether it has a good reputation for honoring obligations stated on the contracts, and whether it has a proven track record of successfully organizing an event with competent staff. In addition, provided sponsor benefits such as free tickets or fan meeting opportunities should be attractive, and fit the marketing objectives of a company. Sponsors can also consider whether cross-promotion opportunities with other participating sponsors are provided or not. Lastly, sponsorship evaluation provided by sponsored entities after an event might be considered in the decision. Sponsored entities should make sure to provide some kind of evidence of sponsorship effectiveness, in order to develop a successful sponsor relationship and to retain their current sponsors for future events.

Cindy Lee
West Virginia University

See Also: Benefits for Sponsors; Image; Official Sponsor; Sponsorship Evaluation Considerations.

Further Readings

Gwinner, Kevin P. and John Eaton. "Building Brand Image Through Event Sponsorship: The Role of Image Transfer." *Journal of Advertising,* v.28/4 (1999).
Howard, Dennis R. and John L. Crompton. *Financing Sport.* Morgantown, WV: Fitness Information Technology, 2004.
Shank, Matthew D. *Sports Marketing: A Strategic Perspective,* 4th Ed. Upper Saddle River, NJ: Prentice Hall, 2008.

Corporate Public Relations, Marketing Public Relations

Every athletic contest needs teams, coaches, a venue, officials, and one more thing: an audience. Athletics in our modern society is a form of popular entertainment, and most contests are intended to be enjoyed by hundreds, thousands, even millions of attendees and viewers. Public relations is an essential tool both for presenting an organization's identity and for marketing that organization's product or service, including an athletic team. Every organization that seeks to win the public's support must take care of its relations with that public. Public relations is the careful and intentional cultivation of goodwill. Marketing is stimulating purchasing decisions. The two processes complement one another; both are necessary for organizational success.

When one markets a product or service to the public there are many things to know. Research must be conducted to determine the wants of potential customers. Competitors must be identified and analyzed, to understand what the consumer's options are and the comparative advantages of your product/service defined. These advantages are part of the process of "positioning," that is, presenting a unique proposition that makes your product/service especially attractive. For example, a clever marketer defined a cold remedy as "the nighttime pain reliever," thus giving that product a point of contrast compared to all other cold remedies. These steps are all part of "inbound" marketing strategies that a company undertakes prior to jumping into the market. Once these decisions are made, the "outbound" process begins, including advertising, promotions, public relations, and sales.

While marketing focuses on "moving the merchandise," public relations aims to create and maintain a positive public image for the organization. The premise is that a product or service can be desirable in itself, but needs the further confirmation that it is offered by a worthwhile organization. Public relations aims to help the public understand the company and its products, often through messages propagated through the media. This understanding can also be promoted as executives join networks where individual and company credibility can be demonstrated.

The corporate Website is another resource for attracting investor and media attention. It should explain the corporate structure, introduce officials, recount the firm's history and growth, and explain company products and services. The goal is to demonstrate and confirm the organization's expertise in its specialties. When circumstances warrant, executives can craft articles to be published on the firm's Website or submitted to authoritative Internet sites. In the latter case, the firm should be sure to build a link from its site to the posting site, to maximize public attention to the message.

Campaigns and Media

Corporate public relations wants to win over customers, but also should attract investors, convince potential employees, placate government officials, and increase public awareness of the company and its products/services—leaving them all with a positive impression of the firm. The ultimate target of the process is creating and maintaining a stainless corporate reputation. Building this sort of public record takes time, and it can be tainted with one product recall, one oil spill, or one airplane crash. The subspecialty of crisis communication is intended to anticipate, and immediately to counter, negative developments that can damage corporate reputation.

Campaigns, whether focused on marketing or public relations, are organized efforts to advance the interests of the firm: in marketing, the goal is increased sales; in public relations, the aim is to burnish a reputation. Any campaign begins with creating an outline and brainstorming to develop a sense of its target. Greater awareness, whether of a specific product/service or of an organization, is the ultimate target of any campaign.

Such campaigns usually involve messages sent through the media. Strategists must decide to focus on local, regional, national, or international media outlets. The media can include newspapers, magazines, radio, television, and Internet outlets. The challenge for any campaign message is to identify why the media outlet would choose to air the company's message; the news media operate in the public interest, not the corporate interest, so finding a news "hook" is a challenge. One particular strategy to create this "hook" is to connect to current news stories and thus serve the media's interest. When the firm offers expert advice or editorial perspective on a topic of public interest, the public and the media are likely to respond favorably. Alternatively, the organization should be certain to make itself easy to find by optimizing its presence on Internet search engines through careful word choices. It is also possible to promote the firm's Web offerings by using a two-line entry with pay-per-click marketing on select search engines.

There are some concerns within the field of public relations that are worthy of attention. In some quarters, the profession and the practice are not held in high esteem. Some accuse the field of promoting "spin," rooted in the notion that truth is relative or "truth is a liquid." Another criticism is of "astroturfing," where industry funds opposition supposedly coming from the public. These front groups serve corporate interests without revealing the source of their staffing and funding.

The Public Relations Society of America (PRSA) is a professional association and credentialing body of 21,000 PR practitioners in the United States. Its code of ethics is touted and intended to counteract concerns about the ethical standards applied in the field. Unfortunately, that code has been designed to emphasize its symbolic value and diminish its deterrent value; observers note that only one member has been sanctioned under it, and that action came after the individual had been convicted of a felony.

John Todd Llewellyn
Wake Forest University

See Also: Competencies; Crisis Management; Positioning; Public Relations.

Further Readings

Heath, Robert L. and Michael J. Palenchar. *Strategic Issues Management: Organizations and Public Policy Challenges.* Thousand Oaks, CA: Sage, 2009.

Sumpter, Randy and James Tankard. "The Spin Doctor: An Alternative Model of Public Relations." *Public Relations Review,* v.20/1 (1994).

Ulmer, Robert R., Timothy L. Sellnow, and Matthew W. Seeger. *Effective Crisis Communication: Moving From Crisis to Opportunity.* Thousand Oaks, CA: Sage, 2009.

Corporate Sponsorship Philosophy

A corporate sponsorship philosophy defines a firm's perspective or view of its participation as a sport sponsor, including the role of sponsorship in the firm's strategy, desired outcomes, and broad boundary-setting guidelines. It is therefore similar in many ways to the sponsorship mission of a firm or the set of principles or high-level policies that guide the sponsorship decisions made by the firm. In this way, the sponsorship philosophy can be viewed as a touchstone or mantra that employees can refer to when faced with choices about which athlete, team, event, stadium, or sporting federation to sponsor, and how to activate or leverage that sponsorship. Within sports management and marketing, corporate sponsorship philosophy is of most relevance to firms that market their offerings through sport sponsorship.

Connecting to Values

Globally, a number of firms have successfully used a well-considered and clearly articulated sponsorship philosophy to guide both internal decision makers and external sponsorship applicants, as well as to differentiate their sport sponsorship activities from category competitors. In Africa, for example, financial services business Nedbank has articulated their sponsorship philosophy in terms of body, mind, and spirit, referring to its investments in sport, art, and the environment. Its sport sponsorships include golf, athletics, and soccer, and its philosophy strongly states the company's belief in the role of sponsorship in translating into bottom line business results, as a tool to sell goods and services.

Meanwhile in Asia, automotive manufacturer Lexus has viewed sponsorship as a brand strategy where support is offered in return for the right to use the sport asset to promote its brand, products, or services. The company's sponsorship philosophy flows from a stated vision to support organizations, events, and causes with a "human purpose." These guidelines, which include eligibility criteria such as not discriminating against minority community groups, result in Lexus sponsorship of rugby union, tennis, and Australian rules football.

Similarly in Europe, financial services businesses Credit-Suisse and ABN Amro Neuflize OBC express their sponsorship philosophies in terms of the fit or alignment between their corporate brand values and the brand or image of the sporting property. For the Swiss-based bank that sponsors soccer, golf, and equestrian sports, the philosophy is one

of long-term collaboration that involves much more than just financial support.

These examples point to an evolution in sport sponsorship philosophy from an overriding belief in the philanthropy or hobby motive, where the purpose may have been disconnected from the business, to a more "hard-nosed" and rational economic returns purpose. Research in China running up to the 2008 Beijing Summer Olympic Games found that over 65 percent of corporate sponsors viewed their sport sponsorship philosophy as more marketing-centered than philanthropically sport-centered.

Academic reviews of sport sponsorship objectives, which flow from a firm's sponsorship philosophy, suggest that three broad categories of objectives feature most often: media exposure and awareness; brand image associations and meaning; and product or service revenues and volumes. Recent research in the United Kingdom, North America, and Australia found a strong emphasis among sponsoring firms on the first two marketing-related objectives, where the sponsorship philosophies view sport sponsorship as a communications tool, with limited evidence of a more strategic purpose. Studies conducted after the 2004 Athens Summer Olympic Games reported similar findings, suggesting a strong focus on bottom line business results from marketing activities, with a limited strategic role for the sponsorship.

Competitive Advantage

Corporate sponsorship philosophies that view sport sponsorship as a source of competitive advantage have been found to be based on three requirements: the sponsorship must be able to significantly increase the value a customer perceives from the sponsoring firm; the sponsorship must differentiate the sponsoring firm from its competitors in a sustainable way; and the sponsorship must provide the space for exploiting the deal in a number of areas of the business, including products, services, employees, and suppliers.

Nike's investment in Michael Jordan since the early 1990s is one example of how a new sponsorship philosophy can revolutionize the organizational and financial performance of a business. Molson Coors Brewing Company's official beer sponsorship of NASCAR auto racing since 2007, where their category exclusivity provides some differentiation, has the potential to provide such competitive advantage in a relatively high-spend media environment. Coors' sponsorship philosophy was expressed as a combination of customer acquisition priorities and a commitment to promote the sport, thereby also meeting the customer value proposition and sponsorship exploitation requirements for competitive advantage.

Most recently, Procter & Gamble's official sponsorship of the National Football League demonstrates the role of a corporate sponsorship philosophy in driving sponsorship objectives and activations to enhance the return on investment achieved by the firm. The corporate philosophy of innovation, challenging conventions, and reinvention guided the creation of a new "locker room product category" sponsorship for 13 of Procter & Gamble's brands, including Old Spice, Gillette, and Head & Shoulders. This approach to sport sponsorship drove the business objective of encouraging multi-brand consumption and, in the case of Old Spice, has seen a viral video activation catapult it to the number one body wash and deodorant brand.

Michael M. Goldman
University of Pretoria

See Also: Marketing Through Sports; Objectives, Sponsorship; Return on Sponsorship Investment.

Further Readings

Amis, John, Trevor Slack, and Tim Berrett. "Sport Sponsorship as Distinctive Competence." *European Journal of Marketing*, v.33/3,4 (1999).
Chadwick, Simon and Des Thwaits. "Managing Sport Sponsorship Programs: Lessons From a Critical Assessment of English Soccer." *Journal of Advertising Research*, v.45/3 (2005).

Co-Sponsor

A co-sponsor is one amongst other sponsors who provides financial, in kind, pro bono know-how or other resources to a sports event, organization, league, team, or player in exchange for a direct association with the respective entity or activity. Because full-sponsorship situations have become rare, the classification into main sponsor, co-sponsor, and other types of partners is widespread (e.g. Gold sponsor, Silver sponsor, and so on). A main-sponsor can make use of a more exclusive range of tactics to leverage the sponsorship, and may even play an influential role in selecting the number and type of co-sponsors and other official partners, suppliers, and supporters (also sometimes interchangeably called "co-sponsors"). In contrast, co-sponsoring packages may be limited in terms of geographical reach, corporate hospitality opportunities, visibility on screen or on a team's Website, and employing players for corporate advertising.

As with other types of sponsoring, an organization that considers engagement in the sporting environment needs to judge potential advantages and disadvantages of the co-sponsoring situation in alignment with its general marketing objectives and its integrated communications mix. Compared to full and main sponsoring, co-sponsoring might be available for significantly less resources. However, the investment can still be very substantial in the case of prestigious events, for example, the Olympics. Hence, the effectiveness depends on active management of the partnership, proper leveraging of the opportunities arising from the sponsorship, and preferably long-term agreements that allow for strong associations to be developed between the sports entity concerned and the co-sponsor's own brand.

In amateur sports in particular, a range of local/regional co-sponsors and supporters is often fundamentally vital in order to organize, promote, and run a sports event or competition by providing technical equipment, media coverage, manpower, and other resources beyond financial assets.

Securing Exclusivity

Both theoretically and practically, a co-sponsor finds itself in a complex situation, because the awareness, relevance, recognition, and impact of its sponsorship is influenced not only by the sports entity concerned, but also its relative position against other co-sponsors in the same sporting context. For example, while company X holds the naming rights for a stadium, company Y appears on the team jerseys, and company Z on the boards along the playing ground. The Beijing Olympic Games featured 12 International Olympic Committee (IOC) Olympic Partners, with exclusive worldwide marketing rights; 11 Beijing 2008 partners; 10 sponsors; 15 exclusive suppliers; and 17 co-exclusive suppliers, with domestic host country marketing rights—making a total of 65 different commercial sponsors.

The sponsorship literature provides evidence that consumers integrate individual sponsors into a holistic cognitive map that, on the one hand, makes it hard for them to remember particular sports-specific sponsorships, but, on the other hand, helps them to recall a web of sponsors when prompted with names of other (co-)sponsors. Consequently, for co-sponsors in particular, it is important to consider one's relative position within the web of different sponsors, because of the comparatively constrained opportunity to exclusively associate itself with the sports entity concerned.

To avoid distraction and allow individual co-sponsors to harness the sponsorship for competitive advantages, the sponsored entity may grant (or, respectively, co-sponsors may demand) a competition clause or "no-touch agreement." In the case of the Olympics, the FIFA World Cup, and most professional sports leagues, comprehensive contracts have become standard that restrict the number of associated organizations from a particular industry or sector to only one. Beyond negotiating appropriate spaces of exclusivity, the use of additional marketing tactics to leverage the sponsorship helps to mitigate potential disadvantages resulting from the web of multiple sponsors.

Conclusion

As a rule of thumb, the more exclusive a sponsorship, the greater the marketing potential—and, consequently, the more expansive that sponsorship. Too many sponsors, or too many noncongruent or competitive sponsors, weaken the marketing potential and impact for individual co-sponsors. Those potentially unfavorable effects are one reason why it is not unusual for the main sponsor(s) to play a role in selecting co-sponsors.

However, a strategically chosen set of main and co-sponsors and other partners can help to facili-

tate sponsor networking and jointly raise the relevance and reach of the sponsored sports entity over time. In such a scenario, traditional sponsorship may extend into a co-branding activity or co-marketing alliance between organizations, serving as a process to create positive spins-offs (i.e., tangible and intangible resources) that can be shared between all parties.

Tim Breitbarth
University of Otago

See Also: Category Exclusivity; Objectives, Sponsorship; Official Sponsor; Sponsorship; Sponsorship Advantages and Disadvantages.

Further Readings

Hermanns, Arnold and Christian Marwitz. *Sponsoring.* Munich, Germany: Vahlen, 2007.
Mullin, Bernard J., Stephen Hardy, and William A. Sutton. *Sport Marketing*, 3rd Ed. Champaign, IL: Human Kinetics, 2007.
Pitts, Brenda and David Stotlar. *Fundamentals of Sport Marketing*, 3rd Ed. Morgantown, WV: Fitness Information Technology, 2007.

Cost per Click

Cost per click (CPC) is one pricing model in the online advertising world. In this case the advertiser pre-negotiates a fee it will pay upon each click of its ads. This is a lucrative pricing model for Websites that have a strong track record in delivering an advertiser's target customer. CPC allows Websites to better predict its advertising revenue compared to cost per action (CPA), where a site only receives revenue if a user performs a certain action (e.g., makes a purchase, opens an account, etc.). Other common online advertising pricing models include cost per thousand (advertisers pay strictly for impressions), barter (exchange of ad space for something of equal value—desirable product or service), sponsorship (advertiser pays a fixed fee for space on a Website for a specified term), and a hybrid model that combines at least two of the aforementioned advertising pricing models.

Similar to advertising rates charged in traditional media (e.g., television, radio, print), two main components will determine the price charged to reach target consumers: ad supply relative to demand, and the success in delivering coveted consumers. For example, if a site gets 1,000 impressions and has a 2 percent CTR, it will generate 20 click-throughs. Assuming a $10 CPM (cost per thousand impressions), then the cost per click is 50 cents. CPC is often used synonymously with the term *pay per click* (PPC). Generally, PPC indicates payment based on click-throughs, while CPC usually suggests measurement of cost on a per click basis for advertising contracts. Many sports related businesses (Web or offline) engage the PPC model.

Content driven sites such as ESPN.com use PPC as a way to maximize revenue on content readership or viewership. The more compelling the content (news stories, sports highlights), the more active the site is in attracting and keeping target consumers. These highly engaged consumers are very valuable to advertisers who are willing to spend top dollar to get their ads in front of them. Advertisers are the full range of product and services providers (e.g., AllState insurance, Hampton Inn hotels), many of which are similar to advertisers that support television programming on the ESPN family of networks.

These ads may incorporate text, image, and rich video (they may also be the same ads shown on television). The critical issue with CPC advertising is contextual relevance. While it is not required that CPC ads are contextually relevant, totally unrelated ads may look odd and out of place on a site that is context incongruent. Many of these ads are selected and placed on Websites though ad networks such as Google AdSense. Whether one has a business that connects with fans via content, such as ESPN.com written and video modes, or is using sports properties such as PGATour.com to connect their brand (e.g., Pepsi) with fans, CPC advertising may be part of the advertising mix.

Conclusion

Online advertising has developed into a successful business for many sports organizations and brands;

it will continue to grow in scope and importance. CPC advertising will perhaps grow as well.

Robert I. Roundtree
University of North Carolina, Charlotte

See Also: Advertising; Internet/Online; Marketing Mix.

Further Readings

Davis, Harold. *Google Advertising Tools.* Sebastopol, CA: O'Reilly Media, 2006.
Laudon, Kenneth C. and Carol Guercio Traver. *E-Commerce: Business, Technology, Society.* Upper Saddle River, NJ: Pearson Prentice Hall, 2010.

Cost per Thousand

Cost per thousand (abbreviated CPM), refers to the cost of reaching 1,000 potential prospects with advertising media. Media planners assess CPM as an efficiency measure. All other things being equal, if a media vehicle can deliver 1,000 exposures at a lower cost than another vehicle, then the vehicle with the lowest CPM is considered the more efficient of the two.

CPM is a simple calculation requiring the media planner to know the total cost of the advertising space or time, along with the number of prospects the media vehicle reaches. Here is the calculation:

$$CPM = \frac{Cost \ of \ advertising \ time \ or \ space \times 1000}{Number \ of \ prospective \ consumers}$$

As a very simple example, consider this scenario: A media planner is considering ads in a magazine charging $1 million for the advertising space. The magazine's circulation is 12 million people. Using the formula detailed above, the CPM for the magazine can be calculated:

$$CPM = \frac{\$1 \ million \times 1000}{12 \ million \ readers} = \$83.33$$

The calculation tells the media planner that the actual cost of reaching 1,000 prospects with that magazine is $83.33. This CPM can be compared to the CPM calculations for other magazines and the efficiency can be assessed. Planners are likely to prefer media vehicles that offer the most prospects at the lowest prices.

Comparisons and Contrasts

CPM can also be calculated for inter-media comparisons. While the example calculated above is for magazines, the CPM can be calculated for all media vehicles and then compared. An advertiser considering placing ads on a sports television broadcast, a sports radio call-in show, or a sports magazine can calculate the CPM for each media vehicle. The planner might then select the most efficient media vehicle, which is the vehicle delivering 1,000 prospects at the lowest cost (the lowest CPM).

Calculating the CPM as an efficiency measure also allows the media planner to level the playing field between media vehicles charging very different prices for the same advertising availability. Assume that the planner is considering placing an ad in two magazines covering college football. One of the magazines is charging $500 for a full-page, four-color ad. The other magazine is charging $500,000 for a full-page, four-color ad. If only the space costs are considered, then the magazine charging $500 appears to be the best value. However, if the magazine has a small circulation, or if the magazine does not reach the brand's potential consumers, then the CPM could actually be higher for the $500 magazine when compared to the $500,000 magazine. While the absolute cost of the space is much higher for one of the magazines, the CPM for the $500,000 magazine might be much more attractive.

The most vivid example of CPM as a cost efficiency measure is the National Football League's annual championship game, the Super Bowl. Year after year, the Super Bowl is the most expensive advertising opportunity in sports media. Brands consistently pay many millions of dollars for a single ad to appear during the game. Brands airing several commercials during the game can easily spend more than $10 million for this single broadcast. Additionally, many brands produce elaborate, exciting commercials to air only during the Super Bowl.

The combined costs of the advertising time and commercial production are very high. However, advertisers are able to justify this expense when the CPM for the Super Bowl is considered. In most years, the Super Bowl draws the largest viewership of any U.S. television broadcast. Rather than considering the ad time and commercial expenses in terms of absolute costs, the advertiser considers these costs to be spread among many millions of viewers. While the absolute cost of advertising on the Super Bowl is very high, the CPM makes this advertising opportunity appear very efficient. CPM is not only considered for single advertising opportunities, inter-media comparisons, or cross-media comparisons. CPM can also be considered for an entire media schedule. Many marketers advertise their brands in multiple media vehicles. Many marketers are also involved with several sports leagues, so the brand advertises all year. Media planners can compare the CPM for alternative plans. The plan delivering the most prospects at the lowest CPM is considered the most efficient plan. Media planning software will provide these CPM estimates. The planner can adjust the plan to bring the average CPM to an acceptable level.

Lance Kinney
University of Alabama

See Also: Advertising Cost, Determination of; Advertising Media; Media Audience.

Further Readings

Pitts, Brenda and David Stotlar. *Fundamentals of Sport Marketing.* Morgantown, WV: Fitness Information Technology, 2007.
Surmanek, Jim. *Media Planning: A Practical Guide.* Chicago: NTC Business Books, 1995.

Cost–Benefit Analysis

Cost–benefit analysis (CBA) is a process by which business decisions are analyzed. The benefits of a given situation or business-related action are summed and then the costs associated with taking that action are subtracted.

Some consultants or analysts also build the model to put a dollar value on intangible items, such as the benefits and costs associated with living in a certain town. Most analysts will also factor opportunity cost into such equations.

In collegiate and professional sports, CBA is commonly employed as a decision-making tool when it comes to modifying existing facilities or constructing new ones. Prudent managers will conduct a cost–benefit analysis as a means of evaluating all of the potential costs and revenues that may be generated if the project is completed. The outcome of the analysis will determine whether the project is financially feasible, or if another project should be pursued.

In governmental planning and budgeting, the attempt is to measure the social benefits of a proposed project in monetary terms and compare them with its costs. The procedure was first proposed in 1844 by Arsène-Jules-Étienne-Juvénal Dupuit, an engineer. It was not seriously applied until the 1936 U.S. Flood Control Act, which required that the benefits of flood-control projects exceed their costs.

Approaches and Parameters

Two basic approaches for CBA are the ratio approach and the net benefit approach. The ratio approach indicates the amount of benefits (or outcomes) that can be realized per unit expenditure on the investment. The choice between a net benefits approach or a benefit/cost approach for CBA can affect findings. The approach selected may depend upon such factors as whether costs must be limited to a certain level, whether the intent is to maximize the absolute level of benefits, whether the intent is to minimize the cost/benefit ratio regardless of the absolute level of costs, etc. Indeed, under certain circumstances, these two basic approaches may yield different preferences among alternative technologies.

A number of different appraisal parameters can be used in CBA. One commonly used parameter is the Net Present Value (NPV) of the project, which is the difference, in monetary terms, between the discounted sums of the costs and benefits of the project. Thus, the value of all future benefits and costs is calculated, using a specified discount rate to calculate the value of such future amounts in cur-

rent terms. The NPV provides a basis on which to determine whether the return on an investment will be positive or negative, and with which to compare different potential investments.

Another parameter used is the Internal Rate of Return (IRR) and the Pay-Back period. The IRR is that discount rate which, when applied to the future streams of costs and benefits the project produces, will produce an NPV of zero. Conversely, the Pay-Back period is the amount of time it takes for the total net benefits of the project to equal the initial investment. There are problems that exist with the use of both the IRR and the Pay-Back period as appraisal criteria. The IRR, for example, does not differentiate between projects of different sizes and scope, because it looks only at the rate of return on the initial outlay, regardless of the size of the outlay.

Uses and Limitations

Internationally, CBA is used in the decision-making processes for programming and facility development in the Olympics. In addition, some sport economists argue that CBA is preferred over economic impact assessments for large-scale sporting events (e.g., World Cup; Commonwealth Games). In practice, an economic impact study does not yield any argument for the government to subsidize the event. Only a cost–benefit analysis can provide the necessary information. Delhi, India, is mandating the use of CBA as it prepares to bid for the 2020 Olympic Games. Delhi officials argue that CBA helps to provide rationale decision making for the upgrading of the city's infrastructure toward the end of ensuring its sport legacy.

Governmental sports authorities frequently use this technique to analyze the public, economic, and social costs and benefits that may be derived from providing government subsidies for the construction of stadia and arenas. Across Major League Baseball, the National Basketball League, the National Football League, and the National Hockey League, staunch economic analysis including CBA is a compulsory tool.

For example, when the New York Yankees approached city, state, and federal officials about partial financing for their new stadium, one of the critical questions surrounding the funding decisions was the economic and social benefits that would be derived from the project, over and above making the Yankees more competitive.

Despite the utility of CBA, there are limitations to its use. First, not everything can be expressed in monetary terms. Social costs are often difficult to quantify, especially in monetary terms. Second, it is impossible to completely predict every result of a policy decision. In other words, not every factor can be taken into account in the analysis. Also, it is not feasible to assess every risk stemming from decisions beforehand. Third, the fact that the concerns of future generations are not always represented in cost–benefit analyses also makes the process less reliable. Overall, CBA is an excellent decision-making tool that has manifold applications for sport organizations.

Steven N. Waller
University of Tennessee, Knoxville

See Also: Balance Sheet; Data Collection; Economic Impact Study; Management Decision-Making Process.

Further Readings

Andreff, Wladimir and Stefan Szymanski. *Handbook of the Economics of Sport.* Cheltenham, UK: Edgar Elgar Publishing, 2006.

Brayley, Russell E. and Daniel D. McLean. *Financial Resource Management: Sport, Tourism, and Leisure Services.* Champaign, IL: Sagamore Publishing, 2008.

Keésenne, Stefan. "Do We Need an Economic Impact Study or a Cost-Benefit Analysis of a Sports Event?" *European Sport Management Quarterly*, v.5/2 (2005).

Masteralexis, Lisa P., Carol A. Barr, and Mary Hums. *Principles And Practice Of Sport Management.* Sudbury, MA: Jones & Bartlett, 2008.

Santo, Charles, A. *Sport and Public Policy: Social, Political and Economic Perspectives.* Champaign, IL: Human Kinetics, 2010.

Sen, Ronojoy. "Events Like CWG Must Be Based on Cost-Benefit Analysis." *The Economic Times.* (September 7, 2010).

Cost-Plus Pricing

Cost-plus pricing is the simplest pricing method and is very common in the sports industry. Using this approach, the price of a sporting good or service is set by adding a desired profit margin to the total costs of production, distribution, and marketing. The major problem of cost-plus pricing is that it ignores demand and competitor prices. Pricing is far more complicated than simply adding a markup to the costs. The way a sport product is priced will have a dramatic influence on the way consumers perceive its value.

The Pricing Process

Suppose a sporting shoe manufacturer had the following costs and expected sales:

Variable cost	$6
Fixed costs	$600,000
Expected unit sales	50,000

Then the manufacturer's cost per shoe is given by:

Unit Cost = Variable Cost + (Fixed Costs / Unit Sales) = $6 + ($600,000 / 50,000) = $18

The price of the shoe is now calculated by adding the desired profit margin of, let's assume 25 percent, to the unit cost:

Price = Unit Cost (1 − Desired Profit Margin) = $18(1 − 0.25) = $24

The manufacturer would charge dealers $24 and make a profit of $6 per unit.

Shortcomings

The first problem of cost-plus pricing arises from calculating the costs. Whereby the calculation of the variable costs is straightforward as they are clearly identifiable with the good or service, this is not the case for the fixed costs (also known as overhead). Apportionment of the overhead according to the costs-by-cause principle is not unequivocally possible if a firm produces more than one good or service.

The second problem is the classic circularity problem of cost-plus pricing. How can the expected unit sales be forecasted when the price is not yet known? After all, according to economic theory, demand is a function of price. The higher the percentage of overhead, the higher the changes in costs per unit with varying expected unit sales. Decreasing unit sales result in fixed costs being spread over a smaller amount of units. This leads to higher prices, which further decreases demand, which again leads to higher prices. This reasoning illustrates that cost-plus pricing neglects the interdependence between quantity of sales, costs per unit, and price. It works only if the calculated price brings in the expected level of sales.

Third, cost-plus pricing is opposed to the marketing approach of satisfying customer needs, for it neglects the value the sporting goods and services present to the customers. Customers usually do not know and do not care about the costs of a firm. So why should costs come into the pricing equation?

Cost-plus pricing may arrive at a price that is above the value or expected benefits as perceived by customers, relative to competing products. In this case neither expected unit sales nor the desired profit margin are achieved. Any attempt to boost sales usually begins with a cut in prices. However, as the manufacturing costs are already established, the expected profitability can never be reached. If a demand-oriented pricing process like value-based pricing had been used instead, the firm would recognize that cost reductions were necessary beforehand.

If, on the other hand, cost-plus pricing arrives at a price that undermines the perceived value that a sport brand holds in consumer perceptions, a profit making opportunity is being lost.

The Alternatives

A further argument against the use of cost-plus pricing is that it is not necessary, as there are a number of pricing methods that take the market (demand and competitors) into account. While cost-plus pricing is a product-driven process, competitor-based and demand-oriented pricing are market and customer driven. Competitor-based pricing considers that consumers usually compare prices and values of goods and services from different brands. A firm then can decide in which price segment it wishes to compete, and try to adjust the costs accordingly.

Demand-oriented pricing adjusts prices according to the prevailing demand. When demand is strong, prices are raised, and they are lowered when demand is weak. Value-based pricing, as a form of demand-oriented pricing, establishes the value a customer assigns to the product. Afterward the marketer calculates if the company can produce the good or service with costs that allow a reasonable profit margin.

Despite all the arguments against cost-plus pricing, there are circumstances when this approach has to be adopted because there is no other option. This occurs when there is no active market with no standard product, and no reference point for assessment of a market price. The most obvious example would be a unique, one-off sport stadium building contract. Cost-plus pricing can also be adopted when introducing a new cutting-edge product, where there is limited information about the possible value it presents to the customer. Moreover, costs, variable or otherwise, set the floor for the price a company can charge.

Christoph Breuer
Pamela Wicker
German Sport University Cologne

See Also: Demand-Oriented Pricing; Pricing Strategies; Supply/Demand Equilibrium.

Further Readings

Anderson, Carol H. and Julian W. Vincze. *Strategic Marketing Management.* Boston: Houghton Mifflin Company, 2004.

Kotler, Philip and Gary Armstrong. *Principles of Marketing.* Upper Saddle River, NJ: Pearson Education, 2006.

Mullin, Bernard J., Stephen Hardy, and William A. Sutton. *Sport Marketing.* Champaign, IL: Human Kinetics, 2007.

Nagle, Thomas, John Hogan, and Joseph Zale. *The Strategy and Tactics of Pricing.* Upper Saddle River, NJ: Prentice Hall, 2010.

Stewart, Bob. *Sport Funding and Finance.* Oxford, UK: Butterworth-Heinemann, 2007.

Warner, Alan and Chris Goodwin. *Pricing for Long-Term Profitability.* Upper Saddle River, NJ: Pearson Education, 2002.

Counterfeit Detection Program

Venues are subject to two kinds of fraud by counterfeiting, both of which have been made more common by the ease of use of sophisticated computers and printers: counterfeit goods (including both tickets and merchandise), and counterfeit currency (occasionally including checks, but since use of personal checks requires personal identification and contact information, this is an easier problem to remedy through police involvement).

Counterfeit tickets are a regular problem at many sports venues, and in all likelihood some of them are never detected. Increasingly, major events like the BCS, the NCAA Final Four, and the World Series are accompanied by reports of counterfeit tickets being discovered at the gate, sometimes in the possession of innocent fans who traveled a long way to see the game. Tickets sold online through Craigslist, eBay, and other forums, where the purchaser cannot physically see them, run a greater risk of being counterfeit—but counterfeiters have been known to scalp tickets in person outside the venue as well, knowing that by the time the buyer finds out (if they ever do), they will be gone. While the easiest way for a buyer to avoid counterfeit tickets is to purchase directly from the venue, this is of no help when a game sells out. Buying from eBay instead of Craigslist offers some additional safety, in that the persistence of identity on eBay and the use of feedback ratings creates a certain degree of accountability: furthermore, there are means of conflict resolution through both eBay and PayPal. However, this does not help the venue itself.

Document fraud, in the form of counterfeit tickets, illegally manufactured fake credit cards and identification, and identity theft, was one of the fastest-growing crimes of the 1990s as a result of the proliferation of affordable and effective technology. One of the remedies that became more popular is one that should still be employed: the use of special paper with overprint patterns, watermarks, and hidden microtext. Large enough organizations can have the paper custom-made for them, and incorporate the anti-counterfeiting features into an overall design, such as using a hologram sticker, an overprint pattern in the team's colors, a watermark of the team or venue's logo, and so on. The difficulty of reproducing tickets like these prices most small-time counterfeiters out of the running. Even the security paper provided by paper goods companies will prevent many would-be counterfeiters. Of course, ticket-takers must know what to look for, and must be diligent in doing so. Enterprising counterfeiters sometimes try to reuse real tickets, altering them to make them appear to be for a later game, but electronic scanning of barcodes can usually be depended on to prevent this from fooling anyone but the unknowing buyer.

Counterfeit merchandise is a problem for any business that owns a brand or relevant intellectual property, and sports brands are especially prone to it. Counterfeit branded goods may include illegal duplicates of goods that the owner of the brand has licensed to another company—such as team jerseys, T-shirts, and other apparel—or illegal uses of the sports brand to promote an illicit company's goods. In both cases, they can often be found for sale from vendors whose legitimacy may be hard to verify, such as flea markets and swap meets, street vendors, and overseas. But legitimate businesses can also be fooled by unscrupulous wholesalers. A typical way of foiling attempts at passing counterfeit merchandise off as legitimate is the use of branded hologram stickers on legitimate authorized products.

In the case of counterfeit currency, various technological means are the best protection. UV LED devices can scan currency for key identifiers that will detect nearly any counterfeit currency; counterfeit detection pens are not quite as accurate, but are much cheaper and are quick to use.

Bill Kte'pi
Independent Scholar

See Also: Brand Protection; Counterfeit Goods; Internet/Online; Knockoffs; Piracy; Trademark, Registered/Infringement/Protection.

Further Readings

Johns, Adrian. *Piracy: The Intellectual Property Wars From Gutenberg to Gates.* Chicago: University of Chicago Press, 2009.

Paradise, Paul R. *Trademark Counterfeiting, Product Piracy, and the Billion Dollar Threat to the U.S. Economy.* Westport, CT: Quorum Books, 1999.

Zimbalist, Andrew S. *The Bottom Line: Observations and Arguments on the Sports Business.* Philadelphia: Temple University Press, 2006.

U.S. Customs and Border Protection uses this mobile laboratory to detect counterfeit goods at U.S. ports.

Counterfeit Goods

Whether referred to as knockoffs or fakes, counterfeit goods in the marketplace continue to plague economies, businesses, and brands. A well-established product, with significant brand recognition and trust, is ripe for counterfeiters to deceptively pass off as a genuine product. The success of marketing a brand is often contingent on the strength of its trademark or patent, which are used to distinguish a company's products from their competitors. Peddling in counterfeit goods is the infringement of a trademark or patent, and on the brand. The act of counterfeiting can steal the identity of a trademark owner and mislead consumers, but industries and governments well versed in the practices deployed by counterfeiters can help strengthen the marketplace.

The rise in the distribution of counterfeit goods is attributed in part to global demand and the move by domestic companies to outsource manufacturing to developing markets where limited intellectual property laws exist.

Now a $600 billion a year industry, counterfeiting grew significantly after World War II in developing countries that lacked local industry. By the late 1960s, advances in technology and globalization made trademark counterfeiting a serious economic threat to industries that had products with high brand recognition, namely the garment industry, including sporting goods and memorabilia.

Countermeasures

The trade in counterfeit sporting goods and memorabilia is a $6.5 billion business that crosses borders, and has affected the business of professional leagues from the National Football League (NFL) to the Professional Golf Association (PGA). The trade in counterfeit sporting goods has received considerable attention from U.S. Immigration and Customs Enforcement (ICE), the largest investigative arm to play a role in targeting criminal organizations responsible for producing, smuggling, and distributing counterfeit products. ICE works with industry partners and other law enforcement agencies to eradicate the distribution of counterfeit goods. For example, in 2010, working with investigators for the NFL and U.S. Customs and Border Protection (CBP), ICE investigated multiple vendors and seized more than 1,400 counterfeit hats, t-shirts, and jerseys worth approximately $210,000. The seizure of counterfeit goods is typically part of joint investigations by ICE and CBP, which track counterfeit products, manufactured abroad and smuggled through ports in the United States.It has become increasingly difficult for authorities to stop the distribution of counterfeit goods in part because of the growing sophistication of counterfeiters, which also makes it harder for consumers to detect a fake. Knowing what to look for can mean the difference between a superior product and a counterfeit. A common technique used by counterfeiters is to import plain clothing from abroad, attach a brand-name label to the product, and then release the product for sale in another country. However, price is a good indicator and can help to determine whether a product is counterfeit or not. In the example of sports memorabilia, authentic jerseys in retail stores cost $200 to $250 on average. A jersey for $75 is most likely to be a counterfeit. If the price is too good to be true, it oftentimes is.

The clandestine nature of distributing counterfeit goods also makes it difficult for companies to manage their brands. As technology advances and the Internet is used as a tool for global commerce, counterfeit online trading continues to be a growing trend. Counterfeiters are leveraging the anonymity of the Internet to profit from counterfeit sales on online auction sites such as eBay. Counterfeit online trading comprises between 5 and 7 percent of world trade, posing a serious threat to a company's global brand.

Several organizations such as the International AntiCounterfeiting Coalition (IACC), the World Intellectual Property Organization (WIPO), and the International Trademark Association (INTA) continue to lobby for stronger legislation and increase awareness to combat counterfeiting.

Elizabeth Candello
University of Oregon

See Also: Brand Protection; Counterfeit Detection Program; Internet/Online; Knockoffs; Piracy; Trademark, Registered/Infringement/Protection.

Further Readings

International AntiCounterfeiting Coalition. "About Counterfeiting." http://www.iacc.org/about-counterfeiting (Accessed September 2010)

Johns, Adrian. *Piracy: The Intellectual Property Wars From Gutenberg to Gates.* Chicago: The University of Chicago Press, 2009.
Paradise, Paul R. *Trademark Counterfeiting, Product Piracy, and the Billion Dollar Threat to the U.S. Economy.* Westport, CT: Quorum Books, 1999.
Spengler, John, Paul Anderson, Daniel Connaughton, and Thomas Baker. *Introduction to Sport Law.* Champaign, IL: Human Kinetics, 2010.

Coupons

Coupons encourage short-term purchase behavior by offering time-sensitive purchase incentives. Each coupon should be printed with an expiration date after which the coupon becomes invalid and the consumer loses the inventive. While coupons are often used by packaged goods and services marketers, sports marketers can also use coupon strategies to great advantage.

Couponing works best as an adjunct to other integrated marketing communication activities. Mass media advertising can deliver brand information to consumers, such as game times, next opponent, ticket availability, and other event-related information. Advertising can also develop attitudes toward a team or sports event. These feelings could include pride in the local team, a sense of community among fans, or shared antipathy for a hated rival.

However, mass media advertising is less successful at influencing immediate behavior. Consumers often receive ads when it is inconvenient or infeasible to purchase. Fans can be exposed to ads in print media, on television, and on the radio. It is unlikely that fans will immediately commit to a purchase and proceed to a Website or other vendor to buy tickets or merchandise.

The most frequent coupon tactic is a temporary reduced-price offer. A coupon can induce fans to upgrade their usual seats by reducing the price of premium seats. Sampling better seating options could result in full-price upgrades for future events. Coupons can attract new or infrequent attendees. A coupon that allows one unpaid or reduced-price admission with each regularly priced admission could result in fans bringing friends. This sampling experience could produce future paid admissions, including season ticket holders.

Coupons can be used to reduce the price of team merchandise at the event or other retail outlets. Coupons can encourage fans to buy concessions in larger quantities while simultaneously reducing the purchase cost. The result could be increased concessions revenue through larger profit margins from larger fan purchases.

Coupons can be used strategically to support select events. A baseball team might use coupons to boost attendance on weekdays. Coupons can be offered for games with rivals where attendance has been consistently low, in an effort to generate crowds and paid admissions.

Coupon strategies are self-selective, rather than comprehensive. The coupon's value is restricted to fans presenting the coupon, while fans without a coupon pay full price. A coupon for reduced-price admission can be distributed as a print ad on the sports page of a local newspaper; reduced-price admission will only be offered to fans presenting the coupon at the time of ticket purchase. Many other attendees, perhaps even the majority of attendees, will not present a coupon.

The Value Question

If coupons or other sales promotions are used too frequently, consumers may begin to devalue the brand. Rather than committing to full price for sports entertainment, value-driven fans may wait until coupons or other promotions are offered. Opportunistic fans may only attend or participate when a compelling coupon promotion is offered.

Eventually, the value of the property and its experience are reduced as fans realize they can postpone the purchase until a better deal is offered. And once a deal becomes common, such as two-for-one admission with a coupon, that deal can become devalued.

Fans will come to expect that admission deal, along with other deals, such as reduced-price concessions or free parking. Occasional coupon offers

protect long-term brand value along with the immediacy of coupon tactics.

Coupons are easily distributed in print media as part of paid advertising insertions. Those wishing to use the coupon can clip and retain it. Coupons can be distributed through conventional postal mail as single mailings or bundled with other coupons. Direct mail firms can supply mailing lists as well as printing services. Fans can download and print coupons with their own devices.

Area vendors can distribute coupons at checkout. Employers often offer coupons for area entertainment attractions as part of their firm's benefits package. Coupons can also be distributed through less conventional means. Teams and events can partner with local convention and visitors bureaus to include coupons in mailings requested by people seeking information about the area; newcomers moving into the market are excellent prospects. Coupons can be delivered on cans or other product packaging that can carry a printed message. Coupons for future events can be distributed to patrons as they exit the venue.

Conclusion

The physical nature of coupons offers easy results measurement. Coupons can be hand counted; coupons with bar codes can be scanned to reduce potential errors from hand counts. Event managers will likely know how many coupons were distributed and how many were returned. Sales figures associated with coupons can be compared to sales from uncouponed events. This allows easy, accurate return-on-investment calculation.

Lance Kinney
University of Alabama

See Also: Integrated Marketing Communication; Price-Based Promotions; Sales Promotions.

Further Readings

Crawford, Garry. *Consuming Sport: Fans, Sport and Culture*. New York: Routledge, 2004.
Fullerton, Sam. *Sports Marketing*. New York: McGraw-Hill, 2010.

Shilbury, David, Hans Westerbeek, Shayne Quick, and Daniel Funk. *Strategic Sport Marketing*, 3rd Ed. London Allen & Unwin Academic, 2009.

Sutton, William A., Mark A. McDonald, and George R. Milne. "Creating and Fostering Fan Identification in Professional Sports." *Sports Marketing Quarterly*, v.6/1 (1997).

Creating a Strong Event, Keys to

An event is an activity that provides opportunities to showcase the strengths of a destination, provides a platform for business development, and generates socioeconomic benefits. A strong event goes further, and provides relevant long-term return beyond expectations to its stakeholders. Such an event also generates additional economic value and organizational strengths to the sustainability of the event itself.

When conceiving and planning the organization of an event, it is of vital importance to apply the "value-for-money" approach to ensure that an appropriate return on investment is in line, or beyond expectations of all the event's stakeholders. In addition, a successful event must also generate relevant preambles to ensure its sustainable longevity, allowing the event itself to provide ongoing strengths both financially and in terms of brand positioning.

Measuring the effectiveness and the overall value of an event can be both a complicated and an onerous task. There are many methods of calculating benefits generated by an event. Briefly, the most commonly used methods are two: one aims at calculating the overall financial outcome—cost-benefit analysis or CBA—and the other one at identifying the event's direct economic benefit—economic impact or EI.

To adopt the CBA method requires the collection of detailed information on specific costs and income strictly related to the production of the event. This method is often used to narrow down specific investments, either from sponsors or public sector organizations, and value the financial outcome directly generated. The EI method looks mainly at the financial impact to the region and the country that is directly generated by hosting of the event.

Often these calculations of benefits are commissioned to experts, to justify actions of support made by politicians and government officials. However, the calculation of these benefits defines some very important elements that are vital to the identification of the beneficiaries of the event, and to securing the right level of financial or other support by sponsors and other financial investors. The measurement of a long-term economic and social impact, in terms of positive outcome generated by productivity as a result of motivation and positive attitude has not been refined yet.

By keeping in mind the various ways of determining the value of an event, it is of vital importance to ensure the delivery beyond expectation to the strategic objectives set by the event's stakeholders prior to the decision to support the event. These stakeholders make up the group of beneficiaries of the event's outcome. A typical list of stakeholders is formed by the following organizations, entities, and groups:

- Central government
- Local government
- Country brand
- Businesses
- Community
- Sponsors

Each of the above stakeholders will obviously set his or her own specific goals. It is important for the stakeholder to be involved with the event's planning and delivery. The level of investment and other kinds of support versus the expected return vary case by case; it does not follow a specific formula. In addition, the level of economic return to the stakeholders directly depends upon the level of their involvement within the organization of the event. Involvement includes taking various actions to maximize the way they leverage opportunities generated by activities as part of the event.

Regardless of the nature of the event itself, whether cultural, sport, or otherwise, the kind of stakeholders generally involved in events and the support they provide are briefly outlined below.

Most central governments provide support in two main areas: financial contribution and government services such as immigration and border facilitation. Major and mega events also see an involvement by governments with contributions such as specifically set-up task forces to support a successful delivery of the event and to implement specific leverage activities. In return, it is expected that event will deliver in the following areas:

- Economic benefits
- Social development opportunities
- Media exposure
- Business development

The support provided by local governments or councils is generally in the form of services related to the organization of the event, such as facilitation in obtaining various and necessary permits, provision of technical and staff support for street closures and traffic management, and official hosting by council representatives for event VIPs and personalities.

In return, councils aim at ensuring that the event delivers incremental revenue for businesses in the city. Typically, councils support the promotion of the city as a tourist destination to ensure hotels, operators, and retailers operate in full capacity.

Country Brand

Brand development is one of the elements that an event could ideally and most effectively support. However, an effective use of an event as vehicle requires a strong coordination of efforts by many relevant entities.

Typically, as not many countries have a centralized brand coordination point, a good result can be achieved by facilitating contributions by experts, and by coordinating brand promotion operations by entities such as the national tourism authority, the national business and trade development agency, and the office of the prime minister or head of state.

Expected return would be the increase of awareness of the destination, the promotion of its culture, and the reinforcement/improvement of the percep-

tion of the country's current brand, resulting in business development in the medium and long term.

Businesses

Direct business income is the most common return events are expected to deliver. The logical assumption is that events bring business opportunities by attracting new customers, whether they are athletes, sponsors, or media people. They provide opportunities to showcase business strengths through media exposure. They can also offer investment showcase opportunities to potential international investors.

The business community within the hosting country provides financial support in exchange for the opportunity to leverage activities within the organization of the event, aiming at generating sales and, where appropriate, export business.

Community

The community contributes by participating directly and indirectly in the activities of the event. This participation is tremendously vital to the success of the event, as it generates income through ticket sales, but also provides a very beneficial atmosphere in the hosting region. However, it implies that an effective marketing of the event by the event producers is in place.

Many other valuable contributions by the community, such as the intangible "embracing the event" one, add an enormous value to the event and often give participants a sense of pride. As alluded to earlier, this creates positive attitude and motivation amongst the local community, which eventually results in incremental productivity.

Another major benefit to the community is the legacy the event leaves behind. There are several attempts in the marketplace on the legacy topic, but the common way of measuring a legacy is to identify how much the event and its activity are either accelerating, improving, or even conceiving the long-term vision and vital social development goals of the hosting country.

Sponsors

Apart from events that solely rely on ticket sales, in many cases this group of stakeholders forms the core financial heart of an event. Sponsors provide financial and/or in-kind support. The level of support is in proportion to the opportunity the event provides to sponsors, and it is normally related to both brand promotion and product sales.

Conclusion
The main features of a strong event are being commercially viable; proving opportunities to the hosting country; being of an assured value to sponsors; and having sound long-term planning in place.

Robert Kaspar
University of Applied Sciences, Tyrol
Vito Lo Iacono
Capo Marketing

See Also: Bid Documents; Mega Sports Events; Olympic Organization; Securing Sports Events; Stakeholders Sports/Teams Events.

Further Readings
Beech, John and Simon Chadwick. *The Business of Sport Management.* Essex, UK: Pearson Education Limited, 2010.
Masterman, Guy. *Strategic Sports Event Management.* Oxford, UK: Elsevier Butterworth-Heinemann, 2006.

Credential Badges

In sport, it is important to provide people who represent official personnel at sporting events with a form of visible identification. By providing photo identification, name, and level of access, symbolized by a credential badge usually worn around the neck on a chain, personnel gain entry denied to those not designated by hosts of the event.

These personnel include athletes, coaches, game officials, sports medicine staff, security, statistics crew, ball personnel, and media. In youth sport, credential badges can be worn by athletes to identify player eligibility, by coaches to verify background checks, and by parents to indicate which team they support.

Generally, those who host a sporting event are responsible for determining and distributing badges to qualified people. A letter of assignment or list of those eligible must be provided to the credentials committee of an event by request. Each person desiring a badge must provide necessary documentation and identification designated by the credentials committee on or before the official deadline. Access to specific levels must be justified and included in each request. For example, the 2008 Beijing Olympic Games limited media credentials to 5,600, the same number as was designated for Athens in 2004 and Sydney in 2000. The value of these credential badges continues to escalate to the degree that controversies ensue about bloggers' abilities to receive media credentials, as they are struggling to earn legitimacy as members of the media.

Members of the media must apply for credentials in order to cover sporting events like the U.S. Olympic Trials and other Olympic qualifying events. Because there are limitations, certain guidelines apply as to who qualifies for credentials.

Each applicant: (1) must be a member in good standing of an officially recognized newspaper, wire service, magazine, photo agency, or broadcast organization; (2) in the case of Internet organizations, must officially represent a news-gathering Internet organization acknowledged by the International Olympic Committee; (3) must agree to guidelines devised by each Olympic Trials national governing body organization; and (4) must make a request for a credential badge through only one organization, generally through its senior or managing editor.

Other criteria that may affect the granting of credential badges for sporting events involve the actual name and background of the publication; publication circulation; evidence of past sport-specific coverage; consistency of coverage of similar sporting events; potential of hometown athletes in future sporting event; ability and eagerness to finance travel for official representative(s); and professional intent.

There are certain rights and obligations that are provided to a credential badge holder. Holders have the right to enter areas as designated on the credential badge. They also have the right to a workplace free from harassment and hostility. They have the obligation to remain courteous and considerate, provide their names and credential badges when requested to do so, and complete their official duties within designated policies and procedures set out by the hosts.

In order to begin the process of gaining a credential badge for a sporting event, the following procedures are recommended. Inform your employer as to the event you want to attend, how it will benefit the organization that you work for, and the location of the event. With approval of your organization, get in touch with the event organizers through appropriate means (phone call, Website, e-mail) to let them know you are interested in getting a credential badge. It is important to check what is allowable upon entry into the venue. Sometimes pocket knives or other potentially harmful objects are not allowed. You can be denied event access by not following the rules. Once you have gained entry into the event, the credential badge must be worn continuously. Be sure to have another photo identification (e.g., a driver's license or passport) with you as well.

Credential badges will continue to be a part of the sport management landscape. Persons holding credentials have proof that the issuer is confident of their professional qualifications. Event management and control play integral roles in the success of sport events.

Darlene A. Kluka
Carl R. Cramer
Barry University

See Also: Entry Control; Event Logistics; Securing Sports Events; Ticketing.

Further Readings

Swedberg, C. "Soccer Fans Use RFID Cards to Gain Admission and Buy Food." http://www.rfidjournal.com/article/view/3985/1 (Accessed January 2011).
Wyld, D. "The Chips Are In: Enhancing Sports Through RFID Technology. *International Journal of Sports Marketing & Sponsorship* (2008).

Credit, Use of

Professional sports teams regularly use both long-term and short-term credit. Long-term credit is often used as part of financing new facilities or the purchase of a team. Short-term credit is often used to meet obligations such as payroll, which are incurred on a regular basis while revenues are received irregularly. In the past decade the major sports leagues have developed credit facilities to give member teams easier access to both long- and short-term credit.

Long-Term Credit

Long-term credit used to finance new facilities or facility upgrades can be for amounts in the tens of millions of dollars or more for terms that span over several decades. New and upgraded facilities and the accompanying luxury and premium seating, improved concessions, and increased nongame day revenue generation have led to significant revenue increases for teams. When all works as planned, the new revenues are enough to both repay the debt and add to the team's bottom line. Teams have used both private lenders and their league's credit facilities for long-term loans to help finance their share of the cost of a new stadium or arena. Public financing of new stadiums and arenas often uses credit in the form of a bond issue. Long-term bonds are sold to creditors and are paid back in a variety of ways depending on how the financing is structured. Revenues generated from special taxes or specific revenues generated by the new facilities can be used to pay back the bonds.

The other common use of long-term credit is to help finance the purchase of a franchise or a partner's share of a franchise. Historically, the value of sports franchises in the four U.S. major leagues has appreciated at a regular, steady rate. Prospective owners often use the share of the franchise that they can finance themselves as collateral for borrowing the rest. If the franchise appreciates in value, the owner is then able to repay the loan. In some cases, such as Tom Hicks's ownership of both MLB's Texas Rangers and the EPL's Liverpool FC, the burden of the debt service on the initial loans used to buy into the teams limited their operational flexibility and eventually led to forced sales of both teams to new ownership groups.

Short-Term Credit

The irregular timing of the receipt of revenues and the regular obligation to meet major expenses such as payroll has always been a distinguishing feature of professional sports. Ticket revenue comes in during the off-season, with season ticket packages, and then comes in irregular bursts prior to each individual event. The NFL, with fewer games and a majority of tickets sold as season ticket packages, faces a much different ticket revenue landscape than sports with a greater number of games and more walk-up ticket sales. Sponsorship and local media revenues are received as negotiated in specific deals and league-shared revenues are often received at the end of the league year.

To bridge the gap between when obligations are due and when the revenue is received, teams turn to short-term credit, due in less than one year. The typical sources are local banks and league credit facilities. In 2010, MLB set up the first league credit facility specifically for short-term loans.

League Credit Facilities

In the 2000s, leagues developed credit facilities that gave member franchises access to larger sums of credit at better terms. The leagues are collectively more creditworthy than the individual teams, which gives them access to better loan terms. The leagues, in turn, offer those terms to individual teams. The leagues have a variety of rules that restrict the amount of debt teams can incur with the amount either being a fixed absolute number or based on the asset values of the borrowing teams. MLB allows a greater amount of borrowing for teams that have recently invested in new facilities.

The use of funds borrowed from the leagues is generally not restricted and can be used on player payroll, to refinance existing debt at better terms, to help finance capital improvements, or be a part of new stadium or arena financing.

Prior to the economic crisis in 2007–08, the league credit facilities were operated on annual renewal terms with banks. In a good credit market, the annual renewals allow for lower interest rates. However, during the credit crunch of 2008, both the NFL and MLB were unable to refinance their loan pool, which triggered tens of millions of amortization costs. Eventually, MLB, the NBA, and the NFL moved to multiyear terms for their credit facilities, which increased the interest rate, but allowed for greater stability.

The NFL was the first league to pool its resources to help individual teams finance new stadium construction with its "G-3" loan fund. In 2000, when the Denver Broncos, New England Patriots, and the Philadelphia Eagles were moving forward on plans to construct new facilities, the NFL borrowed $325 million in the commercial paper market at low rates. Commercial paper is a short-term (one-to-270-day) unsecured loan or promissory note. The NFL worked through Bank of America and Chase Manhattan, which agreed to be backstops, or provide money in case the commercial paper market went bad. None of the teams had the creditworthiness to acquire funds on the commercial paper market on their own. The league pool provided incentives for owners to finance stadiums in their home markets rather than relocate.

Kevin Heisey
Liberty University

See Also: Arena Funding—Public/Private; Debt Service; Facilities Financing.

Further Readings

Brown, M. T., C. D. McEvoy, M. S. Nagel, and D. A. Rascher. *Financial Management in the Sport Industry.* Scottsdale, AZ: Holcomb Hathaway, 2010.

Kaplan, D. "MLB's Short-Term Loan Pool a First for Big Leagues." *Sports Business Journal,* v.13/20 (September 20, 2010).

Rosner, S. R. and K. L. Shropshire, eds. *The Business of Sports.* Sudbury, MA: Jones & Bartlett Learning, 2011.

Crisis Management

The potential for a crisis confronts the sport manager on a regular basis. The stadium manager is advised that a set of bleachers just collapsed, sending several spectators to the hospital. A prominent athlete is arrested and charged with a felony. A hurricane is forecast to hit the local area where a championship game is scheduled. These situations constitute potential crises. How will employees respond to a crisis? A typical error that many sport managers make is thinking that they and their employees will respond effectively and efficiently to a crisis.

Having a formal crisis management plan (CMP) will help prepare an organization in the event of an actual crisis. A comprehensive CMP addresses major potential crises ranging from terrorist threats, litigation against the organization, and major power outages, to natural disasters such as hurricanes.

Numerous problems, incidents, and issues confront the sport manager on a regular basis. For instance, a medical emergency arises when an athlete, spectator, volunteer, or employee suffers a serious injury or illness. While such situations are urgent and often involve the activation of an emergency medical action plan, they typically do not give rise to a crisis, unless they are improperly dealt with. Typical incidents that require organizational resources to respond to are usually manageable, and normal business still occurs while such incidents are being handled. However, these incidents can rapidly escalate into crises if they are not properly addressed, if they result in significant media attention, and/or if they require numerous resources from inside or from outside the organization.

The Nonprofit Risk Management Center has defined a crisis as a sudden situation that threatens an organization's ability to survive: an emergency, a disaster, a catastrophe. A crisis may involve a death or injury, lost access to the use of facilities and/or equipment, disrupted or significantly diminished operations, unprecedented information demands, intense media scrutiny, and irreparable damage to an agency's reputation. A crisis is often an unforeseen situation that can be broad in its scope of disruption and damages to the organization.

Even though a crisis may strike without any warning, other types build up slowly. For instance, the unexpected accidental death of an athlete or employee may come as a complete surprise. In other

Security guards watch over the Major League All-Star Game from above the stands in July 2009.

situations, the actions, or inactions, of key employees may create a crisis over time. A crisis can cause extensive organizational damage that often cannot be very easily or quickly reversed. Crises can threaten an organization's mission, goals, and reputation. They may also have a negative effect on business, fundraising, and overall public perception.

Most crises share common characteristics. Crises are negative. Second, they can create false or distorted perceptions. Crises are also usually disruptive to the organization. Last, a crisis often takes an organization by surprise, placing the organization in a reactive mode. As a result, having a crisis management plan is imperative. Doing so is particularly important for smaller organizations, because they typically have fewer resources to draw from to react to and handle a crisis.

Developing a Plan

The main goal in developing a CMP is to write comprehensive contingency plans based on currently existing resources and operational capabilities that will allow an organization to efficiently and effectively deal with crises. CMPs should not be taken from other organizations, but instead they should be specifically developed for each organization. Every organization has unique factors that must be carefully considered, although there are several general components that form the basis of most CMPs.

The first step in developing and writing a CMP is to create a planning committee that will start the process. Awareness is the initial step to preparedness. A vital process in crisis planning is the identification of potential crises. This committee's main purpose is to identify potential significant crises that may confront the organization.

After significant crisis risks are identified, a crisis assessment is performed. This assessment identifies and prioritizes the risks that would put an organization into crisis mode. Thus, risks that could severely damage the organization's credibility and/or resources become the focus. The next step is to develop an action response plan for the significant crises that may significantly harm the organization. A written action plan carefully considers and provides detailed courses of action that an organization may select when a crisis occurs. When developing these plans, resources that may be utilized in crises should be identified. These include local resources, including but not limited to: local/state offices of the Federal Emergency Management Agency; American Red Cross; local hospital, police, and fire departments; and emergency medical services.

Staffing, Infrastructure, Communication

There are two stages in a CMP related to staffing issues. The first stage outlines the actions to be taken by the personnel in charge of the activity/facility when a crisis occurs. Such personnel should be educated on what immediate actions to take (calling emergency medical services (EMS), activating the CMP, etc. The second stage of staff preparation outlines the subsequent staff actions that should be performed in a crisis situation. The plan should identify, by position title, those staff members who will address, or actively assist with, a crisis.

When developing the CMP, contribution from all organizational levels and affected agencies should be solicited. Both administrative and frontline staff should be consulted, as well as athletes/participants and outside agencies, including groups such as local fire and police departments, EMS, crisis planning and management consultants, and the organization's legal counsel and insurance representative.

Within the CMP, the location of safe shelters; emergency exits; alarm systems; gas, electrical, and water shutoff controls; backup power systems; and firefighting equipment should be clearly identified. Location(s) for meeting EMS and other responding agencies (police, fire, and utility personnel, etc.) should be identified. Evacuation procedures should also be outlined. Identification of the type of equipment available (public address and communication equipment, automated external defibrillators, first aid kits, etc.), where it is stored, and how to access it should also be addressed.

Two major aspects of effective communication are necessary during a crisis. The first is the prompt notification of the proper authorities (e.g., police, medical personnel, or firefighters). Staff must be trained as to where and how to make emergency communications. The location of telephones and other communication devices should be identified, and emergency phone numbers kept available. The second aspect of effective communication involves communicating with organizational constituencies. For instance, an athletic director may need to communicate with EMS, law enforcement, school officials, victims and their families, parents of athletes, news media, counselors, and others after a rioting incident at a sport event.

Dealing appropriately with the news media is also a crucial part of effective communications. Oftentimes, it is adverse publicity, rather than the actual damage from a crisis itself, that severely harms an organization. Therefore, a trained spokesperson from the organization should promptly contact the media. All media requests for information should be directed to this designated spokesperson.

Documentation and Practice

A CMP identifies when and who completes which reports (e.g., incident report forms, insurance forms). Assigned personnel should know how to complete them and to whom the reports should be sent. Policies for filing and retaining reports should be identified. Depending on the crisis and its impact, counseling and/or follow-up with the victims, their families, classmates, colleagues, teammates, as well as with employees may be necessary. Although responses to many crises cannot be easily rehearsed, others can be simulated, practiced, or just discussed, to enhance staff readiness for an actual crisis and to identify any flaws in the CMP. When possible, the plan should be tested in conditions as close to real life as possible. When flaws are noticed, the plan should be modified accordingly. In between such practices, in-service training can help keep the CMP and procedures fresh in the minds of staff. Finally, it is important that the CMP be evaluated and modified after each crisis.

Daniel P. Connaughton
University of Florida

See Also: Assessing Event Risk; Crowd Management/ Control; Event Risk Management Process; Risk Management.

Further Readings

Ajango, Deborah, ed. *Lessons Learned: A Guide to Accident Prevention and Crisis Response.* Anchorage: University of Alaska Anchorage, 2000.

Connaughton, Daniel P. and Thomas A. Baker. "Crisis Management." In Cotten and Wolohan, eds., *Sport Law for Sport and Recreation Managers,* 4th Ed. Dubuque, IA: Kendall/ Hunt, 2007.

Coombs, W. Timothy. *Ongoing Crisis Communication: Planning, Managing, and Responding,* 2nd Ed. Thousand Oaks, CA: Sage, 2007.

Herman, Melanie L. and Barbara B. Oliver. *Vital Signs: Anticipating, Preventing and Surviving a Crisis in a Nonprofit.* Washington, DC: Nonprofit Risk Management Center, 2001.

Stoldt, G. Clayton, Lori I. Miller, Ted D. Ayres, and P. Greg Comfort. "Crisis Management Planning: A Necessity for Sport Managers." *International Journal of Sport Management,* v.4/2 (2000).

Cross-Marketing

Cross-marketing is creating a partnership with another business to market products or businesses together. For example, a male sport league may market a female sport league in addition to the male league's own business; the female sport league will also market both its own business and the male sport league's business. All partners involved will mutually benefit from the cross-marketing. For the cross-marketing to be successful, the partners involved must support one another.

Instruments for cross-marketing may include cross-selling, cross-advertising and cross-promotions, referring to the marketing cooperation of sales channels, advertising, and promotions. The product distribution and promotions take place through the channels of the partners. For example, a sport lottery company tells customers where and when to watch games, while the sport channel company provides information for the audience to buy sport lotteries. Sport managers may adequately use fan information to cross-sell the team's merchandize or do the fundraising.

A more complicated instrument for cross-marketing involves ownership by joint ventures. Two investors may join together to create a joint venture company in which both investors share the ownership and control. For example, a joint venture may be created by a foreign sport professional league and local cable-television operators. By this cooperation, the cable-television operators provide exposure for the league, while the league provides attractive sport programming. Joint ownership may be desirable in an international arena, for the foreign firm may lack resources to undertake the joint venture alone or the local government may require joint ownership to enter the local market. This causes joint ventures to execute cross-marketing across country boundaries.

Further, cross-marketing can occur between a franchise and its owner. For example, when a sport team is owned by a brewery, the beer sales would be promoted by the association with the sport team. Another example is the connection that once linked the Turner network and the Atlanta Braves. The large media company had control of the sport property for home delivery of entertainment. Or when a synergy is obtained in the ownership of sport franchise by the owners of cable networks, the sport contents would offer the significant advantage to meet the need for programming. The cable company, on the other hand, provides revenues and publicity for the sport team. These types of cross-marketing by ownership would create advantages of the owners.

Co-Branding

Co-branding is another instrument for cross-marketing. Two or more brands may be combined into a joint product and marketed together. Co-branding partnerships may be created between sports organizations and multinational company sponsors to extend the audience base globally. Cross-marketing in terms of co-branding can generate greater sales from existing target markets and open opportunities for new markets from the co-branding partners.

For example, the sponsorship relationship between adidas and the New Zealand Rugby Union might help adidas shoes promotions reach the fans of the Rugby Union. In the co-branding strategy, a logical fit in capabilities, values, and goals between the two partner brands may be required, such that the benefits of cross-marketing from the combined brand can be maximized. The benefits include learning more about new consumers, knowing how to approach them, and increasing sales.

In the marketplace of sport, sponsorship is a good opportunity for cross-marketing to increase brand awareness, enhance brand image, and improve sales. Sport footwear companies, beverage, and tobacco manufacturers may use sport sponsorship as a means to communicate with the customers as part of integrated marketing or to circumvent the advertising restrictions. Through the advertising of sporting events such as Formula 1 or the Super Bowl, and the third-party advertising of co-sponsors, alcohol and tobacco brand names may attain visibility to a vast audience. In cross-marketing by sport sponsorship, the brand image of a sponsor might be enhanced in a subtle way by co-sponsors.

Considering the high operating budgets in a major sporting event, multiple sponsors are inevitable. Partnerships might be formed among co-sponsors for a sporting event. This would provide opportunities

to attain visibility through the co-sponsor's advertising. In such third-party advertising, the brand image of a sponsor may be exposed and also enhanced when surrounded by other co-sponsors possessing good symbolic qualities of brands. The dynamics of co-sponsorship in the sport marketplace reveal indirect and implicit benefits of cross-marketing.

Cross-marketing by definition exists to create cooperation between two business units to market business together. The instruments for cross-marketing include cross-selling, cross-advertising, cross-promotions, joint ventures, co-branding, and co-sponsoring.

Li-Shiue Gau
Asia University, Taiwan

See Also: Brand Association; Co-Sponsor; Joint Venture.

Further Readings

Dewhirst, T. and A. Hunter. "Tobacco Sponsorship of Formula One and CART Auto Racing: Tobacco Brand Exposure and Enhanced Symbolic Imagery Through Co-Sponsors' Third Party Advertising." *Tobacco Control*, v.11/1 (2002).
Kotler, Philip and Kevin L. Keller. *Marketing Management*, 13th Ed. Upper Saddle River, NJ: Pearson Education, Inc., 2009.

Cross-Ownership

In business and finance, cross-ownership refers to a company's ownership of stock in the companies with which it does business. In Germany and Japan, cross-ownership is a significant part of the corporate culture, and it is common practice for companies to buy stock in the companies they do business with—vendors, for instance, manufacturers of parts, warehousing companies, transportation providers—in order to shore up a sense of mutual destiny. The benefits of cross-ownership are similar to those of the vertical integration pioneered by 19th-century steel tycoon Andrew Carnegie, who made his business more profitable by buying the companies that supplied his raw materials, keeping his costs lower than those of his competitors. However, Carnegie's motive was what we would now term anticompetitive, and it was exactly such business practices that led to the antitrust reforms of the late 19th and early 20th centuries.

While cross-ownership is not as egregious an anticompetitive practice as vertical integration (which itself is still legal so long as it does not come too close to creating a monopoly), it is a practice that is watched carefully by regulators. It is also in some cases regulated within the sports industry, as in the National Football League (NFL). While the NFL cannot dictate business practices to a company, it does have power over who can and cannot own an NFL franchise, and can take that franchise away.

Vertical Integration

There are examples of vertical integration in sports. For instance, the Tribune Company at one point owned the Chicago Cubs, 13 newspapers including the *Chicago Tribune,* and various television and radio outlets including superstation WGN, which broadcasts the Cubs games. Rather than integrating along the lines of the physical supply of goods—by buying uniform and equipment manufacturers, say—the Cubs organization is integrated along the supply chain of the game broadcast and reportage. This has become a common method, and one that it is argued does not interfere with competitive practices. Unlike Carnegie's vertical integration, for instance, this does not enable the Cubs to offer a product at a price lower than competitors could match.

An early example, critical to the history of baseball, was the purchase of the Atlanta Braves in 1976 by media tycoon Ted Turner, who also owned superstation WTBS, which began broadcasting Braves games. In these early days of cable, the Braves therefore became the first baseball team to enjoy national broadcasts for all of its games, which not only helped to create a nationwide fan base (the Braves billed themselves as "America's Team"), but revitalized the popularity of baseball across the board. Casual fans would watch regardless of who was playing; fans of other teams would watch when their team played the Braves.

In the 21st century, it can be difficult to appreciate the value of an increase in available televised base-

ball games, but in the mid-1970s in-person attendance and the radio were still the only way to catch every game live. The Braves/TBS affiliation was the first step toward today's broadcast saturation.

An interesting modern example of cross-ownership in baseball is New England Sports Ventures (NESV). NESV was formed in 2001 as a consortium of investors interested in buying the Boston Red Sox, a team that had been owned for decades by the same family, the Yawkeys, and later the Yawkey Trust. The deal to purchase the team was concluded in 2002, along with the purchase of Fenway Park, where the team plays its home games. In the next eight years, NESV bought Liverpool F. C. (the English Premier League soccer team), an 80 percent share of the New England Sports Network (which broadcasts Red Sox, Bruins, minor league baseball, and college and high school games), and a 50 percent share of the Roush Fenway Racing NASCAR team.

NESV also established the Fenway Sports Group in 2004, as a sports marketing agency. Between 2004 and 2009, the Fenway Sports Group built up a client base that included not only the Red Sox, but the major intercollegiate sports of Boston College, Professional Bull Riders, the Deutsche Bank PGA golf championship, and a nonexclusive agreement with Major League Baseball (MLB). Further, FSG purchased a Salem, Virginia, High Class A minor league baseball franchise in the Carolina League and renamed it the Salem Red Sox. In addition to all of these affiliations, one of the partners of NESV is the New York Times Company, the media company that owns not only the *New York Times,* but also the *Boston Globe.*

NFL Rule Ramifications

As mentioned, the NFL has rules pertaining to cross-ownership, but their objection is not to situations such as just described in baseball, but rather to NFL franchises being owned by entities that also own a controlling interest in a professional sports team in a competing NFL city. Originally, cross-ownership of other professional sports teams was banned entirely; in the late 1990s, the restriction was loosened. For instance, because there is no NFL team in Portland, the Portland Trailblazers (National Basketball Association) and the Seattle Seahawks (NFL) can be owned by the same entity—but if the Trailblazers were to move to San Diego, a city with an NFL franchise, the NFL would require that the Seahawks be sold to another entity.

Interestingly, the strongest opposition to the original NFL cross-ownership policy came from other sports leagues. As the most profitable sports league, the NFL naturally attracts wealthy owners. It further follows that these owners can afford to own, and may be interested in owning, more than one sports team. By preventing them from doing so, the NFL forces these owners to choose between their league and another—along lines with which smaller leagues cannot compete. This was even condemned as an anticompetitive practice.

The opposition of the North American Soccer League to the NFL's original cross-ownership rules was one of the factors in loosening the restrictions; further, this is one of the reasons why when a smaller professional sports league begins (the XFL, the Arena Football League, Major League Lacrosse), it is in its best interests to open franchises in cities that do not have NFL franchises. Other leagues are not as restrictive. In 2009, the Tampa Bay Rays agreed to purchase a controlling interest in the Florida Tuskers, the new United Football League franchise in Florida. This made them the fifth MLB team involved in cross-league cross-ownership, joining the aforementioned Red Sox, and the pairings of the Chicago White Sox and Bulls, among others.

Bill Kte'pi
Independent Scholar

See Also: Barriers to Entry; Franchise; Ownership, Professional Teams; Sports Networks.

Further Readings

Rosner, Scott, and Kenneth L. Shropshire. *The Business of Sports.* New York: Jones & Bartlett Publishing, 2004.
Staudohar, Paul D, and James A. Mangan. *The Business of Professional Sports.* Chicago: University of Illinois Press, 1991.

Cross-Promotions

Cross-promotions are one of the instruments for cross-marketing, with emphasis on the cooperation of promotions between or among partners. Cross-promotions are one type of marketing tactics wherein two or more business units team up to promote the business jointly and expand each other's customer's base. Cross-promotions refer to advertising a company's product, service, or brand by using another company's channels, resources, or its noncompeting brand through promotional alliances.

Cross-promotions provide another platform whereby a company can gain a presence in new channels through joint efforts with another company or other companies. For example, cross-promotional opportunities might be between a sport organization and a local radio broadcaster. Advertising time for ticket sales and licensed merchandise of the sport organization might be exchanged for advertising space in game programs and outdoor billboard space in the stadium, or for a local radio broadcaster to meet the potential audience. That is, the sport organization and the broadcaster come together to reciprocally carry the promotions for one another.

Bundled Products

Bundled products might be used in cross-promotions for partner businesses to combine products or services together in marketing promotions. For example, sport organizations may promote their tickets bundled with discounted coupons for another firm's beverages or snack products. In sport tourism, marketing managers may promote a golf tournament for golf lovers by using bundled hotel choices.

The bundled product in cross-promotions might work even better for codependent partners whose products or services are integral to each other. For example, in a sponsorship of an outdoor broadcasting activity of the final World Cup game, a sport lottery company sold the lottery at the broadcasting arena for the outcome of the final game in a discounted price. The audience might feel excited to give a try for personal prediction on the game outcome. The audience might buy a lottery entry while watching the broadcast game on a big screen.

In sport sponsorship, cross-promotions are usually encouraged among co-sponsors. Because a major sporting event has a high operating budget, the event holder would try to recruit multiple sponsors to gain sufficient funding for holding the event. This provides opportunities for co-sponsors to create cross-promotional partnerships to capitalize on a sponsorship and expand the scope of their sponsorships. For example, sponsors might be encouraged to use co-sponsor products as prizes for giveaways or a sweepstakes as a means of cross-promotion.

Teaming Up

Another example would be a retail chain of sporting goods stores and a snack goods company teaming up to activate their sponsorships of the Southeastern Conference (SEC) collegiate football games. In their cross-promotions, the two co-sponsors offer the consumers a bundled product with an enhanced value. The snack company offered coupons in 500,000 potato chip bags for a free SEC cap with the purchase of $50 or more from the Authentic SEC Collection at one of the sporting goods chain stores. Meanwhile, the snack company was allowed to carry the coupon promotion in the chain stores. This gave the snack company the opportunity to gain exposure.

A sponsor's promotion would be possibly carried by other co-sponsors to gain exposure in new markets through the marketing channels of co-sponsors and earn positive brand image through association with well-regarded brands of co-sponsors. The cross-promotions among co-sponsors would allow companies to share the cost of sponsorship and promotional execution, and generate more awareness and interest among the sport consumers. When a sponsor and other co-sponsors promote a sponsorship together by adopting cross-promotions, this may double the marketing impact for all the participating sponsors and for the sport property.

In an effort to make cross-promotions work well, sport managers may first analyze which companies would complement their efforts the best; then, they must be clear about what can be gained from cooperating with each other and make sure that the responsibilities are adequately communicated and written in detail.

Cross-promotion involves considering the targeted potential customers, their needs and wants. When incorporated effectively, cross-promotions would expand the customer base, save time while reaching a wider variety of consumers, share the expenses between the partners, and can be more creative than typical promotions of a solo company. After the cross-promotion, assessment and evaluation of the efforts are required. The findings can help create other successful cross-promotional deals.

Further, as an instrument of cross-marketing, cross-promotions can be employed in joint ventures, among teams in the same league, or between a franchise and the owner. For example, in a joint venture, a sport organization and a media company may jointly cross-promote each other's products or programs. Sports teams provide content to promote other products such as television shows; the shows also provide content to promote sports. These benefits of cross-promotion may ultimately encourage media corporations to gain ownership of sport teams.

Li-Shiue Gau
Asia University, Taiwan

See Also: Co-Sponsor; Joint Venture; Promotion.

Further Readings

Baines, Paul, Chris Fill, and Kelly Page. *Marketing.* Oxford, UK: Oxford University Press, 2008.
Masteralexis, Lisa P., Carol A. Barr, and Mary A. Hums. *Principles and Practice of Sport Management.* Sudbury, MA: Jones & Bartlett Publishers, 2009.

Crowd Management/Control

The management of large crowds is an issue of great importance to those hosting major sporting events. Because of the nature of sport, crowds at these events will often be excitable and prone to spontaneous expressions of disappointment and joy. Some fans will be at an unfamiliar venue for the first time, and for sports where there is a culture of heavy alcohol consumption, this brings additional challenges. Managing the influx of these fans to the venue and surrounding environs, their behavior while present, and then their exit—whether planned or emergency—is essential for the staging of a sporting event at which spectators are present.

Hooliganism

In some sports, particularly those where large numbers of visiting supporters are present, there have been problems with crowd disorder and violence. In the sport of soccer, crowd disorder or *hooliganism* has caused considerable concern. Although in the English language hooliganism lacks an accepted definition, it has been generally interpreted to include incidents where fans fight those of rival teams, engage in violence or disorder with police or security officials, or commit mass acts of vandalism. Instances of hooliganism have been recorded as taking place in and around stadiums, in host city centers and train stations, and on journeys to and from sporting events. Widespread disorder has also occurred in and around public screenings of events taking place many thousands of miles away (e.g., in Moscow following Russia's elimination from the 2002 World Cup).

Professional soccer is recognized as the sport where instances of hooliganism are most likely to occur. This is probably because of the large crowds, the tradition of large numbers of supporters traveling to watch the visiting team (creating tensions with supporters of the home team), and the reputation of soccer crowds as being prone to acts of hooliganism (which may in turn draw those with a propensity for violence into the culture and may also lead to hardline policing measures that can exacerbate instances of disorder). However, instances of crowd disorder and rioting can, under certain circumstances, occur at any sports event where large crowds gather, and serious instances of hooliganism have occurred on many occasions in crowds at baseball, cricket, boxing, and rugby league matches.

Control Measures

It is soccer that retains a reputation for unruly, dangerous, and sometimes riotous crowds. From the late 1960s until the mid-1980s, England was perceived to be the home of the problem of hooliganism, with fighting between rival supporters taking place on trains carrying visiting supporters to and from matches, in and around stadiums, and even occasionally on the pitch as games took place. This culminated in the deaths of 39 supporters at the 1985 European Cup Final at Heysel, Belgium, when a wall in the stadium collapsed as fans of Italian club Juventus tried to escape a terrace charge by fans of Liverpool FC.

Hooliganism involving English soccer supporters led to the introduction of a series of strategies, policies, and laws to try and rid the sport of the problem. Soccer in England continues to see instances of violence and disorder, mainly away from soccer stadiums, involving organized gangs of 20–400 hooligans looking to confront each other. However, the problem in and around stadiums is now considered to be under control. Indeed, in terms of measures of crowd control, England has been at the forefront of developments worldwide, and its current practices are much envied and often copied by countries who continue to have widespread problems with hooliganism in their domestic soccer competitions (e.g., Brazil, Argentina, Italy, Poland, Russia, South Africa, and Turkey).

One of the first measures introduced in England to reduce the problem restricted on the alcohol consumption of soccer fans (alcohol could not be consumed within sight of the pitch, and it was made an offense to enter a stadium while drunk). Alcohol has also been banned from soccer matches organized by UEFA, Europe's governing body. Although there is no proven direct pharmacological link between alcohol and violence, there is a significant correlation between violence and disorder and the social consumption of alcohol, and so it was felt that this would have a significant impact upon hooliganism. However, research has shown that fans continue to drink heavily prior to matches and are rarely denied entrance. Furthermore, it is possible that the alcohol restrictions have had a negative impact upon crowd behavior, causing more alcohol to be consumed in the build-up to matches, causing fans to arrive later at stadia (often leading to crowd crushes), and encouraging rival fans to drink in the same pubs and bars before matches.

More significant in terms of successful crowd management and a reduction of hooliganism in and around stadia in England was the regeneration of soccer stadiums following the Hillsborough disaster to improve crowd safety and comfort, the heavy use and advertising of closed-circuit television (CCTV) in stadia, and the use of banning orders to prevent those convicted of soccer-related criminal offenses from attending future matches. This was combined in the late 1980s with a shift in emphasis in police tactics, away from reactionary mass policing methods and toward a more intelligence-led, proactive form of policing that attempted to target those who attended matches to cause trouble, but that treated ordinary fans with respect.

A combination of these factors through the 1990s and 2000s led to increased attendances at English soccer matches (including an increased number of women and families), and a reduction of instances of disorder in and immediately around stadia. Although instances of disorder continue to occur, these typically take place away from the stadium (distant from CCTV, police presence, and the risk of banning orders), and rarely put the safety of normal spectators at risk.

Toward Customer Care

The most important factor in the English experience was the change of emphasis from crowd control to customer care. The pivotal moment here was the Hillsborough disaster of 1989, when 96 Liverpool fans were crushed to death at the start of a match because of policing errors that allowed too many fans to enter one section of a standing terrace, and a perimeter fence that meant they could not escape the crush. Ironically, it was measures designed to prevent hooliganism (fences had been constructed at most grounds to prevent fans fighting with rival supporters or invading the playing area) that led to the biggest loss of life in English football, far more than all the hooligan incidents put together. The subsequent Taylor Report into the disaster blamed the preoccupation with hooliganism as being a key factor in the number of fatalities.

The Hillsborough disaster also demonstrated that the stadium licensing and safety structure in the United Kingdom—based upon codes of practice and local government safety certificates that were enforced in a haphazard way—was not sufficient to ensure either crowd control or spectator safety.

From 1990 onward, far stricter standards and controls were placed upon sports stadia, particularly soccer stadia, in the United Kingdom. Standing terraces were phased out and replaced by all-seater stadia, aging stands were replaced, new state-of-the-art stadia were constructed, and central government took overall control of the implementation of the new safety system.

While new stadia meeting minimum safety standards play an important role in ensuring crowd safety, and the majority of sports stadium disasters around the world continue to take place in older, dilapidated stadia, there is no room for complacency. The Ellis Park disaster of 2001, where 43 soccer fans were killed in a crowd crush in South Africa, took place in a stadium newly renovated for the 1995 Rugby Union World Cup. However, a combination of factors led to the admittance of more fans than the stadium capacity, which led to the disastrous crush. It should also be noted that experience in Germany shows us that new, well-managed terraced areas are not in themselves inherently dangerous or likely to lead to increased crowd disorder.

Progressive Policing

The current dominant sports crowd management theory derives primarily from a number of pan-European sociological, sociolegal, and social psychological studies into the behavior of soccer crowds throughout Europe. These have moved away from previous theories of why sports crowds (or elements within them) become involved in serious incidents of disorder and rioting, which typically were based on individual factors, such as the consumption of alcohol, the emotion of an on-pitch incident, or the presence of hooligans trying to instigate trouble.

Research carried out at two major crowd riots involving English soccer fans at international tournaments (Marseilles at the France World Cup 1998, and Charleroi at the 2000 European Football Championships) revealed that far from being instigated by "known hooligans," around 97 percent of those arrested were unknown to the police, while those suspected of traveling to become involved in disorder were typically not involved. Furthermore, explanations of the violence based on the amount of alcohol consumed did not stand up to scrutiny when compared with other matches where there was similar, or greater, access to alcohol, but violence did not occur.

Current perspectives on soccer crowd behavior in Europe (which also draw upon studies of the behavior of non-sporting crowds) instead suggest that it is in fact the style of crowd management, most notably policing, that plays the most significant role in determining whether large-scale crowd disorder will occur. These theories have been already applied at a number of high-risk soccer matches and international tournaments, including the European Championships of 2004 and 2008, and have demonstrated that where progressive policing strategies are followed, based upon positive interaction, communication, and the setting of clear and achievable tolerance limits with supporters, disorder is unlikely to escalate. This is regardless of access to alcohol, the presence of so-called hooligans, and events on the pitch.

By mingling amongst the crowd, interacting in a positive manner with fans, communicating firmly and clearly with fans whose behavior was breaching tolerance limits, and only taking decisive action in a targeted way against individuals causing trouble, these policing and security strategies severely reduced the risk of disorder occurring.

At Euro 2004, despite an estimated 250,000 English football tourists being present, there was only one arrest at a match venue for disorderly or violent behavior. This compared favorably with more traditional police approaches to soccer crowds where police did not interact with fans, and were typically only seen in large number wearing riot gear. This "show of force" style of policing, often combined with alcohol prohibitions, has continued to lead to serious instances of disorder at soccer matches throughout Europe (e.g., Rome 2007) and South America.

Security guards in high-visibility neon green jackets encircle the perimeter of the crowd at a football game at Gillette Stadium in Foxborough, Massachusetts, in October 2008.

Key Features

The experiences of the European police and governing bodies in responding to the problem of hooliganism at soccer matches have demonstrated that while large sports crowds present a challenge to event organizers, it is possible to manage them in a way that prevents the escalation of inevitable instances of antisocial behavior involving small numbers of fans into large-scale disorder. A focus on the safety and comfort of fans rather than "crowd control" should be the starting point for both police and stadium security/stewards. Stadiums and access points should achieve minimum safety standards to ensure the prevention of crowd crushes, and police and security officials should be familiar with the environment in case of emergency.

Where necessary, fans of rival teams should be segregated, although it needs to be remembered that segregation only inside the stadium can exacerbate problems outside. Positive interaction, communication, and the establishment of clear tolerance limits are vital when managing groups of risky fans, and if individuals need to be ejected or arrested, this should be done with the minimum of force, with communication with surrounding fans, and if possible only after a clear warning. At no stage should police or security take action against a wider group of supporters simply because of the actions of individuals within that group. Finally, research has shown that zero-tolerance and show of force policing and security strategies are likely to increase, rather than reduce, the risk of crowd disorder.

Geoff Pearson
University of Liverpool

See Also: Facilities Management; Fan Attendance, Reasons for; Securing Sports Events; World Cup.

Further Readings

Armstrong, Gary. *Football Hooligans: Knowing the Score.* Oxford, UK: Berg, 1998.
Stott, Clifford and Geoff Pearson. *"Football Hooliganism": Policing and the War on the "English Disease,"* 2nd Ed. London: Pennant Books, 2010.
Stott, Clifford and Steve Reicher. "How Conflict Escalates: The Inter-Group Dynamics of Collective Football Crowd 'Violence.'" *Sociology,* v.32/2 (1998).

Customer Equity

Over the past decade, sports marketing practitioners have begun to alter their perspectives on marketing from that of a product-centered perspective to more of a consumer-oriented focus. Born out of the transition of the global economy to a service-based economy and the spread of service-based industries, *customer equity* refers to the sum total of the discounted lifetime value of a sport organization's current and future potential customers. Grounded in overlapping marketing concepts such as direct marketing, service quality, relationship marketing, and brand equity, the customer equity paradigm recognizes customers as the primary source of an organization's current and future cash flows. Thus, the value of a customer to an organization is viewed in terms of the customer's current profitability as well as the net discounted revenue contribution stream that the organization will realize from the customer over the length of time he or she is a customer.

Each of an organization's customer profitability streams are summed to provide a calculation of the total value of the customer base to that organization. Consider the following example as a simple illustration of customer equity. Suppose the Miami Heat has two customers—Derek and Carly. Derek attends five basketball games a season and contributes roughly $300 per year to profit. He is expected to remain a customer for the next 10 years. Carly is expected to produce $500 in contribution to profit this year, but is not expected to remain a customer. The discounted lifetime value of Derek is (for the Heat's current discounted rate) $1,100. The discounted lifetime value of Carly is $500—the contribution received this year. Therefore, the Heat's total customer equity is $1,100 + $500 = $1,600.

Geared toward growing the long-term value of the firm, customer equity may be thought of as a competitive marketing strategy referring to the value of the resources that customers invest in particular organizations. From this perspective, customer equity is an important asset of the organization, as customer-generated revenues are the basis of an organization's cash flows and represent a significant measure of the value of an organization. So, the ability of an organization to acquire and retain attractive customers is crucial for an organization's success in today's competitive market.

The adoption by sport organizations of a customer-centered orientation has largely been driven by an increase in marketplace competition, which has led to greater financial stakeholder demands for managerial financial accountability. Additionally, because of the emergence of sophisticated technologies, present-day sport organizations have tremendous access to vast amounts of detailed customer information. This has dramatically increased consumer levels of expectations regarding the possibilities of individual-level marketing efforts by the organization.

Conclusion

It is the result of these organizational pressures and marketplace changes that have forced organizations to adapt to, as well as to develop and implement, alternative strategies leading to sustainable profits. The adoption of a customer equity approach enables a sport organization to calculate the value of its customers so that informed, data-driven decisions can be made regarding marketing spending on customer acquisition, retention, and add-on selling. This, in turn, enables the organization to maximize the profitability of each customer over the course of his or her individual customer life cycle.

Daniel R. Sweeney
University of Arkansas at Little Rock

See Also: Brand Equity; Relationship Marketing; Service Quality.

Further Readings

Bauer, Hans H., Nicola E. Sauer, and Philipp Schmitt. "Customer-Based Brand Equity in the Team Sport Industry: Operationalization

and Impact on the Economic Success of Sport Teams." *European Journal of Marketing,* v.39/5–6 (2005).

Blattberg, Robert and John Deighton. "Manage Marketing by the Customer Equity Test." *Harvard Business Review,* v.74/4 (1996).

Hogan, John, Katherine Lemon, and Roland Rust. "Customer Equity Management: Charting New Directions for the Future of Marketing." *Journal of Service Research,* v.5/1 (2002).

Rust, Roland, Katherine Lemon, and Das Narayandas. *Customer Equity Management.* Upper Saddle River, NJ: Pearson Prentice Hall, 2004.

Customer Loyalty Programs

For an organization, attracting new customers is important, but even more important is retaining the existing ones. According to the Pareto principle, 80 percent of sales that an organization makes come from 20 percent of its customers. Keeping this in mind, organizations employ customer loyalty programs (CLPs) to retain the existing or new customers, hence increasing market share, and therefore boosting returns. In general, CLPs are aimed at rewarding the customers for their loyalty and patronage.

Management researcher Barry Berman has provided a typology of CLPs. According to Berman, CLPs can be divided into four main types. The first type of CLP offers discounts to the loyalty program customers when they purchase product of that organization, regardless of any previous purchase history. These CLPs provide instant gratification to the consumers, as they are able to obtain the discount the moment they swipe their membership card to make the purchase. The second type of CLP offers consumers a free item after they have bought a particular number of items at full price. The third type rewards the consumer incrementally, such that member rewards increase disproportionately as the consumer spending level increases. Thus, the customers will need to spend more for obtaining superior rewards. The fourth type of CLP divides the members into categories based on their purchase history. The purchase history is the determinant of offers, promotions, and other rewards that the consumers will receive.

Developing Successful CLPs

Customer loyalty programs are now being used in most industries including sports. We know that fans of sports teams are extremely loyal to their teams. Their commitment to their particular team is often reflected by repeat purchase of products and tickets, and incessant presence at the team matches. These fans provide the sports franchise a competitive advantage over their competitors. As researchers have found, loyalty is important as it not only ensures a team following despite bad performances, but also facilitates the continuous selling of products and services offered by the sports franchise.

Other researchers have promulgated a model that explains how fan identification with their sports team occurs. They state that this attachment progresses through four stages. The first is the awareness stage, where the customer realizes the existence of a sports franchise (e.g., "I know about the Indianapolis Colts"). The second stage is the attraction stage, where customers perceive that their needs are satisfied and they receive benefits from association with their team. At this stage the customer shows a liking toward the team (e.g., "I adore the Indianapolis Colts"). The third stage is the attachment stage, where the customer shows an emotional bond with the sports team (e.g., "I believe I am part of the Indianapolis Colts family"). The final stage is the allegiance stage, where the emotional bond becomes very strong. At this stage the loyalty and devotion of the fan is the highest toward the team and its products (e.g., "I eat, breathe, and exist for the Indianapolis Colts"). CLPs can assist the sports franchises not only in shifting fans from lower stages to higher stages, but also maintaining fans in the higher stages.

Consumption Scale

Other researchers contend that fan identification with teams may influence the success of the loyalty programs. Thus, loyalty programs in sports

mainly concentrate on rewarding the high-identification fan, who generally exhibits high attendance and spends more money to follow his or her team. However, such loyalty programs may not be successful, as they do not alter the purchase behavior of these fans. This view is supported by empirical research conducted by Yuping Liu, who demonstrated that CLPs do not motivate heavy users to consume even more—but the heavy users were most likely to redeem rewards from the loyalty programs. Contrarily, the light users gradually increased their consumption.

Thus, rewarding the highly engaged fans may not necessarily result in successful CLPs. However, the success of CLPs in sports depends on not just on rewarding the high-identification fans, but also providing the access and convenience of enrolling and redeeming rewards for the low-identification fans. Overall, CLPs must augment the overall value proposition of a firm's offering to motivate consumers to purchase over and over again.

In an influential article about CLPs, researchers stated that the value that an organization delivers in CLPs can be classified into five dimensions:

- *Cash value*: the percentage of spending that the consumer is expected to redeem. Customers should perceive that the reward has a substantial value when compared to what they are spending to get the reward
- *Aspirational value*: indicates the attractiveness of the rewards that motivate the customer. It is offering customers something striking and interesting that they will not buy themselves
- *Relevance*: the extent to which a customer feels that the reward is achievable
- *Convenience*: the customers should be able to participate and redeem the reward with ease
- *Choice*: customers should have choices in rewards, so that they can make the decision as to which reward they would like to get once they fulfill the reward conditions

Some researchers have argued that there are four barriers to the success of CLPs. The first barrier is the qualification barrier, where the conditions to redeem the awards are almost impossible to fulfill.

Second is inaccessibility, where the customer cannot redeem the rewards for reasons like unqualified employees or lack of counters to redeem this award in the city, etc. The third barrier is worthlessness, where the customers do not think that the rewards they have received are good enough in comparison to what they have spent to qualify for the reward. The final barrier is redemption costs, where the customers have to spend additional resources (money, time, etc.) to redeem their rewards. These barriers should be avoided, as they can draw very negative sentiments from the customers and hence discourage them.

Dheeraj Sharma
University of Winnipeg

Further Readings

Berman, Barry. "Developing an Effective Customer Loyalty Program." *California Management Review*, v.49/1 (2006).

Gladden, James M. and Daniel C. Funk. "Understanding Brand Loyalty in Professional Sport: Examining the Link Between Brand Associations and Brand Loyalty." *International Journal of Sports Marketing and Sponsorship*, v.3/2 (2001).

Liu, Yuping. "The Long-Term Impact of Loyalty Programs on Consumer Purchase Behavior and Loyalty." *Journal of Marketing*, v.71/4 (2007).

O'Brien, Louise and Charles Jones. "Do Rewards Really Create Loyalty?" *Harvard Business Review*, v.73/3 (1995).

Shilbury, David, Hans Westerbeek, Shayne Quick, and Daniel Funk. *Strategic Sport Marketing*, 3rd Ed. London: Allen & Unwin Academic, 2009.

Stauss, Bernd, Maxie Schmidt, and Andreas Schoeler. "Customer Frustration in Loyalty Programs." *International Journal of Service Industry Management*, v.16/3 (2005).

Sutton, William A., Mark A. McDonald, and George R. Milne. "Creating and Fostering Fan Identification in Professional Sports." *Sports Marketing Quarterly*, v.6/1 (1997).

Customer Relationship Marketing

With constantly changing and improving technology, a business cannot rely solely on offering a service or a product to its customers. Furthermore, with globalization, and increasing competition leading to more choices for the customers, it is very difficult to catch the attention of new customers or hold on to the existing ones. In order for a business to sustain itself in today's ever-changing marketplace, it is imperative to build a long-term relationship with its customers. In his seminal article on CRM, Russell Winer theorized that increasing the customer retention every year even by just a small percentage can result in an exponential increase in revenue for an organization.

Researchers O'Connor and Murphy have contended that in order to improve relations with customers, information systems must be used in today's market. This is particularly crucial with the decrease in computer hardware costs and the increasing ease with which information systems can be accessed.

This is where Customer Relationship Marketing (CRM) comes in. CRM refers to a comprehensive strategy that integrates sales, marketing, and service. Its success depends on the coordination of such actions. Overall, CRM is a tool used to gain a clear understanding of customer needs and behaviors in order to develop and establish long-term relationships with them.

According to Heskett, Sasser, and Schlesinger, customers can be divided into three zones: (1) the zone of defection: customers with the lowest level of satisfaction and maximum hostility; (2) the zone of indifference: customers with medium level of satisfaction and loyalty toward the company; and (3) the zone of affection: customers with maximum loyalty toward the company. CRM aims to transfer any zone 1 customers to the zone 3, and prepare the organization with an approach to retain the newly acquired customers.

In simplistic terms, CRM strives to provide an organization with customer focus. In a journal article, Carolyn Strong defined customer focus as the assurance of an organization to recognize the concerns of a customer regarding the value of the requirements, and to satisfy the requirements in a timely manner. In other words, customer focus allows an organization to recognize and anticipate the demands for new products and services and attempt to meet them.

More specifically, the goals of CRM are to employ integrated information systems so as to further improve the services offered. While doing this, CRM simultaneously puts into practice a more practical solution strategy and uses the current relationships to increase the returns. In summation, CRM's ultimate goal is to instill loyalty among customers.

In recent years, Charles Waltner has noted that CRM has been increasingly employed for attracting and retaining fans by many professional sporting organizations. Concurring in this, Marc Songini has stated in his article that the Orlando Magic basketball sports franchise now employs CRM-based automation to retain and attract sporting fans.

Sport Marketing and CRM

With an increase in sports popularity resulting in an increasing fan base, sports has become a multibillion-dollar industry. And like any other industry, organization with in the sports industry also needs to find a way to sustain and grow its customer base, that is, the fan base, so as to earn profit. Thus, like any traditional organization, professional sporting organizations are now focusing on CRM. This focus has generally helped in marketing sports, and specifically has aided in increasing revenues by pulling more supporters and selling tickets and sports-related products.

As Furuholt and Skutle have documented, the customers of professional sports organizations are remarkably different from those of traditional organizations. The customers of sporting organizations are more loyal to the sport and their particular teams. Patronage and repeat purchase behavior of the customers of a sports organization provides substantial direct income through buying tickets and merchandise, and indirect income through sponsorship and TV agreements. Furthermore, this research team asserts that CRM has provided sports organizations with the ability to establish personalized communication with each of its customers, thus augmenting their direct and indirect income.

Overall, CRM bestows a sports organization with the ability to synchronize its customer data collection activity from multiple sources, to develop a database that will allow it to understand and anticipate customer needs and wants, thus establishing intimate ties with customers.

Components of CRM

CRM ensures that all the information is shared between the front and the back offices and hence throughout the entire organization. Krasnikov, Jayachandran, and Kumar have stated that CRM includes front-office applications that support sales, marketing, service, and the back office. Furthermore, Krasnikov and his colleagues state that CRM assists in optimal and appropriate information flow between an organization and its consumers through reciprocal communications processes. Also, they suggest that CRM enables the routing of information to appropriate employees in sales, marketing, and service components. All the customer information collected from different places (sales, marketing, or service) is stored in a centralized database in the back office. The front-office components of CRM applications assist in integrating and analyzing the data. Overall, CRM allows an organization ways to track the varying needs of customers in an efficient way and, in turn, enhance the organization's decision-making process.

Based on the framework promulgated by Russell Winer in his seminal article on CRM, the following seven components of CRM are proffered:

- *Mission of CRM*: elucidates how the organization should appear to the public. For instance, customer centric, service oriented, market oriented, etc. CRM vision helps in building the CRM strategy. For instance, according to the official Website of the Dallas Cowboys, their mission statement projects the Cowboys as a community-centric organization with a focus on funding programs and facilities dedicated to sports, recreation, and education in its community.
- *CRM database*: Developing a database will not only help in retaining the existing customers, but discovering and attracting new ones. Derek and Susan Nash recommend three

steps for an organization to establish a good database. First, the organization must identify and understand the company's overall vision. Second, the organization must define what information it needs to obtain for providing effective customer service, and making sure that the information is of utmost importance to the company and to each and every department of the company. Third, the organization must ascertain that the database development does not clash with any other business strategies. The development of a CRM database will aid the company in realizing its mission, that is, placing the customers at the heart of the company's activities will help improve customer relationships by being attentive to their needs. This will create a balance of revenues and profits of the company and customer contentment and loyalty. For instance, according to an article written by Wylie Wong, the Dallas Cowboys may not have had a Super Bowl appearance in over a decade, yet the team continues to invest in offering excellent service to its customers. The Dallas Cowboys invested over $1 billion in the new stadium in Arlington, Texas, offering state-of-the-art facilities to consumers. Attention to the needs of consumers can be witnessed in the creation of a system that allows the organization's employees to evaluate inventory and replenish the supply such that if the weather turns cold and sales of fleece pullovers in one end of the stadium skyrocket, the merchandise is replenished at a particular store before it is are sold out. Overall, an organization must realize the importance of customer experiences by taking them into account and also incorporating them into the system. The feedback should be regularly monitored and changes made accordingly.

- *CRM planning*: to bring about changes according to the customer feedback, changes to organizational structures, internal processes, compensation incentives, and employee skills and behavior must be made. Past researchers argue that most people view CRM as a technological solution only. However, CRM is more than just technology—it is a strategy.

Research conducted by the W. P. Carey Business School at Arizona State University contends that the organization must embrace this strategy and refrain from overusing the system for short-term sales gains by over-engaging the customers, for example, with blast e-mail offers. Thus, it may be prudent to put a cap on the number of offers that can be sent to a customer per month and per year. Overzealous use of CRM to engage customers can result in customer resistance.

- *CRM customer targeting*: the relationship with the customer needs should take into account the customer life cycle and hence manage this life cycle. Processes should be created that help meet customer expectations and deliver better customer value. For instance, sports organizations may collect personal information (birthdays and anniversaries) and preferences in sports and ticket-buying behavior information. The collected information can be used to offer discounted tickets, early purchase opportunities, personalized newsletters, and sporting merchandise coupons.

- *CRM building relationships*: successful CRM demands that customer information should be collected, stored, evaluated, distributed, and applied throughout the organization. For instance, in her article, Lisa Picarelli suggests that the customer information must be available to everyone from senior level executives for marketing decisions to a "point of sales" salesperson to accommodate last minute needs of a deserving customer.

- *CRM technology and privacy*: CRM technologies are an essential part of an organization's architecture—but most organizations' CRM technology bases are fragmented. Seamless integration across all parts of the organization (whether CRM or non-CRM technologies or applications) and its partners should be provided. Comcast-Spectacor, owner of the Philadelphia Flyers and Philadelphia 76ers and many other sports and entertainment entities, has used CRM tools to aggregate customer data collected from 5,000 different sources to create an organization-wide system to utilize the collected information. However, the collection of information should not be surreptitious, as it raises important privacy concerns.

- *CRM Metrics*: Measurable CRM objectives must be set and all levels of CRM indicators should be monitored so as to turn customers into assets. For instance, researcher Picarelli provides an example of how the Phoenix Suns successfully employed CRM to make their expensive floor seats available to upper-level, single-game ticket buyers. Further, the Suns allowed and facilitated their ticket holders to resell tickets via the team's Website. This process drove the customers to the Suns Website and exposed them to a variety of offerings.

Applications

Most CRM efforts begin as an attempt to improve customer service, but gradually become an organization-wide philosophy. Sports Alliance, a European marketing services provider that has assisted in CRM application to various soccer team organizations, points to seven steps in the application of a successful CRM effort in the sports marketing domain. First, the organization should endeavor to personalize its interaction with its customers/fans, to augment personal identification with the team. Second, once the organization has recognized its customer base, it must improve the transactional aspect of interaction with the customers: ticketing, merchandise purchases, hospitality etc., should be easy and smooth. Third, customer information and transaction history should be available at all levels of the organization. Fourth, the organization should ensure the timeliness with which data is collected, processed, and made available for use. Specifically, the organization should develop a system to clean and correct the data of all the irregularities and typing errors, and remove redundancy. Fifth, the data collected should be converted into business intelligence such that the manager is efficiently able to contact the supporter and access the supporter's consumption behavior. Sixth, once the manager is outfitted with business intelligence, he/she can convert it into action by developing customer typologies, customer groups, and customer segments. Finally, the customers may be contacted with suitable product and service offerings. The response to offerings is again stored and analyzed to improve future campaigns.

Conclusion

CRM is increasingly becoming essential to compete in today's competitive market. It helps an organization to collect and utilize customer information in a way that helps in retaining existing and attracting new customers—in turn, making profit. CRM is an organization-wide focus on developing, maintaining, and constantly improving not only the product and services, but also the relationship with the customer.

In context with the sports industry, which is a multibillion-dollar field today, CRM can be utilized in the same way as in any mid- to large-size organization. The only major difference here is the loyalty of the customers, that is, the supporters of their particular sports team or club.

Dheeraj Sharma
University of Winnipeg

See Also: Avidity; Behavior; Consumer Behavior; Customer Satisfaction; Fan Avidity; Fan Loyalty Continuum; Marketing Concept, The; Relationship Marketing.

Further Readings

Furuholt, Bjørn and Nils Georg Skutle. "Strategic Use of Customer Relationship Management (CRM) in Sports: The Rosenborg Case." In Gabor Magyar, et al., *Advances in Information Systems Development: New Methods and Practice for Networked Society*. New York: Springer, 2000.

Heskett, James L., Earl Sasser Jr., and Leonard A. Schlesinger. *The Service Profit Chain*. New York: The Free Press, 1997.

Krasnikov, Alexander, Satish Jayachandran, and V. Kumar. "The Impact of Customer Relationship Management Implementation on Cost and Profit Efficiencies: Evidence From the U.S. Commercial Banking Industry." *Journal of Marketing*, v.73/2 (2009).

O'Connor, Peter and Jaime Murphy. "Research on Information Technology in the Hospitality Industry." *International Journal of Hospitality Management*, v.23 (2004).

Customer Satisfaction

When customers purchase a product or service, they expect a certain experience. In general, this experience is presumed to be positive in nature. The customer expectations compared to the outcome (product or service) is how customers evaluate their satisfaction with the experience.

This satisfaction is often called overall customer satisfaction, and can be determined through one transaction experience, or over a series of transactions. Since customer satisfaction is determined by met expectations, if a customer has expectations that are not fulfilled, he or she is likely to have a poor level of satisfaction. Positive customer satisfaction is essential in creating long-term relationships with customers and building brand loyalty.

Managing Expectations

Customer expectations are the key to customer satisfaction. As stated before, high levels of customer satisfaction are obtained when customer expectations are met. Customer expectations are dissected into two types when determining how to meet them. The first is *will* expectations. Will expectations are those preconceived ideas about what will most likely happen during a purchase experience. These expectations can be derived from various sources. For example, a customer attending a professional baseball game may have heard from friends that it was a clean and family-friendly environment. A customer may have previously been to a game and expect the same atmosphere previously experienced.

The second type of expectation is *should* expectations. These are preconceived ideas about what should happen during an experience. These expectations are commonly derived from exterior influencers, such as word-of-mouth from the customer's friends. These types of expectations are sometimes more difficult for the sport organization to meet, because they are the hopes of the customer, which are sometimes lofty in nature.

Within a sport organization, managers frequently examine customer satisfaction across a variety of interactions with the customer. For example, sport organizations might examine the season ticket holder satisfaction with the entire purchase process of their tickets. At the same time, sport organizations may focus the satisfaction examination on customer experiences with concessions or parking. It is not only important to know that consumers are satisfied, but why they are satisfied and with what aspect of the sport organization's business customers are satisfied. In order to provide exemplary customer satisfaction, sport organizations need to know where they are exceeding customer expectations as well as where they are lacking.

Tracking Satisfaction

When determining customer satisfaction, practitioners and researchers acknowledge two types: horizontal and vertical. Horizontal satisfaction addresses the experiences with a single product transaction or event or game. Vertical satisfaction deals with the experiences with the brand or sport organization producing the product or event.

Sport organizations usually measure customer satisfaction through customer surveys. Organizations administer surveys following an experience in order to determine if expectations were met. The two previously mentioned types of satisfaction (horizontal and vertical) are the basis for various satisfaction surveys. For example, sport organizations wanting to determine a satisfied experience with a single event would be a horizontal study. If a marathon event organizing body, for instance, wants to measure the satisfaction its participants experienced, it would want to develop a horizontally based survey. On the other hand, a sport organization evaluating the overall experiences with its organization would be a vertical study. For example, if a professional sports team wanted to determine the satisfaction levels the season ticket holders have toward the organization, it would develop a vertically based survey.

Sport marketers develop two general types of customer satisfaction studies. These two types are similar to horizontal and vertical satisfaction, but distinct in nature. The first is related to the satisfaction the customer has with the product. The sport product can be anything from merchandise to the game experience. This directly relates to the quality of the product the customer is purchasing. Depending on the type of product, the quality is determined by characteristics of the product (e.g., players) and the outcome of the product's consumption (e.g., player performance).

The second type focuses on service the customer experienced. This can be the service the customer experienced during the transaction (e.g., ticket purchasing process) or the service itself (e.g., sport instructional lessons). This is related to the quality of service provided by the sport organization. The overall service quality is determined by the interactions the customer has with the employee as well as the environment in which the transaction takes place, whether online, by telephone, or at the live venue.

Conclusion

One of the primary goals of sport organizations, after the customer has purchased a product or service, is to retain that customer's business. To do this, sport organizations need to increase the customer's intention to repurchase the product or service. Customers, in general, have an increased repurchase intention when they have a high level of satisfaction with their experiences. Increasing customer satisfaction can aid in developing repeat purchases through decreased complaints, as well as increasing potential customer purchases through positive word-of-mouth.

Jason Daniel Reese
Texas A&M University

See Also: Brand Insistence; Event Management; Relationship Marketing; Service Quality; Survey Research; Word-of-Mouth.

Further Readings

Beccarini, Corrado and Alain Ferrand. "Factors Affecting Soccer Club Season Ticket Holders' Satisfaction: The Influence of Club Image and Fans' Motives." *European Sport Management Quarterly*, v.6/1 (2006).

Greenwell, T. Christopher. "Expectations, Industry Standards, and Customer Satisfaction in the Student Ticketing Process." *Sport Marketing Quarterly*, v.16/1 (2007).

Mullin, Bernard J., Stephen Hardy, and William A. Sutton. *Sport Marketing*. Champaign, IL: Human Kinetics, 2000.

Van Leeuwen, Linda, Shayne Quick, and Kerry Daniel. "The Sport Spectator Satisfaction Model: A Conceptual Framework for Understanding the Satisfaction of Spectators." *Sport Management Review*, v.5/2 (2002).

Yoshida, Masayuki and Jeffrey D. James. "Customer Satisfaction With Game and Service Experiences: Antecedents and Consequences." *Journal of Sport Management*, v.24/2 (2010).

Dallas Cowboys

The Dallas Cowboys is one of the most popular teams in the National Football League (NFL). Long known as "America's Team," the Cowboys recorded 20 consecutive winning seasons (1966–85), won five of their record eight Super Bowl appearances, and play their home games in the most extravagant facility in all of American sports. The team has attracted consistent sellout crowds, garnered high television ratings, and been one of the top five sellers of licensed merchandise in the NFL for most of the past 40 years. Owner Jerry Jones has earned both praise and scorn for his groundbreaking marketing initiatives and his confident attitude.

The Cowboys were founded in 1960. Tom Landry coached the Cowboys from their inception and though he was eventually enshrined in the Pro Football Hall of Fame, his first few years as Cowboy coach yielded terrible records. The team had five losing season before finally finishing 7–7 in 1965. Despite the initial on-field failure, Landry had built a solid foundation for future success. In 1966, the Cowboys began a streak of 20 straight winning seasons.

During the late 1960s and 1970s the Cowboys continued to win games and attract fans. Though the team lost numerous heartbreaking playoff games, including the infamous "Ice Bowl" NFL Championship game against the Green Bay Packers in 1967, the team participated in the playoffs for 18 of their 20 consecutive winning seasons. They were able to win Super Bowl VI against the Miami Dolphins and Super Bowl XII against the Denver Broncos. Though the Cowboys' winning records certainly attracted fans, much of their nationwide success can be attributed to general manager Tex Schramm's marketing efforts. Schramm developed the Cowboy brand by marketing the clean-cut image of Tom Landry and popular players such as quarterback Roger Staubach, while also creating and promoting the Dallas Cowboy Cheerleaders.

Though the Cowboys played their initial seasons in the historic Cotton Bowl, by 1971 they had moved into state-of-the-art Texas Stadium. The new facility offered an unprecedented number of luxury suites, which supported the "larger than life" Cowboys image and generated large revenues for the franchise. Even after 30 years Texas Stadium remained one of the highest revenue generating facilities in the NFL.

During the early 1980s, the Cowboys remained one of the best teams in the NFL. However, they were unable to return to the Super Bowl after appearing

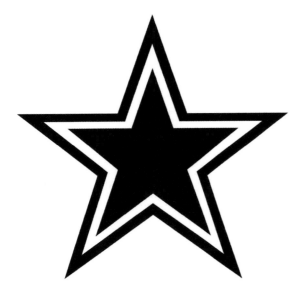

Dallas Cowboys licensed merchandise, much of it featuring the star logo, is often among the top five sellers in the NFL.

five times in the 1970s. The team lost three National Football Conference (NFC) Championship games in a row from 1981 to 1983. In 1985, the team had its last of 20 consecutive winning seasons. By 1986, most of their best players and legendary coach Tom Landry had begun to show their age. From 1986 to 1988, the team became progressively worse, and in 1989, the team was sold to Jerry Jones. One of Jones's first acts as owner was to fire Landry and replace him with University of Miami coach Jimmy Johnson. Though most of the fans knew Landry needed to retire, the move was unpopular among Cowboys fans because of the impact Landry had had upon the team and the entire sport.

The first year under Jones and Johnson was among the worst in NFL history. The 1989 Cowboys finished 1–15 and were the laughingstock of the NFL. However, Johnson used the first year to evaluate all of his players and to establish his philosophy. The team executed a critical trade during the terrible season, sending productive running back Herschel Walker to the Minnesota Vikings for multiple players and draft picks. Though the 1990 team did not make the playoffs, fans realized that Johnson's skillful trades and masterful drafting was building a strong foundation. At the same time, Jones was implementing one of the most aggressive marketing campaigns of any sport organization. The Cowboys signed numerous sponsors and sought any method

to maximize their revenue. When the team made the playoffs after the 1991 season, most NFL observers realized it was only a matter of time before great players such as quarterback Troy Aikman, running back Emmitt Smith, and wide receiver Michael Irvin would dominate the NFL. After the 1992 and 1993 seasons, the Cowboys won the Super Bowl and appeared nearly unstoppable.

Dynasty in Decline

Despite winning two Super Bowls in a row, Johnson and Jones had numerous disagreements. Unfortunately for the Cowboys and their fans, Johnson left the Cowboys before the team had a chance to win an unprecedented third straight Super Bowl. Jones hired Barry Switzer as a replacement, and though Switzer did lead the team to a Super Bowl after the 1995 season, he did not have Johnson's ability to draft top-notch players or to keep the team motivated at the same championship level. During Switzer's years as coach, numerous scandals erupted and the team's performance slowly declined. The NFL's salary cap, which had been implemented in 1994, sped the team's decline, as many of the players Johnson had drafted could not be retained under the new financial rules. From 1997 to 2008, the Cowboys had numerous coaching changes and no playoff victories.

Despite the team's mediocrity in the late 1990s and 2000s, Jerry Jones continued to implement effective marketing strategies, many of which were at odds with most of the other NFL owners. Jones's efforts helped the team remain one of the NFL's top revenue generating franchises. In 2009, the Cowboys opened a new facility that was one of the most spectacular buildings ever constructed. The $1.3 billion retractable-roofed domed stadium instantly became the NFL's landmark facility. Nicknamed "Jerry World," the new facility could host over 100,000 people and offered numerous fan amenities. The facility ensured that the Cowboys would remain one of the highest revenue generating franchises in all of sports.

Mark S. Nagel
University of South Carolina

See Also: Luxury Boxes and Suites; National Football League; Salary Cap; Super Bowl.

Further Readings

Golenbock, Peter. *Landry's Boys*. Chicago: Triumph Books, 2005.

Magee, David. *Playing to Win: Jerry Jones and the Dallas Cowboys*. Chicago: Triumph Books, 2008.

Pearlman, Jeff. *Boys Will Be Boys: The Glory Days and Party Nights of the Dallas Cowboys*. New York: HarperCollins, 2008

Dallas Mavericks

The Dallas Mavericks have become a model of a successfully marketed and managed National Basketball Association (NBA) franchise. However, until the current owner, Mark Cuban, purchased the team, the franchise was highly tumultuous. In 1980, the NBA league owners voted to admit the Dallas Mavericks into the league for a $12 million entry fee. The Mavericks quickly became an established playoff contender in the 1980s, but in the 1990s they were known as one of the worst franchises in the NBA.

In the 1990s, attendance at Mavericks games had declined to the point where Reunion Arena was only at half capacity on average. To make matters worse, the NBA had begun to decline in popularity in the late 1990s, primarily because of the retirement of Michael Jordan and the player lockout at the beginning of the 1998–99 season. In 2000, Mark Cuban, a former Internet mogul, purchased a controlling interest in the Dallas Mavericks for $280 million. Cuban then led one of the more storied franchise turnarounds in NBA history. Under the guidance of Cuban, the Dallas Mavericks routinely began to sell out games, increased their merchandise sales, and were rated number one in customer relations. The team's value increased from $167 million in 1999 to $300 million in 2002.

Management/Marketing Strategies
Unlike the majority of owners in professional sports, Cuban became a recognizable face within the local community and at all Mavericks games. In a somewhat grassroots marketing effort, Cuban orchestrated numerous promotions that were meant to increase his connection with Mavericks fans to enhance the overall image of the franchise. Cuban implemented various promotional strategies in which he was a visible component. In his first few years as owner, Cuban encouraged fans to paint their bodies and faces by offering free tickets to the most elaborately costumed and fanatical fans. Cuban also made appearances at local eateries and fast-food franchises and gave away free food. He regularly sits in the upper-level seating of the American Airlines arena in order to connect with the fans and get their perspectives on improving their experiences at Mavericks games. Cuban's e-mail address is also posted throughout the arena for the fans to offer insight into their experiences or to critique the efforts of the team and arena personnel.

In addition to connecting with the fans, the Mavericks have implemented policies that are meant to ensure that their fans and customers walk away from games having had the best possible game experience. This includes ensuring a high level of customer service from the arena staff and vendors. This focus on the fan experience led to Mavericks games filling the American Airlines Arena to an incredible 103.4 percent capacity, with folding chairs being brought in to create overflow seating areas.

Finally, technology has played an instrumental role in the increased viability of the Mavericks. The Mavericks were the first NBA franchise to print bar codes on their tickets. This has allowed them to track the effectiveness of group sales and free promotional tickets. The Mavericks franchise was also the first to implement a point-of-sale tracking system, which has allowed them to process credit card orders from their merchandise and concession sales more rapidly than other dial-up credit card systems. This system has given team executives multiple years of data so they can accurately predict the proper timing and effectiveness of concession and merchandise promotions while preventing wasted food and drink products. Additionally, each of the luxury suites in American Airlines Arena is equipped with computer systems that are meant to expedite concession and merchandise orders.

In 2010, the Mavericks won a division title and in 2011 went on to win the NBA Finals by defeating the Miami Heat. This marked the team's first NBA Championship in its 31-year history.

The connection of the ownership to the fans, overall commitment to the fan experience, and technological innovations have resulted in the Dallas Mavericks being voted one of the top franchises in the NBA by fans. Moreover, Dallas was named the best NBA city by *The Sporting News*.

Calvin Nite
Texas A&M University

See Also: Barcoding; Concession Pricing; Customer Satisfaction; Fan Attendance, Reasons for; Ownership, Professional Teams; Promotion; Technology in Sports.

Further Readings

Aron, Jamie. *Tales From the Dallas Mavericks.* Champaign, IL: Sports Publishing LLC, 2003.
Cone, Edward. "Dallas Mavericks: Small Companies, Big Return." http://www .baselinemag.com/c/a/Projects-Management/ Dallas-Mavericks-Small-Companies-Big-Returns (Accessed June 2010).
McConnell, Ben and Jackie Huba. *Creating Customer Evangelists: How Loyal Customers Become a Volunteer Sales Force.* Chicago: Dearborn Trade Publishers, 2003.
National Basketball Association. "Mavericks: Mavs History." http://www.nba.com/mavericks/history/ mavs_history.html (Accessed June 2010).

Dallas Stars

The Dallas Stars are a professional National Hockey League (NHL) franchise with a single owner, Thomas O. Hicks. The team plays within the Pacific Division of the NHL's Western Conference. The Dallas Stars Foundation provides community schools and organizations with grants and support, especially for youth programs. The team holds a variety of marketing fundraisers to support the foundation, including the Dr. Pepper Golf Classic, Casino Night, and the holiday "Jingle Jet."

The franchise began in 1967 as the Minnesota North Stars, relocating to Dallas, Texas, before the 1993–94 season. Stars management had the task of building a successful franchise in a nontraditional hockey market, as the NHL sought to increase its presence through expansion into the south along with two new Florida NHL teams. They quickly built a fan base through winning seasons and the acquisition of talented players such as Mike Modano. Team affiliates include the Texas Stars, Idaho Steelheads, and Allen Americans.

The home of the Stars was Reunion Arena from 1993 to 2001, when they moved to their current home, the American Airlines Center. Team highlights include seven Pacific Division titles, two Western Conference titles, and winning the 1998–99 Stanley Cup. The Stars are one of only a few NHL teams that simulcast all games on local television and radio, including Fox Sports Southwest and KTCK. Popular announcers include Ralph Strangis and Daryl "Razor" Reaugh, commonly known to fans as "Ralph and Razor."

Dallas-based billionaire and investor Thomas O. Hicks is the owner and chairman of the board of the Dallas Stars, as well as the chairman and chief financial executive of Hicks Holdings LLC, a Dallas-based investment firm. He purchased the Stars in December 1996. In 1998, Hicks also purchased the Texas Rangers Major League Baseball team. Hicks appointed two ex-NHL players to be in charge of hockey operations: Joe Nieuwendyk is the general manager of the Stars and Brett Hull is the executive vice president. Geoff Moore is the executive vice president of sales and marketing.

Hicks and the executive management staff have acquired some key players over the years to make the Stars a successful franchise. During his tenure as the Stars owner, the team has been very successful, winning seven division championships, making two consecutive trips to the Stanley Cup Finals, and winning the Stanley Cup in 1999. Hicks and the team's management realize that attracting talented and well-known players and building a successful franchise can play an important part in team marketing and fan-based expansion. In June 2009,

Hicks brought in Marc Crawford, another former NHL player and experienced coach, to serve as the team's head coach.

Outreach and Marketing

The team's community outreach organization, the Dallas Stars Foundation, was founded in 1998, although the team has been involved in community service outreach and marketing since the 1993 season. The Stars hold numerous marketing and community events throughout the year, including the Dr. Pepper Golf Classic. The Stars Foundation also markets a Casino Night where fans mingle with the players and get pictures and autographs while playing cards and dining. The foundation then reinvests the proceeds into various community organizations and initiatives. Owner Thomas Hicks also enjoys giving money to local charities and has held a number of charity board memberships.

One of the team's in-game marketing events is the holiday season Mystery Puck Sale. For a $30 donation, fans can buy a gift-wrapped puck. Every puck is autographed, and if it is signed in gold, the winning fan has a chance to attend a Dallas Stars practice and meet the player who signed the winning puck. The Stars have another interesting marketing event during the holiday season, a program called "Jingle Jet."

One of the key goals of the Dallas Stars Foundation is the annual financial support of local children's charities, children's hospitals, children with cancer, youth organizations, food banks, youth emergency shelters, and a variety of other organizations. The Stars also reach out to youth by getting involved with area schools. Every year the club awards scholarships to all-around student athletes from area high schools and hockey and figure skating scholarships to young student athletes. They host reading and media days with area students and schools. The team also donates game tickets to groups that bring children and young adults to the games.

David Trevino
Independent Scholar

See Also: Community Relations; Dallas Cowboys; Dallas Mavericks; National Hockey League.

Further Readings

Dallas Stars Foundation. http://stars.nhl.com/club/page.htm?id=39286 (Accessed September 2010).

Dallas Stars Official Website. http://stars.nhl.com/club (Accessed September 2010).

Duhatschek, Eric. *Hockey Chronicles: An Insider History of National Hockey League Teams.* New York: Checkmark Books, 2001.

Whitson, David and Richard S. Gruneau. *Artificial Ice: Hockey, Culture, and Commerce.* Toronto: Broadview Press, 2006.

Zirin, Dave. *Bad Sports: How Owners Are Ruining the Games We Love.* New York: Scribner, 2010.

Data Collection

In order to effectively craft and spread their messages, public relations and marketing professionals must collect data. Data for a sport marketer may include information or knowledge about one's consumers, markets, suppliers, competitors, economy, political or legal influences, and one's own organization. Without studying their audiences, practitioners will waste valuable time, money, and human resources.

Data collection may be classified in two schools: quantitative and qualitative. Quantitative researchers want to know "what" exists, whereas qualitative researchers seek to determine "how" or "why" it exists. Regardless of the data collection method, two things must be considered: the reliability and validity of the study, and the sampling method chosen for data collection.

Reliability and Validity

Whatever the goal of the data collection research it is important that the methodological design be reliable and valid. Without reliability and validity, there is no way of knowing if the research questions—what it is the professional wants to learn—are being answered with appropriate information.

A reliable study may be repeated with similar findings. This is especially important in data collection for sports. If, for example, a marketing director surveys fans to determine their likes and dislikes regarding game-day promotions, he or she should expect a second survey to provide roughly the same results.

Of equal importance is validity. A valid study measures what the researcher intends to measure. Staying with the fan likes and dislikes example, a valid study will specifically ask questions related to game-day promotions and will seek attitudes and opinions about those promotions, thus answering the researcher's primary questions.

Sampling

The goal of data collection is to provide answers to specific questions. Ideally, a researcher would collect data from every fan or consumer. This, however, is usually unrealistic. Therefore, collecting data from a sample of the population is desirable. Sampling falls in two categories: random and nonrandom sampling.

Nonrandom sampling includes convenience sampling, purposive sampling, and quota sampling. Convenience sampling relies on the selection of readily available units of measurement. The least representative method of sampling, it is the easiest means of gathering data. An example of convenience sampling would be a media relations director looking at clippings from a month of the daily newspaper to determine how much coverage her teams are receiving.

Purposive sampling is used when the researcher is after data from a specific set. A marketing director may want to know the characteristics of fans buying tickets in a particular neighboring town. He is not interested in the characteristics of all fans, but only fans in the particular town so that a specialized ticket-selling campaign may be developed.

Quota sampling is applied when a researcher wants to make sure a certain number of units from specific categories are evaluated. Researchers may be instructed to survey 30 males and 30 females at a sporting event, for example.

Random sampling primarily includes simple, systematic, and stratified random sampling. In this case, all units of the population being studied have an equal chance of being selected. The media relations director would use simple random sampling if he put the names of all the newspapers in the state in a hat and drew out 20 percent of the names. This, then, would be his pool from which to gather data.

Systematic random sampling occurs when the researcher chooses to pick every *xth* unit. In this case, the media relations director would list all the newspapers and then choose, for example, every 10th newspaper on the list.

Stratified sampling is a two-step process. It involves dividing the population into groups, or strata, and then sampling from within these strata. The National Collegiate Athletic Association (NCAA) might choose this type of sampling to compare average length of baseball games of its member institutions. The NCAA could first divide its members into strata, the obvious choice being by division (I, II, or III). It then would randomly pick an equal number (nonproportionate) or an equal percentage (proportionate) of schools from each division.

While random sampling does provide the researcher more of an opportunity to generalize findings, it does take more time and is more complicated.

Quantitative Data Collection

Quantitative measures include survey research (via questionnaires or interviews) and content analysis. Numbers are the focus. The researcher is reducing messages to numbers in search of representative responses. Frequency distributions including mean (average), median (the midpoint in a string of numbers), and mode (the most common occurrence) are sought.

In surveys, lists of questions are presented and numbers are assigned for responses (for example, 1 = strongly agree, 2 = agree, 3 = neutral, 4 = disagree, 5 = strongly disagree). Groups may also be categorized by numbers (1 = age 0–5, 2 = 6–10, 3 = 11–15).

Content analyses may take a similar approach. In most content analyses, however, readily available messages may be utilized. A researcher may count column inches of newspaper articles or count how many times the organization's name was mentioned on ESPN during a given week.

Qualitative Data Collection

In-depth interviewing, focus groups, and ethnographic research all are examples of qualitative research. The goal of qualitative analysis is to find common themes. Messages or responses to open-ended questions are analyzed to determine if individuals have similar attitudes, beliefs, or feelings about the same topic.

In-depth interviewing, as the name suggests, involves presenting a list of open-ended questions and probes that elicit responses from those selected for the study. A focus group, similarly, requires a list of open-ended questions and probes, only instead of interviewing one person at a time a group of people (usually no more than 15) are asked the questions, and they may respond when interested. Ethnographic studies involve the researcher observing individuals for an extended period of time (often weeks or months) as they live and work.

Conclusion

Regardless of the method chosen for data collection it is important to remember that it is a process and that each step is critical to the gathering of data. However, when performed correctly, data collection may yield valuable, detailed information that will help the organization accomplish its goals.

Joe Moore
University of Central Missouri

See Also: Audience Measurement; Customer Relationship Marketing; Economic Impact Study; Evaluation; Fan Market Segmentation; Marketing Objective; Public Relations/Publicity; Qualitative Research; Quantitative Research; Survey Research.

Further Readings

McMillan, J. H. *Educational Research: Fundamentals for Consumers,* 5th Ed. Upper Saddle River, NJ: Pearson, 2008.
Morgan, G. A., J. A. Gliner, and N. Leech. *Research in Applied Settings: An Integrated Approach to Design and Analysis.* Mahwah, NJ: Lawrence Erlbaum Associates, 2009.
Riddick, Carol Cutler and Ruth V. Russell. *Research in Recreation, Parks, Sport, and Tourism,* 2nd Ed. Champaign, IL: Sagamore Publishing, 2008.

Database Management

Database management (DBM) is a technological strategy used by sports teams to capture important information on product usage, demographics, current clients, potential clients, and improving marketing tactics and strategies. DBM uses software to collect information records that are called databases, and it allows users to gather information in an organized and structured manner. DBM is usually used by sales departments in sports teams, but other departments such as service and retention, corporate services, Web departments, and marketing departments also use the information collected by DBM. The reasoning behind using DBM is to acquire new customers, retain current clients, regain former clients, and reduce the costs associated with marketing.

In sport teams, data is collected from season ticket holders (STH), sponsors, and individual ticket buyers. Sport teams use the Customer Relationship Management (CRM) approach to learn everything about its customers' relationships with the organization. Sports teams use CRM software to manage their databases. This approach assists these teams in understanding customer behavior and predicting future behavior. CRM use may help teams acquire better leads, save costs, ensure repeat business, build customer loyalty, increase profitability, and grow customer advocacy. CRM enables sport teams to answer the question: how can we serve the customer better?

Teams implement CRM by selecting the right technology, providing the best data to employees, and making the technology easy for the employees. In properly operating DBM/CRM, information collected must be valid and accurate. The validity of information collected will determine the success or failure of the strategy.

Sports teams use collection of vital information to build their databases, which then serve as a platform for proper CRM. The collection occurs everywhere the fan touches the sport product. For example, sport teams collect data from fans who visit Websites, watch games on television, listen to games on the radio, buy team apparel, complete an All-Star ballot, play in fantasy leagues, or participate in a sweepstakes.

DBM/CRM Systems

Sport organizations come in contact with fans in a myriad of ways: when tickets are purchased, games are watched on television, or team Websites are visited, to name just a few examples. These contact points have made it more important for teams to retain current customers, acquire new customers, and increase the attendance frequency of the average customer. Database management can help teams segment customers by their buying habits, which will assist in targeting specific clients.

By properly managing their database, teams will be able to generate new business, sell tickets to new customers, build loyalty, increase their current customer base, generate more revenue from current clients, and get a higher percentage of renewals for clients. A good DBM system is as good as the data entered into it. Once sport teams have come in contact with fans, they have to enter the data in a manner so that it can be stored for easy retrieval. DBM systems, through proper collection and entering of data, assist teams in making sense of the random activities that occur in their arenas or stadiums. Random activities are those that, without a good DBM system, cannot be tracked and monitored.

Some of the other factors that make DBM important include the following:

• Helps understand customer behavior
• Uses the past to predict future customer behavior
• Automates the prospecting process for sales people
• Generates better leads and eliminates waste of time

The traits of a DBM system include the following:

• *Centralization of data:* all the information should be located in one system and not spread out over different systems. The centralization of data in one location makes the accessibility of information easier and prevents confusion between departments.
• *Integration of databases:* allows for information from different sources to be compared or assembled whenever necessary.

• *Easy retrieval of data:* data must be stored in formats that allow them to be easily read or collected when needed.
• *Integration into e-marketing campaign:* data on all fans and potential fans that visit a team's Website should be captured. The information collected can be on ticket plans, ticket sales, and promotions.

The traits of a CRM system include the following:

• Names of key relationships such as family members and administrators
• Names of childhood teams
• Feedback on positive or negative information
• Work information
• Previous seating location
• Past games attended
• Types of tickets purchased
• Customer surveys
• E-mail permissions

In sport, the benefits of a DBM system are directly tied to how the team uses its CRM. These benefits are what that team gains in the short term and long term from using the CRM, including the following:

• Better tracking of ticket and sponsorship sales
• Improved measurement of marketing efforts
• Maximization of marketing tools
• Greater understanding of customers
• Better decision making
• Full integration of business processes
• Easier access to information between departments
• Assistance in acquiring new business
• Improved retention rates within organization
• Streamlined sales process
• Better targeting of customers
• Enhanced return on investment

Problems with CRM are tied to how teams use their DBM through CRM. They are issues faced by organizations when implementing CRM using the DBM software. They are as follows:

• *Ease of use:* teams/organizations are slow to adopt CRMs because the software system is not easy to use. The systems are made very comprehensive, which sacrifices the ability of employees to easily use the system. This difficulty leads to a low adoption rate among staff in a team.

- *Implementation*: DBM software has to be implemented properly into the organization for the team to benefit from the system.

Some of the causes of implementation problems are as follows:

- *Improper planning*: when organizations do not put enough effort into choosing the right software and incorporating the software into the team's processes.
- *Deficient integration*: when teams fail to properly integrate all their processes.
- *Lack of information sharing*: implementation problems are caused when different departments fail to properly communicate using the DBM software. For instance, a marketing department does not input information into the software that sales would need before approaching a potential customer. This then leads to the salesperson sharing inaccurate or incorrect information to the prospect, which causes problems if the customer decides to make a purchase.

Types

There are several types of database management software in the market that serve different purposes. In sport, the database management software serves CRM and ticketing functions. Examples of CRM solutions providers in the marketplace include: Sage Software, Goldmine, Brainsell, SAP, Sales Net, Stay in Front, Phaseware, Microsoft Dynamics, Infusion CRM, and Netsuite. Some of the CRM solutions providers used by sport organizations include Microsoft Dynamics, Sage Software, Ticketmaster, and Conxeo. Other solutions providers can also serve sport organizations.

Microsoft Dynamics is a line of CRM designed to meet a myriad of business needs and to assist in making important decisions quickly. Microsoft Dynamics has been designed to meet any sales, marketing, or service needs, but it can also meet a number of different demands. Microsoft Dynamics can be accessed through Internet Explorer or Microsoft Outlook. While other browsers can be used to access Dynamics, they are not created by Microsoft and can give mixed results. The benefits of Microsoft Dynamics include that it enables confident decision making, there may be staff familiarity and increased business productivity, and systems compatibility and constant support.

In 2004, The Phoenix Suns decided to use Microsoft CRM, and 50 employees were trained and using the software on a daily basis. The database housed over 270,000 records, and a single view of each record was available to all employees based on security. The system was incorporated into ticket sales, marketing campaigns, and sponsorship sales. Ticket operations and ticket sales and sponsorship sales and service had automated workflow. Inventory management was developed for sponsorship and community relationship programs.

Property Port, which has been developed by Conxeo, is a Web-based application that synchronizes the organization's processes. It allows everyone from the accounting department to the sales team to work off the same application. Property Port gives organizations the ability to organize assets, create customizable proposals and recap reports, and generate reports on their data.

Property Port works closely with entities such as sports teams, fairs, and festivals by assisting in managing their sponsorship assets and sponsorship relationships. The software tracks assets such as signage, ticket backs, media placements, and hospitality tents. It allows sponsorship sales teams to create proposals and recap reports. It also provides reports back to sponsorship management and executives. The benefits of Property Port include better organization of sponsorship assets, increased communication, efficient creation of proposals, improved feedback for sponsors, and better asset inventory identification.

The San Diego Padres use Property Port to create proposals and recap reports for sponsors. Property Port is also used by organizations such as the Chicago Fire and St. Louis Rams. These organizations use Property Port to analyze data, create proposals, recap reports, communicate with other departments, and measure return on investment.

Archtics is a software designed by Ticketmaster that enables clients to customize ticket packages and sell them to fans. It also allows companies to manage billing, renewals, and CRM capabilities. Unlike most other database management systems, Archtics focuses on ticketing, but also has CRM capabilities.

Archtics also has a special tool called Accessmanager. Accessmanager is an access control tool that gives Ticketmaster's clients a look at what happens after the ticket sales process. The benefits of Archtics include easy access to customer data, reduction in manpower and time spent fulfilling ticketing needs, improvement in customer knowledge, and better tracking of customer information.

Archtics is currently being used by professional and college sports teams, arenas, theaters and museums. Professional franchises such as the Washington Capitals and Boston Celtics, to name a few, also use Archtics.

Sage CRM Solutions provides contact and customer manager solutions by tracking the details of customer relationships. Sage ACT is a CRM software that is used to keep track of customer and prospect information in a database that can be viewed by different users. It works well with Internet Explorer, Outlook, and other applications to track client and prospect information. The benefits of ACT include that it captures and manages prospects, promotes well-organized details, improves efficiency, and betters marketing coordination.

Organizations such as the Atlanta Hawks and Atlanta Thrashers use the Sage ACT system to manage their sponsorship prospect information.

Saleslogix is a CRM software that provides a complete view of customer interaction across the sales, marketing, and customer service teams. It is used by 300,000 people and 8,500 companies worldwide. It provides users with the ability to choose their method of access. Users can access Saleslogix via Windows, Web, or mobile without trading functionality, usability, and robust customization capabilities. Saleslogix is ideal for small- to medium-sized businesses and for divisions of larger corporations. The benefits of Sage Saleslogix include that it is easily customizable to specific business needs, reduces time and money spent on training, and promotes integration of information.

Sales force software includes Sales Cloud and Service Cloud. Sales Cloud stores different pieces of information in one place. By easing the access of information, it offers improved communication tools, comprehensive information about prospects and customers, increased number of quality leads, and access through mobile devices.

Service Cloud provides tools for customer service to organizations by assisting companies to tap into conversations taking place between customers online on Web forums, between friends on Facebook, and on Twitter. Service Cloud sifts through tons of information for the client, agent, or partner in the cloud (or community).

Boma Ekiyor
Independent Scholar

See Also: Customer Relationship Marketing; Data Collection; Information Systems, Kinds of.

Further Readings

"Compare CRM: #1 Resource for CRM Buyers." http://www.comparecrm.com/crm-vendors/sage/sage-crm.php (Accessed February 2011).

Harvard Business Review. *Customer Relationship Management*. Cambridge, MA: Harvard Business School Press, 2002.

Irwin, Richard I., William A. Sutton, and Larry M. McCarthy. *Sport Promotion and Sales Management*. Champaign, IL: Human Kinetics, 2008.

Mullin, Bernard J., Stephen Hardy, and William A. Sutton. *Sports Marketing*. Champaign, IL: Human Kinetics, 2007.

Sage CRM Solutions. http://www.sagecrmsolutions.com/Why-Sage-CRM-Solutions (Accessed February 2011).

SportsBusinessWire. "Sponsor Direct Renames Conxeo." http://www.sportsbusinesswire.com/featured-releases/sponsor-direct-renamed-conxeo (Accessed February 2011).

Symes, Steve. "Problems With Microsoft Dynamics CRM." http://www.ehow.com/list_6531737_problems-microsoft-dynamics-crm.html (Accessed February 2011).

Davis Cup

The Davis Cup is the premier men's team event in the sport of tennis. First contested in 1900, the event allows the best players from the member nations of the International Tennis Federation (ITF) the chance to represent their country in a sport where players usually compete as individuals. The tournament was established by a Harvard University student named Dwight Davis. Davis, who at one time was the second-ranked tennis player in the country, originally intended for the match to be a competition between the United States and Great Britain. Davis commissioned a jeweler, Shreve, Crump & Low, to produce a silver trophy, and then captained the U.S. team to a victory against their British opponents during the first match in Boston. The tournament uses a terminology of its own: for example, the word *rubber* is used for match, and the word *tie* is used for a round of competition.

The United States won the first three Davis Cup matches against Great Britain, and then in 1904, teams from Belgium and France took part for the first time. The cup been contested every year since 1911, except for during World War I and World War II. In 1923, the ITF revised the structure of the competition by dividing the world into two zones—American and European—to accommodate the increasing number of teams taking part.

The four nations that host a Grand Slam event in the sport (Australia, France, Great Britain, and the United States) dominated the competition, winning all events up to 1973. However, it should be noted that in early competitions Australia competed as part of an Australasia team alongside New Zealand. For the first seven decades the Davis Cup was only a competition for amateur players, but changed to become an open event in 1973. Since 1974, a number of other nations have won the trophy, with Croatia becoming the most recent first-time victors, winning the cup in 2005. To date, 12 different nations have won the trophy; the United States holds the record for the most victories, with 32 Davis Cup titles to its name.

Over the years, the structure of the competition has changed in order to accommodate the large number of nations that now enter the competition. The most significant change occurred in 1972 when the traditional challenge round was abolished. Teams now comprise three to four players, and nations face off in a best-of-five rubber encompassing four singles and one doubles match-up over a period of three days. The 16 highest-ranked teams are assigned to the World Group and compete annually for the cup. Nations that do not play in the World Group compete in one of three regional zones (Americas, Asia/Oceania, and Europe/Africa) and the competition takes place over the course of four weekends throughout the year. The ITF determines the host countries for matches before each tournament. Nations in the World Group compete in a four-round elimination tournament and are seeded based on a ranking system. The losers of the first-round matches move to the World Group playoff round, where they play along with winners from Group I of the regional zones. The winners of this then enter the World Group for the tournament the following year, and the losers play in Group I of their regional zone.

The global financial group BNP Paribas has been the title sponsor of the event since 2002. Other companies involved as partner sponsors include Hugo Boss, Rolex, and Wilson. The Davis Cup partnership program provides each of these companies with tailored benefits enabling them to achieve their marketing and promotional goals year-round and at every Davis Cup tie. The Davis Cup is primarily shown on terrestrial television, so it allows sponsors to reach a wide audience in a number of different markets.

In 1974, South Africa won their first, and to date only, title without even playing in the final. They were due to meet India to contest the cup but the Indian government boycotted the match in protest against South Africa's system of apartheid. In 2009, the Sweden versus Israel match in Malmo was played in an empty stadium because of security concerns following a "Stop the Match" campaign against Israeli attacks on Gaza. Outside of the stadium protesters clashed with police while the two teams competed.

John Harris
Kent State University

See Also: America's Cup; International Reach; Ryder Cup; U.S. Open Tennis Tournament; Wimbledon Tennis Tournament.

Further Readings

Cateora, Phillip R., et al. *International Marketing.* New York: McGraw-Hill, 2009.

Davis Cup Official Website. http://www.daviscup .com (Accessed October 2010).

Evans, Richard. *The Davis Cup: Celebrating 100 Years of International Tennis.* New York: Universe, 1999.

D.C. United

D.C. United, based in Washington, D.C., is one of the original 10 clubs of Major League Soccer (MLS), and is the strongest team in terms of on-the-field performance in the league's history. In 14 seasons of play, D.C. United has won two U.S. Open Cups, four MLS Cups (the league championship), as well as four supporters shields (the award given to the team with the best regular season ranking).

The choice of Washington, D.C., as the location for an MLS franchise was well in place before the league began play. When the original plans for the MLS were drawn up prior to the U.S. bid for hosting the 1994 World Cup, Washington, D.C., was one of seven cities chosen to have a franchise when the league was formed. However, because of several setbacks in getting the league founded and started, it was not until 1996 when the league began play, and hence, that D.C. United took to the field. D.C. United was chosen to play in the first MLS match on April 6, 1996, in San Jose, in a nationally televised game. Though D.C. United lost the match, they ended up winning the league championship and the U.S. Open Cup in the inaugural MLS season.

The team's colors and name were announced in fall 1995. The team decided on using the name *United* to mimic many of the popular professional soccer clubs in Europe, such as Manchester United and Newcastle United. The team's uniform is black and white, and composed of three stripes that are meant to represent the areas of Washington, D.C., Maryland, and Virginia. In this manner, D.C.

United is similar to many other MLS franchises in choosing to pay tribute to their location through either their team logo or uniform. The team's uniform has evolved over the years and now sports the Volkswagen logo on the front as part of team's current sponsorship deal with the American subsidiary of the German automaker.

Ownership and Sponsors

D.C. United has changed hands between many parties and ownership groups throughout the team's history. Originally, the team was owned by billionaire George Soros, who eventually sold the franchise to Phil Anschutz's sports company, Anschutz Entertainment Group (AEG) in 2001. For several years, AEG owned or operated the most powerful teams in the league, including the Chicago Fire, Los Angeles Galaxy, New York Metrostars, and D.C. United. However, under pressure from league commissioner Don Garber, AEG was encouraged to sell off some of its soccer franchises to allow more new investment to enter the league. In 2007, D.C. United was sold to D.C. United Holdings, a newly formed investment group led by real estate mogul Victor MacFarlane, former NBA player Christian Laettner, and businessman and part owner of the San Francisco Giants William H. C. Chang. Chang eventually bought out all of his other partners in the investment group to become the sole owner of D.C. United.

D.C. United's popularity and strength on the field has made the team attractive to sponsors. This was further heightened in 2003, when the team signed 14-year-old soccer phenomenon Freddy Adu to a contract. Adu was the youngest professional athlete in the past century in American professional sports and was a major selling and marketing point for the franchise, which saw a large spike in attendance during Adu's first season. While Adu left the club via trade in winter 2006, the team was able to profit from Adu's time with them, and has continued to do well in terms of sponsorship.

In recent years, more and more MLS clubs have come to embrace the use of jerseys as a form of advertisement, as is seen in most professional soccer leagues around the world. D.C. United's aforementioned partnership with Volkswagen, which was estimated to be worth around $14 million for a five-

D.C. United playing against the Philadelphia Union in RFK Stadium in August 2010. The players wear black jerseys that feature the logo of Volkswagen, the team's major sponsor, which paid approximately $14 million for the five-year partnership.

year deal, is the second largest shirt sponsorship deal in the league's history. Volkswagen provided an interesting tie-in with this sponsorship deal by providing free parking to the first 50 Volkswagens to arrive at each of the team's home matches.

Stadium

One of the biggest issues for D.C. United in more recent years has been its stadium situation, with the team currently leasing Robert F. Kennedy Memorial Stadium (RFK) as a secondary tenant after the Washington Redskins in 1996 and the Washington Nationals between 2005 and 2007. Having to share RKF stadium with these and other teams and events has caused problems with the quality of the playing surface, as well as with scheduling matches. With the majority of clubs in the rest of the MLS having already constructed their own soccer-specific stadiums, many question why D.C.

United, one of the premier teams in the league, does not have its own stadium.

In 2006, the club came up with a plan to move to Anacostia Park, which was struck down by local government. However, in 2009, a more formalized plan was formed to build a stadium in Prince George's County, Maryland. This plan remained in limbo as of late 2010, as local governments have required more extensive reports and studies to examine the feasibility of building a soccer-specific stadium in this region. Despite these issues, D.C. United has been one of the most popular and successful clubs in the league; the building of their own soccer-specific stadium is likely to further the club's reputation, and continue to mark them as one of the elite of the MLS both on and off the field.

Nicholas M. Watanabe
University of Missouri

See Also: FC Dallas; Major League Soccer; Sponsorship; Washington Nationals; Washington Redskins.

Further Readings

Boehm, Charles. "Chang Assumes Control of D.C. United." http://web.mlsnet.com/news/mls_news.jsp?ymd=20090523&content_id=4901182&vkey=news_mls&fext=.jsp (Accessed October 2010).

D.C. United Official Website. http://www.dcunited.com (Accessed October 2009).

Major League Soccer Official Website. http://web.mlsnet.com/index.jsp (Accessed October 2010).

Nakamura, David. "Talks Fall Apart on Stadium for D.C. Soccer Team." http://www.washingtonpost.com/wp-dyn/content/article/2007/07/20/AR2007072002470_pf.html (Accessed October 2010).

Debt Service

Debt service is the amount of money required to pay back the principal and interest of a loan over a time period specified by a loan agreement. Sport properties regularly take on long-term debt obligations to pay for, or pay for a share of, the construction of a new facility, cover cost overruns in the construction of a new facility, or to pay for other revenue-generating assets such as facility upgrades or suite installations. Teams also take on debt as part of deferred compensation for star athletes. Finally, some purchases of franchises or clubs, such as the Glazer family purchase of a controlling stake in Manchester United, have been significantly financed by debt.

Ideally, sport properties incur debt to invest in assets that will increase revenue. If the actual or expected increase in revenue is enough to cover the debt service then the purchase of the asset is a feasible move and is desirable in the absence of other, more attractive opportunities. This is often how revenue-generating assets such as new facilities with increased amenities, upgrades to existing facilities such as the addition of luxury and premium seating, or

the installation of high-tech, animated video boards that increase advertising inventory are financed. The New York Yankees borrowed over $1.3 billion in tax-exempt bonds, taxable bonds, and private funds to construct the new Yankee Stadium that opened in 2009. For most sport clubs, regular operating income is not adequate to regularly cover debt service. In light of this, long-term annual receipts for facility naming rights are often used to cover annual debt service payments.

Credit availability and debt are essential for the optimal operation of any business endeavor, and sport is no exception. A sport property's debt service coverage ratio, which is the amount of cash flow available to meet the annual interest and principal payments on debts, heavily influences its credit rating and the cost and availability of further financing. Major professional sports leagues typically have debt level limits to keep affordable credit available and to assist league members in maintaining stable financial footing. Leagues also offer credit facilities that allow member clubs to borrow at more affordable terms than would be available otherwise.

Unfortunately, there have been high-profile cases where clubs have been unable to cover their debt service and drastic actions had to be taken. In 2010, Thomas Hicks and his Hicks Sports Group were forced to cede ownership interest in both Major League Baseball's Texas Rangers and the English Premier League's Liverpool Football Club over unmanageable debt. Hicks defaulted on his Rangers debt in 2009 and tried to arrange a sale to an ownership group led by Chuck Greenberg and Nolan Ryan. However, the major creditors objected to the sale and forced the Rangers into bankruptcy court, where they were eventually auctioned off to the highest bidder, which turned out to be the Greenberg and Ryan group at terms more favorable to the creditors. Later in the year, Hicks also lost his interest in Liverpool when the club was unable to refinance a significant debt coming due with the Royal Bank of Scotland. A sale to New England Sports Ventures, the ownership group of the Boston Red Sox, was arranged, which removed most of the club's debt obligations.

The National Football League's Baltimore Ravens moved from Cleveland, where they were the Browns, in 1995 primarily because owner Art

Modell was unable to cover debt service because of the Brown's stadium arrangements in Cleveland. Modell took over operating control of the Cleveland Municipal Stadium in 1974 in the hope that he could turn a profit from the facility. However, the capital costs of carrying out agreed-upon capital upgrades to the aging facility threw Modell into a debt situation that left it difficult to cover the debt service obligations. The state of Maryland offered Modell and the Browns a deal that helped him erase the debt service obligation in exchange for moving the franchise to Baltimore.

Conclusion

The use of debt is part of the normal growth and development of most sport properties. However, organizations have to plan their finances with discipline and foresight to ensure they can cover their debt service. Having adequate debt service coverage guarantees strong financial standing and the availability of additional capital if needed. However, if organizations become overleveraged and their debt service becomes too high, it can result in the forced sale or relocation of a club, reduced on-field competitiveness as a team's ability to commit salary to star players becomes limited, or bankruptcy.

Kevin Heisey
State University of New York College at Cortland

See Also: Arena Funding—Public/Private; Boston Red Sox; Facilities Financing; Venue Naming Rights.

Further Readings

Kaplan, Daniel. "Banker's Gamble Pays Off in Rangers Auction." *The Sports Business Journal* (August 16, 2010).

Kaplan, Daniel. "Henry Joins Liverpool Drama." *The Sports Business Journal* (October 11, 2010).

Kaplan, Daniel. "Yanks Get New Loan for Ballpark." *The Sports Business Journal* (March 16, 2009).

Leone, Marie. "NFL Runs Up the Score." *CFO Magazine* (January 30, 2008).

Munson, Lester. "A Busted Play." *Sports Illustrated* (December 4, 1995).

Demand Elasticity and Inelasticity in Sports

Within economics, the price elasticity of demand (PED) of a good refers to the change in demand for a good in response to a change in the price of that good. This is measured by the percentage change in the amount of a good demanded, divided by the percentage change in price of the good. This concept is often referred to simply as "elasticity" and is a measure of how responsive individuals are to changes in the price of a good. In discussing how elastic certain goods are, there are three basic states that can exist for the good in relation to price: elastic, inelastic, and unitary. Goods that are elastic are those in which changes in the price will cause changes in demand. That is, if a good is elastic and its price increases then the quantity of that good demanded will decrease. An inelastic good, on the other hand, will see relatively little change in the demand for the good even when the price of the good changes. In this situation, a good that is inelastic can have its price increased and see very little change in the demand for the product. Elastic goods can be things such as coffee or sugar, which will have decreased consumption if their price rises, as consumers will choose to purchase other goods as substitutes for these goods. Inelastic goods could be items such as water or medicine; individuals need these items to an extent that even changes in price will not change the quantity the consumer demands.

The reason the examination of elasticity is so important in the management of sports teams is that it is part of a basic understanding of the demand for sports, and how this demand can fluctuate depending upon how much a price changes. There exists a great deal of research examining the price of sport tickets and attempting to find if price is a significant determinant of fan attendance, as well as in what range of elasticity the pricing of tickets to events occurs. Direct implications for sport managers can be gleaned from such research by understanding how consumers will react to changes in the price of tickets to sporting events. From this, sport managers can not only come to an understanding about consumer behavior in choosing to attend sporting events, but also about whether teams can or cannot increase the prices of tickets without hurting the quantity demanded by individuals.

From basic classical microeconomic theory, it is understood that there exists a relationship between the quantity demanded of a good and its price. However, much of the research findings within sports economics indicate that tickets to sporting events are often priced in the inelastic range. That is, they are priced at a level at which there can be changes in the price without having a very large effect on the quantity demanded by consumers.

Research Findings in Sports

The research into the demand for sports can be traced back almost half a century, yet the empirical focus on the effect of price on the demand for sport has been examined only relatively recently. Henry Demmert's work published in 1973 was the first work to truly examine the elasticity of tickets to sporting events. In this work, where data was used on Major League Baseball (MLB) for a two-decade span, findings estimated the elasticity of price during this time period for the MLB was -0.93. With this estimate showing a close to unitary elasticity of demand for MLB tickets, Rodney Fort suggests that this is to be expected when the marginal cost of letting more fans into the game is around zero. In the following year, Roger Noll also examined price elasticity of demand for sport in the MLB and found estimated elasticity of about -0.14, a quite inelastic finding. It is noted by Noll that the pricing point was within one standard deviation of being unitary, and these elasticity estimates are underestimated as ticket price is only part of the overall cost of attending a sporting event. It is also considered that the possibility of inelastic pricing for the sport product as found in his study could be because of the exemption of travel costs.

In order to better understand the effect that other costs such as travel would have on the pricing point for tickets, Peter Bird used data from English soccer that included price and a travel cost variable. Bird's results are very important because they found that even taking into account travel costs, tickets for sporting events were still priced in the inelastic range. This runs counter to the suggestion by Roger Noll that correcting for travel costs would change the range in which tickets were priced. Thus, it be-

came more widely accepted among researchers that ticket prices to sporting events could be priced in the inelastic range.

The question that emerges from the research at this point is not so much focused on whether ticket prices would fall in the inelastic range, but what possible reasons exist to explain these findings. In a 2004 piece Rodney Fort offers propositions as to possible explanations of these consistent findings. In this work, he discusses the potential sources of other revenue such as local television, which if marginally higher than such revenue for other franchises in a league could lead to some teams setting their prices in the inelastic range. Anthony Krautmann and David Berri show that from a theoretical perspective, it is possible for teams to be profit maximizers (that is, they seek to maximize profits before wins) and still price their tickets in the inelastic range. This is done by considering the relationship between concession revenue and ticket revenue, and how by considering the revenues from concessions, owners are able to price the tickets in the inelastic range.

A key point that must be discussed is the relative difficulty in conducting research in regard to the effect of price on the demand for sport. One of the biggest difficulties is in the nature of the data as well as obtaining it from teams. Price data would be much simpler to deal with if teams sold tickets at a single price; however, teams practice price dispersion in that they sell tickets at multiple price points. Because of this practice, some teams can have over a dozen prices for tickets to a single sporting event (not including season ticket prices) making it hard to examine and consider what the actual cost of attending a sporting event is for a consumer. While some researchers have attempted to tackle this problem with different solutions, such as using average price of all tickets, or lowest available ticket price, it still presents some problems for truly understanding the nature of the cost of attending a sporting event. Additionally, because it is difficult to accurately determine the cost of attending a sporting event, it can be difficult for researchers to come to a strong conclusion about whether ticket price truly affects the demand for sport. Despite these issues, the general body of research conducted into the elasticity and price of sport has been very sound in its approach, and thus the results should be considered reliable.

Conclusion

What can truly be understood from the research is that the pricing of sport tickets has consistently (but not always) occurred within the inelastic range. While researchers have sought ways to tease out other effects, these results have generally held strong, and have produced several implications for sport managers. As shown by theoretical models and some empirical research, there may be other sources of revenue that are responsible for allowing teams to price tickets in the inelastic range. Some of these sources include parking fees, concession revenue, and television revenue. While ticket revenue from fans attending the game is still an important part of the revenue for sporting teams, the pricing of these tickets can be placed in the inelastic range because of other sources of revenue. This means that while changes in price of tickets do not necessarily affect the quantity of tickets demanded for a sporting event, sport managers must be aware of all revenue streams and the effects these have on the pricing of tickets to sport events. Some research may be taken to indicate that price has no effect whatsoever on demand; however, this is most certainly not the case. Theory and research implications may show it to have very little effect, but some effect nonetheless. It is therefore prudent for sport managers to understand the price of their goods, revenue brought in from other sources, and at what ranges they can set ticket prices in order to maintain an optimal level of demand for entrance into their sporting events.

Nicholas M. Watanabe
University of Missouri

See Also: Demand for Sports; Demand-Oriented Pricing; Dynamic Pricing; Price Ceilings; Price Determination; Pricing of Tickets; Pricing Strategies; Ticket Price, Secondary Market; Ticket Price, Tiers; Ticket Price, Variable; Yield Management Pricing.

Further Readings

Bird, P. "The Demand for League Football." *Applied Economics*, v.14 (1982).
Demmert, H. *The Economics of Professional Team Sports*. Lexington, MA: Lexington Books, 1973.
Fort, R. D. "Inelastic Sports Pricing." *Managerial and Decision Economics*, v.25 (2004).
Krautmann, A. C. and D. J. Berri. "Can We Find It at the Concessions? Understanding Price Elasticity In Professional Sports." *Journal of Sports Economics*, v.8/2 (2007).
Noll, R. "Attendance and Price Setting." In *Government and the Sports Business*. Washington, DC: Brookings Institute, 1974.

Demand for Sports

The demand for sports can be most simply phrased as the willingness that individuals have to consume various sports products. Demand for sports is one of the more popular topics within the economic literature on sport management and sports economics, and is often intertwined with literature focused upon attendance and viewership at sporting events. While demand for sports is based on economic concepts, this research provides a way for academics and professionals to investigate the various factors that affect consumer decisions to consume sports products.

The focus of the demand for sports can be applied to a wide range of products within the sport industry, including attendance at sporting events, viewership, sporting goods, sports memorabilia, and so forth. Thus, investigation into the demand for sports can prove to be a useful tool for sport managers and researchers in understanding consumer behavior, in addition to surveys and other forms of empirical investigation.

Research into the demand for sports can be traced back to economists Simon Rottenberg and Roger Neale's works into uncertainty of outcome and fan decisions to attend sporting events. Following the theoretical work presented by these two, a large amount of research from both theoretical and empirical standpoints emerged focused on why fans choose to attend/watch live sporting events. From this, much of the demand for sports literature is manifested in the form of studies of the various determinants of demand for live attendance (often called "gate") at sporting matches.

Determinants of Demand

Factors that are considered to be important in determining the demand for sport include, but are not limited to: price and price elasticity, distance traveled, quality of contest, stadium capacity, game-day promotions and giveaways, uncertainty of outcome, competitive balance, presence of star players, and team strength. One factor of primary concern within a demand study is the price of the product, which is theorized in neoclassical economics to affect the demand for the good as price fluctuates. This concept is more commonly referred to as the price elasticity of demand. Despite the theorization that price will affect the demand for sport products, research findings have been rather varied and somewhat inconclusive in regard to the effect of price. More recent findings have indicated the possibility that price is not a significant factor in determining sport attendance, and this finding might be related to the overall cost of attending a game (which includes things such as concessions, parking, and so forth).

While price of tickets and cost of attending have been somewhat inconclusive in findings, there are a number of factors that have been found to affect attendance, and are important in developing an understanding of what affects the fan decision to attend or watch live sporting events. A list and classification of these factors and a more comprehensive overview of the demand for sport literature can be found in Jeffrey Borland and Robert Macdonald's review of the literature on the demand for sport in the *Oxford Review of Economic Policy*. The five categorizations of factors included in their piece are: consumer preferences, economic factors, quality of viewing, sporting contest characteristics, and supply capacity. While these factors are more based on studies into attendance, many of them would most likely be important in the demand for other sport products and services.

The first group, consumer preferences, is one of the more difficult-to-define factors, and includes things such as fan behavior, bandwagon effects, tradition, loyalty, and other factors that are more qualitative. The second group, economics factors, is related directly to economic concerns such as price, per capita income, market size, travel time

and costs, proximity and availability of substitutes, and unemployment rates. Quality of viewing, the third group, considers a variety of factors that revolve around the quality of the viewing experience, including timing of contests, stadium and seating quality, quality of concessions, and so on. Empirical findings regarding this group of factors indicates things such as day of the week, time of day, and the quality of the seats all play a role in the demand for live sport attendance. One interesting piece of research found a lower demand for sporting events in North America when there was bad weather, but found no such change for sporting events in Europe. This finding highlights the fact that different regions/people/markets may behave in different manners in terms of their demand for goods, including sport products and services.

The fourth group of sporting contests is one of the more interesting and highly debated groups, specifically dealing with various ways in which the quality of the match being played can be measured. These include aforementioned factors such as uncertainty of outcome, competitive balance, and team strength. Researchers have spent a great deal of effort investigating the nature of sporting contests, and have found that factors such as uncertainty of outcome are possibly important in fan attendance at sporting events. Uncertainty of outcome is the basic concept that if fans are able to predict the outcome of matches, they will be less likely to attend. Additionally, factors such as competitive balance (parity within a league) and team strength have been found to affect the consumer's willingness to attend sporting events.

The fifth and final group, supply capacity, refers to the amount of tickets that are available and is most commonly measured in the form of stadium capacity. As the capacity is a direct measure of the available supply of seats for individuals wishing to attend a sporting contest, it is directly connected with the demand for the event. Simply put, if there is high demand for an event, and low supply (capacity), it will be that the attendance will equal the stadium capacity; however, the attendance will not be equal to the number of individuals who desire to attend the event. This leads to rationing, in which not everyone who wants to attend an event may do so, and can lead to increased ticket prices, scalping, and other such phenomena.

Without a proper understanding of demand, sports managers will have difficulty making decisions about the amount of supply they should produce for consumption by consumers. For example, Mark McDonald and Daniel Rascher find an increase in attendance for days in which Major League Baseball (MLB) teams hold game-day promotions.

It is important to note that most factors will have different effects between leagues and teams, and it is therefore difficult to make generalized assumptions based on research findings.

However, an understanding of such findings from the research, and principles of demand, allows for managers to not only use such promotions to help increase attendance at games, but also to use these tools to help boost attendance for those times and games that fans may have lower demand for. Thus the demand for sport is a wide-reaching concept that can apply to sport attendance, consumption of sporting goods, and other products and services related to sports.

Nicholas M. Watanabe
University of Missouri

See Also: Demand Elasticity and Inelasticity in Sports; Demand-Oriented Pricing; Dynamic Pricing; Price Ceilings; Price Determination; Pricing of Tickets; Pricing Strategies; Primary Demand; Supply/Demand Equilibrium; Ticket Price, Secondary Market; Ticket Price, Tiers; Ticket Price, Variable.

Further Readings

Borland, J. and R. Macdonald. "Demand for Sport." *Oxford Review of Economic Policy*, v.19/4 (2003).
McDonald, M. and D. Rascher. "Does Bat Day Make Cents? The Effect of Promotions on the Demand for Major League Baseball." *Journal of Sport Management*, v.14/1 (2000).
Neale, W. C. "The Peculiar Economics of Professional Sports." *Quarterly Journal of Economics*, v.78/1 (1964).
Rottenberg, S. "The Baseball Players Market." *Journal of Political Economy*, v.64 (June 1956).

Demand-Oriented Pricing

Pricing methods can be differentiated into cost-based methods and market-based methods. Among the cost-based methods are cost-plus pricing and break-even pricing, whereas market-based methods include demand-oriented pricing and competitor-based pricing.

The central premise of demand-oriented pricing is to charge a high price when demand is strong and a low price when demand is weak. In the sport system this pricing method is common with fitness studios and health clubs. They charge relatively high prices in peak periods (like late afternoon and early evening) and lower prices in off-peak periods (like mid-morning). Value-based pricing, as a form of demand-oriented pricing, goes one step further and takes the value of the product as perceived by the custumer into account.

The in-stadium capacity for most sport events is fixed. That is, there is a fixed number of seats in the venue that cannot be adjusted in the short run. The marketer of the event has to anticipate demand for tickets and set the price accordingly. Demand depends on such things as the day of the week, star power of the athletes, and/or importance of the event. Demand will be highest at the weekend rather than on a weeknight. An Olympic gold medalist will draw more spectators than an unknown athlete, and the Super Bowl will draw more spectators than an ordinary mid-season game. On the other hand, prices should be lowered if these factors are not present. In recent years teams in Major League Baseball (MLB) or the German soccer league (Bundesliga) began to change ticket prices even during the season in order to generate a higher yield.

Price Elasticity of Demand

The responsiveness of demand to a change in price is an important coefficient for setting a demand-oriented price. The price elasticity of demand is a measure of the sensitivity of consumer demand for a product to a change in price. It is calculated by the following formula:

Price Elasticity of Demand = % Change in Quantity Demanded / % Change in Price

Generally, elasticity coefficients bigger than -1 are called elastic, coefficients equaling -1 are unitary elastic, and elasticity coefficients smaller than -1 are inelastic. Suppose demand falls by 15 percent when a sporting goods manufacturer raises its price for shoes by 5 percent. Price elasticity of demand is therefore -3. This means that demand is elastic. The increase in price is overcompensated by the decrease in demand revenue declines. If the change in demand and the change in price are equivalent, then elasticity is -1 and revenue stays the same. If demand falls by 4 percent when the change in price is 8 percent, then elasticity is -0.5 and demand is inelastic, which leads to an increase in revenue.

Studies about price elasticity in spectator sports like the MLB or National Football League (NFL) nearly all document an inelastic demand. Many sport fans are fiercely loyal to their team or their sport. It is almost impossible for them to substitute one sport league, team, or competition for another, which makes them insensitive to changes in price. A second reason for the inelasticity of demand for ticket prices is that ticket prices only account for a fraction of the total costs for visiting a sporting event. Further costs are incurred for transportation, accommodation, food, and/or merchandising. Therefore admission is only a part of the whole budget, and a change in price has only a reduced effect.

Demand and Value

Price elasticity of demand is affected by the perceived value of a product. Value encompasses tangibles like technical features, as well as intangibles like allure of a brand. Demand for a brand with a high value is usually less elastic than demand for a brand with a lower value. A consumer only purchases a sport product if he or she believes that the value will exceed the costs. Therefore it is important for the sport marketer to increase the perceived value of a product in order to charge a higher price. The value of a baseball game, for example, can be increased by modernizing the venue, improving the quality of catering, or integrating side events. Value-based pricing, as a form of demand-oriented pricing, uses the concept of value to set the price for a product. The first step in this process is to determine the perceived value of the product. This is done by the application of marketing research methods such as estimating willingness to pay (WTP) or conjoint measurement. WTP is the maximum price a customer is willing to pay for a good or service. It can be identified by conducting interviews. Whereas WTP is a direct approach, conjoint measurement is an indirect approach. Conjoint measurement is a de-compositional statistical method that allows determining the value of different attributes of a product like color, material, or technical features. The company then combines the attributes with the highest overall value. The next step is to set a price that matches the consumer's perceived value. In the last step the company has to calculate if it can produce the product at costs that are below the given price and allow a reasonable profit margin.

Christoph Breuer
Pamela Wicker
German Sport University Cologne

See Also: Cost-Plus Pricing; Demand Elasticity and Inelasticity in Sports; Demand for Sports; Price Determination; Pricing of Tickets; Pricing Strategies; Supply/Demand Equilibrium; Ticket Price, Secondary Market; Ticket Price, Tiers; Ticket Price, Variable.

Further Readings

Georges, Walter and Robert W. McGee. *Analytical Contribution Accounting. The Interface of Cost Accounting and Pricing Policy.* Westport, CT: Quorum Books, 1987.

Lilien, Gary L., Arvind Rangaswamy, and Arnaud De Bruyn. *Principles of Marketing Engineering.* Victoria, BC: Trafford, 2007.

Pride, William M., Robert J. Hughes, and Jack R. Kapoor. *Business,* 8th Ed. Boston: Houghton Mifflin, 2005.

Pride, William M. and O. C. Ferrell. *Marketing,* 15th ed. Canada: South-Western, 2010.

Rascher, Daniel A., Chad D. McEvoy, Mark S. Nagel, and Matthew T. Brown. "Variable Ticket Pricing in Major League Baseball." *Journal of Sport Management,* v.21 (2007).

Smith, Aaron C. T. *Introduction to Sport Marketing.* Oxford, UK: Butterworth-Heinemann, 2008.

Stewart, Bob. *Sport Funding and Finance*. Oxford, UK: Butterworth-Heinemann, 2007.

Wicker, Pamela. *Price Elasticity in Sport Clubs—Measurement and Empirical Findings*. Saarbrücken, Germany: Südwestdeutscher Verlag für Hochschulschriften, 2009.

Zentes, Joachim, Dirk Morschett, and Hanna Schramm-Klein. *Strategic Retail Management: Text and International Cases*. Wiesbaden, Germany: Gabler, 2007.

Demarketing

The purpose of marketing is usually to induce consumers to buy more and increase sales, profit, or the number of the participating audience. However, occasionally managers may want to reduce the demand for a product or for some services. Achieving this reverse purpose is called demarketing. Demarketing aims to induce consumers to consume less or even cease consumption of a product, service, or experience. Government demarketing campaigns are common in the areas of smoking, binge drinking, and private car usage, which may pose health risks or cause environmental pollution. Demarketing strategies are sometimes used in social marketing by nonprofit or government organizations to try to reduce drug use or prevent drunk driving. Strategies of banning, punishing use, or raising prices may be adopted in demarketing initiatives.

Business managers may want to reduce demands that are greater than their ability to supply. Demarketing strategies may include decreasing advertising or promotions spending, raising fees or prices, or eliminating some benefits of products or services. Demarketing may not be done with the intent to destroy demand, but instead to do selective marketing in areas where marketing efforts may be more profitable and sustainable than other markets. During a downturn, sport managers may want to put limited resources toward those profitable audiences.

Demarketing can strike the unprofitable audience from a correspondence list and pinpoint segments of the population that would not be fulfilled by the offerings. For example, fans who frequently call to complain about the outcome of games but never buy season tickets or licensed merchandise might be considered unprofitable customers. Sport managers may also identify dysfunctional fans whose behavior is antisocial and may disrupt a sporting event or social exchanges surrounding the event. The dysfunctional fan may become a threat to other fans because of violence or hooliganism. Sport marketers can attempt demarketing efforts to shed a risky audience segment or try to channel socially unacceptable behavior into something more acceptable. Managers may separate a group of fans or develop policies for punishing unacceptable behavior.

Demarketing can be applied to tourist management and planning for sustainable sport tourism. For a sporting event, sometimes the demand for travel may exceed the social or environmental carrying capacity. In this situation, demarketing practices can be used to reduce the demand for the sake of ensuring a place's sustainability and reduce visitor numbers to a manageable level. Managers may tell potential tourists to secure accommodations before arriving or inform the tourists of possible crowded situations to deflect visitors. Overall, demarketing is a technique for matching demand with an agency's resources.

Although demarketing may imply doing less or spending less in marketing activities such as advertising or promotions, demarketing can be an active way to adjust a marketing mix's components to dissuade participants from indulging in disruptive activities such as excessive alcohol consumption or illegal gambling. For example, in live games, demarketing may target some dysfunctional fans to dissuade them from using foul language or engaging in violent behavior while supporting their teams.

Conclusion

In short, demarketing is an attempt to reduce demand when demand is too high, or unwholesome, or when satisfying the demand would cost too much. Demarketing strategies include passive and active methods. Passive methods may adopt policies for banning or punishing, increase prices, or simply do fewer promotions or advertising campaigns. Active methods in demarketing may attempt to adjust marketing mix elements to dissuade the audience from socially unacceptable behavior or to change behaviors or intentions.

Li-Shiue Gau
Asia University, Taiwan

See Also: Cause Marketing/Branding; Event Management; Social Marketing; Social Responsibility.

Further Readings

Hunt, Kenneth A., Terry Bristol, and R. Edward Bashaw. "A Conceptual Approach to Classifying Sports Fans." *Journal of Services Marketing*, v.13/6 (1999).
Kotler, Philip and Gerald Zaltman. "Social Marketing: An Approach to Planned Social Change." *Journal of Marketing*, v.35 (1971).
Medway, Dominic and Gary Warnaby. "Alternative Perspectives on Marketing and the Place Brand." *European Journal of Marketing*, v.42/5–6 (2008).

Demographics

The study and analysis of consumer demographics remain an essential part of successful sport marketing. Also known as "state-of-being," demographics are simply the characteristics that make up a specific population. Common basic demographics include age, gender, income level, race, ethnicity, education, occupation, and family life cycle. Demographics continue to play a huge role in market segmentation and meeting the needs and wants of the sport consumer. Since not all consumers have the same background or characteristics, we can also assume that differences exist among demographics in regard to sport consumption. Therefore, demographics continue to be a driving force behind analyzing the sport consumer and identifying trends. In addition, advertisers and sponsors can use de-

mographics as a valued tool to achieve maximum results for their investments.

Unlike psychographics, where the focus is on consumer behavior and purchasing intentions, demographics tend to be more objective and therefore easier to measure. In addition, most demographic variables have standard categories for their values. For example, education is often expressed as highest level earned and includes the categories of some high school, high school or equivalent, associate's degree, some college, bachelor's degree, and postgraduate degree. While specific demographics such as gender, race, and ethnicity tend to remain stable over time within individuals, the demographics of populations can change dramatically.

Understanding the proportion of any given demographic segment that may be available to the sport marketer is essential. For example, if a product is marketed to consumers who are 18–25 years old, it is important to determine how many individuals make up that segment of the population. Fortunately, there are resources that provide the latest demographics of specific populations. The U.S. Census Bureau, which is the main source of the Statistical Abstract of the United States, provides the most comprehensive summary of the growth, distribution, and characteristics of the U.S. population. While the Statistical Abstract focuses on national demographic data, there is also data available on a regional, state, and metropolitan basis.

From a sport marketing standpoint, there are other resources available that may specifically provide linkages between sport and demographics. Scarborough Research and TURNKEY Sports and Entertainment are two organizations that have focused on collecting custom data on the sport fan in order to satisfy specific needs and preferences. Both organizations collect in-depth consumer demographics at the local and national level in order to retain and attract new consumers as well as identify trends in the marketplace.

Determining a population's demographics is important for several reasons in sport marketing. First and foremost, it allows for further examination of the makeup of a population, which can then lead to more effective marketing efforts on all fronts. In regard to sport spectatorship, one may analyze demographic variables in order to retain current spectators as well as recruit new consumer segments. If it is hypothetically found that women's volleyball spectators within a Division I institution are over 50 percent male, Caucasian, and single, then the sport marketer may consider modifying marketing strategies in order to attract more females, ethnicities, and families.

Specific trends in consumer behavior can also be identified by examining demographics. In regard to sponsor brand recall, some research has found that NASCAR sponsor brand recall may be a function of education, age, and gender. Moreover, sponsor brand recall may be higher among younger males who possess some college education. From a marketing and sponsorship standpoint, consideration for those who are not part of the demographics mentioned would be of concern in order to increase brand awareness. Rather than generalizing your consumers or having an "all for one" marketing strategy, proper market segmentation or dividing consumers into smaller groups of people with similar demographics can prove to be invaluable. Often, promotions coincide with demographic variables such as gender, age, family life cycle, and ethnicity. For example, ladies night, kid's day, and family day focus on the demographic variables of gender, age, and family life cycle.

Lastly, demographics also serve a purpose from an advertising and sponsorship standpoint. Understanding the demographic makeup of specific market segments will assist the advertiser or sponsor in determining whether its investment is worthwhile. For example, if a financial investment company is determining whether or not to sponsor a Little League team, it may consider researching the specific demographics making up the spectators and fans for the Little League team. Demographics such as age, income, education, occupation, and family life cycle of the Little League market would help determine whether the potential exists for the financial investment company to possibly gain new clients and increase their revenue.

Laura L. Miller
California University of Pennsylvania

See Also: Psychographics; Segmentation; Target Market.

Further Readings

DeKhill, F. "Understanding Women's Collegiate Volleyball Spectators From the Perspectives of Sociodemographics, Market Demand and Consumption Level." *International Journal of Sport Management & Sponsorship,* v.11/2 (2010).

Kinney, L., S. McDaniels, and L. DeGaris. "Demographic and Psychographic Variables Predicting NASCAR Sponsor Brand Recall." *International Journal of Sport Management & Sponsorship,* v.9/3 (2008).

Mullin, B. J., S. Hardy, and W. A. Sutton. *Sport Marketing,* 3rd ed. Champaign, IL: Human Kinetics, 2007.

Scarborough Research Official Website. http://www.scarborough.com (Accessed September 2010).

TURNKEY Sports & Entertainment Official Website. http://www.turnkeyse.com (Accessed September 2010).

U.S. Census Bureau. http://www.census.gov (Accessed September 2010).

Denver Broncos

The Denver Broncos—through competitive teams, exciting personalities, and deft ownership and management decisions—have developed extremely loyal consumers and captivated the Rocky Mountain region, in particular the 2.5 million residents of the metro Denver area. Over the past few decades this National Football League (NFL) club, which celebrated its 50th anniversary in 2009, has been considered one of the most successful franchises in terms of its on-field product, overall bottom line, and expansive and highly identified fan base. Regarding the team's on-field product, the Broncos have thrived—with only five losing seasons over the past 33 years—throughout the years of the current owner's leadership.

Regarding the team's overall bottom line, by providing a competitive product (e.g., wins, star players) and engaging in savvy deals (e.g., a new stadi-

The highly successful Denver Broncos franchise, which celebrated its 50th anniversary in 2009, has recently been valued at more than $1.1 billion.

um and its luxury boxes; major corporate sponsors such as Anheuser-Busch, U.S. Bancorp, Coca-Cola, Comcast, and Lowe's) Pat Bowlen—the owner and CEO who purchased the club for $78 million in 1984—now has a team that is valued at over $1.1 billion. Regarding the team's fan base, the Broncos have developed a devoted following with a season ticket waiting list of over 28,000 names and an estimated wait time of 13 to 15 years for those on that list.

The team plays in Invesco Field at Mile High, one of the best state-of-the-art facilities in the NFL. Opened in 2001, the stadium was funded through sources both private (Bowlen) and public (tax on retail goods), and has a naming rights deal with Invesco Funds. While the Denver area has strong pro franchises such as the Denver Nuggets, Colorado Avalanche, Colorado Rockies, and Colorado Rapids, and numerous other amateur sport organizations and events, the Broncos are by far the most popular franchise in the region and the only NFL team from Kansas to California. The Bronco's economic and team successes did not always exist, however, as the Denver franchise was a lowly AFL team in the early years and was known more for its ugly uniforms than for its on-field achievements. Failure was common throughout the 1960s and much of the 1970s, but there were a few highlights along the way, including Marlon Briscoe (the first African American starting quarterback in the NFL) and Floyd Little.

Success became the norm—and Broncomania was in full swing—starting with the 1977 season when talented players including Craig Morton and Haven Moses took the Broncos to the Super Bowl. What was most noticeable about the team was its defense, led by such players as Tom Jackson (who became a household name a couple decades later as a sportscaster for ESPN) and Lyle Alzado. The unit was known as the Orange Crush defense, a term that became a marketing slogan and promotional gimmick in the Denver area that is still popular. The Super Bowl marked the arrival of the Denver area on the national scene in terms of the city itself and the team in particular.

While the next few years were not extremely successful, the team was popular and the fanaticism was overwhelming starting in 1983. That was when then owner Edgar Kaiser negotiated with the owner of the Baltimore Colts to trade the Colts's number one pick, John Elway, to the Broncos. The trade, which was conducted between owners, ended in disaster for the Colts (who left Baltimore the next year for Indianapolis) and with immense success for the Broncos.

Elway went on to lead the Broncos to five Super Bowls. The first three Super Bowls were losses under the direction of head coach Dan Reeves. Bowlen then switched to Mike Shanahan, who was given full responsibility for both on-field (coaching) and off-field (player personnel) decisions. This was a new trend in the NFL, and Shanahan was very successful early on. Under Shanahan's leadership, Elway went on to two more Super Bowls, winning both in 1997 and 1998. Elway retired after the last championship, ending his career as the all-time winningest starting quarterback in NFL history.

The Broncos had been unable to find a replacement for Elway from 1998 through 2004. But in 2005, the team drafted quarterback Jay Cutler and by his third season he had started setting records. After the 2008 season, however, Shanahan was fired and Josh McDaniels was hired as the 12th head coach in team history. The relationship between McDaniels and his franchise quarterback was strained early on and ended with the trade of Cutler to the Chicago Bears. In addition to the Cutler saga, the Broncos have had to deal with a variety of crisis management decisions involving incidents such as player insubordination (e.g., Brandon Marshall), questionable draft choices (e.g., character issues surrounding Maurice Clarett), and gun violence (e.g., the death of Darrent Williams).

Paul M. Pedersen
Indiana University

See Also: Colorado Avalanche; Colorado Rockies; Denver Nuggets; Franchise; National Football League.

Further Readings

Denver Broncos Official Website. http://www .denverbroncos.com (Accessed November 2010).

Fatsis, Stefan. *A Few Seconds of Panic: A 5-Foot-8, 170-Pound, 43-Year-Old Sportswriter Plays in the NFL.* New York: Penguin Press, 2008.

Frei, Terry. *'77: Denver, the Broncos, and a Coming of Age.* Lanham, MD: Taylor Trade, 2008.

Martin, Russell. *The Color Orange: A Super Bowl Season ith the Denver Broncos.* New York: Henry Holt, 1987.

Ozanian, Michael K., Kurt Badenhausen, and Dan Bigman. "The Business of Football, 2009." http://www.forbes.com/lists/2009/30/football -values-09_Denver-Broncos_308211.html (Accessed November 2009).

Paige, Jr., Woodrow. *Orange Madness: The Incredible Odyssey of the Denver Broncos.* New York: Thomas Y. Crowell, 1978.

Denver Nuggets

Denver's involvement in professional basketball dates to 1949–50 when the original Nuggets were briefly part of the early National Basketball Association (NBA). In 1967, Denver became a charter franchise in the American Basketball Association (ABA) and the team became known as the Denver Rockets (their original owner named them after his fleet of trucks known as "rockets"). When the franchise anticipated its move back to the NBA as the result of the ABA-NBA merger in 1976, a contest was held to determine a new name (Houston "Rockets" had priority), and once again they became known as the Nuggets.

The Nuggets are owned by Kroenke Sports Enterprises, which also owns the Colorado Avalanche (NHL hockey) and the Pepsi Arena, where both teams play. Mr. E. Stanley Kroenke himself also owns the St. Louis Rams in the NFL.

The Denver ABA franchise hired John McClendon, the first black coach in the ABA, from the AAU for their second season. McClendon was very active in recruiting Spencer Haywood to the 1968 Olympic team, and together they led the team to a gold medal in Mexico City. McClendon then recruited Haywood to the Rockets, although he was still an undergraduate at the University of Detroit. Recruiting undergraduates was against the (unwritten) rules of the NCAA and the rival NBA, and together they sued the Denver franchise—unsuccessfully.

After leading the team to a Western Division title and Rookie of the Year and MVP awards, Haywood left for Seattle for the NBA and a better deal. The ABA struggled, as did the Rockets, and by 1975–76 a merger with the NBA was sought. The New York Nets, Indiana Pacers, and San Antonio Spurs of the ABA, along with Denver, joined the NBA, bringing with them some outstanding ABA players, among them Julius Irving.

During the transition period of 1975–76 and their last season in the ABA, Hall of Famer Larry Brown was coach of a team that included Dan Issel, David Thompson, and Bobby Jones and made the ABA finals. Issel and Thompson, along with Alex English, are the Rocket/Nugget players who are honored in the Basketball Hall of Fame. Their success continued early after entry into the NBA, but after division titles their first two years, continuing success has been difficult to achieve. Doug Moe replaced Larry Brown at the beginning of the 1978–79 season. During their first decade in the NBA the Nuggets were among the most exciting teams in pro basketball, and were known for their "motion offense" led by Alex English and Kiki Vanderweghe. The team established an NBA record 136 consecutive games, scoring more than 100 points. In the 1981–82 season the Nuggets averaged 126.5 points per game, still the NBA record. In 1983 they set the NBA record for points in a single game, winning against Detroit Pistons 186-184 in triple overtime (370 total points was also still the record in 2010). They continue to hold the records for most points scored in a quarter, first half, second half, and for an entire game.

Doug Moe was replaced in 1990 by Paul Westhead, who seemed to care even less about defense than Moe did, and the scoring machines continued. Although they scored many points, the other teams often scored more and writers wryly observed that they were the "Enver Nuggets" since there was no "D" (as in *defense*) by the team. On November 10, 1990, the Phoenix Suns set the NBA record for scoring 107 points—in the first half, against the Nuggets.

The 1990s had a few flashes of success during the time of Dikembe Mutombo and Mahmoud Abdul-Rauf (formerly Chris Jackson). In 1997–98, however, the Nuggets challenged the record for fewest wins in a season, winning only 11 games (the record for fewest is 9 by the 76ers in 1972–73). The 2000s have seen the re-emergence of Nuggets success with division championships in 2006, 2008, and 2010. Carmelo Anthony was drafted in 2003, and in 2008 he was joined by Chauncey Billups. The Nuggets have now accomplished back-to-back 50-win seasons, for the first time in franchise history.

After the single conference title (1976) and three division titles in the ABA (1970, 1975, and 1976) success has been intermittent for the Nuggets. There were two division titles early after joining the NBA (1977 and 1978) and then an additional five in 1985, 1988, 2006, 2009, and 2010. The team holds the NBA record of 20 appearances in the postseason without playing in the NBA finals. There have been no championships in either the ABA or the NBA.

The Nuggets have changed their uniforms almost as often as their rosters. The Rockets uniform featured an animated rocket dribbling the multicolored ball used by the ABA. As they became the Nuggets,

the format has been a variation on the theme of the Rocky Mountains as a backdrop, first with a rainbow logo, and then to the present snow-capped mountain behind the name Denver and NUGGETS in bold gold letters for an overall color combination of white, gold, navy, and powder blue.

Thomas J. Krizek
Saint Leo University

See Also: Colorado Avalanche; Colorado Rockies; Denver Broncos; Franchise; National Basketball Association.

Further Readings

Denver Nuggets Official Website. http://www.nba .com/nuggets (Accessed October 2010).
Frisch, Aaron. *The History of the Denver Nuggets.* Mankato, MN: Creative Education, 2001.
Stewart, Mark. *The Denver Nuggets.* Chicago: Norwood House Press, 2009.

Detroit Lions

In 1929, the Portsmouth Spartans began play as one of many independent teams in the Ohio and Scioto river valleys. In 1930, they joined the National Football League (NFL) after the other independents failed during the Great Depression. Portsmouth was the smallest city in the league, so the owners sold to a Detroit ownership in 1934.

In Detroit, the Lions have won four championships. Their most recent was in 1957, and they are one of only four current teams without a Super Bowl appearance. None of the others have an unbroken existence in the league dating to before 1995. In the years since the 1957 championship, the Lions have made the playoffs only nine times. Since expansion in 2002 to 32 teams, the Lions are the only team in the National Football Conference (NFC) without a playoff appearance.

There were other teams before the Lions in Detroit, but the Lions were the first professional team.

After the Spartans moved, the Lions had six straight winning seasons, including the 1935 championship, the first of their four. In the 1940s, the wins were rare. Bobby Layne became quarterback in 1950 and led seven winning years out of 10, including four championship games and three championships. When the team traded Layne to Pittsburgh in 1958, the fans were outraged, as was Layne, who declared that the Lions would not win for 50 years. This became known as the "Curse of Bobby Layne."

Thirteen years later, the Lions returned to the playoffs, but lost the lowest-scoring game in playoff history. They reappeared in the playoffs in 1982 and 1983 but lost first-round games. In 1991, they won a playoff game, the first since the curse.

Even Barry Sanders and Erik Kramer could not bring a championship, and the four playoff appearances of the 1990s brought four first-round losses. Then they went 0–16 in 2008, the 50th anniversary of the curse. Their half-century record is worst in the league.

The 19-game losing streak from the final 2007 game to September 27, 2009, is second only to the 26-game losing streak put up by the expansion Tampa Bay Buccaneers in 1976–77. The 2008 team lost all 16 games, only the second team since the 1970 merger with not even a tie for a season. The Lions' 24-game road losing streak from 2001 to 2003 is an NFL record.

The Detroit Lions's new logo added more details, such as teeth and a mane, within the previous logo's outline of a lion.

Marketing

The Lions began Thanksgiving Day football in 1934 as an attempt to draw attendees to the new team's games. Owner George A. Richards set up a game with the Chicago Bears for the new Detroit team and had it televised by NBC. The Lions lost the game, but 75 years later the game was still a Detroit tradition, and the Lions had a four-game losing streak in Thanksgiving games.

In 2010, the Lions had what was considered the second best Website in professional sports and provided streaming video of their games. The Lions's Website includes team and player blogs, fan polls, fantasy football, radio- and video-archived game broadcasts, community activities, fan and youth sections, and the usual merchandising and ticket sales. Historical topics covered include profiles of legendary players and the 75th anniversary all-time team.

In 2009, both the state and the team were in dire straits. Michigan was among the hardest hit of the states in the recession, with 13 percent unemployment and Detroit homes going for as little as $10,000. In 2009, the Lions switched marketing firms, bringing in Maingate, Inc., a firm with experience with other NFL teams, including the Browns and Colts. Maingate took over Ford Field merchandising, the pro shop, training camp, internal merchandising, and Web commerce. Speculation then was that there would be a new logo. A month after revealing a new logo and uniforms, the team announced that its new marketing campaign would have no stars and no slogan; the product was to speak for itself.

The Lions introduced their new logo to boost interest in the team and its merchandise and to signal a new beginning for the team after their 0–16 year and history of one playoff victory in 49 years. The new logo meant a new brand posture: the logo had teeth and muscle and a mane—all missing from previous iterations. However, it also referred to the past and did not break with previous logos too significantly. It was expected to increase ticket and merchandise sales for 2010 and indicate that a moribund franchise was making a new start.

John H. Barnhill
Independent Scholar

See Also: Detroit Pistons; Detroit Red Wings; Detroit Tigers; Economic Climate for Sports; Internet/Online; National Football League; Websites, Sports Marketing.

Further Readings

Detroit Lions Official Website. http://www .detroitlions.com/index.html (Accessed October 2010).

Kaplan, Daniel. "No Stars, No Tag Line for Lions' Marketing Campaign Because 'Product Will Speak for Itself.'" http://www.sports businessjournal.com/article/62500 (Accessed October 2010).

Sternberg, Laura. "History and Tradition of Detroit Lions Thanksgiving Day Football." http:// detroit.about.com/od/sportsrecreation/a/Lions _Thanks.htm (Accessed October 2010).

Voiovich, Jason. "Detroit and Its Lions: Looking for a New Roar, State of the Brand." http:// stateofthebrand.com/?p=306 (Accessed October 2010).

Zaroo, Philip. "Does Lions' New Marketing Agreement Mean New Logo?" http://blog.mlive .com/highlightreel/2009/03/does_new_marketing _agreement_m.html (Accessed October 2010).

Detroit Pistons

The Detroit Pistons is a team in the National Basketball Association (NBA) based in Auburn Hills, Michigan, a suburb of Detroit. The team's home arena is the Palace of Auburn Hills. The team was originally founded as the Fort Wayne Pistons as a member of the National Basketball League in 1941. The club joined the NBA in 1948 and moved to Detroit in 1957. In the early history of the franchise the Pistons struggled both on the court and at the box office, with lackluster seasons and low attendance. Starting in 1998, the Pistons have accumulated five Eastern Conference titles, nine Central Division titles, and three NBA championships.

In the 1960s and 1970s, the Pistons became a competitive franchise that featured players such as perennial all-stars Dave DeBusschere, Dave Bing, Walt Bellamy, and Bob Lanier. The franchise's fortunes began to turn with key draft picks and acquisition of players such as Isiah Thomas, Bill Laimbeer, and Vinnie Johnson, who would remain together for more than a decade and form the nucleus for one of the best franchises in professional sports.

In the 1980s, the team added such players as Rick Mahorn, Joe Dumars, Dennis Rodman, John Salley, Adrian Dantley, and Mark Aguirre, along with coach Chuck Daly. It was in this era that the "Motor City Bad Boys" image was born and the Pistons brand was solidified. In 2010, *Sports Illustrated* named the 1988–89 "Bad Boys" number two on the 25 most hated teams in sports history. With historic clashes with the Chicago Bulls, Boston Celtics, and Los Angeles Lakers to their credit, the franchise developed a reputation for playing a hard-nosed brand of basketball and for winning. Under the direction of Joe Dumars, who later became the Pistons president of basketball operations, players such as Chauncey Billups, Richard "Rip" Hamilton, Rasheed Wallace, Ben Wallace, and Tayshaun Prince enabled the Pistons to emerge as consistent contenders again.

Future Concerns

Owner Karen Davidson is seeking to sell the team after the passing of her husband and longtime owner Bill in 2009. *Forbes* recently valued the franchise at $479 million. One of the front-runners for the sale of the Pistons is Mike Ilitch, the Little Caesars pizza mogul who currently owns the Detroit Tigers and Detroit Red Wings. The primary concern for Davidson, Ilitch, and other Michigan-based potential buyers is the possible loss of the franchise to an out-of-town buyer, which some argue would potentially further exacerbate metropolitan Detroit's financial woes. The Pistons, just like the Red Wings, Tigers, and Lions, have a rich and storied tradition in the metro Detroit community. Part of the proposal by Ilitch is to build a new arena in downtown Detroit for the NHL's Red Wings and allow the Pistons to share space.

One of the major concerns confronting the Pistons, Lions, and Red Wings is the continuing collapse of the economy in the region and state. Pistons officials are hypersensitive to ticket pricing and are being more aggressive and creative in their marketing efforts to avert possible backlash from the economic downturn. Full-season, half-season, and other plans offer perks that include upgrade possibilities, gift cards, access to team-sponsored special events, and opportunities for access to the 175 luxury suites or premium seating.

The team also relies heavily upon social networking to keep their fans informed and to maintain their fan base. Sites such as Facebook, Twitter, YouTube and Yahoo! Sports play a major role in Pistons marketing efforts. The Pistons effectively utilize their primary social networking site, called Posting Up, to convey information to fans. Player sites and Pistons play-by-play announcer George Blaha's show *MetroPCS Pistons Weekly* complement their arsenal of social networking tools.

Steven N. Waller
University of Tennessee, Knoxville

See Also: Detroit Lions; Detroit Red Wings; Detroit Tigers; Franchise; National Basketball Association.

Further Readings

Addy, Steve and Jeffrey F. Karzen. *The Detroit Pistons: More Than Four Decades of Motor City Memories.* Champaign, IL: Sport Publishing, 2004.

Berri, David J., Stacey L. Brook, and Martin B. Schmidt. "Does One Simply Need to Score to Score?" *International Journal of Sport Finance,* v.2 (2007).

Detroit News and Chuck Daly. *Detroit Pistons: Champions at Work.* Champaign, IL: Sport Publishing, 2004.

Fanhouse.com. "Mike Ilitch Wants to Buy Detroit Pistons." http://nba.fanhouse.com/2010/08/09/mike-iltch-wants-to-buy-detroit-pistons (Accessed August 2010).

Farrell, Perry A. *Tales From the Detroit Pistons.* Champaign, IL: Sport Publishing, 2004.

Krupa, Greg. "Progress of Sale Pleases Pistons." http://detnews.com/article/20100812/SPORTS0102/8120364/Progress-of-sale-pleases-Pistons#ixzz0zXFDPtBx (Accessed August 2010).

Detroit Red Wings

The Detroit Red Wings is one of the National Hockey League's (NHL) most successful franchises. The team's history can be traced back to the old Western Hockey League, in which the Victoria (British Columbia) Cougars were members until their roster was sold to an investment group from Detroit. Then the group was awarded an NHL franchise on May 15, 1926. Initially, the team struggled on the ice and on the ledger sheet because the new owners inherited more than $80,000 in debt from the Cougars.

Over the life of the franchise, the Red Wings have found the formula for success after winning 11 Stanley Cups, six conference championships, and 18 division championships. The modern Red Wings began their resurgence in 1982 when current owners and pizza barons Mike and Marian Ilitch purchased the team. In the years that followed, the Ilitches acquired perennial team captain Steve Yzerman, defensemen Nicklas Lidstrom and Vladimir Konstantinov, forward Sergei Fedorov, and the NHL's winningest coach, Scotty Bowman, to strengthen the team. In 1995, Detroit reached the finals for the first time in nearly 30 years only to be swept by the New Jersey Devils.

After falling to the Colorado Avalanche in a rivalry-creating conference final in 1996, Detroit added Brendan Shanahan and veteran defenseman Larry Murphy to make a run at the Stanley Cup in 1997. The Red Wings swept the Philadelphia Flyers in the finals to claim their first cup in 42 years. The revamped Red Wings dominated the 2001–02 season and fought back from early playoff scares before eliminating the Colorado Avalanche in a seven-game Western Conference Final series that included shutouts by Dominik Hasek in games 6 and 7, when Detroit was facing elimination. The Wings faced the Carolina Hurricanes in the Stanley Cup Finals, and after the Hurricanes surprised the hockey world with an overtime win in game 1, Detroit won four consecutive games to secure their third Stanley Cup in six years. In 2008, the Red Wings claimed their 11th Stanley Cup with a 4–2 series win over the Pittsburgh Penguins.

With the collapse of the automobile industry in the metropolitan Detroit area, the Red Wings also felt the pinch. When unemployment hovered at 7 percent and Detroit's economy first began to dip in 2007, the Detroit Red Wings were the first team to feel the economic slide among the professional sport franchises in Detroit. The NBA's Detroit Pistons played to capacity, and the Detroit Tigers baseball team's attendance increased, while Red Wings attendance slipped to 94.2 percent of capacity and hockey's perennial winners failed to sell out the playoffs. Ultimately, with a declining economy and less discretionary income that could be spent for sport consumption, Red Wings fans had to make tough economic choices. Red Wings top brass attributed this shift in the marketplace to the economy.

The Red Wings responded immediately and began to offer giveaways for the first time. They also hired senior executive Steve Violetta from the Nashville Predators to manage the team's business operations. Those moves and others have put the team a step ahead of its peers in dealing with the economic devastation in Detroit. The Red Wings still face challenges. Full-season ticket equivalents are 8–10 percent behind the previous year, and the team hopes to make up the gap with a combination of individual and group ticket sales, an area where the team was seventh in the league last year. To encourage ticket purchases, the Red Wings kept prices flat for 2009–10 despite another Stanley Cup finals appearance. Additionally, the team expanded its payment plan system, allowing buyers to spread payments over six installments. On the group sales front, the Red Wings launched a series of mini-ticket packages, including a nine-game package, a 19-game package, and a new children's mini-ticket plan.

Major corporate sponsors include Molson Coors, AT&T, Kroger, Bank of America, Comerica, and Motor City Casino. Current media partners include FSN Detroit (television) and WXYT-AM/97.1 (radio). The team also relies heavily upon social networking to keep their fans informed and to maintain their fan base. Sites such as Facebook, LinkedIn, MySpace, Twitter, and YouTube play a major role in Red Wings marketing efforts. The Red Wings have also used WingCast podcasts to keep their fan base informed.

With the area's unemployment rate climbing upward of 16 percent, an aging Joe Louis Arena, and less discretionary income in the market, the Red Wings have an uphill battle to sustain their brand and franchise greatness.

Steven N. Waller
University of Tennessee, Knoxville

See Also: Detroit Lions; Detroit Pistons; Detroit Tigers; Franchise; National Hockey League.

Further Readings

DetroitHockey.net. "Red Wings History." http://www.detroithockey.net/history (Accessed July 2010).
Fischler, Stan. *Detroit Red Wings Greatest Moments and Players*. Champaign, IL: Sports Publishing, 2002.
Forbes.com. "NHL Team Valuations: #4 Detroit Red Wings." http://www.forbes.com/lists/2009/31/hockey-values-09_Detroit-Red-Wings_314898.html (Accessed July 2010).
Goodman, Michael E. *The Story of the Detroit Red Wings*. Mankato, MN: The Creative Company, 2008.
Sporting News. "Red Wings Get Creative in Down Economy." http://www.sportingnews.com/nhl/story/2009-10-06/red-wings-get-creative-down-economy (Accessed July 2010).
Trickle, Mickle. "The Detroit Red Wings and Their Marketing Plan." http://www.kuklaskorner.com/index.php/hockey/comments/the_detroit_red_wings_their_marketing_plan (Accessed August 2010).

Detroit Tigers

The Tigers, established in 1896, were a charter member of the American League (AL). They are one of the four AL charter teams still based in their original cities (the others being the Boston Red Sox, Chicago White Sox, and Cleveland Indians) and the only member of the AL-predecessor Western League to be in its original city. The team is owned by Detroit Tigers, Inc., which also markets memo-

The Detroit Tigers playing in the 2006 World Series helped them make the 2008 list of top 10 teams in attendance.

rabilia, tickets, merchandise, and apparel through the company Website. The Tigers have won four World Series and 10 American League championships, but have had many lackluster seasons.

During low years, the Tigers have marketed their glory years. In 2003, nostalgia was a popular theme in baseball marketing, with 16 of the 30 baseball teams incorporating it into their marketing plans that year. At the time, baseball was losing fans to other pastimes and to disenchantment with dismal performances. The strategy of harkening back to team heritage had the potential to show that the Tigers were sincere in wanting to improve on 2002's 106 losses, which had added to a string of losing seasons since 1993. For opening day in 2003 they brought out old-timers from the 1984 team—Alan Trammell, Kirk Gibson, and Lance Parrish. Trammell was the new manager that year, and the rebuilding team's season schedule and other printed material featured the old-timers rather than current players. The team slogan, "We Come to Play," seemed an admission that the team wasn't expecting to win many games but was going to play with pride and effort. The Tigers supplemented the

nostalgia campaign with a renewed emphasis on attracting youngsters through more theme nights, two-for-one tickets, camping on the field and running the bases, and other promotions. In 2003, they set an AL record for most losses with a 43–119 record, one short of the Mets's major league record.

Winning (other than for consistent teams such as the Yankees and Boston Red Sox) and affordable tickets by themselves do not fill ballparks. The 2008 *Sports Illustrated* ballpark ranking survey, conducted online with fans from each team, indicated fan satisfaction with the team, venue, concessions, and atmosphere. Although the number-one park was the home of the low-attendance Cleveland Indians, the Tigers were the highest rated of only four teams returning to the top 10 from the preceding year, ranking fourth in the poll and ninth in attendance. Top 10 teams in attendance need an attractive stadium in a good location. Like other top 10 teams, the Tigers had a new or refurbished park; in 1999, they left Tiger Stadium for Comerica Park and its Ferris wheel, waterfall, and pedestrian museum.

Other Marketing Activities

The Tigers have a star player, Curtis Granderson, noted for his community involvement as well as his sports prowess, and they market him extensively through appearances and memorabilia. Fans have access to him through his Website and e-mail, and can also request 5 x 7 cards. The site offers his bio, his training techniques, and other information about the star. He gives motivational speeches and appears or sponsors trade shows, camps, and clinics. He is also available for product endorsements, paid appearances, and other moneymaking opportunities.

In 2009, Granderson was a featured player in the Major League Baseball (MLB) marketing effort, appearing in a spot called "Beyond a Leadoff Man" in his various roles as a ballplayer at Detroit's Comerica Park and a speaker at public schools in support of reading and staying in school. The commercials sought to show how baseball influences everyday American life and culture. Granderson was the team's leading home run and stolen base getter and batted 266 a third of the way through the season.

The Detroit Tigers's promotional activities for the 10 months from February through November 2008 included on-field youth clinics, giveaways during games, the Detroit Tigers Kids Club, and promotional nights such as Motown, 1970s, 1980s, and country-themed nights, with pregame parties, prizes, banners, and other material. The Tigers's mascot appears often at venues other than the stadium.

In 2009, the Tigers arranged with Comcast and Fox Sports Detroit to offer on-demand games and related action to fans throughout the state. For an extra fee, consumers could receive full replay of Tigers games anytime they wanted, starting two hours after the end of the game and for a limited time.

In 2006 the Tigers returned to the World Series for the first time since 1984, but did not win. As of 2010, they had not been back to the playoffs.

John H. Barnhill
Independent Scholar

See Also: Detroit Lions; Detroit Pistons; Detroit Red Wings; Major League Baseball, Player as Brand; World Series.

Further Readings

Carranza, Lamar. "The History of the Detroit Tigers." http://article-niche.com/launch/The -History-Of-The-Detroit-Tigers.htm (Accessed October 2010).

Crainsdetroit.com. "Tigers' Curtis Granderson Focus of New Baseball Marketing Campaign TV Spots." http://www.crainsdetroit.com/ article/20090619/FREE/906199969/crains-blog -tigers-curtis-granderson-focus-of-new-baseball -marketing-campaign-tv-spots# (Accessed October 2010).

"Detroit Tigers, Inc. Company Overview." Businessweek.com. http://investing.business week.com/research/stocks/private/snapshot .asp?privcapId=4420508 (Accessed October 2010).

Greenberg, Jon. "*Sports Illustrated* Ranks Ballparks With Help From TMR." http://www .teammarketing.com/blog/index.html?article _id=14 (Accessed October 2010).

Smith, Jennette. "'84 Success Pitched to Connect With Tiger Fans; Marketing Shifts to Nostalgia." *Crain's Detroit Business* (March 31, 2003).

Development League

Development leagues were formed by professional sports executives as a way to train players and prepare them for the major leagues once there had been improvement in a player's skills or there was a need for that player at the higher level. Major League Baseball (MLB) has established many minor league franchises all over the United States to develop players. The National Hockey League (NHL) also has a history of development leagues and teams. In Europe, club teams have academies that serve as a way to develop younger players in the sports of basketball, hockey, and soccer. The Professional Golf Association (PGA) uses a tour sponsored at some point by companies like Nike, Nationwide, and the Hooters restaurant chain. This tour serves as a way to develop golfers similarly to the minor leagues in baseball and hockey and the club academies in Europe.

Leagues, teams, and their executives have also used these minor leagues, development leagues, or academies to groom executives, train coaches, and also try out innovative marketing practices to attract fans to games. Many members of MLB have borrowed ideas they have discovered at the minor league level relating to in-game entertainment, season ticket marketing ideas, creative advertising, and other unique business practices. Holding night games in the sport of baseball was an idea that originated in the minor leagues. The idea came from the general manager of the Cincinnati Reds, who cut his teeth in the minor leagues. The Cincinnati Reds became the first MLB team to install lights.

The National Basketball Association (NBA) Developmental League, or the D-League as it is fondly called, now has 16 franchises located in cities all over the United States. There are franchises in Springfield, Massachusetts, and Portland, Maine. On the opposite side of the country are the Idaho Stampede and the Utah Flash. The most recent D-League Champs are the Vipers from Rio Grande Valley in Texas, who feature the league's leading scorer and MVP, Michael Harris. The D-League drew over 1 million fans in the 2009–10 season. The league is religiously scouted by NBA executives looking for players to call up to the big leagues. Teams from China, Japan, the Philippines, and some of the best basketball clubs in Europe also regularly send scouts to the D-League.

All of the NBA teams have some formal relationship with at least one of the D-League franchises. A few of the NBA teams actually own a D-League team, and there are also some teams that share affiliation with one or two other NBA teams. For example, the San Antonio Spurs own the Austin Toros, and the Oklahoma City Thunder own the Tulsa 66ers. The Fort Wayne Mad Ants are affiliated with the Detroit Pistons, Indiana Pacers, and Milwaukee Bucks. The New Mexico T-Birds have an agreement with New Orleans and the Orlando Magic. The Rio Grande Valley team is privately owned, but they have an exclusive management agreement with the Houston Rockets. The Dallas Mavericks and Mark Cuban own the Texas Legends.

These affiliation agreements help to provide access to professional basketball business experience for these teams as well as a ready source for players from one of the parent teams. A parent can decide to send down one of their first- or second-year players who may need seasoning or more playing time. As the NBA has drafted more and more players with less or no college experience, the need for seasoning in a professional league, staffed with quality coaches, has increased. The Memphis Grizzlies created quite a stir in the NBA and the D-League when they sent their first-round draft pick and second overall pick, Hasheem Thabeet, down to the Dakota Wizards during the 2009–10 season. The Grizzlies had two centers ahead of Hasheem on the depth chart, so management decided Thabeet could develop faster by playing in the D-League, rather than sitting on the bench for their team. A fifth of the NBA's players in the 2009–10 season had some D-League experience. There are also many coaches who have D-League coaching experience. It is worth noting that the Golden State Warriors have hired a former D-League head coach to be their replacement for Don Nelson for the 2010–11 season. Keith Smart not only coached in the D-League, but played in the precursor to that league, the old Continental Basketball Association (CBA). Phil Jackson, the Los Angeles Lakers coach with all of the NBA Championship rings, was a head coach in that same CBA for several years before he became an assistant coach in the NBA with the Chicago Bulls.

D-League teams sell some of the same merchandise as their NBA counterparts; each D-League team has a full complement of trademarked sweatshirts, T-shirts, hats, keychains, and pennants. All of these items are available on each team's professionally designed Website, as well as at the arenas. The D-League has a community service program modeled after the NBA Cares program called D-League Cares. Many of the teams also operate basketball camps for kids during the season and in the summer. Each of the teams sells sponsorships, and the league has some partnerships with the NBA and the Women's National Basketball Association (WNBA) where a sponsor has access to fans of all three leagues. For the 2010–11 season, two D-League teams have sold sponsors space on their uniforms, following a practice that was started in the WNBA. Also, the league will serve as a laboratory for two rules experiments: one relating to the offensive goal tending rule from FIBA (the world governing body for basketball) and the other, a shortened overtime.

Craig Esherick
George Mason University

See Also: Farm Team System; Leagues, Major; Leagues, Minor; National Basketball Association; Player Development.

Further Readings

Benbow, Julian. "Developing Nicely." http://www.boston.com/sports/basketball/articles/2009/01/11/developing_nicely/?page=3 (Accessed October 2010).

Feinstein, John. *Tales From Q School*. New York: Little, Brown and Company, 2007.

Lombardo, John. "D League Teams Secure Jersey Sponsorships." http://www.sportsbusinessjournal.com/article/66394 (Accessed October 2010).

NBA.com. "D-League Draws 1 Million Fans." http://www.nba.com/2010/news/04/06/dleague.attendance.ap/index.html (Accessed October 2010).

White, G. Edward. *Creating the National Pastime*. Princeton, NJ: Princeton University Press, 1996.

Differentiation

Theoretically, anything that is valued by a customer and that he or she is motivated and capable of paying for can be used to differentiate a product or service. In practice, differentiators usually revolve around combinations of the following:

- Superior quality
- Unusual, unique, or, at best, proprietary features
- Better customer service
- Rapid product innovation
- Engineering or design excellence
- Additional features as "add-ons"
- An image of prestige, status, and exclusivity

A differentiation strategy relies on delivering better value to the customer in a format that the customer appreciates and wants. This type of strategy is not just about being different—differentiators must be based on what potential customers will truly value. As such, rigorous attention to the process of segmentation and targeting (ST) must be paid within marketing research. Once the ST process has been completed, differentiators can be built into the product and the marketing communications to achieve the positioning of the product offering. The concept of strategy through differentiation is thus intimately linked with environmental scanning and the matching of internal resources to the external opportunities in the market to derive a positioning that is sustainable and valued by the market to be served.

Companies following a differentiation strategy are often characterized by the almost constant innovation (based on market needs) or invention of new products to keep their differential advantage in the market. There is no better example than the constant churn of new products in the laundry detergent market, where the major companies are forever reinventing and relaunching old brands and products alongside new ones in an effort to keep their market shares.

Differentiation strategy is also closely linked to product theory, where the differentiators are often built in layers around a core product to create an augmented product, which also often includes elements of service in contemporary markets.

Note that those who differentiate actively control their value chains and those of their suppliers in order to continuously innovate and improve their differential advantage in the marketplace. This has key implications as to how differentiators are managed as a business, as opposed to those trying to be lowest cost, who squeeze their value chains.

Differentiation Strategy

Strategy is fundamentally about two things: deciding where you want your business to go, and deciding how to get there. A strategic plan is often compared to planning a journey: you know where you want to go to and from where you are starting; how you choose to travel depends on the resources and timescales you have in which to complete the journey. This is what a business's strategic plan does: it lays out where the business is heading in terms of targets and goals, where it currently is and what resources it intends to use, at what time and with what expected result, to get there. A more complete definition is based on an understanding of competitive advantage and the mechanisms by which such advantage is created and communicated to the target audience. According to Michael Porter in his 1985 book *Competitive Advantage*, these are the objectives of most corporate strategy:

> Competitive advantage grows out of value a firm is able to create for its buyers that exceeds the firm's cost of creating it. Value is what buyers are willing to pay, and superior value stems from offering lower prices than competitors for equivalent benefits or providing unique benefits that more than offset a higher price. There are two basic types of competitive advantage: cost leadership and differentiation.

A firm's relative position within an industry is given by its choice of competitive advantage (cost leadership versus differentiation) and its choice of competitive scope. Competitive scope distinguishes between firms targeting broad industry segments and firms focusing on a narrow segment. Generic strategies are useful because they characterize strategic positions at the simplest and broadest level. Porter maintains that achieving competitive advantage requires a firm to make a choice about the type and scope of its competitive advantage. There are different risks inherent in each generic strategy, but trying to be all things to all people is a sure recipe for mediocrity.

Andrew J. Whalley
Royal Holloway University of London

See Also: Barriers to Entry; Brand Preference; Branding; Product Life Cycle; Strategic Management; Total Product Concept.

Further Readings

de Chernatony, Leslie and Malcolm McDonald. *Creating Powerful Brands in Consumer Service and Industrial Markets*, 3rd Ed. Oxford, UK: Butterworth Heinemann, 2003.
Fullerton, Sam. *Sports Marketing*. New York: McGraw Hill, 2007.
Keller, Kevin L. *Strategic Brand Management*, 2nd Ed. Upper Saddle River, NJ: Prentice Hall, 2003.
Porter, Michael E. *Competitive Advantage*. New York: Free Press, 1985.
Porter, Michael E. *Competitive Strategy: Techniques for Analyzing Industries and Competitors*. New York: The Free Press, 1980

Diffusion of Innovation

Diffusion of innovation describes the process by which innovations are introduced and move through a particular environment. Everett Rogers was a pioneer in the diffusion of innovation research. He proposed that five stages exist in the diffusion of innovations: knowledge, persuasion, decision, implementation, and confirmation. Individuals first become aware of the innovation in the knowledge stage but possess little to no information about it. During the persuasion stage, they express interest in the innovation and gather related information. This information helps them decide whether to adopt or reject the innovation in the decision stage. In the event of adoption, individuals begin using the in-

novation during the implementation stage. Finally, individuals who reach the confirmation phase continue using the innovation for its intended purpose.

Innovations represent the deliberate use of resources to create something new, whether a new product, process, policy, or procedure. Numerous innovations have diffused through the sports industry. Sports facilities have adopted innovations like synthetic turf, luxury boxes and personal seat licenses, and naming rights. Sports television broadcasting has incorporated innovations such as the yellow line indicating a first down in football and the use of the instant replay across all sports. Online social networks like Twitter and Facebook as sports-related innovations have transformed the way fans, athletes, and teams interact in the online sports environment.

Sporting goods manufacturers have also developed a variety of innovations. They sell over $87 billion in sports-related equipment annually and dedicate countless hours and economic resources to creating innovations touted to improve performances for professional and amateur athletes alike. For example, Callaway spends $25 million a year on research and development to design and produce its golf clubs. In total, golf manufacturers were awarded patents for over 8,000 products within a five-year period. Innovations like face masks, helmets, and sports bras have increased the protection and comfort of athletes at all levels. Sporting goods manufacturers create innovations that can change the way sports are played.

The diffusion of innovations like sporting goods can be quantified via consumer product sales. Potential consumers can be placed into one of five groups: innovators, early adopters, early majority, late majority, and laggards. Innovators purchase the innovation first. They are willing to take risks and possess the financial means to buy the innovation. Early adopters follow the innovators and purchase the innovation next. Like innovators, they also have the necessary purchasing power plus a wide variety of social connections. They can influence an individual's decision to adopt or reject an innovation. Consumers in the early majority will purchase the innovation after they receive positive feedback from innovators and early adopters. The late majority possesses greater skepticism about the innovation and will only purchase the innovation after the majority of consumers have done so. As the final group, the laggards are the last to purchase the product, if at all.

The innovation sales trend can be depicted with an S-curve. Innovators and early adopters purchase the innovation first, and sales grow slowly at the outset. Consumers in the early majority begin to purchase the innovation as they receive positive feedback from innovators and early adopters. The early majority and late majority follow, and sales grow at an exponential rate, creating a critical mass. Finally, laggards make their purchases, and the innovation saturates the market. The S-curve reflects the initial consumer interest in the innovation, followed by burgeoning interest in and adoption of the innovation, and later declines in both sales and interest as the innovation reaches market saturation.

The diffusion of innovations can be illustrated using an example from the sport of rodeo kayaking. Rodeo kayakers perform tricks in whitewater conditions. As the sport progressed, kayakers paddled in increasingly challenging settings but found their boats lacked the requisite maneuverability. A smaller subset of kayakers developed new kayaks to address the shortcomings, making the boats shorter and more streamlined. Kayakers as innovators and early adopters saw and purchased the innovations. They reported improved performances, including more wins at competitive events. Other kayakers expressed interest in the redesigned kayaks after witnessing the successes of the innovators and early adopters. Sporting goods manufacturers began to mass produce the boats to meet the increasing demands of kayakers from the early majority, late majority, and laggard groups. Eventually, the innovations saturated the kayaking marketplace.

Innovation Failures
The consumer products market emphasizes a pro-innovation approach where newer equals better. Manufacturers spend time and resources developing and introducing innovations to meet consumer demands. Yet their efforts do not always translate into commercial success. Six out of every seven product ideas fail to become actual products. Furthermore, up to 80 percent of commercially available products fail. Innovations may fail to diffuse for a number of reasons, including lack of consumer support. Consum-

ers targeted to receive the innovation must be willing and ready to accept it. Without this support, an innovation will not diffuse, no matter how meritorious.

Sometimes innovations lack support because they are perceived as too new. Innovations lie on a continuum from continuous—simple modifications to existing products—to discontinuous—significant breakthroughs that go well beyond current product offerings. Discontinuous innovations may require consumers to learn new technologies or make significant modifications to their current lifestyles and routines. One such product was a synthetic basketball introduced by the National Basketball Association for the 2006–07 season. The players complained about the damage the new basketball did to their hands, playing styles, and athletic performances. They balked at using the innovation. The basketball failed to diffuse, and the league returned to the traditional leather basketball three months into the season.

In addition to being too new, innovations may fail to diffuse because they are perceived as creating an unfair advantage. Innovative swimsuits introduced by Speedo were developed through collaborations with professional swimmers and the aerospace industry. During a 17-month period, which included the 2008 Olympics, athletes using the swimsuits broke more than 130 major swimming records. Some swimmers sponsored by other swimsuit manufacturers demanded similar suits from their product sponsors. Other participants asked for a complete ban of the swimsuits. The international swimming governing body FINA (Fédération Internationale de Natation) responded by banning the suits permanently, beginning with the 2010 season. Here, the diffusion of an innovation failed after a governing body banned the innovation to maintain competitive balance.

Opinion Leaders
An innovation may also fail to diffuse because consumers are simply not aware it exists. Individuals must know about the innovation and have an interest in learning more about it. Communication and the spread of innovation information are important to the diffusion of innovations. Potential consumers gain knowledge by contacting sources who can offer in-depth innovation information. Opinion

leaders often serve as information sources. They possess extensive knowledge about an innovation and express a willingness to share this information with others. Opinion leaders can influence an innovation's marketability. Early majority and late majority consumers often wait for positive reviews from opinion leaders before making purchases of their own. Upon receipt of favorable information, the majority of consumers will then purchase the innovation, helping it to diffuse more rapidly.

Sporting goods manufacturer Dunlop provides an example of opinion leaders at work. Dunlop watched one of its tennis shoe brands lose its cachet over time and languish in discount stores. Trendy adolescents as opinion leaders later discovered the shoes and began wearing them to popular nightspots and other events. Receiving a stamp of approval from trendsetters, the shoes increased in popularity, and more adolescents began purchasing them. The underground communications reignited sales, and Dunlop responded by introducing a mass-market campaign to promote the shoes to a larger audience.

Conclusion

Sporting goods manufacturers spend millions of dollars each year developing and marketing innovations for their consumers. They must identify and avoid impediments to the successful diffusion of innovations. The diffusion of innovations begins with the innovation itself. Athletes as consumers must support the new product. They must know it exists, want to learn more about it, and make a decision to adopt it. Other athletes must learn about and adopt the innovation at increasing rates until the innovation saturates the market. Positive information helps an innovation diffuse if the information convinces athletes to purchase and tell others about the innovation. Conversely, negative information may suppress the diffusion of innovations if individuals choose to reject the new product. The collection and spread of innovation information precedes and then aids or hinders the diffusion. Thus, initial innovation support, favorable innovation information, and product sales are necessary ingredients for the successful diffusion of innovations in the sporting goods industry.

Marion E. Hambrick
University of Louisville

See Also: New Product; New Product Development Process; Technology in Sports; Word-of-Mouth.

Further Readings

Franke, Nikolaus and Sonali K. Shah. "How Communities Support Innovative Activities: An Exploration of Assistance and Sharing Among End Users." *Research Policy*, v.32 (2003).
Hienerth, Christoph. "The Commercialization of User Innovations: The Development of the Rodeo Kayak Industry." *R&D Management*, v.36 (2006).
Lüthje, Christian. "Characteristics of Innovating Users in a Consumer Goods Field." *Technovation*, v.23 (2003).
Rogers, Everett M. *Diffusion of Innovations*, 5th ed. New York: Free Press, 2003.

Direct Foreign Investment

Direct foreign investment, or foreign direct investment (FDI), is long-term investment by entities of one country in companies in another country through joint ventures, management, or transfer of technology. Foreign ownership of a factory is a common example; when an American corporation opens an auto factory in Mexico or a Japanese corporation opens one in the United States, that is FDI. The greatest flow of FDI is among the industrialized countries of North America, Western Europe, and Japan, where foreign ownership of assets and multi-company joint ventures are common. In recent years, FDI flows to developing countries have risen steadily and rapidly. FDI is *direct* investment in contrast to the *indirect* investment of shareholding: purchasing stock in a foreign company is not an example of FDI.

FDI occurs in all sectors of the economy, including the sports industry and sports equipment industry. Government incentives exist to encourage FDI in some countries, including loan guarantees, land subsidies, low corporate tax rates, tax holidays and other concessions, preferential tariffs, infrastructure subsidies to encourage new industrialization, and in the case of big projects, derogation from regulations. The United States is the world's largest recipient of FDI, and the Department of Commerce operates its Invest in America initiative to promote FDI.

American involvement in sports-team FDI began with FDI outflow. Several Premier League European soccer teams have been purchased by American owners, including the Liverpool FC owned by New England Sports Ventures, the owners of the Boston Red Sox. Such purchases inspired Dallas Mavericks owner Mark Cuban to ask in a 2008 essay on his blog, "When will foreign ownership of U.S. sports teams start?" "It's going to happen," he wrote. "The money will be too big for a current owner to say no." As he pointed out, the recent economic gains in China and creation of a Chinese billionaire class created a demand for investments as well.

Cuban was right. Foreign-owned U.S. sports had actually already begun, when the group of Seattle businessmen who bought the Mariners in 1992 included 60 percent owner Hiroshi Yamauchi, a Japanese Nintendo executive. The restrictions placed on the deal by Major League Baseball (MLB) effectively insulated Yamauchi from the day-to-day operations of the team, reducing his role to revenue-sharer. MLB had a policy against foreign ownership at the time, though current commissioner Bud Selig is not believed to be as strongly opposed to it as 1992's commissioner Fay Vincent was.

Foreign ownership in sports has caught on in the rest of the world before the United States. Russian billionaire Roman Abramovich became the George Steinbrenner of the Premier League when he purchased the Chelsea FC in 2003. Sparing no expense to attract talent, the Abramovich-owned Chelsea won eight trophies, but went through seven managers in the same period. The Manchester City FC was purchased in 2007 by former Thai prime minister Thaksin Shinawatra, but was sold a year later when Shinawatra's vast expenditures failed to secure a win. The team's next owner was Sheikh Mansour bin Zayed Al Nahyan of Abu Dhabi, who

The English soccer team Manchester United, which has been owned by American businessman Malcolm Glazer since 2005, is shown here in a match against Arsenal in the 2008–09 UEFA Champions League tournament on April 29, 2009.

has made a point of tweaking the team's cross-town rival, Manchester United—which since 2005 has been owned by American Malcolm Glazer, who also owns the Tampa Bay Buccaneers.

In 2010, Russian billionaire Mikhail Prokhorov was given permission by the NBA to purchase the New Jersey Nets for $200 million. Prokhorov is expected to spend heavily on turning the once great but troubled club into a playoff contender, much as Mark Cuban's expenditures transformed the Mavericks. Prokhorov's Nets were involved in the summer 2010 bidding war for free agents LeBron James and Dwyane Wade, albeit unsuccessfully. At 45 years old, Prokhorov is the second-richest Russian, and his purchase may well open the door to an incoming flood of sports-team FDI.

Bill Kte'pi
Independent Scholar

See Also: Global Market Expansion; Global Sports Expansion: Baseball, Basketball, NASCAR, Football; Global Sports Structure; Globalization of Sports; International Reach.

Further Readings

Rosner, Scott, and Kenneth L. Shropshire. *The Business of Sports.* Sudbury, MA: Jones & Bartlett Publishing, 2004.
Sauvant, Karl P., Wolfgang A. Maschek, and Geraldine A. McAllister, eds. *Foreign Direct Investments From Emerging Markets: The Challenges Ahead.* New York: Palgrave Macmillan, 2010.
Weesterbeek, H. and A. Smith. *Sport Business in the Global Marketplace.* New York: Palgrave Macmillan, 2003.

Direct Mail

Direct marketing is defined by the Direct Marketing Association (DMA) as an interactive system of marketing that uses one or more advertising media to affect a measurable response and/or transaction at any location. Direct mail is a subset of this broader category and is delivered by the postal service to homes and businesses. Consumers are given the means to reply by return mail, by phone, online, or even at a sports facility or business location.

Direct mail literally puts information into potential customers' hands. Effective use of direct mail includes techniques that help sporting organizations reach the most likely customer, tailor an offer, and create a way for the customer to respond. The success of the mailing is regulated by several factors. First, there is the accuracy of the mailing list. Next is ascertaining the appropriateness of the product for the target market. The cost of the mailing is a factor, as is creating a direct mail piece that stands out in a sea of unwanted commercial "junk" mail. Regulations developed to prevent invasion of the consumer's privacy also play a part.

Mailing List

At the heart of direct mail is the mailing list. Success is directly attributable to getting the right piece into the hands of the right consumer, so the list is one of the most important parts of the mailing. The database requires almost continuous clean-up, as addresses, demographics, customer interests, and even names change.

Mailing lists are either internal or external. Internal lists are the sports organization's own customers, subscribers, and donors or potential customers who have inquired about the business. This list allows organizations to cultivate their own customers, continuing and expanding the services and opportunities offered to them.

An external list can be purchased or rented from list compilers and brokers. The list can be specific—such as all female runners over the age of 35 in the Cincinnati area, or general, such as the names and addresses of potential sponsors living in an affluent ZIP code in Menomonee Falls, Wisconsin. List brokers can provide either printed labels or merge lists that work with the sports organization's computers and printers.

An enhanced mailing list consists of the internal list combined with a targeted external list. Enhanced lists may combine internal and external lists sorted together by demographic, geodemographic, psychographic, or behavioral data fields.

Target and Offer

The old adage that the best customer is the customer you already have certainly applies to direct mail. Every person who has attended a game or been a part of a team can be on the mailing list if the names and addresses are captured. The more fields that are listed, the more information is available for the mailing. If the database shows that a football fan has purchased season tickets, that fan is a prospect for a direct mail offer for box seats, special offers, and merchandise. Each response to a direct mailing creates a field in the database by leaving a data trail.

The first rule of direct mail is "don't waste your money on people who don't want your mail." Resistance to direct mail is limited somewhat by allowing potential customers to opt in or opt out of the mailings. Opt-in mail is sent with the recipient's consent; when an opt-out response is received, a field is blocked in the database so opt-out consumers do not receive the mailings. That consumer may be permanently removed from the database.

The direct mail piece makes a specific, targeted offer that promises a reward. It could be a special discount or price or a bonus product such as a free team T-shirt with tickets. The offer may only be available for a limited time to motivate the recipient to take action and respond. The best offer is something that generates sales or encourages trials of a new product by an already predisposed audience. Teaser copy may broadcast the offer on the outside of the envelope or mailer to lure the consumer inside.

Format

Direct mail formats vary widely and may include a letter in an envelope, a double postcard, a multicomponent mailer, a brochure or catalog.

A personalized letter with an offer is the simplest form. The standard A10 business envelope looks like personal mail and may be enhanced with teaser copy that invites the reader inside. The mailing address and the return address are often designed to look like regular, nonbulk correspondence. The letter makes a proposal tailored to the consumer and offers a method of response such as a fill-in-the blank card and an addressed return envelope with return postage.

Multi-component mailers, brochures, and catalogs are designed for people who have moved up the hierarchy of listings from prospectives who have never purchased to customers who have registered for events, bought tickets or merchandise, or indicated an interest in the team or sports activity. Inserts, samples, promotional materials, photos, and descriptions of merchandise make the mailing worth its hefty price.

A less expensive format is the double postcard (DPC) that consistently outperforms more elaborate mailers. The 8.5-inch by 5-inch card is half of a letter-size page and cheaper than cards requiring more or odd-size cuts. The front of the card has photos, art, logos, and slogans that may be part of an integrated marketing campaign. The other side has space for a personalized mailing address, the sports organization's address, a stamp or indicia, and a bar code that contains postal information.

Mailing

As postage costs increase, direct mailers have been forced to cut their lists, reduce the size of the mailers, and look for ways to spend less on postage. Getting a bulk mail permit from the postal service allows a greatly reduced cost. The bulk mail indicia, or printed stamp, has prescribed wording that indicates the mail is presorted standard by ZIP code or is from a nonprofit organization, with the words "U.S. postage paid" and the official bulk mail permit number. Most organizations pay the rate for postage that allows incorrectly addressed letters to be returned to sender so that the mailing list may be updated with address changes.

Because the return card will not be part of a bulk mailing, postage costs more per piece than the original mailing. Rather than putting a stamp on the return envelope, most organizations use a postal permit with a bar code and the words "no postage necessary if mailed in the United States." Then the organization is only charged for postage on the cards that are sent back.

Bulk mail regulations are particularly stringent for more elaborate mailers, including a stipulation that two sides of the piece must be taped so it won't snag in the bulk mail equipment.

The vehicle for response may be a reply card with a return envelope; an order sheet that can be mailed, faxed, or e-mailed; a page or coupon in a brochure or catalog that can be cut or torn along perforations; an 800-number; the URL for a Website, or a hashtag for texting.

Objections to Direct Mail

Direct mail is synonymous with junk mail, but it is still a viable part of sports marketing. Direct Marketing Association figures indicate that in 2009 more than 70 percent of Americans shopped direct, generating more than $686 billion in sales. More than 80 percent of U.S. households read some or all of their advertising mail. More than 300,000 small businesses across the country relied on direct mails for part of their sales. And nonprofit organizations raised nearly $200 billion from generous donors through direct mail.

There are strong consumer support groups that object to the volume of paper products, often unwanted, that appears in mailboxes across the nation. Junk mail is considered a nuisance and even an environmental concern. A study by the U.S. Postal Service showed that junk mail in the United States adds up to over 100 billion pieces of mail each year—about 30 percent of all the mail delivered in the world. Each year, American households receive a total of 104.7 billion pieces of junk mail, or 848 pieces of junk mail per household, requiring 6.5 million tons of paper. The average American will spend eight months of his or her lives dealing with junk mail.

Figures like these have led to regulations that limit direct mail and provide a way for consumers to stop receiving it. The U.S. Federal Trade Commission has developed guidelines to prevent invasion of privacy and has offered them as voluntary provisions for marketers who use direct mail. The Data Mining and Invasion of Privacy study of the potential impact of technological advances on society with specific reference to targeted direct mailings (junk mail) and Internet spam has led to creation of data removal sites such as the Do Not Mail Organization and the Privacy Rights Clearinghouse.

Conclusion

Sports organizations that use direct mail effectively target their mailings to consumers who have made a commitment to the sport by buying tickets, attending or sponsoring events, or purchasing merchandise. They let prospective customers opt in for more opportunities—tailor-made for their mailboxes.

Linda Thorsen Bond
Stephen F. Austin State University

See Also: Advertising; Database Management; Direct Marketing Association; Marketing Mix; Publicity; Target Market.

Further Readings

Altstiel, T. and Jean Grow. *Advertising Creative: Strategy, Copy, Design*, 2nd Ed. Thousand Oaks, CA: Sage, 2010.
Direct Marketing Association. http://www.the-dma.org (Accessed October 2010).
Do Not Mail Organization. "The Issues." http://www.donotmail.org/the-issues (Accessed October 2010).
O'Guinn, Thomas C., Chris T. Allen, and Richard J. Semenik. *Promo*. Mason, OH: South-Western, Cengage Learning, 2011.
Privacy Rights Clearinghouse, http://www.privacyrights.org/fs/fs4-junk.htm (Accessed October 2010).

Direct Marketing Association

Direct marketing has come a long way since the days of telemarketing and direct mail. Today, direct marketing encompasses a variety of methods to create brand awareness, inform potential customers, solicit donations, and encourage targeted behavior. The media used today in direct marketing include Websites, catalogs, television, inserts, mobile, magazines, e-mail, and search engines, and are used by business-to-business marketers as well as direct to consumer. The Direct Marketing Association (DMA) is the primary source of information about direct marketing activities for both academics and practitioners about direct marketing practices and self-regulation. Because of the nature of direct marketing and concerns for privacy and security, the DMA has become the leading global trade association of businesses and nonprofit organizations in the field.

DMA advocates industry standards for responsible direct marketing, promotes relevance as the key to reaching consumers with desirable offers, and provides research, education, and networking opportunities to improve results throughout the end-to-end direct marketing process.

Founded in 1917, DMA now represents companies from many industries in the United States as well as 48 other nations. DMA members include nearly half of the Fortune 100 companies, the travel and hospitality industry, as well as nonprofit organizations. The DMA is headed up by newly appointed CEO Lawrence Kimmel and is embracing its role with new media. The organization launched an updated Website in October 2010 to reflect this progress.

DMA is headquartered in New York City and has a robust lobbying arm in Washington, D.C. The organization represents member interests at the state and national level. Active in following legislation, DMA represents its members and the industry on Capitol Hill, at the Federal Trade Commission, the Federal Communications Commission, and other agencies such as the U.S. Postal Service. Each year DMA tracks thousands of proposed laws and regulations in Washington, D.C., and across the nation and addresses key federal and state policy issues that affect the direct marketing community.

Some of the issues that DMA has been active in monitoring include behavioral marketing, data security, privacy, postal reform, Do Not Mail legislation (DNM), the Streamlined Sales and Use Tax Agreement (SSUTA), and others.

Education and professional development opportunities provided by DMA for their members include specialized seminars, Webinars, in-house training, certificate programs, access to direct marketing databases and information, a library and resource center; as well as case studies, white papers, in-depth analyses, performance benchmarks, thought-leader trend briefings, and research reports.

In response to public criticism and to head off federal regulation, DMA launched the Website DMAchoice.org in October 2008 to enable consumers to opt out of commercial mailings they are not interested in receiving and opt in to those mailings they do want. Because self-regulation and responsible marketing are so important to the overall health of the direct marketing community, DMA's Corporate & Social Responsibility (CSR) department hosts free compliance briefings for DMA members. Topics range from self-regulation and privacy/ethics to environment and international affairs. The organization's mission statement reads as follows:

DMA's goal is to keep all marketing channels open and economically viable, as well as maintain the flow of data that fuels multichannel marketing. DMA advocates with legislators and regulators, provides reputation management, cutting-edge research and education, as well as networking and market making opportunities to improve results throughout the end-to-end direct marketing process.

DMA's members can be categorized into three broad segments: marketers, vendors and suppliers to the direct marketing community, and nonprofit organizations. Membership is made up of businesses that are both users of direct marketing (consumer and business-to-business marketers) and suppliers of the various services such as Website developers, printers, graphic designers, advertising agencies, and publishers. DMA provides a database of vendors and companies that offer direct marketing assistance and services for the sports industry.

DMA provides its members with news of key legislation and current trends and issues in the industry. The Website offers additional benefits such as a job bulletin board, member directory, issues briefs, and a corporate responsibility resource center. The Corporate Responsibility Center provides information on the organization's guidelines on ethical practices, environmental resources, and a public list of the companies not in compliance with DMA's ethical practices guidelines.

Nancy E. Furlow
Marymount University

See Also: Advertising; Direct Mail; Marketing Publications; Publicity.

Further Readings

Carson, Erik and Pradeep Korgaonkar. "The Broadened Concept of Direct Marketing Advertising." *Marketing Management Journal* (Spring 2001).

Direct Marketing Association and the Federation of European Direct and Interactive Marketing. *Directory of International Direct and E-Marketing: A Country-by-Country Sourcebook of Providers, Legislation and Data*, 7th ed. London: Kogan Page, 2003.

Direct Marketing Association. http://www.newdma .org (Accessed September 2010).

Direct Marketing Association. "What Is the Direct Marketing Association?" http://www.the-dma .org/aboutdma/whatisthedma.shtml (Accessed September 2010).

Rapp, Stan. "A Call to Reinvent the DMA: Why We Need a Name Change Now. 'iDirect Marketing' Would Symbolize the Interactive, Informed and Immediate Way the Industry Operates Today." *Advertising Age* (October 19, 2010).

DirecTV

DirecTV is an integral part of Rupert Murdoch's News Corporation sports media distribution empire. As the leading direct broadcast satellite (DBS) service, with 18 million subscribers, it offers viewers nearly 300 channels. DirecTV is the sole provider of a number of exclusive sports programming packages. Most notably, the National Football League's (NFL) Sunday Ticket allows viewers in any market to watch every NFL Sunday game, in contrast to the limited schedule viewers were accustomed to based on the decisions made by their local broadcast affiliates. The Sunday Ticket has over 2 million subscribers paying a $300 fee on top of their regular monthly fees. DirecTV also has similar packages

for NCAA tournament basketball and NASCAR. Murdoch has always valued sports as vital programming to attract male consumers. Throughout the 1990s, Murdoch coveted ownership of a cable operator to ensure carriage of the many Fox-related networks. Unable to secure one, Murdoch turned to the emerging DBS News Corporation and purchased DirecTV from Hughes Communications, then part of General Motors, in 2003. In 2008, John Malone and his Liberty Media acquired a 41 percent interest in the DirecTV Group. The company also owns the highly profitable DirecTV Latin America with its 6 million viewers.

DirecTV traces its origins back to 1990 when it teamed with United States Satellite Broadcasting (USSB) to develop the first DBS system. Even though it provided competition to the cable monopoly, there was a major hurdle the company needed to overcome. Hesitant consumers had to first purchase satellite dishes and then have them installed on their residence. This limited potential customers in major urban areas such as New York City where apartment and condo owners did not like the idea of satellite dishes being affixed to their property. Also, dishes need a clear view of the southern sky. These are issues the company and its customers still deal with today.

DirecTV launched the Sunday Ticket in 1994 and immediately satisfied the hunger of football fans demanding out-of-market contests. A year later, DirecTV had over 1 million customers. That number surpassed 15 million a decade later. After its contract with the NFL for exclusive rights to the Sunday Ticket ended in 2004, cable providers made a serious run at the package. However, DirecTV retained the rights with a deal for $3.5 billion that lasted through the 2010 season, and DirecTV now holds the Sunday Ticket rights through the 2014 season.

Even though the company focuses much of its marketing toward sporting events, DirecTV currently faces a new wave of competition in the pay-television market. Telecom companies such as Verizon now offer subscription television programming, while Internet content continues to attract more viewers.

DirecTV, in an effort to remain the leading DBS provider, is once again focusing on sports to gain more viewers. In summer 2010, DirecTV made the Sunday Ticket available online and on PDAs for users who were unable to install a satellite dish at their home and for mobile users.

Aaron J. Moore
Rider University

See Also: Broadcast Rights; Pay-per-View Sports; Sports Networks; Televised Sports.

Further Readings

DirecTV. "The Official Site of DirecTV." http://www.directv.com (Accessed August 2010).

Flint, Joe. "DirecTV to Offer Sunday Ticket Football Package Online to Some Non-Subscribers." *Los Angeles Times* (August 25, 2010).

Gomery, Douglas. The Making of a Satellite Behemoth." *American Journalism Review*, v.21/2 (May 1999).

La Monica, Paul. *Inside Rupert's Brain*. New York: Portfolio, 2009.

Neel, K. C. "DirecTV Grows Latin America Business." *Multichannel News* (August 24, 2009).

Sandomir, Richard. "DirecTV's N.F.L Games to Be Online." *New York Times* (August 24, 2010).

Shawcross, William. *Murdoch*. New York: Simon & Schuster, 1997.

Discrimination

Prejudice and discrimination are prevalent in the sport and physical activity context. Prejudice is psychologically based and refers to bias against (or preference for) certain groups. It is seen as an antecedent of discrimination, which is more of a sociologically based construct and refers to the behaviors in which people engage that privilege one group over another. Theories of discrimination abound, but perhaps the two most prevalent are Gary Becker's economics model of discrimination and Jeffrey

Greenhaus, Saroj Parasuraman, and Wayne Wormley's conceptualizations of access and treatment discrimination. Examination of this construct is critical given that discrimination has a serious, negative effect on those who experience it.

Economics Model

From an economics perspective (i.e., the taste for discrimination), three types of discrimination can apply to sport and physical activity: employer, employee, and consumer. Employer discrimination occurs when persons in leadership roles, such as coaches, general managers, or owners, favor a certain group so much that they are willing to make sacrifices in order to have employees of that group. For instance, a coach with a preference for white players will primarily recruit white players for the team, even if it costs the team future success. As another example, an athletic director with a preference for heterosexual coaches will not hire sexual minorities, even if it means giving up victories to do so.

Employee discrimination occurs when employees refuse to work with members of another social group, or when they require additional compensation to do so. For instance, members of athletic teams in the mid-1900s often refused to play with persons of a different race. The "color barrier" in Major League Baseball is illustrative of this phenomenon. Today, these preferences might not influence willingness to play with one another, but they do impact the manner in which players interact with one another. For instance, hockey teams with high nationality diversity have been shown to have fewer assists than do their more homologous counterparts, suggesting that players might not cooperate well with persons from a different country.

Finally, consumer discrimination occurs when fans of a team prefer to see members of certain groups perform over others. One prevalent example of this is in major college football programs and among the boosters who financially support them. Most of the boosters of these programs are white, and some believe that these boosters prefer same-race coaches; thus, if the school were to hire a head coach of color, then donations might cease. This dynamic would explain the severe underrepresentation of coaches of color in NCAA Football Bowl Subdivision teams.

Access and Treatment Discrimination

From a different perspective, discrimination can be conceived as a two-dimensional construct. Access discrimination occurs when members of a particular social group are prevented from obtaining a position. This occurs when they are looking for a job or membership on an athletic team. Women coaches, for example, face discrimination in the hiring process, especially when the athletic director is a man.

Similarly, African American assistant coaches are under-represented on athletic teams when compared to the proportion of available coaches. These effects are particularly salient when the head coach is white, but not when the head coach is African American. Finally, access discrimination can also impact how people are treated during interviews, as persons from under-represented groups are not given as much time to interview and are often treated in hostile manners.

Whereas access discrimination occurs before people are on a team or in a sport organization, treatment discrimination takes place once people are employed. This form of discrimination occurs when people from a particular group receive fewer rewards, opportunities, and resources than they duly deserve based on their on-the-job performance. Thus, the discrimination occurs because of their membership in a group (e.g., religious minority) rather than their actual performance. Research suggests that persons different from the typical majority in sport—that is, those who are not white, able-bodied, heterosexual, Protestant, or male—are likely to face treatment discrimination.

Outcomes

Both access and treatment discrimination negatively influence persons who experience them. Because access discrimination denies people opportunities to join a team, workplace, or profession based on their (perceived) membership in a particular social group, one of the most obvious outcomes is the limitation placed on jobs and careers one can pursue. These effects can also influence people not yet in the field, such as athletes, as anticipated discrimination in a given profession is likely to deter people from pursuing that path.

Treatment discrimination influences a number of tangible and subtle outcomes. With respect to tangible outcomes, persons who face discrimination receive less on-the-job training, have fewer social contacts, are paid less for equal work, and receive fewer returns for their work-related investments. They are also more likely than their counterparts to have strained relationships with their supervisors or coaches. More subtle outcomes include integration into a group, supervisor support, and job discretion.

Furthermore, treatment discrimination can, over time, result in self-limiting behaviors, such that people experience decreased motivation and job-related self-efficacy because of the continued negative feedback. As might be expected, when self-limiting behavior takes place, subsequent task performance might suffer, and stereotypes about

Discrimination may cause minorities and women in sports, like this female coach, to receive less training, support, or pay.

the under-represented group then become confirmed. In short, both access and treatment discrimination have serious detrimental effects on persons from under-represented groups.

George B. Cunningham
Texas A&M University
Claudia Benavides Espinoza
Universidad Autónoma de Nuevo León

See Also: Americans with Disabilities Act; Diversity in Sport; Employee Development; Employee Relations; Gender Diversity; Gender Equity; Paralympics.

Further Readings

Becker, Gary S. *The Economics of Discrimination.* Chicago: University of Chicago Press, 1957.

Grant, Randy R., John Leadley, and Zenon Zygmont. *The Economics of Intercollegiate Sport.* Singapore: World Scientific Publishing, 2008.

Greenhaus, Jeffrey H., Saroj Parasuraman, and Wayne M. Wormely. "Effects of Race on Organizational Experiences, Job Performance Evaluations, and Career Outcomes." *Academy of Management Journal,* v.33 (1990).

Hebl, Michelle R., Jessica B. Foster, Laura M. Mannix, and John F. Dovidio. "Formal and Interpersonal Discrimination: A Field Study of Bias Toward Homosexual Applicants." *Personality and Social Psychology Bulletin,* v.28 (2002).

Sartore, Melanie, L. "Categorization, Performance Appraisals, and Self-Limiting Behavior: The Impact on Current and Future Performance." *Journal of Sport Management,* v.20 (2006).

Dispute Resolution/ Arbitration

Increasing legal intervention in sport has traditionally taken the form of courts in the state legal system enforcing established legal rights founded in contract, tort, or property, or sanctioning an infringement of criminal law. Initially, this was acceptable as vindicating the notion that sports governing bodies and athletes are subject to legal rules and enforcement processes in the same way as other organizations and individuals. Over the past 20 years, the relentless increase in sports litigation in developed legal systems has brought about a re-think: the drawbacks of such intervention in terms of costs, delays, antagonism, and emerging legalism has prompted a shift toward alternative dispute resolution (ADR) as preferred policy. ADR is a powerful and pervasive international movement well entrenched in labor relations, family disputes, and commercial law. It has now successfully established itself in sport as a cheap, informal, flexible, and effective alternative to the official court system.

Types of ADR in Sport

A variety of different ADR techniques exist in sport, and it is possible to combine a number of them in a single institution. Mediation is essentially a private voluntary dispute resolution process in which a neutral third party seeks to promote an agreed solution. The mediator takes an active role but lacks the power to enforce a settlement. Where agreement is reached it does not have to reflect the strict legal position. Mediation is rapidly developing into the most popular form of ADR in sport based on the fact it is quick, cheap, confidential, informal, can embrace issues beyond the immediate interests of the parties, and permits the parties to retain control of the dispute. Also, it is without prejudice in the sense that negotiations may be frank, but if a solution is not possible either side retains the right to subsequently commence litigation. Perhaps its greatest advantage is that solutions can be closely tailored to the commercial needs and expectations of both parties. Court-ordered remedies and arbitration awards lack this flexibility. Likewise, it is conducive to continuing harmonious relations between governing bodies and athletes.

Arbitration in essence involves the parties subscribing to a formal written agreement to submit their dispute to binding resolution by a third party who is normally a lawyer. Arbitrations are usually formal court-like hearings, and the arbitrator's award is governed by legal rules. Compared with mediation, it is expensive and adversarial. Moreover, arbitrator rulings are binding and enforceable via both the legal system in which they are conducted and in overseas legal systems. National rules on arbitration frequently provide for a right of appeal, but this is normally narrowly confined to correction of material errors of law. Its advantage over the courts lies in its relative cheapness and confidentiality, which avoids the embarrassing publicity generated by litigation. Resort to arbitration is secured either by inserting a provision requiring its use into governing bodies' rulebooks or by ad hoc agreement. External arbitration services specific to sport are now available on an organized basis in the United Kingdom and Australia.

In conciliation, an independent third party intervenes with the aim of bringing the parties together to discuss the dispute. This is useful when diametrically opposed positions have been adopted, but differs from mediation in that the parties reach their own solution.

"Med–arb" is a combined technique of mediation followed by arbitration involving a binding settlement. The mediation is designed to take the heat out of the situation and identify common ground. This can be done by a trusted nonlawyer third party with the arbitrator completing the process by determining the dispute according to legal rules.

A mini-trial is a formal trial-type hearing but in a private forum. The procedure is voluntary and typically involves presenting the issues before senior officials of each side who are assisted by a neutral expert able to proffer advice on technical and legal issues and on the likely outcome if the matter proceeds to litigation. Unlike arbitration, this process is not binding but it is useful in commercial disputes since it permits the consideration of business and technical issues. Its great benefit is to avert an escalating legal dispute proceeding to court and redirect it instead into a private business-resolution forum.

Neutral evaluation is when a neutral third-party expert is assigned the task of evaluating the facts/evidence and providing an opinion designed to assist the parties to reach a settlement. This is useful in complex disputes involving technical issues and can speed up protracted negotiations that have become mired in factual or technical disputes.

The Court of Arbitration for Sport

Headquartered in Lausanne, Switzerland, with regional offices in Sydney, Australia, and New York, the Court of Arbitration for Sport (CAS) is an international arbitration body that operates principally to resolve disputes between athletes (and commercial organizations) and those international federations belonging to the International Olympic Movement. CAS is independent of the International Olympic Committee in terms of its funding, administration, and arbitration decisions. This has been confirmed on two separate occasions by the Swiss Federal Tribunal. Arbitrators are selected from a pool of 150 individuals with established reputations in sports law who are required to display conspicuous independence in reaching their decisions. CAS awards cannot in general be further appealed against or reviewed, and they are rendered enforceable in 100 states throughout the world by virtue of the New York Convention on the Recognition and Enforcement of Foreign Arbitral Awards (1958).

CAS hears cases in private, although the format is broadly similar to that of commercial arbitrations with parties normally legally represented. Publicity may attach to its awards provided both parties consent. It has started to distill key principles from its case law in a published digest. The main sources of law used are the Code of Sports-Related Arbitration and World Anti-Doping Code. These are supplemented by the constitutions of the International Federations, parties' contractual commitments, national legal rules, and its own case law, which is not binding but which it normally follows in the interest of consistency.

Types of cases heard by CAS include ordinary cases, which are decided by a panel of three arbitrators, two nominated by the parties, and the other by these two arbitrators. A single arbitrator may be used with the consent of the parties. The entire process takes between six and nine months from the initial filing of the request for arbitration. Appeal cases are heard before three arbitrators and take about four months from the initial request. The dispute is decided in accordance with the law chosen by the parties or that of the seat of the International Federation.

Ad hoc divisions are CAS arbitrators sitting at major global events such as the Olympic and

Commonwealth Games. They reach decisions within 24 hours, are free, and decide cases in accordance with the Olympic Charter, any relevant regulations, general principles of law, and any other rules it deems appropriate. Athletes wishing to participate in these events are required to assent to use of the CAS Ad Hoc Divisions in preference to the local courts as a means of dispute resolution. This consent, it could be argued, is procured under duress and therefore these are not valid international arbitrations.

The work of CAS has historically been dominated by doping disputes involving the application of so-called strict liability offenses, that is, where the offense is deemed committed simply upon the prohibited substance being found to be in the athlete's bloodstream or urine. Most panels have tended to uphold these even in cases where the outcome and penalty appears draconian. In other words, pure strict liability is applied with no room for a defense of lack of intention or negligence. In more recent arbitrations, however, a minority of panels have been prepared to mitigate these offenses by enabling athletes to escape liability on proof they were not at fault or by means of a rebuttable presumption whereby an athlete is provisionally guilty if the prohibited substance is found in his or her body, but this is capable of being rebutted if he or she adduces evidence of lack of intention or negligence. Much turns on the precise wording of the offense and overall facts. Advisors should consult the CAS digest and its Website for detailed guidance.

In addition, CAS delivers arbitrations on the entire range of sports issues including eligibility, selection, technical event rules, intellectual property rights, allocation of broadcasting rights, and interpretation of contracts generally. It also offers nonbinding conciliation and advisory opinion services. Its long-term objective is to become the pre-eminent global sports dispute resolution agency.

Philip E. Morris
Independent Scholar

See Also: Breach of Contract; Contract, Key Factors in a; Doping; Drug Use in Sports; Ethical Conduct; Ethics in Sport; Legal Considerations in Sport; Misbehavior by Athletes; Olympic Organization.

Further Readings

Blackshaw, I. *Mediating Sports Disputes: National and International Perspectives*. The Hague, Netherlands: TMC Asser Press, 2002.
Court of Arbitration for Sport Official Website. http://www.tas-cas.org (Accessed April 2010).
Gardiner, S., et al. *Sports Law*. London: Cavendish Publishing, 2005.
Gearhart, S. "Sporting Arbitration and the International Olympic Committee's Court of Arbitration for Sport." *Journal of International Arbitration*, v.6 (1989).
Polivino, A. "Arbitration as Preventative Medicine for Olympic Ailments: The International Olympic Committee Court of Arbitration for Sport and the Future of the Settlement of International Sporting Disputes." *Emory International Law Review*, v.8 (1994).

Distributed Ownership

Distributed ownership is a professional sports league organizational structure that is used in the major North American professional sports. In this structure the individual clubs in a league are owned independently by ownership groups or individuals. The clubs form together as a closed group, with any new teams or owners needing approval of the existing membership. The leagues are governed by associations of the clubs that govern the league office.

In the distributed ownership league model, revenues can be broadly classified as shared and unshared revenue. Individual clubs typically generate revenue in their local markets that they get to keep as their own, and league-wide revenues are shared equally among all teams. Currently, each Major League Baseball (MLB) team contributes 31 percent of its defined local market revenues to a revenue sharing pot from which all teams draw an equal share. All of the major sports leagues share national broadcasting revenues equally among teams, with the broadcasting revenue making up the majority of National Football League (NFL) revenue and a much less significant portion of revenue for the other sports. Other revenue that is typically shared is league licensed merchandise, which is shared among teams and the players unions. The revenue sharing schemes must be collectively bargained with the respective players unions.

All of the major sport league offices, except for the National Basketball Association (NBA), are structured as tax-exempt, not-for-profit associations whose members consist of the teams in the league. The league offices are governed collectively by the group of teams in the league, with the commissioners being selected by a vote among the teams. Teams also vote on issues such as rule changes, expansion, and the approval of team relocations and ownership transfers. They agree on defined exclusive market territories or to compensate existing teams in a market that a new team moves into.

The individual clubs are structured as general partnerships, sole proprietorships, limited liability corporations, or nonprofits. Leagues currently proscribe clubs from being publicly owned corporations that issue shares, but many clubs were wholly or partially shareholder owned in the past.

The distributed ownership structure does lead to conflict between the associated clubs, often with the lines being drawn between large- and small-market clubs. The various revenue sharing systems employed by the leagues have the effect that the wealthier teams subsidize the poorer teams. Conflict arises between the wealthy, mostly large-market, teams, who feel that they are being penalized for effective management and note that the initial cost of owning a franchise in a large market is significantly higher, and the poor, mostly small-market, teams, who feel that they cannot effectively compete. This tension is particularly present in the NFL where the successful, large-market teams are now playing in new stadiums that allow them to capitalize on their large market status. Premium seating, sponsorship, concession, and nongame revenues all increase in the new stadiums, and none of those revenue streams are shared. Under the collective bargaining agreement that expires in 2011, team payroll costs are relatively even while the disparity between revenue among teams is increasing to levels that have not been seen in years.

The league structure has legal implications. The two primary ways of organizing a league are by distributed ownership or as a single entity. Single entity ownership is where the league is owned as a whole by one entity or group of owners with teams and players being assigned and controlled by the league. The main legal difference between the two structures is that courts have consistently ruled that teams organized in a distributed ownership structure are limited in how closely they can work together without violating antitrust statutes. This means that outside of a collective bargaining agreement, players have the right to move from team to team and to work for the club that will pay the most. If teams in a distributed ownership structure are found to be working together, or colluding, to restrict salaries outside of a collective bargaining agreement, they can be successfully sued and legally punished by the courts.

While cooperation among clubs and "league think" are essential to successful leagues, there is an inherent tension between the goals of the league and the goals of the individual clubs. If the league is organized so that the goal is team equality, there is little incentive for individual clubs to take risks to improve or expand their business since gains are often shared with the league. On the other hand, there is a great deal of incentive for clubs to free ride. They free ride by enjoying the benefits, through league sharing, of the clubs who are more successful, while avoiding risk themselves. However, the benefit of league think within a distributed ownership model is greater stability in the overall league and the individual teams' ability to achieve stable cost structures.

Kevin Heisey
Liberty University

See Also: Antitrust Laws and Sports; Collective Bargaining Agreement; Commissioner System; Competitive Balance; League Structure; Ownership, Professional Teams; Revenue Sharing.

Further Readings

Cotten, D. and J. Wolohan. *Law for Recreation and Sport Managers*, 4th Ed. Dubuque, IA: Kendall/Hunt, 2007.

Foster, George, Stephen Greyser, and Bill Walsh. *The Business of Sports.* Mason, OH: Thomson-South-Western, 2006.

Quirk, Charles. *Sports and the Law.* New York: Garland Publishers, 1996.

Distribution (Spectator)

The distribution of spectators is an issue sports organizations put a great deal of thought into. With the exception of baseball (which predates radio), most professional sports organized at a time when fans had the choice of either attending in person or being a home spectator through various media: first radio, then broadcast and cable television, and now streaming media on the Internet or even cell phones. But revenue, among other factors, varies according to where a fan sees the game.

Revenues from broadcast contracts negotiated at the league level—which includes most national television broadcasts—are generally shared by the league, regardless of which teams are competing. Revenues from local broadcasts accrue to the team. Local broadcasts include radio, local television channels, and regional cable sports channels like NESN or YES. Streaming media has not yet become common enough to generalize about; the games offered by MLB.com are paid for by subscription, the revenues of which are shared. For the time being, streaming media broadcasts can fairly be considered to have no impact on other audiences: in other words, it seems unlikely any spectators are choosing to watch a game on the Internet instead of attending in person or watching it on television. Far more common are online viewers who have no other means of watching: they're at work, they don't live near the site of the game, or tickets were sold out. As bandwidth issues are settled so that high-definition broadcasts can be streamed without a noticeable buffer, especially if they can be piped to a television or streamed through an Internet-compatible set-top device, this may no longer be the case.

Broadcast revenues are dependent in part on ratings. Just as with other television programs, ratings do not directly impact revenues in a short-term time frame. But they influence sponsor decisions about how much they are willing to pay for an advertisement, and sponsor willingness to pay for advertising affects a network's willingness or ability to pay for a broadcast contract. In some cases there are intangibles providing benefits to the network beyond advertising dollars. There is prestige attached to possessing sports broadcast rights, particularly to events like the Super Bowl or the National Collegiate Athletic Association (NCAA) Final Four for which there are no analogues. In some cases it may be desirable to have broadcast rights simply to prevent another network from having them. The broadcast rights may be important to the network's identity, as was the case for various sports broadcast rights over the past 30 to 40 years for both NBC and ABC; though this is likely to dovetail with advertising dollars, there may be a demographic appeal to the broadcast contract. For instance, a network seeking men of a certain age may be more invested in a sports broadcast independent of the revenue from it, in order to build that segment of its audience; or a network catering to or looking to attract female viewers may be disproportionately interested in signing a broadcast contract for the Women's National Basketball Association (WNBA) or women's softball. In some cases it can be safely assumed that broadcast rights will continue to be renewed regardless of ratings, as with the Red Sox games on NESN, Yankees games on YES, or various golf tournaments on the Golf Channel. Further, many regional sports networks such as those operated by Comcast need to offer broadcasts of whatever local sports games are not otherwise available on television—in the New England area, this means Boston Celtics games—as part of their *raison d'être*.

Broadcasting and Attendance
The concern with television broadcasts has long been that local fans will watch on TV for free or the cost of a cable subscription, rather than attending in person. While broadcast revenue is important, ticket revenue is heavily relied on by a team franchise. Ticket revenues are handled slightly differently by each league. In the National Football

League (NFL), one-third of ticket revenue is shared with the league, with the remainder kept by the team; in Major League Baseball (MLB), 30 percent is shared; in the National Hockey League (NHL) and National Basketball Association (NBA), ticket revenue is kept entirely by the team. Since the NHL, for example, is the least media-rich of these leagues, it is especially key to team franchises that they not sacrifice ticket revenue for the sake of their share of broadcast revenue.

The leagues have adopted various blackout policies as a result. A blackout is when a game cannot be televised in a particular media market, in order to encourage ticket purchasing or for other purposes. In the MLB, many blackouts are actually done to divert viewers to local broadcasts. When a game is televised on a local broadcast (or local cable station like NESN or YES), that telecast takes precedence over a national broadcast as long as the national broadcaster does not have exclusive rights, and so the ESPN or MLB Network telecast will be blacked out in the local market. Fox has exclusive nationwide rights on Saturdays from 3:55 P.M. to 7:00 P.M. (EST), while ESPN has those rights for Sunday nights after 8:00 P.M. Games that begin during that window can only be broadcast by the network holding the exclusive rights. The NHL's policy is similar, while the NBA only blacks out games broadcast on NBA TV, doing so in markets within 35 miles of the home team's market.

The NFL's policy, on the other hand, is based on attendance. This is perhaps an effect of the NFL's media richness, or the fact that the schedule offers so few games compared to other sports. Any broadcaster whose signal reaches within 75 miles of an NFL stadium may broadcast a game only if it is a road game, or if the game sells out 72 hours or more before the game begins. Time extensions are sometimes granted if a game is close to being sold out by the deadline. Broadcasters are also required to broadcast the road games for their market. The blackout is such an issue—NFL ratings being typically quite high—that broadcasters have been known to buy up the remaining hundreds of seats in order to be able to broadcast, which is perfectly allowed by the policy. The problem with the NFL policy is that it is based on the assumption that television viewership is stealing from in-person attendance. This may be true in some cases, to some limited degree. But the overall financial failure of the Los Angeles Rams, who relocated to St. Louis in 1995, was due in part to their inability to sell out games during their final years in Los Angeles—which meant games were not being broadcast either, leading to a gradual attrition of the fanbase.

Bill Kte'pi
Independent Scholar

See Also: Audience Measurement; Blackouts; Broadcast Rights; Fan Attendance, Reasons for.

Further Readings

Igel, Lee. "Time to Abandon the Blackout Rule, Pro Football's Sacred Cow." http://blogs.forbes.com/sportsmoney/2010/09/13/time-to-abandon-the-blackout-rule-pro-footballs-sacred-cow (Accessed October 2010).

Jozsa, Frank P. *American Sports Empire: How the Leagues Breed Success*. Westport, CT: Greenwood Press, 2003.

Quirk, James P., and Rodney D. Fort. *Pay Dirt: The Business of Professional Sports*. Princeton, NJ: Princeton University Press, 1997.

Diversity in Sport

Diversity is a term used to acknowledge divergence from a host society's dominant cultural values, physical traits, intellectual development, sexual preferences, and lifestyle choices. Issues associated with diversity include access, equity, inclusion, exclusion, difference, prejudice, and discrimination. Diversity has an impact on individual, team, and sport organization effectiveness and performance. This impact can be positive and create value for the sport, the community, or the individual, or it can lead to negative outcomes and less than optimal performance. The outcomes of embracing diversity and fostering inclusion are an enhanced understanding of community needs and better provision of sport services.

Sport has many beneficial outcomes in terms of quality of life, and everyone should have equal access to sporting opportunities.

Perceptions of being different and the subsequent consequences, as much as the actual differences between people and groups of people, are important to recognize. Perceptions of diversity can relate to demographic differences and psychological differences. The former include attributes such as age, sex, sexual preference, race, religion, or physical disability—aspects that can be visible to others. Psychological differences such as values, beliefs, attitudes, knowledge, and experience are not so easily observable.

In the past 30 or so years, there have been significant changes for women, people with disabilities, ethnic and racial minority groups, gays and lesbians, and other minority groups. These changes have improved the social, economic, and political position of many individuals and challenged traditional conceptions of power, privilege, and practice that previously marginalized or excluded some groups in society and made sport more inclusive. Inclusion is the social, environmental, emotional, economic, and cultural understanding and valuing of individuals. Inclusive sport provision means taking a proactive approach to addressing diversity issues across all dimensions of community and organizational practices.

However, inequity in access and opportunity in sport participation and employment in sport organizations still exists. The notion of a "level playing field" is still alien to many individuals and subgroups within society whose needs are largely invisible outside their own cohort and who face major obstacles in gaining access to the field of play. While direct institutional discrimination and formal exclusion have largely dissipated in recent years, under the threat of legal retribution, many underlying forms of discrimination and informal exclusion are still evident.

Many groups have risen to the inequity challenge and used discriminatory and exclusionary practices as a starting point to strengthen bonds and unite individuals in a common cause. In these instances sport participation has provided an avenue for the group members to develop a sense of pride and identity and allow for a celebration of diversity.

Diversity at Different Levels

Diversity in sport can be evidenced at each of the three levels of a sport enterprise—the societal and sport industry level, the sport organization level, and the level at which sport is personally experienced (i.e., the playing field).

Issues pertaining to diversity are prominent in general society, but historically many equity- and equality-related matters have been prominently evident in the sport context. For instance, female sport participation has been significantly lower than that of males in all areas of sport from participants to senior administrators. People with disabilities face many accessibility issues, and racial and ethnic minority groups have faced discrimination and prejudicial treatment to the extent of formal exclusion from certain sport clubs.

There have been many United Nations and other global-level declarations, conventions, resolutions, and charters relating to sport that encompass principles on gender, cultural diversity, racial discrimination, and disability areas. For example, the Brighton Declaration on Women and Sport covers all governments, public authorities, organizations, businesses, educational and research establishments, women's organizations, and individuals who are responsible for, or who directly or indirectly influence the conduct, development, or promotion of sport, or who are in any way involved in the employment, education, management, training, development, or care of women in sport. This declaration is meant to complement all sporting, local, national, and international charters, laws, codes, rules, and regulations relating to women or sport. The overriding aim is to develop a sporting culture that enables and values the full involvement of women in every aspect of sport.

At the national level many countries have specific laws and legislation that enshrines the rights of certain groups of people. For example, many Western countries will have some form of a disability discrimination act that makes it unlawful for sports clubs to treat disabled people less favorably for a reason related to their disability. Organizations must also make reasonable adjustments for disabled people, such as providing extra help, making changes to the way they provide their services, or adapting the physical features of their premises to overcome physical barriers to access.

At the sport organization level inequalities that result from bias and discrimination have been addressed with policies, programs, and practices that seek to eliminate structural and procedural impediments to accessing workplace employment, promotion, and success. Equal opportunity programs, affirmative action, and quota systems are examples of such initiatives. There has been a shift away from such approaches, which can be seen as deficiency based (accentuating the negative), to approaches that value differences. Valuing diversity means embracing and celebrating variations.

At the individual or personal level diversity considerations may impact the involvement of sport participants, coaches, officials, volunteers, and administrators. Participation in sport is influenced by the extent, variety, and accessibility of sport programs and facilities and how people are treated when involved in sport. Many sports have introduced initiatives that target particular under-represented diversity groups to encourage greater participation from these sections of the community. Additionally, codes of conduct that respect the rights, dignity, and worth of each and every person and treat each equally within the context of the sport can set out principles of inclusion for players, coaches, parents, and spectators.

Barriers and Facilitators

Facilitating inclusion and challenging discrimination in sport can require taking actions to break down barriers. There are many different ways to promote inclusion, depending on the nature of the diversity, including the following:

- Set standards and establish strategic frameworks that prioritize participation of diversity groups
- Develop and implement diversity policies at the national, community, and organization levels
- Adopt diversity-sensitive language and appropriate behaviors that value diversity
- Challenge prejudice and discrimination
- Break down negative stereotype roles and expectations
- Check access of facilities for explicit and implicit barriers and provide family-friendly facilities

- Provide relevant education and information to the general public that demonstrates the importance of including all groups of people
- Promote sport and sporting organizations as diverse and welcoming
- Reinforce the health and quality-of-life benefits of sport
- Promote the sporting achievements of people from diverse backgrounds and establish role models
- Educate sport administrators (at national and community levels) about how to inclusively engage diverse groups
- Develop specific resources or training modules relating to best practices in working with diverse populations
- Establish formal partnerships and collaborations between sport and diversity-related organizations

Diversity in sport has moved beyond the rhetoric of quotas and affirmative action to the celebration and valuing of diversity on the sporting field and in the workplace. Evidence clearly shows that sport can help build inclusion, express different forms of diversity, and promote better social relations within communities. In the longer term the sustainability of sport depends upon its ability to embrace diversity and fully realize the benefits. A diverse sport population can supply a greater variety of talent, skills, perspectives, and experiences. The success and competitiveness of sport will be enhanced if it can be inclusive of all members of society.

Tracy Taylor
University of Technology, Sydney

See Also: Americans with Disabilities Act; Discrimination; Gender Diversity; Gender Equity; Paralympics.

Further Readings

Becker, Gary S. *The Economics of Discrimination.* Chicago: University of Chicago Press, 1957.
Cunningham, G. B. *Diversity in Sport Organizations.* Scottsdale, AZ: Holcomb Hathaway, 2007.

Knoppers, A. and A. Anthonissen. *Making Sense of Diversity in Organizing Sport (The Business of Sports)*. Oxford, UK: Meyer & Meyer, 2006.

Sartore, Melanie, L. "Categorization, Performance Appraisals, and Self-Limiting Behavior: The Impact on Current and Future Performance." *Journal of Sport Management*, v.20 (2006).

Doping

Doping is a reality of sport, and has been throughout recorded history. In the conjoined histories of sport and performance enhancement, the goal of victory and the social or economic capital that victory brings to the athlete have provided the motivation for athletes to intentionally alter their physiological functioning for a level of functioning that will promote winning. The term *doping* has a varied etymology that has been the subject of much debate. One source suggests it comes from 18th-century South Africa, where *dop* was an alcohol-based sacrament used in ceremonial rituals. Another suggests that the word comes to us from an American adaptation of the Dutch word *doop*. The Dutch term refers to a "thick dipping sauce," but the Americanized term *dope* referred to jimson weed, which was thought to be used by thieves to sedate their victims prior to robbery. A more recent and relevant use comes from the late 1800s and early 1900s, when it referred to the thick opiate paste that was smoked in that era. In modern usage, *doping* is defined as the use of a substance to enhance performance.

Even though many people "dope" as part of their daily lives, doping has become a subject of public and academic interest as it relates to sport. While some see doping as an emerging threat to sport, the history of doping is as old as the history of sport itself. For example, Milo of Croton, a celebrated athlete of the ancient Olympics, is said to have consumed a pre-competition meal of 10 pounds of lamb specifically for performance enhancement. In ancient times distance runners also consumed hallucinogenic fungi to numb themselves to pain, fatigue, and discomfort. Galen, the ancient Greek father of present-day Western medicine, reported that stimulant use among Greek athletes was common. The motivation for doping then was similar to the motivations of today's athlete—the spoils of victory. At the ancient Olympics, the motto was στεφανι η θανατος ("wreath or death"), the wreath being the award signifying victory in the ancient games.

Doping re-emerged into the public consciousness in the late 1800s, when athletes began to perish from their performance-enhancing methods. The 1886 Paris to Bordeaux bicycle race was overshadowed by the death of 24-year-old Arthur Linton, who fatally miscalculated his usage of the stimulant trimethyl. Cycling was a popular testing ground for new doping methods in the late 1800s, and some would say even to the present day. Caffeine, cocaine, heroin, ether, digitalis, alcohol, strychnine, opium, and oxygen were all deployed alone or in combination to attempt to improve endurance.

The first recorded case of doping in the modern Olympic Games came in 1904, when Thomas Hicks collapsed immediately after winning the marathon. Investigations into the reasons for Hicks's collapse revealed that he had been kept on the path to victory with numerous doses of brandy, albumen, and strychnine administered by trainers who drove alongside him in a car.

The emergence of doping the late 1800s is not coincidental. The original interest in enhancing sporting performance actually relates to nonsporting contexts. Physicians such as Charles-Édouard Brown-Séquard and Serge Voronoff, among others, were seeking a treatment for the growing incidence of fatigue and virility issues among men who found themselves increasingly urbanized and subject to the working conditions of industrialization. In the 1930s, several research teams isolated testosterone as a treatment for testosterone deficiency (hypogonadism). German chemist Adolf Butenandt lays claim to being the first to develop anabolic steroids, and won the Nobel Prize for his work in hormone therapies.

There are numerous anecdotal claims about Nazi use of steroids to promote aggression, particularly on the eastern front. The rumors claim that Hitler himself was treated for hypogonadism through anabolic steroids, but these are unsubstantiated.

Recent Incidents

Doping returned to the forefront of sport in the 1950s and 1960s with the emergence of the Eastern Bloc sporting dynasties (Russia, East Germany, Romania, and Bulgaria). There were widespread rumors and discussions about Communist use of steroids to dominate the sports of strength and power (e.g., weightlifting, discus, shot put), and this caused some concern among the International Olympic Committee (IOC) members. What initiated the current level of vigilance against doping was the death of a cyclist from stimulant abuse. On opening day of the Rome Games of 1960, Knud Jensen died competing in the 100-km time trial, while two of his teammates were hospitalized, all with acute intoxication of amphetamines and nicotinyl nitrate.

In the aftermath of Jensen's death, the IOC established the Medical Committee on June 21, 1961. The first experiment with doping control policies took place at the Mexico City Games of 1968; while there were many firsthand accounts of drug use by athletes, no athlete tested positive.

Doping was a reality of sport but of little public interest until the Ben Johnson scandal of 1988. Doping returned to the forefront of public concern in 1998 when the Tour de France bicycle race was rocked with scandal regarding the use of performance-enhancing drugs.

It was the so-called Festina affair that prompted the International Olympic Committee to invest heavily in their antidoping policies to protect their image and their business interests. This move begat the World Anti-Doping Agency (WADA), which was founded and predominantly funded by the IOC to lead a multifaceted campaign against doping in sport. Headed by IOC member Richard W. Pound, WADA is now an independent agency that administers drug testing and enforces penalties against violators. With the introduction of WADA, doping in sport has received even greater public attention. In sports such as Major League Baseball in North America, the drama created by Congressional hearings on the subject, as well as by the Mitchell Report, indicated the scope of doping in baseball.

While the effectiveness of doping control is highly suspect, there are some new forms of doping in the immediate future, such as genetic modification for performance enhancement, or "gene doping,"

that demonstrate that doping will remain a factor in high-performance sport for the foreseeable future.

Kenneth Kirkwood
University of Western Ontario

See Also: Drug Testing; Drug Use in Sports; Ethical Conduct; Ethics in Sport; Misbehavior by Athletes.

Further Readings

Hoberman, John. *Mortal Engines: The Science of Performance and the Dehumanization of Sport.* Toronto: Macmillan Canada 1992.
Mottram, David R., ed. *Drugs in Sport*, 3rd Ed. New York: Routledge, 2003.
Ungerleider, Steven. *Faust's Gold: Inside the East German Doping Machine.* New York: St. Martin's Press, 2001.

Draft System

Each of the major professional sports leagues in North America has been using a draft system to allocate new players as they enter the leagues for at least the past 40 years. The systems were developed to equitably allocate players across teams and to combat bidding wars for unsigned talent. The oldest draft system among the major sports was introduced by the National Football League (NFL) in 1936 by then Philadelphia Eagles owner and future commissioner Bert Bell. This was one year after teams fought a bidding war over the right to sign University of Minnesota fullback Stan Kostka. The fullback signed with the Brooklyn Dodgers for $5,000. The last of the major sport leagues to implement a draft system was Major League Baseball (MLB) in 1966. A year earlier, outfielder Rick Reichardt received a $200,000 bonus from the Los Angeles Angels as a result of a bidding war that broke out over his services. The National Basketball Association (NBA) had a player draft system from its inception in 1946, and the National Hockey League (NHL) held its first player draft in 1963.

A common characteristic across all of the drafts is that teams finishing with poorer records generally get to choose players before the stronger teams. The NBA and NHL hold a lottery drawing to determine the order of selection among the weakest clubs. The lotteries are in place to reduce the incentive struggling teams have to intentionally lose games to improve their draft standing.

Major League Baseball

The MLB first-year player draft, held in June, is the only one among the major sports that occurs while the league is in season. It is extremely rare for a drafted player to begin playing immediately in the major leagues. The selections are ordered in each round so the team with the worst win-loss record in the most recently completed regular season selects first with subsequent selections assigned in order of worst to best record. The selections are assigned by win-loss record without regard to which league, American or National, the team belongs. Teams cannot negotiate or trade selection slots nor trade a drafted player until at least one year after the player is drafted.

Over 1,500 players can be selected in the MLB first-year player draft, which has had as many as 50 rounds. Only a small minority of the players selected will ever play in a major league game, but their rights are assigned to a major league team, and they are assigned to one of the more than 200 minor league baseball clubs. There is a "sandwich" round of picks between the first and second round that consists of compensatory picks awarded to teams who lost a Class A (top 20 percent at his position) or Class B (between the top 20 percent and 40 percent at his position) free agent the previous year. Teams who lose Class A free agents also receive a draft pick from the signing team.

Players who are eligible for the first-year player draft are from the United States, including territories such as Puerto Rico, and Canada. International players, regardless of where they are from, become part of the draft if they enrolled in high school or college in the United States. Additional requirements are being a high school graduate who has not enrolled in college or junior college, a college player who has completed his junior or senior year or is 21 years old or older, or being a junior college player. After the selection, teams retain the rights to the player until August 15 or the player enters or returns to college on a full-time basis. It is not unusual for a drafted player to not sign, go on to college, and be drafted again in a later year.

There are no restrictions on bonuses, pay, or salary for players selected in the MLB draft. The unlimited pay and inability to trade draft picks often leads to the consensus best players not being selected with the earliest picks. Teams must consider how much money it will take to sign a selection before choosing, because if the player goes unsigned, they lose the pick. Since 2009, teams who fail to sign players from the first three rounds have been given relatively equivalent compensatory picks the next year.

National Basketball Association

Since the NBA was established in 1946, when it was known as the Basketball Association of America (BAA), new players entered the league through a draft. The BAA merged with the National Basketball League to become the NBA. The initial NBA drafts were unique in that each team had a territorial pick that gave it the right to any player in its immediate area. If a team used its territorial pick it then forfeited its first-round pick. In the days before widespread television coverage it was hoped that a team's ability to bring in a local star would give it a more attractive product for the local fans.

Currently, the annual NBA draft must occur prior to July 10, and consists of two rounds. The first three selections are assigned by a lottery among the worst 14 nonplayoff teams, and the remaining selections are assigned based on the inverse order of the teams' win-loss records from the previous season. The lottery to determine the first three picks is organized in such a way that the worst team has the highest chance (25 percent) to get the first pick, while the team with the best record among the nonplayoff teams has the lowest chance (0.6 percent). Teams can trade their position in the draft.

Players eligible for the draft include athletes from the United States and the rest of the world. Players must be at least 19 years old. Players who have played one season of college basketball or played professionally in a league other than the NBA can apply to the draft as early entry players.

Draft picks in the NBA face rigid salary restrictions. For example, the contract of the first pick in the NBA draft for the 2010–11 season calls for an approximately $4.3 million salary for the first season. The team is committed to the player for two seasons and has an option to extend for a third and fourth season. Levels of raises are limited by the collective bargaining agreement so that if the team exercises its options to retain the number-one pick through four seasons, the player's fourth season salary will be approximately $6.2 million. Those numbers are for the first selection. The assigned salaries decrease for each later selection. The ninth player chosen in 2010–11 earned less than half of what the first pick earned, and the 24th player earned half yet of that. This serves to rigidly control the salaries of all successful players for the first four years of their career based on the pick with which they were originally selected.

Both the NBA draft lottery, which is held more than a month prior to the draft, and the draft have become televised media events on cable sports broadcasters. The lottery occurs in the midst of the league playoffs and can serve as a reason for fans of nonplayoff teams to stay engaged with the league through the playoffs and finals as the sport competes with both MLB and the NHL for viewers. The draft is held soon after the championship series and serves to rapidly turn fans' attention to team efforts to acquire talent for the subsequent season.

Commissioner of the National Football League Roger Goodell speaking in Radio City Music Hall during the 2008 draft.

National Football League

The NFL's draft has led the way in creating a media event out of its selection and assignment of new players into the league. Radio City Music Hall in New York City has been the site of the NFL draft since 2006, and the now three-day event (as of 2010) is televised on both ESPN and the NFL Network.

The draft is held between February 14 and May 2 and consists of seven rounds with as many selections per round as there will be teams in the upcoming season. In 1977, the number of rounds in the draft was reduced from 17 to 12 until 1993, when there were eight rounds, dropping to the current seven the next year.

Selection order is generally based on the reverse order of the teams' win-loss records from the previous season. If an expansion team is entering the league, it automatically receives the first selection. If there are no expansion teams, the first 20 selections are assigned such that the team with the worst record chooses first, followed by the team with the next worst record, and so on. Selections 21 through 24 are assigned to the four teams eliminated during the previous season's Wild Card playoff round. Selections 25 through 28 are assigned to the four teams eliminated during the divisional playoff round. Selections 29 and 30 are assigned to the teams eliminated during the conference championship round. The final two selections go to the Super Bowl runner-up and champion in that order. The same order is followed for subsequent rounds with the exception that groups of teams finishing with identical records cycle the order of selection within that group. Clubs can trade positions in the draft in deals that may include draft picks, other players, both, or even coaches. Prior to the 2002 draft, head coach Jon Gruden was traded from the Oakland Raiders to the Tampa Bay Buccaneers for a number of high draft picks over the subsequent three drafts.

To be eligible for the NFL draft, three NFL seasons must have begun and finished since the prospective player's high school graduation or the graduation of the class in which he entered high school. In effect this means that the NFL draft consists almost entirely of college players who have used their collegiate eligibility, finished their junior year football season, or who are redshirt sophomores (players who have been in college three years but have only used two years of football eligibility).

Each team is allotted a specified dollar salary limit that it cannot go over when signing its pool of draftees. The actual amount differs for each team and is based on the order and number of selections each team has. Within the rookie salary pool, teams negotiate individual contracts with players but they generally have to stay within a narrow salary associated with each player's draft slot if they want to sign all of their picks.

Rounds three through seven of the NFL draft include compensatory selections that are assigned to compensate teams for the loss of veteran players in free agency the previous season. The round that the compensatory picks are assigned is based on the quality of the player lost as determined roughly by salary, playing time, and awards or honors. If a team gained as many free agents of approximately the same quality as it lost the previous season, it would not be awarded compensatory selections. The picks are only awarded to teams that lost more players in free agency than they gained, or that lost a higher-quality player than the one they gained.

National Hockey League

The NHL Entry Draft, previously known as the NHL Amateur Draft, has been held in a different city each year since 1984 after being held in Montreal, Quebec, from 1963 to 1984. The NHL's draft was held in private prior to 1980. It is currently held every June on a date to be determined by the commissioner of the NHL.

The order of selection in the NHL Entry Draft is determined by a weighted lottery for the first 14 selections and by playoff results for the remaining 16 selections. The lottery for the first 14 picks is held among the 14 teams that failed to advance to the playoffs. The teams with poorer records have a better chance of winning the lottery than the teams with better records. Teams failing to qualify for the playoffs are originally placed in order from the worst record to the best to determine their lottery chances. Ultimately, winning the lottery allows a team to advance four selections ahead of its ranking by record. For example, if a team had the 10th worst record in the league the previous season and won the lottery, it would be assigned the sixth selection in the draft. This means that only the four teams with the worst records can be assigned the first selection.

The remaining selections are decided; first, by the round of the playoffs in which the teams were eliminated the previous season, with those who were eliminated early being assigned an early selection and second, by regular season record. For example, among the eight teams eliminated during the first round of the playoffs, the team with the worst regular season record would be assigned the earliest selection, and the team with the best regular season record would be assigned the latest. The draft consists of seven rounds with the same order of selection for each round.

North American players between the ages of 18 and 20 and non–North American players over the age of 20 are eligible for the NHL entry draft. Players who are drafted but do not sign with the team that selected them can re-enter the draft after two years if they are under 20 years old. If they are over 20, they become unrestricted free agents and can sign with any team they choose. Teams who draft NCAA collegiate players retain the rights to those players up until 30 days after the player leaves college.

Entry level, or Group 1, players have maximum salary restrictions scheduled to be $925,000 in 2011. A Group 1 player signed between the ages of 18 and 21 is subject to the entry-level compensation limit for the first three years of the contract. Those first signed between the ages of 22 and 23 are subject to the limit for two years. Those who sign at age 24 are subject to the limit for one year. Players who enter the league at age 25 or older are not considered Group 1 players or part of the entry-level system and are not subject to compensation limits.

In addition to the seven rounds of selections, the NHL Entry Draft provides compensatory selections. The number of compensatory selections can be no more than the number of teams in a given year. If a team loses its rights to an unsigned draft choice it is awarded a compensatory selection in the subsequent year's draft that is slotted in the same numerical order, but one round later than the original selection.

Kevin Heisey
Liberty University

See Also: Collective Bargaining Agreement; Player Acquisition; Reverse Order Entry Draft.

Further Readings

Christensen, R. *Ray Christensen's Gopher Tales.* Champaign, IL: Sports Publishing, 2002.
Koppett, L. "Baseball's New Draft." *New York Times* (February 28, 1965).
MLB. "Basic Agreement 2007–2011." http://mlbplayers.mlb.com/pa/pdf/cba_english.pdf (Accessed January 2011).
NBA Players Association. "2005 Collective Bargaining Agreement." http://www.nbpa.org/cba/2005 (Accessed January 2011).
NFL. "NFL Collective Bargaining Agreement, 2006–2012." http://images.nflplayers.com/mediaResources/files/PDFs/General/NFL%20COLLECTIVE%20BARGAINING%20AGREEMENT%202006%20-%202012.pdf (Accessed January 2011).
NHL Players Association. "Collective Bargaining Agreement, 2005." http://www.nhlpa.com/About-Us/CBA (Accessed January 2011).
Pro Football Hall of Fame. "History: Pro Football Draft History." http://www.profootballhof.com/history/general/draft/index.aspx (Accessed January 2011).

Drug Testing

Performance-enhancing drug use scandals involving high-profile athletes such as Marion Jones, Alex Rodriguez, and Jason Giambi, among others, demonstrate the pervasive nature of drug use within sports. The use of performance-enhancing drugs (PEDs) in competitive sports has a long history, and sport programs and organizations have turned to drug testing as a means of combating the problem. Drug testing occurs at the interscholastic, intercollegiate, and professional levels in the United States as well as at the Olympic level internationally.

Athletic administrators and sport organizations argue for the necessity of drug testing for two main reasons. The first surrounds protecting the health and safety of athletes. Sport organizations do not want their athletes using PEDs for their own well-being, and drug testing can be used as a deterrent to athletes who may feel peer pressure to use such substances in order to compete. In addition, the use of PEDs can pose a risk to other athletes competing against a drug user, as such substances have been shown to exhibit a marked increase in aggression in users. The second reason relates to protecting the sanctity and integrity of the sport itself as well as ensuring fairness in competition. Many see drug use in sport as a form of cheating by which one athlete gains an unfair advantage over others, thus rendering his or her achievement meaningless and undermining the integrity of the sport itself.

Despite support for drug testing from many directions, not all agree that drug testing should be undertaken by athletic administrators and sport organizations. Those opposing drug testing argue that it represents a substantial invasion of an athlete's privacy. Most drug tests occur through urinalysis, and requiring athletes to submit to such testing can be embarrassing. In addition, athletes often question why they are being singled out for such testing. Why not the school chess club or cheerleading team? Considering that submitting to drug testing is a condition for participation in athletics at many educational institutions and professional sport organizations, the question becomes whether athletes really have any choice in the matter.

When examining drug testing, constitutional law comes into play, as drug testing involves search (of a person's body) and seizure (e.g., urine), which is governed by the Fourth Amendment to the U.S. Constitution. For a search, and thus a drug test, to be constitutional under the Fourth Amendment, it must be deemed reasonable. In order to determine the reasonableness of such a test, a court will balance the intrusion on an athlete's Fourth Amendment rights (i.e., privacy) against the promotion of a compelling state interest (i.e., legitimate reason/need for the drug test). Factors considered by a court will likely include the privacy expectation of those tested (e.g., student athletes), the character of the intrusion (i.e., how the test is conducted), and the nature and immediacy of the governmental concern (i.e., whether the intrusion is outweighed by the need for the test). Thus, a court will look at whether there is a legitimate privacy expectation by those being tested, whether this privacy expectation is being infringed upon, and whether the infringement is outweighed by the necessity of the test. At the interscholastic level, the U.S. Supreme Court established in *Vernonia School District 47J v. Acton* (1995) that random, suspicion-less drug testing of high school student athletes was not in violation of the Constitution because student athletes have a lessened expectation of privacy than their student peers, and problems involving drug use among athletes necessitated such testing.

Currently, drug testing of high school athletes occurs across the United States, but not in every state or school district. Some states with drug testing programs are reconsidering testing because of the high financial costs associated with such testing.

At the collegiate level, testing is regulated by the National Collegiate Athletic Association (NCAA), which conducts random drug testing of athletes throughout the year, depending on the institutional level and the sports offered. Many institutions that offer collegiate sports also have their own internal drug-testing program. The NCAA's drug testing policy was challenged in 1994 by a group of student athletes at Stanford University. In ruling against the athletes, the court held that the NCAA's interest in protecting the health and safety of athletes and the integrity of its athletic programs outweighed the athletes' privacy interests, and thus the NCAA's drug testing policy was constitutional (*Hill v. NCAA*, 1994).

At the professional level, drug-testing policies exist for each of the four main professional sport leagues (i.e., MLB, NFL, NBA, NHL), with MLB instituting a policy in 2003 following the threat of Congressional intervention. Each of the drug-testing policies is governed by the collective bargaining agreement (CBA) for each league, which represents the contract between the players, represented by the players association (e.g., NLFPA), and the team owners. At the Olympic level, the World Anti-Doping Agency is responsible for drug testing. A consolidated drug-testing program for all international sports was designed in 2003 and implemented in 2004. The need for such a plan stemmed from inconsistencies in various national drug-testing policies and procedures for Olympic athletes up to that point. The program was revised in 2009 in the midst of criticism regarding its inflexibility and strict liability stance regarding positive test results.

Conclusion

Sport organizations and athletic administrators face a tough battle in the future related to drug testing. First, drug-testing policies and procedures must be designed in such a way that they are constitutionally valid and do not violate the Fourth Amendment. Second, new and innovative ways of substance abuse are developing alongside testing procedures. As such, the challenge will be to develop drug-testing policies and procedures capable of detecting new "designer" drugs created to be undetectable (e.g., EPO) as well as "natural" performance enhancement, such as blood doping, in which an athlete uses his or her own blood and not any artificial substances in order to gain a performance boost.

Michael S. Carroll
University of Southern Mississippi

See Also: Doping; Drug Use in Sports; Ethical Conduct; Ethics in Sport; Misbehavior by Athletes.

Further Readings

Kucharson, M. C. "NOTE: Please Report to the Principal's Office, Urine Trouble: The Effect of *Board of Education v. Earls* on

America's Schoolchildren." *Akron Law Review,* v.37 (2004).

Hill v. NCAA, 865 P.2d 633 (Cal. 1994).

Vernonia School District 47J v. Acton, 515 U.S. 646 (1995).

Wolohan, J. T. and G. Gordon. "Drug Testing." In D. J. Cotten and J. T. Wolohan, eds., *Law for Recreation and Sport Managers,* 5th Ed. Dubuque, IA: Kendall-Hunt, 2010.

Drug Use in Sports

The use of performance-enhancing drugs (PEDs) in sport, also termed *doping,* while historically evident in some ancient sports and games, has in the past half century become characterized as the dark side of a larger, high-stakes antidoping "war." With the ever-increasing commercialization and political prominence of sport, and the incredible technical advances of sport performance research, the stakes have never been higher for athletes, nations, and sport organizations. These pressures entice competitors and sport organizations to seek a wide variety of aids for performance advantages. The implications for sport managers and marketers are that they must clearly understand how the culture and institutional structures of sport can help engender or mitigate publicly derided doping transgressions. This importance may be simply from a risk-management concern, especially in sport contexts that are heavily reliant on corporate sponsorship and maintaining a "clean" image. The negative consequences of sport corruption in the form of drug use and abuse could potentially be severe and long term.

The arguments for and against the prohibition of drug use in sports have been thoroughly discussed in terms of science, morality, and ethics. Many sport governors adhere to hard-line stances based on preserving the spirit of sport, fairness, and health, while many scientists, academics, and social science researchers argue for a variety of more critical and often humanizing perspectives. While the latter do not condone the breaking of

sporting rules or governing law, they do push for a critical review of the origins and justifications of the prohibitions. Although the debate could easily continue over the policy of prohibition of performance enhancing substances, the recent formation (1999) of the World Anti-Doping Agency (WADA) and many national-level antidoping agencies such as the U.S. Anti-Doping Agency (USADA) have signaled that antidoping efforts will be with us for the foreseeable future and have a momentum all their own.

Nevertheless, if policy-makers and scholars agree that the use of prohibited substances in sports is a wrong choice to make for athletes under present rules, then why do we see continued efforts by individual athletes to beat the system and circumvent the rules? Additionally, why would we see evidence of systematic and widespread doping practices? The answer to these questions may be found in basic economic theory. When considering the consequences of choosing to use or not to use PEDs in their sport, the athlete is ultimately forced to weigh those alternatives based on his/her expected outcomes. These outcomes, however, are also clearly dependent on choices of the other participants in the athletic contests. One athlete's payoffs are intimately linked with the choices of all of the others while at the same time that athlete cannot observe their choice beforehand. This essentially gives rise to a strategic game of incomplete information that can be directly analogous to the classic "prisoner's dilemma." Under those circumstances game players end up making choices that lead them to outcomes that are jointly suboptimal. Depending on the potential payoffs, which can clearly be great in Olympic and professional competition, athletes can essentially be "trapped" into strategic choices that involve systematic circumvention of the rules, doping in particular.

To perhaps shine a positive light on this morbid game, we might take solace in the fact that competitive advantages may not necessarily be gained with widespread drug use in sport. Because we may generally assume the athletes' choices are symmetric and all face similar payoffs, all of them will be selecting similar strategies, i.e., all will dope, or all will compete clean. This symmetry potentially debunks the unfair advantage argument and might reassure us as sports consumers that the pure comparative performances of athletes are on display, if not the "cleanest" absolute level of performance.

Despite this point, issues still remain with health and wellness, as well as the coercive nature of such a game structure, that is, an athlete who values honesty more than other competitors is at a disadvantage in terms of his or her eventual payoffs. It is this commitment to the honest athlete and the health and wellness of participants that the way forward for antidoping is most clearly mapped.

History

There has been evidence, going back centuries, that humans have consistently ingested a variety of medicinal aids, potions, and foods to help them perform more work, and with the development of sport, to compete at a higher level. The most commonly cited stories emerge from the ancient Olympic Games, where competitors were not only said to be professionalized, but were also ingesting herbal medications, wine potions, and hallucinogens, as well as animal hearts and testicles, all in a search for potency and enhanced performance. Roman gladiators also made use of these types of substances as well as strychnine to aid in their fighting and fatigue resistance.

These types of efforts have persisted into modern athletics. The era of drug use in modern sports, beginning in the late 19th century and continuing to the present day, includes several periods (some overlapping) leading up to what we know as the modern war between performance enhancers and antidoping agents. These eras in many cases included characteristic substances and techniques unique during their time:

1. The early years of global sport development: the concoctions (mid-1800s to 1920s)
2. The boom of exercise science and postwar spillovers: amphetamines (1920s–1976)
3. The Cold War and steroid developments (1950s–1980)
4. The great evasion: blood doping, EPO, HGH, and designer drugs (1980–2003)
5. Globalized antidoping efforts: WADA (1999–present)
6. Genetically modified athletes (the future?)

There was no historically obvious outcry against PEDs in sport for many centuries and leading into the early 20th century. In fact, the use of medicinal aids, elixirs, and concoctions was an open public practice. One of the most telling examples of this is the success of Thomas Hicks in the Olympic Marathon of 1904. In this case, on the way to winning the event, Hicks was stumbling and struggling but was repeatedly administered doses of strychnine and brandy by his handlers to fuel him to continue. While a clear scandal unfolded when the first competitor to cross the finish line, Fred Lorz, was disqualified after completing a portion of the course in a motorcar, Hicks's open use of medicinal support was viewed as nothing short of ordinary.

With the push to help people battle fatigue and improve industrial productivity, science, industry, and the military forged ahead into pharmacological methods. The formalization of the study of exercise science took place most prominently with the founding of the Harvard Fatigue lab in 1927. The alarm that was sounded as many enlisting soldiers failed to meet performance criteria was countered with a push toward physiological study and enhancement. During World War II, the widespread use of stimulants and amphetamines by soldiers became common. Without the stigma that is attached today to such practices, the public perception remained that these pharmaceutical aids were welcome, if not necessary, because of the demands of modern warfare.

While some antidoping authorities of the present day sometimes aim to paint the picture of these drugs emerging and being perpetrated by fascist Nazi regimes, historical evidence clearly shows that this push for enhancement came from both sides of the battle. In particular, soldiers returning from the war brought many of these techniques with them, and the public dissemination of many of the advancements in exercise science research fueled the sport practices of the postwar period. Amphetamine use was ubiquitous in sport and persisted through at least the late 1960s. The clearest evidence of this emerged from professional cyclists via numerous public statements and ultimately the circumstances surrounding the dramatic deaths of Knut Jensen in the 1960 Summer Olympics, and Tom Simpson in the 1967 Tour de France (both had amphetamines in their systems, and Simpson was an admitted habitual user).

It was during the 1950s through 1970s that the antidoping movement began to take shape. The invention of the first steroids and synthetic testosterone occurred during this time, and in many ways they created a stark visual representation of drugs in sports, particularly among the female competitors. Such practices were railed against as abominations, government "program" female athletes, primarily from the former East Germany and China, suffered ridicule and continue to feel the effects today through long-term health problems, side effects, and birth defects. In many ways, this lent itself to being framed in terms of Cold War rhetoric. Because the world's political powers began to tap into the emotional and nationalistic reserves of the Olympic movement, much government support and research was poured into elite sport performance.

While the prohibition of PEDs had taken off during the middle of the 20th century, antidoping authorities encountered their most enormous challenges toward the close of the century from about 1980 to 1999. While techniques were available to detect nearly any substance in an athlete's urine or blood, unfortunately, new derivatives of banned substances were being developed, used, and often withstood legal challenges on the appeal of a positive test. For example, an athlete might test positive for elevated testosterone levels, but because the substance found in her system was not listed on the prohibited list, that is, a "designer" steroid, the Court of Arbitration for Sport often cleared the athlete of the charges.

Additionally, this period was characterized by the adoption of some of medical science's most promising advancements in clinical care by athletes seeking undetectable advantages. Erythropoietin (EPO), developed to treat anemia, and human growth hormone (HGH) treatments, developed to counter developmental growth deficiencies and muscle wasting disorders, were both rapidly adopted by athletes seeking the next promising and undetectable enhancement. Whereas steroids and synthetic testosterone detection were possible through effective urine testing, EPO and HGH were essentially undetectable because they occur naturally in the body. The practice of blood-doping was also developed and widely credited for the success of nearly all of the U.S. cycling athletes at the 1984 Los Angeles Olympic Games.

The 1998 Tour de France played host to the largest unmistakable revelation of systematic doping programs in cycling when customs officials stopped team staff traveling with hundreds of grams of anabolic steroids, EPO, and syringes. Following this affair, antidoping efforts reached a tipping point and sprinted into independent testing and oversight. No longer would it be sufficient for international sport federations to try to police themselves. This big change came primarily with the formation of the WADA, and also through increased criminalization of doping-related offenses in many countries, that is, where the possession of PEDs and equipment was deemed illegal and severely punished. Additionally, the scope of testing and investigations would be broadened far beyond the post-event test. Athletes began to be tested out of competition, with blood tests, and most recently through athlete biological markers. The development of a test for EPO and blood transfusion detection techniques was a clear advancement as a cascade of would-be champions began being caught in the antidoping net. Professional cycling is the leader of this dubious count with over 100 athletes being subject to sanctions from 2000 to 2010.

Despite previous efforts, the feeling that antidoping authorities are in a high-stakes game of "whack-a-mole" continues. The next frontier in sport enhancements is predicted to be genetic enhancements, therapies, and manipulation. Again, the benevolent efforts by medical scientists to develop techniques to fight disease and illness have created vast technical knowledge and resources for sport scientists and trainers to exploit. With some extended sport-specific investments or simply by trial and error, these ambitious sport scientists can push human performance to new levels and open up entirely new ethical questions. The International Cycling Union (UCI) is beginning to lay the groundwork for such a chase with its new "biological passport" system to track changes in athletes' biological makeup. However, these personal intrusions will surely be challenged on human rights and privacy grounds.

Arguments

The classic arguments for the prohibition of PEDs center around two main themes, (1) seeking fairness and leveling the playing field, and

(2) safeguarding the health and wellness of sport participants and the public. While the latter is a continuing issue that encompasses the issues of side-effects, overdose, addiction, as well as role-modeling effects for youth sport, the former has only in the past 50 years become the battle cry and the primary fuel for the antidoping movement. While there have also been some other arguments put forth that center on maintaining the authenticity of sport performances for fans, there has been far less convincing empirical evidence in this vein, and the promotion of this point is often included as hand-waving arguments in the mass media, and is an addendum to the antidoping agencies' two primary pushes.

On the flip side, opponents to the prohibition of PEDs in sport also make some consistently repeated points. These include: (1) promoting the ability of sport participants to exercise their free will and choose whether or not to use performance-enhancing substances, (2) arguing that the rules of sport should be changed to be more in line with the reality and inevitability of performance-enhancing practices, (3) questioning the meaninglessness of arbitrary prohibition of some performance enhancing activities, but not others, (4) emphasizing the need to protect athletes through decriminalization and promotion of open, and presumably safer, medically supervised performance-enhancing practices, and (5) arguing for the important appeal of maximizing human potential and technological advancement.

Much of what is required for a fair view of this debate returns to the central "meaning" of sport. Antidoping authorities will proudly carry the flag of the "spirit" of sport while the opponents to these prohibitions simply question the existence of such a concept, characterizing the "spirit of sport" as a social and cultural construction. However, the above debate is ultimately about whether or not the prohibition of drug use in sport is the correct policy choice for sport generally and the public at large.

Undoubtedly, both sides of this argument agree that as the present rules are in place, it is wrong to use or participate in the use of PEDs in violation of those rules. As such, the increasing focus is on enforcement and growing antidoping efforts both in scope and sophistication.

Modern Antidoping Efforts

The establishment of global antidoping efforts and the WADA has led to vast resources being directed at the deterrence and detection of performance enhancement transgressions. It is important to note, however, that the antidoping war and WADA have had very little success penetrating many professional sport institutions, especially outside the purview of the International Olympic Committee. The U.S. professional sport leagues in particular have generally chosen to keep their doping controls in-house and resist the outside involvement of independent authorities. These internal efforts have had the limited effectiveness one might expect, and Major League Baseball has had the most public failings in recent history. Following many years of mere lip service to antidoping efforts, the prevalence of player use and abuse of PEDs has become more apparent during the broad federal (BALCO affair) and Congressional investigations (Mitchell Report). Similarly, international professional soccer has chosen to internalize its antidoping efforts and refused to allow out-of-competition testing. This has been to the disdain of WADA, and could potentially threaten the sport's inclusion in the Olympic Games.

Testing

Drug tests are primarily conducted as a urine test or blood test. At the collection of the sample, it is coded to conceal the athlete's identity to testers and divided into two specimens, an A and a B sample. Upon a positive finding in the A sample, the B specimen can be tested on the request of the athlete. Athletes have been known to attempt to cheat or invalidate the tests at collection by substituting another person's (clean) urine or by contaminating the sample with other chemicals. The former can be achieved through catheterization or using a prosthetic penis for males. These efforts have led to strict and somewhat invasive observation to detect such activities.

Prisoner's Dilemma

The present antidoping code, likelihood of detection, access to new clandestine techniques, and the size of commercial payoffs all must go into the calculus of the decision-making process of the modern athlete with concern about the choice to use prohibited performance-enhancing techniques. Probably one of the most often neglected considerations when people consider the doping athlete is the expected behavior of fellow competitors. It is because of the interaction of the actors' choices and payoffs that we can consider the structural problems with current antidoping efforts.

The classic prisoner's dilemma puts forth the concept of a strategic game with incomplete information. In the scenario, two prisoners involved in a crime together are separated upon apprehension. Prosecuting authorities have insufficient evidence to convict either for anything but minor charges. If at least one of the prisoners confesses, they will have enough evidence for a full conviction of the other. The authorities offer each prisoner the opportunity to cooperate in the investigation in exchange for leniency. If one of the prisoners chooses to deny involvement in the face of the other's confession, he will be subject to the most severe punishment. If they both cooperate with the authorities, both will receive some reduced level of punishment. By forcing the subjects to choose independently whether to cooperate or remain silent about the other elements of their crime, authorities can actually exploit the payoff structure of the prisoners' options in order to solicit full confessions from both criminals.

First consider prisoner A's alternatives. If he expects prisoner B to confess, he is strictly better off confessing himself (five years in jail is preferred to 10). Alternatively, if A expects B to deny involvement in the crime, suspect A is strictly better off choosing to confess (going free is preferred to one year in jail). Choosing to confess is clearly a dominant strategy. Furthermore, prisoner B's alternatives are identical, and therefore symmetric, so he will inevitably make the same choice. This constitutes what is referred to by economists as Nash equilibrium. So we can see that even though they would both be better off denying involvement (only one year in jail each), they end up in a jointly suboptimal outcome of five years served in jail.

Relating this scenario to drug use in sport is relatively straightforward. By replacing the alternatives with "to dope" or "not to dope" (clean), we can consider the payoffs that might lead us to the undesirable Nash equilibrium outcome of Dope-Dope for athletes A and B.

In a more general form, of the payoff matrix for two athletes with approximately equal natural ability and the composition of the payoffs can be placed in the context of sports to consider the following consequences of changes to the system:

- E: the "edge," or temptation, represents the payoff garnered with a competitive edge by using drugs against a clean opponent. This is the highest payoff available to an individual in the game. In sports this is particularly high because a majority of the spoils go to the winner. Of course, this expected payoff is reduced by the chance and consequences of being detected as well as the side effects of drug use. We might consider these to be very small and the net payoff will likely still be larger than C.
- C: represents the payoff an athlete receives if both athletes cooperate and compete without PEDs. The cooperative clean payoff would be the best possible joint payoff and would pay both athletes roughly equal rewards without any risk of detection (no doping).
- D: represents the payoffs if both athletes choose to use PEDs. The joint doping payoffs are strictly less than the clean payoffs because although the earnings and accolades are distributed evenly, both athletes suffer the extra risk of loss from being detected and other side effects. Although these may be small, each player's payoff is still strictly lower than that of the joint clean choice.
- S: the "sucker's" payoff for not using drugs while one's competitor does. The sucker's payoff is the lowest payoff in sport, as the doping opponent "steals" the accolades away from the clean athlete. The athlete will likely be strictly better off earning an equal share of the winnings through doping than the little or nothing from staying clean.

For a true prisoner's dilemma analog where the dominant choices result in suboptimal outcome, we must see that $E > C > D > S$. If these inequalities hold, despite Clean-Clean being the jointly optimal outcome, the athletes will both choose to Dope based on their uninformed independent alternatives.

As long as athletes are highly rewarded for winning, the detection of at least some performance-enhancing substances is not likely, and side effects are not severe, athletes' incentives induce them to gravitate toward doping practices. Despite this dismal statement, there are some caveats that leave room for some optimism. For instance, the better the detection techniques get, the more discounted the doping payoffs become. This is also compounded because the more likely detection is, the higher the "sucker's" payoff becomes. If these payoff changes are large enough so S may exceed D and the sanctions are severe enough so that C exceeds E, the dominant strategy for both players would be to compete clean.

Very often we see antidoping purists characterizing doping offenses as a problem of individual judgment, poor personal choice, and/or weakness of "character," but we can see that the structural problem that is presented to an athlete can potentially be altered as well. With direct application to our "doper's dilemma" we have seen several avenues for changing expected payoffs and subsequent dominant strategies. In this model, there are several salient areas that hold promise for enticing behavioral change. These include but are not limited to: (1) improving detection probabilities, (2) increasing severity of penalties, and (3) reduction in unequal distribution of rewards based on performance.

One can easily extend this to any number of players (as we see many in individual sports such as cycling and track and field). With that, one may find how the multidimensional payoff matrix even further exacerbates the doping incentives. Additionally, athletes can have more information about expected behavior and reputations over time introducing dynamic interactions. The complexity with which these systems of reaction and interaction can be considered is tremendous, but what remains clear is the key to the dominant suboptimal Nash equilibrium of athletes choosing to dope: exceedingly large payoffs for winning, small probabilities of detection, and relatively weak punishments.

Therapeutic Use Exemptions

Athletes can sometimes, albeit rarely, be granted exceptions for taking drugs that would otherwise be considered doping. The criteria are: (1) the athlete would experience significant health problems without taking the prohibited substance or method, (2) the therapeutic use of the substance would not produce significant enhancement of performance, and (3) there is no reasonable therapeutic alternative to the use of the otherwise prohibited substance or method. All of these criteria must be met to be granted a therapeutic use exemption. These exceptions are granted by the antidoping authority for international federations of particular sports, but there have been efforts made to make them consistent across sport.

Daniel J. Larson
University of Georgia

See Also: Doping; Drug Testing; Misbehavior by Athletes; Olympics; Olympic Organization.

Further Readings

Andreff, Wladimir and Stefan Szymanski. *Handbook on the Economics of Sport.* Northampton, MA: Edward Elgar, 2006.

Bahrke, Michael S. and Charles Yesalis. *Performance-Enhancing Substances in Sport and Exercise.* Champaign, IL: Human Kinetics, 2002.

Dimeo, Paul. *A History of Drug Use in Sport 1876–1976: Beyond Good and Evil.* New York: Routledge, 2007.

Mas-Colell, Andreu, Michael Dennis Whinston, and Jerry R. Green. *Microeconomic Theory.* New York: Oxford University Press, 1995.

Murray, Thomas H., Karen J. Maschke, and Angela A. Wasunna. *Performance-Enhancing Technologies in Sports: Ethical, Conceptual, and Scientific Issues.* Baltimore, MD: Johns Hopkins University Press, 2009.

Rosen, Daniel M. *Dope: A History of Performance Enhancement in Sports From the Nineteenth Century to Today.* Westport, CT: Praeger, 2008.

Tyrrell, William Blake. *The Smell of Sweat: Greek Athletics, Olympics, and Culture.* Wauconda, IL: Bolchazy-Carducci, 2004.

U.S. Congress. House Committee on Oversight and Government Reform. *The Mitchell Report.* Washington, DC: U.S. Government Printing Office, 2010.

Dynamic Pricing

The increasing use of dynamic pricing by sport franchises is revolutionizing how sport managers think about pricing tickets. Rather than print a traditional face value price, organizations using dynamic pricing employ a system where prices are posted electronically and constantly updated based on changing demand for tickets. Franchises benefit from increased revenue from both an increase in tickets sold and the concessions, merchandising, and parking spending that accompany extra people attending a game. Dynamic ticket pricing is a natural extension of the variable ticket pricing that was increasingly used over the past decade and the development of a formal secondary market for tickets.

Face value ticket pricing results in two types of market inefficiencies. The first is if the face value price is set too high, there will be empty seats. If the price can adjust to reflect the demand, the empty seats can be filled and the franchise can benefit from additional ancillary spending that goes with game attendance. The second type of inefficiency is a result of the face value price being set too low. The result is a sold-out event, but unless the face value price perfectly reflected the market, a sold-out event indicates that the franchise could have increased ticket revenue by charging a higher price. Static prices that are set prior to the season necessarily result in loss of revenue because of the inefficiencies described above and constantly changing demand for tickets.

An intermediate step in the movement from static to dynamic pricing is variable ticket pricing. With variable pricing, face value prices are set at the beginning of the season with different prices set for different games based on predicted demand. Main factors used in predicting demand for variable pricing are opponent, day of the game, and time of the season. Variable pricing increases the efficiency of a standard, static price for all games, but the prices are based on predictions made far in advance. Player acquisitions, emerging stars, injuries, unforeseen game outcomes, records, and milestones all can drastically affect demand for tickets to a specific game, but they cannot be foreseen prior to the season. Variable ticket pricing improves efficiency by adjusting for predictable variability in demand for tickets based on event characteristics that are known prior to a season. The improvement in efficiency is limited in that it cannot account for changes in demand that occur within a season.

Traditionally, sports marketers worried that reducing ticket prices for events that had lower demand would undermine how fans value tickets and reduce a franchise's ability to charge higher prices for high demand events. The downside of reduced ancillary game revenue, lost potential ticket revenue, and the loss of a marketing opportunity to develop fans who might not otherwise attend was often not seen as enough of a reason to lower prices for low-demand games.

Sports marketers also worried that increasing prices for high-demand events would be seen as price gouging and result in negative publicity that could harm the organization's long-term relationship with its fan base. The public release of ticket prices is always accompanied by newspaper coverage and opinion regarding the price level. For many years some teams appeared to keep ticket prices lower than what the market demanded in acknowledgement of the public relations effect of ticket prices that might be perceived as being too high. The emergence of the secondary market and companies such as StubHub and eBay as significant players in the sports ticket marketplace increased transparency in the marketplace and created an environment where fans are more accustomed to seeing higher prices associated with high-demand tickets. Before the emergence of formal league and team partnerships with the major secondary ticket companies and the development of dynamic ticket pricing, teams that had printed tickets with a $50 face value received no extra benefit if those tickets were selling on the secondary market for $100. With fans having easy access to the online secondary ticket market, they are aware of the prices that high-demand tickets are bringing sellers, whether those sellers are season ticket holders or secondary market dealers. This has created an environment in which it is becoming more acceptable to the fans for the teams themselves to benefit from the higher prices for the games that create the highest demand.

Dynamic pricing changes the element of risk that tickets inherently have. Since a game or event is something that is happening in the future, the holder of a ticket carries the risk. For the sport franchise it is the risk that the ticket will not be sold. For the fan it is the risk that the game might not be as attractive as originally anticipated or that there may be a development that causes the ticket holder to miss the game. Without dynamic pricing, the risk aspect only had a downside for teams, and it was in their best interest to sell tickets as quickly as possible. With dynamic pricing, unsold tickets can potentially end up benefiting the team in the event of a previously unanticipated increase in demand because of the team performing better than expected or the debut of a star prospect or newly acquired player. In those cases unsold ticket inventory would benefit the team as the increased demand would allow it to sell at prices much higher than it could have before the positive developments. This effect will require teams to adopt formal technical models to not just analyze the market and manage dynamic prices, but to also assess risk and reward and create strategies for optimal timing in selling tickets.

Early adopters of dynamic pricing are the San Francisco Giants in Major League Baseball, the Dallas Stars in the National Hockey League, and the Cleveland Cavaliers in the National Basketball Association. The Giants and Stars work with Qcue Inc., and the Cavaliers work with Veritix, companies that developed dynamic algorithms to estimate demand and set optimal ticket prices.

Kevin Heisey
Liberty University

See Also: Demand Elasticity and Inelasticity in Sports; Demand for Sports; Demand-Oriented Pricing; Price Determination; Price Discrimination; Pricing of Tickets; Pricing Strategies; Supply/Demand Equilibrium; Ticket Price, Secondary Market; Ticket Price, Tiers; Ticket Price, Variable.

Further Readings

Fisher, Eric. "Ticketing's Changeup." *Sports Business Journal* (May 31, 2010).
Noll, R. "Attendance and Price Setting." In *Government and the Sports Business.* Washington, DC: Brookings Institute, 1974.
Stewart, Bob. *Sport Funding and Finance.* Oxford, UK: Butterworth-Heinemann, 2007.
Zentes, Joachim, Dirk Morschett, and Hanna Schramm-Klein. *Strategic Retail Management: Text and International Cases.* Wiesbaden, Germany: Gabler, 2007.

Earnhardt Ganassi Racing

The merger of Dale Earnhardt, Inc. (DEI) and Chip Ganassi Racing after the 2008 NASCAR season was a marriage of two of the more storied names in auto racing. The union, which created a new organization called Earnhardt Ganassi Racing with Felix Sabates, was also a marriage made of necessity.

DEI was formed by Dale and Theresa Earnhardt in 1980. The company won over 100 races in three NASCAR series (cup, nationwide, and truck). Included among DEI's victories were 24 races at the cup level, including three Daytona 500 wins. Theresa, Dale's third wife, inherited the company after Dale was killed during the last lap of the 2001 Daytona 500. It was the second merger in two years for DEI, which merged with Ginn Racing in July 2007.

Chip Ganassi made his mark in IndyCar and Rolex Grand-Am Series before moving on to NASCAR. He started his first IndyCar team in 1990 and has won six championships and 64 races since 1994. He purchased a controlling interest in SABCO Racing from Felix Sabates during the 2001 season and quickly showed that his success was transferable from open wheel racing to stock cars, as his NASCAR teams have won 12 races and three Rookie of the Year titles.

The merger of DEI and Ganassi Racing came during a time when mergers were rampant in NASCAR. Teams were desperate for sponsorship, and DEI and Ganassi Racing were no exceptions. Both teams had fallen on hard times in the years leading up to the merger and neither team won a cup race in 2008. Both teams were losing sponsors—and drivers—for 2009. DEI ran four cup cars in 2008, but only had one guaranteed sponsor for 2009. Ganassi had fielded three cup cars to start the 2008 season but folded one during the season when sponsorship failed to materialize.

In the first year of competition following the merger, Earnhardt Ganassi intended to run four cup cars. But the lack of sponsorship resulted in starting the season with three cars, only two of which—the #1 Bass Pro Shops Chevrolet driven by Martin Truex, Jr., and the #42 Target Chevrolet driven by Juan Pablo Montoya—were fully sponsored. The #8 driven by Aric Almirola started the season but dropped out after seven races for lack of sponsorship. Almirola brought suit against Earnhardt Ganassi, claiming they breached their contract with him to run a full season. Truex finished 24th in the final 2009 point standings. Montoya was the only Earnhardt Ganassi driver to make the Chase for the Sprint Cup—the top 12 cars after the first 26 races

Cars sponsored by Bass Pro Shops and Target, among other companies, in the Earnhardt Ganassi race shop on January 29, 2011.

of the season. Montoya finished sixth in the year-end standings.

Montoya had raced for Ganassi's IndyCar team for a number of years, winning the Indianapolis 500 and a CART Championship before moving on to F1 racing. He left F1 and reunited with Ganassi in 2006. Montoya is one of the few crossover drivers who have experienced success in both open wheel and stock car racing. The Colombia native gives Earnhardt Ganassi a marketing force in the Latino community, something that other NASCAR teams cannot duplicate. He also has given NASCAR's diversity efforts a tremendous boost, as one of the sanctioning body's avowed goals is to increase the fan base beyond its traditional support.

Dale Earnhardt, Jr., raced for his father's company beginning in 1985 and won back-to-back nationwide titles (when it was called Busch), one level below cup competition, in 1998 and 1999, before moving up to cup in the #8 car. After his father's death, Junior's relationship with his stepmother—never good—became even more difficult. Despite his success in cup races, he longed for a piece of his father's company. Theresa would not relent and the

animosity between the two became palpable. After making an offer to purchase DEI that Theresa rejected, Junior decided to leave DEI for Hendrick Motorsports after the 2007 season. That move spelled the beginning of the end for DEI as a stand-alone company. After Junior's departure, DEI was unable to retain his top two sponsors, Budweiser and the U.S. Army.

Despite her marriage to the sport's biggest icon, Theresa Earnhardt was always looked upon as an outsider in NASCAR. After Dale's death, Theresa appeared to be more interested in burnishing and marketing her late husband's name and legacy than she was in winning races.

After the DEI-Ganassi merger, Chip Ganassi became the manager of the new entity. Theresa spent most of her time at the old DEI headquarters promoting her late husband's agenda and marketing his name. By some accounts, Dale sold more merchandise in death than he did when he was alive. Theresa was involved with the Dale Earnhardt Foundation, an organization dedicated to education, children, the environment, and wildlife.

Midway through the 2009 season, Martin Truex announced that he was leaving Earnhardt Ganassi for a new ride with Michael Waltrip Racing in 2010. In November 2009, it was announced that Jamie McMurray would replace Truex in the #1 Chevrolet for Earnhardt Ganassi for the 2010 season, reuniting him with Chip Ganassi, his first team owner as a cup driver. The primary sponsor was not announced. Bass Pro Shops had only a one-year contract to sponsor Truex, which expired after the 2009 season. The addition of McMurray will allow Earnhardt Ganassi to run two cars at the cup level for the 2010 season.

Target has been a sponsor of Ganassi cars for over 20 years, which ranks as one of the longest-running relationships in motorsports history. In addition to Target, the primary sponsor of Montoya's car, other Earnhardt Ganassi sponsors include TomTom, the world's leading navigation solutions provider, Tracker Boats, Tums, Guitar Hero, Gillette, Microsoft, Energizer, Mercury, Polaroid, and Memorex.

Jordan I. Kobritz
Eastern New Mexico University

See Also: EM Motorsports; Michael Waltrip Racing; National Association for Stock Car Auto Racing; SPEED Channel.

Further Readings

Earnhardt Ganassi Racing With Felix Sabates. http://www.earnhardtganassi.com (Accessed October 2010).
ESPN.com. "DEI and Chip Ganassi Will Merge Next Season to Form Earnhardt Ganassi Racing." http://sports.espn.go.com/rpm/nascar/cup/news/story?id=3698603 (Accessed October 2009).
NASCAR Official Website. http://www.nascar.com (Accessed October 2009).
Target Chip Ganassi Racing. http://www.chip ganassiracing.com (Accessed October 2009).

e-Commerce

From a broad perspective, e-commerce may be described as a subset of e-marketing. Whereas e-marketing involves any marketing activities that are conducted through the Internet (such as advertising, providing product information, responding to customer e-mail inquiries, marketing research, and so forth), e-commerce focuses on revenue-generating Internet transactions. E-commerce may be defined as a business approach whereby real-time transactions are conducted by customers and merchants in different geographical areas through telecommunications networks. It includes virtual browsing for goods and services, selecting what to buy, and payment methods.

After initially utilizing the Internet mostly to offer free content, the sports world has aggressively embraced it as a mechanism to generate additional revenue—in some instances, a lot more revenue. Sports teams, athletes, the media, leagues, retailers, and other entities and individuals—of all types and sizes—now recognize the vast sales potential of the Internet. In some cases, e-commerce is used to increase sales of traditional items such as game programs, sweatshirts, balls, and equipment. In other cases, new revenue streams are being developed by the online selling of fan club membership, memorabilia, DVDs, special access to restricted content (such as ESPN's *Insider* magazine), after-market tickets, and a lot more.

Scope and Goals

When organizations or individuals first began offering sports-related Websites about a decade or so ago, they tended to engage almost exclusively in non-revenue-generating activities—e-marketing—rather than in e-commerce. They sought greater exposure for their sports or themselves, offered free insights to fans and the general public, fostered better customer relations, and encouraged site visitors to attend events and to buy sports items at traditional stores. The most popular sports Website is ESPN.com, which attracts 30 million unique visitors monthly.

More recently, organizations and individuals have used e-commerce to generate several billion dollars in annual sports-related revenues. The U.S. Census Bureau reports that e-commerce accounts for significant sales in these categories: sporting goods, sports videos and games, books and magazines, and apparel. And a large proportion of sports-related tickets are bought online. Despite the 2008–09 economic downturn, comScore found that online sales for sports-related goods and services showed substantial growth. During the 2008 holiday shopping season, online sales for sport and fitness items rose by 18 percent even though most categories saw sharp declines because of the economic recession. Online sales of sports video games such as *Madden NFL Football* have been especially popular.

When a Website increases the popularity of a sports organization or individual in a way that later leads to offline sales, e-commerce is not involved—even though the health of the sport is vastly strengthened. For example, many U.S. teams are able to sell more merchandise internationally because of the attractiveness of league Websites. The National Basketball Association attracts nearly one-half of the visitors to NBA.com from outside North America.

It is difficult to gauge the true impact of e-commerce because many organizations and individuals do not break out online sales data, such as ticket sales, separately. There is also an under-reported element of e-commerce. When a person shops for tickets, memorabilia, sports games, and so forth online, but picks up (or completes the purchase of those items) in a store, the revenues are often not included as e-commerce. In addition, online transactions between private parties tend not to be reported.

Uses of E-Commerce in Sports

One way to illustrate the widespread uses of e-commerce in sports is to present several diverse examples. An example of a sports team's use of e-commerce is the Philadelphia Phillies Website (http://www.phillies.com), which is operated by Major League Baseball. At this site, a visitor can buy a gift certificate; purchase a travel package to spring training in Florida; be connected to StubHub to acquire regular season tickets; shop for jerseys, caps, DVDs, and other items; and participate in online auctions for baseball cards, baseballs, bats, jerseys, photos, and "game used items."

The National Football League (http://www.nfl.com) conducts e-commerce in three main categories. It has links for both regular season and postseason ticket sales, sells team and league merchandise through its own dedicated shopping site (http://www.nflshop.com), and offers online "game access." With the latter, a visitor can purchase a "field pass" to listen live to games and buy videos and other downloads via links to iTunes store and Amazon.com. The NFL also offers "game rewind" so fans can buy access to replays of popular games.

Individual sports personalities are also making use of e-commerce. Tennis star Roger Federer has a site for his charity where visitors can make contributions (http://www.rogerfedererfoundation.org/en.html). Baseball manager Joe Torre has a site for his Safe at Home foundation where contri-

butions can be made (http://www.joetorre.org). NASCAR driver Jeff Gordon has two Websites, one for his children's foundation (http://www.jeffgordonfoundation.org) where visitors can donate and purchase items to benefit the foundation and another for an online store for his fans (http://jeffgordon.com/store).

At the sports network site ESPN.com, the primary goal is e-marketing to foster the network's image as the leader in sports broadcasting. Nonetheless, ESPN.com also sells products at its ESPN Shop site (http://www.espnshop.com)—"real gear for real fans"—and *Insider* magazine online subscriptions (http://insider.espn.go.com) for the most intense fans.

Dick's Sporting Goods is a bricks-and-clicks retailer that relies on both traditional stores and its expanding, ever more important Website (http://www.dickssportinggoods.com) to maximize revenues and reach customers anywhere at any time. It has invested heavily in its site with customer-friendly features such as "quick info," "shop by brand," "product browser," and a "mini cart."

In fantasy sports, participants select teams of real-life athletes whom they hope will generate the best future statistics. They use a predefined scoring system that assigns a certain amount of points based upon the actual statistical results of the athletes they choose.

The fantasy competition typically takes into account multiple games and a "season." Although some fantasy sport leagues are free, many also charge an online entry fee and award prizes (sometimes in cash). Head2Head (http://www.head2head.com), founded in 1994, is a popular online operator that requires entry fees.

Ticket Sales

Among the leading secondary market ticket sellers are StubHub (http://www.stubhub.com), RazorGator (http://www.razorgator.com), Ticketmaster's TicketsNow (http://www.ticketsnow.com), and Coast to Coast Tickets (http://www.coasttocoasttickets.com). These sites typically offer tickets at prices above their face value. The scope of their online offerings can be quite broad. According to its Website, StubHub is "the world's largest ticket marketplace" and provides ticketing to "tens of thousands of sports, concert, theater, and other live entertainment events."

The most controversial aspect of sports e-commerce involves online gambling because of the possibilities of underage gambling and betting beyond a person's means.

In October 2006, a federal law was enacted, which is known as the Unlawful Internet Gambling Enforcement Act of 2006. The most significant restriction of this law is the ban on the use of a credit card to gamble online by persons accessing the Web from within the United States.

Planning Considerations

To succeed in e-commerce, sports organizations and individuals need to undertake a number of activities. This list of questions for the potential e-commerce planner is derived from the work of the authors Barry Berman and Joel Evans:

- What are the e-marketing versus e-commerce goals? At what point is it expected that the site will be profitable?
- What budget will be allocated to developing and maintaining a Website?
- Who will develop and maintain the Website, the organization itself or an outside specialist?
- What is the role of the league relative to individual teams in site development and maintenance?
- Should third parties be utilized (such as ticket resellers)?
- What party is responsible for inventory handling and management?
- What features will the Website have? What level of customer service will be offered?
- What information will the Website provide? In what format?
- What is the proper goods and services assortment?
- Will the Website offer benefits not available elsewhere?
- Will prices reflect a good value for the consumer?
- How fast will the user be able to download the text and images from the Website?
- How often will Website content be changed?

- What staff will handle Web inquiries and transactions? How fast will turnaround time be?
- How will the firm coordinate online and offline transactions and customer interactions?
- How easy will it be for shoppers to enter and complete orders, including shipping choices?
- What online payment methods will be accepted?
- How will the site be promoted: (1) on the Web and (2) by the organization?
- How will Web data be stored and arranged?
- How will the organization ensure secure (encrypted) transactions and consumer privacy?
- How will returns and customer complaints be handled?

When engaging in e-commerce, there are various "don'ts" to keep in mind:

- Don't have obsolete material on the site, such as dated information or products not in stock.
- Don't slow down the site by having an excessive amount of bells and whistles.
- Don't do e-mail blasts unless visitors give permission to be contacted (opt-in e-mail).
- Don't present a site that is inconsistent with the organization's image.
- Don't hide shipping and handling fees until a customer gets to the final stage of a purchase.
- Don't use an insecure section of the site to gather personal information.
- Don't treat online shoppers poorly if they want to make an in-store return.

Joel R. Evans
Hofstra University
Stacey B. Evans
American Conference Institute

See Also: Banner Ads; Click-Through Rate; Cost per Click; Electronic Marketing; Internet Bulletin Board; Internet Revenue From Sports Websites; Internet/Online; Keyword Buys; Links to Other Websites; m-Commerce; Online Advertising; Online Communities; Online Gaming; Online Research; Pop-Up Ads; Search Engines; Ticketmaster; Virtual

Advertising; Virtual Communities; Webcasts; Websites, Sports Marketing; Websites for Tickets.

Further Readings

Berman, Barry and Joel R. Evans. *Retail Management: A Strategic Approach*, 11th Ed. Upper Saddle River, NJ: Pearson Prentice Hall, 2010.

Businesstown.com. "The Definition of E-Commerce." http://www.businesstown.com/internet/ecomm-definition.asp (Accessed November 2010).

comScore.com "Professional North American Sports League Sites Draw Attractive Audiences From Around the Globe." http://www.comscore.com/Press_Events/Press_Releases (Accessed November 2010).

Datamonitor. *Online Retail in the United States*. New York: Datamonitor, 2009.

E-Commerce Times. http://www.ecommercetimes.com (Accessed November 2010).

FantasySportsBusiness.com. http://www.fantasysportsbusiness.com (Accessed November 2010).

Institute for Telecommunication Services. http://www.its.bldrdoc.gov (Accessed November 2009).

U.S. Census Bureau. "E-Stats." http://www.census.gov/econ/estats (Accessed November 2010).

Vandelay Design. "25 Well Designed Sports E-Commerce Sites." http://vandelaydesign.com/blog/galleries/25-well-designed-sports-e-commerce-sites (Accessed November 2010).

Economic Climate for Sports

The term *economic climate* generally refers to the state of being of the economy, with a bad economic climate usually being during times of depression and recession, and a good climate during times of boom in growth. In relation to sport management, economic climate has garnered very little attention from academics and practitioners. This, however, seems set to change with the widespread economic downturn and recession that began in 2008 and plagued much of the globe, especially countries in North America, Europe, and Asia. Previously, much of the sports industry, especially professional sports, had been described as being "recession-proof"— that is, the professional sports industry around the world was considered to be strong and resilient enough to not be negatively impacted by the recession in either a financial or organizational manner. During recessions, organizations often experience a shortfall of revenue and profits because of reduced consumer expenditures. In turn, the lack of revenue forces many organizations to lay off employees, reduce salaries, and make other cuts. Sport organizations have proven to be no different than other organizations during the most recent recession.

Recession and Professional Sport Leagues

With the recent recession, leagues and teams across the world have been hit hard, and as the scholar Dennis Howard pointed out in 1999, the sports industry also experienced decline in the 1990s. Along with the author Daniel Mahoney, he has also explored the future of the sports business, noting the industry's ever-increasing dependence on revenue from sponsors. With the economic recession of 2008–09, many sport leagues found that sponsorship and attendance revenues decreased, affecting the operations and payroll of franchises. One league that was among the hardest hit was the Arena Football League (AFL), which was forced to cancel its 2009 season, and suspend the league indefinitely.

Larger major professional sports leagues also suffered from the effects of the recession. The National Basketball Association (NBA) felt the need to take out a total of around $200 million in loans to help support basketball operations for the 2008–09 season. These loans were distributed among 15 different franchises that requested financial help, as the NBA predicted shortfalls in many major revenue sources for teams in the league. The recession not only hit NBA franchises in the pocketbooks, but also forced some teams to limit the number of players they brought onto their roster. Other professional sport leagues have had to find different ways of dealing with the recession, including laying off employees, reducing the price of tickets and products, and other creative cost-cutting and revenue-generating methods. What is clear is that the axiom that sports is recession-proof is clearly false, and that it is important for professional sport leagues to take into account possible periods of recession or economic downturn, and how their operations may be impacted by the economic climate.

Recession and the National Collegiate Athletic Association

It was not just the professional sports leagues and franchises that were negatively impacted by the recession that began in 2008. The National Collegiate Athletic Association (NCAA) also reported widespread financial losses among a large number of its member institutions. The problems faced by Division One (D-I), Division Two (D-II), and Division Three (D-III) schools can be traced to the shortfall of $30 billion that states faced, which was estimated to possibly rise to over $350 billion over the two years following 2009. Because of this shortfall of state revenues, many individual states have been forced to cut budgets, including money for institutions of higher education and the athletic programs in these schools as well. This shortfall caused schools to not only start trying to cut costs, but also to halt the building or renovation of facilities, a key link to revenues for many of these athletic programs.

Another channel through which athletic programs have traditionally received money has been boosters and donors. With the recent recession many schools came to rely on this group more and more to help bring in revenue for them to be able to maintain a relatively competitive level of operations with other schools. However, even large donations from boosters and alumni do not necessarily translate into guaranteed financial success for programs. While many donations programs receive are checks, they also receive a large number of donations in the form of stocks and options, which were hit hard by the recession. Probably the biggest example of a large loss by a university athletic program was that of Oklahoma State University.

In the winter of 2005, Texas oilman T. Boone Pickens, one of the richest investors in America and a loyal Oklahoma State University fan, gave $165 million to a charity to help the sports programs at Oklahoma State University. Previously, under his guidance, the

university's athletic program had turned a $6 million investment into $31 million. However, when the recession hit, the $165 million gift, as well as another $37 million given by other donors, was invested in a hedge fund that Pickens managed called BP Capital Management. The losses for Pickens personally were over $1 billion, and the money the university had invested virtually disappeared overnight. Because of this, the school, which had planned to build an athletic village, had to put construction of this project on hold. While Pickens is still worth billions of dollars and has pledged to make more donations to make up for all the lost investments, not all donors have been able to re-pledge the money that athletic departments lost during the recession.

Conclusion

It is clear from the most recent recession that much of the sport industry's feeling of recession-proof was indeed a fallacy. Many leagues have failed, fallen into financial crisis, been forced to borrow money, and cut costs. While the recession has been a negative for the sports industry at all levels, it is important to consider the positive lessons that can be learned from this period to provide implications for the better managing of sport. As mentioned earlier, academics have pointed out the need for sport organizations to understand economic cycles and be aware of the real possibility of downturns. With this in mind, sport managers can better plan and prepare for such eventualities in order to not only survive, but find ways to be more responsible organizations in any economic climate.

Nicholas M. Watanabe
University of Missouri at Columbia

See Also: Change in Sports Management; Credit, Use of; Demand for Sports; Embracing Change; Risk Management; Sports Industry.

Further Readings

Howard, D. R. "The Changing Fanscape for Big-League Sports: Implications for Sport Managers. Earle F. Zeigler Lecture." *Journal of Sport Management*, v.13 (1999).

Lemke, T. "NBA Gets a Loan." http://www .washingtontimes.com/news/2009/feb/26/nba-set -to-acquire-175-million-line-of-credit (Accessed November 2010).

Mahony, D. F. and D. R. Howard. "Sport Business in the Next Decade: A General Overview of Expected Trends." *Journal of Sport Management*, v.15 (2001).

Pickle, David. "NCAA Schools Adjust to Harsh Economic Climate." http://www.ncaa.org/ wps/ncaa?key=/ncaa/ncaa/ncaa+news/ncaa+news +online/2009/association-wide/ncaa+schools +adjust+to+harsh+economic+climate+-+1-16 -09+-+ncaa+news (Accessed November 2010).

Storm, S. "Billionaire Gives a Big Gift but Still Gets to Invest It." *New York Times*. http://www .nytimes.com/2006/02/24/national/24pickens .html?_r=1&ex=1140930000&en=da19748d91 540a35&ei=5070 (Accessed November 2010).

Economic Impact Study

An economic impact study is a formal investigation into the net benefits of a specific event. In sports, popular topics for economic impact studies include new venues, hosting mega-events such as the Olympics or a Super Bowl, or hosting a new franchise. In the broader arena of tourism and economic development, economic impact studies have investigated various tourism draws such as fishing, skiing, boating, basketball, soccer, and softball tournaments.

One way to delineate economic impact studies is between those undertaken on behalf of a local government, developer, or other interested party, and those undertaken for academic purposes. Studies sponsored by developers or cities are most often completed long before the investigated event actually takes place.

In other words, the studies are prospective in nature. On the other hand, most, if not all, academic studies are undertaken after the event has happened and generally make fewer untested assumptions. In other words, the studies are retrospective in nature.

Therefore, a useful taxonomy is to distinguish between *ex ante* economic impact studies, undertaken before the event, and *ex post* studies, undertaken after the event.

Both types of studies try to answer the same questions and share many commonalities. However, given different timing and methodologies, many times the different studies differ dramatically in their assumptions and conclusions.

Ex Ante Studies

There are generally two types of *ex ante* economic impact studies. The first are based on regional input-output models, which deterministically measure the impact of a given amount of new spending, such as that associated with tourists coming to a city for a big sporting event, across a large number of sectors of the regional economy. While new spending by tourists might be directly spent in the hospitality and transportation industry, this spending is ultimately diffused throughout the local and regional economy as the firms that receive the direct spending purchase inputs (e.g., labor, materials, energy) from other sectors. These additional expenditures, in turn, lead those sectors to hire more inputs, and so on. Input-output models capture how new spending spreads through the regional economy and calculate the total impact.

Input-Output Models

Input-output models can seem somewhat complicated to the layperson because they cover a large number of industries, many of which are indirectly related to the sector that receives the new direct spending. However, this is one of the theoretical benefits of input-output models: they capture less obvious, more nuanced but nevertheless real impacts that should be accounted. On the other hand, the broad scope of input-output models can also be a liability: some of the benefits attributed to a tourism event may seem far afield from the hospitality-entertainment sector and the total benefits may seem overstated. Notwithstanding the pros and cons of the input-output methodology, the approach is very popular among regional economists and urban planners.

The three most popular models are RIMS II (the Regional Input-Output Modeling System, developed by the U.S. Department of Commerce), IM-PLAN (Impact analysis for PLANning, developed by the Minnesota IMPLAN Group), and REMI (developed by Regional Economics Modeling, Inc.). While all three have methodological idiosyncrasies, RIMS II and IMPLAN are closely related in methodology. All three use data generated by federal, state, and local governments concerning the amount of inputs hired and output produced in several hundred subsectors of the economy (the data mostly come from the Bureau of Economic Analysis, the Bureau of the Census, and the Bureau of Labor Statistics). However, the RIMS II and IMPLAN models take these data as given and proceed to calculate total impacts in a deterministic fashion. On the other hand, the REMI model uses the data to estimate a multiple-equation econometric model that specifies, for instance, the technology used by the firms, the distribution of final products, the direct demand for products, and the derived demand for inputs. The results of the econometric specifications are then used as parameters to estimate a regional input-output model.

The RIMS and IMPLAN methodologies are very popular with many consulting firms and academics because of the breadth of the economy included and their relative ease of use. Unfortunately, because these models include so many different sectors, there are a large number of (essentially unchecked) assumptions made in order to calculate the estimated economic impact of an event using the input-output methodology. For instance, the data employed might reflect regional economic conditions, which might differ from local economic conditions, for example, unemployment rates or industrial concentration. If, say, the assumptions made about the local transportation industry are incorrect, these mistakes might spill over to other sectors, potentially contaminating the calculated total economic impact of an event.

On the other hand, the econometric-based REMI model holds considerable appeal to academic economists because it accommodates (and hopefully mitigates) any measurement error inherent in the government-provided data. However, it too faces criticism as econometric models are vulnerable to incorrect assumptions about the statistical nature of the data used.

Net Benefit Calculation

An alternative to the multisector input-output model is a net benefit calculation that estimates the total benefits and costs (both private and public) of hosting an event and determines the difference between the two. Usually net benefit analyses use relatively simple-to-understand aggregation techniques. While the calculations are simplified and perhaps easier to convey to the layperson, one downside with the approach is that it cannot pinpoint exactly which sectors of the local economy will be impacted the most.

Ex ante aggregation studies most often have one or more of the following six elements:

- Definition of the relevant geographic market
- An estimate for the new direct spending associated with the event
- An estimate for the induced spending associated with the event
- A set of multipliers applied to the direct and induced spending
- An estimate for the implicit benefits associated with the event
- An estimate for the total economic impact associated with the event

An economic impact study of this type might also include estimated impacts on hotel occupancy rates and prices, local job creation and employment earnings associated with the event, the impact of the event on local property values and tax revenues, local and state sales and excise tax revenues, and host-city notoriety.

Relevant Geographic Market

The relevant geographic market is important to identify as the extent of the market reflects how widespread the impacts of the event are anticipated to be. Generally, the relevant geographic market is the actual host city but might extend to a larger metropolitan area. The greater the assumed relevant geographic market, the larger any estimated impacts will be because the larger geographic market reduces the amount of leakages from the local economy. However, the greater the assumed relevant geographic market, the less likely it is that any particular portion of the market is directly impacted by the event; far-flung areas of the geographic market might not experience any increase in economic activity attributable to the event. The relevant geographic market ideally would reflect the reasonable approximation for the actual geographic region directly impacted by the event. However, it is likely that the choice of the relevant geographic market is contextual; the geographic market for a local marathon is likely much smaller than the geographic market associated with the Olympics.

Direct, Induced, Indirect, and Implicit Benefits

Direct spending is defined as dollars spent specifically because of the event and, ideally, reflects only money that would not have been spent but for the event, so-called *new* spending. Direct spending might include access to the event, lodging, food, local transportation, and spending at other tourism and entertainment venues in the local market. To avoid double counting, it is important that only new spending associated with the event be included; spending that is shifted from other entertainment events should not be counted as new spending. For example, if recreational and entertainment spending in the city would have been $500,000 in the absence of an event but is anticipated to be $750,000 with the event, only $250,000 in direct spending should be credited to the event.

Induced spending is new spending associated with carrying out the event that would not have happened but for the event. Induced spending is generally undertaken by the event promoter, for example, a sports franchise or a convention bureau, and the host city. For example, if the host city paves roads surrounding the event venue, and would not have done so otherwise, then the money spent on the paving can be considered induced spending. However, if the money would have been spent by the host city in another area then it should not be considered "new" induced spending. Another example would be a stadium operator or franchise purchasing additional food and beverage for a postseason playoff game that would otherwise not have happened. Only the induced spending in the local economy should be counted in the total economic impact; that which is spent outside of the local economy is considered a leakage.

Multipliers account for the additional rounds of local spending created after the direct and induced spending has been completed (see the entry on the Multiplier Effect). Many studies will assume a single multiplier for all direct and induced spending; however, it is not uncommon to see a different multiplier for each type of spending. The appropriate multiplier for direct spending is different than that for induced spending if direct and induced spending have different amounts of leakages from the local economy, face different tax structures, or have different geographic scopes. It is important to use a multiplier of appropriate magnitude. Some studies use multipliers as high as five whereas economists estimate that multipliers should be less than two, and conservative multipliers less than 1.5. The implicit benefits are admittedly difficult-to-measure benefits that accrue to the local citizenry and business community because of hosting the event. These benefits include civic pride, quality of life advancements, and "advertising benefits," which improve the city's regional, national, or international image and which might increase tourism, migration, and business relocation in the future. While it is notoriously difficult to obtain accurate estimates for implicit benefits, they are commonly included in economic impact studies.

Total Estimated Economic Impact

Combining the direct, induced, indirect, and implicit benefits yields the total estimated economic impact of a tourist-drawing event. The total estimated economic impact is often found to be in the tens or hundreds of millions of dollars. Because of the number of assumptions made in the aggregation technique, the estimates from these studies are often simultaneously met with skepticism from those opposed to using public resources to host events and with optimism by those who are in favor. To avoid ideological battles and debating individual assumptions, one possible gauge to whether the total estimated economic impact of an event is "too high" or "just right" is to measure the estimated impact of the event against the already-existing local economy: just how much does the estimated economic impact represent of the existing economy? For example, if the local economy is $2 billion per year in total activity and the estimated impact of an event is $500 million, this would represent 25 percent of the local economy. This might not seem credible when one considers that the total impact would represent either a 25 percent across all sectors of the economy, including those that are not related to the event, or a more than 25 percent increase in the sectors directly impacted by the economy. Neither possibility may seem credible and might bring into question the results of the study. On the other hand, if an event was estimated to have a $50 million impact on a $2 billion local economy, this would represent 2.5 percent of the local economy, a percentage which might seem more credible.

The aggregation technique has come under criticism by academic studies because they seem overly sensitive to assumptions about the level of direct and induced spending, the amount of leakages from the local economy, and the multipliers employed. Many times the questionable assumptions are hard to identify by the layperson and there is some concern that the incentives facing those undertaking the analyses are potentially in conflict with conservative assumptions. A stylized example might serve to prove the sensitivity of economic impact studies to the assumptions made.

Assume a city plans to bid on hosting a nationally important sporting event. The event is anticipated to attract 70,000 individuals in total, 50,000 of which will come from outside the metropolitan area; the remaining 20,000 people are locals who will not spend any new dollars associated with the event. Those coming from outside of town are assumed to plan an average stay of three nights and four days. Three-fifths of the individuals coming from out of town are flying and all are staying in metro-area hotels. The metro area has 15,000 hotels at an average rate of $100 per night and 80 percent of the hotel rooms are owned and operated by national and multinational firms. When the event is scheduled to take place, the average number of tourists is 30,000 people, hotel occupancy entails 9,000 rooms at $100 per night, and on average each individual spends $75 daily on food and entertainment. It is anticipated that each individual attending the event will spend $150 a day in food and entertainment, will spend $150 per night on lodging, and will spend $500 attending the event. The induced spending on the event, perhaps on additional concessions and other services, is assumed to be $10,000,000. It

is assumed the local citizenry enjoys $1,000,000 in implicit benefits. The study assumes a multiplier effect on direct sending of 1.5 and on induced spending of 1.3. The municipality will incur costs of hosting the event of approximately $5 million, including overtime for police and firefighters, beautification efforts, and other public services.

What is the estimated total economic impact of the event? To assess, it is important to recognize what has been embedded in the assumptions and what new spending is correctly attributable to the event. First, many studies will not formally mention that without the event taking place there might be individuals already staying in the local area and spending money. The new direct spending associated the event can be enumerated as follows:

Hotel spending: $0.20 \times (9000) \times (\$150-\$100) + 0.20 \times (6000) \times (\$150) = \$270,000 \times 3$ nights $810,000

Additional spending: $30,000 \times (\$150-\$75) + 20,000 \times (\$150) = \$5,250,000 \times 4$ days = $21,000,000

Total new direct spending in local economy: $21,810,000

Indirect spending caused by new direct spending: $21,810,000 \times (1.5-1) = \$10,905,000$

Total economic impact of direct spending = $32,715,000

The assumptions state that 80 percent of the hotel rooms in the metro area are owned and operated by national and multinational corporations. The remaining 20 percent of hotel rooms are locally owned and operated. A conservative estimate is to assume that all the dollars spent at the non-locally owned hotel rooms represents a leakage from the local economy, that is, the money is immediately remitted out of town. On the other hand, the assumption that all money spent at locally owned and operated hotel rooms stays in the local economy might be a bit strong. Because the average hotel rate increases from $100 to $150 per night, only the difference, $50, applied to the 9000 hotel rooms that would normally be let had the event not taken place can be considered new direct spending. The additional 6,000 rooms let during the event will be credited the full $150 per night. For each of these groups of rooms, 20 percent of the spending is assumed to stay in the local economy. Each night there is an estimated total spending of 0.20 x (6000 x $150 + 9000 x $50) = $270,000 that will impact the local economy. Over three nights the total local impact from the hotel industry is $810,000.

The additional direct spending associated with the event is calculated in a similar fashion. Without the event it is assumed 30,000 people were spending $75 per day on local entertainment and food; with the event 50,000 out-of-towners spend $150 per day on the same items. Therefore, for 30,000 people only $75 can be credited as new spending in the local economy. For the other 20,000 individuals, their $150 in daily spending is considered new spending in the local economy. For the remaining 20,000 locals who attend the event the study's assumption was that those individuals would not spend any new money on attending the event, that is, these people substitute entertainment dollars from other pastimes to the event in question. The total new direct spending (beyond the lodging) is therefore estimated to be $21,000,000.

The direct spending is assumed to have a multiplier effect of 1.5, which incorporates leakages from the local economy in the form of profits, rents, wages, and spending on material and energy remitted to non-locals. The total impact of the direct spending is therefore calculated by multiplying the total direct spending by 1.5. The total indirect spending caused by the new direct spending on lodging, food, and entertainment is therefore 0.5 (= 1.5–1) times the total direct spending. In this case the indirect spending $10,905,000. Combined, the indirect and direct spending comprise the total impact of the direct spending and is calculated to be $32,715,000.

Induced Spending
The induced spending is that which is spent on hosting the event, for example, additional concessions, hiring vendors, additional parking attendants, and so forth. The study assumes the induced spending to be $10,000,000 with an associated multiplier effect of 1.3, which also accounts for (potentially greater) leakages from the local economy. The total impact of the induced spending is $10,000,000 × 1.3 or $13,000,000. The indirect spending associated with the induced spending is therefore $10,000,000 × (1.3-1) = $3,000,000.

Implicit Benefits
The implicit benefits are assumed to be $1 million. Because these benefits are nonmonetary they do not carry a multiplier effect. To the extent that the implicit benefits are correctly measured, they are credited toward the gross benefits of the event.

Total Gross Economic Impact
The total gross benefit of the event is the sum of the total economic impact of the direct spending, the total economic impact of the induced spending, and the implicit benefits. In this case the total gross impact is therefore calculated to be $46,715,000. If, instead, the analysis had treated all 50,000 out-of-towners as new tourists, had ignored the potential leakage of the majority of the hotel expenditure, and had treated all of the out-of-towner spending as new spending (as opposed to being somewhat offset by what would have happened if the event didn't take place), then the total gross economic impact of the study would have been $69,125,000. The mistaken calculation of the new direct spending would have inflated the estimated gross impact of the event by almost 48 percent.

Total Net Economic Impact
A subtle mistake made in some economic impact studies is to estimate only the gross benefits of the event, ignoring any costs the host city might incur in hosting the event, including public services such as fire, police, and EMT protection, beautification such as planting trees and flowers, repaving roads, and so forth. In our stylized example the city is expected to incur $5 million in expenses putting on the event. To calculate the net economic impact, then, it is appropriate to subtract the $5 million in out-of-pocket costs from the gross benefit. This, in turn, makes the net impact of the event $41,015,000.

Other Areas of Interest
There are other areas that impact studies might also investigate. Some might attempt to estimate

the number of jobs associated with the event. While this is an important metric for many, for transitory events it is unlikely that many permanent jobs are created; most jobs will be temporary. Indeed, if the study has already accounted for the induced spending, much of the jobs impact will have already been correctly accounted for there. Additionally, some studies will provide an estimate of the fiscal impact of the event for the local government, that is, the tax revenues generated by the new spending associated with the event. If the local sales tax were 2 percent, then the total gross impact of the event in the stylized example would contribute $934,300 to local tax revenues. This would partially offset the $5 million public expenditure for the event.

This extended numerical example shows the basic construct of the aggregation approach. Unlike the input-output approach the total economic impact is "lump sum" and does not indicate which sectors will receive more or less of the total impact. The important lesson is that the stylized example incorporated a number of assumptions that are common to many studies. For instance, the following critical assumptions were made: the number of people coming from out of town, their length of stay, their average daily expenditures, the multipliers applied, and the implicit benefits. Tourist spending is often estimated from the results of small surveys, perhaps taken in another city or surrounding a different event, and may not be an accurate estimate of what individuals will spend in a particular host city.

Overall, while *ex ante* economic impact studies can be useful and valuable tools for local planners and those interested in bidding for and hosting sporting events or franchises, there is a healthy skepticism about these studies in the academic community. This skepticism has two primary sources. First, the studies are, by definition, prospective in nature and therefore run the risk of being incorrect while simultaneously influencing public policy. Second, while there are credible analyses that make conservative assumptions, all too often the studies make assumptions that seem difficult to justify, employ numbers that seem inflated, and often fail to account for substitution effects and out-of-pocket costs for the host city. As a result, many studies seem to overstate the net benefits of an event.

Ex Post Studies

There is a growing academic literature investigating the impact of hosting mega-events and sports teams. Rather than predicting what might happen if an event is hosted, these studies try to estimate what did happen when an event was hosted. These studies are retrospective or *ex post* in nature and most often entail econometric models. Numerous studies have investigated the impacts of mega-events, such as the Summer and Winter Olympics, the NFL Super Bowl, the MLB All-Star Game, the NBA All-Star Game, or political conventions. Still other studies have looked at the impact of hosting regular season professional games, regular season college football games, and postseason college football games. These studies generally focus on a select few variables of interest such as wages, employment, unemployment, land values, or taxable activity. Counter to the *ex ante* studies, the vast majority of retrospective studies find rather modest, and sometimes negative, impacts of these events (outside of the Super Bowl).

Why might *ex post* econometric studies consistently find that hosting seemingly big and important sporting and tourism events carry such a small net impact, even while the *ex ante* studies predict tens or hundreds of millions of dollars in benefits? One possibility is that the *ex ante* studies make assumptions that are not consistent with the economy when the event takes place. If so, the *ex ante* studies would not be expected to correspond with the *ex post* studies. Another possible explanation is that the incentives facing the authors of *ex post* studies mirror those of the authors of *ex ante* studies, that is, academic writers have an incentive to find small impacts in order to increase the chances of publication. This "publication bias" would be in the opposite direction of any upward bias introduced by the way *ex ante* studies are commissioned.

However, there are legitimate potential explanations for the vast differences between the *ex ante* and *ex post studies*. One possibility is that the data employed in the econometric studies are not appropriate. For instance, perhaps the overall average wage of a metro area is not impacted by hosting a mega-event even as the average wage in the hospitality sector increases. Thus, using an economy-wide average wage might suggest no positive impact when it actually exists. Another possibility is that the correct data are being employed but the wrong time period is investigated. For example, perhaps an increase in wages in the hospitality industry occurs during the two weeks before and immediately after hosting a mega-event. If the data employed measure quarterly average wages in the hospitality industry, it is possible that the increase (and subsequent decrease) would suggest no impact of the event in an econometric study. Another possibility is that econometricians look for impacts in the wrong geographic areas. Perhaps average wages in the hospitality industry increase in the area immediately around a mega-event's venue but only data for the entire local economy is available. In this case, even if wages increase proximate to the venue, these increases might not be large enough to significantly alter the overall metro average wage.

Another explanation for the wide disparity between *ex ante* and *ex post* studies is that the *ex post* econometric studies generally measure *net* rather than *gross* effects. *Ex ante* studies should include only net new spending but all too often fail to do so.

Thus, while *ex post* studies implicitly account for dynamic decisions by local residents of a host city and potential tourists to the host city, *ex ante* studies do not. Local residents have three possible responses to their city hosting a mega-event. The first is to join the fun and contribute new local spending toward attending the event. A second is to "hunker down" and avoid spending money in the local economy while the event is happening. A third is to "skedaddle" and leave town during the event, thereby spending money in another city. Only the first would contribute new spending to the local economy. The "hunker down" effect would offset any new spending taking place during the event but these individuals might transfer local spending to the future, thereby creating an ambiguous net impact on the local economy. The "skedaddle" effect would represent a leakage from the local economy, which would offset on a dollar-per-dollar basis new spending generated by the event. Would-be tourists also make decisions that are not directly observed but are reflected in the data employed by *ex post* studies. For example, a couple might consider a va-

The National Aquatics Center in Beijing, China, was built for swimming meets during the 2008 Summer Olympics. The total economic impact of the 1996–2004 Summer Olympiads has been estimated at a combined $15 billion for their host cities.

cation to a particular city but might divert their tourism to another city when learning of the event taking place. While these tourists might be replaced by others, the amount of spending attributed to the would-be and the actual tourists might differ. These differences are not directly estimated by the *ex post* studies but would be reflected in the *net* estimated benefits. To the extent that the skedaddle and hunker-down effects of the locals and the diversion effects of would-be tourists are reflected in the data employed in *ex post* studies, the *net* impact of events would differ from those estimated in *ex ante* studies.

There are two final reasons econometric studies might not yield the same positive results *ex ante* studies suggest. First, the net effects of the event might be positive but so small that it is (nearly) impossible to detect the effects in a meaningful way using modern statistical techniques. Houston (TX) hosted the 2004 Super Bowl. A study commissioned by the NFL estimated the impact of the Super Bowl to be $336 million. In that year, according to the Bureau of Economic Analysis, the Houston Metropolitan Statistical Area (MSA) economy was approximately $175 billion per year. Therefore, even if the NFL's estimate was correct, the impact would only represent about 0.19 percent of Houston's annual economy. While the absolute magnitude of the event seems large, its relative impact is small and might not be detectable given the state of the art in econometric analysis.

A final reason why *ex post* studies fail to find meaningful impacts of hosting events is that the positive impacts might not exist. This is controversial because *ex ante* studies almost always predict large impacts and it can seem to be overly skeptical to contradict those claims. However, the large number of studies that find little or no impacts of hosting events suggests that this might be the case, notwithstanding the hard work done on the *ex ante* studies.

Mega Events

It should be noted that there are some *ex post* studies that find positive benefits from hosting mega-events, most notably the Olympics, the Super Bowl, and the NBA All-Star game. These three events have one commonality: they are multiday or multiweek events that attract thousands of relatively affluent people from out of town and therefore might generate enough new spending over a long enough period of time to be detectable by econometric techniques. Studies have estimated that the total impact of the summer Olympiads between 1996 and 2004 might have been as high as $15 billion for the host cities (combined). Studies suggest that the Super Bowl might add $45–$60 million in *net* new spending in the host city and that, while many day-to-day regular-season professional sporting events do not offer a lot of "bang" to host cities, postseason play does generate noticeable *net* increases in local spending. Thus, there seems to be a growing consensus among *ex post* studies that the biggest events might have a modest positive *net* impact on the host city but nothing near what *ex ante* studies suggest.

Craig A. Depken, II
University of North Carolina, Charlotte

See Also: Data Collection; Marketing Research Process; Mega Sports Events.

Further Readings

Gratton, Chris and Ian Jones. *Research Methods for Sport Studies*. Florence, KY: Psychology Press, 2004.

Hamakawa, Curt and Elizabeth Elam. "Beijing Olympics: Games of Epic Proportion." *Journal of Business Cases and Applications*, v.3 (2010).

Jozsa, Frank P. *Sports Capitalism*. London: Ashgate Publishing, 2004.

Edmonton Oilers

The Edmonton Oilers is a hockey franchise that, despite early team success, has had to develop innovative marketing strategies to compensate for the team's small market size. The team started as the Alberta Oilers, one of the original 12 teams that formed the World Hockey Association (WHA) in 1972. The team played in the WHA for seven years.

In 1979 the Oilers, along with three other WHA teams, merged with the National Hockey League (NHL) and were charged a $6 million expansion fee to enter the league.

Once in the NHL the Oilers began to distinguish themselves as a young, talented team. The Oilers were led by Wayne Gretzky, arguably the best hockey player to play the game. By 1984, only five years after they entered the league, the Oilers won the Stanley Cup. Over seven years the Oilers won five Stanley Cups. Only three other franchises in the NHL have won the Stanley Cup more than the Oilers.

At the height of the Oilers dynasty, however, the economics of professional sport forced the team to trade Wayne Gretzky to the Los Angeles Kings for three players, draft picks, and $15 million. The trade was precipitated by the financial difficulties of owner Peter Pocklington. Pocklington's decision to sell his star player signaled that escalating player salaries were placing severe financial pressures on the franchise because of the small size of its market.

Currently, the Oilers are owned by Darryl Katz of Rexall Pharmacies. Katz purchased the franchise for over $200 million in 2008. Katz is now attempting to build a new arena for the Oilers and has offered to contribute $100 million of his own money to kick-start the project.

Management and Marketing Innovations

Prior to the NHL lockout of 2004–05, the Edmonton Oilers were considered a franchise at risk because of the small size of their consumer market. As a result, the franchise employed a number of creative strategies to help expand the team's fan base. The best example of this was the Heritage Classic outdoor hockey game. The Oilers organized the first outdoor game in NHL history. The game was modeled after the "cold war" between Michigan and Michigan State in NCAA Hockey. The event was played in Commonwealth Stadium in Edmonton and drew over 57,000 fans, which, at the time, was a single-game attendance record for the NHL. The event featured an NHL regular season game between the Edmonton Oilers and the Montreal Canadiens. Nevertheless, the true draw of the event was the Oldtimers Game held prior to the actual game. In this game many players from the Oilers Stanley Cup championship teams returned to the city to play. The Heritage Classic was so successful that the NHL now holds an annual outdoor game called the "Winter Classic."

Some of the other creative marketing initiatives include the Oilers third jersey, designed by Todd McFarlane, owner of the *Spawn* comic book and former Oilers owner. The franchise has cultivated a strong relationship with the Canadian military with their promotion "Tickets for the Troops." The team has also worked to build markets outside of the local area. The team held their training camp in different northern Alberta cities and once went as far north as Yellowknife in the Northwest Territories.

The result of these marketing initiatives combined with a league-wide salary cap and a strong Canadian dollar has seen the franchise enjoy relative financial health for a number of years. At present season ticket sales are strong. The financial crisis of 2008 has had some effect on the revenue of the franchise. However, going forward, the Edmonton Oilers are in a stable financial position because of their strong marketing initiatives and their ability to extend their fan base.

William M. Foster
University of Alberta

See Also: Creating a Strong Event, Keys to; Event Marketing; Franchise; National Hockey League.

Further Readings

Foster, W. M. and C. Hyatt. "Inventing Team Tradition: A Conceptual Model for the Strategic Development of Fan Nations." *European Sport Management Quarterly,* v.8/3 (2008).

Gzowski, P. *The Game of Our Lives,* Rev. Ed. Toronto: MacClelland and Stewart, 1982.

Hunter, D. *The Glory Barons: The Saga of the Edmonton Oilers.* Toronto: Viking, 1999.

Ramshaw, G. and T. Hinch. "Place Identity and Sport Tourism: The Case of the Heritage Classic Ice Hockey Event." *Current Issues in Tourism,* v.9/4–5 (2006).

Willes, E. *The Rebel League: The Short and Unruly Life of the World Hockey Association.* Toronto: M & S, 2004.

Eduselling

Eduselling is the practice of educating the consumer about the different aspects of a sponsorship property in order to develop a partnership. With the growing concern about how money is utilized, sponsoring corporations have become increasingly savvy about marketing and promotional budgets, and the onus is now on sport organizations to inform the buyer how to best capitalize on a sponsorship investment and the entitlements associated with it. Therefore, eduselling may be defined as the systematic and continuous dissemination of knowledge and assistance to the prospective decision maker to enhance his or her knowledge about the product's benefits, and to establish a sense of partnership between a sport property and sponsoring organization.

The Eduselling process is a dynamic, continuous, and longitudinal process that may enhance the buyer's perspective on the outcome of sponsoring a sport organization. Concentrating on the relationship's life span—something not traditionally rewarded in the sport sales environment—eduselling may be viewed as a step-by-step process; however, steps may occur simultaneously or in a nonlinear way.

The first step is identifying the prospect, which is viewed as the key to a successful sales campaign. In this step, sport managers generate relevant research about a potential group of organizations or potential sponsors. The sport manager should identify the prospect's business objectives in terms of sponsorship to determine its level of exposure and common patterns. The salesperson should also identify any regulatory concerns, which may make sponsoring a sport organization a more or less viable option. Finally, the key decision maker for the prospect should be identified to eliminate wasted time and resources. Methods for attaining new leads may come from current sponsors, business networking opportunities, and business periodicals, among others.

The second step is preparing a how-to guide. The how-to guide should include information about the sport property, audience/fan profile, key benefits derived from the relationship, media partners and anticipated media coverage, current sponsor roster and testimonials, and contact information. This executive summary may be sent prior to face-to-face meetings to increase the prospect's awareness about the sport property, or placed on the sport property's Website to engender sales leads.

Developing a partnership is the third step. This is considered one of the most difficult steps because the salesperson is attempting to gain the decision maker's trust. By demonstrating his or her awareness and understanding of the prospect's business, the salesperson may enhance the partnership. Some sport properties have used coaches, players, or hall of famers to initiate the partnership and enhance the prospect's attention and response.

Next, the sport property should offer a product-sampling experience. For some sport properties this is difficult because their event occurs infrequently. In other cases, however, the sport property may invite potential sponsors to an event so they may gain a better understanding about the product, its use, and how the sponsor may benefit from the partnership. When the event occurs infrequently, some sport properties have signed sponsors to smaller deals and demonstrated the benefit they received from the current sponsor level, and the benefits they would have received at a higher level.

Once the prospect has tested the product, salespeople should design appropriate follow-up procedures. This step occurs when the salesperson creates customized presentations for prospects indicating how the relationship benefits them. The sales presentation's success should be based on the learning that took place, and the congruency between the sponsorship and marketing objectives.

The sixth step—making the offer—may be the most difficult for salespeople. The offer should include an introductory paragraph, audience demographics, relevant inventory highlights, fee structure, and a call to action. Next, the salesperson should attempt to close the deal: reaching an agreement between the sport property and prospect.

The last two steps occur once the sponsorship has been agreed upon. The first is planning, activating, and fulfilling the agreed-upon sponsorship entitlements. This is followed closely by completing an evaluation and providing feedback to the sponsor. This stage could be used to attract the sponsor to renew or reactivate at the current level or even a higher level of sponsorship.

Thomas J. Aicher
Northern Illinois University

See Also: Personal Selling; Unique Selling Proposition; Up-Selling.

Further Readings

Futtrell, C. M. *Fundamentals of Selling: Customers for Life Through Selling.* New York: McGraw-Hill, 2004.

Irwin, R. L., W. A. Sutton, and L. M. McCarthy. *Sport Promotion and Sales Management*, 2nd Ed. Champaign, IL: Human Kinetics, 2008.

Jowdy, E. and M. McDonald. "The Futures Golf Tour Case Study: Sponsorship Sales and Eduselling." *Sport Marketing Quarterly,* v.11/4 (2002).

Mullin, B., S. Hardy, and W. Sutton. *Sport Marketing*, 3rd Ed. Champaign, IL: Human Kinetics, 2007.

Effective Teamwork, Management

The need for effective teamwork has become a requirement in business. Workgroups that function as teams have evolved as part of the "total quality management" concept. The evolution of teamwork within management systems was initiated with the belief that employees will be most productive when they identify with the success of an organization, and a small group will have more perceived success while fitting into a larger-scale organization. Thus, managers must be trained to take the role of a coach or facilitator and set goals for the work teams to achieve. Establishing the expectation of effective teamwork and supporting team members should increase the rate of goal attainment.

Many organizations attempt to develop their work teams in the same manner as sports teams. Management intent on developing effective teamwork must deliberately develop an environment where the elements of teamwork can be practiced and perfected. This takes strategy and discipline. In sport management, the idea is not foreign to managers in many organizations, but they may not have

the same opportunities to develop teamwork in practice situations as a sport team. Many organizations place a group of workers together and ask them to work as a team. The newly formed team is then expected to succeed or fail at their given task. Management must be cognizant of the process for developing effective teamwork and what contributes to effective teams.

The context of each group can vary significantly, but groups also share similar characteristics. In management there are a number of different team categorizations. The most common types are work teams, project teams, and management teams. Each has a nuanced difference that affects the context of the team; work teams are general teams, project teams are time-limited, and management teams generally supervise subunits of work teams.

The scholars Albert V. Carron and Heather A. Hausenblas have identified five categories that define groups/teams: common fate, mutual benefit, social structure, group processes, and self-categorization. The first category, a common fate, serves as the basis for effective teamwork. The end result is reflected on all group members equally. Once a common fate is established, members must rely upon one another and receive support from one another for a mutual benefit, which is the second category. Social structures, the third category, are established within the group. Group norms and roles are negotiated and accepted within the social structure. Group processes must also be present, specifically communication within the group, cooperative interactions for the task at hand, and social interactions. Finally, the fifth category, known as self-categorization, occurs when the members of the team begin to identify themselves as a collective that is different and distinct from other teams.

Effective teamwork is the result of a number of factors, all generally related to the ability of the group to work within the previously mentioned categories as a single cohesive unit. Effective teamwork is more than just individuals participating in coordinated actions; it begins with a set of common goals, beliefs, and purposes enacted with the dependence on and best interests of the team over that of the individual. According to the authors Susan G. Cohen and Diane E. Bailey, the measurement of effective teamwork encompasses three very specific dimensions: (1) quality and/or quantity of outputs, (2) behavioral outcomes, and (3) attitudes of team members.

The quantity and quality of output for work teams can usually be measured in an objective way. The measurement is typically assessed through accuracy, speed, and creativity, among others. Behavioral outcomes are somewhat more difficult to measure but may include organizational commitment, trust among group members, perceived cohesiveness, unified communication, and feelings of empowerment. The attitudes of team members may be evaluated with such concepts as group efficacy, group identity, role acceptance, and shared values.

While effective teamwork does have specific dimensions of measurement, there are also specific factors that contribute to the ability of the team to work effectively. These factors include group size, homogeneity or heterogeneity of group members, competition with other groups, perceived or measured success, and exclusivity. Group size has been hypothesized to work most efficiently when kept small, ideally between five and 10 members. Heterogeneity or homogeneity of the team can have a positive or negative effect depending on the team's charges. People typically get along with and communicate most easily with those who are similar to themselves. A homogenous team generally shares attitudes, values, and common experience; these elements typically predict a more effective team. However, heterogeneity can improve effectiveness by encouraging mutual learning or increasing the group's variable strength. Competition with other teams can also enhance effective teamwork as it supports the concept of self-categorization of a certain team. Success also increases effective teamwork as a successful team becomes especially attractive to the team members, which increases cohesiveness, empowerment, and other positive effects. Exclusivity can increase effectiveness of presenting the members of the team the opportunity to increase their prestige or social status, which increases their commitment to belonging to their team.

Conclusion

Effective teamwork in management has to be developed and planned in accordance with the aforementioned factors and concepts. The context of the

success of each group will provide information for its effectiveness, but as more organizations design their structure-utilizing work teams, the development and measurement of effectiveness of such teams must occur.

Craig Paiement
Ithaca College

See Also: Centralization Versus Decentralization of Authority; Employee Development; Employee Relations; Human Resources Management; Structure and Strategy.

Further Readings

Carron, A. V. and H. A. Hausenblas. *Group Dynamics in Sport,* 2nd Ed. Morgantown, WV: Fitness Information Technology, 1998.

Cleland, D. I. *Strategic Management of Teams.* Hoboken, NJ: John Wiley & Sons, 1996.

Cohen, S. G. and D. E. Bailey. "What Makes Teams Work: Group Effectiveness Research From the Shop Floor to the Executive Suite." *Journal of Management,* v.23/3 (1997).

Luthans, F. "The Need for and Meaning of Positive Organizational Behavior." *Journal of Organizational Behavior,* v.6 (2002).

Spencer, B. "Models of Organizational and Total Quality Management: A Comparison and Critical Evaluation." *Academy of Management Review,* v.19/3 (1994).

Electronic Marketing

In today's sports world, the Internet is being used to facilitate every aspect of sports management and marketing. There are thousands of Websites that deliver a vast range of sports content, team and league information, e-commerce capabilities, access to online sports gambling, and fantasy sports, to name a few. The following sections discuss some of the more common uses of the Internet to market sports events, apparel and equipment, and related sports services. The revenue models common to these sports business sites will be also be addressed.

Sports Content Sites

Content in sports typically incorporates a large base of information that users can consult to find sports news, scores, and analysis. Many content sites are associated with major television organizations, which can be local, national, or international in reach and scope (e.g., CNN, ESPN, or BBC). The largest of these sites tend to be broad in their coverage of sport and its content; however, recently organizations such as ESPN have attempted to localize content to fit specific geographic regions (e.g., ESPNChicago.com, ESPNLosAngeles.com); sites like these attempt to customize the user experience to what's locally relevant and thus attract more frequent users, while keeping them there for longer periods of time.

In the past five years or so, sports organizations have increasingly used the Internet as a distribution channel for live content or archived footage. For example, in their 2010 offerings, Major League Baseball (MLB.TV) offers a full range of content that includes a premium package experience that gives the fan ultimate control of what, when, and where the fan sees it. It includes many of the functions found on cable and satellite packages (including DVR controls to pause and rewind live action). The key distinction, however, is the portability of the content offering; fans may view games on any computer as well as many portable devices and smartphones whenever they choose. The National Basketball Association has a similar offering for the 2010–11 NBA season.

Several organizations (e.g., syndicatedsports.com; sbrtools.com; sportsdirectinc.com) provide services whereby they syndicate sports content to websites devoted to sports news, niche Web portals, sports wagering, and fantasy sports. The content these companies syndicate covers all major professional team sports as well as college football and basketball. The basic content feed is free and a customized service is also available. With regular updates, sports-themed Websites remain relevant by keeping fresh content that is valued by their target users. This service is invaluable to small startup sports related businesses that need to have relevant and timely sports information in order to satisfy the appetite of millions of sports-hungry fans.

Sports Teams and Leagues Sites

These sites typically represent amateur and professional teams and leagues. Some leagues have created portals of sorts for their league and have almost complete uniformity within the individual team sites. The National Basketball Association (NBA.com) and Major League Baseball (MLB.com) do an excellent job of this and choose to exercise more control while displaying uniformity over the message and experiences their fans receive. In contrast, the National Football League has a portal site for fans of its teams but also allows teams to create a unique experience for their fans. For example, the Dallas Cowboys official team site (DallasCowboys.com) is separate from the league and provides more online community and overall experience that goes beyond the facts, dates and stats associated with their page on NFL.com.

Many amateur governing bodies (e.g., USOC, NCAA, FIFA USOC, SEC) and teams (e.g., University of Florida's Gatorzone.com) also have a significant online presence. For example, the U.S. Olympic Committee's TeamUSA.com site provides rich information about Olympic athletes, teams, stats and events. While Web traffic on a site such as this spikes during the Olympic season, it is available year-round for fans to access archive footage and other content as well as become involved in its online community. At the collegiate level, the University of Florida uses Gatorzone.com to build community around all of its sports teams. While football and basketball are their most prominent sports, Gator alumni, fans, and Boosters can find Gator information and a source for community connection to all of their favorite sports.

E-Commerce/Retail Sites

Sports related e-commerce businesses for products and services have proliferated over the past decade. These types of sites have been started and are run by sports leagues and teams, sporting goods retailers, ticket brokers, auction sites as well as product manufacturers. Products that bear the official names and trademarks of leagues and teams are typically sold through a licensing agreement with licensee manufacturers (e.g., Champion Athletic Wears). The resulting products (e.g., caps, t-shirts, or sweatshirts) in turn are sold through a retailer (e.g., Dick's Sporting Goods) or directly on the Website of a team or league There are manufacturer brands, such as Nike, that sell at the retail level (e.g., Footlocker.com) and directly to consumers online for a more customized product and buying experience. The proliferation of the Internet has made mass customization of sports-related products (e.g., footwear, golf clubs, tennis racquets) possible and is a growing market of product offerings.

Other e-commerce businesses that are popular with sports fans involve the purchase and sale/re-sale of sports tickets. Traditional companies like Ticketmaster.com have long been in the business of selling sports tickets. It is recently that start-ups like StubHub.com (purchased by eBay.com) created a more efficient secondary market for sports and entertainment tickets. Leagues like the NFL recently tried to gain some control over the secondary ticket market by starting their own online marketplace. Finally, sports memorabilia and collectibles is still a booming business for casual and professional collectors. For over a decade, eBay has provided a fairly efficient marketplace for people seeking a market to either buy or sell a piece of sports history.

Gambling Sites

Gambling on sports has grown tremendously in the first decade or so of the Internet. While these types of businesses are discouraged by teams, leagues, and governing bodies of mainstream sports and events, they have played a significant role in increasing interest and popularity of some sports. Sport betting is an international business and is legal in many countries around the world but is significantly limited in the United States to places like Las Vegas, Nevada. For this reason, many who choose to gamble on sport often wager on them either illegally or through online bookmakers—located off the shores of the United States. Bets on high-profile events such as the Super Bowl and the Daytona 500 generate significant revenue for these online gambling businesses (e.g., Sportsbetting.com) and are very financially lucrative online ventures. It should

be noted that while gambling on sports may not be sanctioned by sports teams and their leagues, for some fans it does heighten their interest in following sports events live, on radio and television, and on the Internet.

Fantasy Sports Sites

Fantasy sports is a relatively new online sports phenomena and is an estimated $3.8 billion business. An estimated 25 million Americans play fantasy sports (and many more outside of the United States) with the average player spending more than $150 per year on fantasy games and related products. This is a financial bonanza for independent entrepreneurs (e.g., footballguys.com) and large corporate entities (e.g., Yahoo! and CBS) alike. This industry has grown primarily as a result of the Internet's ability to connect sports fans and quickly collect and aggregate game and player statistics.

One of the larger players in online fantasy sports is Fantasy Sports Ventures, which owns and is affiliated with more than 400 sites on the Internet. This network of sites provides coverage of football, basketball, baseball, hockey, and college sports to name a few. While many of these sites deliver content to sports fans (e.g., NBADraft.net, Probasketballnews.com) much of their growth has been in the fantasy sports area. Fantasy sports has become so large that it has spawned a new industry—fantasy sports insurance. FantasySportsInsurance.com was created in 2008 as "a disability insurance policy that protects a fantasy team owner's investment in their team should a key player(s) suffer a season-changing injury."

Other innovations that capitalize on the popularity of the fantasy sports industry may also be in development. Teams and leagues clearly see the value fantasy sports have in keeping and building interest in sports contests. Many followers of fantasy sports have kept interest in games long after their teams have been eliminated from playoff contention. During the final weeks of what may be a meaningless season for their losing teams, they may continue to follow the games because they have interest in the performance outcomes of individual players. In the next sections, the common revenue models associated with these aspects of sports electronic marketing will be discussed.

Overview of Revenue Model Definition

A firm's revenue model describes how the firm will earn revenue, earn a profit, and ultimately generate an acceptable return on investment. A revenue model is but one component of a firm's business model, which includes all of the planned activities designed to result in delivering some value to the marketplace and its customers. Many online businesses will engage in several revenue models in order to maximize revenue potential and ensure that they have a diversified stream of revenue. The following sections will discuss some common revenue models used by various sports site businesses.

Content Sites Revenue Models

Revenue for these types of sites are usually created to take advantage of the volume of traffic that flows to these types of sites. An advertising revenue model is very common on these sites because sports content tends to not only attract a large readership or viewership but can also be very "sticky"; stickiness often refers to the ability of the Website and its content to retain user attention. Game highlight footage and blog discussions about content tend to be very sticky and thus increase the value of ads placed on these types of sites. Much of the content on many of these sites is free since they are ad supported. However, many sites also offer premium content for subscription fees. The revenue generated through advertising may vary depending on the levels of traffic on a site. Sponsorship revenue, however, tends to be a little more stable than advertising (in the short run) but also runs the risk of going away without fresh content to drive traffic.

On these sites, content will always be "king" and thus has to be managed diligently for quality. Since many content sites provide much of their content for free the main objective of their business models is to generate traffic and provide incentive for users to stay as long as possible. With this business model the amount charged for advertisements by content providers (often referred to as "publishers" in the online advertising world) depends on the amount of traffic generated by each site. Banner ads are a very common form of ad displays that usually commands ad revenue based on a cost-per-thousand (CPM) approach. In some cases publishers may charge on a click-through rate (CTR); while this

is a popular approach, the CPM approach is still more common. Factors such as size, type, location of the ad, and demographic audience reach are all used to determine the amount to be paid for a display ad; basic economic principles of supply and demand for the ad inventory greatly figures into ad pricing as well.

Content sites may also act as "affiliates" for other sites (usually online retailers) who are trying to sell products and services to the users of these sites. ESPN.com and CBSSports.com offer direct sales of licensed merchandise for major sports leagues (e.g., Super Bowl locker room shirts and caps) and generate revenue for themselves by collecting a commission (affiliate revenue) based on a percentage of the retail sales revenue directed to the online retailers. These commissions can range from 1 percent to 8 percent or more depending upon the volume of business that is directed to a specific retailer.

Teams and Leagues

Revenue on these sites covers a very broad range. The traffic on these sites tends to be substantial and seasonal. For example, during baseball season the New York Yankees Website is very active and fans can visit it to see game highlights as well as purchase game tickets and licensed Yankee apparel. They generate revenue from each sale and also sell advertising space to businesses that wish to connect their product with Yankees fans. The ads on this site tend to be from organizations and brands that have a sponsorship relationship with the Yankees and/or Major League Baseball. It is very common these days to have ads on a team or league site as part of an overall sponsorship package sold by the teams/leagues. It should be noted that sales revenue generated on this site and all other Major League Baseball team sites is done directly on MLB.com's site. Fans click on the sales merchandise button and they are sent to MLB for shopping and purchase.

Subscription fees are also a key revenue source for game content found on team and league sites. Access to premium content can cost several hundred dollars depending on the level the fan chooses and the sport. The National Basketball Association, for example, offers two tiers of access to its games on NBA.com: the full offering (about $190) gives fans access to all games for all teams throughout the season (similar to the League Pass offering on Satellite and Cable). The lower-level package (about $120) limits you to your selection of only seven of your favorite teams to follow. A key point is they have two subscription levels that aims to satisfy the broadest NBA fans as well as the avid fans of a specific team or two.

E-Commerce/Retail Sites

e-commerce sites typically earn revenue through sales transactions. Nike, for example uses its site to enable customers to create a custom Nike shoe. Customization for Nike's shoes is limited to several designs and colors; even with these limitations it does give the customer the impression that their shoe is made just for them and helps drive sales on the site. Columbia Sportswear (Columbia.com) creates an excellent experience for its customers; the site primarily caters to outdoor enthusiasts. Columbia uses its Website to educate existing and potential customers on the unique benefits of the Columbia brand. For example, winter sports enthusiast can enjoy a customized experience that is different from someone who is an avid fisherman. Much of the experience revolves around a specific sports activity that helps to achieve the goal of a sales transaction online or increase foot traffic in a retail store. Sites like Nike and Columbia serve to transact business directly with the customer and also drive traffic to its retail store partners either online or in a city where one lives. One such partner is Dick's Sporting Goods, which has stores throughout the United States and a strong presence on the Internet. DicksSportingGoods.com's primary goal is to transact business online and drive traffic to its physical stores. Many of the promotions it runs are exclusive to the Web and entice consumers to make purchase decisions immediately. The revenue model breadth for retail businesses is typically limited to sales transactions; however, other e-commerce businesses use other sources of revenue.

An online ticket broker like StubHub.com is a strong player in secondary market for buying and selling sport event tickets. StubHub generates revenue by taking a fee for the transactions it enables with buyer and seller. The resale of sports tickets has become such a lucrative business the National Football League started the NFL Ticket Exchange

"The Official Ticket Exchange of the NFL." It is providing this service to NFL fans through a partnership with Ticketsnow.com and Ticketmaster. The NFL too is charging a transaction fee for bringing buyer and seller together. Online auction sites such as Steiner Sports offer a service for sports memorabilia enthusiast who needs a market to buy and sell their collectibles. While eBay may have pioneered the online auction and exchange, many Web-based businesses have sprung up to serve the sports collectible niche market. Much of the revenue generated on these type of sites are transaction-fee-based with very little risk for the broker.

Gambling Sites and Fantasy Sports

Sports gambling sites primarily operate like an offline casino whereby they make their revenue through bets being placed and a profit being made off the spread between what they take in and what they pay out on wagers. Sites like Betus.com and Sports.com engage in all types of sports book gambling as well as casino games. Sports.com estimates that it takes in $2 billion worth of wagers each year—of which sports gambling is a significant portion. Sports betting is a lucrative business online but is probably outdistanced by the amount and scope of sports gambling that goes unrecorded and is illegal.

Fantasy sports sites are a rapidly growing industry where interest in fantasy sports has crossed into just about every major team sport. These sites primarily make their revenue through transaction fees with fantasy league team and individual players. For example, CBSSports.com's Fantasy business has multilevel offerings for sports fans. They offer a free version which is an organized game where anyone can join. Their premium games offer three levels of competition, which range in fees from $29.99 to $249.99 to start a team. These premium games offer live chat and instant messaging for players and live updates and point scoring for games. Many other sites have similar offerings covering a wide range of sports fan market segments and their sport's needs.

Conclusion

Electronic marketing touches every aspect of sports business online. The Internet enables delivery of live and archived game content via the Web, purchase of tickets to see live events, promotion of games and special events, gambling on sports events, fan community and connection with other fans (e.g., fantasy sports), and purchases of new and used merchandise and collectibles. Each activity touches one or more segments of sports fans who appreciate: a level of convenience for customers; access to sports content and related sports information; and exposure to a breadth of sports-related products and service never seen before. As the Internet matures and grows, both fans and businesses alike will find more creative and innovative ways to use technology to make sports fan experiences more enjoyable and convenient.

Robert I. Roundtree
University of North Carolina, Charlotte

See Also: e-Commerce; Internet/Online; Websites, Sports Marketing.

Further Readings

Fullerton, Sam. *Sports Marketing*. New York: McGraw Hill/Irwin, 2010.

Laudon, Kenneth and Carol Guercio Traver. *E-Commerce: Business, Technology, Society*. Upper Saddle River, NJ: Pearson Prentice Hall, 2010.

Wertime, K. and I. Fenwick. *DigiMarketing: The Essential Guide to New Media & Digital Marketing*. Singapore: John Wiley & Sons Asia, 2008.

EM Motorsports

EM Motorsport LTD is an independent automotive racing research, development, and manufacturing company established in 2003. The company entered the motorsports industry in the same year and quickly became a leading supplier. EM Motorsport products have been used in various racing circuits, including the FIA F1 Championship, the GP2 Series, the British F3 International and F3,

the Euroseries, the GP3 Series, the GP2 Asia (from 2004 to 2009), and the DPM. EM Motorsport is best known for its flagship product, the Formula 1 Marshalling System as well as its cutting edge technology and ability to custom design and manufacture hardware and software to meet its customers' specific needs.

EM Motorsport is currently headquartered in Church Farm House, Holton, Oxford in the United Kingdom. The company's product research and development takes place largely at its research and manufacturing center in Italy. EM Motorsport is involved in auto club racing all the way up to Formula 1 racing and has had much global success, winning a number of single-seater championships. They also delve into other aspects of the racing industry, including motorbikes and touring cars as well as powerboats. EM Motorsport is a member of the Motorsport Industry Association.

EM Motorsport began its corporate career as the sole agency for Magneti Marelli Motorsport products in the United Kingdom, the United States, and Japan, an exclusive relationship that ended in 2005. In that same year, the company started to develop safety devices for motorsport. EM Motorsport works with Italian-based prototyping and manufacturing partners the ART Group, Temis, and Il Pischiello in order to offer a variety of standard and custom products and services. They also actively collaborate with research universities to maintain their reputation for cutting-edge technological development. EM Motorsport products and services have contributed to numerous domestic and international-level championships.

The company's main goals include improving safety for both cars and drivers as well as the race circuits and race marshals, the development of new safety devices, the development of technologically advanced products that are also affordable, and the provision of expert customer service and support. EM Motorsport products include the FAI approved F1 Marshalling System, the FIA homologated Surveillance Data Recorder, the FIA homologated Accident Data Recorder, the FIA approved Electronic Flag System, the FAI approved Start Light System, the FIA approved Start Light/Pit-Entry/Pit-Exit, the Personal Marshalling Device, the GdiX GDI/Diesel ECU, sensors, the Paddle-Shift Steering Wheel, Image acquisition and distribution technology (also HD), telemetry systems, and GPS systems.

EM Motorsport also creates custom designs and prototypes of electronic hardware and software and provides track support from its race engineers. The company develops and manufactures custom-made products, including an ear-plug accelerometer, the GP2 Asia paddle-shift steering wheel, custom accelerometers and LED pit-exit lights, an Engine Tone Generator, a narrow band telemetry system, and an electronic flag for the karting circuit. The company's Italian research and manufacturing center allows custom hardware and software to be built on-site.

EM Motorsport has been able to market itself through its involvement in the safety devices of racing cars. One of its most marketable and ingenious devices is the Formula 1 Marshalling System, the company's flagship product. This is a GPS-based two-way telemetry system. The Formula I Marshalling System specializes in race control by providing full view of the GPS location of the other cars on the track during the racing sessions. It has been used in F1 championships since 2007. In 2009, EM Motorsports won an award for the Best Safety Innovation of the Year. The award was part of the Professional Motorsport World Expo Awards.

David Trevino
Independent Scholar

See Also: National Association for Stock Car Auto Racing; Technology in Sports; Trade, Marketing to the.

Further Readings

The ART Group. http://www.artgroup-srl.it (Accessed October 2010).
Burgess Wise, David. *The Ultimate Race Car*. New York: DK Press, 1999.
EM Motorsport LTD. http://www.emmotorsport .com/index.html (Accessed October 2010).
Jenkins, Mark, Ken Pasternak, and Richard West. *Performance at the Limit: Business Lessons From Formula 1 Motor Racing*. New York: Cambridge University Press, 2005.
Motorsport Industry Association. http://www.the -mia.com (Accessed October 2010).

Embracing Change

In order to be successful in the 21st century business climate, sport organizations are recognizing that it is no longer sufficient to conduct business as usual, and that they must embrace change in order to survive and remain competitive and viable as business entities. As the external environment becomes increasingly more turbulent for organizations, the pace of change is increasing with no sign of slowing. For sport organizations to survive and grow, they must adapt quickly and nimbly to changes in strategy, size, environment, and technology. External pressures for change can involve fluctuating economic situations, technology advances in manufacturing of sport equipment, globalization of sport, and increased societal interest in sport and leisure. Internal pressures for change can include a renewed emphasis on service quality, changing work climates, declining effectiveness, the move to self-managed teams, and demand for flexible operating procedures. Thus, sport organizations at all levels, from grassroots youth sport leagues to intercollegiate athletics to professional and international sport, need to embrace change to most effectively achieve organizational outcomes.

Organizational change can be a planned, deliberate attempt to alter an organization in some fashion, or an unplanned occurrence, where change is imposed upon the organization and is unforeseen. Change can be triggered by a crisis, it can be reactive as a response to environmental or internal conditions, or it can be pre-emptive, where the change is undertaken to avoid potentially negative consequences for the organization. Additionally, organizational change can be broad or narrow in scope. For instance, change can involve slight revisions to a policy and procedural manual or remodeling the office space, or it can be more radical and large-scale, such as shifting strategy and philosophy, or undergoing a major downsizing. Change can also take place within the competitive teams of a sport organization, where constant shifts of strategy and team composition are undertaken to maximize competitive advantage.

Thus, organizational change can occur in four functional areas in sport organizations: technology, structures and systems, people, and productivity and

Change in sport organizations must be embraced by every level of the group from coaches and employees to players.

services. Sport organizations that adapt and embrace change in these areas are better able achieve the mission and goals of the organization. For example, prior to 1952, the National Collegiate Athletic Association (NCAA) did not have any regulatory power over its member institutions. However, because of public disclosures of unethical recruiting, illegal payments to student athletes, point-shaving in college basketball and tampering with student transcripts, there was concerted pressure for the NCAA to take action. The NCAA moved quickly to develop a system under which sanctions against member institutions could be invoked.

Thus, the fundamental role of the NCAA changed from being a passive observer and consultant to one of exercising power to penalize member institutions. Also, the Canadian National Sport Organizations (NSOs) underwent drastic organizational changes in the 1990s. Under pressure from the national sport governing body, NSOs shifted from volunteer-organized to professional and bureaucratic organizational designs to enhance their effectiveness in administering sport at the national level. As can be seen, both the NCAA and NSOs embraced change to remain effective and viable entities.

Readiness for Change

The conditions in an organization contribute to whether or not change is embraced by the organi-

zation. An organization must have a visible need for change in order for the change to be effective and elicit widespread acceptance throughout the organization. This visible need for change should be recognized by most employees. If conditions in the organization are not such as to permit change because of the environment, culture, climate, or leadership, or if change is just being enacted for change's sake, the change initiative runs the risk of failure or producing a negative effect on organizational outcomes, such as lower job satisfaction, decreased commitment to the organization, and greater intent to leave the organization on the part of employees. Also, employee's sense of their ability to accomplish change, and their participation in the change process, contribute to readiness for change in the organization and its ability to embrace change. Readiness for change is the extent to which employees hold positive views about the need for organizational change, coupled with the extent to which employees believe that such changes will have positive implications for themselves and the organization as a whole. Employee perceptions of the risks of organizational change will influence one's readiness for change. If change poses a threat to an individual's job security, level of decision making that one has in the organization, one's intrinsic rewards derived from the job, or increases one's emotional exhaustion and stress to a great degree, that individual will experience reduced readiness for change. If employees are not ready for change, it will be difficult for the sport organization to fully embrace change.

In many sport organizations, the natural response to proposed change initiatives by employees is resistance or ambivalence. Change is difficult, as it disrupts the status quo and comfortable work routines, systems, and processes. In order to effectively manage change in this environment, the astute change agent should first strive to communicate a visible need for change to all employees, and then garner support for change by fostering a shared vision. This is best accomplished in many instances through transformational leadership, where vision, empowerment, and participatory decision making are advanced to facilitate change acceptance.

Managers who involve their employees in the change process, valuing their opinions, will enhance acceptance of change and allow the organization to achieve better organizational outcomes through embracing change, even in organizations where there is pronounced initial resistance or ambivalence. Along these lines, organizations that foster a relational rather than a competitive or hierarchal culture will experience greater change acceptance from employees and other stakeholders.

Creativity and risk taking among employees should also be encouraged. Sport managers must also pay attention to the pace of change implementation in order to mitigate resistance. If major change is implemented too quickly, resistance can calcify, as employees may feel that there is no firm ground to stand upon during the process. Thus, sport managers must balance the need for change with a comfortable pace of implementation that will allow employees to adjust to major disruptions and new routines and processes. When these facets are in place, sport organizations can fully embrace change and achieve better outcomes.

Jon Welty Peachey
Texas A&M University

See Also: Economic Climate for Sports; Flexible Models of Organizational Design; Implementing a Change Process; Organizational Design.

Further Readings

Hinings, C. R. and R. Greenwood. *The Dynamics of Strategic Change.* Oxford, UK: Basil Blackwood, 1988.

Jick, T. and M. Peiperl. *Managing Change: Cases and Concepts.* New York: McGraw-Hill, 2003.

Jones, R., N. Jimmieson, and A. Griffiths. "The Impact of Organizational Culture and Reshaping Capabilities on Change Implementation Success: The Mediating Role of Readiness for Change." *Journal of Management Studies*, v.42/2 (2005).

Slack, T. and C. R. Hinings. "Understanding Change in National Sport Organizations: An Integration of Theoretical Perspectives." *Journal of Sport Management*, v.6 (1992).

Slack, T. and M. Parent. *Understanding Sport Organizations: The Application of Organization Theory.* Champaign, IL: Human Kinetics, 2006.

Emergencies: Athletes/Fans/Volunteers

Sporting events pose a risk of injury to all those involved. Specifically, athletes (participants), spectators, and volunteer workers may be susceptible to an increased risk of harm. Whether an individual is participating in the sport activity, is a spectator at an event, or is volunteering as an event staff member, the risk of injury can be significant. As such, organizations that sponsor sporting events have a legal obligation to provide emergency care (competent medical assistance) to injured parties, or summon such assistance in a timely fashion. Emergency care has been defined as "the provision of medical assistance to an injured person in an urgent, immediate, or unexpected circumstance." Additionally, emergency care includes forecasting emergencies that are likely to occur so that the organization can fulfill its legal obligations for emergency preparedness.

Elements of Emergency Care

Whether a sport organization is emergency planning for participants, spectators, or volunteers, the organization must consider the four elements of emergency care: emergency planning, appropriate personnel and injury assessment, adequate certifications and equipment, and implementing emergency procedures. First, the organization must participate in emergency planning, which is attempting to identify foreseeable emergencies before they occur. While not all emergencies can be forecast, emergency planning requires organizations to anticipate events that have a reasonable likelihood of occurring.

Common foreseeable emergencies for athletes, fans, or volunteers could include medical emergencies such as heat exhaustion or cardiac arrest, as well as facility-related risks, such as fire or weather emergencies. Further, organizations should forecast emergencies stemming from crowd management situations. Once foreseeable emergencies are identified, emergency planning requires the organization to develop an emergency response plan according to the needs of each individual scenario. General planning is insufficient, and will likely result in poor handling of the emergency by organization personnel. Each forecast emergency situation requires a specific emergency response plan.

Second, an organization must consider appropriate personnel and injury assessment; appropriate first responders must be determined for any given emergency. Responders must be designated based on their ability to assess injury and implement proper treatment measures. Further, responders must follow a chain of command, and know who is specifically responsible for summoning emergency personnel and maintaining crowd control. In addition to assisting the victim, identified responders must follow the chain of command determined for the specific emergency, maintaining control and order until the situation is resolved. Typically, each forecast emergency will be assigned multiple responders, each with specific responsibilities, to ensure that the emergency is handled as effectively and efficiently as possible.

The third element of emergency care requires organizations to ensure that responders have adequate certifications and equipment. Although many injuries to participants, spectators, or volunteers require professional emergency medical assistance, the responder (identified in the second phase) must care for the injured individual until such emergency personnel arrive. Providing this interim care is most successful when the responder is at least certified in basic first aid and CPR, and able to use an automated external defibrillator (AED). Beyond certifications, all organizations should ensure that responders have quick access to adequate medical equipment, such as a first-aid kit, slings, splints, and Ace wraps.

Most importantly, organizations should consider having an AED available. While there is no current legal mandate requiring AEDs in all facilities offering sport participation opportunities, some states have adopted legislation that mandates AEDs in school buildings, as well as in fitness clubs. Specifically, Colorado, Florida, Georgia, Illinois, Maryland, Nevada, New York, Ohio, Pennsylvania, and South Carolina require some schools to have AEDs on the premises, although the extent to which AEDs are required varies. Regarding fitness facilities, Arkansas, California, Illinois, Indiana, Louisiana, Massachusetts, Michigan, New York, New Jersey, Oregon, Rhode Island, and the District of Columbia require AEDs. All sport organizations must be aware of the statutory re-

States are beginning to require that schools and fitness centers have automated external defibrillators like this one.

quirements within their state, so as to be adequately equipped for an emergency.

Lastly, organizations must consider implementing the emergency procedures. Emergency planning is only successful in limiting organization liability if the plans are properly executed. Proper implementation includes distributing the emergency plans and training staff on how each of the specific plans should be executed. An organization must never assume that plans will be administered correctly absent specific training. Further, plans must be accessible to employees. Distribution of emergency plans in employee training materials can work, as can uploading copies of the plans to an organization Website. This electronic method also allows plans to be quickly revised or replaced, should circumstances warrant. Finally, evaluation and potential revision of the emergency plans is essential to the implementation phase. Emergency plans cannot remain stagnant; they must evolve as an organization does. Any significant change in human or financial resources should result in a re-evaluation of emergency plan documents.

Conclusion

As noted, emergency planning must be done specifically for common foreseeable emergencies that may be encountered by athletes, fans, and volunteers. In addition, certain types of sport organizations must be aware of activity- or facility-specific risks that may occur, and any additional legal duties that may result. For example, aquatic facilities are specifically regulated by each state. Organizations sponsoring aquatic programming must be aware of the proper state regulatory codes that indicate what facilities must maintain regarding safety equipment, personnel, and certifications. Organizations that provide participation opportunities for special populations such as children, seniors, and disabled individuals may have heightened responsibilities regarding emergency planning.

Kristi Schoepfer
Winthrop University

See Also: Acts of God; Assessing Event Risk; Contingency Planning; Control for Safety of Fans/Athletes/Volunteers; Crisis Management; Crowd Management/Control; Event Risk Management Process; Insurance Against Risks; Legal Considerations in Sport; Medical Safety; Murphy's Law; Negligence; Officials, Legal Responsibilities; Risk Management; Securing Sports Events.

Further Readings

Cotton, Doyice J. and John T. Wolohan. *Law for Recreation and Sport Managers.* Dubuque, IA: Kendall Hunt, 2010.

McGregor, Ian and Joseph MacDonald. *Risk Management Manual for Sport and Recreation Organizations.* Corvallis, OR: NIRSA, 2000.

Schoepfer, Kristi L. "Emergency Care." In Doyice J. Cotton and John Wolohan, eds., *Law for Recreation and Sport Managers.* Dubuque, IA: Kendall Hunt, 2010.

Employee Benefits

Employee benefits (also called fringe benefits, perquisites, or perks) refer to nonwage compensation provided to employees in addition to their normal wages or salaries.

These benefits are designed to promote economic stability and enhance living standards by providing specific services. Historically, employee benefits were initiated by the government to ensure U.S. companies provided economic security for their workers. As organizations became more concerned for the general well-being of their employees and realized the advantages these programs could bring, firms began to offer a variety of voluntary employment-based benefit programs.

There are two basic types of employee benefits: voluntary benefits and mandatory benefits. Many employment-based benefits (i.e., retirement plans and health insurance) are provided voluntarily by businesses. The government supports these voluntary employment-based benefits by granting favorable tax treatment both to the employers that sponsor them and to the workers who receive them. Certain other benefits, including Social Security, unemployment insurance, worker's compensation, and family and medical leave, are mandatory under federal or state law.

Some of the benefits organizations now offer include housing (employer-provided or employer-paid), pensions, health insurance, profit sharing, funding of education, miscellaneous employee discounts, wellness programs, and other specialized benefits. It is common within the sport industry to see employees receive complimentary tickets to athletic events, access to premier events, opportunities to network with elite athletes, clothing stipends, and athletic equipment allotments. Coaches within intercollegiate athletics are also afforded considerable benefits. At the NCAA Division I level, head coach positions are sometimes associated with complimentary cars, apparel endorsements, country club memberships, or additional opportunities to generate income—such as offering youth summer camps or hosting local television/radio shows. These additional sources of revenue lower the base salary for head coaches and can provide ways to supplement assistant coaches' salaries.

Oftentimes employees may not wish to receive all the benefits that are offered to them by the organizations. To ensure employees do not have to incur the costs of unwanted benefits, employers have implemented cafeteria-style benefit packages. This allows employees to select the mix of benefits that they prefer without increasing cost for the individual and the organization. In most cases, these plan are funded by both the employees and the employer.

Professional Sports

One area within the sport industry where employee benefits become an important issue is in professional sports. An inevitable reality of being a professional athlete is that the physical demands necessitate constant turnover. Whether it is through injury, competition, or aging players leaving on their own terms, the professional sports world continues to churn active players into former players at an extraordinary rate. This is made evident if we consider that almost 425 players on active NFL rosters in 2010 will be out of the league by the start of the 2011 season. Consequently, professional athletes have become more adamant that the league they play for offers them some sort of financial security once their active playing time has ended.

Each professional league typically has a players union that lobbies on behalf of the players to ensure athletes are justly compensated for their service. For example, the NFL Players Association was instrumental in reaching an agreement in 2006 with the league office that increased the benefits for retired and current players. The new agreement ensured former players would receive nearly $60 million a year in retirement benefits. Specifically, this deal increased costs approximately $120 million per year, which, in turn, increased the annual cost of NFL players benefits to $700 million per year.

Other benefits that are now provided to ensure economic stability and an increased living standard for players include the NFL Player Care Foundation and the "88 Plan" for dementia benefits. The NFL Player Care Foundation was started in 2007 and primarily conducts medical research and national health screenings for NFL alumni. What is unique about the foundation is that it provides monetary support for former players who are experiencing economic hardships. This allows these players to receive joint replacement surgery, spine treatment, or neurological care that they would not be able to afford otherwise. The "88 Plan" grants retired players up to $88,000 per year for medical care related to dementia. This program is the first of its kind and demonstrates the NFL's renewed commitment to supporting its players after their playing careers have ended.

Conclusion

When implemented correctly and with the employee's best interest in mind, these benefit packages not only enhance the lives of employees, but can also make an organization more attractive to position applicants, thus creating a competitive advantage for the organization in the marketplace.

E. Nicole Melton
Texas A&M University

See Also: Compensation; Employee Development; Employee Relations; Wage and Human Capital.

Further Readings

Ebri.org. "Education." http://www.ebri.org/education/?fa=cts (Accessed June 2010).
Ebri.org. "FAQs About Benefits." http://www.ebri.org/publications/benfaq/index.cfm?fa=overfaq (Accessed June 2010).
Rynes, S. L. and A. E. Barber. "Applicant Attraction Strategies: An Organizational Perspective." *Academy of Management Review*, v.15/2 (1990).

Employee Development

Managerial practice indicates that human resources are the most valuable resource in an organization. To that end, organizations have discovered the value of employee development and have created human resource departments to focus on that outcome. There are a myriad of benefits for an organization to place significance on the development of the employee and numerous ways to accomplish this development. Effects like job satisfaction, employee morale, and production help the organization reach for success. Orientation, training, and motivation are some of the ways in which the development can take place.

The process of employee development begins in the hiring and staffing stage. One Major League Baseball organization uses interest inventories and personality assessment tools to understand its future employees. Not only does it use the information in hiring, the organization uses these tests to place the employee in the right setting for his or her success. Further, the information from these tests is used in the development process. The supervisor and human relations department work in tandem to ensure the communication with the employee is efficient and effective.

Benefits

Organizations that show a concern for the employee's professional development and provide opportunities for the employee to grow tend to have a workforce that displays discretionary effort. A supportive learning environment along with training and development can lead to improved employee satisfaction, retention, and motivation. Increased job satisfaction helps to improve morale among employees and volunteers. High satisfaction and morale will lead to less job turnover of employees and volunteers. (We talk of volunteers in this section because numerous sport organizations have and deal with volunteer workers.) As turnover is reduced, an organization is able to improve competencies in how things are completed and the ways in which they are completed.

Effective training and development benefits the individual, other employees, volunteers, and managers. The training should help in the alignment of the employee with the strategic direction of the sport organization. Relationships among the workforce should improve as they work together and pull in the same direction. Organizational success needs to increase the morale and motivation among the employees.

Tools

Once an employee has been hired, he or she needs to be assimilated into the organization. A good orientation is vital for an employee to get started in the right direction as he or she begins their new position. There should be a formal and informal process to the orientation. The formal process should include things like the history, the mission, policies, procedures, benefits, job expectations, and other important information. The informal process should include things like a tour of the facility, introduction to other employees, discussions about the job, creating a positive impression, and other information to help the new employee feel comfortable. Assigning a mentor can be an excellent way for an employee to get acquainted with the job and organization. However, following up with the new employee is imperative for a successful orientation. It may even take a few months for the new hire to be completely acclimated.

After the orientation portion has been addressed, the next step is to ensure the employee is properly trained for his or her job. The employee needs to have the knowledge, skills, and abilities or competencies to be successful. Training should occur when an individual begins a new position; this could be as a new hire or after a promotion or transfer of an existing employee. Training could include the development of new attitudes or new behaviors within the organization. For instance, when a professional baseball team that has underachieved hires a new general manager, there will be changes requiring new attitudes or new behaviors.

Feedback is necessary for an individual to continue his or her improvement and reduce uncertainty as a member of the organization. One way this feedback can take place is through performance appraisals. The appraisal can be used as a developmental tool or an evaluative tool. As a developmental tool the focus is on the employee and his or her growth as a worker for the company. This can even include a focus on employee career development and advancement. If the appraisal is used as an evaluative tool, the focus will be geared toward his or her performance, achieving goals, and accomplishing tasks. Giving out feedback needs to occur frequently. If the feedback is given out yearly, then performance improvements can be expected yearly. Feedback should be received by an employee from his or her supervisor, peers, staff, coworkers, and clients or customers.

The organization benefits from feedback because it are able to identify performance successes and needs. It will reduce its risk of discrimination if managers are giving feedback to all of their employees throughout the process. Customer service should improve as feedback is received from the consumer. Through this feedback, the organization will be equipped to assess areas within the organization and current employees that need further training.

Future

An area for employee development that needs to be examined is emotional intelligence. Emotional intelligence is recognizing the importance of emotions within the workplace and how they impact decision making, people, and customers. Daniel Goldman, an expert on emotional intelligence, found that emotional intelligence is a better predictor of success than IQ. It is an attachment between feelings and the thinking process. Developing this area within your employees and organization could lead to an increased depth and success in the sport arena.

Organizations that are constantly looking for ways to improve and are structured for that learning are called learning organizations. Administration, management, and employees of these organizations are constantly and purposely learning new ways to enhance the organization and surpass their goals. This can occur through adopting new technologies, improving the products, improving the processes, or improving the work environment. Learning organizations should provide a supportive learning environment that can lead to employee satisfaction.

Paul Keiper
Texas A&M University

See Also: Flexible Models of Organizational Design; Organizational Design; Wage and Human Capital.

Further Readings

Caruth, D., G. Caruth, and S. Pane Haden. "Getting Off to a Good START." *Industrial Management,* v.52/2 (2010).

Linderbaum, B. A. and P. E. Levy. "The Development and Validation of the Feedback Orientation Scale (FOS)." *Journal of Management,* v.36/6 (2010).

Lussier, R. N. and D. C. Kimball. *Applied Sport Management Skills.* Champaign, IL: Human Kinetics, 2009.

Slack, T. and M. M. Parent. *Understanding Sport Organizations: The Application of Organization Theory.* Champaign, IL: Human Kinetics, 2006.

Taylor, T., A. Doherty, and P. McGraw. *Managing People in Sport Organizations: A Strategic Human Resource Management Perspective.* Oxford, UK: Butterworth-Heinemann, 2008.

Employee Relations

Employee relations refers to employer–employee relationships that contribute to satisfactory productivity, motivation, and morale. Employee relations is concerned with preventing and resolving problems involving individuals that arise out of or affect work situations. Supervisors are given advice on how to correct poor performance and employee misconduct.

On the other hand, employees are given information on how to promote a better understanding of the company's goals and policies. Advice is given to employees about applicable regulations, legislation, and bargaining agreements.

The unitary theory proposes that the employment relationship is a harmonious relationship between employer and employee in order to achieve performance. The theory emphasizes employers and employees working together. In contrast, pluralism recognizes there are conflicts between employers and employees. Thus, it is necessary to develop procedures to resolve those conflicts. System theory suggests the world of employment is a system, which suits the requirements of the society at that time.

The formal contract that employees may have with their employers covers the tangible aspects of work includes working hours and working conditions. Those tangible aspects form an area that was traditionally negotiated with the trade union. The psychological contract goes beyond the tangible contract and considers the expectations of the relationship that employee and employers have of one another.

The individual employee is usually in a weaker position than the prospective employer. Employers are free to choose the employee, and it is rare for employees to choose different employers. Also, by accepting an offer of employment, the employee works under the authority of an employer.

Employees seek the best possible available package of monetary and nonmonetary employment conditions. The monetary aspects include wage, hours of work, paid holidays, pension scheme, paid sick leave, bonus, double pay, childcare facilities, and flexible working arrangements. The nonmonetary aspects include employment security, working environment, promotion, training, respect, job satisfaction, and fair treatment.

Some employees attempt to enhance their interest through professional associations, staff associations, and trade unions by presenting a collective front to their employers. In very small companies, a close relationship exists between employers and employees. As the size of organization grows, staff representatives are needed to negotiate with the employers. Trade unions are the best known form of employee representative organization. They are formed to promote the interests of employees against employers.

Scholars have proposed that collective bargaining is not only an employee relations process for determining employment conditions but also a system of industrial governance in which unions and employers jointly reach decisions concerning the employment relationship. Collective bargaining is a problem-solving mechanism but can only take place if employees are organized and if the employer is prepared to recognize the trade union for collective bargaining purposes.

The ability to identify which employee relations policies are suitable and which are unsuitable for sports organizations is an important skill for the employee relations professional to develop. External and internal factors should be taken into consideration in drafting employee relations policies and then implementing them. External factors include existing and future legislative constraints, and policies in the similar sports organizations. Internal factors include business strategies and organizational cultures.

If agreements cannot be reached in the collective bargaining process and negotiations break down, there are a number of choices available to the employers and employees. The matter can be referred to the dispute procedure, in which attempts may be made to resolve the dispute. Arbitration, mediation, and third-party intervention are the other methods.

In order to improve employee relations, employee participation, involvement, and engagement are encouraged. Employee participation is sharing some degree of power in relation to organizational decision making. Employee involvement through making of suggestions offers employees limited influence over decision making. Employee engagement is an employee's involvement with, commitment to, and satisfaction with work. This integrates the classic constructs of job satisfaction and organizational commitment.

Employees are one of the important stakeholders of an organization because, for example, more employee commitment will lead to improved performance. Employees are often better informed about their work tasks and processes than their managers. Employee participation, involvement, and engagement provide employees with greater intrinsic rewards from work. The rewards will in turn increase job satisfaction and enhance employee motivation to achieve new goals.

Participative decision making is likely to lead to better-quality management decisions, so that empowerment represents a win-win situation with gains available to both employers, as increased working efficiency, and to employees, as job satisfaction.

Tai Ming Wut
Hong Kong Polytechnic University

See Also: Dispute Resolution/Arbitration; Employee Benefits; Employee Development; Labor Law; Labor Stability; Wage and Human Capital.

Further Readings

Gennard, John and Graham Judge. *Employee Relations*. London: The Chartered Institute of Personnel and Development, 2005.

Hollinshead, Graham, Peter Nicholls, and Stephanie Tailby. *Employee Relations*. Upper Saddle River, NJ: Prentice Hall, 2003.

Lewis, Philip, Adrian Thornhill, and Mark Saunders. *Employee Relations*. London: Financial Times/Prentice Hall, 2003.

Wilkinson, A. "Employment." In T. Redman and A. Wilkinson, *Contemporary Human Resources Management: Text and Cases*. London: Financial Times/Prentice Hall, 2001.

Williams, Steve and Derek Adam-Smith. *Contemporary Employment Relations*. Oxford, UK: Oxford University Press, 2010.

Endorsement

Product endorsements have been an integral part of marketing plans since the creation of advertising. Endorsements in sport are thought to date as far back as the ancient Olympic Games. Competitors from Greek city-states were often provided with free housing, meals, and training support in preparation for the games and as compensation for athletic performances. The return of successful athletes to their hometowns may have also brought many opportunities to associate with local business people and their wares. Athletes today are often used to influence the attitudes of consumers. In 1918, early in the modern era of athlete endorsements, a basketball player named Chuck Taylor helped popularize Converse shoes for use in basketball. The popularity of the shoes led to their appearance in the 1936 Olympics, and they are still being manufactured today. The true explosion of athlete endorsements came during the 1950s and 1960s, primarily through tennis and golf, and ostensibly because of television. Spectators and consumers could easily identify athletes they had seen on television and associate them with products.

Star power sells in today's sport industry. Corporations spend more than $12 billion on multiyear athlete endorsements, with more than $1.6 billion committed by Nike alone. Some professional athletes make more money annually from endorsement deals than from their salaries. In 2006, the top 10 professional athletes who endorse products earned over $220 million all together. Leading the way was Tiger Woods, who earned over $85 million from endorsement deals alone in 2006 and had multi-year endorsement contracts of $105 million and $40 million with Nike and Buick, respectively. Endorsement opportunities may also continue past the end of an athlete's playing career.

Celebrities in Advertising

The use of sport celebrities in advertising campaigns is an important aspect in marketing to a target market of sport fans. Sports celebrities are widely used in product advertising to drive sales by improving consumer product recall and positively influencing their brand choice behavior. Such endorsements enhance consumer recognition and image awareness of brands the athletes represent.

Celebrity endorsements have enormous financial implications, and the investments have been getting bigger. For example, in 1984 National Basketball Association (NBA) star Michael Jordan signed a five-year, $2.5 million contract with Nike. Then, in 2003, Nike signed high school student (and future NBA star) LeBron James to a $90 million, multi-year deal. That fact that LeBron had never played in a National Basketball Association game was not an issue; it was about perception and LeBron's anticipated ability to market the Nike brand.

American society tends to place elite athletes upon a social pedestal, and many consumers thus buy products that are associated with their favorite celebrity athlete in order to feel a connection to that athlete or sports team. An effective endorser inspires fans to desire to be like them. The "be like Mike" slogan used by Gatorade in 1991, featuring playful impressions of Michael Jordan sticking his tongue out, encouraged millions to play like Jordan. Michael Phelps noted that this campaign had inspired him to greatness as a youngster.

Scholars have identified traits of successful athlete endorsers, such as being physically attractive and having a perceived expertise and trustworthiness, exciting personalities, accepted public images, and high creditability. Some argue that trustworthiness is the most important trait because it gives a consumer confidence in the endorser's ability to provide information about a product in an objective and honest manner.

Researchers have found that consumers may be less likely to buy a product linked to someone who has had negative connotations associated with his or her persona. A recent example of this is golfer Tiger Woods, who lost an estimated $22 million in endorsement deals after rumors of his extramarital affairs were made public.

Through endorsements, products may become closely tied to an athlete's public image, and athletes can be negatively affected by association with inappropriate products. More specifically, athletes who associate their names with products that the public perceives as unhealthy may experience a significant negative impact on their image. Endorsements of tobacco or alcohol, for example, may have a negative effect on an endorser's image. One study found that someone who endorsed chewing tobacco had a significantly lower evaluation among those surveyed than a person who endorsed orange juice. The study also found that the negative impact was greater for an athlete versus a nonathlete endorser. Athletic endorsers do better when focusing on products with generic or inoffensive images. An example of such product endorsements would be Michael Jordan and tennis shoes or Kobe Bryant and the Sprite beverage.

Endorsements are believed to help companies capture the attention of consumers, change or reinforce brand image, reinforce brand name, provide message credibility, and increase brand loyalty; they do not necessarily guarantee a company's success. For example, Interbrand, the world's leading brand consultancy, lists the top global brands annually. In 2009, the top 10 included Intel, Google, Microsoft, Nokia, and Coca-Cola, none of which used a celebrity endorser.

There has been some excessive saturation of athletes associated with signature products. While Nike stock did rise by 75 percent on the day it was announced that the company had signed LeBron James, research has shown that this is not the norm for all companies. A 2008 study suggested that a company's returns from signing a celebrity endorser are comparable to the cost of obtaining the endorsement; this raises the question of whether a company can be just as successful without relying on celebrity endorsers.

Branding and Effectiveness

The scholar Philip Kotler defines a brand as "a name, term, sign, symbol, or design, or combination of them which is intended to identify the goods and services of one seller or group of sellers and to differentiate them from those of competitors." In essence, a brand is represented as an image that has been developed and that exists in the minds of consumers. Therefore, since a celebrity endorser is essentially a bundle of meanings that combine to form an overall image, a celebrity endorser can also be considered a brand. For example, Nike produced the first pair of Air Jordan basketball shoes. Now, "Jordan" is a brand in itself and even hires other celebrities to endorse the brand. For example, the boxer Roy Jones was one of the Jordan brand's first additional celebrity endorsers; this afforded the Jordan label the opportunity to gain exposure outside the sport of basketball.

Not all celebrity endorsements end in success. In the case of scandals, especially those that involve illegal or unethical acts, bring in multiple parties over a sustained period of time, and/or whose impact affects the integrity of the sport with which a celebrity is associated, the endorser has the potential to harm the reputation of the product he or she endorses. Some scholars believe that a onetime violation by an admired sports celebrity will carry less impact with the consumer than repeated illegal or unethical events. For example, some celebrities are able to recover by speaking out against undesirable behaviors that he or she may have been involved with at one point in time. However, others who repeat illegal and unethical behaviors may permanently damage their reputations, hindering them from ever being the face of a product line again. Other researchers argue that incidents involving "celebrities gone bad" are part of the fun for consumers; they question whether scandals truly do serious damage to consumer views of the endorsed brand.

Advertisements and Sponsorship

Advertisement and sponsorship are two different promotional procedures, although they have many common aspects in theory and practice. The common underlying objective of each is to influence consumer rate of consumption and interaction with the product. According to a theoretical model known as AIDA (which stands for attention, interest, desire, and action), consumers receive information from commercials; formulate or renew interest based on previous experience, individual attitude, and personal beliefs; develop desire by filtering the information and formulating favorable dispositions; and take action through cognitive, affective, and behavioral involvement with a brand.

Advertising plays a key role in generating and increasing awareness of a brand, communicating information about the brand, developing or changing the brand image or personality, associating a brand with feelings and emotions, creating reference groups, and causing behavioral action. Without the effects of sponsorships and advertising, there would be no need for celebrity athletes to endorse goods or products. This means that an entire segment of the sport industry would not even exist. Television commercials during athletic events are among the most common forms of advertising. Sports have a wide audience, as almost 75 percent of Americans watch televised sports at least once a week. Corporations have recognized this and are thus willing to advertise during TV programs that appeal to their target audiences.

Conclusion

To maximize persuasive communication in advertisements, practitioners need to recognize the importance of a good fit between celebrity endorsers and endorsed products. Credibility, attractiveness, and trustworthiness are especially important factors that should be considered when selecting celebrity athlete endorsers. Celebrity endorsers play a key role in generating and increasing awareness of a brand. They are employed to help develop the brand's image and in some cases change the image of a brand; at best, associating their personality with a brand may arouse feelings, emotions, and a sense of attachment in consumers.

Aaron Livingston
West Virginia University
Kerry Grant
Grambling State University

See Also: Athletes as Sponsors; Brand Image; Branding; Corporate Criteria for Sponsor Evaluation; Corporate Sponsorship Philosophy; Endorser Effectiveness; Image; Misbehavior by Athletes.

Further Readings

Behr, A. and A. Beeler-Norrholm. "Fame, Fortune, and the Occasional Branding Misstep: When Good Celebrities Go Bad." *Intellectual Property & Technology Law Journal,* v.18 (2006).

Bush, A. F., C. A. Martin, and V. D. Bush. "Sports Celebrity Influence on the Behavioral Intentions of Generation Y." *Journal of Advertising Research,* v.44 (2004).

Carlson, B. D. and D. T. Donavan. "Concerning the Effect of Athlete Endorsements on Brand and Team-Related Intentions." *Sport Marketing Quarterly,* v.17 (2008).

Cianfrone, B. A. and J. J. Zhang. "Differential Effects of Television Commercials, Athlete Endorsements and Venue Signage During a Televised Action Sports Event." *Journal of Sport Management,* v.20 (2006).

Horrow, R. "Marketing and Representing the Professional Athlete." http://www.pbfn.org/about/ezine/june2005/art5.htm (Accessed April 2007).

Hughes, S. and M. Shank. "Defining Scandal in Sports: Media and Corporate Sponsor Perspectives." *Sport Marketing Quarterly,* v.14/4 (2005).

Keller, K. L. *Strategic Brand Management: Building, Measuring, and Managing Brand Equity.* Upper Saddle River, NJ: Prentice-Hall, 1998.

Lyons, R. and E. N. Jackson. "Factors That Influence African-American Gen-Xers to Purchase Nikes." *Sport Marketing Quarterly,* v.10/2 (2001).

Shuart, J. "Heroes in Sport: Assessing Celebrity Endorser Effectiveness." *International Journal of Sport Marketing and Sponsorship,* v.8/2 (2007).

Stotlar, D. K. "Sponsorship Evaluation: Moving From Theory to Practice." *Sport Marketing Quarterly,* v.13/1 (2004).

Till, B. "Managing Athlete Endorser Image: The Effect of Endorsed Product." *Sport Marketing Quarterly,* v.10/1 (2001).

Endorser Effectiveness

Present-day consumers are bombarded by advertising; in fact, it is estimated the average consumer is exposed to 600–1,500 advertising messages per day from a variety of media sources such as television, radio, billboards, new media, etc. Such advertising "clutter" makes it very difficult for a company to effectively inform consumers about its product or service. Athlete endorsers are used as a strategy to cut through this advertising clutter and make the product or service stand out among competing brands. Because of sport's ubiquitous appeal, successful athletes garner incredible media attention. As such, they are among the most widely recognized celebrities, often surpassing movie stars, models, business leaders, politicians, and musicians in their recognition and appeal. Thus, companies hope coupling their products and services with a successful athlete will enable them to stand out in a crowded marketplace and the athlete's characteristics will "rub off" onto their product or service. Athlete endorsers have also been found to assist in the establishment of distinct brand personalities.

In 1905, Honus Wagner became one of the first athlete endorsers when he contracted with the Hillerich & Bradsby Company, makers of the Louisville Slugger brand, to sign a bat, the Honus Wagner. The bat was a top seller for years and an example of a sport star using his successful image to assist companies in selling their products. Athlete endorsements occur when corporate clients selling goods and services contract with successful athletes in an attempt to bolster their sales. The results of studies regarding the effectiveness of athlete endorsers on actual purchasing behavior are equivocal, yet companies spend millions to use athletes as their spokespeople. Throughout the years, the practice has proliferated to such an extent that successful athletes often earn much more money through endorsements than they do through their playing contracts or tournament winnings. Female athletes are also beginning to cash in on the endorsement game. Although far fewer female athletes are chosen as endorsers, and they typically do not garner the same amount of endorsement money as their male counterparts, several female athletes presently earn millions of dollars in endorsement revenue.

The use of athlete endorsers as a marketing strategy is quite common today, but it does pose risks. Athlete endorsers involved in crimes or public controversies can result in negative images for their sponsoring companies; athletes often get injured, which takes them out of the spotlight; and the most well-recognized athletes often endorse multiple products, which can produce confusion among consumers.

Theories of Endorser Effectiveness

Several theories have been forwarded to predict and explain the effectiveness of celebrity endorsers. The source attractiveness model contends that the effectiveness of the message relayed by the celebrity endorser will depend on his or her likeability, familiarity, and similarity as perceived by the consumer. The more the endorser embodies these characteristics, the more attractive the endorser to the consumer and the greater his or her persuasive powers. The source credibility model suggests the effectiveness of the endorser will be dependent upon his or her credibility with the intended audience. The source of such credibility is typically thought to stem from the endorser's attractiveness, expertise, or trustworthiness. The more credible the source in the eyes of the consumer, the more effective he or she will be in selling the product or service. The meaning transfer model suggests the endorser's multidimensional image, that is, the entire cultural image personified by the endorser, can be transferred to the product or service through advertisements. Thus, different endorsers embody different images, and successful endorsements occur when the endorser's persona is transferred onto the product or service.

One of the most widely used theories to predict and explain endorser effectiveness is the match-up hypothesis. It suggests endorsers will be most effective when there is a "fit" between them and the products or services they endorse. Thus, an attractive endorser would be more effective in selling products or services related to attractiveness (e.g. make-up, perfume/cologne) than those not related to attractiveness. Similarly, an endorser considered an expert in a certain area (e.g., Bill Gates and business) should be more effective selling products or services related to that area than a merely attractive endorser. Thus, Tiger Woods should be a more

Tiger Woods was the highest earner among athlete endorsers in 2009, earning $92 million from endorsements.

effective endorser for Nike golf products than he is for Buick automobiles because there is a more natural "fit" between him and golf.

However, considering that endorsers embody entire personas, nonsport products and services can also be effectively matched with athletes. Sport celebrities become "brands" themselves and portray a certain set of qualities. Thus, companies should try to find athletes who possess the same product attributes they hope to highlight in their own products or services. For example, Canon coupled with Maria Sharapova to endorse its PowerShot digital camera to highlight the camera's qualities of being powerful, precise, and stylish—all qualities Sharapova also possesses. Companies that do all they can to leverage or create the fit between the athlete's brand

image and the image they hope to portray in their product will be the most successful.

Rating systems of endorsers have also been developed to determine who might be the most effective choices among celebrities. For example, the Q score was developed in 1963 and identifies the familiarity of the celebrity endorser as well as his or her likeability among those consumers who do recognize the endorser. A more recently devised rating method, the Davie-Brown index (DBI), was developed in 2006. It purports to be more thorough in its analysis of endorser effectiveness as it has participants rate celebrities on eight key aspects: appeal, notice, trendsetter, influence, trust, spokespersonability, aspiration, and awareness. In April 2009, Tiger Woods and David Beckham were the top ranked athletes on the DBI list.

Cost

In order to link themselves with athletes, companies typically must spend a great deal of money. In fact, the cost of endorsement deals has skyrocketed in recent decades. Consider, for example, that in 1954 Arnold Palmer signed a three-year endorsement deal with Wilson Sporting Goods that paid him $5,000 per year. Compare that to Tiger Woods, the highest earner among athlete endorsers, who in 2009 earned $92 million in endorsement money alone. It is estimated that companies spend nearly $1 billion a year on athlete endorsements.

Before Tiger Woods, Michael Jordan was considered the king of athlete endorsements, most notably for his endorsement deal with Nike. In 1985, he signed a deal with Nike to endorse a new brand of shoes, Air Jordans. That deal provided Jordan $2.5 million for five years plus royalties. Additionally, the deal spurred what has been termed the "Sneaker Wars," a fight among athletic shoe companies to gain and keep market shares. The competition has been particularly fierce between Nike and Reebok, although other brands of shoes have become involved. At the height of the competition for market share, companies clamored for the most talented athletes to endorse their shoes. For example, before becoming the first draft pick in the National Basketball Association (NBA) in 2003, LeBron James signed a seven-year shoe endorsement contract with Nike for $90 million. Reebok signed the talented

Chinese basketball player Yao Ming to a $70 million endorsement deal in an attempt to better capture a global market share. And although Jordan is retired, he still earns $40 million per year in endorsement income.

However, high-paid athlete endorsement deals are not limited to shoes or other athletic products. Athletes endorse all types of products and services from underwear and cologne to consulting agencies and financial services. As such, many athletes earn more money through their endorsements than they do through their contracts or event prize money. Tiger Woods's $92 million in endorsement earnings in 2009 was nearly 12 times the amount he earned through his tournament winnings. Phil Mickelson was second in endorsement earnings in 2009 with $46.6 million, which is more than seven times the amount he earned playing in golf tournaments. LeBron James ($28 million, NBA), Dale Earnhardt, Jr. ($22 million, NASCAR), Jeff Gordon ($15 million, NASCAR), Shaquille O'Neil ($15 million, NBA), Peyton Manning ($13 million, National Football League [NFL]), Dwyane Wade ($12 million, NBA), Dwight Howard ($12 million, NBA), and Jim Furyk ($11 million, Professional Golf Association) round out the top 10 paid U.S. athletes relative to endorsement contracts. The highest-earning international athletes are soccer player David Beckham, Formula 1 racecar driver Kimi Raikkonen, and boxer Manny Pacquio Pacquiao. Athletes in sports with the greatest international appeal (e.g., golf, tennis, Formula 1 racing, soccer, and basketball) tend to have more opportunities for endorsement earnings as they can reach a much larger market than those playing a sport that has a mainly "American" appeal, such as American football.

Female athletes are also beginning to cash in on endorsement deals, although far fewer female athletes obtain endorsement deals and those who do typically earn less than their most popular male athlete counterparts. In 2000, Venus Williams signed the highest endorsement deal for a female athlete up to that point, a reported $40 million, five-year deal. However, the top-paid female athletes do not earn nearly as much as their male counterparts. As of 2008, Maria Sharapova was the highest-paid female athlete, earning $26 million in endorsements and tennis prize money.

Rounding out the top 10 paid female athletes in endorsements and prize money are: Serena Williams ($14 million, tennis); Venus Williams ($13 million, tennis); Justine Henin ($12.5 million, tennis); Michelle Wie ($12 million, golf); Annika Sorenstam ($11 million, golf); Lorena Ochoa ($10 million, golf); Danica Patrick ($8 million, Formula 1 racing); Ana Ivanovic ($6 million, tennis); and Paula Creamer ($6 million, golf). Noticeably absent from the list are any female athletes in team sports. Although the Women's National Basketball Association (WNBA) has been in existence for 13 years, its athletes do not garner the sort of endorsement attention that its NBA counterpart does. And, unlike their male counterparts, companies often choose female athletes for their sex appeal as much as for their athletic expertise.

Marketing campaigns relative to female athletes focus on sex appeal to a much greater extent than those designed for male athletes. Thus, oftentimes the most successful female athlete endorsers must also be physically attractive. As a result, the most athletically talented female athletes are not always chosen for endorsements. For example, in 2002, Anna Kournikova earned between $20 million and $40 million in endorsement money yet had never won a major tennis tournament. In contrast, Lindsay Davenport, the number one ranked player in the world and U.S. Open, Wimbledon, and Australian Open champion, earned far less money for endorsements than Kournikova.

Risks

The research relative to the impact of athlete endorsers on actual consumer purchases has been ambivalent. Most experts agree that athlete endorsers typically provide a positive image and aid in brand recall; however, that does not always translate into purchasing behavior. Often consumers do not believe the endorser actually uses the product. In fact, aspects of the product or service such as quality, price, and consumer experience with the brand typically have more impact on consumer purchases than the athlete endorser. Recent studies show that business leaders are the most persuasive celebrity endorsers, although athletes ranked second in persuasiveness. Athletes were ranked first with younger (i.e., age 18–24) consumers.

Beyond the equivocal research results relative to increased consumer purchases of athlete-endorsed products and services, athlete endorsers also pose several proven risks. For example, athletes who endorse multiple products run the risk of losing credibility and likeability and diminish the uniqueness and impact of each product association. Athletes are also more exposed to injury than other types of celebrity endorsers—such injuries can reduce performance, playing time, and visibility, which, in turn, diminishes the endorsement. Some athletes garner so much attention that they may overshadow the product or service they are endorsing. Perhaps the biggest risk posed by the athlete endorser is the chance that he or she may become involved in a controversy and create negative publicity for the company. Research indicates such situations can result in negative attitudes about the brand. However, studies also indicate companies can be negatively impacted when they choose to cancel the endorsement contracts of athletes involved in a controversy.

Thus, companies are left in precarious positions to determine whether to keep or drop athletes involved in some sort of public scandal. Often this decision will be determined by the nature of the scandal and/or the product/s the athlete endorses. For example, nearly all companies utilizing Michael Vick as an endorser canceled or suspended their contracts with the NFL quarterback when he pled guilty to illegal dogfighting. It is estimated that Vick lost $2 million to $3 million per year in endorsements when he lost deals with Rawlings, Nike, Upper Deck, and Donruss. Even the NFL itself suspended the sale of all Vick merchandise for a period of time.

After Olympic swimming sensation Michael Phelps was captured in a picture smoking marijuana at a party, Kellogg (makers of the cereal Kellogg's Corn Flakes) dropped him as an endorser, costing Phelps a reported $500,000. The company indicated his behavior was not consistent with the image they wanted to portray. However, while not condoning Phelps's behavior, Visa, Speedo, and Omega retained Phelps as an endorser.

Janet S. Fink
University of Connecticut

See Also: Athletes as Sponsors; Brand Image; Branding; Image; Marketing Through Sports; Misbehavior by Athletes; Positioning.

Further Readings

Charbonneau, J. and R. Garland. "Celebrity or Athlete? New Zealand Advertising Practitioners Views on Their Use as Endorsers." *International Journal of Sports Marketing and Sponsorship*, v.7/1 (2005).

Fink, J. S., G. B. Cunningham, and L. J. Kensicki. "Using Athletes as Endorsers to Sell Women's Sport: Attractiveness vs. Expertise." *Journal of Sport Management*, v.18/4 (2004).

Freedman, J. "The 50 Highest Earning American Athletes." http://sportsillustrated.cnn.com/more/specials/fortunate50/2009 (Accessed November 2009).

Freedman, J. "The Top Earning Non-American Athletes." http://sportsillustrated.cnn.com/more/specials/fortunate50/2009/index.20.html (Accessed November 2009).

Gilbert, S. J. "Marketing Maria: Managing the Athlete Endorsement." http://hbswk.hbs.edu/item/5607.html (Accessed July 2009).

Kamins, M. A. "An Investigation Into the Match-up Hypothesis in Celebrity Advertising: When Beauty May Only Be Skin Deep." *Journal of Advertising*, v.19/1 (1990).

McCracken, Grant. "Who Is the Celebrity Endorser? Cultural Foundations of the Endorsement Process." *Journal of Consumer Research*, v.16/3 (1989).

Ohanian, R. "Construction and Validation of a Scale to Measure Celebrity Endorsers' Perceived Expertise, Trustworthiness, and Attractiveness." *Journal of Advertising Research*, v.19/3 (1990).

Till, B. D. and M. Busler. "The Match-Up Hypothesis: Physical Attractiveness, Expertise, and the Role of Fit on Brand Attitude, Purchase Intent, and Brand Beliefs." *Journal of Advertising*, v.29/3 (2000).

Till, B. D. and T. A. Shimp. "Endorsers in Advertising: The Case of Negative Celebrity Information." *Journal of Advertising*, v.27/1 (1998).

Entrepreneurship

Entrepreneurship involves the creation of new organizations outright or within existing organizations. This innovative activity is undertaken by entrepreneurs who see and understand customer needs, find and combine resources, develop innovative solutions, take risks, and strive to make a profit. The rates of entrepreneurial activity vary by local and national environment, industry, and other factors. Compared to the rest of the population, entrepreneurs tend to have a stronger need for achievement, higher risk-taking propensity, greater perseverance, more commitment to a task, bigger vision, higher creativity, and more tolerance for ambiguity. Individuals who want to become entrepreneurs also tend to have more positive attitudes toward risk and independence. Entrepreneurs keen to start high-potential projects often seek venture capital or angel funding to raise necessary capital. Serial entrepreneurs are individuals who start a number of entrepreneurial efforts over time.

At the firm level, corporate entrepreneurship is an effort by enterprises with large, established businesses to discover new opportunities. Entrepreneurial orientation describes an organization's ability to promote autonomy, innovativeness, proactiveness, competitive aggressiveness, and risk taking. There are many subspecialties within entrepreneurship, including international entrepreneurship, social entrepreneurship, and sports entrepreneurship.

Broadly defined, the field of sports entrepreneurship describes the study of how, by whom, and with what effects opportunities to create future goods and services are discovered, evaluated, and exploited within the sports industry. This entry provides an overview of entrepreneurs, new ventures, and corporate entrepreneurship and innovation in the sports industry.

The Sports Industry

There is preliminary evidence across entrepreneurship, sports management, and psychology literatures that athletes possess many of the desired qualities of entrepreneurs, including self-efficacy, self-leadership, persistence, fitness levels, and team skills. Self-efficacy describes individuals' beliefs about their ability to produce high levels of task performance and how they think about themselves. Highly self-efficacious individuals approach tasks as challenges, even under stressful situations, and treat failures as opportunities to acquire new knowledge/skills. Low self-efficacy individuals doubt their abilities, are unmotivated to pursue difficult tasks/activities and, facing failure, recover slowly/lose motivation. Sports psychology research demonstrates clear linkages between self-efficacy and sports success. Although athlete-entrepreneurs draw strength from past success, albeit in a different domain, this confidence may sow the seeds of failure and athletes may find that they need to work harder to be successful in business. Reputation effects may be fleeting, and self-efficacy can be task-specific. Self-leadership is a process of influencing oneself to establish the self-motivation and self-direction needed to perform a task. Self-leaders often employ self-dialog, project mental images of success that lead to performance improvements, and focus on "opportunity thinking" about the positive options rather than "obstacle thinking" about potentially insurmountable challenges. Another quality frequently attributed to both athletes and entrepreneurs is persistence. Research indicates that individuals who attain their goals are likely to stay motivated and continue to follow their entrepreneurial drive. Fourth, research has shown a link between an individual's fitness and various measures of entrepreneurial and business performance. Fifth, entrepreneurial ventures are most often the product of teams of two or more individuals who provide complementary resources. Athletes frequently develop team skills.

There are countless examples of athletes who pursued entrepreneurial careers, including retired gymnast/Olympic medalist Li Ning, whose namesake athletic footwear/apparel company outsells Nike and adidas in China. An example of a serial entrepreneur is Sally Edwards, a triathlete, runner, and ultrarunner who co-founded Fleet Feet, a specialty running store, in a Victorian-style house in Sacramento, California, when she was 28 years old. After expanding the franchise to 40 locations in 15 states, Sally sold Fleet Feet. She later started Yuba Shoe Sports Snowshoes, selling it three years later. After that, she founded Heart Zones, a fitness education company that teaches people how to use heart rate monitors to stay healthy.

Many athletes who transition to entrepreneurship establish new ventures in areas in which they have expertise. For example, former U.S. Olympic athletes Alan and Shayne Culpepper established Solepepper, a running store in Louisville, Colorado. Former gymnasts Valeri Liukin and Evgeny Marchenko run a successful gymnastics center in Plano, Texas. Other athletes pursue social entrepreneurship, such as retired WNBA/three-time Olympic gold medalist Dawn Staley, who launched an ambitious Philadelphia-based social venture to improve at-risk students' chances of attending college.

New Sports Industry Ventures

There are many examples of new ventures in the sports industry, including firms (e.g., Under Armour, Golf Channel), sports (e.g., ultradistance and extreme action such as freestyle motocross), events (e.g., X Games), and organizations (e.g., the Hansons-Brooks project). The brothers Keith and Kevin Hanson established the Hansons-Brooks Original Development Program (ODP) in Rochester Hills, Michigan, in 1999. The Hanson brothers were keen to start a unique grassroots training program for postcollegiate American athletes to allow them to live in a supportive environment, and that provide employment (at the Hansons' specialty running store), housing, coaching, healthcare, and running gear. The brothers established their new organization based on four principles: (1) create an opportunity for successful college athletes to continue training beyond their college years, (2) provide an environment in which training can be the focus of those postcollegiate athletes (without the financial necessity of working full time or chasing after money in road races), (3) develop a center for those athletes to train together as a team, and (4) incorporate the team members in local community activities to foster excitement for the sport of distance running, and motivate future distance runners. ODP has launched the postcollegiate careers of many outstanding distance runners including Brian Sell and Desiree Davila.

Corporate Innovation

The sports industry is very dynamic, with constantly shifting customer demands, frequent introductions of new technology, and influences from globalization. To survive, existing firms try to develop an entrepreneurial orientation and offer innovative products and services.

Athletics manufacturer Nike has pioneered many innovations in the industry, including the mass-customization range of NIKEiD shoes, the Nike Pre-Cool Vest to keep athletes' body temperatures low before events, and the integration of iPod technology into shoes. Another example of corporate entrepreneurship and innovation in the athletic footwear and apparel arena is Washington-based Brooks Sports' history of innovation in footwear. The company has managed to develop groundbreaking products year after year, most recently "BioMoGo," a biodegradable midsole compound with high levels of cushioning, energy return, and stability.

Siri Terjesen
Indiana University

See Also: Diffusion of Innovation; Leadership Styles; New Product; New Product Development Process.

Further Readings

Gartner, W. B. "A Conceptual Framework for Describing the Phenomenon of New Venture Creation." *Academy of Management Review,* v.10/4 (1985).

Global Entrepreneurship Monitor. *2008 Executive Report.* Wellesley, MA: Babson College, 2009.

Goldsby, M. G., D. F. Kuratko, and J. W. Bishop. "Entrepreneurship and Fitness: An Examination of Rigorous Exercise and Goal Attainment Among Small Business Owners." *Journal of Small Business Management,* v.43/1 (2005).

Huff, A., S. Floyd, H. Sherman, and S. Terjesen. *Strategic Management: Logic and Action.* Hoboken, NJ: John Wiley & Sons, 2008.

Neck, C. P. and K. H. Cooper. "The Fit Executive: Exercise and Diet Guidelines for Enhancing Performance." *Academy of Management Executive,* v.14/2 (2000).

Neck, C. P. and C. C. Manz. "Thought Self Leadership: The Influence of Self Talk and Mental Imagery on Performance." *Journal of Organizational Behavior,* v.13/7 (1992).